THE
FIREARMS
PRICE
GUIDE

BOOKS BY DAVID BYRON

The Firearms Price Guide
Gunmarks

THE FIREARMS PRICE GUIDE

SECOND EDITION

BY DAVID BYRON

A HERBERT MICHELMAN BOOK

Crown Publishers, Inc. / New York

Inquiries should be addressed to Crown Publishers, Inc., One Park Avenue, New York,
New York 10016

Printed in the United States of America

Published simultaneously in Canada by General Publishing Company Limited

Library of Congress Cataloging in Publication Data

Byron, David.
  The Firearms Price Guide.

  "A Herbert Michelman Book."
  1. Firearms—Catalogs. I. Title.
TS534.7.B95 1980   683.4′029′473   79-27231
ISBN: 0-517-540657

10 9 8 7 6 5 4 3 2

INTRODUCTION

HOW TO USE THIS GUIDE

The Values listed in this guide are based on the national average retail price for modern firearms ranging from *N.R.A. Very Good* to *N.R.A. Excellent* for modern arms, and from *N.R.A. Very Good* to *N.R.A. Fine* for antiques. Unless otherwise noted the price quoted is for the most common variant of a particular gun.

For the sake of simplicity the following organization has been adopted for this book:

1. Manufacturer, importer, or brand name
2. Type of gun
3. Type of action
4. Model
5. Caliber or gauge

To find your gun in this guide first look under the name of the manufacturer, importer, or brand name, then look under the subdivision "type of gun" (i.e., rifle, handgun, etc.). For instance if you want to find a "General Hood Centennial" Colt Scout .22 l.r.r.f. single action revolver, look for:

COLT; Handgun; Revolver; General Hood Centennial, .22 l.r.r.f.

If nothing is known about the origin of a particular gun, an approximation of the value can be determined by checking the categories of: "type of action" (wheel lock, percussion, cartridge weapon, etc.), "Unknown Mtaker." A section on "custom firearms" has been added to this edition and follows the same format.

FACTORS AFFECTING PRICE

Condition

Strict grading of condition following N.R.A. guidelines is essential.

Antique firearms in excellent to new condition add 25% to 100% to the "fine" price depending on scarcity and demand. Antiques in good condition, deduct 30% to 35% from "very good."

Modern firearms in good condition deduct 20% to 25% from "very good"; fair condition, deduct 45% to 55%.

Any collectable firearm, no matter how poor the condition (so long as it hasn't been crushed or melted), should fetch 20% to 30% of the "very good" price. As the saying goes, "Old guns never die, they just get reblued."

Ornamentation

Engraving:

It's hard to generalize about art, and that is what engraving is. You must examine a number of examples to learn to judge the quality of the work.

Crude engraving: sparse, add about 25%; medium coverage, add 50% to 75%; full coverage add 100% to 125%.

High quality engraving: sparse, add 50% to 100%; medium coverage, add 150% to 200%; full coverage, add 300% up.

Ornate, high quality work with gold inlays, etc., add 400% up.

Wood carving and marquetry (stock inlays):

This is also in the realm of art, and you should try to look at as many specimens as possible to compare craftsmanship.

Carvings: simple, add $5 to $25 each depending on the quality of execution; complex, add $40 to $125. Full coverage, good quality, add $100 up. Remember that poor carving (such as crude initials) will detract from value.

Inlays: simple, add $5 to $15 each; ornate, add $35 up. Exotic materials, such as ivory or mother-of-pearl, can double the value of the inlay. The value of wire inlays depends as much on the coverage as the execution. Simple wire inlays using brass or German silver should start at $25 each, doubling that if silver is used, and multiplying by 10 if gold is used. Initial shields that are unmarked and not standard equipment on the gun add $3; $7 for sterling silver, $20 for 14k gold.

Heat carving, stampings, and woodburnings are becoming increasingly common and should not be confused with real carving. These should add about $15 if done well.

Custom checkering:

As with carving, craftsmanship is paramount. A poorly done checkering job will lower the value of a gun. Nicely executed patterns on a long gun, add $15 to $20. Fine, complex patterns with wide coverage, add $40 up.

Gold damascening:

The is the art of applying gold leaf or gold plate in a fancy pattern, usually in conjunction with engraving, and should not be confused with gold inlay. Simple patterns, add $40 to $60; fancy patterns, add $225 to $300.

Location of sale

As this guide lists average national prices, several regional factors must be considered.

Antiques: If a particular arm was made in your area, or saw wide service there, there should be more interest in it. This increased market demand will run prices 10% to 15% higher than listed. The converse is also true.

Modern: Much depends on the type of area you live in. In wide-open places where long-range shooting is possible, high-powered rifles may bring 10% over value listed, whereas shotguns will be 15% less. In wooded areas the reverse will occur. In high crime areas, handguns for home protection will bring premiums. Trap and skeet generally stay constant. Wherever you are, judge the type of hobby shooting most prevalent, and the types of guns used for it will follow the above pattern.

Special markings and limited editions (commemoratives)

Standard firearms of most all companies have at some time been ordered or issued with special markings, special features, or as commemoratives. The important consideration in this section is that all deviations from the norm be factory original.

Governments, law enforcement agencies, and stores have ordered the factory to put special marks on guns, and the main requirement in adding value to a gun with these marks is that the gun itself be collectable. The percentage additions shown reflect "common" variations. Rare marks on already very scarce guns may run five to ten times that percentage; however, caution is advisable since this particular market is limited and highly specialized, and as always with rare items, when you get out of your field it's best to consult an expert.

Police or agency markings in lieu of regular marks (not overstamps or extra stamps), add 25% to 50%; trade marks of stores in exotic locales (Rhodesia, etc.), add 50% to 75%; foreign military marks, add 50% to 75%.

Mismarked guns: No stamps, upside-down stamps, wrong markings, etc., add 100% up depending on the collectability of the gun itself.

Special features: This section applies to custom modifications done by the factory and not listed under a particular manufacturer elsewhere in this guide.

Special sights, add 10% to 15%; special metal finish (nickel, etc.), add 10% to 15%; extra-fancy wood on long guns, add 15% to 25%; special barrel lengths, add 20% to 30%.

Commemoratives: One very important question to ask yourself: Is this gun a standard mass-produced item with just an extra stamp or applied token, or is it actually limited production and different from standard in style and embellishment? If your gun falls into the first category, appreciation will be quite slow; if the latter, than the value will rise sharply for the first two or three years, thereafter leveling off to a little better than the inflation rate. For the value to be maintained, commemoratives should be kept in new condition in original packaging with all papers and accessories. Shooting, and subsequent wear, drastically affect the price. Current values are listed under the manufacturer of the individual item.

Historic relics

Documentation is the key word in connecting an old gun with a historic event or famous person. Saying "it used to belong to grandpa and he was so and so" just isn't enough. To be absolutely certain of a weapon's ownership or use, records contemporary with its use must be available. They can be factory records showing the gun's disposition, wills, diaries, etc. Lacking that, if there is strong evidence of ownership such as a name engraved and some documentation showing that the person could have owned it, then it should be labeled "probably." "Grandpa" testimony without supporting evidence can be labeled "possibly." The value of a historic relic transcends the worth of the gun, and depends on the fame (or infamy) of the owner, the artistic value, the location of the sale, and the intangible "mood" of the public as to what period of history is "in."

A plain Colt Single Action Army revolver belonging to Bat Masterson brought $36,000 at auction. A very ornate flintlock fowler made for Louis XIII fetched $300,000 as a work of art several years ago. Although these prices are the exception rather than the rule, if you have an authentic relic it would be worth your while to contact an expert for an appraisal.

An arm with the label "probably" would bring anywhere between 25% and 75% of the "definite's" price depending on buyer belief in its authenticity. "Possibly" may bring only double the value of the gun alone.

Trends

Since the last edition of this guide, the market in the turn-of-the-century "Suicide Specials" has stabilized, and the values are now rising just a bit faster than inflation. Obsolete military arms are rising steadily, with the obscure variations being extremely volatile. Guns with Damascus steel barrels are starting to catch on, but they can still be had at reasonable prices.

Continental European weapons made prior to World War II have been leapfrogging in price due to a very heavy buying pressure from Europe, but the market is not neccessarily firm and there have been wide price swings. This is the area for the speculator, with the best bets being pre-1898 military revolvers, and high quality, low production, pistols. As the availability of guns diminishes, also look for the myriad Spanish pocket pistols of the World War I era to climb, as well as high-grade American shotguns from the lesser known makers, and obsolete .22 rifles.

The market has been virtually flooded with commemorative arms of every description, and many collectors have paused to catch their breaths. The prices of the "standard" commemoratives have stabilized, while the very limited high grade guns have enjoyed a reasonable increase.

Prices of collectable guns, in general, should rise 15% to 25% per year. As always, seasonal adjustments should be made on the common guns, checking the type of sport shooting in your area and deducting 10% to 15% for arms "out of season."

LEGAL CLASSIFICATIONS

There are four classifications of firearms used by the Bureau of Alcohol, Tobacco, and Firearms of the Treasury Department.

Antique: Any firearm manufactured in or before 1898, and replicas that do not fire rim-fire or center-fire cartridges readily available in commercial trade. Antiques are exempt from federal regulation.

Modern: Firearms manufactured after 1898, excluding Replica Antiques, and with special regulations for Class III arms.

Curios and Relics: Certain modern firearms that can be sent interstate to licensed collectors.

Class III Arms: This includes machine guns, silencers, short (under 18") shotguns, short (under 16") rifles, modern smoothbore handguns, and modern arms with a rifled bore diameter greater than .50".

All of the above may be legally owned, notwithstanding federal regulations and local restrictions in a few areas. For further information, contact your local office of the Bureau of Alcohol, Tobacco, and Firearms.

A Special Note about Legal Classifications

Curios: This is a subdivision of "modern" and pertains to arms that may be sent interstate to licensed collectors. However, there is a great deal of confusion as to what constitutes a "curio". The B.A.T.F. issues a yearly list of arms so classified, which is constantly changing and, by virtue of time and space limitations, is incomplete.

Since this guide followed the curio list in force at the time of writing, far more arms are "curios" than are described as such.

The following is the federal guideline to use to determine if a specific firearm or cartridge is a "curio". It must:

1. have been manufactured at least 50 years prior to the current date, but not including replicas therof; or

2. be certified by the curator of a municipal, state, or federal museum that exhibits firearms to be curios or relics of museum interest; or

3. derive a substantial part of its monetary value from the fact that it is novel, rare, or bizarre, or from the fact of its association with some historical figure, period, or event.

Collectors wishing to obtain a curio or relic determination from ATF on a specific firearm or round of ammunition should submit a letter to the Chief of the Firearms Technology Branch, Bureau of Alcohol, Tobacco, and Firearms, Washington, D.C. 20226. The letter should include a complete physical description of the firearm or ammunition, reasons that the collector believes that the firearm or ammunition in question merits such classification, and supporting data concerning the history of the firearm or ammunition, including production figures, if available, and market value.†

Antiques: Many arms listed in this guide were produced between dates overlapping the "antique" determination date. In cases where experts have given a recognized serial number cutoff for "antiques" I have tried to include it. In other instances where arms have no numbers, or where no number is generally recognized as the magic one, I have classified them as modern and leave it to a specialist to make an individual determination.

N.R.A. Condition Guidelines

NEW: Not previously sold at retail, in same condition as current factory production.

NEW-DISCONTINUED: Same as New, but discontinued model.

The following definitions will apply to all secondhand articles:

PERFECT: In new condition in every respect.

EXCELLENT: New condition, used but little, no noticeable marring of wood or metal, bluing perfect (except at muzzle or sharp edges).

VERY GOOD: In perfect working condition, no appreciable wear on working surfaces, no corrosion or pitting, only minor surface dents or scratches.

GOOD: In safe working condition, minor wear on working surfaces, no broken parts, no corrosion or pitting that will interfere with proper functioning.

FAIR: In safe working condition, but well worn, perhaps requiring replacement of minor parts or adjustments, which should be indicated in advertisement, no rust, but may have corrosion pits which do not render article unsafe or inoperable.

Another set of standards applies to "antique" arms as follows:

FACTORY NEW: 100% original finish and parts, everything perfect.

EXCELLENT: All parts and 80%-100% finish original; all letters, numerals, designs sharp; unmarred wood, fine bore.

FINE: All parts and over 30% finish original; all letters, numerals, designs sharp; only minor wood marks, good bore.

VERY GOOD: Up to 30% original finish, all original parts; metal surfaces smooth, with all edges sharp; clear letters, numerals, designs, wood slightly scratched or bruised; bore on collector items disregarded.

† *1977 Guide to Firearms Regulation,* Department of the Treasury, Bureau of Alcohol, Tobacco, and Firearms, p. 99.

GOOD: Only minor replacement parts; metal smoothly rusted or lightly pitted in places; cleaned or reblued; principal letters, numerals, designs legible; wood refinished, scratched, bruised, or with minor cracks repaired; mechanism in good working order.

FAIR: Some major parts replaced; minor replacements; metal may be lightly pitted all over, vigorously cleaned or reblued, edges partly rounded; wood scratched, bruised, cracked or repaired; mechanism in working order. ‡

NOTE: Because each entry in the price guide was computer-sorted, entries whose principal designation is a number do not appear in a regular numerical sequence but are listed in the order of their first digit, second digit, and so on. Thus "Model 78" would be listed before "Model 8," "Model 175" before "Model 18," etc.

---

‡ Firearm Grading Standards reprinted from the *American Rifleman,* courtesy of the National Rifle Association.

ACKNOWLEDGMENTS

The prices listed in this guide were gathered from dealers, collectors, auctions, and ads in collectors' publications. They were then computer sorted and double-checked to ensure maximum reliability.

I wish to extend to the following people, companies, organizations, and especially the many unnamed people who helped, my sincere gratitude for the assistance they freely gave, for without it this guide would not be.

Bob Hills of Browning
Bill Mrock of the B.A.T.F.
Tim Pancurak of Thompson-Center
Nadine Ljutic of Ljutic Industries
Jim Casillo and Fred Paddock of Navy Arms
Vicky Barton of Universal
Fred Karp of Sears, Roebuck & Co.
Rich Sledziona of Hi Standard
Charley Gara of Charter Arms
Nolen Jackson of Wichita Engineering & Supply
Sharon Cunningham of Dixie Gun Works
Sandy Reardon of Colt
Pegi Quatrochi of Ruger
Judy Schroepfer of Kreighoff
Jinny Sundius of Marlin
Earl Harrington of Savage
Fred Hill of Dan Wesson

Barbara Seibert of Heckler & Koch
James R. Steffey of Detonics
Tol Cherry
Duncan Barnes, Lori Alessi, and John Nassif of Winchester
Bruce Hacker of Ventura Imports
Debbie Dean of Weatherby's
I.W. Walentiny of Tradewinds
Marian Partridge of Ithaca
Syd Rachwal
Robert Simpson
Sam Constanzo
Don Valenti
Herb Gopstein
Peter Potter
Alvin Snaper
Bill Drollinger
Dick Sherk
Heinrich Schiefer of Collector Guns
Roger Simonet of W. Glaser Waffen

I also want to give a special thanks to Bob and Herb Michelman for their support, encouragement, and fine ideas, which I have incorporated in this volume.

A & R Sales
South El Monte, Calif. Current

Handgun, Semi-Automatic
Government, .45 ACP, Lightweight, Clip Fed "Parts Gun" Modern   145   195

Rifle, Semi-Automatic
Mark IV Sporter, .308 Win., Clip Fed, Version of M-14, Adjustable Sights,
  Modern   250   350

Abbey, George T
Chicago, Ill. 1858-75

Rifle, Percussion
.44, Octagon Barrel, Brass Furniture, Antique   350   500
.44, Double Barrel, Over-Under, Brass Furniture, Antique   600   800

Abbey, J F & Co
Chicago, Ill. 1871-75. Also made by Abbey & Foster

Rifle, Percussion
Various Calibers, Antique   225   325

Shotgun, Percussion
Various Gauges, Antique   275   400

Acier Comprime
Tradename on Revolvers Made by Apaolozo Hermanos

Handgun, Revolver
Various Calibers, 6 Shot, Modern   65   100

Acme
Made by Hopkins & Allen, Sold by Merwin & Hulbert C. 1880

Handgun, Revolver
.22 Short R.F., 7 Shot, Spur Trigger, Solid Frame, Single Action, Antique   80   145
.32 Short R.F., 5 Shot, Spur Trigger, Solid Frame, Single Action, Antique   85   150

Acme Arms
Maker unknown, sold by J. Stevens Arms Co. C. 1880

Handgun, Revolver
.22 Short R.F., 7 Shot, Spur Trigger, Solid Frame, Single Action, Antique   80   140
.32 Short R.F., 5 Shot, Spur Trigger, Solid Frame, Single Action, Antique   85   150

Shotgun, Double Barrel, Side by Side
12 Gauge, Damascus Barrel, Antique   90   160

Acier Comprime .25 ACP

Acme Hammerless
Made by Hopkins & Allen for Hulbert Bros. 1893

Handgun, Revolver

.32 S & W, 5 Shot, Top Break, Hammerless, Double Action, 2½" Barrel, Antique	55	95
.38 S & W, 5 Shot, Top Break, Hammerless, Double Action, 3" Barrel, Antique	55	95

Action
Modesto Santos; Eibar, Spain

Handgun, Semi-Automatic

Model 1920, .25 ACP, Clip Fed, Modern	65	115
#2; .32 ACP, Clip Fed, Modern	125	175

Adams
Made by Deane, Adams, & Deane, London, England

Handgun, Percussion

.38, M1851, Revolver, Double Action, 4½" Barrel, Antique	450	775
.38, M1851, Revolver, Double Action, 4½" Barrel, Cased with Accessories, Antique	625	900
.44, M1851, Revolver, Double Action, 6" Barrel, Antique	325	550
.44, M1851, Revolver, Double Action, 6" Barrel, Cased with Accessories, Antique	400	675
.500, M1851, Dragoon, Revolver, Double Action, 8" Barrel, Antique	375	700
.500, M1851 Dragoon, Revolver, Double Action, 8" Barrel, Cased with Accessories, Antique	600	950

Adams, Joseph
Birmingham, England 1767-1813

Rifle, Flintlock

.65, Officers Model Brown Bess, Musket, Military, Antique	800	1,100

Adamy Gebruder
Suhl, Germany 1921-39

Shotgun, Double Barrel, Over-Under

16 Ga., Automatic Ejector, Double Trigger, Engraved, Cased, Modern	1,250	1,600

Adirondack Arms Co.
Plattsburg, N.Y. 1870-74. Purchased by Winchester 1874

Rifle, Lever Action

Robinson 1875 Patent, Various Rimfires, Octagon Barrel, Open Rear Sight, Antique	725	1200
Robinson Patent, Various Calibers, Octagon Barrel, Antique	700	1100

Adler
Engelbrecht & Wolff; Zella St. Blasii, Germany

Handgun, Semi-Automatic

7.25 Adler, Modern	1,500	2,500

Aerts, Jan
Maastricht, Holland C.1650

Handgun, Flintlock

Ornate Pair, Very Long Ebony Full Stock, Silver Inlay, High Quality, Antique		60,000

Aetna
Made by Harrington & Richardson C.1876

Handgun, Revolver

.22 Short R.F., 7 Shot, Spur Trigger, Solid Frame, Single Action, Antique	80	140
Aetna, .32 Short R.F., 5 Shot, Spur Trigger, Solid Frame, Single Action, Antique	85	150
Aetna 2, .32 Short R.F., 5 Shot, Spur Trigger, Solid Frame, Single Action, Antique	85	150
Aetna 2½, .32 Short R.F., 5 Shot, Spur Trigger, Solid Frame, Single Action, Antique	85	150

Aetna Arms Co.
N.Y.C. C.1880

Handgun, Revolver

.22 Short R.F., 7 Shot, Spur Trigger, Tip-Up, Antique	225	325
.32 Short R.F., 5 Shot, Spur Trigger, Tip-Up, Antique	225	350

Ajax Army
Maker Unknown, Sold By E. C. Meacham Co. C.1880

Handgun, Revolver

.44 Short R.F., 5 Shot, Spur Trigger, Solid Frame, Single Action, Antique	175	275

Akrill, E.
Probably St. Etienne, France C.1810

Rifle, Flintlock

.69, Smoothbore, Octagon Barrel, Damascus Barrel, Breech Loader, Plain, Antique	950	1,700

Alaska
Made by Hood Firearms, Sold by E. C. Meacham Co. 1880

Handgun, Revolver

.22 Short R.F., 7 Shot, Spur Trigger, Solid Frame, Single Action, Antique	85	140

Albrecht, Andrew
Lancaster, Pa. 1779-82. See Kentucky Rifles and Pistols

Albright, Henry
Lancaster, Pa. 1740-45. See Kentucky Rifles and Pistols

Aldenderfer, M.
Lancaster, Pa. 1763-84. See Kentucky Rifles and Pistols

Alert
Made by Hood Firearms Co. C.1874

Handgun, Revolver

.22 Short R.F., 7 Shot, Spur Trigger, Solid Frame, Single Action, Antique	85	140

Alexia
Made by Hopkins & Allen C.1880

Handgun, Revolver

.22 Short R.F., 7 Shot, Spur Trigger, Solid Frame, Single Action, Antique	85	140
.32 Short R.F., 5 Shot, Spur Trigger, Solid Frame, Single Action, Antique	85	150
.38 Short R.F., 5 Shot, Spur Trigger, Solid Frame, Single Action, Antique	95	170
.41 Short R.F., 5 Shot, Spur Trigger, Solid Frame, Single Action, Antique	140	225

Alexis
Made by Hood Firearms Co., Sold by Turner & Ross Co. Boston, Mass.

Handgun, Revolver

.22 Short R.F., 7 Shot, Spur Trigger, Solid Frame, Single Action, Antique	85	140

Alkar
See Alkartasuna

Alkartasuna
Spain Made by Alkartasuna Fabrica De Armas 1910-22

Handgun, Semi-Automatic

Alkar 1924, .25 ACP, Cartridge Counter, Grips, Clip Fed, Modern	200	325
Pocket, .32 ACP, Clip Fed, Long Grip, Modern	95	150
Pocket, .32 ACP, Clip Fed, Short Grip, Modern	95	150
Vest Pocket, .25 ACP, Clip Fed, Cartridge Counter, Modern	90	135
Vest Pocket, .25 ACP, Clip Fed, Modern	85	140

Allegheny Works
Allegheny, Pa. 1836-75. See Kentucky Rifles and Pistols

Allen
Made by Hopkins & Allen C. 1880

Handgun, Revolver

22 Short R.F., 7 Shot, Spur Trigger, Solid Frame, Single Action, Antique	85	140

Allen & Thurber
Grafton, Mass. 1837-42, Norwich, Conn. 1842-47

Handgun, Percussion

.28 (Norwich,) Pepperbox, 6 Shot, 3" Barrel, Antique	225	350
.31, Pepperbox, 6 Shot, 3½" Barrel, Antique	275	400
.31, (Norwich,) Pepperbox, 6 Shot, 3" Barrel, Antique	225	300
.31, (Norwich,) Singleshot, 3" Barrel, Antique	120	175
.36, Singleshot, 4" Barrel, Half-Octagon Barrel, Antique	120	175
.36, Singleshot, 2½" Barrel, Half-Octagon Barrel, Antique	100	150
.36, Singleshot, 3½" Barrel, Half-Octagon Barrel, Antique	125	200
.36, Pepperbox, 6 Shot, 5¼" Barrel, Antique	275	400

Allen & Thurber
Worcester, Mass. 1855-56

Handgun, Percussion

.31, Pepperbox, 6 Shot, Various Barrel Lengths, Antique	250	325
.31, Pepperbox, 6 Shot, Hammerless, 3" Barrel, Antique	275	375
.34, Pepperbox, 5 Shot, 3" Barrel, Antique	275	350
.34, Pepperbox, 6 Shot, 4½" Barrel, Antique	200	275
.36, Under-Hammer, Half-Octagon Barrel, 4" Barrel, Antique	135	200
.36, Under-Hammer, Half-Octagon Barrel, 4" Barrel, Antique	135	200
.36, Singleshot, 3" Barrel, Antique	145	220
.36, Target Pistol, 10" Barrel, Adjustable Sights, Half-Octagon Barrel, Antique	200	280
.36, Pepperbox, 6 Shot, 5" Barrel, Antique	250	325
.38, Target Pistol, I0" Barrel, Adjustable Sights, Half-Octagon Barrel, Antique	200	300

Rifle, Percussion

.43, Singleshot, Sporting Rifle, Antique	400	550

Allen & Wheelock
Worcester, Mass. 1856-65

Handgun, Percussion

.25, Repeater, Octagon Barrel, 5¾" Barrel, 5 Shot, Engraved Cylinder, Antique	300	400
.28, .31, Repeater, Octagon Barrel, 2¼" Barrel, 5 Shot, Antique	95	145
.28, .31, Repeater, Octagon Barrel, 4" Barrel, 5 Shot, Antique	100	150
.31, Pepperbox, 5 Shot, 2⅞" Barrel, Antique	260	350
.31, Repeater, Octagon Barrel, 4" Barrel, 6 Shot, Antique	260	350
.31, Repeater, Octagon Barrel, 7½" Barrel, 6 Shot, Antique	275	375
.32, Repeater, Octagon Barrel, 5¾" Barrel, 5 Shot, Engraved Cylinder, Antique	250	350
.36, Pepperbox, 4 Shot, 2⅞" Barrel, Antique	275	395
.36, Repeater, Octagon Barrel, 4" Barrel, 5 Shot, Antique	250	325
.36, Revolver, Various Barrel Lengths, 6 Shot, Military, Antique	275	400
.36, Revolver, Various Barrel Lengths, 6 Shot, Center Hammer, Military, Antique	285	425
.41, Repeater, Octagon Barrel, 5" Barrel, 5 Shot Engraved Cylinder, Antique	300	450
.44, Repeater, Military, 6 Shot, 7" Barrel, Antique	275	400

Handgun, Revolver

.22 Short R.F., 7 Shot, Side Hammer, Solid Frame, Antique	110	175
.25 L.F., 7 Shot, Side Hammer, Solid Frame, Antique	275	400
.32 L.F., 6 Shot, Side Hammer, Solid Frame, Antique	300	425
.32 Short R.F., 6 Shot, Side Hammer, Solid Frame, Antique	95	145
.38 L.F., 6 Shot, Side Hammer, Solid Frame, Antique	375	500
.38 Short R.F., 6 Shot, Side Hammer, Solid Frame, Antique	100	175
.44 L.F., 6 Shot, Side Hammer, Solid Frame, Antique	500	625
.44 Short R.F., 6 Shot, Side Hammer, Solid Frame, Antique	140	200

Handgun, Singleshot

.22 Short R.F., Derringer, Spur Trigger, Antique	150	225
.32 Short R.F., Derringer, Spur Trigger, Antique	95	160
.41 Short R.F., Derringer, Spur Trigger, Antique	250	350

Rifle, Percussion

.31 Allen Patent, Carbine, Breech Loader, Antique	400	600
.36 Allen Patent, Sporting Rifle, Breech Loader, Antique	350	450
.44, Revolver, Carbine, 6 Shot, Antique	1,750	2,500

Rifle, Singleshot

.62 Allen R.F., Falling Block, Sporting Rifle, Antique	250	375
.64 Allen R.F., Falling Block, Sporting Rifle, Antique	250	375

Allen, C. B.
Springfield, Mass. 1836-41 Also See U.S. Military

Handgun, Percussion

.36 Cochran Turret, 7 Shot, 4¾" Barrel, Antique	5,000	7,500
.40 Cochran Turret, 7 Shot 5" Barrel, Antique	6,750	8,500
.54 Elgin Cutlass, Octagon Barrel, with Built-in Knife, Smoothbore, Antique	4,500	6,500

Rifle, Percussion

.44 Cochran Turret, 7 Shot, Octagon Barrel, Antique	5,000	7,500
.44 Cochran Turret, 8 Shot, Octagon Barrel, Antique	5,000	7,500

Allen, Ethan
Grafton, Mass. 1835-37

Handgun, Percussion

Various Calibers, Various Barrel Lengths, Singleshot, Antique	100	150
.31, Singleshot, Under-Hammer, Half-Octagon Barrel, 7" Barrel, Antique	125	175

.31, Pepperbox, 6 Shot, 3" Barrel, Antique	300	425
.36, Pepperbox, 6 Shot, 5" Barrel, Antique	250	375

Handgun, Revolver

.22 Short R.F., 7 Shot, Side Hammer, Sheath Trigger, Antique	125	200
.32 Short R.F., 6 Shot, Side Hammer, Sheath Trigger, Antique	110	185

Handgun, Singleshot

Derringer, .32 Short R.F., Side-Swing Barrel, Round Barrel, Antique	90	145
Derringer, .32 Short R.F., Side-Swing Barrel, Half-Octagon Barrel, Antique	90	150
Derringer, .41 Short R.F., Side-Swing Barrel, Half-Octagon Barrel, Antique	90	160
Derringer, .41 Short R.F., Side-Swing Barrel, Round Barrel, Antique	90	160
Derringer, .41 Short R.F., Side-Swing Barrel, Octagon Barrel, Antique	90	170

Rifle, Singleshot

Various Rimfires, Sporting Rifle, Antique	350	475

Allies
Spain, Unknown Maker

Handgun, Semi-Automatic

Model 1924, .25 ACP, Clip Fed, Modern	85	125
Pocket, .32 ACP, Clip Fed, Modern	85	125
Vest Pocket, .25 ACP, Clip Fed, Modern	75	115
Vest Pocket, .32 ACP, Clip Fed, Short Grip, Modern	85	125

America
Made by Bliss & Goodyear C.1878

Handgun, Revolver

.22 Short R.F., 7 Shot, Spur Trigger, Solid Frame, Single Action, Antique	90	150

America
Made by Norwich Falls Pistol Co. C.1880

Handgun, Revolver

.32 Long R.F., Double Action, Solid Frame, Modern	60	95

American Arms Co.
Boston, Mass. 1873-93, Milwaukee, Wisc. 1893-1901 Purchased by Marlin 1901

Handgun, Double Barrel, Over-Under

Wheeler Pat. .22 Short R.F., 32 Short R.F., Brass Frame, Spur Trigger, Antique	425	650
Wheeler Pat, .32 Short R.F., Brass Frame, Spur Trigger, Antique	300	450
Wheeler Pat, .41 Short R.F., Brass Frame, Spur Trigger, Antique	375	650

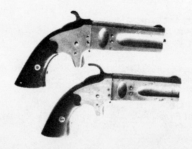

American Arms Wheeler Pat. Pistols - .22/32; .32/32

Shotgun, Double Barrel Side by Side
12 Ga., Semi-Hammerless, Checkered Stock, Antique	250	400
Whitmore Patent, 10 Ga., 2⅞", Hammerless, Checkered Stock, Antique	250	400
Whitmore Patent, 12 Ga., Hammerless, Checkered Stock, Antique	300	450

Shotgun, Singleshot
12 Ga., Semi-Hammerless, Checkered Stock, Antique	150	225

American Barlock Wonder
Made by Crescent for Sears-Roebuck & Co.

Shotgun, Double Barrel, Side by Side
Various Gauges, Outside Hammers, Damascus Barrel, Modern	80	150
Various Gauges, Hammerless, Steel Barrel, Modern	95	175
Various Gauges, Hammerless, Damascus Barrel, Modern	75	150
Various Gauges, Outside Hammers, Steel Barrel, Modern	90	175

Shotgun, Singleshot
Various Gauges, Hammer, Steel Barrel, Modern	45	75

American Boy
Made by Bliss & Goodyear for Townley Hdw. Co.

Handgun, Revolver
.32 Short R.F., Single Action, Solid Frame, Spur Trigger, 7 Shot, Antique	75	130

American Bulldog
Made by Johnson, Bye & Co.; Worcester, Mass. 1882-1900

Handgun, Revolver
.22 Short R.F., 7 Shot, Spur Trigger, Solid Frame, Single Action, Antique	90	160
.32 S & W, 5 Shot, Spur Trigger, Solid Frame, Single Action, Modern	80	130
.32 Short R.F., 5 Shot, Spur Trigger, Solid Frame, Single Action, Antique	90	I60
.38 S & W, 5 Shot, Spur Trigger, Solid Frame, Single Action, Modern	80	135
.38 Short R.F., 5 Shot, Spur Trigger, Solid Frame, Single Action, Antique	95	160
.41 Short C.F., 5 Shot, Spur Trigger, Solid Frame, Single Action, Antique	95	175

American Champion

Shotgun, Singleshot
M1899, 12 Gauge, Plain, Modern	55	95

American Eagle
Made by Hopkins & Allen 1870-1898

Handgun, Revolver
.22 Short R.F., 7 Shot, Spur Trigger, Solid Frame, Single Action, Antique	90	160
.32 Short R.F., 5 Shot, Spur Trigger, Solid Frame, Single Action, Antique	90	170

American Firearms Co.
San Antonio, Texas

Handgun, Semi-Automatic
.25 ACP, Clip Fed, Blue, Modern	45	75
.25 ACP, Clip Fed, Stainless Steel, Modern	50	90
.380 ACP, Clip Fed, Stainless Steel, Modern	100	175

American Gun Co.
Made by Crescent Firearms Co. Sold by H. & D. Folsom Co.

Handgun, Revolver
.32 S & W, 5 Shot, Double Action, Top Break, Modern	50	115
.32 S & W, 5 Shot, Double Action, Top Break, Modern	50	115

Shotgun, Double Barrel, Side by Side
Various Gauges, Outside Hammers, Damascus Barrel, Modern	80	150
Various Gauges, Hammerless, Steel Barrel, Modern	95	175
Various Gauges, Hammerless, Damascus Barrel, Modern	75	150
Various Gauges, Outside Hammers, Steel Barrel, Modern	90	175

Shotgun, Singleshot
Various Gauges, Hammer, Steel Barrel, Modern	45	75

American Standard Tool Co.
Newark, N.J. 1865-70

Handgun, Revolver
.22 Short R.F., 7 Shot, Spur Trigger, Tip-Up, Antique	175	325

Americus
Made by Hopkins & Allen 1870-1900

Handgun, Revolver
.22 Short R.F., 7 Shot, Spur Trigger, Soli Frame, Single Action, Antique	90	150
.32 Short R.F., 5 Shot, Spur Trigger, Solid Frame, Single Action, Antique	90	160

Amsden, B. W.
Saratoga Springs, N.Y. 1852

Combination Weapon, Percussion
.40-16 Ga., Double Barrel, Rifled, Antique	700	900

Rifle, Percussion
.40, Octagon Barrel, Set Trigger, Rifled, Antique	375	550
.44, 3 Shot, 2 Nipples, Single Barrel, Rifled, Antique	1,500	2,250

AMT
Arcadia Machine & Tool; Arcadia, Calif.

Handgun, Semi-Automatic
Hardballer, .45 ACP, Stainless Steel, Clip Fed, Adjustable Sights, Modern	225	360
Skipper, .45 ACP, Stainless Steel, Clip Fed, Adjustable Sights, Modern	250	375
Combat Skipper, .45 ACP, Stainless Steel, Clip Fed, Fixed Sights, Modern	225	350
Longslide, .45 ACP, Stainless Steel, Clip Fed, Adjustable Sights, Modern	375	500
Parts Gun, .45 ACP, made with Stainless Steel Frame, Modern	150	225
Back Up, .380 ACP, Stainless Steel, Clip Fed, Modern	135	195

Angstadt, A. & J.
Berks County, Pa. 1792-1808 See Kentucky Rifles and U.S. Military

Angush, James
Lancaster County, Pa. 1771 See Kentucky Rifles and Pistols

Anschutz
See Savage Arms Co.

Anschutz, E.
Philadelphia, Pa. C.1860

Rifle, Percussion
.36, Schutzen Rifle, Octagon Barrel, Target, Antique	1,400	1,900

Anstadt, Jacob
Kurztown, Pa. 1815-17, See Kentucky Rifles and Pistols

Argentine Military Mannlicher Model 1905

Argentine Military Modelo 1927 .45 ACP

Apache
Made by Ojanguren y Vidosa; Eibar, Spain

Handgun, Semi-Automatic
.25 ACP, Clip Fed, Modern   75   125

Argentine Military

Automatic Weapon, Assault Rifle
FN-FAL, .308 Win., Clip Fed, Class 3   1,000   1,300

Automatic Weapon, Submachine Gun
C-3, .45 ACP, Class 3   200   325
C-4, Hafdasa, .45 ACP, Class 3   200   325
M E M S, 9mm Luger, Class 3   450   600
M1943, .45 ACP, Class 3   200   325
M1946, .45 ACP, Class 3   200   325
P A M, 9mm Luger, Class 3   350   600
Star M D, 9mm Luger, Class 3   475   750

Handgun, Revolver
Colt M 1985, Double Trigger, Solid Frame, Swing-out Cylinder, Military,
    Modern   90   145

Handgun, Semi-Automatic
Ballester-Molina, .45 ACP, Clip Fed, Modern   150   250
Ballester-Rigaud, .45 ACP, Clip Fed, Modern   160   275
Mannlicher M1905, 7.63 Mannlicher, Curio   150   225
Modelo 1916 (Colt 1911), .45 ACP, Clip Fed, Modern   200   300
Modelo 1927 (Colt 1911A1), .45 ACP, Clip Fed, Modern   275   425

Rifle, Bolt Action
M 1908/09, 7.65 Argentine, Carbine, Open Rear Sight, Full-Stocked
    Military, Modern   130   175
M 1891, 7.65 Argentine, Rifle, Full Stocked Military, Modern   75   110
M 1891, 7.65 Argentine, Carbine, Open Rear Sight, Full Stocked
    Military, Modern   85   125
M 1909, 7.65 Argentine, Rifle, Full Stocked Military, Modern   75   115

Rifle, Singleshot
M1879, .43 Mauser, Rolling Block, Antique   225   325

Aristocrat
Made by Hopkins & Allen for Suplee Biddle Hardware 1870-1900

Handgun, Revolver
.22 Short R.F., 7 Shot, Spur Trigger, Solid Frame, Single Action, Antique   95   160
.32 Short R.F., 5 Shot, Spur Trigger, Solid Frame, Single Action, Antique   90   175

Aristocrat
Made by Stevens Arms

Shotgun, Double Barrel, Side by Side
M 315, Various Gauges, Hammerless, Steel Barrel, Modern   90   150

Arizaga, Gaspar
Eibar, Spain

Handgun, Semi-Automatic
.32 ACP, Clip Fed, Modern 90   125

Armalite
Costa Mesa, Calif.

Automatic Weapon, Assault Rifle
AR-10, .308 Win., Clip Fed, Commercial, Class 3   2,400   3,000
AR-18, .223 Rem., Clip Fed, Commercial, Class 3   500   625
AR-18, .223 Rem., Clip Fed, Folding Stock, Class 3   600   800

Rifle, Semi-Automatic
AR-180, .223 Rem., Clip Fed, Folding Stock, Modern   250   375
Explorer, .22 L.R.R.F., Clip Fed, Modern   50   85
Explorer Custom, .22 L.R.R.F., Checkered Stock, Clip Fed, Modern   60   95

Shotgun, Semi-Automatic
AR-17, 12 Ga., Lightweight, Modern   350   500

Arminius
Herman Weihrauch Sportwaffenfabrik, Mellrichstadt/ Bayern, West Germany; for Current Models, See F.I.E.

Handgun, Revolver
HW-3, .22 L.R.R.F., Modern   15   30
HW-3, .32 S & W Long, Modern   20   35
HW-5, .22 L.R.R.F., Modern   15   30
HW-5, .32 S & W Long, Modern   20   30
HW-7, .22 L.R.R.F., Modern   15   30
HW-9, .22 L.R.R.F., Adjustable Sights, Modern   30   40

Arminius
Friederich Pickert; Zella-Mehlis, Germany 1922-39

Handgun, Revolver
.22 L.R.R.F., Target, Modern   30   55
Model 10, .32 ACP, Hammerless, Modern   85   125
Model 3, .25 ACP, Hammerless, Folding Trigger, Modern   85   125
Model 8, .320 Revolver, Hammerless, Folding Trigger, Modern   75   115
Model 9, .32 ACP, Modern   80   130

Handgun, Singleshot
Model 1, .22 L.R.R.F., Target, Adjustable Sights, Modern   125   200
Model 2, .22 L.R.R.F., Target, Adjustable Sights, Set Trigger, Modern   175   275

Armsport
Current Importers, Miami, Fla.

Handgun, Flintlock

Kentucky, .45, Reproduction, Antique	45	75

Handgun, Percussion

New Remington Army, .44, Stainless Steel, Brass Trigger Guard, Reproduction, Antique	80	125
New Remington Army, .44, Blue, Brass Trigger Guard, Reproduction, Antique	60	90
Whitney, .36, Solid Frame, Brass Trigger Guard, Reproduction, Antique	60	90
Spiller & Burr, .36, Solid Frame, Brass Frame, Reproduction, Antique	45	65
1851 Colt Navy, .36, Brass Frame, Reproduction, Antique	45	70
1851 Colt Navy, .44, Brass Frame, Reproduction, Antique	45	70
1851 Colt Navy, .36, Steel Frame, Reproduction, Antique	55	85
1851 Colt Navy, .44, Steel Frame, Reproduction, Antique	55	85
1860 Colt Army, .44, Brass Frame, Reproduction, Antique	50	80
1860 Colt Army, .44, Steel Frame, Reproduction, Antique	60	95
New Hartford Police, .36, Reproduction, Antique	45	80
1847 Colt Walker, .44, Reproduction, Antique	75	115
Corsair, .44, Double Barrel, Reproduction, Antique	50	80
Kentucky, .45 or .50, Reproduction, Antique	45	70
Patriot, .45, Target Sights, Set Triggers, Reproduction, Antique	60	100

Rifle, Bolt Action

Tikka, Various Calibers, Open Sights, Checkered Stock, Clip Fed, Modern	250	350

Rifle, Lever Action

Premier 1873 Winchester, Various Calibers, Rifle, Engraved, Reproduction, Modern	700	900
Premier 1873 Winchester, Various Calibers, Carbine, Engraved, Reproduction, Modern	600	775

Rifle, Flintlock

Kentucky, .45, Reproduction, Antique	100	145
Deluxe Kentucky, .45, Reproduction, Antique	150	200
Hawkin, .45, Reproduction, Antique	120	160
Deluxe Hawkin, .50, Reproduction, Antique	130	170

Rifle, Percussion

Kentucky, .45 or .50, Reproduction, Antique	95	140
Deluxe Kentucky, .45, Reproduction, Antique	130	185
Hawkin, Various Calibers, Reproduction, Antique	110	150
Deluxe Hawkin, Various Calibers, Reproduction, Antique	120	160

Combination Weapon, Over-Under

Tikka Turkey Gun, 12 Ga. and .222 Rem., Vent Rib, Sling Swivels, Muzzle Break, Checkered Stock, Modern	400	550

Rifle, Double Barrel, Side by Side

Emperor, Various Calibers, Holland and Holland Type Sidelock, Engraved, Checkered Stock, Extra Barrels, Cased, Modern	8,000	9,500
Emperor Deluxe, Various Calibers, Holland and Holland Type Sidelock, Fancy Engraving, Checkered Stock, Extra Barrels, Cased, Modern	11,500	14,500

Rifle, Double Barrel, Over-Under

Emperor, Various Calibers, Checkered Stock, Engraved, Extra Barrels, Cased, Modern	6,000	7,500
Express, Various Calibers, Checkered Stock, Engraved, Modern	1,500	2,250

Shotgun, Percussion

Hook Breech, Double Barrel, Side by Side, 10 and 12 Gauges, Reproduction, Antique	150	225

Shotgun, Double Barrel, Side by Side

Goose Gun, 10 Ga. 3½" Mag., Checkered Stock, Modern	350	450
Side by Side, 12 and 20 Gauges, Checkered Stock, Modern	300	400
Express, 12 and 20 Gauges, Holland and Holland Type Sidelock, Engraved, Checkered Stock, Modern	2,000	2,750
Western Double, 12 Ga. Mag. 3", Outside Hammers Double Trigger, Modern	275	375

Shotgun, Double Barrel, Over-Under

Premier, 12 Ga., Skeet Grade, Checkered Stock, Engraved, Modern	1,000	1,350
Model 2500, 12 and 20 Ga., Checkered Stock, Adjustable Choke, Single Selective Trigger, Modern	400	525
Special, 410 Ga., Checkered Stock, Double Trigger, Modern	70	100

Shotgun, Singleshot

Monotrap, 12 Ga., Two Barrel Set, Checkered Stock, Modern	1,500	2,000
Monotrap, 12 Ga., Checkered Stock, Modern	1,000	1,350

Armstrong, John
Gettysburg, Pa. 1813-17 Also See Kentucky Rifles and Pistols

Asheville Armory
Asheville, N.C. 1861-64

Rifle, Percussion

.58 Enfield Type, Rifled, Brass Furniture, Military, Antique	1,300	1,900

Astra
Made by Unceta Y Cia., Spain

Automatic Weapon, Machine-Pistol

Model 901, 7.63 Mauser, Holster Stock, Class 3	700	1,000
Model 902, 7.63 Mauser, Holster Stock, Class 3	700	1,000
Model 903, 7.63 Mauser, Holster Stock, Class 3	700	1,000
Model F, 9mm Bayard Long, Holster Stock, Class 3	700	1,000

Handgun, Revolver

Cadix, .22 L.R.R.F., Modern	80	125
Cadix, .38 Special, Modern	85	130
Constable, .357 Magnum, Modern	125	190

Handgun, Semi-Automatic
Chrome Plating Add $20-$35
Light Engraving Add $50-$90

Constable, Various Calibers, Blue, Modern	125	200
Model 100, .32 ACP, Modern	100	150
Model 1911, .32 ACP, Modern	95	150
Model 1915, .32 ACP, Modern	80	140
Model 1916, .32 ACP, Modern	85	160

Astra Model 1911 .32 ACP

Astra Model 1921 9mm

Model 1921, 9mm Bayard Long, Clip Fed, Commercial, Modern	175	225
Model 1924, .25 ACP, Modern	80	140
Model 200, .25 ACP, Modern	80	125
Model 200 Firecat, .25 ACP, Modern	90	135
Model 2000 Camper, .22 Short R.F., Modern	90	140
Model 2000 Cub, .22 Short R.F., Modern	90	140
Model 2000 Cub, .25 ACP, Modern	90	130
Model 300, .32 ACP, Modern	115	175
Model 300, .32 ACP, Nazi-Proofed, Curio	275	375
Model 300, .380 ACP, Modern	125	175
Model 300, .380 ACP, Nazi-Proofed,Curio	275	375
Model 3000 (Late), .380 ACP, Modern	100	150
Model 400, .32 ACP, Modern	225	325
Model 400, 9mm Bayard Long, Nazi-Proofed, Curio	400	500
Model 400, 9mm Bayard Long, Modern	150	225
Model 4000 Falcon, Conversion Unit Only $65-$95		
Model 4000 Falcon, .22 L.R.R.F., Modern	140	200
Model 4000 Falcon, .32 ACP, Modern	130	190
Model 4000 Falcon, .380 ACP, Modern	130	190
Model 600, .32 ACP, Modern	140	200
Model 600, 9mm Luger, Nazi-Proofed, Curio	200	300
Model 600, 9mm Luger, Modern	125	190
Model 700 Special, .32 ACP, Modern	400	525
Model 900, 7.63 Mauser, Holster Stock, Modern	800	1,200

Astra Model 200 .25 ACP with Long Clip

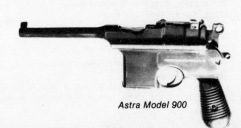

Astra Model 900

Model 900, 9mm Luger, Modern	1,000	1,400
Model 902, 9mm Bayard Long, Holster Stock, Curio	1,100	1,600
Model 903E, .38 Super, Modern	1,100	1,600
Model 903E, 7.63 Mauser, Holster Stock, Modern	800	1,100
Model 903E, 9mm Bayard Long, Modern	750	1,100

Rifle, Semi-Automatic

Model 1000, .32 ACP, Modern	300	425
Model 3000 (Early), .32 ACP, Modern	100	150
Model 3000 (Late) .22 L.R.R.F., Modern	90	140
Model 3000 (Late), .32 ACP, Modern	90	140
Model 800 Condor, 9mm Luger, Curio	450	575
Model 902, 7.63 Mauser, Modern	1,000	1,400

Atis
Ponte S. Marco, Italy

Shotgun, Semi-Automatic

12 Ga., Lightweight, Vent Rib, Modern	150	200
12 Ga., Lightweight, Vent Rib, Left-Hand, Modern	200	260

Aubrey
Made by Meridan Arms Co., Sold by Sears-Roebuck 1900-30

Handgun, Revolver

.32 S & W, 5 Shot, Double Action, Top Break, Modern	50	95
.38 S & W, 5 Shot, Double Action, Top Break, Modern	50	95

Audax
Tradename of Manufacture D'Armes Des Pyrenees, Hendaye, France, Marketed by La Cartoucherie Francaise, Paris 1931-39

Handgun, Semi-Automatic

.25 ACP, Clip Fed, Magazine Disconnect, Grip Safety, Modern	65	125
.32 ACP, Clip Fed, Magazine Disconnect, Modern	70	130

Austrian Military

Automatic Weapon, Assault Rifle

FN FAL, .308 Win., Class 3	1,200	1,600

Automatic Weapon, Submachine Gun

MP Solothurn 34, 9mm Mauser, Clip Fed, Class 3	950	1,300
MP 34, 9mm Luger, Class 3	500	650

Handgun, Flintlock

.64 Dragoon, with Shoulder Stock, Singleshot, Antique	450	650

Handgun, Percussion

.64 Dragoon, with Shoulder Stock, Singleshot, Antique	275	400

Handgun, Revolver

M1898 Rast Gasser, 8mm Rast-Gasser, Modern	175	300

Handgun, Semi-Automatic

M1907 Roth Steyr, 8mm Roth-Steyr, Modern	175	275
M1908 Steyr, 8mm Roth-Steyr, Modern	175	275
M1912 Steyr, 9mm Steyr, Modern	150	225
Mannlicher 1901, 7.63 Mannlicher, Modern	175	300
Mannlicher 1905, 7.63 Mannlicher, Curio	150	250

Handgun, Singleshot

Werder Lightning, 11mm, Antique	225	350

Rifle, Bolt Action

M1883 Schulhof, 11.15 x 58R Werndl, 8 Shot, Antique	325	450
M1885 Steyr, 11.15 x 58R Werndl, Straight-Pull, Antique	275	400

Austrian Military Steyr M1912

M1886 Steyr, 11.15 x 58R Werndl, Straight-Pull Bolt, Antique	80	150
M1888, 8 x 50R Mannlicher, Antique	80	140
M1888/90, 8 x 50R Mannlicher, Antique	60	95
M1890, 8 x 50R Mannlicher, Carbine, Antique	60	95
M1895, 8 x 50R Mannlicher, Carbine, Modern	60	95
M1895, 8 x 50R Mannlicher, Modern	55	90
M1895 Stutzen, 8 x 50R Mannlicher, Modern	75	145

Auto Mag
Pasadena, Calif., Started about 1968. Made by T D E, Jurras Associates, and High Standard

Handgun, Semi-Automatic

Shoulder Stock Only, Class 3, Add $225-$325		
First Model (Calif.), .357 AMP, Clip Fed, Stainless Steel, Hammer, Adjustable Sights Cased, Modern	850	1,250
First Model (Calif.), .44 AMP, Clip Fed, Stainless Steel, Hammer, Adjustable Sights, Cased, Modern	700	925
Model 160, .357 AMP, Clip Fed, Stainless Steel, Hammer, Adjustable Sights, Cased, Modern	500	750
Model 170, .41 JMP, Clip Fed, Stainless Steel, Hammer, Adjustable Sights, Cased, Modern	500	750
Model 260, .357 AMP, Clip Fed, Stainless Steel, Hammer, Adjustable Sights, Cased, Modern	450	700
Model 280, .44 AMP, Clip Fed, Stainless Steel, Hammer, Adjustable Sights, Cased, Modern	450	700

Automatic
Made by Hopkins & Allen C.1900

Handgun, Revolver

.32 S & W, 5 Shot, Top Break, Hammerless, Double Action, Modern	60	95
.38 S & W, 5 Shot, Top Break, Hammerless, Double Action Modern	60	95

Automatic Hammerless
Made by Iver Johnson C.1900

Handgun, Revolver

.22 L.R.R.F., 7 Shot, Double Action, Top Break, Hammerless, Modern	55	95
.32 S & W, 5 Shot, Top Break, Hammerless, Double Action, Modern	60	110
.38 S & W, 5 Shot, Top Break, Hammerless, Double Action, Modern	60	110

Automatic Pistol .25 ACP

Automatic Pistol
Spain, Maker Unknown

Handgun, Semi-Automatic
Pocket, .32 ACP, Clip Fed, Modern   60   95

Automatic Police
See Forehand & Wadsworth

Auto-Ordinance Corp.
See Thompson

Auto-Pointer
Made by Yamamoto Mfg. Co., Imported by Sloans

Shotgun, Semi-Automatic
12 and 20 Gauges, Tube Feed, Checkered Stock, Modern   175   275

Avenger

Handgun, Revolver
.32 Long R.F., 5 Shot, Single Action, Spur Trigger, Antique   90   140

AYA
Aguirre Y Aranzabal, Spain. Now Imported by Ventura

Shotgun, Double Barrel, Over-Under
Model 37 Super, Various Gauges, Single Selective Trigger, Automatic
  Ejector, Fancy Checkering, Fancy Engraving, Sidelock, Modern   1,200   1,600

Shotgun, Double Barrel, Side by Side
Bolero, Various Gauges, Single Trigger, Checkered Stock, Modern   170   225
Matador, Various Gauges, Single Selective Trigger, Checkered Stock,
  Selective Ejector, Modern   175   250
Matador II, Various Gauges, Single Selective Trigger, Checkered Stock,
  Selective Ejector, Vent Rib, Modern   225   325
Model 1, 12 and 20 Gauges, Automatic Ejector, Sidelock, Fancy
  Checkering, Engraved, Lightweight, Modern   725   850
Model 117, 12 and 20 Gauges, Sidelock, Single Selective Trigger,
  Engraved, Checkered Stock, Modern   375   500
Model 2, 12 and 20 Gauges, Automatic Ejector, Sidelock, Engraved,
  Checkered Stock, Double Trigger, Modern   475   675
Model 53E, 12 and 20 Gauges, Sidelock, Single Selective Trigger, Fancy
  Checkering, Fancy Engraving, Modern   800   1,150
Model 56, 12 and 20 Gauges, Sidelock, Raised Matted Rib, Fancy
  Checkering, Fancy Engraving, Modern   725   850
Model 76, 12 and 20 Gauges, Automatic Ejector, Single Selective
  Trigger, Engraved, Checkered Stock, Modern   275   400
Model XXV/SL, 12 Ga., Sidelock, Automatic Ejector, Engraved
  Checkered Stock, Modern   575   700

A y A Model 53E
Courtesy of Ventura Imports

Azanza Y Arrizabalaga
Spain C.1910

Handgun, Semi-Automatic
M1916, .32 ACP, Clip Fed, Long Grip, Modern   65   100

Babcock
Maker Unknown C.1880

Handgun, Revolver
.32 Short R.F., 5 Shot, Spur Trigger, Solid Frame, Single Action, Antique   90   160

Baby Bulldog

Handgun, Revolver
.22 L.R.R.F., Double Action, Hammerless, Folding Trigger, Modern   85   130
.32 Short R.F., Double Action, Hammerless, Folding Trigger, Modern   80   120

Baby Russian
Made by American Arms Co. C.1890

.38 S & W, 5 Shot, Single Action, Spur Trigger, Top Break, Modern   120   160

Backup
See T D E, and A M T

Bacon Arms Co.

Handgun, Percussion
6 Shot, Fluted Barrel, Pepperbox, Under-Hammer, Pocket Pistol, Antique   550   700

Bacon Mfg. Co.
Norwich, Conn. 1852-91

Handgun, Revolver
.22 Short R.F., 7 Shot, Spur Trigger, Solid Frame, Single Action, Antique   90   160
.32 Short R.F., 5 Shot, Spur Trigger, Solid Frame, Single Action, Antique   90   160
.32 Short R.F., 6 Shot, Solid Frame, Spur Trigger, Single Action, Antique   110   175
.32 Short R.F., 6 Shot, Solid Frame, Single Action with Trigger Guard,
  Antique   80   120

Bacon Mfg. Co. Navy 2nd Type

"Navy," .38 Long R.F., 6 Shot, 7½" Barrel, Solid Frame, Spur Trigger,
  Single Action, Antique   175   250

Baker Gun & Forging Co.
Batavia, N.Y. 1886-1919, Purchased by Folsom 1919

Rifle, Semi-Automatic
Batavia, .22 Short, Clip Fed, Modern   200   300

Shotgun, Double Barrel, Side by Side
Single Trigger, Add $75-125
Deduct 50% for Damascus Barrels
Automatic Ejectors, Add $75-150
Batavia Leader, Various Gauges, Sidelock, Double Trigger, Checkered
  Stock, Modern   275   400
Batavia Leader Special, Various Gauges, Sidelock, Double Trigger,
  Checkered Stock, Automatic Ejector, Modern   350   500
Black Beauty, Various Gauges, Sidelock, Double Trigger, Checkered
  Stock, Modern   350   475
Black Beauty Special, Various Gauges, Sidelock, Double Trigger,
  Checkered Stock, Automatic Ejector, Modern   425   550
Deluxe ($1,000 Grade), Various Gauges, Sidelock, Fancy Wood, Fancy
  Engraving, Fancy Checkering, Automatic Ejector, Modern   7,500 10,000
Deluxe ($300 Grade), Various Gauges, Sidelock, Fancy Wood, Fancy
  Engraving, Fancy Checkering, Automatic Ejector, Modern   2,500   3,500
Expert, Various Gauges, Sidelock, Fancy Wood, Fancy Engraving,
  Fancy Checkering, Automatic Ejector, Modern   1,850   2,250
Grade A, Various Gauges, Sidelock, Hammerless, Engraved, Damascus
  Barrels, Modern   160   225
Grade B, Various Gauges, Sidelock, Hammerless, Engraved, Damascus
  Barrels, Modern   160   225
Grade C Batavia, Various Gauges, Boxlock, Hammerless, Engraved,
  Damascus Barrels, Modern   140   200
Grade H Deluxe, Various Gauges, Sidelock, Fancy Engraving, Modern   2,250   3,000
Grade L Pigeon, Various Gauges, Sidelock, Fancy Engraving, Modern   1,100   1,600
Grade N Krupp Trap, 12 Ga., Sidelock, Engraved, Modern   750   1,000
Grade R, Various Gauges, Sidelock, Light Engraving, Modern   300   425
Grade S, Various Gauges, Sidelock, Light Engraving, Modern   275   400
Model 1896, 10 and 12 Gauges, Hammers, Modern   150   225
Model 1897, Various Gauges, Hammers, Modern   150   225
New Baker Model, 10 and 12 Gauges, Hammers, Modern   140   200
Paragon, Various Gauges, Sidelock, Double Trigger, Engraved, Fancy
  Checkering, Modern   650   875
Paragon, Various Gauges, Sidelock, Double Trigger, Engraved, Fancy
  Checkering, Automatic Ejector, Modern   750   950
Paragon Special, 12 Ga., Sidelock, Fancy Wood, Fancy Engraving,
  Modern   850   1300

Shotgun, Singleshot
Elite, 12 Ga., Vent Rib, Fancy Engraving, Modern   600   750

Sterling, 12 Ga., Vent Rib, Light Engraving, Modern	425	550
Superba, 12 Ga., Trap Grade, Fancy Wood, Fancy Engraving, Fancy Checkering, Automatic Ejector, Modern	1,700	2,250

Baker Gun Co.
Made in Belgium for H & D Folsom Arms Co.

Shotgun, Double Barrel, Side by Side

Various Gauges, Outside Hammers, Damascus Barrel, Modern	80	150
Various Gauges, Hammerless, Steel Barrel, Modern	95	175
Various Gauges, Hammerless, Damascus Barrel, Modern	75	150
Various Gauges, Outside Hammers, Steel Barrel, Modern	90	175

Shotgun, Singleshot

Various Gauges, Hammer, Steel Barrel, Modern	45	75

Baker, Ezekiel
London, England 1784-1825

Handgun, Percussion

.58, Holster Pistol, Round Barrel, Light Ornamentation, Antique	350	425

Baker, W. H. & Co.
Marathon, N.Y. 1870; Syracuse, N.Y. 1878-86

Combination Weapon, Drilling

Hammer Drilling, Various Gauges, Damascus Barrels, Front Trigger Break, Antique	300	450

Rifle, Percussion

.60, Brass Furniture, Scope Mounted, Target, Octagon Barrel, Antique	1,700	2,200

Shotgun, Double Barrel, Side by Side

Hammer Double, 10 and 12 Gauges, Damascus Barrels, Front Trigger Break, Antique	200	300

Ball & Williams
Worcester, Mass. 1861-66

Rifle, Singleshot

Ballard, .44 Long R.F., Military, Carbine, Falling Block, Antique	525	675
Ballard, .46 Long R.F., Kentucky Rifle, Falling Block, Antique	675	800
Ballard, Various Rimfires, Falling Block, Sporting Rifle, Antique	350	475
Ballard, Various Rimfires, Military, Falling Block, Antique	600	800
Merwin & Bray, .54 Ballard R.F., Military, Carbine, Falling Block, Antique	525	675
Merwin & Bray, Various Rimfires, Falling Block, Sporting Rifle, Antique	450	600

Ballard Rifle
Made by Ball & Williams 1861-66, Merrimack Arms & Mfg Co. 1866-69, Brown Mfg Co. 1869-73, J.M. Marlin from 1875

Rifle, Singleshot

#1½ Hunter (Marlin), .40-65 Ballard Everlasting, Falling Block, Sporting Rifle, Open Rear Sight, Antique	500	700
#1 Hunter (Marlin), .44 Long R F/C F, Falling Block, Sporting Rifle, Recoil Pad, Antique	500	700
#2 (Marlin), .44-40 WCF, Falling Block, Sporting Rifle, Open Rear Sight, Antique	525	750
#2 (Marlin), Various Calibers, Falling Block, Sporting Rifle, Recoil Pad, Early Model, Antique	500	700
#3½ (Marlin), .40-65 Ballard Everlasting, Falling Block, Target Rifle, Target Sights, Octagon Barrel, Antique	725	900
#3 Gallery (Marlin), .22 Short R.F., Falling Block, Target Rifle, Early Model, Antique	325	400

#4½ (Marlin), .40-65 Ballard Everlasting, Falling Block, Mid-Range Target Rifle, Checkered Stock, Antique	700	900
#4½ (Marlin), .45-70 Government, Falling Block, Sporting Rifle, Antique	675	875
#4½ (Marlin), Various Calibers, Falling Block, Sporting Rifle, Antique	600	800
#4½ (Marlin), Various Calibers, Falling Block, Mid-Range Target Rifle, Target Sights, Fancy Wood, Antique	800	1,100
#4 Perfection (Marlin), Various Calibers, Falling Block, Target Rifle, Target Sights, Set Trigger, Early Model, Antique	550	750
#5 Pacific (Marlin), .45-70 Government, Falling Block, Target Rifle, Open Rear Sight, Set Trigger, Octagon Barrel, Antique	550	750
#5 Pacific (Marlin), Various Calibers, Falling Block, Target Rifle, Open Rear Sight, Set Trigger, Octagon Barrel, Antique	450	625
#6½ (Marlin), .40-65 Ballard Everlasting, Falling Block, Off-Hand Target Rifle, Target Sights, Set Trigger, Antique	700	900
#6½ (Marlin), Various Calibers, Falling Block, Mid-Range Target Rifle, Antique	550	700
#6 Pacific (Marlin), Various Calibers, Falling Block, Schutzen Rifle, Target Sights, Fancy Wood, Set Trigger, Antique	1,300	1,650
#7A-1 (Marlin), .44-75 Ballard Everlasting, Falling Block, Creedmore Long Range, Target Sights, Fancy Wood, Set Trigger, Antique	1,800	2,250
#7A (Marlin), .44-100 Ballard Everlasting, Falling Block, Long Range Target Rifle, Target Sights, Set Trigger, Antique	700	900
#7A-1 (Marlin), .44-100 Ballard Everlasting, Falling Block, Long Range Target Rifle, Target Sights, Set Trigger, Fancy Wood, Antique	1,000	1,350
#7A-1 Extra Deluxe, .44-100 Ballard Everlasting, Falling Block, Long Range Target Rifle, Target Sights, Set Trigger, Fancy Wood, Antique	1,600	2,000
#8 (Marlin), .44-75 Ballard Everlasting, Falling Block, Creedmore Long Range, Target Sights, Pistol-Grip Stock, Set Trigger, Antique	1,400	1,800
#9 (Marlin), .44-75 Ballard Everlasting, Falling Block, Creedmore Long Range, Target Sights, Set Trigger, Antique	1,300	1,700
(Ball & Williams), .44 Long R.F., Military, Carbine, Falling Block, Antique	525	675
(Ball & Williams), .46 Long R.F., Kentucky Rifle, Falling Block, Antique	675	850
(Ball & Williams), .54 Ballard R.F., Military, Carbine, Falling Block, Antique	550	700
(Ball & Williams), Various Rimfires, Falling Block, Sporting Rifle, Antique	375	475
(Ball & Williams), Various Rimfires, Military, Falling Block, Antique	600	800
1½ Hunter (Marlin), .45-70 Government, Falling Block, Sporting Rifle, Open Rear Sight, Antique	550	775
1¾ Far West (Marlin), .40-65 Ballard Everlasting, Falling Block, Sporting Rifle, Open Rear Sight, Set Trigger, Antique	525	725
1¾ Far West (Marlin), .45-70 Government, Falling Block, Sporting Rifle, Open Rear Sight, Set Trigger, Antique	575	800
5½ Montana (Marlin), .45-100 Sharps, Falling Block, Sporting Rifle, Octagon Barrel, Antique	675	850
Brown Mfg. Co., .44 Long R.F., Falling Block, Mid-Range Target Rifle, Antique	700	900
Hunter, .44 Long R F/C F, Falling Block, Sporting Rifle, Recoil Pad, Antique	450	575
Merrimack Arms, .44 Long R.F., Falling Block, Carbine, Antique	525	700
Merrimack Arms, .46 Long R.F., Falling Block, Military, Antique	650	800
Merrimack Arms, .56-52 Spencer R.F., Falling Block, Carbine, Antique	525	700
Merrimack Arms, Various Rimfires, Falling Block, Sporting Rifle, Antique	500	675
Merwin & Bray, Various Rimfires, Falling Block, Sporting Rifle, Antique	450	600

Ballard & Co.
Worcester, Mass 1861-71; Also See U.S. Military

Rifle, Singleshot

#2 (Marlin), Various Calibers, Falling Block, Sporting Rifle, Antique	500	700
#3 Gallery (Marlin), Various Calibers, Falling Block, Target Rifle, Antique	550	675
#3 Gallery (Marlin), Various Rimfires, Falling Block, Target Rifle, Antique	475	575

#3-F Gallery (Marlin), .22 Long R.F., Falling Block, Target Rifle, Fancy Wood, Antique	600	750
#4 Perfection (Marlin), Various Calibers, Falling Block, Target Rifle, Target Sights, Set Trigger, Octagon Barrel, Antique	800	950

Bang-Up
Made by Hopkins & Allen C.1880

Handgun, Revolver
.22 Short R.F., 7 Shot, Spur Trigger, Solid Frame, Single Action, Antique	90	160

Banister, T.
England, C.1700

Handgun, Flintlock
Pocket Pistol, Screw Barrel, Steel Mounts, Engraved, High Quality, Antique	1,000	1,500

Barker, F.A.
Fayettesville, N.C. 1860-64; Also see Confederate Military

Barker, T.
Made by Crescent; Also Made in Belgium

Shotgun, Double Barrel, Side by Side
Various Gauges, Outside Hammers, Damascus Barrel, Modern	80	150
Various Gauges, Hammerless, Steel Barrel, Modern	95	175
Various Gauges, Hammerless, Damascus Barrel, Modern	75	150
Various Gauges, Outside Hammers, Steel Barrel, Modern	90	175

Shotgun, Singleshot
Various Gauges, Hammer, Steel Barrel, Modern	45	75

Barlett, J. & Bro.
N.Y. 1825-47. See Kentucky Rifles

Barlow, J.
Moscow, Ind. 1836-40. See Kentucky Rifles

Barnett & Son
London, England 1750-1832

Rifle, Flintlock
.75, 3rd. Model Brown Bess, Musket, Military, Antique	800	1,200

Barnett, J. & Sons
London, England 1835-75

Rifle, Percussion
.577, C.W. Enfield, Rifled, Musket, Military, Antique	350	500

Barrett, J.
Wythesville, Va. 1857-65. See Confederate Military

Bauer Firearms
Fraser, Mich.

Handgun, Semi-Automatic
22-SS, .22 L.R.R.F., Clip Fed, Pocket Pistol, Stainless Steel Hammerless, Modern	65	85
25-Bicentennial, .25 ACP, Clip Fed, Pocket Pistol, Stainless Steel, Hammerless, Engraved, Modern	170	225

25-SS, .25 ACP, Clip Fed, Pocket Pistol, Stainless Steel, Hammerless,
  Modern   65   80

Bauer, George
Lancaster, Pa. 1770-81. See Kentucky Rifles

Bay State Arms Co.
Uxbridge & Worcester, Mass. 1873-74

Rifle, Singleshot
.32 Long R.F., Dropping Block, Antique   90   140
Various Calibers, Target Rifle, Antique   575   750

Shotgun, Singleshot
Davenport Patent, 12 Ga., Antique   150   200

Bayard
Belgium. Made by Anciens Etablissments Pieper C.1900

Handgun, Semi-Automatic
Model 1908 Pocket, .25 ACP, Blue, Clip Fed, Modern   85   145
Model 1910 Pocket, .32 ACP, Blue, Clip Fed, Modern   100   185
Model 1923 Pocket, .25 ACP, Blue, Clip Fed, Modern   85   150
Model 1923 Pocket, .32 ACP, Blue, Clip Fed, Modern   100   185
Model 1930 Pocket, .25 ACP, Blue, Clip Fed, Modern   100   185

Beattie, James
London, England 1835-65

Handgun, Percussion
.40 Six Shot, Revolver, Octagon Barrel, Fancy Wood, Fancy Engraving,
  Cased with Accessories, Antique   2,750   3,400

Beck, Gideon
Lancaster, Pa. 1780-88. See Kentucky Rifles and Pistols

Beck, Isaac
Miffinberg, Pa. 1830-40

Rifle, Percussion
.47, Octagon Barrel, Brass Furniture, Antique   725   850

Beholla
Germany. Made by Becker & Hollander C.1910

Handgun, Semi-Automatic
.32 ACP, Clip Fed, Commerical, Modern   90   140
.32 ACP, Clip Fed, Gering, Modern   90   140
.32 ACP, Clip Fed, Military, Modern   120   175

Bayard Model 1910 .32 ACP

Beholla "Gering" .32 ACP

Belgian Military
Also see Browning, FN

Rifle, Bolt Action

M 1924, Various Calibers, Military, Modern	95	170
M 1930, Various Calibers, Military, Modern	95	170
M 1934/30, Various Calibers, Military, Modern	95	170
M 1950, .30-06 Springfield, Military, Modern	150	225
M1889 Mauser, Military, Modern	75	100
M1889 Mauser, Carbine, Military, Modern	75	100
M1935 Mauser, Military, Modern	95	150
M1936 Mauser, Military, Modern	85	130

Rifle, Semi-Automatic

M 1949, .30-06 Springfield, Military, Modern	325	450
M 1949, Various Calibers, Military, Modern	275	375

Bellmore Gun Co.
Made by Crescent C.1900

Shotgun, Double Barrel, Side by Side

Various Gauges, Outside Hammers, Damascus Barrel, Modern	80	150
Various Gauges, Hammerless, Steel Barrel, Modern	95	175
Various Gauges, Hammerless, Damascus Barrel, Modern	75	150
Various Gauges, Outside Hammers, Steel Barrel, Modern	90	175

Shotgun, Singleshot

Various Gauges, Hammer, Steel Barrel, Modern	45	75

Benelli
Italy, Diana Import Co.

Shotgun, Semi-Automatic

Engraved Model, 12 and 20 Gauges, Checkered Stock, Modern	350	475
Standard Model, 12 and 20 Gauges, Checkered Stock, Modern	275	375

Benfer, Amos
Beaverstown, Pa. C.1810. See Kentucky Rifles and Pistols

Beretta, Giovanni
Brescia, Italy C.1700

Handgun, Snaphaunce

Belt Pistol, Engraved, Carved, Light Ornamentation, Antique	3,000

Beretta
Pietro Beretta; Gardone V.T., Italy

Automatic Weapon, Assault Rifle

Model 70, .223 Rem., Clip Fed, Plastic Stock, Class 3	500	800
Model BM59, .308 Win., Clip Fed, Bipod, Class 3	600	850
Model SC70L, .223 Rem., Clip Fed, Folding Stock, Class 3	450	600
Model SC70S, .223 Rem., Clip Fed, Folding Stock, Short Barreled Rifle, Class 3	475	650

Benelli Model 121

Beretta Model 1915 .32 ACP

Automatic Weapon, Submachine Gun

Model 12, 9mm Luger, Clip Fed, Folding Stock, Class 3	300	400
Model 38/49, 9mm Luger, Clip Fed, Wood Stock, Class 3	300	400
Model MP38/44, 9mm Luger, Clip Fed, Military, Class 3	700	850
Model MP38A, 9mm Luger, Clip Fed, Military, Wood Stock, Class 3	600	750
Model MP38A, 9mm Luger, Clip Fed, Commercial, Wood Stock, Class 3	750	900

Handgun, Semi-Automatic

1915, .32 ACP, Clip Fed, Military, Modern	155	225
1915, .380 ACP, Clip Fed, Military, Modern	225	300
1915/1919, .32 ACP, Clip Fed, Military, Modern	200	250
1919 V P, .25 ACP, Clip Fed, Modern	90	145
Cougar, .380 ACP, Clip Fed, Modern	125	200
Jaguar, .22 L.R.R.F., Clip Fed, Modern	90	145
Jetfire, .25 ACP, Clip Fed, Modern	90	145
Model 100, .32 ACP, Clip Fed, Modern	90	140
Model 101, .22 L.R.R.F., Clip Fed, Adjustable Sights, Modern	95	155
Model 1923, 9mm Luger, Clip Fed, Military, Modern	200	275
Model 1923, 9mm Luger, Clip Fed, Military, with Detachable Shoulder Stock, Curio	600	750

Beretta Model 1931 .32 ACP

Beretta Model 1935 .32 ACP

Model 1931 Navy, .32 ACP, Clip Fed, Military, Modern	175	250
Model 1934, .380 ACP, Clip Fed, Military, Modern	90	145
Model 1934, .380 ACP, Clip Fed, Commercial, Modern	125	200
Model 1935, .32 ACP, Clip Fed, Commercial, Modern	95	160
Model 1935, .32 ACP, Clip Fed, Military, Modern	90	150
Model 318, .25 ACP, Clip Fed, Modern	90	145
Model 418, .25 ACP, Clip Fed, Modern	90	145
Model 420, .25 ACP, Clip Fed, Chrome, Light Engraving, Modern	150	222
Model 421, .25 ACP, Clip Fed, Gold Plated, Fancy Engraving, Modern	225	325
Model 70S, .380 ACP, Clip Fed, Modern	95	150
Model 70T, .32 ACP, Clip Fed, Adjustable Sights, Modern	95	160
Model 76, .22 L.R.R.F., Clip Fed, Adjustable Sights, Modern	145	225
Model 81, .32 ACP, Clip Fed, Double Action, Modern	160	250
Model 84, .380 ACP, Clip Fed, Double Action, Modern	160	250
Model 90, .32 ACP, Clip Fed, Double Trigger, Modern	165	225
Model 92, 9mm Luger, Clip Fed, Double Action, Modern	225	325
Model 948, .22 L.R.R.F., Clip Fed, Lightweight, Modern	75	110
Model 949 Olympic, .22 L.R.R.F., Clip Fed, Target Pistol, Modern	175	250
Model 949 Olympic, .22 Short R.F., Clip Fed, Target Pistol, Modern	175	250
Model 950 Minx, .22 Short R.F., Clip Fed, 2″ Barrel, Modern	75	110
Model 950B Minx, .22 Short R.F., Clip Fed, 4″ Barrel, Modern	75	110
Model 951 Brigadier, 9mm Luger, Clip Fed, Commercial, Modern	175	275
Model 951 Egyptian, 9mm Luger, Clip Fed, Military, Curio	400	600
Model 951 Israeli, 9mm Luger, Clip Fed, Military, Curio	400	600
Puma, .32 ACP, Clip Fed, Modern	90	140

Rifle, Semi-Automatic

Silver Gyrfalcon, .22 L.R.R.F., Checkered Stock, Modern	75	120

Shotgun, Double Barrel, Over-Under

Golden Snipe, 12 and 20 Gauges, Single Trigger, Automatic Ejector, Engraved, Fancy Checkering, Modern	325	425
Golden Snipe, 12 and 20 Gauges, Single Selective Trigger, Automatic Ejector, Engraved, Fancy Checkering, Modern	350	450
Golden Snipe Deluxe, 12 and 20 Gauges, Single Selective Trigger, Automatic Ejector, Fancy Engraving, Fancy Checkering, Modern	375	475
Model ASEL, 12 and 20 Gauges, Single Trigger, Checkered Stock, Modern	550	700
Model BL 1, 12 Ga., Field Grade, Double Trigger, Checkered Stock, Modern	200	275

Beretta Model 950 .22

Model BL 2, 12 Ga., Field Grade, Single Selective Trigger, Checkered Stock, Modern	250	325
Model BL 3, 12 Ga., Trap Grade, Single Selective Trigger, Checkered Stock, Light Engraving, Vent Rib, Modern	350	425
Model BL 3, Various Gauges, Skeet Grade, Single Selective Trigger, Checkered Stock, Light Engraving, Vent Rib, Modern	350	425
Model BL 3, Various Gauges, Field Grade, Single Selective Trigger, Checkered Stock, Light Engraving, Vent Rib, Modern	325	400
Model BL 4, 12 Ga., Trap Grade, Single Selective Trigger, Selective Ejector, Engraved, Vent Rib, Modern	450	575
Model BL 4, Various Gauges, Skeet Grade, Single Selective Trigger, Selective Ejector, Engraved, Vent Rib, Modern	425	575
Model BL 4, Various Gauges, Field Grade, Single Selective Trigger, Selective Ejector, Engraved, Vent Rib, Modern	400	500
Model BL 5, 12 Ga., Trap Grade, Single Selective Trigger, Selective Ejector, Fancy Engraving, Vent Rib, Modern	600	750
Model BL 5, Various Gauges, Skeet Grade, Single Selective Trigger, Selective Ejector, Fancy Engraving, Vent Rib, Modern	600	750
Model BL 5, Various Gauges, Field Grade, Single Selective Trigger, Selective Ejector, Fancy Engraving, Vent Rib, Modern	575	675
Model BL 6, 12 Ga., Trap Grade, Single Selective Trigger, Selective Ejector, Fancy Engraving, Vent Rib, Modern	750	900
Model BL 6, Various Gauges, Field Grade, Single Selective Trigger, Selective Ejector, Fancy Engraving, Vent Rib, Modern	700	850
Model BL 6, Various Gauges, Skeet Grade, Single Selective Trigger, Selective Ejector, Fancy Engraving, Vent Rib, Modern	750	900
Model S02, 12 Ga., Sidelock, Selective Ejector, Single Trigger, Checkered Stock, Engraved, Modern	1,200	1,600
Model S03, 12 Ga., Sidelock, Automatic Ejector, Single Selective Trigger, Fancy Engraving, Fancy Wood, Modern	1,600	2,100
Model S03 EELL, 12 Ga., Sidelock, Automatic Ejector, Single Selective Trigger, Fancy Engraving, Fancy Wood, Modern	3,300	4,000
Model S03 EL, 12 Ga. Sidelock, Automatic Ejector, Single Selective Trigger, Fancy Engraving, Fancy Wood, Modern	2,200	2,800
Model S04, 12 Ga., Sidelock, Automatic Ejector, Single Trigger, Fancy Engraving, Fancy Wood, Modern	2,000	2,500
Model S05, 12 Ga., Sidelock, Selective Ejector, Single Trigger, Fancy Engraving, Fancy Checkering, Modern	3,300	3,900
Model S55B, 12 and 20 Gauges, Single Selective Trigger, Automatic Ejector, Vent Rib, Checkered Stock, Modern	375	475
Model S56E, 12 and 20 Gauges, Single Selective Trigger, Automatic Ejector, Engraved, Checkered Stock, Modern	400	500
Model S58, 12 Ga., Trap Grade, Automatic Ejector, Single Selective Trigger, Engraved, Checkered Stock, Modern	525	650
Model S58, 12 and 20 Gauges, Skeet Grade, Automatic Ejector, Single Selective Trigger, Engraved, Checkered Stock, Light Engraving, Modern	525	650
Silver Snipe, 12 and 20 Gauges, Single Trigger, Checkered Stock, Light Engraving, Modern	250	325
Silver Snipe, 12 and 20 Gauges, Single Selective Trigger, Checkered Stock, Light Engraving, Modern	275	350
Silver Snipe, 12 and 20 Gauges, Single Trigger, Checkered Stock, Light Engraving, Vent Rib, Modern	250	325
Silver Snipe, 12 and 20 Gauges, Single Selective Trigger, Light Engraving, Vent Rib, Modern	450	575

Shotgun, Double Barrel, Side by Side

Model 409PB, Various Gauges, Double Trigger, Light Engraving, Checkered Stock, Modern	300	375
Model 410 Early, 10 Ga. 3½", Double Trigger, Engraved, Checkered Stock, Modern	400	500
Model 410 Late, 10 Ga. 3½", Modern	675	800
Model 410E, Various Gauges, Double Trigger, Engraved, Checkered Stock, Automatic Ejector, Modern	400	500

Model 411E, Various Gauges, Double Trigger, Engraved, Fancy
  Checkering, Automatic Ejector, Modern   550   750
Model 424, 12 and 20 Gauges, Double Trigger, Light Engraving,
  Checkered Stock, Modern   350   450
Model 426E, 12 and 20 Gauges, Single Selective Trigger, Automatic
  Ejector, Engraved, Checkered Stock, Modern   525   650
Model GR 2, 12 and 20 Gauges, Double Trigger, Checkered Stock, Light
  Engraving, Modern   225   350
Model GR 3, 12 and 20 Gauges, Single Selective Trigger, Checkered
  Stock, Light Engraving, Modern   275   375
Model GR 4, 12 Ga., Single Selective Trigger, Selective Ejector,
  Checkered Stock, Engraved, Modern   350   475
Silver Hawk, 10 Ga. 3½", Double Trigger, Magnum, Modern   350   450
Silver Hawk, 12 Ga., Mag. 3", Double Trigger, Magnum, Modern   275   350
Silver Hawk, 12 Ga. Mag. 3", Magnum, Modern   325   400
Silver Hawk, Various Gauges, Double Trigger, Lightweight, Modern   225   300
Silver Hawk, Various Gauges, Single Trigger, Lightweight, Modern   275   350

Shotgun, Semi-Automatic
Gold Lark, 12 Ga., Vent Rib, Light Engraving, Checkered Stock, Modern   150   250
Model A301, 12 Ga., Slug, Open Rear Sight, Modern   210   275
Model A301, 12 Ga., Trap Grade, Vent Rib, Modern   210   280
Model A301, 12 and 20 Gauges, Field Grade, Vent Rib, Modern   190   270
Model A301, 12 and 20 Gauges, Skeet Grade, Vent Rib, Modern   190   260
Model A301, 12 Ga., Mag. 3", Field Grade, Vent Rib, Modern   250   325
Model AL 1, 12 and 20 Gauges, Checkered Stock, Modern   125   200
Model AL 2, 12 Ga., Vent Rib, Trap Grade, Checkered Stock, Modern   180   220
Model AL 2, 12 and 20 Gauges, Vent Rib, Checkered Stock, Modern   160   210
Model AL 2, 12 and 20 Gauges, Vent Rib, Skeet Grade, Checkered
  Stock, Modern   180   225
Model AL 3, 12 Ga., Vent Rib, Checkered Stock, Light Engraving, Trap
  Grade, Modern   225   300
Model AL 3, 12 and 20 Gauges, Vent Rib, Checkered Stock, Light
  Engraving, Modern   200   260
Model AL3, 12 and 20 Gauges, Vent Rib, Checkered Stock, Light
  Engraving, Skeet Grade, Modern   225   300
Model AL 3, 12 Ga. Mag. 3", Vent Rib, Checkered Stock, Light
  Engraving, Modern   225   300
Ruby Lark, 12 Ga., Vent Rib, Fancy Engraving, Fancy Checkering,
  Modern   225   325
Silver Lark, 12 Ga., Checkered Stock, Modern   95   160

Shotgun, Singleshot
Campanion FS 1, Various Gauges, Folding Gun, Modern   60   85
Model TR 1, 12 Ga., Trap Grade, Vent Rib, Light Engraving, Checkered
  Stock, Monte Carlo Stock, Modern   120   190

Shotgun, Slide Action
Gold Pigeon, 12 Ga., Vent Rib, Checkered Stock, Engraved, Modern   130   200
Gold Pigeon, 12 Ga., Vent Rib, Fancy Engraving, Fancy Checkering,
  Modern   225   350
Model SL 2, 12 Ga., Vent Rib, Checkered Stock, Modern   125   180
Ruby Pigeon, 12 Ga., Vent Rib, Fancy Engraving, Fancy Checkering,
  Modern   350   450
Silver Pigeon, 12 Ga., Light Engraving, Checkered Stock, Modern   95   160

Bergmann
Gaggenau, Germany 1892-1944; Company Renamed Bergmann Erben 1931.

Handgun, Semi-Automatic
Model 1894, 5mm, Blow Back, Clip Fed, Antique   10,000
Model 1894, 8mm, Blow Back, Clip Fed, Antique   6,000
Model 1896 #2, 5mm, Small Frame, Clip Fed, Modern   750   1,000

Bergmann Model 1896 #3

Model 1896 #3, 6.5mm, Clip Fed, Modern	800	1,200
Model 1896 #4, 8mm, Military, Clip Fed, Modern	1,000	1,600
Model 1897 #5, 7.8mm, Clip Fed, Modern	1,200	1,800
Simplex, 8mm, Clip Fed, Modern	400	600
Bergmann Mars, 9mmB, Clip Fed, Modern	1,500	2,000
Bergmann/Bayard, Model 1908, 9mmB, Clip Fed, Modern	400	600
Bergmann/Bayard, Model 1910, 9mmB, Clip Fed, Modern	400	650
Bergmann/Bayard, Model 1910/21, 9mmB, Clip Fed, Modern	350	500
Model 2, .25 ACP, Clip Fed, Modern	125	200
Model 2A, .25 ACP, Einhand, Clip Fed, Modern	175	250
Model 3, .25 ACP, Long Grip, Clip Fed, Modern	125	200
Model 3A, .25 ACP, Einhand, Long Grip, Clip Fed, Modern	195	275
Erben Special, .32 ACP, Clip Fed, Modern	175	275
Erben Model I, .25 ACP, Clip Fed, Modern	150	235
Erben Model II, .25 ACP, Clip Fed, Modern	175	250

Rifle, Semi-Automatic

Model 1897, Karabiner, 7.8mm, Long Barrel, Detachable Stock, Modern	2,500	4,000

Berlin, Abraham
Caston, Pa. 1773-86. See Kentucky Rifles and Pistols

Bergmann Bayard Model 1910/21 9mm

Bernardelli
Vincenzo Bernardelli; Gardone V.T., Italy

Handgun, Semi-Automatic

M1956, 9mm Luger, Clip Fed, Curio	750	950
Model 100, .22 L.R.R.F., Clip Fed, Blue, Target Pistol, Modern	160	210
Model 60, .22 L.R.R.F., Clip Fed, Blue, Modern	75	95
Model 60, .22 L.R.R.F., Clip Fed, Blue, 8" Barrel, Detachable Front Sight, Adjustable Sights, Modern	200	300
Model 60, .32 ACP, Clip Fed, Blue, Modern	70	100
Model 60, .380 ACP, Clip Fed, Blue, Modern	75	115
Model 80, .22 L.R.R.F., Clip Fed, Blue, Modern	85	125
Model 80, .22 L.R.R.F., Clip Fed, Blue, 6" Barrel, Modern	80	130
Model 80, .32 ACP, Clip Fed, Blue, Modern	80	125
Model 80, .380 ACP, Clip Fed, Blue, Modern	80	125
Model V P, .22 L.R.R.F., Clip Fed, Blue, Modern	110	175
Model V P, .25 ACP, Clip Fed, Blue, Modern	85	150
Standard, .22 L.R.R.F., Clip Fed, Blue, Modern	80	120
Standard, .22 L.R.R.F., Clip Fed, Blue, 6" Barrel, Detachable Front Sight, Modern	115	150
Standard, .22 L.R.R.F., Clip Fed, Blue, 8" Barrel, Detachable Front Sight, Modern	135	200
Standard, .22 L.R.R.F., Clip Fed, Blue, 10" Barrel, Detachable Front Sight, Modern	225	300
Standard, .32 ACP, Original 17 Shot Clip only, Add $25-$40		
Standard, .32 ACP, Clip Fed, Blue, Modern	125	175
Standard, .32 ACP, Clip Fed, Blue, 6" Barrel, Detachable Front Sight, Modern	175	250
Standard, .32 ACP, Clip Fed, Blue, 8" Barrel, Detachable Front Sight, Modern	225	325
Standard, .32 ACP, Clip Fed, Blue, 10" Barrel, Detachable Front Sight, Modern	275	375
Standard, .380 ACP, Clip Fed, Blue, Modern	125	175
Standard, 9mm Luger, Clip Fed, Blue, Modern	225	325

Rifle, Double Barrel, Over-Under

Various Calibers, Checkered Stock, Engraved, Modern	700	950

Shotgun, Double Barrel, Side by Side

Brescia, 12 and 20 Gauges, Checkered Stock, Hammer, Modern	425	550
Elio, 12 Ga., Checkered Stock, Light Engraving, Lightweight Selective Ejector, Modern	575	725
Game Cock, 12 and 20 Gauges, Checkered Stock, Double Trigger, Modern	400	575
Game Cock Premier, 12 and 20 Gauges, Checkered Stock, Single Trigger, Selective Ejector, Modern	550	675
Holland, Various Gauges, Sidelock, Engraved, Checkered Stock, Automatic Ejector, Modern	1.000	1,250
Holland Deluxe, Various Gauges, Sidelock, Fancy Engraving, Fancy Checkering, Automatic Ejector, Modern	1,100	1,450
Holland Presentation, Various Gauges, Sidelock, Fancy Engraving, Fancy Checkering, Automatic Ejector, Modern	1,500	2,000
Italia, 12 and 20 Gauges, Checkered Stock, Hammer, Light Engraving, Modern	425	550
Roma #3, Various Gauges, Engraved, Checkered Stock, Automatic Ejector, Modern	375	500
Roma #4, Various Gauges, Fancy Engraving, Fancy Checkering, Automatic Ejector, Modern	475	600
Roma #6, Various Gauges, Fancy Engraving, Fancy Checkering, Automatic Ejector, Modern	625	750
St. Uberto F.S., 12 and 16 Gauges, Checkered Stock, Double Trigger, Automatic Ejector, Modern	325	425
Wesley Richards, Various Gauges, Checkered Stock, Light Engraving, Double Trigger, Modern	650	850

Wesley Richards, Various Gauges, Fancy Checkering, Fancy Engraving,
   Single Trigger, Selective Ejector, Vent Rib, Modern   1,250   1,700

Bernardon-Martin
St. Etienne, France

Handgun, Semi-Automatic
Automatique Francais, .32 ACP, Clip Fed, Modern   175   250

Bertuzzi
Gardone V.T., Italy; Imported by Ventura

Shotgun, Double Barrel, Over-Under
Zeus, 12 Ga., Sidelock, Automatic Ejector, Single Selective Trigger, Fancy
   Checkering, Fancy Engraving, Modern   1,800   2,300
Zeus Extra Lusso, 12 Ga., Sidelock, Automatic Ejector, Single Selective
   Trigger, Fancy Checkering, Fancy Engraving, Modern   3,800   4,600

Bicycle
Bicycle by Harrington & Richardson C.1895

Handgun, Revolver
.22 L.R.R.F., Top Break, Double Action, Modern   60   95
.32 S & W, 5 Shot, Double Action, Top Break, Modern   60   95

Bicycle
French, Maker Unknown

Handgun, Singleshot
.22 L.R.R.F., Auto Styling, Modern   225   300

Big Bonanza
Made by Bacon Arms Co. C.1880

Handgun, Revolver
.22 Short R.F., 7 Shot, Spur Trigger, Solid Frame, Single Action, Antique 90   160

Big Horn Arms Co.
Watertown, S.D.

Handgun, Singleshot
Target Pistol, .22 Short, Plastic Stock, Vent Rib, Modern   75   125

Shotgun, Singleshot
12 Ga. Short, Plastic Stock, Modern   50   90

Billinghurst, William
Rochester, N.Y. 1843-80

Combination Weapon, Percussion
.36, 12 Ga., Double Barrel, Antique   1,200   1,600

Bertuzzi Zeus Extra Lusso
Courtesy of Ventura Imports

Rifle, Percussion
.36, Revolver, 7 Shot, Octagon Barrel, Antique   1,800   2,400
.40, Revolver, 7 Shot, Octagon Barrel, Antique   1,550   2,000

Rifle, Pill Lock
.40, 7 Shot, Octagon Barrel, Antique   1,800   2,400
.40, Carbine, 7 Shot, Octagon Barrel, Antique   1,800   2,400

Bisbee, D. H.
Norway, Me. 1835-60

Rifle, Percussion
.44, Octagon Barrel, Silver Inlay, Antique   1,400   1,900

Bison
Handgun, Revolver
.22 LR/.22 WMR Combo, Adjustable Sights, Western Style, Single Action,
  Modern   25   35
.22 L.R.R.F., Adjustable Sights, Western Style, Single Action, Modern   20   30

Bittner, Gustav
Vejprty, Bohemia, Austria-Hungary C.1893

Handgun, Manual Repeater
Model 1893, 7.7mm Bittner, Box Magazine, Checkered Stocks, Antique   1,400   2,100

Blanch, John A.
London, England 1809-35

Handgun, Percussion
.68 Pair, Double Barrel, Side by Side, Officer's Belt Pistol, Engraved, Silver
  Inlay, Steel Furniture, Cased with Accessories, Antique   3,800   4,400
Pair, Pocket Pistol, Converted from Flintlock, High Quality, Cased with
  Accessories, Antique   1,800   2,400

Bland, T. & Sons
London & Birmingham, England from 1876

Shotgun, Double Barrel, Side by Side
12 Ga., Boxlock, Adjustable Choke, Color Case Hardened Frame,
  Engraved, Modern   1,000   1,350

Blangle, Joseph
Gratz, Styria, Austria, C.1670

Rifle, Wheel-Lock
Brass Furniture, Engraved, Silver Inlay, Light Ornamentation, Full-
  Stocked, Antique   4,500   6,000

Bleiberg
London, England C.1690

Handgun, Flintlock
Holster Pistol, Engraved, Silver Inlay, High Quality, Antique   8,500

Blickensdoerfer & Schilling
St. Louis, Mo. 1871-75

Rifle, Percussion
.48, Octagon Barrel, Fancy Wood, Brass Furniture, Antique   800   1,100

Bloodhound
Made by Hopkins & Allen C.1880

Handgun, Revolver
.22 Short R.F., 7 Shot, Spur Trigger, Solid Frame, Single Action, Antique   85   140

Blue Jacket
Made by Hopkins & Allen C.1880

Handgun, Revolver
Model 1, .22 Short R.F., 7 Shot, Spur Trigger, Solid Frame, Single Action,
Antique   85   140
Model 2, .32 Short R.F., 5 Shot, Spur Trigger, Solid Frame, Single Action,
Antique   85   150

Blue Whistler
Made by Hopkins & Allen C.1880

Handgun, Revolver
.32 Short R.F., 5 Shot, Spur Trigger, Solid Frame, Single Action, Antique   85   150

Blunt, Orison & Syms
N.Y.C. 1837-65

Rifle, Percussion
.37, Octagon Barrel, Brass Furniture, Antique   450   600

Bonanza
Made by Bacon Arms Co.

Handgun, Revolver
Model 1½, .22 Short R.F., 7 Shot, Spur Trigger, Solid Frame, Single
Action, Antique   85   150

Bond, Edward
London, England 1800-30

Handgun, Flintlock
.68, Pair Officers' Type, Holster Pistol, Brass Furniture, Plain, Antique   1,900   2,650

Bond, Wm.
London, England 1798-1812

Handgun, Flintlock
Pair, Folding Bayonet, Belt Pistol, Box Lock, Cannon Barrel, Brass Frame
and Barrel, Cased with Accessories, Antique   4,000   5,000

Bonehill, C. G.
Birmingham, England

Rifle, Double Barrel, Side by Side
.450 N.E. 3¼", Under-Lever, Recoil Pad, Plain, Modern   700   950

Boowles, R.
London, England C.1690

Handgun, Flintlock
Holster Pistol, Engraved, Iron Mounts, Medium Quality, Antique   650   1,100

Boss & Co. Ltd.
London, England 1832 to Date

Shotgun, Double Barrel, Over-Under
12. Ga., Single Selective Trigger, Straight Grip, Vent Rib, Trap Grade,
Cased, Modern   14,000   18,000

| 16 Ga., Double Trigger, Plain, Modern | 5,000 | 6,500 |
| 20 Ga., Single Selective Trigger, Vent Rib, High Quality, Modern | 16,500 | 21,000 |

Shotgun, Double Barrel, Side by Side

| 12 Ga., Vent Rib, Fancy Wood, Fancy Checkering, Fancy Engraving, Modern | 4,500 | 6,000 |
| Pair, 12 Ga., Straight Grip, Plain, Cased, Modern | 8,500 | 12,000 |

Boston Bulldog
Made by Iver Johnson, Sold by J.P. Lovell & Sons; Boston, Mass.

Handgun, Revolver

.22 Short R.F., 7 Shot, Double Action, Solid Frame, Modern	45	85
.32 S & W, 5 Shot, Double Action, Solid Frame, Modern	45	80
.32 Short R.F., 5 Shot, Double Action, Solid Frame, Modern	45	75
.38 S & W, 5 Shot, Double Action, Solid Frame, Modern	45	80
.38 Short R.F., 5 Shot, Double Action, Solid Frame, Modern	35	75

Boyington, John
S. Coventry, Conn. 1841-47

Rifle, Percussion

| .50, Octagon Barrel, Brass Furniture, Antique | 600 | 800 |

Boy's Choice
Made by Hood Firearms Co. C.1875

Handgun, Revolver

| .22 Short R.F., 7 Shot, Spur Trigger, Solid Frame, Single Action, Antique | 90 | 150 |

Breda
Italy, Diana Import Co., Current

Shotgun, Double Barrel, Over-Under

| .410 Ga., Light Engraving, Checkered Stock, Modern | 250 | 325 |

Shotgun, Semi-Automatic

"Magnum", 12 Ga., Mag. 3", Checkered Stock, Vent Rib, Lightweight, Modern	300	375
Grade 1, 12 Ga., Checkered Stock, Vent Rib, Lightweight, Engraved, Modern	350	425
Grade 2, 12 Ga., Fancy Checkering, Vent Rib, Lightweight, Fancy Engraving, Modern	425	550
Grade 3, 12 Ga., Fancy Checkering, Vent Rib, Lightweight, Fancy Engraving, Modern	500	625
Standard, 12 Ga., Checkered Stock, Plain Barrel, Lightweight, Modern	175	240
Standard, 12 Ga., Checkered Stock, Vent Rib, Lightweight Modern	185	250

B.R.F.
Successor to Pretoria Arms Factory, South Africa, about 1957.

Handgun, Semi-Automatic

| "Junior," .25 ACP, Clip Fed, Blue, Modern | 200 | 300 |

B.R.F. .25 ACP

"Junior," .25 ACP, Clip Fed, Factory Chrome Plated, Modern   300   400
"Junior," for Cocking Indicator, Add $75-$125

Briggs, William
Norristown, Pa. 1848-75

Shotgun, Percussion
12 Ga., Under-Hammer, Antique   175   250

British Bulldog
Made by Forehand & Wadsworth

Handgun, Revolver
.32 S & W, 7 Shot, Double Action, Solid Frame, Antique   45   85
.38 S & W, 6 Shot, Double Action, Solid Frame, Antique   45   85
.44 S & W, 5 Shot, Double Action, Solid Frame, Antique   60   125

British Bulldog
Made by Johnson, Bye, & Co. Sold by J. P. Lovell 1881-82

Handgun, Revolver
.32 S & W, 5 Shot, Double Action, Solid Frame, Modern   45   85
.38 S & W, 5 Shot, Double Action, Solid Frame, Modern   45   85
.44 S & W, 5 Shot, Double ACtion, Solid Frame, Modern   60   125

British Military

Automatic Weapon, Assault Rifle
Sterling-AR18S, .223 Rem., Clip Fed, Short Rifle, Class 3   750   950

Automatic Weapon, Heavy Machine Gun
M1906 Marlin, .303 British, Belt Fed, Tripod, Potato Digger, Military,
    Class 3   1,250   1,600
Vickers Mk I, .303 British, Belt Fed, Tripod, Class 3   4,500   5,500

Automatic Weapon, Light Machine Gun
Bren Mk II, .303 British, Clip Fed, Bipod, Class 3   4,000   5,000
Hotchkiss Mk I*, .303 British, all Metal, Tripod, Class 3   950   1,400
Lewis Gun, .303 British, Drum Magazine, Bipod, Class 3   1,250   1,600

Automatic Weapon, Submachine Gun
Lanchester Mk I*, 9mm Luger, Wood Stock, Clip Fed, Military, Class 3   500   650
Lanchester Mk I*, 9mm Luger, Wood Stock, Dewat, Clip Fed, Military,
    Class 3   275   350
Sten Mk II, 9mm Luger, all Metal, Clip Fed, Military, Class 3   400   550
Sten Mk II S, 9mm Luger, Clip Fed, all Metal, Military, Silencer, Class 3   550   800
Sten Mk III, 9mm Luger, Clip Fed, all Metal, Military, Class 3   450   600
Sterling L2A3, 9mm, Clip Fed, all Metal, Military, Class 3   600   800
Sterling L3A1, 9mm, Clip Fed, all Metal, Military, Silencer, Class 3   675   875
Thompson M1928, .45 ACP, Clip Fed, with Compensator, Lyman Sights,
    Finned Barrel, Class 3   2,500   3,000

Handgun, Flintlock
.58, New Land M1796 Tower, Long Tapered Round Barrel, Belt Hook,
    Brass Furniture, Antique   1,000   1,400
.67, George III Tower, Calvary Pistol, Military, Tapered Round Barrel,
    Brass Furniture, Antique   725   975
.80, Modified M1796 Spooner, Holster Pistol, Plain Brass Furniture,
    Antique   900   1,300

Handgun, Revolver
#2 Mk I, .38 S & W, Military, Top Break, Modern   80   120
#2 Mk I R.A.F., .38 S & W, Military, Top Break, Modern   90   135
S & W M38/200, .38 S & W, Solid Frame, Swing-Out Cylinder, Double
    Action, Military, Modern   95   145

Webley Mk I, .455 Revolver Mk I, Top Break, Round Butt, Military, Antique	175	250
Webley Mk I*, .455 Revolver Mk I, Top Break, Round Butt, Military, Antique	165	240
Webley Mk I**, .455 Revolver Mk I, Top Break, Round Butt, Military, Modern	125	175
Webley Mk II, .455 Revolver Mk I, Top Break, Round Butt, Military, Modern	160	220
Webley Mk II*, .455 Revolver Mk I, Top Break, Round Butt, Military, Modern	125	175
Webley Mk II**, .455 Revolver Mk I, Top Break, Round Butt, Military, Modern	125	175
Webley Mk III, .455 Revolver Mk I, Top Break, Round Butt, Military, Modern	160	220
Webley Mk IV, .455 Revolver Mk I, Top Break, Round Butt, Military, Modern	150	200
Webley Mk V, .455 Revolver Mk I, Top Break, Round Butt, Military, Modern	160	220
Webley Mk VI, .455 Revolver Mk I, Top Break, Square Butt, Military, Modern	125	175

Handgun, Semi-Automatic

M1911A1 Colt, .455 Webley Auto., Clip Fed, Military, Modern	275	375

Rifle, Bolt Action

#1 Mk III*, .303 British, Tangent Sights, Military, Ishapore, Modern	80	135
#3 Mk I* (1914 Enfield,) .303 British, Military, Modern	95	150
Lee Metford Mk I, .303 British, Clip Fed, Carbine, Modern	125	190
Lee Metford Mk I, .303 British, Clip Fed, Modern	120	175
Lee Metford MK 1 *, .303 British, Clip Fed, Carbine, Modern	95	175
Lee Metford MK II, .303 British, Clip Fed, Modern	95	175
Lee Metford MK II *, .303 British, Clip Fed, Modern	125	190
M1896 Lee Metford, .303 British, Clip Fed, Military, Carbine, Modern	90	160
MK V Jungle Carbine, .303 British, Peep Sights, Military, Modern	135	200
Pattern 14 (U.S.), .303 British, Modern	120	175
S M L E #1 MK III, .303 British, Military, Modern	90	150
S M L E #1 MK III*, .303 British, Military, Modern	80	135
S M L E #2 MK IV, .22 L.R.R.F., Singleshot, Training Rifle, Modern	95	160
S M L E #4 MK I*, .303 British, Military, Lightweight, Modern	90	145
S M L E #4 MK I*, .303 British, Military, Modern	80	125
S M L E #7, .22 L.R.R.F., Singleshot, Training Rifle, Modern	125	175
S M L E #8, .22 L.R.R.F., Singleshot, Training Rifle, Modern	125	175

Rifle, Flintlock

.75, 1st Model Brown Bess, Musket, Brass Furniture, Antique	2,500	3,000
.75, 2nd Model Brown Bess, Musket, Military, Antique	1,150	1,750
.75, 3rd Model Brown Bess, Musket, Military, Antique	900	1,300

Rifle, Percussion

.58 Snider-Enfield, Military, Musket, Antique	275	425
.60 M 1856 Tower, Military, Musket, Antique	225	350
.60 M 1869 Enfield, Military, Musket, Antique	250	375

British Military #1 Mk.III

36

Rifle, Singleshot
Martini-Henry, .303 British, Carbine, Antique	95	175
Martini-Henry, .303 British, Antique	125	185
Martini-Henry, .577/.450 Martini-Henry, Carbine, Antique	95	170
Martini-Henry, .577/.450 Martini-Henry, Antique	125	190
Martini-Henry, .577/.450 Martini-Henry, Long Lever, Antique	90	170

BRNO
Czechoslovakia, by Ceska Zbrojovka

Rifle, Bolt Action
2I H, Various Calibers, Sporting Rifle, Express Sights, Cheekpiece, Checkered Stock, Set Trigger, Modern	450	650
22 F, Various Calibers, Sporting Rifle, Express Sights, Mannlicher, Checkered Stock, Set Trigger, Modern	475	675
Model I, .22 L.R.R.F., Sporting Rifle, Express Sights, 5 Shot Clip, Checkered Stock, Set Trigger, Modern	175	325
Model II, .22 L.R.R.F., Sporting Rifle, Express Sights, 5 Shot Clip, Fancy Wood, Set Trigger, Modern	200	375
Z-B Mauser, .22 Hornet, Sporting Rifle, Express Sights, 5 Shot Clip, Checkered Stock, Set Trigger, Modern	475	675

Brockway, Norman S.
Bellows Falls, Vt. From 1867

Rifle, Percussion
Various Calibers, Target Rifle, Antique	1,250	2,000

Bronco
Imported by Garcia

Combination Weapon, Over-Under
.22/.410, Skeleton Stock, Modern	40	60

Rifle, Singleshot
Skeleton Stock, Modern	30	45

Shotgun, Singleshot
.410 Ga., Skeleton Stock, Modern	40	55

Bronco
Spain Unknown Maker C.1910

Handgun, Semi-Automatic
1918 Vest Pocket, .32 ACP, Clip Fed, Modern	85	135
Vest Pocket, .25 ACP, Clip Fed, Modern	60	100
Vest Pocket, .25 ACP, Clip Fed, Light Engraving, Modern	80	135

Bronco .25 ACP

Brooklyn Arms Slocum Revolver

Brooklyn Arms Co.
Brooklyn, N.Y., C. 1863

Handgun, Revolver

Slocum Patent, .32 R.F., 5 Shot Cylinder with Sliding Chambers, Spur Trigger, Single Action, Engraved, Antique	175	300

Brown Mfg. Co.
Newburyport, Mass. 1869-73 Also see Ballard Rifles

Rifle, Bolt Action

1853 Long Enfield, .58 U.S. Musket, Converted from Percussion, Brass Furniture, Antique	400	550
U.S. M1861 Musket, .58 U.S. Musket, Converted from Percussion, Brass Furniture, Antique	400	550

Rifle, Singleshot

Ballard, .44 Long R.F., Falling Block, Mid-Range Target Rifle, Antique	700	900

Brown, John & Sons
Poplin & Fremont, N.H. 1840-71

Rifle, Percussion

Various Calibers, Sporting Rifle, Antique	675	1,200
.50, Target Rifle, Scope Mounted, Set Trigger, Antique	1,200	1,750

Browning
Established 1870 in St. Louis, Mo., now at Morgan, Utah

Handgun, Semi-Automatic

Various Calibers, Baby-.380-Hi Power Set, Renaissance, Nickel Plated, Engraved, Modern	1,750	2,500
380 Auto, .380 ACP, Clip Fed, Renaissance, Nickel Plated, Engraved, Modern	475	625
380 Auto, .380 ACP, Clip Fed, Adjustable Sights, Modern	95	155
380 Auto Standard, .380 ACP, Clip Fed, Modern	95	135
Baby, .25 ACP, Clip Fed, Lightweight, Nickel Plated, Modern	190	250
Baby, .25 ACP, Clip Fed, Renaissance, Nickel Plated, Engraved, Modern	350	475
Baby Standard, .25 ACP, Clip Fed, Modern	125	200

Browning Baby

Browning Renaissance Challenger

Hi Power

Medalist

BDA 380, .380 ACP, Clip Fed, Double Action, Fixed Sights, Modern	175	225
BDA 45, .45 ACP, Clip Fed, Double Action, 7 Shot, Modern	240	285
BDA 9, 9mm Luger, Clip Fed, Double Action, 9 Shot, Modern	230	275
Challenger, .22 L.R.R.F., Clip Fed, Checkered Wood Grips, Adjustable Sights, Modern	135	200
Challenger, .22 L.R.R.F., Clip Fed, Renaissance, Checkered Wood Grips, Fancy Engraving, Nickel Plated, Modern	375	550
Challenger, .22 L.R.R.F., Clip Fed, Checkered Wood Grips, Gold Inlays, Engraved, Modern	350	500
Challenger II, .22 L.R.R.F., Clip Fed, Adjustable Sights, Modern	95	145
Hi Power, 9mm, Clip Fed, Military, Tangent Sights, Curio	375	500
Hi Power, 9mm, Clip Fed, Military, Tangent Sights, with Detachable Shoulder Stock, Curio	650	850
Hi Power, 9mm, Clip Fed, Military, Curio	350	475
Hi Power, 9mm, Clip Fed, Military, with Detachable Shoulder Stock, Curio	525	700
Hi Power Inglis #1 Mk I, 9mm, Tangent Sights, Slotted for Shoulder Stock, Military, Modern	600	900
Hi Power Inglis #1 Mk I*, 9mm, Tangent Sights, Slotted for Shoulder Stock, Military, Modern	500	800
Hi Power Inglis #2 Mk I, 9mm, Fixed Sights, Military, Modern	475	700

Browning Challenger II

Browning Inglis Mk.I* 9mm

Hi Power Inglis #2 Mk I*, 9mm, Tangent Sights, Slotted for Shoulder Stock, Military, Modern	350	550
Hi Power Louis XVI, Fancy Engraving, Nickel Plated, Fixed Sights, Cased, Modern	600	900
Hi Power Louis XVI, Fancy Engraving, Nickel Plated, Adjustable Sights, Cased, Modern	625	925
Hi Power, 9mm, Clip Fed, Renaissance, Nickel Plated, Engraved, Modern	700	950
Hi Power, 9mm, Clip Fed, Renaissance, Nickel Plated, Engraved, Adjustable Sights, Modern	750	975
Hi Power, 9mm, Clip Fed, with Lanyard Ring Hammer, Renaissance, Nickel Plated, Engraved, Modern	725	1,000
Hi Power Standard, 9mm, Nickel Plating, Add $30-$45		
Hi Power Standard, 9mm, Clip Fed, with Lanyard Ring Hammer, Modern	250	350
Hi Power Standard, 9mm, Clip Fed, with Spur Hammer, Modern	200	300
Hi Power Standard, 9mm, Clip Fed, with Spur Hammer, Adjustable Sights, Modern	225	325
Model 1900, .32 ACP, Clip Fed, Modern	95	175
Model 1900, .32 ACP, Clip Fed, Military, Modern	125	225
Model 1903, 9mm Browning Long, Clip Fed, Modern	140	225
Model 1903, 9mm Browning Long, Clip Fed, Cut for Shoulder Stock, Military, Modern	325	500
Model 1910, .32 and .380 ACP, Clip Fed, Modern	90	150
Model 1922, .32 and .380 ACP, Clip Fed, Modern	95	160

Browning Model 1903

Browning Model 1910 .32 ACP

Browning Medalist .22 Cased

Model 1922, .32 ACP, Nazi-Proofed, Clip Fed, Military, Modern	125	200
Medalist, .22 L.R.R.F., Clip Fed, Checkered Wood Target Grips, Wood Forestock, Target Sights, Modern	300	500
Medalist, .22 L.R.R.F., Clip Fed, Renaissance, Checkered Wood Target Grips, Fancy Engraving, Target Sights, Modern	625	850
Medalist, .22 L.R.R.F., Clip Fed, Checkered Wood Target Grips, Wood Forestock, Gold Inlays, Engraved, Modern	575	800
Medalist International, .22 L.R.R.F., Clip Fed, Checkered Wood Target Grips, Target Sights, Modern	250	400
Medalist International, .22 L.R.R.F., Clip Fed, Checkered Wood Target Grips, Gold Inlays, Engraved, Target Sights, Modern	475	700
Medalist International, .22 L.R.R.F., Clip Fed, Renaissance, Checkered Wood Target Grips, Fancy Engraving, Target Sights, Modern	500	750
Nomad, .22 L.R.R.F., Clip Fed, Plastic Grips, Adjustable Sights, Modern	125	175

Rifle, Bolt Action

Medallion Grade, .458 Win. Mag., Long Action, Fancy Wood, Fancy Checkering, Engraved, Open Rear Sight, Modern	700	950
Medallion Grade, Various Calibers, Short Action, Fancy Wood, Fancy Checkering, Engraved, Modern	675	800
Medallion Grade, Various Calibers, Long Action, Fancy Wood, Fancy Checkering, Engraved, Modern	675	850
Medallion Grade, Various Calibers, Long Action, Magnum, Fancy Wood, Fancy Checkering, Engraved, Modern	725	975
Olympian Grade, .458 Win. Mag., Long Action, Fancy Wood, Fancy Checkering, Engraved, Modern	1,350	2,000
Olympian Grade, Various Calibers, Short Action, Fancy Wood, Fancy Checkering, Fancy Engraving, Modern	950	1,600
Olympian Grade, Various Calibers, Medium Action, Fancy Wood, Fancy Checkering, Fancy Engraving, Modern	950	1,600
Olympian Grade, Various Calibers, Long Action, Fancy Wood, Fancy Checkering, Fancy Engraving, Modern	1,200	1,800
Olympian Grade, Various Calibers, Long Action, Magnum, Fancy Wood, Fancy Checkering, Fancy Engraving, Modern	1,250	1,900
Safari Grade, Various Calibers, Short Action, Checkered Stock, Modern	350	600
Safari Grade, Various Calibers, Medium Action, Checkered Stock, Modern	425	650
Safari Grade, Various Calibers, Long Action, Checkered Stock, Modern	475	750
Safari Grade, Various Calibers, Long Action, Magnum, Checkered Stock, Modern	575	800
T-Bolt T-1, .22 L.R.R.F., 5 Shot Clip, Plain, Open Rear Sight, Modern	50	90
T-Bolt T-1, .22 L.R.R.F., 5 Shot Clip, Plain, Open Rear Sight, Left-Hand, Modern	55	100
T-Bolt T-2, .22 L.R.R.F., 5 Shot Clip, Checkered Stock, Fancy Wood, Open Rear Sight, Modern	60	115
BBR, Various Calibers, Long Action, Clip Fed, Checkered Stock, Modern	225	300

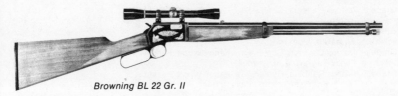

Browning BL 22 Gr. II

Browning BLR

Rifle, Lever Action

BL-22, .22 L.R.R.F., Belgian Mfg., Add 10%-20%

BL-22 Grade 1, .22 L.R.R.F., Tube Feed, Checkered Stock, Modern	90	140
BL-22 Grade 2, .22 L.R.R.F., Tube Feed, Checkered Stock, Light Engraving, Modern	95	160
BLR, Various Calibers, Center-Fire, Plain, Clip Fed, Checkered Stock, Modern	175	250
Model 92, .44 Mag., Tube Feed, Open Sights, Modern	165	225
Model 92 Centennial, Tube Feed, Open Sights, Commemorative, Modern	250	375

Rifle, Percussion

J Browning Mountain Rifle, Various Calibers, Singleshot, Octagon Barrel, Open Rear Sight, Single Set Trigger, Brass Finish, Reproduction, Antique	200	300
J Browning Mountain Rifle, Various Calibers, Singleshot, Octagon Barrel, Open Rear Sight, Single Set Trigger, Browned Finish, Reproduction, Antique	200	300

Rifle, Semi-Automatic

Auto-Rifle, .22 L.R.R.F., Belgian Mfg., Add 10%-20%

Auto-Rifle Grade I, .22 L.R.R.F., Tube Feed, Takedown, Open Rear Sight, Checkered Stock, Modern	95	150
Auto-Rifle Grade I, .22 Short, Tube Feed, Takedown, Open Rear Sight, Checkered Stock, Modern	95	150
Auto-Rifle Grade II, .22 L.R.R.F., Tube Feed, Takedown, Open Rear Sight, Satin Chrome Receiver, Engraved, Modern	165	225
Auto-Rifle Grade III, .22 L.R.R.F., Takedown, Satin Chrome Receiver, Fancy Wood, Fancy Checkering, Fancy Engraving, Modern	425	550
BAR, .22 L.R.R.F., Checkered Stock, Modern	95	145

BAR, Various Calibers, Center-Fire, Belgian Mfg., Add 10%-20%

BAR, Various Calibers, Center-Fire, Add 10% for Magnum Calibers

BAR Grade 1, Various Calibers, Center-Fire, Checkered Stock, Plain, Modern	250	375

Browning .22 Auto Rifle Gr. II

BAR Grade 2, Various Calibers, Center-Fire, Checkered Stock, Light
Engraving, Modern   300   450
BAR Grade 3, Various Calibers, Center-Fire, Fancy Wood, Fancy
Checkering, Engraved, Modern   450   675
BAR Grade 4, Various Calibers, Center-Fire, Fancy Wood, Fancy
Checkering, Fancy Engraving, Modern   850   1,300
BAR Grade 5, Various Calibers, Center-Fire, Fancy Wood, Fancy
Checkering, Fancy Engraving, Gold Inlays, Modern   1,450   2,000

Rifle, Singleshot
Model 78, Various Calibers, Various Barrel Styles, Checkered Stock,
Modern   250   325
Model 78, 45-70 Govt., Bicentennial Commemorative, Checkered Stock,
Modern   1,250   1,950

Rifle, Double Barrel, Over-Under
Superposed Continental, 20 Ga. and 30/06, Engraved, Fancy Wood, Fancy
Checkering, Modern   2,750   3,500
Express Rifle, 30/06 or .270 Win., Engraved, Fancy wood, Fancy
Checkering, Cased, Modern   2,200   2,750
Centennial Superposed, 20 Ga. and 30/06, Engraved, Fancy Checkering,
Fancy Wood, Cased, Commemorative, Modern   5,000   7,250

Rifle, Slide Action
BPR, .22 L.R.R.F., Grade I, Checkered Stock, Modern   95   150
BPR, .22 Mag., Grade I, Checkered Stock, Modern   100   160
BPR, .22 Mag., Grade II, Checkered Stock, Engraved, Modern   150   225

Browning B-78 Rifle

Browning BPR .22 Rifle

Shotgun, Double Barrel, Over-Under
Citori, 12 Ga., Trap Grade, Vent Rib, Checkered Stock, Modern   350   475
Citori, 12 and 20 Gauges, Field Grade, Vent Rib, Checkered Stock,
Modern   325   425
Citori, 12 and 20 Gauges, Skeet Grade, Vent Rib, Checkered Stock,
Modern   325   425
Citori International, 12 Ga., Trap Grade, Vent Rib, Checkered Stock,
Modern   375   475
Citori Grade II, Various Gauges, Hunting Model, Engraved, Checkered
Stock, Single Selective Trigger, Modern   550   800
Citori Grade II, Trap and Skeet Models, Add 10%
Citori Grade V, Various Gauges, Fancy Engraving, Checkered Stock,
Single Selective Trigger, Modern   800   1,250
Citori Grade V, Trap and Skeet Models, Add 10%
Citori International, 12 Ga., Skeet Grade, Vent Rib, Checkered Stock,
Modern   375   475

Superposed, 12 Ga., Broadway Trap Model, Presentation Grade 4, Fancy Engraving, with Sideplates, Gold Inlays, Fancy Checkering, Fancy Wood, Modern	5,500	7,250
Superposed, 12 Ga., Lightning Trap Model, Presentation Grade 4, Fancy Engraving, with Sideplates, Gold Inlays, Fancy Checkering, Fancy Wood, Modern	5,400	7,150
Superposed, 12 Ga., Broadway Trap Model, Presentation Grade 4, Fancy Engraving, with Sideplates, Fancy Checkering, Fancy Wood, Modern	4,750	6,250
Superposed, 12 Ga., Lightning Trap Model, Presentation Grade 4, Fancy Engraving, with Sideplates, Fancy Checkering, Fancy Wood, Modern	4,650	6,150
Superposed, 12 Ga., Broadway Trap Model, Presentation Grade 3, Fancy Engraving, Gold Inlays, Fancy Checkering, Fancy Wood, Modern	4,250	5,500
Superposed, 12 Ga., Lightning Trap Model, Presentation Grade 3, Fancy Engraving, Gold Inlays, Fancy Checkering, Fancy Wood, Modern	4,150	5,400
Superposed, 12 Ga., Broadway Trap Model, Presentation Grade 2, Fancy Engraving, Fancy Checkering, Fancy Wood, Modern	2,750	3,400
Superposed, 12 Ga., Lightning Trap Model, Presentation Grade 2, Fancy Engraving, Fancy Checkering, Fancy Wood, Modern	2,650	3,300
Superposed, 12 Ga., Broadway Trap Model, Presentation Grade 2, Fancy Engraving, Gold Inlays, Fancy Checkering, Fancy Wood, Modern	3,000	4,000
Superposed, 12 Ga., Lightning Trap Model, Presentation Grade 2, Fancy Engraving, Gold Inlays, Fancy Checkering, Fancy Wood, Modern	3,000	4,000
Superposed, 12 Ga., Broadway Trap Model, Presentation Grade 1, Engraved, Gold Inlays, Fancy Checkering, Fancy Wood, Modern	2,250	3,000
Superposed, 12 Ga., Lightning Trap Model, Presentation Grade 1, Engraved, Gold Inlays, Fancy Checkering, Fancy Wood, Modern	2,200	2,950
Superposed, 12 Ga., Broadway Trap Model, Presentation Grade 1, Engraved, Fancy Checkering, Fancy Wood, Modern	2,000	2,750
Superposed, 12 Ga., Lightning Trap Model, Presentation Grade 1, Engraved, Fancy Checkering, Fancy Wood, Modern	1,950	2,700
Superposed, 12 and 20 Gauges, Lightning Skeet Model, Presentation Grade 4, Fancy Engraving, with Sideplates, Gold Inlays, Fancy Checkering, Fancy Wood, Modern	4,250	6,800
Superposed, 12 and 20 Gauges, Super-Light Hunting Model, Presentation Grade 4, Extra Barrels, Fancy Engraving, with Sideplates, Gold Inlays, Fancy Checkering, Fancy Wood, Modern	6,000	7,500
Superposed, 12 and 20 Gauges, Lightning Hunting Model, Presentation Grade 4, Fancy Engraving, with Sideplates, Gold Inlays, Fancy Checkering, Fancy Wood, Extra Barrels, Modern	6,000	7,500
Superposed, 12 and 20 Gauges, Lightning Skeet Model, Presentation Grade 4, Fancy Engraving, with Sideplates, Fancy Checkering, Fancy Wood, Extra Barrels, Modern	5,000	7,000
Superposed, 12 and 20 Gauges, Super-Light Hunting Model, Presentation Grade 4, Fancy Engraving, with Sideplates, Fancy Checkering, Fancy Wood, Extra Barrels, Modern	5,000	7,000
Superposed, 12 and 20 Gauges, Lightning Hunting Model, Presentation Grade 4, Fancy Engraving, with Sideplates, Fancy Checkering, Fancy Wood, Extra Barrels, Modern	5,000	7,000
Superposed, 12 and 20 Gauges, Lightning Skeet Model, Presentation Grade 3, Fancy Engraving, Gold Inlays, Fancy Checkering, Fancy Wood, Modern	3,400	4,750
Superposed, 12 and 20 Gauges, Super-Light Hunting Model, Presentation Grade 2, Fancy Engraving, Fancy Checkering, Fancy Wood, Extra Barrels, Modern	2,900	4,400
Superposed, 12 and 20 Gauges, Lightning Hunting Model, Presentation Grade 2, Fancy Engraving, Fancy Checkering, Fancy Wood, Extra Barrels, Modern	2,900	4,400
Superposed, 12 and 20 Gauges, Lightning Skeet Model, Presentation Grade 2, Fancy Engraving, Gold Inlays, Fancy Checkering, Fancy Wood, Modern	3,000	4,000
Superposed, 12 and 20 Gauges, Super-Light Hunting Model, Presentation Grade 2, Fancy Engraving, Gold Inlays, Fancy Checkering, Fancy Wood, Extra Barrels, Modern	3,850	5,350

Superposed, 12 and 20 Gauges, Lightning Hunting Model, Presentation Grade 2, Fancy Engraving, Gold Inlays, Fancy Checkering, Fancy Wood, Extra Barrels, Modern	3,850	5,350
Superposed, 12 and 20 Gauges, Lightning Skeet Model, Presentation Grade 1, Engraved, Gold Inlays, Fancy Checkering, Fancy Wood, Modern	2,300	3,150
Superposed, 12 and 20 Gauges, Super-Light Hunting Model, Presentation Grade 1, Engraved, Gold Inlays, Fancy Checkering, Fancy Wood, Modern	2,250	3,100
Superposed, 12 and 20 Gauges, Lightning Hunting Model, Presentation Grade 1, Engraved, Gold Inlays, Fancy Checkering, Fancy Wood, Modern	2,200	3,100
Superposed, 12 and 20 Gauges, Lightning Skeet Model, Presentation Grade 1, Engraved, Fancy Checkering, Fancy Wood, Modern	2,100	2,800
Superposed, 12 and 20 Gauges, Super-Light Hunting Model, Presentation Grade 1, Engraved, Fancy Checkering, Fancy Wood, Modern	2,100	2,800
Superposed, 12 and 20 Gauges, Lightning Hunting Model, Presentation Grade 1, Engraved, Fancy Checkering, Fancy Wood, Modern	2,000	2,700
Superposed, 28 Ga. or .410 Ga., Lightning Skeet Model, Presentation Grade 4, Fancy Engraving, with Sideplates, Gold Inlays, Fancy Checkering, Fancy Wood, Modern	4,950	6,550
Superposed, 28 Ga. or .410 Ga., Lightning Hunting Model, Presentation Grade 4, Fancy Engraving, with Sideplates, Gold Inlays, Fancy Checkering, Fancy Wood, Modern	4,900	6,500
Superposed, 28 Ga. or .410 Ga., Lightning Skeet Model, Presentation Grade 4, Fancy Engraving, with Sideplates, Fancy Checkering, Fancy Wood, Modern	4,300	5,800
Superposed, 28 Ga. or .410 Ga., Lightning Hunting Model, Presentation Grade 4, Fancy Engraving, with Sideplates, Fancy Checkering, Fancy Wood, Modern	4,300	5,700
Superposed, 28 Ga. or .410 Ga., Lightning Skeet Model, Presentation Grade 3, Fancy Engraving, Gold Inlays, Fancy Checkering, Fancy Wood, Modern	3,800	5,000
Superposed, 28 Ga. or .410 Ga., Lightning Hunting Model, Presentation Grade 3, Fancy Engraving, Gold Inlays, Fancy Checkering, Fancy Wood, Modern	3,750	4,950
Superposed, 28 Ga. or .410 Ga., Lightning Skeet Model, Presentation Grade 2, Fancy Engraving, Fancy Checkering, Fancy Wood, Modern	2,600	3,450
Superposed, 28 Ga. or .410 Ga., Lightning Hunting Model, Presentation Grade 2, Fancy Engraving, Fancy Checkering, Fancy Wood, Modern	2,550	3,400
Superposed, 28 Ga. or .410 Ga., Lightning Skeet Model, Presentation Grade 2, Fancy Engraving, Gold Inlays, Fancy Checkering, Fancy Wood, Modern	3,100	4,150
Superposed, 28 Ga. or .410 Ga., Lightning Hunting Model, Presentation Grade 2, Fancy Engraving, Gold Inlays, Fancy Checkering, Fancy Wood, Modern	3,000	4,100
Superposed, 28 Ga. or .410 Ga., Lightning Skeet Model, Presentation Grade 1, Engraved, Gold Inlays, Fancy Checkering, Fancy Wood, Modern	2,450	3,250
Superposed, 28 Ga. or .410 Ga., Lightning Hunting Model, Presentation Grade 1, Engraved, Gold Inlays, Fancy Checkering, Fancy Wood, Modern	2,400	3,200
Superposed, 28 Ga. or .410 Ga., Lightning Skeet Model, Presentation Grade 1, Engraved, Fancy Checkering, Fancy Wood, Modern	2,150	2,900
Superposed, 28 Ga. or .410 Ga., Lightning Hunting Model, Presentation Grade 1, Engraved, Fancy Checkering, Fancy Wood, Modern	2,000	2,750
Superposed, Various Gauges, Presentation Grade 4, Extra Sets of Barrels, Add for each: $1,100-$1,600		
Superposed, Various Gauges, Presentation Grade 3, Extra Sets of Barrels, Add for each: $950-$1,500		
Superposed, Various Gauges, Presentation Grade 2, Extra Sets of Barrels, Add for each: $850-$1,250		

Superposed, Various Gauges, Presentation Grade 1, Extra Sets of Barrels,
Add for each: $800-$1,100
Superposed, Various Gauges, Lightning Skeet, Add 5%-10%
Superposed, Various Gauges, Extra Barrel, Add 35%-40%
Superposed, Various Gauges, 4-Barrel, Skeet Set, Add 275%-300%
Superposed, Various Gauges, Raised Solid Rib, Pre-War, Add $50-$75
Superposed, Various Gauges, Vent Rib, Pre-War, Add 10%-15%
Superposed, Various Gauges, Super-Light Lightning, Add 15%-20%
Superposed, Various Gauges, Lightning Trap Model, Add 5%-10%
Superposed, Various Gauges, Broadway Trap Model, Add 8%-13%

Superposed, Various Gauges, Super Exhibition Grade, Fancy Wood, Fancy Checkering, Fancy Engraving, Gold Inlays, Modern		30,000
Superposed, Various Gauges, Field Grade, Engraved, Checkered Stock, Vent Rib, Single Selective Trigger, Modern	950	1,450
Superposed, Various Gauges, Pointer Grade, Fancy Engraving, Fancy Checkering, Single Selective Trigger, Modern	1,650	2,350
Superposed, Various Gauges, Pigeon Grade Hunting Model, Satin Nickel-Plated Frame, Fancy Engraving, Fancy Checkering, Fancy Wood, Modern	1,400	2,000
Superposed, Various Gauges, Diana Grade Hunting Model, Satin Nickel-Plated Frame, Fancy Engraving, Fancy Checkering, Fancy Wood, Modern	1,750	2,500
Superposed, Various Gauges, Midas Grade Hunting Model, Fancy Engraving, Fancy Checkering, Fancy Wood, Gold Inlays, Modern	2,650	3,850
Superposed Bicentennial, Fancy Engraving, Gold Inlays, Fancy Wood, Fancy Checkering, Cased, Commemorative, Modern		10,000
Grand Liege, 12 Ga., Engraved, Single Trigger, Checkered Stock, Modern	500	700
Liege, 12 Ga., Engraved, Single Trigger, Checkered Stock, Modern	350	550
ST-100, 12 Ga., Trap Special, Engraved, Checkered Stock, Modern	1800	2400

Browning Superposed, Pigeon Grade

Browning Superposed, Diana Grade

Browning Superposed, Midas Grade

Browning BSS Shotgun

Shotgun, Double Barrel, Side by Side

B-SS. 12 and 20 Gauges, Checkered Stock, Field Grade, Modern	250	325
B-SS, 12 and 20 Gauges, Checkered Stock, Grade II, Engraved, Modern	450	625

Shotgun, Semi-Automatic

Auto-5, Add for Belgian Make, 5%-10%		
Auto-5, I2 Ga., Trap Grade, Vent Rib, Checkered Stock, Modern	275	375
Auto-5, 12 and 20 Gauges, Magnum, Checkered Stock, Light Engraving, Plain Barrel, Modern	250	350
Auto-5, 12 and 20 Gauges, Skeet Grade, Checkered Stock, Light Engraving, Vent Rib, Modern	275	375
Auto-5, 16 Ga. 2$\frac{9}{16}$", Pre-WW2, Checkered Stock, Light Engraving, Plain Barrel, Modern	225	300
Auto-5, Various Gauges, Lightweight, Checkered Stock, Light Engraving, Plain Barrel, Modern	250	350
Auto-5, Various Gauges, Buck Special, Checkered Stock, Light Engraving, Plain Barrel, Modern	300	375
Auto-5, Various Gauges, Vent Rib, Add $30-$45		
Auto-5, Various Gauges, Raised Solid Rib, Pre-WW2, Add $20-$35		
Auto-5, Various Gauges, Diana Grade, Pre-WW2, Plain Barrel, Fancy Engraving, Modern	700	1,000
Auto-5, Various Gauges, Midas Grade, Pre-WW2, Plain Barrel, Fancy Engraving, Gold Inlays, Modern	900	1,350
Double-Auto, I2 Ga., Trap Model, Add 10-15%		
Double-Auto, I2 and 20 Gauges, Lightweight, Checkered Stock, Engraved, Plain Barrel, Modern	225	300
Double-Auto, I2 and 20 Gauges, Vent Rib, Add $30-$35		
Double-Auto, I2 and 20 Gauges, Skeet Model, Add 10-15%		
Model 2000, I2 Ga., Trap Grade, Vent Rib, Tube Feed, Checkered Stock, Modern	285	365
Model 2000, 12 and 20 Gauges, Vent Rib, Tube Feed, Checkered Stock, Modern	225	300
Model 2000, 12 and 20 Gauges, Buck Special, Open Rear Sight, Tube Feed, Checkered Stock, Modern	225	320
Model 2000, 12 and 20 Gauges, Skeet Grade, Vent Rib, Tube Feed, Checkered Stock, Modern	285	365

Browning 2000 Auto Shotgun

Browning BT 99 Competition

Shotgun, Singleshot
BT-99, 12 Ga., Trap Grade, Vent Rib, with extra Single Trap Barrel,
   Checkered Stock, Engraved, Modern   500   575
BT-99, 12 Ga., Pigeon Grade, Checkered Stock, Engraved, Vent Rib,
   Modern   750   1,000
BT-99, 12 Ga., Trap Grade, Vent Rib, Checkered Stock, Engraved, Modern   290   350

Shotgun, Slide Action
BPS, 12 Ga., Checkered Stock, Vent Rib, Modern   150   225
BPS, 12 Ga., Buck Special, Rifle Sights, Modern   175   250

Brutus
Made by Hood Firearm Co. C.1875-76

Handgun, Revolver
.22 Short R.F., 7 Shot, Spur Trigger, Solid Frame, Single Action, Antique   90   160

BSA
Birmingham Small Arms, Ltd, England. From 1885 to Date

Automatic Weapon, Light Machine Gun
Lewis Gun, .303 British, Drum Magazine, Bipod, Class 3   1,250   1,750

Rifle, Bolt Action
Imperial, Various Calibers, Sporting Rifle, Muzzle Brake, Checkered
   Stock, Open Rear Sight, Modern   125   200
Imperial, Various Calibers, Sporting Rifle, Muzzle Brake, Checkered
   Stock, Open Rear Sight, Lightweight, Modern   140   225
Majestic Deluxe, .458 Win. Mag., Sporting Rifle, Muzzle Brake,
   Lightweight, Checkered Stock, Open Rear Sight, Modern   165   250
Majestic Deluxe, Various Calibers, Sporting Rifle, Muzzle Brake,
   Lightweight, Checkered Stock, Open Rear Sight, Modern   145   225
Majestic Deluxe, Various Calibers, Sporting Rifle, Checkered Stock, Open
   Rear Sight, Modern   130   210
Monarch Deluxe, Various Calibers, Sporting Rifle, Checkered Stock,
   Open Rear Sight, Modern   150   235
Monarch Deluxe, Various Calibers, Varmint, Heavy Barrel, Checkered
   Stock, Open Rear Sight, Modern   165   245

Rifle, Singleshot
#12 Martini, .22 L.R.R.F., Target, Target Sights, Checkered Stock, Modern   150   225
#12/15 Martini, .22 L.R.R.F., Target, Target Sights, Target Stock, Modern   175   275
#12/15 Martini, .22 L.R.R.F., Target, Target Sights, Target Stock, Heavy
   Barrel, Modern   200   315
#13 Martini, .22 Hornet, Sporting Rifle, Checkered Stock, Modern   195   300
#13 Martini, .22 L.R.R.F., Target, Target Sights, Checkered Stock,
   Modern   150   225
#13 Martini, .22 L.R.R.F., Sporting Rifle, Checkered Stock, Modern   140   215
#15 Martini, .22 L.R.R.F., Target, Target Sights, Target Stock, Modern   260   350
Centurion Martini, .22 L.R.R.F., Target, Target Sights, Target Stock,
   Target Barrel, Modern   190   295
International Martini, .22 L.R.R.F., Target, Target Sights, Heavy Barrel,
   Target Stock, Modern   195   325
International MK 2 Martini, .22 L.R.R.F., Target, Target Sights, Target
   Stock, Modern   215   345

International MK 2 Martini, .22 L.R.R.F., Target, Target Sights, Target Stock, Heavy Barrel, Modern	195	325
International MK 3 Martini, .22 L.R.R.F., Target, Target Sights, Target Stock, Heavy Barrel, Modern	225	350
Mark V, .22 L.R.R.F., Heavy Barrel, Target Rifle. Target Sights, Target Stock, Modern	275	400
Martini I S U, .22 L.R.R.F., Target Rifle, Target Sights, Target Stock, Modern	275	400

Budischowsky
Made by Norton Armament (Norarmco), Mt. Clemens, Mich.

Handgun, Semi-Automatic

TP-70, .22 L.R.R.F., Clip Fed, Double Action, Pocket Pistol, Stainless Steel, Hammer, Modern	200	300
TP-70, .25 ACP, Clip Fed, Double Action, Pocket Pistol, Stainless Steel, Hammer, Presentation, Custom Serial Number, Curio	750	1,000
TP-70, .25 ACP, Clip Fed, Double Action, Pocket Pistol, Stainless Steel, Hammer, Modern	150	250

Bufalo
Gabilondo y Cia., Elgoibar, Spain

Handgun, Semi-Automatic

.32 ACP, Clip Fed, Modern	65	100

Buffalo Bill
Maker Unknown, Sold by Homer Fisher Co.

Handgun, Revolver

.22 Short R.F., 7 Shot, Spur Trigger, Solid Frame, Single Action, Antique	90	160

Bull Dozer
Made by Norwich Pistol Co., Sold by J. McBride & Co. C.1875-83

Handgun, Revolver

.22 Short R.F., 7 Shot, Spur Trigger, Solid Frame, Single Action, Antique	90	160
.38 Short R.F., 5 Shot, Spur Trigger, Solid Frame, Single Action, Antique	95	175
.41 Short R.F., 5 Shot, Spur Trigger, Solid Frame, Single Action, Antique	125	200
.44 Short R.F., 5 Shot, Spur Trigger, Solid Frame, Single Action, Antique	175	250

Bullard Repeating Arms Co.
Springfield, Mass. 1887-89

Rifle, Lever Action

Military, Full Stocked, with Bayonet, Open Rear Sight, Antique	1,600	2,500
Military, Full Stocked, with Bayonet, Open Rear Sight, Carbine, Antique	1,600	2,500
Various Calibers, Small Frame, Tube Feed, Round Barrel, Plain, Open Rear Sight, Sporting Rifle, Antique	375	625

Budischowski .25 ACP

Various Calibers, Tube Feed, Round Barrel, Plain, Open Rear Sight, Sporting Rifle, Antique	450	700
Various Calibers, Light Engraving, Add $50-$150		
Various Calibers, Medium Engraving, Add $200-$400		
Various Calibers, Ornate Engraving, Add $750-$1,000		
Various Calibers, Full Nickel Plating, Add $50-$75		
Various Calibers, for Fancy Wood, Add $25-$45		
Various Calibers, for Standard Checkering, Add $30-$45		
Various Calibers, Fancy Checkering, Add $70-$100		
Various Calibers, Octagon Barrel, Add $25-$50		
Various Calibers, Half-Octagon Barrel, Add $30-$60		
Various Calibers, Target Sights, Add $125-$175		
Various Calibers, for Lyman Sights, Add $40-$70		
Various Calibers, for Express Sights, Add $100-$150		

Rifle, Singleshot

Military, Full-Stocked, with Bayonet, Open Rear Sight, Antique	850	1,250
Military, Full-Stocked, with Bayonet, Open Rear Sight, Carbine, Antique	850	1,250
Various Calibers, Schuetzen Target Rifle, Octagon Barrel, Target Sights, Swiss Buttplate, Checkered Stock, Antique	750	1,750
Various Calibers, Sporting Rifle, Octagon Barrel, Open Rear Sight, Antique	450	700
Various Rimfires, Target Rifle, Octagon Barrel, Target Sights, Swiss Buttplate, Checkered Stock, Antique	500	800
Various Rimfires, Sporting Rifle, Octagon Barrel, Open Rear Sight, Antique	400	750

Bulldog
Made by Forehand & Wadsworth

Handgun, Revolver

.32 S & W, 7 Shot, Double Action, Solid Frame, Modern	45	85
.38 S & W, 6 Shot, Double Action, Solid Frame, Modern	45	85
.44 S & W, 5 Shot, Double Action, Solid Frame, Modern	60	115

Bulls Eye
Maker Unknown C.1875

Handgun, Revolver

.22 Short R.F., 7 Shot, Spur Trigger, Solid Frame, Single Action, Antique	90	150

Bulwark
Beistegui Hermanos, Eibar, Spain

Handgun, Semi-Automatic

.25 ACP, External Hammer, Clip Fed, Blue, Curio	175	250
.25 ACP, Hammerless, Clip Fed, Blue, Curio	75	125
.32 ACP, External Hammer, Clip Fed, Blue, Curio	150	225
.32 ACP, Hammerless, Clip Fed, Blue, Curio	75	125

Bumford
London, England 1730-60

Handgun, Flintlock

.38, Pocket Pistol, Box Lock, Queen Anne Style, Screw Barrel, Silver Inlay, Antique	400	650

Burgess, Andrew
Oswego, N.Y. 1874-1877

Rifle, Lever Action
Model 1876, .45-70 Government, Tube Feed, Octagon Barrel, Antique 675 1,500

Shotgun, Slide Action
12 Ga., Takedown, Solid Rib, Light Engraving, Antique 175 350

Bushmaster
Gwinn Arms Co., Winston-Salem, N.C.

Automatic Weapon, Machine-Pistol
.223 Rem., Clip Fed, Commercial, Class 3 375 500

Handgun, Semi-Automatic
Bushmaster, .223 Rem., Clip Fed, Modern 225 325

Rifle, Semi-Automatic
.223 Rem., Clip Fed, Wood Stock, Modern 200 300

Busoms
Spain C.1780

Handgun, Miquelet-Lock
.70 Pair, Belt Pistol, Belt Hook, Engraved, Brass Furniture, Antique 1,750 2,250

Bustindui, Augustin
Toledo, Spain C.1765

Handgun, Miquelet-Lock
Pair, Locks by Guisasola, Half-Octagon Barrel, Antique 4,500

Bustindiu, Juan Esteban
Eibar, Spain C.1775

Handgun, Miquelet-Lock
Pair, Half-Octagon Barrel, Silver Inlay, Light Ornamentation, Antique 3,500

Cadet
Sold by Maltby-Curtis Co.

Handgun, Revolver
.22 Long R.F., 7 Shot, Single Action, Solid Frame, Spur Trigger, Antique 80 135

Calderwood, William
Phila., Pa. 1808-16. See Kentucky Rifles and Pistols, U.S. Military

Canadian Military

Handgun, Semi-Automatic
Hi Power Inglis #1 Mk I, 9mm, Tangent Sights, Slotted for Shoulder Stock,
 Military, Modern 600 900
Hi Power Inglis #1 Mk I*, 9mm, Tangent Sights, Slotted for Shoulder
 Stock, Military, Modern 500 800
Hi Power Inglis #2 Mk I, 9mm, Fixed Sights, Military, Modern 475 700
Hi Power Inglis #2 Mk I*, 9mm, Tangent Sights, Slotted for Shoulder
 Stock, Military, Modern 350 550

Rifle, Bolt Action
1907 MK 2 Ross, .303 British, Full-Stocked, Military, Modern 125 175

Capt. Jack
Made by Hopkins & Allen 1871-75

Handgun, Revolver

.22 Short R.F., 7 Shot, Spur Trigger, Solid Frame, Single Action, Antique	85	150

Caroline Arms
Made by Crescent Firearms Co. 1892-1900

Shotgun, Double Barrel, Side by Side

Various Gauges, Outside Hammers, Damascus Barrel, Modern	80	150
Various Gauges, Hammerless, Steel Barrel, Modern	95	175
Various Gauges, Hammerless, Damascus Barrel, Modern	75	150
Various Gauges, Outside Hammers, Steel Barrel, Modern	90	175

Shotgun, Singleshot

Various Gauges, Hammer, Steel Barrel, Modern	45	75

Carpenter, John
Lancaster, Pa. See Kentucky Rifles

Carroll, Lawrence
Philadelphia, Pa. 1786-90. See Kentucky Rifles

Cartridge Firearms
Unknown Maker

Handgun, Revolver

11mm Pinfire, Lefaucheux Military Style, Antique	150	225
11mm Pinfire, Lefaucheux Military Style, Engraved, Antique	200	350
7mm Pinfire, Pocket Pistol, Folding Trigger, Engraved, Antique	75	125
.22 Short, Small Pocket Pistol, Folding Trigger, Modern	50	90
.22 Short, Small Pocket Pistol, Double Action, Modern	40	75
Belgian Proofs, Various Calibers, Top Break, Double Action, Medium Quality, Modern	55	85
Belgian Proofs, Various Calibers, Top Break, Double Action, Engraved, Medium Quality, Modern	75	100
Belgian Proofs, Various Calibers, Top Break, Double Action, Folding Trigger, Medium Quality, Modern	50	75
Chinese Copy of S & W M-10, .38 Special, Double Action, Solid Frame, Swing-Out Cylinder, Low Quality, Modern	45	70
Chinese Copy of S & W M-10, 9mm Luger, Double Action, Solid Frame, Swing-Out Cylinder, Low Quality, Modern	45	80
Copy of Colt SAA, Various Calibers, Western Style, Single Action, Low Quality, Modern	60	100
Copy of Colt SAA, Various Calibers, Western Style, Single Action, Medium Quality, Modern	75	125
Copy of S & W Russian Model, Various Calibers, Break, Single Action, Low Quality, Antique	65	125
Copy of S & W Russian Model, Various Calibers, Top Break, Single Action, Medium Quality, Antique	100	200

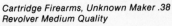

Cartridge Firearms, Unknown Maker .38 Revolver Medium Quality

Copy of S & W Russian Model, Various Calibers, Top Break, Single Action, High Quality, Antique	325	475
Montenegrin Copy, 11mm, 6 Shot, Solid Frame, Antique	75	125
Spanish Copy of S & W M-10, .32-20 WCF, Double Action, Solid Frame, Swing-Out Cylinder, Low Quality, Modern	55	80
Spanish Copy of S & W M-10, .38 Special, Double Action, Solid Frame, Swing-Out Cylinder, Low Quality, Modern	45	70
Various Centerfire Calibers, Folding Trigger, Open Top Frame, Modern	60	100
Various Centerfire Calibers, Bulldog Style, Double Action, Solid Frame, Modern	50	90
Various Centerfire Calibers, Small Pocket Pistol, Hammerless, Folding Trigger, with Safety, Modern	60	100
7.62mm Nagent, Nagent Style Gas Seal, Solid Frame, Double Action, Modern	75	150
Various Centerfire Calibers, European Military Style, Double Action, Solid Frame, Modern	75	150
Various Centerfire Calibers, Warnant Style, Top Break, Double Action, Modern	80	150
Various Centerfire Calibers, Gasser Style, Solid Frame, Double Action, Modern	80	150
Velo-Dog Pistols, Various Calibers, Double Action, Modern	80	125

Cartridge Firearms, Unknown Maker .44 Break Top

Cartridge Firearms, Unknown Maker Montenegrin Copy

Cartridge Firearm, Unknown Maker, Velo Dog

*Cartridge Firearm, Unknown Maker 10 Shot
Velo Dog*

Handgun, Semi-Automatic

Chinese Broomhandle, 7.63 Mauser, Low Quality, Modern	75	140
Chinese Pocket Pistols, Various Calibers, Clip Fed, Low Quality, Modern	60	95
Copy of Colt M1911, .45 ACP, Clip Fed, Military, High Quality, Modern	125	200
Spanish Pocket Pistols, .25 ACP, Clip Fed, Low Quality, Modern	60	95
Spanish Pocket Pistols, .32 ACP, Clip Fed, Low Quality, Modern	65	115

Handgun, Singleshot

Flobert Style, Various Configurations, Modern	45	85
.22 Short, Target Pistol, Tip-Up Barrel, Plain, Modern	65	120
.22 Short, Fancy Target Pistol, Tip-Up Barrel, Engraved, Set Triggers, Modern	125	200
.22 R.F., Fancy Target Pistol, Hammerless, Set Triggers, Modern	200	350

Rifle, Bolt Action

Various Rimfire Calibers, Singleshot, Checkered Stock, European, Modern	30	50
Arabian Copies, Various Calibers, Military, Reproduction, Low Quality, Modern	45	75

Rifle, Singleshot

Various Calibers, Flobert Style, Checkered Stock, Modern	55	95
Various Calibers, Warnant Style, Checkered Stock, Modern	70	125
Belgian Proofs, .22 Long R.F., Tip-Up, Octagon Barrel, Medium Quality, Antique	70	95

Shotgun, Double Barrel, Side by Side

Belgian Proofs, Various Gauges, Damascus Barrel, Low Quality, Outside Hammers, Modern	60	90
Belgian Proofs, Various Gauges, Damascus Barrel, Low Quality, Outside Hammers, Modern	60	100
English Proofs, Various Gauges, Damascus Barrel, Low Quality, Outside Hammers, Modern	80	125
No Proofs, Various Gauges, Damascus Barrel, Low Quality, Outside Hammers, Modern	50	90
Various Gauges, American, Outside Hammers, Damascus Barrel, Modern	80	150
Various Gauges, American, Hammerless, Steel Barrel, Modern	95	175
Various Gauges, American, Hammerless, Damascus Barrel, Modern	75	150
Various Gauges, American, Outside Hammers, Steel Barrel, Modern	90	175

Shotgun, Singleshot

Various Gauges, American, Hammer, Steel Barrel, Modern	45	75
Various Gauges, Warnant Style, Checkered Stock, Modern	40	70
"Zulu," 12 Ga., Converted from Perc. Musket, Trap Door Action, Antique	75	125

Centennial
Made by Derringer Rifle & Pistol Works 1876

Handgun, Revolver

.22 Short R.F., 7 Shot, Spur Trigger, Tip-Up, Antique	200	300

.32 Short R.F., 5 Shot, Spur Trigger, Solid Frame, Single Action, Antique	90	160
.38 Short R.F., 5 Shot, Spur Trigger, Solid Frame, Single Action, Antique	95	175
Centennial '76, .38 Long R.F., 5 Shot, Single Action, Spur Trigger, Tip-Up, Antique	250	325
Model 2, .32 R.F., 5 Shot, Single Action, Spur Trigger, Tip-Up, Antique	200	275

Central
Made by Stevens Arms

Shotgun, Double Barrel, Side by Side

Model 315, Various Gauges, Hammerless, Steel Barrel, Modern	90	145
Model 215, 12 and 16 Gauges, Outside Hammers, Steel Barrel, Modern	85	150
Model 311, Various Gauges, Hammerless, Steel Barrel, Modern	90	160

Shotgun, Singleshot

Model 94, Various Gauges, Takedown, Automatic Ejector, Plain Hammer, Modern	35	55

Central Arms Co.
Made by Crescent, For Shapleigh Hardware Co., C.1900

Shotgun, Double Barrel, Side by Side

Various Gauges, Outside Hammers, Damascus Barrel, Modern	80	150
Various Gauges, Hammerless, Steel Barrel, Modern	95	175
Various Gauges, Hammerless, Damascus Barrel, Modern	75	150
Various Gauges, Outside Hammers, Steel Barrel, Modern	90	175

Shotgun, Singleshot

Various Gauges, Hammer, Steel Barrel, Modern	45	75

Challenge
Made by Bliss & Goodyear, C.1878

Handgun, Revolver

.32 Short R.F., 5 Shot, Spur Trigger, Solid Frame, Single Action, Antique	90	160

Champion
Unknown Maker C.1870

Handgun, Revolver

.22 Short R.F., 7 Shot, Spur Trigger, Solid Frame, Single Action, Antique	90	160

Champlin Firearms
Enid, Oklahoma

Rifle, Bolt Action

Various Calibers, with Quarter Rib, Express Sights, Add $150-$200		
Various Calibers, Fancy Wood, Add $40-$75		
Various Calibers, Fancy Checkering, Add $20-$30		
Basic Rifle, Various Calibers, Adjustable Trigger, Round or Octagon Tapered Barrel, Checkered Stock, Modern	1,350	1,750

Shotgun, Double Barrel, Over-Under

12 Ga., Extra Barrels, Add $150-$225		
Model 100, 12 Ga., Field Grade, Checkered Stock, Vent Rib, Single Selective Trigger, Engraved, Modern	475	750
Model 100, 12 Ga., Trap Grade, Checkered Stock, Vent Rib, Single Selective Trigger, Engraved, Modern	525	800
Model 100, 12 Ga., Skeet Grade, Checkered Stock, Vent Rib, Single Selective Trigger, Engraved, Modern	525	800
Model 500, 12 Ga., Field Grade, Checkered Stock, Vent Rib, Single Selective Trigger, Engraved, Modern	750	1,100
Model 500, 12 Ga., Skeet Grade, Checkered Stock, Vent Rib, Single Selective Trigger, Engraved, Modern	800	1,250
Model 500, 12 Ga., Trap Grade, Checkered Stock, Vent Rib, Single Selective Trigger, Engraved, Modern	825	1,275

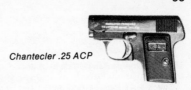

Chantecler .25 ACP

Shotgun, Singleshot
Model SB 100, 12 Ga., Trap Grade, Checkered Stock, Vent Rib, Single
    Selective Trigger, Engraved, Modern   500   775
Model SB 500, 12 Ga., Trap Grade, Checkered Stock, Vent Rib, Single
    Selective Trigger, Engraved, Modern   800   1,200

Chantecler
Mre. d'Armes des Pyrenees

Handgun, Semi-Automatic
Vest Pocket, .25 ACP, Clip Fed, Modern   80   110

Charles Daly
Imported by Sloans, N.Y.C. Early "Prussian Daly's" are worth a premium.

Combination Weapon, Drilling
Diamond, Various Calibers, Fancy Engraving, Fancy Checkering, Modern   2,500   4,000
Regent Diamond, Various Calibers, Fancy Engraving, Fancy Checkering,
    Fancy Wood, Modern   4,250   6,500
Superior, Various Calibers, Engraved, Modern   1,800   3,000

Rifle, Bolt Action
.22 Hornet, 5 Shot Clip, Checkered Stock, Modern   475   750

Shotgun, Double Barrel, Over-Under
For 28 Ga., Add 10%-15%
12 Ga., for Wide Vent Rib, Add $20-$30
Various Gauges, Field Grade, Light Engraving, Single Selective Trigger,
    Automatic Ejector, Post-War, Modern   275   375
Commander 100, Various Gauges, Automatic Ejector, Checkered Stock,
    Double Trigger, Modern   300   400
Commander 100, Various Gauges, Automatic Ejector, Checkered Stock,
    Single Trigger, Modern   350   450
Commander 200, Various Gauges, Double Trigger, Modern   450   550
Commander 200, Various Gauges, Automatic Ejector, Checkered Stock,
    Engraved, Single Trigger, Modern   500   625
Diamond, 12 Ga., Trap Grade, Selective Ejector, Single Selective Trigger,
    Post-War, Modern   425   700
Diamond, 12 and 20 Gauges, Field Grade, Trap Grade, Selective Ejector,
    Single Selective Trigger, Post-War, Modern   425   750
Diamond, 12 and 20 Gauges, Skeet Grade, Trap Grade, Selective Ejector,
    Single Selective Trigger, Post-War, Modern   425   750
Diamond, Various Gauges, Double Trigger, Automatic Ejector, Fancy
    Engraving, Fancy Checkering, Modern   2,900   5,000
Empire, Various Gauges, Double Trigger, Automatic Ejector, Checkered
    Stock, Engraved, Modern   2,500   4,000
Superior, 12 Ga., Trap Grade, Automatic Ejector, Single Selective Trigger,
    Post-War, Modern   300   425
Superior, Various Gauges, Field Grade, Trap Grade, Automatic Ejector,
    Single Selective Trigger, Post-War, Modern   300   425
Superior, Various Gauges, Skeet Grade, Trap Grade, Automatic Ejector,
    Single Selective Trigger, Post-War, Modern   300   425
Venture, 12 Ga., Trap Grade, Single Trigger, Monte Carlo Stock, Post-
    War, Modern   250   340

Venture, 12 and 20 Gauges, Field Grade, Single Trigger, Trap Grade,
Post-War, Modern   245   325
Venture, 12 and 20 Gauges, Skeet Grade, Single Trigger, Trap Grade,
Post-War, Modern   250   340

Shotgun, Double Barrel, Side by Side
Diamond, Various Gauges, Double Trigger, Fancy Engraving, Fancy
Checkering, Fancy Wood, Automatic Ejector, Modern   2,500   3,900
Empire, Various Gauges, Double Trigger, Engraved, Checkered Stock,
Automatic Ejector, Modern   1,250   2,000
Empire, Various Gauges, Vent Rib, Single Trigger, Checkered Stock,
Engraved, Post-War, Modern   225   300
Regent Diamond, Various Gauges, Double Trigger, Fancy Engraving,
Fancy Checkering, Fancy Wood, Automatic Ejector, Modern   3,000   5,250
Superior, Various Gauges, Double Trigger, Light Engraving, Checkered
Stock, Modern   850   1,550

Shotgun, Semi-Automatic
Novamatic, 12 Ga., Takedown, Trap Grade, Vent Rib, Checkered Stock,
Monte Carlo Stock, Modern   165   225
Novamatic, 12 and 20 Gauges, Takedown, Plain Barrel, Checkered
Stock, Lightweight, Modern   130   175
Novamatic, 12 and 20 Gauges, Takedown, Vent Rib, Checkered Stock,
Lightweight, Modern   150   195
Novamatic, 12 and 20 Gauges, Takedown, Plain Barrel, Checkered
Stock, Lightweight, Interchangeable Choke Tubes, Modern   140   185
Novamatic, 12 and 20 Gauges, Takedown, Vent Rib, Checkered Stock,
Lightweight, Interchangeable Choke Tubes, Modern   160   210
Novamatic, 12 Ga. Mag. 3″, Takedown, Vent Rib, Checkered Stock,
Magnum, Modern   170   220
Novamatic, 20 Ga., Takedown, Checkered Stock, Magnum, Lightweight,
Modern   145   200
Novamatic Super Light, 12 and 20 Gauges, Takedown, Plain Barrel,
Checkered Stock, Modern   130   190
Novamatic Super Light, 12 and 20 Gauges, Takedown, Plain Barrel,
Checkered Stock, Interchangeable Choke Tubes, Modern   140   210
Novamatic Super Light, 12 and 20 Gauges, Takedown, Vent Rib,
Checkered Stock, Modern   150   225

Shotgun, Singleshot
Empire, 12 Ga., Trap Grade, Fancy Engraving, Fancy Wood, Automatic
Ejector, Modern   3,000   4,250
Sextuple Empire, 12 Ga., Trap Grade, Fancy Checkering, Fancy
Engraving, Fancy Wood, Automatic Ejector, Modern   2,900   4,600
Sextuple Regent Diamond, 12 Ga., Trap Grade, Fancy Checkering,
Fancy Engraving, Fancy Wood, Automatic Ejector, Modern   4,800   6,400
Superior, 12 Ga., Trap Grade, Monte Carlo Stock, Selective Ejector,
Engraved, Post-War, Modern   275   375

Charola-Anitua
Garate, Anitua y Cia. Eibar, Spain

Handgun, Semi-Automatic
Charola, 5mm Clement, Locked Breech, Box Magazine, Belgian Made,
Curio   350   500
Charola, 5mm Clement, Locked Breech, Box Magazine, Spanish Made,
Curio   475   675

Charter Arms
Stratford, Conn.

Handgun, Revolver
Milestone Limited Edition, .44 Special, Bulldog, Engraved, Silver Plated,
Cased with Accessories, Modern   1,750   2,500

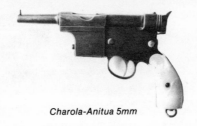

Charola-Anitua 5mm

Bulldog, .357 Magnum, Double Action, Blue, Adjustable Sights, Modern	90	130
Bulldog, .44 Special, Double Action, Blue, Modern	90	125
Bulldog, .44 Special, Double Action, Nickel Plated, Modern	95	140
Pathfinder, .22 L.R.R.F., Adjustable Sights, Bulldog Grips, Double Action, Modern	85	135
Pathfinder, .22 L.R.R.F., Adjustable Sights, Square-Butt, Double Action, Modern	80	130
Pathfinder, .22 WMR, Adjustable Sights, Double Action, Bulldog Grips, Modern	90	140
Pathfinder, .22 WMR, Adjustable Sights, Double Action, Square-Butt, Modern	90	140
Police Bulldog, .38 Special, Double Action, Blue, Adjustable Sights, Modern	95	135
Target Bulldog, .357 Magnum, Double Action, Blue, Adjustable Sights, Modern	95	145
Target Bulldog, .44 Special, Double Action, Blue, Adjustable Sights, Modern 95	145	
Undercover, .38 Special, Double Action, Blue, Modern	70	115
Undercover, .38 Special, Double Action, Blue, Bulldog Grips, Modern	75	120
Undercover, .38 Special, Double Action, Blue, Square-Butt, Modern	70	115
Undercover, .38 Special, Double Action, Nickel Plated, Modern	70	115
Undercover, .38 Special, Double Action, Nickel Plated, Bulldog Grips, Modern	75	120
Undercover, .38 Special, Double Action, Nickel Plated, Square-Butt, Modern	75	120
Undercoverette, .32 S & W Long, Double Action, Blue, Modern	65	110

Charter Arms Bulldog .44

Charter Arms Pathfinder .22

58

Charter Arms Undercoverette .32

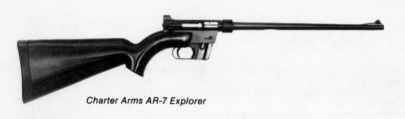

Charter Arms AR-7 Explorer

Undercoverette, .32 S & W Long, Double Action, Blue, Bulldog Grips,
   Modern   75   115
Undercoverette, .32 S & W Long, Double Action, Blue, Square-Butt,
   Modern   65   110

Rifle, Semi-Automatic
Explorer, .22 L.R.R.F., Clip Fed, Takedown, Modern   50   65

Chase, William
Pandora, Ohio 1854-60

Combination Weapon, Percussion
Various Calibers, Double Barrel, Antique   650   1,100

Cherokee Arms Co.
Made by Crescent, C.M. McClung & Co. Tennessee C.1900

Shotgun, Double Barrel, Side by Side
Various Gauges, Outside Hammers, Damascus Barrel, Modern   80   150
Various Gauges, Hammerless, Steel Barrel, Modern   95   175
Various Gauges, Hammerless, Damascus Barrel, Modern   75   150
Various Gauges, Outside Hammers, Steel Barrel, Modern   90   175

Shotgun, Singleshot
Various Gauges, Hammer, Steel Barrel, Modern   45   75

Cherrington, Thomas P.
Cattawissa, Pa. 1847-58

Rifle, Pill Lock
.40, Revolver, Octagon Barrel, Antique   1,800   2,300

Chesapeake Gun Co.
Made by Crescent C.1900

Shotgun, Double Barrel, Side by Side
Various Gauges, Outside Hammers, Damascus Barrel, Modern   80   150
Various Gauges, Hammerless, Steel Barrel, Modern   95   175

Various Gauges, Hammerless, Damascus Barrel, Modern	75	150
Various Gauges, Outside Hammers, Steel Barrel, Modern	90	175

Shotgun, Singleshot
Various Gauges, Hammer, Steel Barrel, Modern	45	75

Chicago Arms

Handgun, Revolver
.38 S & W, Top Break, Hammerless, Double Action, Grip Safety, Modern	80	125

Chicago Arms Co.
Sold by Fred Bifflar Co. Made by Meriden Firearms Co. 1870-1890

Handgun, Revolver
.32 S & W, 5 Shot, Double Action, Top Break, Modern	45	95
.38 S & W, 5 Shot, Double Action, Top Break, Modern	45	95

Chicago Fire Arms Co.
Chicago, Ill. 1883-94

Handgun, Palm Pistol
.32 Extra Short R.F., Blue, Antique	600	800

Chicnester
Made by Hopkins & Allen C.1880

Handgun, Revolver
.38 Short R.F., 5 Shot, Spur Trigger, Solid Frame, Single Action, Antique	95	170

Chieftain
Made by Norwich Pistol Co. C.1880

Handgun Revolver
.32 Short R.F., 5 Shot, Spur Trigger, Solid Frame, Single Action, Antique	90	160

Chinese Military

Automatic Weapon, Heavy Machine Gun
Type 24, 8mm Mauser, Belt Fed, Tripod, Class 3	3,500	4,500

Handgun, Semi-Automatic
Makarov, 9mm Mak., Clip Fed, Modern	450	625
Tokarev, 7.62mm Tokarev, Clip Fed, Modern	150	225

Rifle, Bolt Action
Type 53 (Nagent), 7.62 x 54R Russian, Modern	85	150

Rifle, Semi-Automatic
SKS, 7.62 x 39 Russian, Folding Bayonet, Military, Modern	150	225

Chinese Nationalist Military

Automatic Weapon, Submachine Gun
Sten MK II, 9mm Luger, all Metal, Clip Fed, Class 3	550	750

Chicago Palm Pistol

Handgun, Semi-Automatic

Hi Power, 9mm Luger, Clip Fed, Military, Tangent Sights, Curio	375	500
Hi Power, 9mm Luger, Clip Fed, Military, Tangent Sight, with Detachable Shoulder Stock, Curio	650	800

Rifle, Bolt Action

Kar 98k Type 79, 8mm Mauser, Modern	90	145
M1871 Mauser, .43 Mauser, Carbine, Antique	75	150
M1888 Hanyang, 8mm Mauser, 5 Shot, Modern	75	125
M98 Mukden, 8mm Mauser, Modern	125	200

Churchill, E. J. & Robert
London, England 1892 to Date

Rifle, Bolt Action

One of 1,000, Various Calibers, Checkered Stock, Recoil Pad, Express Sights, Cartridge Trap, Modern	700	850
One of 1,000, Various Calibers, Fancy Checkering, Engraved Express Sights, Cartridge Trap, Cased with Accessories, Modern	1,600	2,200

Shotgun, Double Barrel, Side by Side

Utility Model, Various Gauges, Boxlock, Double Triggers, Color Case Hardened Frame, Engraved, Modern	2,400	3,250
Hercules Model XXV, Various Gauges, Hammerless Sidelock, Engraved, Fancy Checkering, Fancy Wood, Cased, Modern	3,750	5,000
Field Model, Various Gauges, Hammerless Sidelock, Fancy Checkering, Automatic Ejectors, Engraved, Modern	6,500	7,750
Imperial Model XXV, Various Gauges, Hammerless Sidelock, Fancy Checkering, Automatic Ejectors, Engraved, Modern	6,500	7,750
Premier Quality, Various Gauges, Hammerless Sidelock, Fancy Checkering, Automatic Ejectors, Engraved, Modern	7,500	8,750
Regal Model XXV, Various Gauges, Hammerless Sidelock, Fancy Checkering, Automatic Ejectors, Engraved, Modern	3,000	4,000
For Single Selective Trigger Add $350-$500		

Shotgun, Double Barrel, Over-Under

Premier Quality, Various Gauges, Hammerless Sidelock, Fancy Checkering, Automatic Ejectors, Engraved, Modern	10,000	13,500
Premier Quality, Add for Single Selective Trigger, $400-$500		
Premier Quality, Add for Raised Vent Rib, $350-$500		

Chylewski
Made by S.I.G.

Handgun, Semi-Automatic

Einhand, .25 ACP, Clip Fed, Curio	350	500

Clarkson, J.
London, England 1680-1740

Handgun, Flintlock

.32, Pocket Pistol, Queen Anne Style, Box Lock, Screw Barrel, Silver Furniture, Antique	350	550

Chylewski .25 ACP

Classic Arms
Palmer, Mass. Current

Handgun, Percussion

.36 Duckfoot, 3 Shot, Brass Frame, Reproduction, Antique	25	40
.36 Twister, 2 Shot, Brass Frame, Reproduction, Antique	25	40
.36 Ethan Allen, Pepperbox, 4 Shot, Brass Frame, Reproduction, Antique	25	40
.36 Snake-Eyes, Double Barrel, Side by Side, Brass Frame, Reproduction, Antique	20	35
.44 Ace, Rifled, Brass Frame, Reproduction, Antique	15	25
.44 Ace, Smoothbore, Brass Frame, Reproduction, Antique	15	25

Clement, Charles
Belgium

Handgun, Semi-Automatic

M1903, 5mm Clement, Clip Fed, Curio	275	400
M1907, .25 ACP, Clip Fed, Modern	150	225
M1907, .32 ACP, Clip Fed, Modern	175	275
M1908, .25 ACP, Clip Fed, Modern	175	275
M1909, .25 ACP, Clip Fed, Modern	150	225
M1909, .32 ACP, Clip Fed, Modern	175	245

Clement, J.B.
Belgium

Shotgun, Double Barrel, Side by Side

Various Gauges, Hammerless, Steel Barrel, Modern	95	175
Various Gauges, Outside Hammers, Steel Barrel, Modern	90	175

Clement Model 1903 5mm

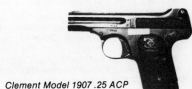

Clement Model 1907 .25 ACP

Clement, J.B. Double Barrel Shotgun

Clerke
Santa Monica, Calif.

Handgun, Revolver

32-200, .32 S & W, Nickel Plated, Modern	10	20
CF200, .22 L.R.R.F., Nickel Plated, Modern	10	20

Rifle, Singleshot

Hi-Wall, Various Calibers, Fancy Wood, Modern	175	250
Hi-Wall Deluxe, Various Calibers, Octagon Barrel, Fancy Wood, Modern	200	300
Hi-Wall Deluxe, Various Calibers, Octagon Barrel, Set Trigger, Fancy Wood, Modern	225	350

Clipper
Maker Unknown C.1880

Handgun, Revolver

.22 Short R.F., 7 Shot, Spur Trigger, Solid Frame, Single Action, Antique	85	150

Climas
Made by Stevens Arms

Shotgun, Singleshot

Model 90, Various Gauges, Takedown, Automatic Ejector, Plain Hammer, Modern	35	55

Cody Manufacturing Co.
Chicopee, Mass. 1957-59

Handgun, Revolver

Thunderbird, .22 R.F., 6 Shot, Double Action, Aluminium with Steel Liners, Modern	100	160

Cogswell & Harrison
London, England 1770 to Date; Branch in Paris 1924-38

Handgun, Revolver

S & W Victory, .38 Special, Double Action, Swing-Out Cylinder, Refinished and Customized. Rebored from .38 S & W. May be unsafe with .38 Spec., Modern	65	110

Rifle, Bolt Action

BSA-Lee Speed, .303 British, Sporting Rifle, Express Sights, Engraved, Checkered Stock, Commercial, Modern	450	700

Shotgun, Double Barrel, Side by Side

Avant Tout (Konor), Various Gauges, Box Lock, Automatic Ejector, Fancy Checkering, Fancy Engraving, Double Trigger, Modern	1,900	2,850
Avant Tout (Konor), Various Gauges, Box Lock, Automatic Ejector, Fancy Checkering, Fancy Engraving, Single Trigger, Modern	2,250	3,100
Avant Tout (Konor), Various Gauges, Box Lock, Automatic Ejector, Fancy Checkering, Fancy Engraving, Single Selective Trigger, Modern	2,400	3,200
Avant Tout (Rex), Various Gauges, Box Lock, Automatic Ejector, Checkered Stock, Light Engraving, Double Trigger, Modern	1,100	2,000
Avant Tout (Rex), Various Gauges, Box Lock, Automatic Ejector, Checkered Stock, Light Engraving, Single Trigger, Modern	1,300	2,200
Avant Tout (Rex), Various Gauges, Box Lock, Automatic Ejector, Checkered Stock, Light Engraving, Single Selective Trigger, Modern	1,400	2,350
Avant Tout (Sandhurst), Various Gauges, Box Lock, Automatic Ejector, Fancy Checkering, Engraved, Double Trigger, Modern	1,700	2,500
Avant Tout (Sandhurst), Various Gauges, Box Lock, Automatic Ejector, Fancy Checkering, Engraved, Single Trigger, Modern	1,900	2,700
Avant Tout (Sandhurst), Various Gauges, Box Lock, Automatic Ejector, Fancy Checkering, Engraved, Single Selective Trigger, Modern	2,000	2,800
Huntic, Various Gauges, Sidelock, Automatic Ejector, Checkered Stock, Double Trigger, Modern	2,200	3,200

Huntic, Various Gauges, Sidelock, Automatic Ejector, Checkered Stock, Single Trigger, Modern	2,450	3,450
Huntic, Various Gauges, Sidelock, Automatic Ejector, Checkered Stock, Single Selective Trigger, Modern	2,550	3,550
Markor, Various Gauges, Box Lock, Automatic Ejector, Checkered Stock, Double Trigger, Modern	1,000	1,950
Markor, Various Gauges, Box Lock, Checkered Stock, Double Trigger, Modern	800	1,700
Primic, Various Gauges, Sidelock, Automatic Ejector, Fancy Engraving, Fancy Checkering, Double Trigger, Modern	3,000	4,200
Primic, Various Gauges, Sidelock, Automatic Ejector, Fancy Engraving, Fancy Checkering, Single Trigger, Modern	3,250	4,400
Primic, Various Gauges, Sidelock, Automatic Ejector, Fancy Engraving, Fancy Checkering, Single Selective Trigger, Modern	3,350	4,550
Victor, Various Gauges, Sidelock, Automatic Ejector, Engraved, Checkered Stock, Double Trigger, Modern	4,900	6,250
Victor, Various Gauges, Sidelock, Automatic Ejector, Engraved, Checkered Stock, Single Trigger, Modern	5,100	6,500
Victor, Various Gauges, Sidelock, Automatic Ejector, Engraved, Checkered Stock, Single Selective Trigger, Modern	5,200	6,650

Colon
Antonio Azpiri

Handgun, Semi-Automatic

Vest Pocket, .25 ACP, Clip Fed, Modern	80	110

Colt
Patterson N.J. 1836-41. Whitneyville, Conn. 1847-48. Hartford, Conn. 1848 to Date; London, England 1853-64. Also See U.S. Military.

Automatic Weapon, Assault Rifle

AR-15, .223 Rem., Clip Fed, Early Model, Class 3	650	950
M16-M A C, .22 L.R.R.F., Clip Fed, Conversion Unit only, Class 3	70	110
MI6A1, .223 Rem., Clip Fed, Commercial, Class 3	550	800
M1919 BAR, .30-06 Springfield, Clip Fed, Commercial, Finned Barrel, with Compensator, Curio, Class 3	2,750	3,200

Automatic Weapon, Heavy Machine Gun

M1906 Colt, .30-06 Springfield, Belt Fed, Tripod Potato Digger, Military, Class 3	1,500	2,000
M2 Browning, .50 BMG, Belt Fed, Heavy Barrel, Military, Class 3	1,800	2,250
M2 Browning, .50 BMG, Belt Fed, Heavy Barrel, Commercial, Class 3	2,300	2,900

Automatic Weapon, Light Machine Gun

Benet-Mercie U.S.N. 1912, .30-06 Springfield, Clip Fed, Dewat, Class 3	2,300	3,000

Automatic Weapon, Submachine Gun

XM177E2, .223 Rem., Clip Fed, Folding Stock, Silencer, Short Rifle, Military, Class 3	1,200	1,800

Combination Weapon, Drilling

Various Calibers, Engraved, Fancy Checkering, Modern	1,150	1,600

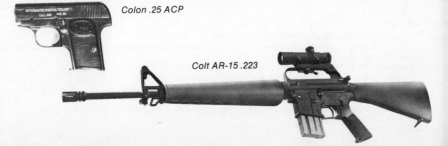

Colon .25 ACP

Colt AR-15 .223

Colt Model 1855 Root

Handgun, Percussion

.28 Model 1855 Root, Full Fluted Cylinder, Side Hammer, Spur Trigger, Revolver, Octagon Barrel, Antique	350	625
.28 Model 1855 Root, Full Fluted Cylinder, Side Hammer, Spur Trigger, Revolver, Round Barrel, Antique	350	650
.28 Model 1855 Root, Round Cylinder, Side Hammer, Spur Trigger, Revolver, Octagon Barrel, Antique	325	600
.28 Model 1855 Root, Round Cylinder, Side Hammer, Spur Trigger, Revolver, Round Barrel, Antique	375	650
.28 Model Patterson (Baby), 5 Shot, Various Barrel Lengths, Octagon Barrel, no Loading Lever, Antique	1,750	3,000
.28 Model Patterson (Baby), 5 Shot, Various Barrel Lengths, Octagon Barrel, with Factory Loading Lever, Antique	2,250	3,400
.31 Model 1848 Revolver, Baby Dragoon, 5 Shot, Various Barrels Lengths, no Loading Lever, no Capping Groove, Antique	1,500	2,400
.31 Model 1848 Revolver, Baby Dragoon, 5 Shot, Various Barrels Lengths, no Loading Lever, Stagecoach Cylinder, Antique	900	1,750
.31 Model 1848 Revolver, Baby Dragoon, 5 Shot, Various Barrels Lengths, no Loading Lever, Antique	1,100	2,000
.31 Model 1848 Revolver, Baby Dragoon, 5 Shot, Various Barrel Lengths, with Loading Lever, Antique	1,200	2,100
.31 Model 1849 Revolver, Wells Fargo, 5 Shot, no Loading Lever, Pocket Pistol, Antique	1,000	1,500
.31 Model 1849 Revolver, Pocket Pistol, with Loading Lever, 5 Shot, Round-backed Trigger Guard, Large, 1-Line N.Y. Address, Brass Frame, Antique	325	450
.31 Model 1849 Revolver, Pocket Pistol, with Loading Lever, 5 Shot, Large Round-Backed Trigger Guard, 1-Line Hartford Address, Brass Frame, Antique	400	600
.31 Model 1849 Revolver, Pocket Pistol, with Loading Lever, 5 Shot, Round-backed Trigger Guard, Large, 1-Line Hartford Address, Iron Frame, Antique	425	650
.31 Model 1849 Revolver, Pocket Pistol, with Loading Lever, 5 Shot, Large Round-backed Trigger Guard, 1-Line London Address, Iron Frame, Antique	550	800
.31 Model l849 Revolver, Pocket Pistol, with Loading Lever, 5 Shot, Round-backed Trigger Guard, Small, 2-Line N.Y. Address, Iron Frame, Antique	350	475
.31 Model 1849 Revolver, Pocket Pistol, with Loading Lever, 5 Shot, Round-Backed Trigger Guard, Small, 2-Line N.Y. Address, Brass Frame, Antique	350	475
.31 Model 1849 Revolver, Pocket Pistol, with Loading Lever, 5 Shot, Square-Backed Trigger Guard, Small, 2-Line N.Y. Address, Antique	700	1,150
.31 Model 1849, For 5″ Barrel, Add 10%-15%		
.31 Model 1849, For 6″ Barrel, Add 15%-25%		
.31 Model 1849, 6 Shot (Model 1850), Add 15%-25%		
.31 Baby Dragoon, Late, Unfluted Cylinder, Reproduction, Antique	125	200
.31 Model 1855 Root, Full Fluted Cylinder, Side Hammer, Spur Trigger, Revolver, Octagon Barrel, Antique	400	675

.31 Model 1855 Root, Full Fluted Cylinder, Side Hammer, Spur Trigger, Revolver, Round Barrel, Antique	425	700
.31 Model 1855 Root, Round Fluted Cylinder, Side Hammer, Spur Trigger, Revolver, Octagon Barrel, Antique	450	725
.31 Model 1855 Root, Round Fluted Cylinder, Side Hammer, Spur Trigger, Revolver, Round Barrel, Antique	500	800
.31 Model 1855, For 4½" Barrel, Add 10%-15%		
.31, .28 Model 1855, London Markings, Add 50%-75%		
.31 Model Patterson (Baby), 5 Shot, Octagon Barrel, Various Barrel Lengths, no Loading Lever, no Capping Groove, Antique	1,850	3,200
.31 Model Patterson (Baby), 5 Shot, Octagon Barrel, Various Barrel Lengths, with Factory Loading Lever, Antique	2,250	3,750
.31, .34 Model Patterson (Pocket), 5 Shot, Octagon Barrel, Various Barrel Lengths, no Loading Lever, no Capping Groove, Antique	2,500	3,750
.31 Model Patterson (Pocket), 5 Shot, Octagon Barrel, Various Barrel Lengths, with Factory Loading Lever, Antique	3,000	4,250
.31 Model Patterson (Belt), 5 Shot, Octagon Barrel, Various Barrel Lengths, no Loading Lever, no Capping Groove, Straight Grip, Antique	2,500	4,000
.31 Model Patterson (Belt), 5 Shot, Octagon Barrel, Various Barrel Lengths, no Loading Lever, no Capping Groove, Flared Grip, Antique	3,000	4,500
.31 Model Patterson (Belt), Factory Loading Lever Add 10%-15%		
.36 M1851 Grant-Lee Set, Revolver, Commemorative, Cased Reproduction, Antique	750	1,100
.36 M1851 Late, Revolver, 6 Shot, Reproduction, Antique	125	225
.36 M1851 R.E. Lee, Revolver, Commemorative, Cased Reproduction, Antique	225	375
.36 M1851 U.S. Grant, Revolver, Commemorative, Cased Reproduction, Antique	225	375
.36 Model 1851, Half-Fluted, Rebated Cylinder, Add 25%-40%		
.36 Model 1851 Navy, Revolver, with Loading Lever, Square-Backed Trigger Guard, 1st Type, Under #1250, 6 Shot, Antique	2,000	3,250
.36 Model 1851 Navy, Revolver, with Loading Lever, Square-Backed Trigger Guard, 2nd Type, #1250 to #3500, 6 Shot, Antique	1,200	1,900
.36 Model 1851 Navy, Revolver, with Loading Lever, 6 Shot, Small Round-Backed Guard, Small Loading Cut, Antique	650	1,200
.36 Model 1851 Navy, Revolver, with Loading Lever, 6 Shot, Small Round-Backed Guard, Large Loading Cut, Antique	650	1,200
.36 Model 1851 Navy, Revolver, with Loading Lever, 6 Shot, Round-Backed Trigger Guard, Large Loading Cut, London Address, Iron Frame, Antique	700	1,250
.36 Model 1851 Navy, Revolver, with Loading Lever, 6 Shot, Round-Backed Trigger Guard, Small Loading Cut, London Address, Iron Frame, Antique	850	1,600
.36 Model 1851 Navy, Revolver, with Loading Lever, 6 Shot, Large Round-Backed Guard, Large Loading Cut, N.Y. Address, Antique	450	800
.36 Model 1851 Navy, Revolver, with Loading Lever, 6 Shot, Large Round-Backed Guard, Large Loading Cut, Hartford Address, Antique	550	900
.36 Model 1851 Navy, Revolver, with Loading Lever, 6 Shot, Large Round-Backed Guard, Cut for Shoulder Stock, Iron Backstrap, Antique	1,600	2,750
.36 Model 1851 Navy, Revolver, with Loading Lever, 6 Shot, Large Round-Backed Guard, with Detachable Shoulder Stock, Iron Backstrap, Antique	3,250	5,000
.36 Model 1862 Navy, Revolver, New Navy Pocket Pistol 4½" Barrel, Rebated Cylinder, Antique	450	750
.36 Model 1862 Navy, Revolver, New Navy Pocket Pistol 5½" Barrel, Rebated Cylinder, Antique	500	850
.36 Model 1862 Navy, Revolver, Late New Navy Pocket Pistol 5½" Barrel, Rebated Cylinder, Reproduction, Antique	125	200
.36 Model 1862 Navy, Revolver, New Navy Pocket Pistol 1861, 6½" Barrel, Rebated Cylinder, Antique	450	750
.36 Model 1861 Navy, Revolver, Round Barrel, Military Model, no Cuts for Shoulder Stock, Antique	1,500	2,500

.36 Model 1861 Navy, Revolver, Round Barrel, Civilian Model, no Cuts for
   Shoulder Stock, Antique   650   1,200

.36 Model 1861 Navy, Revolver, Late, Round Barrel, Civilian Model, no
   Cuts for Shoulder Stock, Reproduction, Antique   125   225

.36 Model 1861 Navy, Revolver, Round Barrel, Military, Cut for Shoulder
   Stock, Antique   1,750   3,750

.36 Model 1861 Navy, Revolver, Round Barrel, Military, With Shoulder
   Stock, Antique   2,750   6,250

.36 Model 1862 Police, Revolver, Half-Fluted Rebated Cylinder, Antique   400   750

.36 Model 1862 Police, Revolver, Late, Half-Fluted Rebated Cylinder,
   Reproduction, Antique   125   200

.36 Model 1862 Police, for Hartford Marks Add 10%-20%

.36 Model 1862 Police, for London Marks Add 10%-20%

.36 Model Patterson (Holster), 5 Shot, Octagon Barrel, Various Barrel
   Lengths, no Loading Lever, no Capping Groove, Antique   5,750   9,000

.36 Model Patterson (Holster), 5 Shot, Octagon Barrel, Various Barrel
   Lengths, with Factory Loading Lever, Antique   7,500   12,500

.44 Model 1847, Revolver, Whitneyville Walker (U.S.M.R.), Square-Backed
   Trigger Guard, 6 Shot, Antique   14,000   20,000

.44 Model 1847 Revolver, Dragoon, (Hartford) Horizontal Loading Lever
   Latch, 6 Shot, Antique   4,000   8,500

.44 Model 1847, Revolver, Dragoon, (Hartford) Vertical Loading Lever
   Latch, Square-Backed Trigger Guard, 6 Shot, Antique   2,500   4,250

.44 Dragoon 1st Model, Revolver, 6 Shot, Civilian, Antique   1,250   3,750

.44 Dragoon 1st Model, Revolver, 6 Shot, Military, Antique   1,500   4,250

.44 Dragoon 1st Model, Revolver, 6 Shot, Military, Cut for Shoulder Stock,
   Antique   1,750   4,750

.44 Dragoon 1st Model, Revolver, 6 Shot, Military, With Shoulder Stock,
   Antique   3,500   7,250

.44 Dragoon 1st Model, Revolver, 6 Shot, Reproduction, Antique   165   235

.44 Dragoon 1st Model, Revolver, 6 Shot, Fluck Variation, Antique   2,000   4,000

.44 Dragoon 2nd Model, Revolver, 6 Shot, Civilian, Antique   1,000   3,250

.44 Dragoon 2nd Model, Revolver, 6 Shot, Military, Antique   1,200   3,500

.44 Dragoon 2nd Model, Revolver, 6 Shot, Military, Cut for Shoulder
   Stock, Antique   2,000   4,750

.44 Dragoon 2nd Model, Revolver, 6 Shot, Military, With Shoulder Stock,
   Antique   4,000   8,000

.44 Dragoon 2nd Model, Revolver, 6 Shot, Militia, Antique   1,500   4,000

.44 Dragoon 3rd Model, Revolver, 6 Shot, Civilian, Antique   900   2,500

.44 Dragoon 3rd Model, Revolver, 6 Shot, Military, Antique   1,100   2,750

.44 Dragoon 3rd Model, Revolver, 6 Shot, Military, Cut for Shoulder Stock,
   Antique   1,500   3,500

.44 Dragoon 3rd Model, Revolver, 6 Shot, Military, With Shoulder Stock,
   Antique   2,250   5,000

.44 Statehood Dragoon 3rd Model, Revolver, 6 Shot, Fancy Engraving,
   Gold Inlays, Ivory Stocks, Commemorative, Reproduction, Antique   10,000   13,500

.44 Model 1860 Army, Revolver, Cut for Shoulder Stock, Antique   600   950

.44 Model 1860 Army, Revolver, Cut for Shoulder Stock, Four-Screw
   Frame, Antique   750   1,250

Colt .44 Dragoon, 1st Model

.44 Model 1860 Army, Revolver, Cut for Shoulder Stock, Four-Screw
Frame, with Shoulder Stock, Antique 2,600   3,500
.44 Model 1860 Army, Revolver, Cut for Shoulder Stock, Four-Screw
Frame, Fluted Cylinder, Antique 1,000   1,700
.44 Model 1860 Army, Revolver, Cut for Shoulder Stock, Four-Screw
Frame, Fluted Cylinder, Hartford Address, Antique 1,500   1,950
.44 Model 1860 Army, Revolver, Cut for Shoulder Stock, Four-Screw
Frame, Fluted Cylinder, Hartford Address, with Shoulder Stock, Antique   3,000   4,200
.44 Model 1860 Army, Revolver, Cut for Shoulder Stock, Civilian Model,
Antique 600   950
.44 Model 1860 Army, Revolver, Cut for Shoulder Stock, London
Markings, Add 50%-75%

Handgun, Cartridge Conversions

Model 1851 Navy, .38 R.F. or C.F., Richards-Mason, Antique	300	500
Model 1851 Navy, .36 Thuer, Theur Style, Antique	1,500	3,000
Model 1860 Army, .44 Thuer, Theur Style, Antique	1,500	3,000
Model 1860 Army, .44 Colt, Richards, Antique	400	750
Model 1860 Army, .44 Colt, Richards-Mason, Antique	500	900
Model 1861 Navy, .36 Thuer, Theur Style, Antique	2,000	3,800
Model 1862 Pocket Navy, .36 Thuer, Theur Style, Antique	1,800	3,500
Model 1862 Pocket Navy, .38 R.F., no Ejector, Octagon Barrel, Antique	250	500
Model 1862 Pocket Navy, .38 R.F., no Ejector, Round Barrel, Antique	250	500
Model 1862 Pocket Navy, .38 R.F., with Ejector, Round Barrel, Antique	275	600

Handgun, Revolver
Add $15-$25 for Nickel Plating

".357 Magnum," .357 Magnum, 6 Shot, Various Barrel Lengths, Adjustable
Sights, Target Hammer, Target Grips, Modern 185   300
".357 Magnum," .357 Magnum, 6 Shot, Various Barrel Lengths, Adjustable
Sights, Modern 165   275
125th Anniversary, .45 Colt, Single Action Army, Commemorative, Blue,
with Gold Plating, Cased, Curio 350   525
Agent, .38 Special, 6 Shot, Blue, 2" Barrel, Lightweight, Modern . . 120   165
Agent, .38 Special, 6 Shot, Nickel Plated, 2" Barrel, Lightweight, Modern . 130   180
Agent Early, .38 Special, 6 Shot, 2" Barrel, Lightweight, Modern . . 130   185
Alabama Sesquicentennial, .22 L.R.R.F., Frontier Scout S.A.,
Commemorative, Gold Plated, with Nickel Plating, 4¾" Barrel, Cased,
Curio 175   275
Alamo Model, .22 L.R.R.F., Frontier Scout S.A., Commemorative, Blue,
with Gold Plating, 4¾" Barrel, Cased, Curio 150   225
Alamo Model, .22 L.R.R.F., and .45 Colt Set, Frontier Scout and S.A.A.,
Commemorative, Blue, with Gold Plating, Cased, Curio 575   850
Alamo Model, .45 Colt, Single Action Army, Commemorative, Blue, with
Gold Plating, 5½" Barrel, Cased, Curio 375   600
Abercrombie & Fitch, .45 Colt, Trailblazer New Frontier S.A.,
Commemorative, New York, 7½" Barrel, Cased, Curio 1,100   1,650
Abercrombie & Fitch, .45 Colt, Trailblazer New Frontier S.A.,
Commemorative, Chicago, 7½" Barrel, Cased, Curio 1,100   1,650

Colt Agent

Abercrombie & Fitch, 45. Colt, Trailblazer New Frontier S.A., Commemorative, San Francisco, 7½" Barrel, Cased, Curio — 1,100 — 1,650

Appomattox Centennial, .22 L.R.R.F., Frontier Scout S.A., Commemorative, Blue, With Nickel Plating, 4¾" Barrel, Cased, Curio — 155 — 225

Appomattox Centennial, .22 L.R.R.F., and .45 Colt Set, Frontier Scout and S.A.A., Commemorative, Blue, with Nickel Plating, Cased, Curio — 525 — 850

Appomattox Centennial, .45 Colt, Single Action Army, Commemorative, Blue, with Nickel Plating, 5½" Barrel, Cased, Curio — 400 — 600

Argentine M1895, Double Trigger, Solid Frame, Swing-Out Cylinder, Military, Modern — 95 — 145

Arizona Ranger, .22 L.R.R.F., Frontier Scout S.A., Commemorative, Blue, Color Case, Hardened Frame, 4¾" Barrel, Cased, Curio — 150 — 225

Arizona Territorial Centennial, .22 L.R.R.F., Frontier Scout S.A., Commemorative, Blue, with Gold Plating, 4¾" Barrel, Cased, Curio — 150 — 225

Arizona Territorial Centennial, .45 Colt, Single Action Army, Commemorative, Blue, with Gold Plating, 4¾" Barrel, Cased, Curio — 400 — 600

Arkansas Territorial Sesquicentennial, .22 L.R.R.F., Frontier Scout S.A., Commemorative, Blue, 4¾" Barrel, Cased, Curio — 145 — 200

Army Special, .32-20 WCF, 6 Shot, Various Barrel Lengths, Modern — 145 — 250

Army Special, .38 Special, 6 Shot, Various Barrel Lengths, Modern — 145 — 200

Army Special, .41 Long Colt, 6 Shot, Various Barrel Lengths, Modern — 155 — 225

Banker's Special, .22 L.R.R.F., 6 Shot, 2" Barrel, Modern — 375 — 550

Banker's Special, Fitzgerald Trigger Guard Add $150-$250

Banker's Special, .38 S & W, 6 Shot, 2" Barrel, Modern — 200 — 300

Battle of Gettysburg Centennial, .22 L.R.R.F., Frontier Scout S.A., Nickel Plated, Blue, with Gold Plating, 4¾" Barrel, Cased, Curio — 150 — 225

Bicentennial Set, Python, SAA, Dragoon, Commemorative, Cased, Curio — 1,900 — 2,500

California Bicentennial, .22 L.R.R.F., Frontier Scout S.A., Commemorative, Gold Plated, with Nickel Plating, 6" Barrel, Cased, Curio — 150 — 225

California Gold Rush, .22 L.R.R.F., Frontier Scout S.A., Commemorative, Gold Plated, 4¾" Barrel, Cased, Curio — 175 — 275

California Gold Rush, .45 Colt, Single Action Army, Commemorative, Gold Plated, 5½" Barrel, Cased, Curio — 550 — 875

Carolina Charter Tercentennial, .22 L.R.R.F., Frontier Scout S.A., Commemorative, Blue, with Gold Plating, 4¾" Barrel, Cased, Curio — 200 — 300

Carolina Charter Tercentennial, .22 L.R.R.F., and .45 Colt Set, Frontier Scout & S.A.A., Commemorative, Blue, with Gold Plating, 4¾" Barrel, Cased, Curio — 500 — 800

Chamizal Treaty, .22 L.R.R.F., Frontier Scout S.A., Commemorative, Blue, with Gold Plating, 4¾" Barrel, Cased, Curio — 150 — 225

Chamizal Treaty, .22 L.R.R.F., and .45 Colt Set, Frontier Scout and S.A.A., Commemorative, Blue, with Gold Plating, Cased, Curio — 1,000 — 1,650

Chamizal Treaty, .45 Colt, Single Action Army, Commemorative, Blue, with Gold Plating, 5½" Barrel, Cased, Curio — 800 — 1,150

Cherry's 35th Anniversary, .22 L.R.R.F., and .45 Colt Set, Frontier Scout and S.A.A., Nickel Plated, Gold Plated, 4¾" Barrel, Cased, Curio — 725 — 975

Cobra, .38 Special, Blue, 2" Barrel, 6 Shot, Lightweight, Modern — 125 — 170

Cobra, .38 Special, Nickel Plated, 2" Barrel, 6 Shot, Lightweight, Modern — 135 — 185

Cobra, .38 Special, 6 Shot, 5" Barrel Military, Lightweight, Modern — 95 — 165

Colt Army Special .38

Colt Commando .38 Special

Cobra Early, .38 Special, 6 Shot, 2" Barrel. Lightweight, Modern	125	185
Cobra Early, .38 Special, 6 Shot, 4" Barrel, Lightweight, Modern	130	190
Cobra Early, .38 Special, 6 Shot, 2" Barrel, Lightweight, Hammer Shroud, Modern	130	190
Cobra Early, .38 Special, 6 Shot, 4" Barrel, Lightweight, Hammer Shroud, Modern	135	195
Col. Sam Colt Sesquicentennial, .45 Colt, Single Action Army, Commemorative, Blue, Silver-Plated Gripframe, 7½" Barrel, Cased, Curio	475	650
Col. Sam Colt Sesquicentennial, .45 Colt, Single Action Army, Commemorative, Blue, Silver-Plated Gripframe, 7½" Barrel, Cased, Curio	750	1,100
Col. Sam Colt Sesquicentennial, .45 Colt, Single Action Army, Commemorative, Blue, Silver-Plated Gripframe, 7½" Barrel, Cased, Curio	1,950	2,950
Colorado Gold Rush, .22 L.R.R.F., Frontier Scout S.A., Commemorative, Gold Plated, with Nickel Plating, 4¾" Barrel, Cased, Curio	150	225
Columbus Sesquicentennial, .22 L.R.R.F., Frontier Scout S.A., Commemorative, Gold Plated, 4¾" Barrel, Cased, Curio	375	495
Commando, .38 Special, 6 Shot, Military, Modern	95	145
Courier, .22 L.R.R.F., 6 Shot, 2" Barrel, Lightweight, Modern	375	550
Courier, .32 S & W Long, 6 Shot, 2" Barrel, Lightweight, Modern	375	550
Dakota Territory, .22 L.R.R.F., Frontier Scout S.A., Commemorative, Blue, with Gold Plating, 4¾" Barrel Cased, Curio	150	225
Detective Special, .38 Special, 6 Shot, 4" Barrel, Heavy Barrel, Modern	200	300
Detective Special Early, .32 S & W, 6 Shot, 2" Barrel, Modern	100	145
Detective Special Early, .38 S & W, 6 Shot, 2" Barrel, Modern	100	145
Detective Special Early, .38 Special, 6 Shot, 2" Barrel, Modern	115	155
Detective Special Late, .38 Special, 6 Shot, 2" Barrel, Blue, Modern	125	175
Detective Special Late, .38 Special, 6 Shot, 2" Barrel, Nickel Plated, Modern	135	190
Diamondback, .22 L.R.R.F., Blue, Vent Rib, 6 Shot, Modern	155	225
Diamondback, .38 Special, Blue, Vent Rib, 6 Shot, Modern	150	220
Diamondback, .38 Special, Nickel Plated, Vent Rib, 6 Shot, Modern	165	245
Florida Sesquicentennial, .22 L.R.R.F., Frontier Scout S.A., Commemorative, Blue, Color Case, Hardened Frame, 4¾" Barrel, Cased, Curio	150	225
Fort Findlay Sesquicentennial, .22 L.R.R.F., Frontier Scout S.A., Commemorative, Gold Plated, 4¾" Barrel, Cased, Curio	375	500
Fort Findlay Sesquicentennial Pair, .22LR/.22 WMR Combo, Frontier Scout S.A., Commemorative, Gold Plated, 4¾" Barrel, Cased, Curio	1,750	2,500
Fort Stephenson Sesquicentennial, .22 L.R.R.F., Frontier Scout S.A. Nickel Plated, Blue, with Nickel Plating, 4¾" Barrel, Cased, Curio	375	500
Forty-Niner Miner, .22 L.R.R.F., Frontier Scout S.A., Commemorative, Blue with Gold Plating, 4¾" Barrel, Cased, Curio	150	225
Frontier Scout, .22 L.R.R.F., Single Action, Western Style, 6 Shot, Various Barrel Lengths, Modern	90	150

Frontier Model 1878 Double Action, Various Calibers, Various Barrel Lengths, with Ejector, Curio	200	375
Frontier Model 1878 Double Action, Sheriff's Model, Various Calibers, Various Barrel Lengths, no Ejector, Curio	250	425
Frontier Model 1878 Double Action, Phillipine Model, .45 Colt, 6" Barrel, Large Trigger Guard, Curio	275	500
Frontier Model 1878 Double Action, Serial #'s under 39,000 are Antique		
Gen. J.H. Morgan Indian Raid, .22 L.R.R.F., Frontier Scout S.A., Nickel Plated, Blue, with Gold Plating, 4¾" Barrel, Cased, Curio	450	650
Gen. Nathan Bedford Forrest, .22 L.R.R.F., Frontier Scout S.A., Commemorative, Blue, with Gold Plating, 4¾" Barrel, Cased, Curio	150	225
Gen. Hood Centennial, .22 L.R.R.F., Frontier Scout S.A., Commemorative, Blue, with Gold Plating, 4¾" Barrel Cased, Curio	150	225
Gen. Meade Campaign, .22 L.R.R.F., Frontier Scout S.A., Commemorative, Blue, with Gold Plating, 4¾" Barrel, Cased, Curio	150	225
Gen. Meade Campaign, .45 Colt, Single Action Army, Commemorative, Blue, with Gold PLating, 5½" Barrel Cased, Curio	450	575
Golden Spike, .22 L.R.R.F., Frontier Scout S.A., Commemorative, Blue, with Gold Plating, 6" Barrel, Cased, Curio	150	225
H. Cook 1 of 100, .22 L.R.R.F., and .45 Colt Set, Commemorative, Nickel Plated, Blue Frame, Cased, Curio	675	925
House Pistol, .41 Short R.F., Cloverleaf-Cylinder, Model 1871, 4 Shot, 3" Barrel, Round Barrel, Spur Trigger, Antique	300	400
House Pistol, .41 Short R.F., Cloverleaf-Cylinder Model 1871, 4 Shot, 1½" Barrel, Round Barrel, Spur Trigger, Antique	425	550
House Pistol, .41 Short R.F., Cloverleaf-Cylinder Model 1871, 4 Shot, 1½" Barrel, Octagon Barrel, Spur Trigger, Antique	575	800
House, Pistol, .41 Short R.F., Round Cylinder Model of 1871, 5 Shot, 2⅝" Barrel, Round Barrel, Spur Trigger, Antique	325	450
Idaho Territorial Centennial, .22 L.R.R.F., Frontier Scout S.A., Nickel Plated, Blue, with Nickel Plating, 4¾" Barrel, Cased, Curio	220	325
Indiana Sesquicentennial, .22 L.R.R.F., Frontier Scout S.A., Commemorative, Blue, with Gold Plating, 4¾" Barrel, Cased, Curio	150	225
Joaquin Murietta, .22 L.R.R.F., and .45 Colt Set, Frontier Scout and S.A.A., Commemorative, Blue, with Gold Plating, Cased, Curio	675	950
Kansas Centennial, .22 L.R.R.F., Frontier Scout S.A., Commemorative, Gold Plated, Walnut Grips, Cased, Curio	150	225
Kansas Cowtown: Abilene, .22 L.R.R.F., Frontier Scout S.A., Commemorative, Gold Plated, 4¾" Barrel, Cased, Curio	175	275
Kansas Cowtown: Coffyville, .22 L.R.R.F., Frontier Scout S.A., Commemorative, Blue, with Gold Plating, 4¾" Barrel, Cased, Curio	175	275
Kansas Cowtown: Dodge City, .22 L.R.R.F., Frontier Scout S.A., Commemorative, Blue, with Gold Plating, 4¾" Barrel, Cased, Curio	175	275
Kansas Cowtown: Wichita, .22 L.R.R.F., Frontier Scout S.A., Commemorative, Gold Plated, 4¾" Barrel, Cased, Curio	175	275
Kansas Fort Hays, .22 L.R.R.F., Frontier Scout S.A., Commemorative, Blue, with Nickel Plating, 4¾" Barrel, Cased, Curio	150	225
Kansas Fort Larned, .22 L.R.R.F., Frontier Scout S.A., Commemorative, Blue, with Nickel Plating, Cased, Curio	150	225
Kansas Fort Riley, .22 L.R.R.F., Frontier Scout S.A., Commemorative, Blue, with Nickel Plating, 4¾" Barrel, Cased, Curio	150	225
Kansas Fort Scott, .22 L.R.R.F., Frontier Scout S.A., Commemorative, Blue, with Nickel Plating, 4¾" Barrel, Cased, Curio	150	225
Kansas: Chisholm Trail, .22 L.R.R.F., Frontier Scout S.A., Commemorative, Blue, with Nickel Plating, 4¾" Barrel, Cased, Curio	150	225
Kansas: Pawnee Trail, .22 L.R.R.F., Frontier Scout S.A., Commemorative, Blue, with Nickel Plating, 4¾" Barrel, Cased, Curio	150	225
Kansas: Santa Fe Trail, .22 L.R.R.F., Frontier Scout S.A., Commemorative, Blue, with Nickel Plating, 4¾" Barrel, Cased, Curio	150	225
Kansas: Shawnee Trail: .22 L.R.R.F., Frontier Scout S.A., Commemorative, Blue, with Nickel Plating, 4¾" Barrel, Cased, Curio	150	225
Lawman MK III, .357 Magnum, Various Barrel Lengths, Blue, 6 Shot, Modern	145	175

Lawman MK III, .357 Magnum, Various Barrel Lengths, Nickel Plated, 6
  Shot, Modern — 155 — 190
Lawman: Bat Masterson, .22 L.R.R.F., Frontier Scout S.A.,
  Commemorative, Nickel Plated, 4¾" Barrel, Cased, Curio — 175 — 275
Lawman: Bat Masterson, .45 Colt, Single Action Army, Commemorative,
  Nickel Plated, 4¾" Barrel, Cased, Curio — 375 — 600
Lawman: Pat Garrett, .22 L.R.R.F., Frontier Scout S.A., Commemorative,
  Gold Plated, with Nickel Plating, 4¾" Barrel, Cased, Curio — 175 — 275
Lawman: Pat Garrett, .45 Colt, Single Action Army, Commemorative, Gold
  Plated, with Nickel Plating, 5½" Barrel, Cased, Curio — 375 — 550
Lawman: Wild Bill Hickock, .22 L.R.R.F., Frontier Scout S.A.,
  Commemorative, Blue, with Nickel Plating, 6" Barrel, Cased, Curio — 175 — 275
Lawman: Wild Bill Hickock, .45 Colt, Single Action Army,
  Commemorative, Blue, with Nickel Plating, 7½" Barrel, Cased, Curio — 375 — 550
Lawman: Wyatt Earp, .22 L.R.R.F., Frontier Scout S.A., Commemorative,
  Blue, with Nickel Plating, Cased, Curio — 190 — 295
Lawman: Wyatt Earp, .45 Colt, Single Action Army, Commemorative, Blue,
  with Nickel Plating, 16⅛" Barrel, Cased, Curio — 775 — 995
Lightning Model 1877, .38 Colt, 6 Shot, Double Action, Standard Model,
  Modern — 175 — 300
Lightning Model 1877, .38 Colt, 6 Shot, Double Action, Sheriff's Model,
  Modern — 175 — 325
Lightning Model 1877, Serial Numbers under 105,123 are Antique
M1909 Army, .45 Colt, 6 Shot, Military, 5½" Barrel, Modern — 175 — 350
M1909 U.S.M.C., .45 Colt, 6 Shot, 5½" Barrel, Modern — 275 — 525
M1909 U.S.N., .45 Colt, 6 Shot, Military, 5½" Barrel, Modern — 225 — 475
M1917 Army, .45 Auto-Rim, 6 Shot, Military, 5½" Barrel, Modern — 140 — 275
Maine Sesquicentennial, .22 L.R.R.F., Frontier Scout S.A.,
  Commemorative, Gold Plated, with Nickel Plating, 4¾" Barrel, Cased,
  Curio — 150 — 225
Marshal, .38 Special, 6 Shot, Round Butt, Modern — 155 — 195
Metropolitan MK III, .38 Special, 4" Barrel, 6 Shot, Modern — 125 — 165
Missouri Sesquicentennial, .22 L.R.R.F., Frontier Scout S.A.,
  Commemorative, Blue, with Gold Plating, 4¾" Barrel, Cased, Curio — 150 — 225
Missouri Sesquicentennial, .45 Colt, Single Action Army, Commemorative,
  Blue, with Gold Plating, 5½" Barrel, Cased, Curio — 375 — 575
Model 1872 Army, .44 Henry R.F., Open-Top Frontier Single Action, Army
  Style Gripframe, Antique — 1,350 — 1,850
Model 1872 Army, .44 Henry R.F., Open-Top Frontier Single Action, Navy
  Style Gripframe, Antique — 1,600 — 2,250
Model 1889, .38 Long Colt, 6 Shot, Commercial, Various Barrel Lengths,
  Double Action, Swing-Out Cylinder, Antique — 125 — 250
Model 1889, .41 Long Colt, 6 Shot, Commercial, Various Barrel Lengths,
  Double Action, Swing-Out Cylinder, Antique — 125 — 250
Model 1889 Navy, .38 Long Colt, 6 Shot, Military, 6" Barrel, Double
  Action, Swing-Out Cylinder, Antique — 175 — 350

Colt Lightning Sheriff's Model

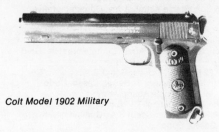

Colt Model 1902 Military

Model 1892 New Army,.38 Long Colt, 6 Shot, Military, 6" Barrel, Double Action, Swing-Out Cylinder, Antique	135	225
Model 1892 New Navy, .38 Long Colt, 6 Shot, Military, 6" Barrel, Double Action, Swing-Out Cylinder, Antique	160	275
Model 1892 New Navy, .38 Long Colt, 6 Shot, Commercial, Various Barrel Lengths, Double Action, Swing-Out Cylinder, Antique	125	200
Model 1892 New Navy, .41 Long Colt, 6 Shot, Commercial, Various Barrel Lengths, Double Action, Swing-Out Cylinder, Antique	125	200
Model 1894 New Army, .38 Long Colt, 6 Shot, Military, 6" Barrel, Double Action, Swing-Out Cylinder, Antique	125	200
Model 1894 New Navy, .38 Long Colt, 6 Shot, Military, 6" Barrel, Double Action, Swing-Out Cylinder, Antique	150	240
Model 1895 New Army, .38 Long Colt, 6 Shot, Military, 6" Barrel, Double Action, Swing-Out Cylinder, Antique	125	200
Model 1895 New Navy, .38 Long Colt, 6 Shot, Military, 6" Barrel, Double Action, Swing-Out Cylinder, Antique	150	250
Model 1896 New Army, .38 Long Colt, 6 Shot, Military, 6" Barrel, Double Action, Swing-Out Cylinder, Antique	125	200
Model 1896 New Navy, .38 Long Colt, 6 Shot, Military, 6" Barrel, Double Action, Swing-Out Cylinder, Antique	150	225
Model 1901 New Army, .38 Long Colt, 6 Shot, Military, 6" Barrel, Double Action, Swing-Out Cylinder, Antique	125	195
Model 1902 Army, .45 Colt, 6 Shot, Military, 6" Barrel, Double Action, Modern	300	450
Model 1903 New Army, .38 Long Colt, 6 Shot, Military, 6" Barrel, Double Action, Swing-Out Cylinder, Modern	120	190
Model 1903 New Navy, .32-20 WCF, 6 Shot Commercial, Various Barrel Lengths, Double Action, Swing-Out Cylinder, Modern	165	250
Model 1903 New Navy, .38 Long Colt, 6 Shot, Commercial, Various Barrel Lengths, Double Action, Swing-Out Cylinder, Modern	155	245
Model 1903 New Navy, .38 Long Colt, 6 Shot, Commercial, Various Barrel Lengths, Double Action, Swing-Out Cylinder, Modern	135	220

Colt Model 1903 .38 ACP

Model 1905 U.S.M.C., .38 Long Colt, 6 Shot, Military, 6" Barrel, Swing-Out Cylinder, Modern	375	550
Model 1905 U.S.M.C., .38 Long Colt, 6 Shot, Commercial, 6" Barrel, Swing-Out Cylinder, Modern	400	600
Montana Territory Centennial, .22 L.R.R.F., Frontier Scout S.A., Commemorative, Blue, with Gold Plating, 4¾" Barrel, Cased, Curio	150	225
Montana Territory Centennial, .45 Colt, Single Action Army, Commemorative, Blue, with Gold Plating, 7½" Barrel, Cased, Curio	375	600
Nebraska Centennial, .22 L.R.R.F., Frontier Scout S.A., Commemorative, Gold Plated, 4¾" Barrel, Cased, Curio	150	225
Ned Buntline, .45 Colt, New Frontier Single Action Army, 12" Barrel, Commemorative, Modern	700	950
Nevada Battle Born, .22 L.R.R.F., Frontier Scout S.A., Commemorative, Blue, with Nickel Plating, 4¾" Barrel, Cased, Curio	150	225
Nevada Battle Born, .22 L.R.R.F. and .45 Colt Set, Frontier Scout and S.A.A., Commemorative, Blue, with Nickel Plating, Cased, Curio	1,150	1,750
Nevada Battle Born, .45 Colt, Single Action Army, Commemorative, Blue, with Nickel Plating, 5½" Barrel, Cased, Curio	750	1,100
Nevada Centennial, .22 L.R.R.F., Frontier Scout S.A., Commemorative, Blue, with Nickel Plating, 4¾" Barrel, Cased, Curio	150	225
Nevada Centennial, .22 L.R.R.F. and .45 Colt Set, Frontier Scout and S.A:A., Nickel Plated, Blue, with Nickel Plating, Cased, Curio	525	775
Nevada Centennial, .22 L.R.R.F. and .45 Colt Set, Frontier Scout and S.A.A., Commemorative, Blue, with Nickel Plating, with Extra Engraved Cylinder, Cased, Curio	625	875
Nevada Centennial, .45 Colt, Single Action Army, Nickel Plated, Blue, with Nickel Plating, 5½" Barrel, Cased, Curio	400	600
New Frontier, .22LR/.22WMR Combo, Various Barrel Lengths, Blue, 6 Shot, Adjustable Sights, Modern	95	175
New Frontier, .22R/.22 WRM Combo, 7½" Barrel, Blue, 6 Shot, Adjustable Sights, Modern	100	185
New Jersey Tercentenary, .22 L.R.R.F., Frontier Scout S.A., Commemorative, Blue, with Nickel Plating, 4¾" Barrel, Cased, Curio	150	225
New Jersey Tercentenary, .45 Colt, Single Action Army, Commemorative, Blue, with Nickel Plating, 5½" Barrel, Cased, Curio	400	600
New Line, .38 Long Colt, Police and Thug Model, with Ejector, 5 Shot, Spur Trigger, Standard, Antique	350	575

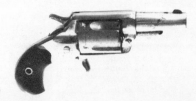

Colt New Line .38

New Line, .32 or .41 C.F., Police and Thug Model, with Ejector, 5 Shot, Spur Trigger, Antique	425	825
New Line, .38 Long Colt, House Civilian Model, with Ejector, 5 Shot, Spur Trigger, Antique	175	300
New Line, .38 Long Colt, House Civilian Model, no Ejector, 5 Shot, Spur Trigger, Antique	175	300
New Line, .41 Short C.F., House Civilian Model, with Ejector, 5 Shot, Spur Trigger, Antique	190	350
New Line, .41 Short C.F., House Civilian Model, no Ejector, 5 Shot, Spur Trigger, Antique	160	300
New Line Pocket, Locking Notches, Cylinder Periphery, Add 20%-30%		
New Line Pocket, .22 Long R.F., the Little Colt, 7 Shot, Spur Trigger, Antique	130	225
New Line Pocket, .30 Long R.F., the Pony Colt, 5 Shot, Spur Trigger, Antique	150	275
New Line Pocket, .32 Long R.F. or .32 Long Colt, Add for 4" Barrel 100%-150%		
New Line Pocket, .32 Long Colt, the Ladies Colt, 5 Shot, Spur Trigger, Antique	135	225
New Line Pocket, .32 Long R.F., the Ladies Colt, 5 Shot, Spur Trigger, Antique	135	225
New Line Pocket, .38 Long Colt, the Pet Colt, 5 Shot, Spur Trigger, Antique	160	250
New Line Pocket, .38 Long R.F. the Pet Colt, 5 Shot, Spur Trigger, Antique	150	240
New Line Pocket, .41 Long R.F., the Big Colt, 5 Shot, Spur Trigger, Antique	250	345
New Line Pocket, .41 Short C.F., the Big Colt, 5 Shot, Spur Trigger, Antique	260	370
New Mexico Golden Anniv., .22 L.R. R.F., Frontier Scout S.A., Commemorative, Blue, with Gold Plating, 4 3/4" Barrel, Cased, Curio	175	295
New Pocket, .32 Long Colt, 6 Shot, Various Barrel Lengths, Modern	150	245
New Pocket, .32 S & W Long, 6 Shot, Various Barrel Lengths, Modern	150	220
New Police, .32 Long Colt, 6 Shot, Various Barrel Lengths, Modern	160	255
New Police, Serial Numbers under 7,300 are Antique		
New Police, .32 S & W Long, 6 Shot, Various Barrel Lengths, Modern	150	220
New Police Target, .32 Long Colt, 6 Shot, 6" Barrel, Adjustable, Modern	175	275
New Police Target, .32 S & W Long, 6 Shot, 6" Barrel, Adjustable Sights, Modern	175	275
New Service, .357 Magnum, 6 Shot, Commercial, Various Barrel Lengths, Modern	225	375
New Service, .38 Special, 6 Shot, Commercial, Various Barrel Lengths, Modern	175	250
New Service, .38-40 WCF, 6 Shot, Commercial, Various Barrel Lengths, Modern	200	325
New Service, .38-44, 6 Shot, Commercial, Various Barrel Lengths, Modern	225	375
New Service, .44 Special, 6 Shot, Commercial, Various Barrel Lengths, Modern	250	400
New Service, .44-40 WCF, 6 Shot, Commercial, Various Barrel Lengths, Modern	250	400
New Service, .45 Auto-Rim, 6 Shot, Commercial, Various Barrel Lengths, Modern	175	275
New Service, .45 Colt, 6 Shot, Commercial, Various Barrel Lengths, Modern	200	325
New Service, .455 Colt, 6 Shot, Commercial, Various Barrel Lengths, Modern	225	350
New Service Target, .44 Special, 6 Shot, Commercial, 7½" Barrel, Adjustable Sights, Modern	350	500
New Service Target, .45 Auto-Rim, 6 Shot, Commercial, 7½" Barrel, Adjustable Sights, Modern	325	475
New Service Target, .45 Colt, 6 Shot, Commercial, 7½" Barrel, Adjustable Sights, Modern	325	400

Colt Officer's Model

New Service Target, .455 Colt, 6 Shot, Commercial, 7½" Barrel, Adjustable
    Sights, Modern   325   500
NRA Centennial, .357 Mag. or .45 Colt, Single Action Army,
    Commemorative, Blue, Color Case, Hardened Frame, Various Barrel
    Lengths, Cased, Curio   375   575
Officer's Model, .38 Special, 6 Shot, Adjustable Sights, with Detachable
    Shoulder Stock, Curio   750   1,200
Officer's Model Match, .22 L.R.R.F., 6 Shot, Adjustable Sights, 6" Barrel,
    Target Grips, Target Hammer, Modern   170   240
Officer's Model Match, .22 W.M.R., 6 Shot, Adjustable Sights, 6" Barrel,
    Target Grips, Target Hammer, Modern   400   575
Officer's Model Match, .38 Special, 6 Shot, Adjustable Sights, 6" Barrel,
    Target Grips, Target Hammer, Modern   160   225
Officer's Model Special, .22 L.R.R.F., 6 Shot, Adjustable Sights, 6" Barrel,
    Heavy Barrel, Modern   150   225
Officer's Model Special, .38 Special, 6 Shot, Adjustable Sights, 6" Barrel,
    Heavy Barrel, Modern   160   235
Officer's Model Target, .22 L.R.R.F., 6 Shot, Adjustable Sights, 6" Barrel,
    Second Issue, Modern   195   275
Officer's Model Target, .32 S & W Long, 6 Shot, Adjustable Sights, 6"
    Barrel, Second Issue, Modern   200   300
Officer's Model Target, .38 Special, 6 Shot, Adjustable Sights, 6" Barrel,
    Modern   175   250
Officer's Model Target, .38 Special, 6 Shot, Adjustable Sights, 6" Barrel,
    Second Issue, Modern   200   300
Official Police, .22 L.R.R.F., 6 Shot, Various Barrel Lengths, Modern   150   215
Official Police, .32-20 WCF, 6 Shot, Modern   175   275
Official Police, .38 Special, 6 Shot, Modern   125   190
Official Police, .41 Long Colt, 6 Shot, Modern   145   185
Oklahoma Territory, .22 L.R.R.F., Frontier Scout S.A., Commemorative,
    Blue, with Gold Plating, 4¾" Barrel, Cased, Curio   150   225
Old Fort Des Moines, .22 L.R.R.F., Frontier Scout S.A., Commemorative,
    Gold Plated, 4¾" Barrel, Cased, Curio   175   275

Colt Official Police .38 Special

Colt Old Line .22

Old Fort Des Moines, .22 L.R.R.F. and .45 Colt Set, Frontier Scout S.A. and S.A.A., Commemorative, Gold Plated, Cased, Curio	600	795
Old Fort Des Moines, .45 Colt, Single Action Army, Commemorative, Gold Plated, 5½" Barrel, Cased, Curio	375	550
Old Line Pocket, .22 Short R.F., Open Top, First Model with Ejector, 7 Shot, Spur Trigger, Antique	500	750
Old Line Pocket, .22 Short R.F., Open Top, Second Model, No Ejector, 7 Shot, Spur Trigger, Antique	175	295
Oregon Trail, .22 L.R.R.F., Frontier Scout S.A., Commemorative, Blue, with Gold Plating, 4¾" Barrel, Cased, Curio	150	225
Peacemaker, .22LR/.22 WMR Combo, Various Barrel Lengths, Blue, 6 Shot, Modern	95	150
Peace Maker, .22LR/.22 WMR Combo, 7½" Barrel, Blue, 6 Shot, Modern	95	160
Peacemaker Centennial, .44-40 WCF, Single Action Army, Commemorative, Blue, Color Case, Hardened Frame, 7½" Barrel, Cased, Curio	375	550
Peacemaker Centennial, .44-40 and .45 Colt Set, Single Action Army, Commemorative, Blue, Color Case, Hardened Frame, 7½" Barrel, Cased, Curio	875	1,350
Peacemaker Centennial, .45 Colt, Single Action Army, Commemorative, Blue, Color Case, Hardened Frame, 7½" Barrel, Cased, Curio	375	550
Pocket Positive, .32 Long Colt, 6 Shot, Various Barrel Lengths, Modern	140	195
Pocket Positive, .32 S & W Long, 6 Shot, Various Barrel Lengths, Modern	145	200
Police Positive, .22 L.R.R.F., 6 Shot, Various Barrel Lengths, Modern	125	175
Police Positive, .22 WRF, 6 Shot, Various Barrel Lengths, Modern	140	195
Police Positive, .32 Long Colt, 6 Shot, Various Barrel Lengths, Modern	95	170
Police Positive, .32 S & W Long, 6 Shot, Various Barrel Lengths, Modern	95	180
Police Positive, .38 S & W, 6 Shot, Various Barrel Lengths, Modern	95	175
Police Positive Late, .38 Special, Blue, 4" Barrel, Modern	125	175
Police Positive Late, .38 Special, Nickel Plated, 4" Barrel, 6 Shot, Modern	130	185
Police Positive Special, .32 S & W Long, 6 Shot, Various Barrel Lengths, Modern	90	175
Police Positive Special, .32-20 WCF, 6 Shot, Various Barrel Lengths, Modern	150	245
Police Positive Special, .38 S & W, 6 Shot, Various Barrel Lengths, Modern	85	165
Police Positive Special, .38 Special, Shot, Various Barrel Lengths, Modern	95	175
Police Positive Target, .22 L.R.R.F., 6 Shot, 6" Barrel, Adjustable Sights, Modern	175	325
Police Positive Target, .22 WRF, 6 Shot, 6" Barrel, Adjustable Sights, Modern	200	350
Police Positive Target, .32 Long Colt, 6 Shot, 6" Barrel, Adjustable Sights, Modern	175	275
Police Positive Target, .32 S & W Long, 6 Shot, 6" Barrel, Adjustable Sights, Modern	185	295
Police Positive Target, .38 S & W Long, 6 Shot, 6" Barrel, Adjustable Sights, Modern	175	275
Pony Express Centennial, .22 L.R.R.F., Frontier Scout S.A., Commemorative, 4¾" Barrel, Gold Plated, Cased, Curio	325	475

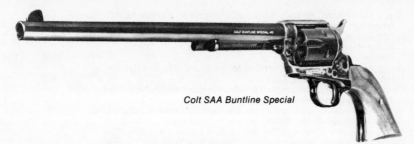

Colt SAA Buntline Special

Pony Express Presentation, .45 Colt, Single Action Army, Commemorative, Nickel Plated, 7½" Barrel, Cased, Curio	575	825
Python, .357 Magnum, 2" Barrel, Blue, Vent Rib, Adjustable Sights, 6 Shot, Modern	225	325
Python .357 Magnum, 4" Barrel, Blue, Vent Rib, 6 Shot, Adjustable Sights, Modern	225	335
Python, .357 Magnum, 4" Barrel, Nickel, Vent Rib, 6 Shot, Adjustable Sights, Modern	235	340
Python, .357 Magnum, 6" Barrel, Blue, Vent Rib, 6 Shot, Adjustable Sights, Modern	225	325
Python, .357 Magnum, 6" Barrel, Nickel, Vent Rib, 6 Shot, Adjustable Sights, Modern	235	340

(Handgun, Revolver)

S.A.A. Buntline Special, .45 Colt, 12" Barrel, Blue, Modern	225	350
S.A.A. Buntline Special New Frontier, .45 Colt, 12" Barrel, Blue, Adjustable Sights, Modern	225	350
Sheriff's Model, .45 Colt, Single Action Army, Commemorative, Blue, Color Case, Hardened Frame, 3" Barrel, Curio	750	1,100
Sheriff's Model, .45 Colt, Single Action Army, Commemorative, Nickel Plated, 3" Barrel, Curio	2,500	3,450
Shooting Master, .357 Magnum, 6 Shot, Commercial, 6" Barrel, Adjustable Sights, Modern	440	600
Shooting Master, .38 Special, 6 Shot, Commercial, 6" Barrel, Adjustable Sights, Modern	375	475
Shooting Master, .44 Special, 6 Shot, Commercial, 6" Barrel, Adjustable Sights, Modern	450	600
Shooting Master, .45 Auto-Rim, 6 Shot, Commercial, 6" Barrel, Adjustable Sights, Modern	375	500
Shooting Master, .45 Colt, 6 Shot, Commercial, 6" Barrel, Adjustable Sights, Modern	375	550
Single Action Army Late, .357 Magnum, Various Barrel Lengths, Blue, 6 Shot, Modern	215	300
Single Action Army Late, .357 Magnum, 7½" Barrel, Blue, 6 Shot, Modern	220	315
Single Action Army Late, .44 Special, 7½" Barrel, Blue, 6 Shot, Modern	220	315
Single Action Army Late, .45 Colt, 7½" Barrel, Blue, 6 Shot, Modern	210	300
Single Action Army Late, .45 Colt, Various Barrel Lengths, Blue, 6 Shot, Modern	200	290
Single Action Army Late, .45 Colt, 7½" Barrel, Nickel Plated, 6 Shot, Modern	250	345
Single Action Army Late New Frontier, .357 Magnum, Various Barrel Lengths, Blue, 6 Shot, Adjustable Sights, Modern	250	350
Single Action Army Late New Frontier, .44 Special, 7½" Barrel, Blue, 6 Shot, Adjustable Sights, Modern	235	340
Single Action Army Late New Frontier, .45 Colt, Various Barrel Lengths, Blue, 6 Shot, Adjustable Sights, Modern	235	340
Single Action Army, .44-40 WCF, Frontier Six Shooter, Commercial, 5½" Barrel or 6½" Barrel, Antique	700	1,150

Single Action Army, .45 Colt, Standard Cavalry Model # Under 15,000,
 Screw-Retained Cylinder Pin, Blue, Military, 7½" Barrel, Antique   950   2,150
Single Action Army, .45 Colt, Indian Scout Model, #'s Under 30000,
 Screw-Retained Cylinder Pin, Nickel Plated, Military, 7½" Barrel,
 Antique   1,250   2,250
Single Action Army, .45 Colt, Artillery Model, Screw-Retained Cylinder
 Pin, Military, 5½" Barrel, Antique   850   1,500
Single Action Army, Various Calibers, Storekeeper's Model, No Ejector,
 Short Barrel, Commercial, Antique   1,250   2,250
Single Action Army, Various Calibers, Standard Peacemaker, Calibers: .45
 Colt, .44-40, .38-40, .41, .32-20, Commercial, Antique   475   850
Single Action Army, Various Calibers, for Rare Calibers Add 50%-200%
Single Action Army, Various Calibers, Folding Rear Sight, Long Barrel,
 Add $1,850-$2,750
Single Action Army, Various Calibers, Target Model (Flat-Top), Add
 $950-$2,000
Single Action Army, Various Calibers, 8" or 9" Barrel, Add $250-$400
Single Action Army, Various Calibers, for 12" Barrel, Add $375-$550
Single Action Army, Various Calibers, for 16" Barrel, Add $500-$850
Single Action Army, Various Calibers, Shoulder Stock, Add $850-$1,400
Single Action Army, Various Calibers, #'s over 182,000 are Modern, #'s
 under 165,000 Black Powder Only
Single Action Army, Various Calibers, Nickel Plating, Add 10%-20%
Single Action Army, Various Calibers, Rimfires Add 100%-125%
Single Action Army, Various Calibers, Long-Fluted Cylinder #'s 330,000 to
 331,379, Commercial, Curio   850   1,250
Single Action Bisley, Various Calibers, Standard Model, Calibers:, 32-20,
 38-40, 41, 41-40, 45, Target Trigger, Modern   600   950
Single Action Bisley, Various Calibers, Target Model, (Flat-Top), Modern   950   1,950
Single Action Bisley, Various Calibers, Add for other than Standard
 Calibers 50%-100%
Single Action Bisley, Various Calibers, Non-Standard Barrel Lengths, Add
 20%-30%

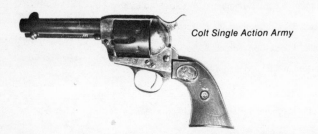

Colt Single Action Army

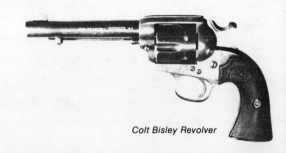

Colt Bisley Revolver

Single Action Bisley, Various Calibers, No Ejector Housing, Add 25%-35%

St. Augustine Quadricentennial, .22 L.R.R.F., Frontier Scout S.A., Commemorative, Blue, with Gold Plating, 4¾" Barrel, Cased, Curio	175	275
St. Louis Bicentennial, .22 L.R.R.F., Frontier Scout S.A., Commemorative, Blue, with Gold Plating, 4¾" Barrel, Cased, Curio	150	225
St. Louis Scout, .22 L.R.R.F. and .45 Colt Set, Frontier Scout and S.A.A., Commemorative, Blue, with Gold Plating, Cased, Curio	550	725
St. Louis Bicentennial, .45 Colt, Single Action Army, Commemorative, Blue, with Gold Plating, 5½" Barrel, Cased, Curio	350	475
Texas Ranger, Standard, .45 Colt, Single Action Army, Commemorative, Blue, Color Case Hardened Frame, Cased, Curio	750	1,100
Thunderer Model 1877, .41 Colt, 6 Shots, Double Action, Standard Model, Modern 175	300	
Thunderer Model 1877, .41 Colt, 6 Shots, Double Action, Sheriff's Model, Modern	180	325
Trooper, .22 L.R.R.F., 6 Shot, Adjustable Sights, Target Grips, Target Hammer, Modern	170	250
Trooper, .357 Magnum, 6 Shot, 4" Barrel, Adjustable Sights, Modern	175	250
Trooper, .357 Magnum, 6 Shot, Adjustable Sights, Target Grips, Target Hammer, Modern	190	275
Trooper, .38 Special, 6 Shot, 4" Barrel, Adjustable Sights, Modern	165	225
Trooper, .38 Special, 6 Shot, Adjustable Sights, Target Grips, Target Hammer, Modern	175	240
Trooper MK III, .22 L.R.R.F., 4" Barrel, Blue, 6 Shot, Adjustable Sights, Modern	150	215
Trooper MK III, .22 W.M.R., 4" Barrel, Blue, 6 Shot, Adjustable Sights, Modern	150	215
Trooper MK III, .22 L.R.R.F., 6" Barrel, 6 Shot, Adjustable Sights, Modern	150	215
Trooper MK III, .22 W.M.R., 6" Barrel, 6 Shot, Adjustable Sights, Modern	150	215
Trooper MK III, .357 Magnum, 4" Barrel, Blue, 6 Shot, Adjustable Sights, Modern	150	215
Trooper MK III, .357 Magnum, 4" Barrel, Nickel Plated, 6 Shot, Adjustable Sights, Modern	160	225
Trooper MK III, .357 Magnum, 6" Barrel, 6 Shot, Adjustable Sights, Modern	150	215
Trooper MK III, .357 Magnum, 6" Barrel, Nickel Plated, 6 Shot, Adjustable Sights, Modern	165	235
Viper, .38 Special, Nickel Plated, 4" Barrel, 6 Shot, Lightweight, Modern	145	185
Viper, .38 Special, Blue, 4" Barrel, 6 Shot, Lightweight, Modern	125	170
West Virginia Centennial, .22 L.R.R.F., Frontier Scout S.A., Commemorative, Blue, with Gold Plating, 4¾" Barrel, Cased, Curio	150	225
West Virginia Centennial, .45 Colt, Single Action Army, Commemorative, Blue, with Gold Plating, 4¾" Barrel, Cased, Curio	375	575
Wyatt Earp Buntline, .45 Colt, Single Action Army, Commemorative, Gold Plated, 12" Barrel, Cased, Curio	900	1,400
Wyoming Diamond Jubilee, .22 L.R.R.F., Frontier Scout S.A., Commemorative, Blue, with Nickel Plating, 4¾" Barrel, Cased, Curio	150	225
Second Amendment, .22 L.R.R.F., Frontier Scout, Cased, Curio	190	295

Handgun, Semi-Automatic

Ace, .22 L.R.R.F., Clip Fed, Adjustable Sights, Target Pistol, Curio	500	850
Ace 45-22 Conversion Unit, .45 ACP, Clip Fed, Adjustable Sights, Target Pistol, Curio	125	225
Ace Service Model, .22 L.R.R.F., Clip Fed, Adjustable Sights, Target Pistol, Curio	525	900
Challenger, .22 L.R.R.F., Clip Fed, Modern	90	175
Combat Commander, .38 Super, Clip Fed, Blue, Modern	165	240
Combat Commander, .45 ACP, Clip Fed, Blue, Modern	160	235
Combat Commander, .45 ACP, Clip Fed, Satin Nickel, Modern	160	245
Combat Commander, 9mm Luger, Clip Fed, Blue, Modern	160	235

Colt Commander

Colt Government Model .45 ACP

Commander, .45 ACP, Clip Fed, Blue, Lightweight, Modern	150	225
Conversion Unit, .22 L.R.R.F., Clip Fed, Blue, Adjustable Sights, Modern	75	110
Gold Cup, .45 ACP, Clip Fed, Adjustable Sights, Target Pistol, Military Style Stock, Modern	275	400
Gold Cup MK III, .38 Special, Clip Fed, Adjustable Sights, Target Pistol, Military Style Stock, Modern	325	450
Gold Cup MK IV, .45 ACP, Clip Fed, Blue, Target Trigger, Modern	240	325
Gold Cup NRA Centennial, .45 ACP, Commemorative, Target Pistol, Light Engraving, Cased, Curio	275	400
Government, .45 ACP, Clip Fed, Commercial, Modern	200	325
Government 1911 English, .455 Webley Auto., Clip Fed, Military, Curio	350	450
Government BB 1911A1, .45 ACP. Clip Fed, Curio	275	400
Government M1911, M1911A1, .45 ACP, Also See U.S. Military		
Government M1911, .45 ACP, Clip Fed, Commercial, Curio	225	375
Government M1911, .45 ACP, Clip Fed, Military, Curio	200	325
Government M1911A1, .45 ACP, Clip Fed, Military, Modern	175	275
Government M1911A1, .45 ACP, Clip Fed, Military, with Detachable Shoulder Stock, Class 3	900	1,500
Government MK IV, .38 Super, Clip Fed, Blue, Modern	175	245
Government MK IV, .45 ACP, Clip Fed, Blue, Modern	175	240
Government MK IV, .45 ACP, Clip Fed, Nickel Plated, Modern	190	255
Government MK IV, 9mm Luger, Clip Fed, Blue, Modern	165	225
Junior, .22 Short R.F., Clip Fed, Modern	85	150
Junior, .25 ACP, Clip Fed, Modern	80	145
M 1911A1 (British), .455 Webley Auto., Clip Fed, Military, Modern	275	375
M1905/07 U.S., .45 ACP, Clip Fed, Blue, Military, Curio	1,300	1,800
Model 1900, .38 ACP, Clip Fed, 6" Barrel, Commercial, Safety Sight, Curio	600	1,100
Model 1900, .38 ACP, Clip Fed, 6" Barrel, Commercial, Foward Slide Serrations, Curio	450	650
Model 1900, .38 ACP, Clip Fed, 6" Barrel, Commercial, Curio	375	500
Model 1900 U.S. Army, .38 ACP, Clip Fed, 6" Barrel, Military, Curio	500	800
Model 1900 U.S. Navy, .38 ACP, Clip Fed, 6" Barrel, Military, Curio	550	900
Model 1902, .38 ACP, Clip Fed, 6" Barrel, Foward Slide Serrations, Commercial, Curio	325	450

Colt Junior .25 ACP

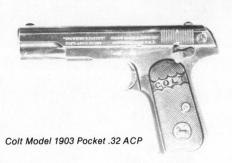

Colt Model 1903 Pocket .32 ACP

Colt Model 1902 Commercial

Model 1902, .38 ACP, Clip Fed, 6″ Barrel, Commercial, Curio	375	550
Model 1902 Military, .38 ACP, Clip Fed, 6″ Barrel, Foward Slide Serrations, Curio	375	500
Model 1902 Military, .38 ACP, Clip Fed, 6″ Barrel, Curio	325	450
Model 1902 Military U.S. Army, .38 ACP, Clip Fed, 6″ Barrel, Curio	450	750
Model 1903 Round Hammer, .38 ACP, Clip Fed, Curio	200	300
Model 1903 Spur Hammer, .38 ACP, Clip Fed, Curio	175	275
Model 1905, .45 ACP, Clip Fed, Curio	350	550
Model 1905, .45 ACP, Clip Fed, Adjustable Sights, with Detachable Shoulder Stock, Curio	1,750	3,250
Model 1903 Pocket 1st Type, .32 ACP, Clip Fed, Barrel Bushing, Commercial, Curio	140	230
Model 1903 Pocket 2nd Type, .32 ACP, Clip Fed, Commercial, Curio	135	225
Model 1903 Pocket 3rd Type, .32 ACP, Clip Fed, Commercial, Magazine Disconnect, Modern	125	215
Model 1903 Pocket 1st Type, .380 ACP, Clip Fed, Barrel Bushing, Commercial, Curio	145	235
Model 1903 Pocket 2nd Type, .380 ACP, Clip Fed, Commercial, Curio	140	230
Model 1903 Pocket 3rd Type, .380 ACP, Clip Fed, Commercial, Magazine Disconnect, Modern	135	220
Model 1903 U.S., .32 ACP, Clip Fed, Military, Magazine Disconnect, Curio	275	400
Model 1903 U.S., .380 ACP, Clip Fed, Military, Magazine Disconnect, Curio	275	400
Model 1908 Pocket, .25 ACP, Clip Fed, Hammerless, Curio	175	250
Model 1908 Pocket, .25 ACP, Clip Fed, Hammerless, Magazine Disconnect, Modern	150	222
National Match, .45 ACP, Clip Fed, Target Pistol, Adjustable Sights, Modern	450	600
National Match, .45 ACP, Clip Fed, Target Pistol, Modern	350	475

Colt Pony

Pony, .380 ACP, Clip Fed, Hammer, Modern	600	900
Super, .38 Super, Clip Fed, Commercial, Modern	175	300
Super Match, .38 Super, Clip Fed, Adjustable Sights, Target Pistol, Modern	375	500
Super Match, .38 Super, Clip Fed, Target Pistol, Modern	275	400
Super Mexican Police, .38 Super, Clip Fed, Military, Modern	250	375
WWI Battle of 2nd Marne, .45 ACP, Commemorative, M1911, Light Engraving, Cased, Curio	250	400
WWI Battle of 2nd Marne Deluxe, .45 ACP, Commemorative, M1911, Engraved, Cased, Curio	675	1,100
WWI Battle of 2nd Marne Special Deluxe, .45 ACP., Commemorative, M1911, Fancy Engraving, Cased, Curio	1,350	2,250
WWI Belleau Wood, .45 ACP, Commemorative, M1911, Light Engraving, Cased, Curio	250	400
WWI Belleau Wood Special Deluxe, .45 ACP, Commemorative, M1911, Fancy Engraving, Cased, Curio	1,350	2,250
WWI Belleau Wood Deluxe, .45 ACP, Commemorative, M1911, Engraved, Cased, Curio	675	1,100
WWI Chateau Thierry, .45 ACP, Commemorative, M1911, Light Engraving, Cased, Curio	250	400
WWI Chateau Thierry Deluxe, .45 ACP, Commemorative, M1911, Engraved, Cased, Curio	675	1,100
WWI Chateau Thierry Special Deluxe, .45 ACP, Commemorative, M1911, Fancy Engraving, Cased, Curio	1,350	2,250
WWI Meuse-Argonne, .45 ACP, Commemorative, M1911, Light Engraving, Cased, Curio	250	400
WWI Meuse-Argonne Deluxe, .45 ACP, Commemorative, M1911, Engraved, Cased, Curio	675	1,100
WWI Meuse-Argonne Special Deluxe, .45 ACP, Commemorative, M1911, Fancy Engraving, Cased, Curio	1,350	2,250
WWII E.T.O., .45 ACP, Commemorative, M1911A1, Light Engraving, Cased, Curio	250	400
WWII P.T.O., .45 ACP, Commemorative, M1911A1, Light Engraving, Cased, Curio	250	400
Woodsman, .22 L.R.R.F., Clip Fed, Adjustable Sights, with Detachable Shoulder Stock, Curio	750	1,250
Woodsman Huntsman, .22 L.R.R.F., Clip Fed, Blue, Adjustable Sights, Modern	95	175
Woodsman Match Target 1st Type, .22 L.R.R.F., Clip Fed, Extended Target Grips, Modern	350	525
Woodsman Match Target 2nd Type, .22 L.R.R.F., Clip Fed, Blue, Adjustable Sights, Modern	145	225

Colt Woodsman .22

Woodsman N & S, .22 L.R.R.F., Clip Fed, Adjustable Sights, with Detachable Shoulder Stock, Curio	950	1,500
Woodsman Sport 1st. Type, .22 L.R.R.F., Clip Fed, Adjustable Sights, Modern	225	350
Woodsman Sport, .22 L.R.R.F., Clip Fed, Blue, Adjustable Sights, Modern	95	185
Woodsman Target 1st Type, .22 L.R.R.F., Clip Fed, Adjustable Sights, Modern	175	295
Woodsman Target 1st Type, .22 L.R.R.F., Clip Fed, Adjustable Sights, with Extra Mainspring Housing, Modern	225	325
Woodsman Target 2nd. Type, .22 L.R.R.F., Clip Fed, Adjustable Sights, Modern	200	295
Woodsman Target 3rd Type, .22 L.R.R.F., Clip Fed, Blue, Adjustable Sights, Modern	125	225
Woodsman Targetsman, .22 L.R.R.F., Clip Fed, Blue, Adjustable Sights, Modern	95	175

Handgun, Singleshot

#1 Deringer, .41 Short R.F., all Metal, Spur Trigger, Light Engraving, Antique	450	650
#2 Deringer, .41 Short R.F., "Address Col. Colt," Wood Grips, Spur Trigger, Light Engraving, Antique	500	850
#2 Deringer, .41 Short R.F., Wood Grips, Spur Trigger, Light Engraving, Antique	300	475
#3 Deringer Thuer, .41 Short R.F., Wood Grips, Spur Trigger, 1st Issue, Contoured Swell at Pivot, High-Angled Hammer, Antique	450	800
#3 Deringer Thuer, .41 Short R.F., Wood Grips, Spur Trigger, 2nd Issue, Angled Frame, no Swell, High Angled Hammer, Antique	275	425
#3 Deringer Thuer, .41 Short R.F., Wood Grips, Spur Trigger, 3rd Issue, Straight Thick Frame, High-Angled Hammer, Antique	220	325
#3 Deringer Thuer, .41 Short R.F., Wood Grips, Spur Trigger, London Marked, Antique	500	650
#4 Deringer, .22 Short R.F., Geneseo Anniversary Commemorative, Spur Trigger, Curio	300	450
#4 Deringer, .22 Short R.F., Fort McPherson Commemorative, Spur Trigger, Curio	150	225
#4 Deringer, .22 Short R.F., Spur Trigger, Modern	45	65
#4 Deringer, .22 Short R.F., Spur Trigger, Cased Pair, Modern	90	140
#4 Lord Deringer, .22 Short R.F., Spur Trigger, Cased Pair, Modern	80	125
#4 Lady Deringer, .22 Short R.F., Spur Trigger, Cased Pair, Modern	90	135
#4 Lord and Lady Deringers, .22 Short R.F., Spur Trigger, Cased Pair, Modern	85	130

Colt Camp Perry .22

Camp Perry 1st Issue, .22 L.R.R.F., Adjustable Sights, Target Pistol,
   Modern   450   600
Camp Perry 2nd Issue, .22 L.R.R.F., Adjustable Sights, Target Pistol,
   Modern   550   850
Civil War Centennial, .22 Short R.F., ⅞ Scale 1860 Army Replica,
   Commemorative, 6" Barrel, Blue, Cased, Curio   45   80
Civil War Centennial Pair, .22 Short R.F., ⅞ Scale 1860 Army Replica,
   Commemorative, 6" Barrel, Blue, Cased, Curio   100   170
Rock Island Arsenal Centennial, .22 Short R.F., ⅞ Scale 1860 Army
   Replica, Commemorative, 6" Barrel, Blue, Cased, Curio   80   140

Rifle, Bolt Action
Colteer 1-22, .22 L.R.R.F., Singleshot, Plain, Modern   20   35
Colteer 1-22, .22 WMR, Singleshot, Plain, Modern   30   50
Coltsman Custom (FN), Various Calibers, Sporting Rifle, Fancy Wood,
   Light Engraving, Checkered Stock, Monte Carlo Stock, Modern   225   300
Coltsman Custom (Sako), Various Calibers, Sporting Rifle, Fancy Wood,
   Checkered Stock, Monte Carlo Stock, Modern   275   350
Coltsman Deluxe (FN), Various Calibers, Sporting Rifle, Checkered Stock,
   Monte Carlo Stock, Modern   190   245
Coltsman Deluxe (Sako), Various Calibers, Sporting Rifle, Checkered
   Stock, Monte Carlo Stock, Modern   225   300
Coltsman Standard (FN), Various Calibers, Sporting Rifle, Checkered
   Stock, Modern   175   225
Coltsman Standard (Sako), Various Calibers, Sporting Rifle, Checkered
   Stock, Modern   190   250
Sauer, Various Calibers, Clip Fed, Checkered Stock, Short Action,
   Modern   375   600
Sauer, Various Calibers, Clip Fed, Checkered Stock, Magnum Modern   425   650
Sauer, Various Calibers, Clip Fed, Checkered Stock, Modern   400   625

Colt Colteer Autoloader

Colt Sauer Grand African

Colt Colteer Stagecoach

Sauer Grand African, .458 Win. Mag., Clip Fed, Fancy Wood, Modern	475	700
Sauer Grand Alaskan, .375 H & H Mag., Clip Fed, Checkered Stock, Magnum, Modern	450	650

Rifle, Semi-Automatic

AR-I5, .223 Rem., Clip Fed, Modern	250	325
AR-I5, .223 Rem., Clip Fed, Collapsible Stock, Modern	290	375
Colteer 22 Autoloader, .22 L.R.R.F., Tube Feed, Plain, Modern	45	70
Colteer Stagecoach, .22 L.R.R.F., Tube Feed, Light Engraving, Modern	50	80

Rifle, Percussion

1st Model Ring Lever, Various Calibers, 8 or 10 Shot Revolving Cylinder, with Topstrap, Antique	3,750	6,500
2nd Model Ring Lever, .44, 8 or 10 Shot Revolving Cylinder, no Topstrap, Antique	3,250	6,000
Model 1839, 6 Shot Cylinder, with Hammer, Antique	2,750	4,500
Model 1855 Sporting Rifle, .36, 6 Shot Revolving Cylinder, Sidehammer, no Forestock, Spur Triggerguard, Antique	1,500	3,000
Model 1855 Sporting Rifle, Various Calibers, 6 Shot Revolving Cylinder, Sidehammer, Halfstock, Scroll Triggerguard, Antique	1,250	2,250
Model 1855 Sporting Rifle, Various Calibers, 6 Shot Revolving Cylinder, Sidehammer, Full Stock, Scroll Triggerguard, Antique	1,400	2,400
Model 1855 Carbine, Various Calibers, 6 Shot Revolving Cylinder, Sidehammer, no Forestock, Antique	1,200	2,200
Model 1855 Military Rifle, Various Calibers, 6 Shot Revolving Cylinder, Sidehammer, Full Stock, U.S. Military, Antique	2,000	4,000
Model 1861 Musket, .58, Military Contract Musket, Antique	400	700

Rifle, Singleshot

Sharps, Various Calibers, Fancy Wood, Fancy Checkering, Cased with Accessories, Modern	1,250	1,750

Colt Sharps Rifle

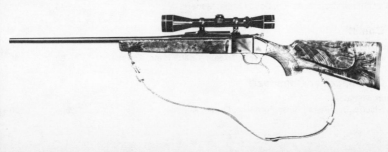

Rifle, Slide Action

Lightning, .22 R.F., Small Frame (Numbers over 35,300 are Modern),
Antique 200 325
Lightning, Various Calibers, Medium Frame (Numbers over 84,000 are
Modern), Antique 225 350
Lightning Carbine, Various Calibers, Medium Frame (Numbers over
84,000 are Modern), Antique 275 450
Lightning Baby Carbine, Various Calibers, Medium Frame (Numbers over
84,000 are Modern), Antique 325 500
Lightning, Various Calibers, Large Frame, Antique 275 450
Lightning Carbine, Various Calibers, Large Frame, Antique 500 850
Lightning Baby Carbine, Various Calibers, Large Frame, Antique 650 1,100

Shotgun, Double Barrel, Side by Side

Custom, 12 and 16 Gauges, Double Trigger, Automatic Ejector,
Checkered Stock, Beavertail Forend, Hammerless, Modern 175 275
Model 1878 Standard, Various Gauges, Outside Hammers, Damascus
Barrel, Antique 275 450
Model I883 Standard., Various Gauges, Hammerless, Damascus Barrel,
Antique 325 525

Shotgun, Semi-Automatic

Various Gauges, Add $10-$20 for Solid Rib
Various Gauges, Add $20-$30 for Vent Rib
Ultra-Light, 12 and 20 Gauges, Checkered Stock, Takedown, Modern 135 170
Ultra-Light Custom, I2 and 20 Gauges, Checkered Stock, Light Engraving,
Takedown, Modern 145 200
Ultra-Light Magnum, I2 and 20 Gauges 3", Checkered Stock, Takedown,
Modern 145 195
Ultra-Light Magnum Custom, I2 and 20 Gauges 3", Checkered Stock,
Light Engraving, Takedown, Modern 155 220

Shotgun, Slide Action

Coltsman Custom, Various Gauges, Takedown, Checkered Stock, Vent
Rib, Modern 125 185
Coltsman Standard, Various Gauges, Takedown, Plain, Modern 85 140

Columbia Armory
Tenn. Maltby & Henley Distributers 1890

Handgun, Revolver

New Safety, .22 L.R.R.F., 7 Shot, Double Action, Solid Frame, Grip Safety,
Modern 55 95
New Safety, .32 S & W, 5 Shot, Double Action, Solid Frame, Grip Safety,
Modern 65 120
New Safety, .38 S & W, 5 Shot, Double Action, Solid Frame, Grip Safety,
Modern 70 120

Columbian
Made by Foehl & Weeks, Philadelphia, Pa. C.1890

Handgun, Revolver

.32 S & W, 5 Shot, Double Action, Solid Frame, Modern 40 75
.38 S & W, 5 Shot, Double Action, Solid Frame, Modern 40 75

Comet

Handgun, Revolver

.32 Long R.F., 7 Shot, Single Action, Spur Trigger, Solid Frame, Antique 80 I35

Cominazzo or Cominazzi

Handgun, Flintlock

.54, Mid-I600's, Belt Pistol, Brass Furniture, Ornate Antique 2,500 3,500

Handgun, Wheel-Lock
Ebony Full Stock, Ivory Pom, Holster Pistol, German Style, Military,
   Engraved, Antique   3,500   4,500

Commando Arms
Knoxville, Tenn. Current

Rifle, Semi-Automatic

Commando MK III, .45 ACP, Clip Fed, Horizontal Forend, with Compensator, Carbine, Modern	85	125
Commando MK III, .45 ACP, Clip Fed, Vertical Forend, with Compensator, Carbine, Modern	90	125
Commando MK 9, 9mm Luger, Clip Fed, Horizontal Forend, with Compensator, Carbine, Modern	85	115
Commando MK 9, 9mm Luger, Clip Fed, Vertical Forend, with Compensator, Carbine, Modern	95	130
Commando MK 45, .45 ACP, Clip Fed, Horizontal Forend, with Compensator, Carbine, Modern	85	115
Commando MK 45, .45 ACP, Clip Fed, Vertical Forend, with Compensator, Carbine, Modern	95	130

Commander

Handgun, Revolver
.32 Long R.F., 7 Shot, Single Action, Spur Trigger Solid Frame, Antique   80   135

Commercial
See Smith, Otis A.

Compeer
Made by Crescent for Van Camp Hardware C.1900

Shotgun, Double Barrel, Side by Side

Various Gauges, Outside Hammers, Damascus Barrel, Modern	80	150
Various Gauges, Hammerless, Steel Barrel, Modern	95	175
Various Gauges, Hammerless, Damascus Barrel, Modern	75	150
Various Gauges, Outside Hammers, Steel Barrel, Modern	90	175

Shotgun, Singleshot
Various Gauges, Hammer, Steel Barrel, Modern   45   75

Cone, D. D.
Washington, D.C.

Handgun, Revolver

.22 Long R.F., 7 Shot, Single Action, Spur Trigger, Solid Frame, Antique	90	150
.32 Long R.F., 6 Shot, Single Action, Spur Trigger, Solid Frame, Antique	95	160

Confederate Military

Handgun, Percussion

.36 Columbus, Revolver, Brass Trigger Guard, 6 Shot, Antique	3,000	9,000
.36 Dance Bros., Revolver, Iron Frame, 6 Shot, Antique	3,000	7,500
.36 Griswald & Gunnison, Revolver, Brass Frame, 6 Shot, Serial No. is the Only Marking, Antique	2,200	3,400
.36 Leech & Co., Revolver, Brass Grip Frame, 6 Shot, Antique	2,500	3,400
.36 Leech & Rigdon, Revolver, Brass Grip Frame, 6 Shot, Antique	1,750	2,750
.36 Rigdon & Ansley, Revolver, Brass Grip Frame, 6 Shot, Antique	2,000	3,500
.36 Shawk & McLanahan, Revolver, Brass Frame, 6 Shot, Antique	3,750	8,000
.36 Spiller & Burr, Revolver, Brass Frame, 6 Shot, Antique	2,000	3,500
.36 T. W. Cofer, Revolver, Brass Frame, 6 Shot, Antique	7,500	15,000
.44 Dance Bros., Revolver, Brass Grip Frame, 6 Shot, Antique	3,000	4,500

.44 Tucker & Sherrod, Revolver, Copy of Colt Dragoon, Serial Number is
the Only Marking, Antique   4,000   9,000
.54 Palmetto, Singleshot, Brass Furniture, Antique   750   1,500
.58 Fayetteville, Singleshot, Rifled, Antique   900   1,500
.58 Fayetteville, Singleshot, Rifled, with Shoulder Stock, Antique   1,500   2,500
.60 Sutherland, Singleshot, Brass Barrel, Converted from Flintlock,
Antique   575   850

Rifle, Percussion
.52, "P", Tallahassee, Breech Loader, Carbine, Antique   2,000   3,750
.52, Tarpley, Breech Loader, Carbine, Brass Breech, Antique   3,000   7,500
.54, L.G. Sturdivant, Brass Furniture, Rifled, Serial No. is the Only
Marking, Antique   1,000   1,750
.54, Wytheville-Hall, Muzzle Loader, Rifled, Brass Frame, Antique   1,200   1,925
.57, Texas Enfield, Brass Furniture, Antique   2,500   4,000
.58, Musketoon, Brass Furniture, Military, Antique (Cook & Brother)   1,500   2,500
.58, Military, Carbine, Antique, (Dickson, Nelson & Co.)   1,750   4,000
.58, Military, Antique, (Dickson, Nelson & Co.)   1,500   2,500
.58, Artillery, Brass Furniture, Military, Antique (Cook & Brother)   1,750   3,000
.58, D. C. Hodgkins & Co., Iron Mounts, Rifled, Carbine, Antique   1,750   3,500
.58, Enfield Type, Brass Furniture, Military, Antique (Cook & Brother)   1,350   2,400
.58, Enfield Type, Rifled, Brass Furniture, Military, Antique   1,200   2,200
.58, Fayetteville, Brass Furniture, 2 Bands, Rifled, Antique   1,250   2,750
.58, Georgia, Brass Furniture, Rifled, Antique   1,200   2,400
.58, H. C. Lamb & Co., Brass Furniture, 2 Bands, Rifled, Antique   2,250   4,000
.58, Palmetto, Musket, Antique   1,000   2,000
.58, Richmond, Carbine, Antique   950   1,750
.58, Richmond, Musket, Rifled, Antique   750   1,500
.58, Tallahassee, Carbine, Brass Furniture, 2 Bands, Antique   2,500   4,500
.58, Whitney, Rifled, Musket, Antique   350   600
.61, Whitney Enfield, Rifled, Brass Furniture, Antique   350   700
.62, Richmond Navy, Musketoon, Smoothbore, Antique   950   2,000

Rifle, Singleshot
.50, S. C. Robinson, Brass Furniture, Breech Loader, Carbine, Imitation
Sharps, Antique   975   2,000
.69, Morse, Smoothbore, Carbine, Breech Loader, Antique   1,200   2,250
.69, Morse, Smoothbore, Breech Loader, Antique   900   1,750

Conn. Arms Co.
Norfolk, Conn. 1862-69

Handgun, Revolver
Wood's Patent, .28 T.F., Tip-Up Barrel, 6 Shot, Spur Trigger, Antique   100   225

Conn. Arms & Mfg. Co.
Naubuc, Conn. 1863-69

Handgun, Singleshot
Hammond Patent Bulldog, .44 R.F., Pivoting Breechblock, Hammer, Spur
Trigger, Antique   150   225
Hammond Patent Bull-Dozer, .44 R.F., Pivoting Breechblock, Hammer,
Spur Trigger, Antique   175   275

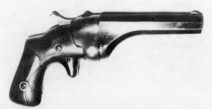

Connecticut Arms Bulldozer .44

Connecticut Valley Arms (C.V.A.)
Haddon, Conn. Current (Prices reflect Factory Assembled Guns, not Kits)

Handgun, Flintlock

.45 Kentucky, Brass Furniture, Reproduction, Antique	30	40

Handgun, Percussion

.45 or .50 Mountain Pistol, Brass Furniture, Reproduction, Antique	30	50
.45 Kentucky, Brass Furniture, Reproduction, Antique	25	40
.45 Tower Pistol, Brass Furniture, Reproduction, Antique	25	35
.45 Colonial Pistol, Brass Furniture, Reproduction, Antique	15	30
.45 Philadelphia Derringer, Reproduction, Antique	15	25

Rifle, Flintlock

.45 or .50 Mountain Rifle, German Silver Furniture, Reproduction, Antique	75	125
.45 Kentucky Rifle, Brass Furniture, Reproduction, Antique	45	80

Rifle, Percussion

.45, .50, .54, or .58 Mountain Rifle, German Silver Furniture, Reproduction, Antique	80	125
.45 or .50 Frontier Rifle, Brass Furniture, Reproduction, Antique	60	100
.45 Kentucky Rifle, Brass Furniture, Reproduction, Antique	40	75
.58 Zouave, Brass Furniture, Reproduction, Antique	80	125

Conquerer
Made by Bacon Arms Co. C.1880

Handgun, Revolver

.22 Short R.F., 7 Shot, Spur Trigger, Solid Frame, Single Action, Antique	85	160
.32 Short R.F., 5 Shot, Spur Trigger, Solid Frame, Single Action, Antique	85	160

Constable, Richard
Philadelphia, Pa. 1817-51

Handgun, Percussion

Dueling Pistols, Cased Pair, with Accessories, Antique	1,500	3,000

Rifle, Percussion

.44, Octagon Barrel, Brass Furniture, Antique	750	1,500

Contento
See Ventura Imports

Continental
Made by Stevens Arms

Rifle, Bolt Action

Model 52, .22 L.R.R.F., Singleshot, Takedown, Modern	30	40

Shotgun, Double Barrel, Side by Side

Model 315, Various Gauges, Hammerless, Steel Barrel, Modern	90	145
Model 215, 12 and 16 Gauges, Outside Hammers, Steel Barrel, Modern	85	145
Model 311, Various Gauges, Hammerless, Steel Barrel, Modern	95	160

Shotgun, Singleshot

Model 90, Various Gauges, Takedown, Automatic Ejector, Plain Hammer, Modern	35	55

Continental
Made by Hood Firearms Co., Successors to Continental Arms Co.; Sold by Marshall Wells Co., Duluth, Minn. C.1870

Handgun, Revolver

.22 Short R.F., 7 Shot, Spur Trigger, Solid Frame, Single Action, Antique	85	160
.32 Short R.F., 5 Shot, Spur Trigger, Solid Frame, Single Action, Antique	90	170

90

Continental

Handgun, Semi-Automatic
Hammer, .25 ACP, Clip Fed, Modern 100 140
Hammerless, .25 ACP, Clip Fed, Modern 80 120

Continental Arms Co.
Norwich, Conn. 1866-67

Handgun, Pepperbox
Continental 1, .22 R.F., 7 Shot, Spur Trigger, Solid Frame, Antique 200 325
Continental 2, .32 R.F., 5 Shot, Spur Trigger, Solid Frame, Antique 225 375

Copeland, T.
Made by T. Copeland, Worcester, Mass. 1868-74

Handgun, Revolver
.22 Short R.F., 7 Shot, Spur Trigger, Solid Frame, Single Action, Antique 95 175

Coq
Spain, Unknown Maker C.1900

Handgun, Semi-Automatic
K-25, .25 ACP, Clip Fed, Modern 50 75

Cornforth
London, England 1725-60

Handgun, Flintlock
Pair, Belt Pistol, Brass Barrel, Brass Furniture, Plain, Antique 2,400 3,500

Continental .25 ACP with Hammer

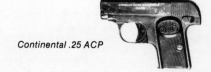
Continental .25 ACP

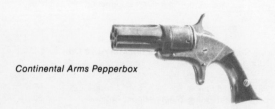
Continental Arms Pepperbox

Cosens, James
Gunmaker in Ordinary to Charles II England, Late 1600's

Handgun, Flintlock
Pair, Holster Pistol, Silver Furniture, Engraved Silver Inlay, High Quality,
Antique   14,500

Cosmi
Made for Abercrombie & Fitch C.1960

Shotgun, Semi-Automatic
12 or 20 Gauges, Magazine in Buttstock, Top Break, Fancy Engraving,
Fancy Wood, Modern   1,000   1,750

Cosmopolitan Arms Co.
Hamilton, Ohio 1860-65; Also see U.S. Military

Rifle, Percussion
.45, Sporting Rifle, Antique   600   900
.50, Carbine, Antique   550   850

Craft Products

Handgun, Semi-Automatic
.25 ACP, Clip Fed, Modern   65   100

Crescent
Made by Norwich Falls Pistol Co. C.1880

Handgun, Revolver
.32 Short R.F., 5 Shot, Spur Trigger, Solid Frame, Single Action, Antique   85   160

Crescent Fire Arms Co.
*Norwich, Conn., 1892; Purchased by H & D Folsom in 1893, and Absorbed by
Stevens Arms & Tool 1926*

Handgun, Singleshot
.410 Ga., Top Break, Class 3   125   200

Shotgun, Double Barrel, Side by Side
Various Gauges, Outside Hammers, Damascus Barrel, Modern   80   150
Various Gauges, Hammerless, Steel Barrel, Modern   95   175
Various Gauges, Hammerless, Damascus Barrel, Modern   75   150
Various Gauges, Outside Hammers, Steel Barrel, Modern   90   175

Shotgun, Singleshot
Various Gauges, Hammer, Steel Barrel, Modern   45   75

Cowels & Smith
Chicopee, Mass. 1863-76. Became Cowels & Son 1871

Handgun, Singleshot
.22 R.F., Side-Swing Barrel, Hammer, Spur Trigger, Antique   125   200
.30 R.F., Side-Swing Barrel, Hammer, Spur Trigger, Antique   140   220

Creedmore
Made by Hopkins & Allen C.1870

Handgun, Revolver
#1, .22 Short R.F., 7 Shot, Spur Trigger, Solid Frame, Single Action,
Antique   85   160

Crown Jewel
Made by Norwich Falls Pistol Co. C.1880

Handgun, Revolver

.32 Short R.F., 5 Shot, Spur Trigger, Solid Frame, Single Action, Antique	85	160

Crucelegui
Spain, Imported by Mandall Shooting Supplies, Scotsdale, Ariz.

Shotgun, Dougle Barrel, Side by Side

Model 150, 12 and 20 Gauges, Outside Hammers, Double Trigger, Modern	120	150

Cruso
Made by Stevens Arms

Rifle, Bolt Action

Model 53, .22 L.R.R.F., Singleshot, Takedown, Modern	30	40

Shotgun, Singleshot

Model 90, Various Gauges, Takedown, Automatic Ejector, Plain Hammer, Modern	35	55

Cumberland Arms Co.
Made by Crescent for Hibbard-Spencer Bartlett Co. C.1900

Shotgun, Double Barrel, Side by Side

Various Gauges, Outside Hammers, Damascus Barrel, Modern	80	150
Various Gauges, Hammerless, Steel Barrel, Modern	95	175
Various Gauges, Hammerless, Damascus Barrel, Modern	75	150
Various Gauges, Outside Hammers, Steel Barrel, Modern	90	175

Shotgun, Singleshot

Various Gauges, Hammer, Steel Barrel, Modern	45	75

CZ
Czechoslovakia from 1918 to Date; Ceska Zbrojovka Brno

Handgun, Semi-Automatic

CZ1922, .25 ACP, Clip Fed, Modern	250	350
CZ1922, .380 ACP, Clip Fed, Modern	135	225
CZ1936, .25 ACP, Clip Fed, Modern	95	145
Duo, .25 ACP, Clip Fed, Modern	100	175
Fox, .25 ACP, Clip Fed, Modern	225	325
M1938, .380 ACP, Clip Fed, Double Action, Modern	90	150
Niva, .25 ACP, Clip Fed, Modern	175	250
PZK, .25 ACP, Clip Fed, Modern	150	225
Vest Pocket CZ 1945, .25 ACP, Clip Fed, Modern	95	150
VZ NB 50 Police, .32 ACP, Clip Fed, Double Action, Curio	175	275
VZ1922, .380 ACP, Clip Fed, Modern	135	225
VZ1924, .380 ACP, Clip Fed, Modern	90	145
VZ1924 Navy, .380 ACP, Clip Fed, Nazi-Proofed, Curio	145	200
VZ1938, .380 ACP, Clip Fed, Double Action, Nazi-Proofed, Curio	150	220
VZ1938, .380 ACP, Clip Fed, Double Action, Curio	125	195
VZ27, .22 L.R.R.F., Clip Fed, Nazi-Proofed, Modern	350	500
VZ27, .32 ACP, Clip Fed, Commercial, Modern	95	150
VZ27, .32 ACP, Clip Fed, Barrel Extension for Silencer, Curio, Class 3	350	500
VZ27 Luftwaffe, .32 ACP, Clip Fed, Nazi-Proofed, Modern	90	145
VZ27 Navy, .32 ACP, Clip Fed, Nazi-Proofed, Curio	135	200
VZ27 Police, .32 ACP, Clip Fed, Nazi-Proofed, Modern	90	150
VZ50, .32 ACP, Clip Fed, Double Action, Curio	145	200
VZ52, 7.62mm Tokarev, Clip Fed, Double Action, Curio	500	950

Handgun, Singleshot

Drulov, .22 L.R.R.F., Top Break, Target Pistol, Target Sights, Modern	200	300
Model P, .22 L.R.R.F., Top Break, Target Pistol, Modern	150	225
Model P, 6mm Flobert, Top Break, Target Pistol, Modern	120	175

VZ1924, .380

VZ1938, .380

Czar
Made by Hood Firearms C.1876

Handgun, Revolver
.22 Short R.F., 7 Shot, Spur Trigger, Solid Frame, Single Action, Antique   85   160

Czar
Made by Hopkins & Allen C.1880

Handgun, Revolver
.22 Short R.F., 7 Shot, Spur Trigger, Solid Frame, Single Action, Antique   85   160
.32 Short R.F., 5 Shot, Spur Trigger, Solid Frame, Single Action, Antique   90   170

Czechoslovakian Military
Also see German Military, CZ

Automatic Weapon, Light Machine Gun
ZB-VZ26, 8mm Mauser, Finned Barrel, Clip Fed, Bipod, Class 3   2,500   3,250

Rifle, Bolt Action
GEW 33/40, 8mm Mauser, Military, Nazi-Proofed, Carbine, Modern   125   225
Gewehr 24 T, 8mm Mauser, Military, Nazi-Proofed, Curio   120   200
VZ 24, 8mm Mauser, Military, Modern   90   175
VZ 33, 8mm Mauser, Military, Carbine, Modern   90   175

Daisy
Made by Bacon Arms Co. C.1880

Handgun, Revolver
.22 Short R.F., 7 Shot, Spur Trigger, Solid Frame, Single Action, Antique   85   160

94

Dakin Gun Co.
San Francisco, Calif. C.1960

Shotgun, Double Barrel, Over-Under
Model 170, Various Gauges, Light Engraving, Checkered Stock, Double
  Triggers, Vent Rib, Modern   225   375

Shotgun, Double Barrel, Side by Side
Model 100, 12 or 20 Gauges, Boxlock, Light Engraving, Double Triggers,
  Modern   125   200
**Model 147, Various Magnum Gauges, Boxlock, Light Engraving, Double
Triggers, Vent Rib, Modern**   175   275
Model 160, 12 or 20 Gauges, Single Selective Trigger, Ejectors, Vent Rib,
  Modern   200   300
Model 215, 12 or 20 Gauges, Sidelock, Fancy Engraving, Fancy Wood,
  Ejectors, Single Selective Trigger, Vent Rib, Modern   350   700

Dalby, David
Lincolnshire, England C.1835

Handgun, Flintlock
.50, Pocket Pistol, Box Lock, Screw Barrel, Folding Trigger, Silver Inlay,
  Antique   450   700

Daly Arms Co.
N.Y.C. C.1890

Handgun, Revolver
.22 Long R.F., 6 Shot, Double Action, Ring Trigger, Solid Frame, Antique   160   225
Peacemaker, .32 Short R.F., 5 Shot, Spur Trigger, Solid Frame, Single
  Action, Antique   90   160

Dan Wesson Arms
Monson, Mass.

Handgun, Revolver
Model 11, .357 Magnum, Double Action, 3-Barrel Set, Satin Blue, Modern   145   190
Model 11, .357 Magnum, Double Action, 3-Barrel Set, Nickel Plated,
  Modern   155   200
Model 11, .357 Magnum, Various Barrel Lengths, Satin Blue, Double
  Action, Modern   70   100
Model 11, .357 Magnum, Various Barrel Lengths, Nickel Plated, Double
  Action, Modern   85   120
Model 11, .38 Special, Various Barrel Lengths, Satin Blue, Double Action,
  Modern   65   100
Model 11, .38 Special, Various Barrel Lengths, Nickel Plated, Double
  Action, Modern   75   110
Model 12, .357 Magnum, Double Action, 3-Barrel Set, Satin Blue,
  Adjustable Sights, Modern   150   210
Model 12, .357 Magnum, Double Action, 3-Barrel Set, Nickel Plated,
  Adjustable Sights, Modern   200   275
Model 12, .357 Magnum, Various Barrel Lengths, Double Action, Blue,
  Adjustable Sights, Modern   80   115
Model 12, .357 Magnum, Various Barrel Lengths, Double Action, Nickel
  Plated, Adjustable Sights, Modern   90   130
Model 12, .38 Special, Various Barrel Lengths, Double Action, Blue,
  Adjustable Sights, Modern   80   110
Model 12, .38 Special, Various Barrel Lengths, Double Action, Nickel
  Plated, Adjustable Sights, Modern   85   120
Model 14, .357 Magnum, Double Action, 3-Barrel Set, Satin Blue, Modern   135   170
Model 14, .357 Magnum, Double Action, 3-Barrel Set, Nickel Plated,
  Modern   175   225
Model 14, .357 Magnum, Various Barrel Lengths, Double Action, Satin
  Blue, Modern   75   120

Model 14, .357 Magnum, Various Barrel Lengths, Double Action, Nickel Plated, Modern	85	130
Model 14, .38 Special, Various Barrel Lengths, Double Action, Satin Blue, Modern	75	100
Model 14, .38 Special, Various Barrel Lengths, Double Action, Nickel Plated, Modern	80	110
Model 14-2, .357 Magnum, Various Barrel Lengths, Double Action, Satin Blue, Modern	80	115
Model 14-2, .357 Magnum, Double Action, 4-Barrel Set, Blue, Modern	175	235
Model 15, .357 Magnum, Various Barrel Lengths, Double Action, Nickel Plated, Adjustable Sights, Modern	95	130
Model 15, .357 Magnum, Double Action, 3-Barrel Set, Satin Blue, Adjustable Sights, Modern	175	250
Model 15, .357 Magnum, Double Action, 3-Barrel Set, Nickel Plated, Adjustable Sights, Modern	220	275
Model 15, .357 Magnum, Double Action, 3-Barrel Set, Blue, Adjustable Sights, Modern	190	260
Model 15, .357 Magnum, Various Barrel Lengths, Double Action, Satin Blue, Adjustable Sights, Modern	90	140
Model 15, .357 Magnum, Various Barrel Lengths, Double Action, Blue, Adjustable Sights, Modern	95	150
Model 15, .38 Special, Various Barrel Lengths, Double Action, Nickel Plated, Adjustble Sights, Modern	95	160
Model 15, .38 Special, Various Barrel Lengths, Double Action, Satin Blue, Adjustable Sights, Modern	85	130
Model 15, .38 Special, Various Barrel Lengths, Double Action, Blue, Adjustable Sights, Modern	90	120
Model 15-2, .357 Magnum or .22 L.R.R.F., Various Barrel Lengths, Double Action, Blue, Adjustable Sights, Modern	125	180
Model 15-2, .357 Magnum or .22 L.R.R.F., Double Action, 4-Barrel Set, Blue, Adjustable Sights, Modern	225	300

Dan Wesson 14-2 Set

Dan Wesson 15-2H Set

Model 15-2H or .22 L.R.R.F., .357 Magnum, Various Barrel Lengths,
   Double Action, Blue, Adjustable Sights, Heavy Barrel, Modern   130   190
Model 15-2H, .357 Magnum or .22 L.R.R.F., Double Action, 4-Barrel Set,
   Blue, Adjustable Sights, Heavy Barrel, Modern   275   350
Model 15-2V, .357 Magnum or .22 L.R.R.F., Various Barrel Lengths,
   Double Action, Blue, Adjustable Sights, Vent Rib, Modern   140   200
Model 15-2V, .357 Magnum or .22 L.R.R.F., Double Action, 4-Barrel Set,
   Blue, Adjustable Sights, Vent Rib, Modern   290   380
Model 15-2VH, .357 Magnum or .22 L.R.R.F., Various Barrel Lengths,
   Double Action, Adjustable Sights, Heavy Barrel, Vent Rib, Modern   150   215
Model 15-2VH, .357 Magnum or .22 L.R.R.F., Double Action, 4-Barrel Set,
   Blue, Adjustable Sights, Heavy Barrel, Vent Rib, Modern   300   425
Extra Barrel Assemblies Add:
   15" 15-2 $75-$110; 15-2H $95-$135; 15-2V $95-$135; 15-2VH $120-$160
   12" 15-2 $50-$80; 15-2H $75-$110; 15-2V $75-$110; 15-2VH $95-$140
   10" 15-2 $45-$70; 15-2H $55-$85; 15-2V $55-$85; 15-2VH $70-$100
   Others 15-2, $20-$40; 15-2H, $35-$55; 15-2V, $35-$55; 15-2VH, $40-$70

Dan Wesson 15-2V Set

Dan Wesson 15-2VH Set

Ronge Revolver

Danish Military

Automatic Weapon, Submachine Gun
Madsen M50B, 9mm Luger, Clip Fed, Wood Stock, Military, Class 3 — 550 — 800

Handgun, Revolver
9.1mm Ronge 1891, Military, Top Break, Hammer-Like Latch, Antique — 175 — 275

Handgun, Semi-Automatic
S.I.G. SG/8 9mm Luger, Clip Fed, Military, Modern — 1,000 — 1,750

Rifle, Bolt Action
M1889 Krag, 8 x 54 Krag-Jorgensen, Carbine, Antique — 200 — 300

Danton
Made By Gabilondo y Cia., Elgoibar, Spain

Handgun, Semi-Automatic
Pocket, .25 ACP, Clip Fed, Modern — 80 — 130
Pocket, .32 ACP, Clip Fed, Modern — 90 — 145

Dardick
Hamden, Conn.

Handgun, Revolver
Series 1100, .38 Dardick Tround, Double Action, Clip Fed, 3" Barrel, 11
  Shot, Modern — 350 — 475
Series 1500, .30, Double Action, Clip Fed, 4¾" Barrel, Modern — 575 — 750
Series 1500, .38 Dardick Tround, Double Action, Clip Fed, 6" Barrel, 15
  Shot, Modern — 350 — 475
Series 1500, .22, Double Action, Clip Fed, 2" and 11" Barrels, Modern — 600 — 800
For Carbine Conversion Unit .38, Add $175-$250
For Carbine Conversion Unit .22, Add $200-$325

Danton .32 ACP

Darne
St. Etienne, France

Shotgun, Double Barrel, Side by Side

Bird Hunter, Various Gauges, Sliding Breech, Ejectors, Double Triggers, Checkered Stock, Modern	325	425
Hors Serie #1, Various Gauges, Sliding Breech, Ejectors, Fancy Engraving, Checkered Stock, Modern	2,000	3,000
Magnum, 12 or 20 Gauges 3", Sliding Breech, Ejectors, Double Triggers, Checkered Stock, Modern	600	850
Pheasant Hunter, Various Gauges, Sliding Breech, Ejectors, Light Engraving, Checkered Stock, Modern	575	725
Quail Hunter, Various Gauges, Sliding Breech, Ejectors, Engraved, Checkered Stock, Modern	650	1,000

Davenport, W. H.
Providence, R.I. 1880-83, Norwich, Conn. 1890-1900

Shotgun, Double Barrel, Side by Side

8 Ga., Modern	350	460

Shotgun, Singleshot

Various Gauges, Hammer, Steel Barrel, Modern	45	60

Davidson
Spain Mfg. by Fabrica de Armas, Imported by Davidson Firearms Co.

Shotgun, Double Barrel, Side by Side

73 Stagecoach, 12 or 20 Gauges, Magnum, Checkered Stock, Modern	110	160
Model 63B, 10 Ga. 3½", Magnum, Engraved, Nickel Plated, Checkered Stock, Modern	145	195
Model 63B, 12 and 20 Gauges, Magnum, Engraved, Nickel Plated, Checkered Stock, Modern	130	175
Model 63B, Various Gauges, Engraved, Nickel Plated, Checkered Stock, Modern	125	165
Model 69 SL, 12 and 20 Gauges, Sidelock, Light Engraving, Checkered Stock, Modern	135	200

Davis, N.R. & Co.
Freetown, Mass. 1853-1917. Merged with Warner Co. of Norwich, Conn. and became Davis-Warner Arms Co. It was not active between 1920-22, but in 1930 started again as Crescent-Davis Arms Co., Norwich. This included Crescent Firearms Co. Davis relocated in Springfield, Mass. 1931-32. and was taken over in 1932 by Stevens Arms.

Rifle Percussion

.45, Octagon Barrel, Antique	375	550

Shotgun, Percussion

#1 Various Gauges, Double Barrel, Side by Side Damascus Barrel, Outside Hammers, Antique	275	400
#3, Various Gauges, Double Barrel, Side by Side Damascus Barrel, Outside Hammers, Antique	200	300

Shotgun, Double Barrel, Side by Side

Various Gauges, Outside Hammers, Damascus Barrel, Modern	80	150
Various Gauges, Hammerless, Steel Barrel, Modern	95	175
Various Gauges, Hammerless, Damascus Barrel, Modern	75	150
Various Gauges, Outside Hammers, Steel Barrel, Modern	90	175

Shotgun, Singleshot

Various Gauges, Hammer, Steel Barrel, Modern	45	75

Day Arms Co.
San Antonio, Tex.

Handgun, Semi-Automatic
Conversion Unit Only, .22 L.R.R.F., For Colt M1911, Clip Fed, Modern   75   110

Dead Shot
L.W. Pond Co.

Handgun, Revolver
.22 Long R.F., 6 Shot, Single Action, Solid Frame, Spur Trigger, Antique   155   225

Debatir

Handgun, Semi-Automatic
.25 ACP, Clip Fed, Modern   125   185
.32 ACP, Clip Fed, Modern   135   225

Deberiere, Henry
Phila., Pa. 1769-74, See Kentucky Rifles & Pistols

Defender
Made by Iver-Johnson, Sold by J.P. Lovell Arms 1875-95

Handgun, Revolver
.22 Short R.F., 7 Shot, Spur Trigger, Solid Frame, Single Action, Antique   95   160
.32 Short R.F., 5 Shot, Spur Trigger, Solid Frame, Single Action, Antique   95   170
#89, .22 Short R.F., 7 Shot, Spur Trigger, Solid Frame, Single Action,
   Antique   90   155
#89, .32 Short R.F., 5 Shot, Spur Trigger, Solid Frame, Single Action,
   Antique   90   165

Defiance
Made By Norwich Fall Pistol Co. C.1880

Handgun, Revolver
.22 Short R.F., 7 Shot, Spur Trigger, Solid Frame, Single Action, Antique   85   150

Dehuff, Abraham
Lancaster, Pa. C.1779 See Kentucky Rifles & Pistols

Delphian
Made by Stevens Arms

Shotgun, Single Shot
Model 90, Various Gauges, Takedown, Automatic Ejector, Plain Hammer,
   Modern   35   55

Debatir .25 ACP

Deringer .32 Pocket Revolver

Delu
Fab. d'Armes Delu & Co.

Handgun, Semi-Automatic
.25 ACP, Clip Fed, Modern   125   175

Demro

Rifle, Semi-Automatic
T.A.C. Model 1, .45 ACP or 9mm Luger, Clip Fed, Modern   200   300

Deringer Rifle and Pistol Works
Philadelphia, Pa. 1870-80

Handgun, Revolver
Centennial '76, .38 Long R.F., 5 Shot, Single Action, Spur Trigger, Tip-up,
  Antique   225   325
Model 1, .22 Short R.F., 7 Shot Spur Trigger, Tip-up, Antique   200   300
Model 2, .22 Short R.F., 7 Shot, Spur Trigger, Tip-up, Antique   195   275
Model 2, .32 Long R.F., 5 Shot, Single Action, Spur Trigger, Tip-up,
  Antique   195   285

Deringer, Henry, Sr.
Richmond, Va. & Philadelphia, Pa. 1768-1814 See Kentucky Rifles & Pistols; U.S. Military

Derr, John
Lancaster, Pa. 1810-44, See Kentucky Rifles & Pistols

Despatch
Made by Hopkins & Allen C.1875

Handgun, Revolver
.22 Short R.F., 7 Shot, Spur Trigger, Solid Frame, Single Action, Antique   85   160

Destroyer
Made in Spain by Isidro Gaztanaga 1914-36

Handgun, Semi-Automatic
.25 ACP, Clip Fed, Modern   80   135
.32 ACP, Clip Fed, Long Grip, Modern   85   150

Destroyer .25 ACP

Destroyer .32 ACP

Destructor
Iraola Salaverria, Eibal, Spain

Handgun, Semi-Automatic

.25 ACP, Clip Fed, Modern	70	125
.32 ACP, Clip Fed, Modern	80	135

Detonics
Seattle, Washington Current

Handgun, Semi-Automatic

"45" Combat, .45 ACP, Combat Modifications, Clip Fed, Pocket Pistol, Blue, Modern	225	300
"45" Combat, .45 ACP, Combat Modifications, Clip Fed, Pocket Pistol, Nickel, Modern	250	325
Green Beret Series, .45 ACP, Combat Modifications, Clip Fed, Pocket Pistol, Engraved, Cased, Modern	1,000	1,500
Royalty Series, .45 ACP, Combat Modifications, Clip Fed, Pocket Pistol, Fancy Engraving, Cased, Modern	3,000	4,500
Signature Series, .45 ACP, Combat Modifications, Clip Fed, Pocket Pistol, Customized, Modern	450	650

Diamond
Made by Stevens Arms

Shotgun, Singleshot

Model 89 Dreadnaught, Various Gauges, Hammer, Modern	45	60
Model 90, Various Gauges, Takedown, Automatic Ejector, Plain Hammer, Modern	35	55
Model 95, 12 and 16 Gauge, Takedown, Modern	35	55

Diane
Made by Wilkinson Arms

Handgun, Semi-Automatic

Standard Model, .25 ACP, Clip Fed, Modern	150	250
Lightweight Model, .25 ACP, Clip Fed, Modern	550	800

Dickson
Italy American Import Co. until 1968

Handgun, Semi-Automatic

Detective, .25 ACP, Clip Fed, Modern	60	95

Detonics .45

Dixie Gun Works Flintlock Tower Pistol

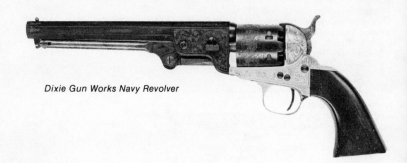

Dixie Gun Works Navy Revolver

Dictator
Made by Hopkins & Allen C.1880

Handgun, Revolver

.22 Short R.F., 7 Shot, Spur Trigger, Solid Frame, Single Action, Antique	85	160
.32 Short R.F., 5 Shot, Spur Trigger, Solid Frame, Single Action, Antique	85	160
#2, .32 Short R.F., 5 Shot, Spur Trigger, Solid Frame, Single Action, Antique	85	175

Dixie Gun Works
Union City, Tenn. Current

Handgun, Flintlock

Tower, .67, Brass Furniture, Reproduction, Antique	15	25

Handgun, Percussion

Army, .44, Revolver, Buntline, Reproduction, Antique	50	65
Navy, .36, Revolver, Buntline, Brass Frame, Reproduction, Antique	20	35
Navy, .36, Revolver, Buntline, Brass Frame, Engraved, Reproduction, Antique	25	40
Spiller & Burr, .36, Revolver, Buntline, Brass Frame, Reproduction, Antique	30	50
Wyatt Earp, .44 Revolver, Buntline, Brass Frame, Reproduction, Antique	30	45
Wyatt Earp, .44 Revolver, Buntline, Brass Frame, With Shoulder Stock, Reproduction, Antique	50	75

Rifle, Flintlock

1st Model Brown Bess, .75, Military, Reproduction, Antique	250	340
2nd Model Brown Bess, .74, Military, Reproduction, Antique	125	190
Coach Guard, .95, Blunderbuss, Brass Furniture, Reproduction, Antique	75	120
Coach Guard Blunderbuss, .95, Steel Barrel, Brass Fittings, Reproduction, Antique	65	90

Dixie Gun Works Second Model Brown Bess

Dixie Gun Works Coach Guard Blunderbuss

Day Rifle, .45, Double Barrel, Over-under, Swivel Breech, Brass Furniture, Reproduction, Antique	250	345
Deluxe Pennsylvania, .45, Kentucky Rifle, Full-Stocked, Brass Furniture, Light Engraving, Reproduction, Antique	185	250
Deluxe Pensylvania, .45, Kentucky Rifle, Full-Stocked, Brass Furniture, Reproduction, Antique	175	245
Kentuckian, .45, Kentucky Rifle, Full-Stocked, Brass Furniture, Reproduction, Antique	80	120
Kentuckian, .45, Kentucky Rifle, Full-Stocked, Brass Furniture, Reproduction, Carbine, Antique	80	120
Musket, .67 Smoothbore, Reproduction, Carbine, Antique	45	75
Squirel Rifle, .45, Kentucky Rifles, Full-Stocked, Brass Furniture, Reproduction, Antique	150	195
York County, .45, Kentucky Rifle, Full-Stocked, Brass Furniture, Reproduction, Antique	85	125

Rifle, Lever Action

Win. 73 (Italian), .44-40 WCF, Tube Feed, Octagon Barrel, Carbine, Modern	120	175
Win 73 (Italian), .44-40 WCF, Tube Feed, Octagon Barrel, Color Cased Hardened Frame, Engraved, Modern	170	245

Rifle, Percussion

Day Rifle, .45, Double Barrel, Over-under, Swivel Breech, Brass Furniture, Reproduction, Antique	150	235
Deluxe Pennsylvania, .45, Kentucky Rifle, Full-Stocked, Brass Furniture, Reproduction, Antique	160	225
Deluxe Pensylvania, .45, Kentucky Rifle, Full-Stocked, Brass Furniture, Light Engraving, Reproduction, Antique	175	245
Dixie Hawkin, .45, Half-Stocked, Octagon Barrel, Set Trigger, Brass Furniture, Reproduction, Antique	100	150
Dixie Hawkin, .50, Half-Stocked, Octagon Barrel, Set Trigger, Brass Furniture, Reproduction, Antique	100	150
Enfield Two-Band, .577, Musketoon, Military, Reproduction, Antique	80	145
Kentuckian, .45, Kentucky Rifle, Full-Stocked, Brass Furniture, Reproduction, Antique	70	115

*Dixie Gun Works Percussion Pennsylvania
Rifle*

Dixie Gun Works Percussion Plains Rifle

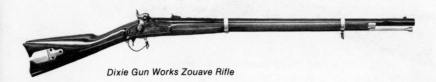

Dixie Gun Works Zouave Rifle

Kentuckian, .45, Kentucky Rifle, Full-Stocked, Brass Furniture, Reproduction, Carbine, Antique	70	115
Musket, .66, Smoothbore, Reproduction, Antique	40	70
Plainsman, .45, Half-Stocked, Octagon Barrel, Reproduction, Antique	80	135
Plainsman, .50, Half-Stocked, Octagon Barrel, Reproduction, Antique	80	135
Squirrel Rifle, .45, Kentucky Rifle, Full-Stocked, Brass Furniture, Reproduction, Antique	135	190
Target, .45, Half-Stocked, Octagon Barrel, Reproduction, Antique	40	70
York County, .45, Kentucky Rifle, Full-Stocked, Brass Furniture, Reproduction, Antique	75	120
Zouave M 1863, .58, Military, Reproduction, Antique	70	120

Shotgun, Flintlock

Fowling Piece, 14 Gauge, Single Barrel, Reproduction, Antique	45	75

Shotgun, Percussion

12 Gauge, Double Barrel, Side by Side, Double Trigger, Reproduction, Antique	85	130
28 Gauge, Single Barrel, Reproduction, Antique	25	45

Dobson, T.
London, England C.1780

Handgun, Flintlock

.64, Presentation, Holster Pistol, Gold Inlays, Engraved, Half-octagon Barrel, High Quality, Antique	2,500	3,250

Domino
Made in Italy, Imported by Mandell Shooting Sports

Handgun, Semi-Automatic

Model O.P. 601, .22 Short, Target Pistol, Adjustable Sights, Target Grips, Modern	400	600
Model S.P. 602, .22 L.R.R.F., Target Pistol, Adjustable Sights, Target Grips, Modern	400	600

Dreadnaught
Made by Hopkins & Allen C.1880

Handgun, Revolver

.22 Short R.F., 7 Shot, Spur Trigger, Solid Frame, Single Action, Antique	90	150
.32 Short R.F., 5 Shot, Spur Trigger, Solid Frame, Single Action, Antique	95	170

Dreyse Model 1907 .32 ACP

Dreyse
Dreyse Rheinische Metallwaren Machinenfabrik, Sommerda, Germany

Handgun, Semi-Automatic
M1907, .32 ACP, Clip Fed, Early Model, Modern	120	170
M1907, .32 ACP, Clip Fed, Modern	80	125
M1910, 9 MM Luger, Clip Fed, Curio	450	600
Rheinmetall, .32 ACP, Clip Fed, Modern	175	275
Vest Pocket, .25 ACP, Clip Fed Modern	95	170

Drippard, F.
Lancaster, Pa. 1767-73, See Kentucky Rifles & Pistols.

Driscoll, J.B.
Springfield, Mass. C.1870

Handgun, Singleshot
.22 R.F., Brass Frame, Spur Trigger, Antique	150	250

DuBiel Arms Co.
Sherman, Tex. Since 1978

Rifle, Bolt Action
Custom Rifle, Various Calibers, Various Styles, Fancy Wood, Modern	900	1,300

Dumaresd, B.
Marseille, France, Probably C.1730

Handgun, Flintlock
Holster Pistol, Engraved, Horn Inlays, Ornate, Silver Furniture, Antique	900	1,500

Dumoulin Freres et Cie
Belgium From 1849

Rifle, Bolt Action
Grade I, Various Calibers, Fancy Checkering, Engraved, Modern	650	950
Grade II, Various Calibers, Fancy Checkering, Engraved, Fance Wood, Modern	950	1,400
Grade III, Various Calibers, Fancy Checkering, Fancy Engraving, Fancy Wood, Modern	1,450	2,000

Rifle, Double Barrel, Side by Side
Various Calibers, Fancy Checkering, Engraved, Fancy Wood, Modern	1,300	1,800

Duo
Czechoslovakia 1926-48. F. Dusek from 1948 to date.

Handgun, Semi-Automatic
.25 ACP, Clip Fed, Modern	100	175

Dutch Military

Handgun, Revolver
Model 1871 Hemberg, 9.4 MM, Military, Antique 75 125

Rifle, Bolt Action
Beaumont-Vitale M1871/88, Military, Antique 75 110

Rifle, Flintlock
.70, Officers Type, Musket, Brass Furniture, Antique 650 950

Dutton, John S.
Jaffrey, N.H. 1855-1870

Rifle, Percussion
.36, Target Rifle, Swiss Buttplate, Octagon Barrel, Target Sights, Antique 750 1,200

DWM
Germany. Deutche Waffen und Munitionsfabrik. Also See Luger

Handgun, Semi-Automatic
Pocket, .32 ACP, Clip Fed, Modern 125 200

Eagle
Made by Iver-Johnson C.1879-86

Handgun, Revolver
.22 Short R.F., 7 Shot, Spur Trigger, Solid Frame, Single Action, Antique 85 150
.32 Short R.F., 5 Shot, Spur Trigger, Solid Frame, Single Action, Antique 85 150
.38 Short R.F., 5 Shot, Spur Trigger, Solid Frame, Single Action, Antique 95 175
.44 Short R.F., 5 Shot, Spur Trigger, Solid Frame, Single Action, Antique 170 250

Eagle Arms Co.
N.Y.C. C.1865

Handgun, Revolver
.28 Cup Primed Cartridge, 6 Shot, Single Action, Spur Trigger, Solid
Frame, Antique 150 275
.28 Cup Primed Cartridge, 6 Shot, Single Action, Spur Trigger, Tip-up,
Antique 175 300
.30 Cup Primed Cartridge, 6 Shot, Single Action, Spur Trigger, Solid
Frame, Antique 140 260
.30 Cup Primed Cartridge, 6 Shot, Single Action, Spur Trigger, Tip-up,
Antique 175 300
.42 Cup Primed Cartridge, 6 Shot, Single Action, Spur Trigger, Solid
Frame, Antique 135 250
.42 Cup Primed Cartridge, 6 Shot, Single Action, Spur Trigger, Tip-up,
Antique 200 350

Eagle Arms Co. .28 Cup-Fire

Eagle Gun Co.
Stratford, Conn. C.1965

Rifle, Semi-Automatic
.45 ACP, Clip Fed, Carbine, Class 3 ... 110 ... 170
9 MM Luger, Clip Fed, Carbine, Class 3 ... 160 ... 220

Earlhood
Made by E.L. Dickinson Co. Springfield, Mass. 1870-80

Handgun, Revolver
.32 Short R.F., 5 Shot, Spur Trigger, Solid Frame, Single Action, Antique ... 90 ... 165

Early, Amos
Dauphin Co. Pa. See Kentucky Rifles

Early, Jacob
Dauphin Co. Pa. See Kentucky Rifles

Earthquake
Made by E.L. Dickinson Co. Springfield, Mass. 1870-80

Handgun, Revolver
.32 Short R.F., 5 Shot, Spur Trigger, Solid Frame, Single Action, Antique ... 90 ... 170

Eastern
Made by Stevens Arms

Shotgun, Double Barrel, Side By Side
Model 311, Various Gauges, Hammerless, Steel Barrel, Modern ... 95 ... 150

Shotgun, Singleshot
Model 94, Various Gauges, Takedown, Automatic Ejector, Plain Hammer,
Modern ... 35 ... 50

Eastern Arms Co.
Made by Meriden Firearms, Sold by Sears-Roebuck

Handgun, Revolver
.32 S & W, 5 Shot, Double Action, Top Break, Modern ... 50 ... 95
.38 S & W, 5 Shot, Double Action, Top Break, Modern ... 50 ... 95

Eastfield
See Smith & Wesson

Echaberria, Artura
Spain, C.1790

Handgun, Miquelet-Lock
Pair, Holster Pistol, Plain, Brass Furniture, Antique ... 2,750 ... 3,750

Echasa
Echave, Arizmendi Y Cia. Spain

Handgun, Semi-Automatic
Model GZ Mab, .22 L.R.R.F., Clip Fed, Hammer Modern ... 65 ... 110
Model GZ Mab, .25 ACP, Clip Fed, Hammer, Modern ... 70 ... 120
Model GZ Mab, .32 ACP, Clip Fed, Hammer, Modern ... 60 ... 110

Eclipse
Made by Johnson, Bye & Co.

Handgun, Singleshot
.25 Short R.F., Derringer, Spur Trigger, Antique ... 50 ... 85

Egyptian Military Tokagypt Model 58

Edgeson
Lincolnshire, England, 1810-30

Handgun, Flintlock
.45, Pair, Box Lock, Screw Barrel, Pocket Pistol, Folding Trigger, Plain
  Antique   850   1,250

Edmonds, J.
See Kentucky Rifles

Egg, Durs
London, England 1770-1840. See British Military

Handgun, Flintlock
.50, Duelling Type, Holster Pistol, Octagon Barrel, Steel Furniture, Light
  Ornamentation, Antique   750   1,250

Handgun, Percussion
6 Shot, Pepperbox, Fluted Barrel, Pocket Pistol, Engraved, Antique   850   1,150

Egyptian Military

Handgun, Semi-Automatic
Tokagypt M-58, 9 MM Luger, Clip Fed, Curio   300   400

Rifle, Semi-Automatic
Hakim, 8 MM Mauser, Military, Modern   425   550

84 Gun Co.
Eighty Four, Pa. C.1973

Rifle, Bolt Action
Classic Rifle, Various Calibers, Checkered Stock, Standard Grade,
  Modern   200   300
Classic Rifle, Various Calibers, Checkered Stock, Grade 1, Modern   275   400
Classic Rifle, Various Calibers, Checkered Stock, Grade 2, Modern   400   600
Classic Rifle, Various Calibers, Checkered Stock, Grade 3, Modern   800   1,300
Classic Rifle, Various Calibers, Checkered Stock, Grade 4, Modern   1,200   2,000
Lobo Rifle, Various Calibers, Checkered Stock, Standard Grade, Modern   200   300
Lobo Rifle, Various Calibers, Checkered Stock, Grade 1, Modern   275   400
Lobo Rifle, Various Calibers, Checkered Stock, Grade 2, Modern   400   600
Lobo Rifle, Various Calibers, Checkered Stock, Grade 3, Modern   800   1,300
Lobo Rifle, Various Calibers, Checkered Stock, Grade 4, Modern   1,200   2,000
Pennsy Rifle, Various Calibers, Checkered Stock, Standard Grade,
  Modern   200   300
Pennsy Rifle, Various Calibers, Checkered Stock, Grade 1, Modern   275   400
Pennsy Rifle, Various Calibers, Checkered Stock, Grade 2, Modern   400   600
Pennsy Rifle, Various Calibers, Checkered Stock, Grade 3, Modern   800   1,300
Pennsy Rifle, Various Calibers, Checkered Stock, Grade 4, Modern   1,200   2,000

El Faisan

Shotgun, Double Barrel, Side by Side
El Faisan, .410 Gauge, Folding Gun, Double Trigger, Outside Hammers,
  Modern   50   75

El Tigre

Rifle, Lever Action
Copy of Win M 1892, .44-40 WCF, Tube Feed, Modern   150   200

Elector
Made by Hopkins & Allen, C.1880

Handgun, Revolver
.22 Short R.F., 7 Shot, Spur Trigger, Solid Frame, Single Action, Antique   90   160
.32 Short R.F., 5 Shot, Spur Trigger, Solid Frame, Single Action, Antique   95   170

Electric
Made by Forehand & Wadsworth 1871-80

Handgun, Revolver
.32 Short R.F., 5 Shot, Spur Trigger, Solid Frame, Single Action, Antique   90   160

Elgin Arms Co.
Made by Crescent for Fred Bifflar & Co. Chicago

Shotgun, Double Barrel, Side by Side
Various Gauges, Outside Hammers, Damascus Barrel, Modern   80   150
Various Gauges, Hammerless, Steel Barrel, Modern   95   175
Various Gauges, Hammerless, Damascus Barrel, Modern   75   150
Various Gauges, Outside Hammers, Steel Barrel, Modern   90   175

Shotgun, Singleshot
Various Gauges, Hammer, Steel Barrel, Modern   45   75

E.M.F.
(Early and Modern Firearms) Studio City, Calif. Current

Handgun, Revolver
Dakota, Various Calibers, Single Action, Western Style, Modern   90   140
Dakota, Various Calibers, Single Action, Western Style, Engraved, Modern   135   200
Super Dakota, Various Calibers, Single Action, Western Style, Magnum,
  Modern   95   170
Thermodynamics, .357 Magnum, Solid Frame, Swing-out Cylinder, Vent
  Rib, Stainless Steel, Modern   95   155

Handgun, Singleshot
Baron, .22 Short R.F., Derringer, Gold Frame, Blue Barrel, Wood Grips,
  Modern   15   25
Baron, Count, Etc. .22 Short R.F., Derringer, if Cased Add $7-$15
Baroness, .22 Short R.F., Derringer, Gold Plated, Pearl Grips, Modern   20   30
Count, .22 Short R.F., Derringer, Blue, Wood Grips, Modern   15   25
Countess, .22 Short R.F., Derringer, Chrome, Pearl Grips, Modern   20   30

Rifle, Semi-Automatic
AP-74 Military, .22 L.R.R.F., Clip Fed, Carbine, Modern   40   70
AP-74 Sport, .22 L.R.R.F., Clip Fed, Carbine, Modern   55   85
AP-74 Military, .32 ACP, Clip Fed, Carbine, Modern   50   80
AP-74 Sport, .32 ACP, Clip Fed, Carbine, Modern   60   95

Empire
Made by Jacob Rupertus 1858-88

Handgun, Revolver
.22 Short R.F., 7 Shot, Spur Trigger, Solid Frame, Single Action, Antique   90   160

.38 Short R.F., 5 Shot, Spur Trigger, Solid Frame, Single Action, Antique	95	190
.41 Short R.F., 5 Shot, Spur Trigger, Solid Frame, Single Action, Antique	125	220

Empire Arms
Made by Meriden, Distributed by H. & D. Folsom

Handgun, Revolver

.32 S & W, 5 Shot, Double Action, Top Break, Modern	45	95
.38 S & W, 5 Shot, Double Action, Top Break, Modern	45	95

Empire Arms Co.
Made by Crescent for Sears Roebuck & Co. C. 1900

Shotgun, Double Barrel, Side by Side

Various Gauges, Outside Hammers, Damascus Barrel, Modern	80	150
Various Gauges, Hammerless, Steel Barrel, Modern	95	175
Various Gauges, Hammerless, Damascus Barrel, Modern	75	150
Various Gauges, Outside Hammers, Steel Barrel, Modern	90	175

Shotgun, Singleshot

Various Gauges, Hammer, Steel Barrel, Modern	45	75

Empire State
Made by Meriden Firearms, Distributed by H & D Folsom

Handgun, Revolver

.32 S & W, 5 Shot, Double Action, Top Break, Modern	45	95
.38 S & W, 5 Shot, Double Action, Top Break, Modern	45	95

Empress
Made by Jacob Rupertus C. 1858-88

Handgun, Revolver

.32 Short R.F., 5 Shot, Spur Trigger, Solid Frame, Single Action, Antique	90	160

Encore
Made by Johnson-Bye, Also Hopkins & Allen 1847-87

Handgun, Revolver

.22 Short R.F., 7 Shot, Spur Trigger, Solid Frame, Single Action, Antique	90	160
.32 Short R.F., 5 Shot, Spur Trigger, Solid Frame, Single Action, Antique	95	170
.38 R.F., 5 Shot, Spur Trigger, Solid Frame, Single Action, Antique	95	190

Enders Oakleaf
Made by Crescent for Shapleigh Hardware Co., St. Louis, Mo.

Shotgun, Double Barrel, Side by Side

Various Gauges, Outside Hammers, Damascus Barrel, Modern	80	150
Various Gauges, Hammerless, Steel Barrel, Modern	95	175
Various Gauges, Hammerless, Damascus Barrel, Modern	75	150
Various Gauges, Outside Hammers, Steel Barrel, Modern	90	175

Shotgun, Singleshot

Various Gauges, Hammer, Steel Barrel, Modern	45	75

Enders Royal Service
Made by Crescent for Shapleigh Hardware Co., St. Louis, Mo.

Shotgun, Double Barrel, Side by Side

Various Gauges, Outside Hammers, Damascus Barrel, Modern	80	150
Various Gauges, Hammerless, Steel Barrel, Modern	95	175
Various Gauges, Hammerless, Damascus Barrel, Modern	75	150
Various Gauges, Outside Hammers, Steel Barrel, Modern	90	175

Shotgun, Singleshot

Various Gauges, Hammer, Steel Barrel, Modern	45	75

Enterprise
Made by Enterprise Gun Works, Pittsburgh, Pa. C.1875

Handgun, Revolver

#1, .22 Short R.F., 7 Shot, Spur Trigger, Solid Frame, Single Action, Antique	90	160
#2, .32 Short R.F., 5 Shot, Spur Trigger, Solid Frame, Single Action, Antique	95	170
#3, .38 Short R.F., 5 Shot, Spur Trigger, Solid Frame, Single Action, Antique	95	190
#4, .41 Short R.F., 5 Shot, Spur Trigger, Solid Frame, Single Action, Antique	125	220

Erbi

Shotgun, Double Barrel, Side By Side

Deluxe Ejector Grade, 12 and 20 Gauge, Raised Matted Rib, Double Trigger, Checkered Stock, Beavertail Forend, Automatic Ejector, Modern	145	200
Field Grade, 12 and 20 Gauge, Raised Matted Rib, Double Trigger, Checkered Stock, Modern	125	165

Erma
Germany made by Erma-Werke, Current

Automatic Weapon, Submachine Gun

EMP, 9mm Luger, Clip Fed, Class 3	700	950

Handgun, Semi-Automatic

EP-22, .22 L.R.R.F., Clip Fed, Modern	60	95
EP-25, .25 ACP, Clip Fed, Modern	60	90
ET-22 Navy, .22 L.R.R.F., Clip Fed, Modern	85	135
ET-22 Navy, .22 L.R.R.F., Clip Fed, With Conversion Kit, Cased With Accessories, Modern	125	185
FB-1, .25 ACP, Clip, Modern	40	60
KGP-68 (Baby), .32 ACP, Clip Fed, Modern	70	115
KGP-68 (Baby), .380 ACP, Clip Fed, Modern	80	125
KGP-69, .22 L.R.R.F., Clip Fed, Modern	65	115
LA-22 PO 8, .22 L.R.R.F., Clip Fed, Modern	75	125

Rifle, Lever Action

EG-71, .22 L.R.R.F., Tube Feed, Modern	65	110
EG-712, .22 L.R.R.F., Tube Feed, Modern	75	125
EG-712 L, .22 L.R.R.F., Tube Feed, Octagon Barrel, Nickel Silver Receiver, Modern	125	200
EG-73, .22 W.M.R., Tube Feed, Modern	90	145

Rifle Semi-Automatic

EM-1, .22 L.R.R.F., Clip Fed, Modern	60	110
EGM-1, .22 L.R.R.F., Clip Fed, Modern	60	110
ESG22, .22 L.R.R.F., Clip Fed, Modern	70	125
ESG22, .22 W.M.R., Clip Fed, Modern	95	175

Essex
Made by Crescent for Belknap Hardware Co. Louisville, Ky.

Shotgun, Double Barrel, Side by Side

Various Gauges, Outside Hammers, Damascus Barrel, Modern	80	150
Various Gauges, Hammerless, Steel Barrel, Modern	95	175
Various Gauges, Hammerless, Damascus Barrel, Modern	75	150
Various Gauges, Outside Hammers, Steel Barrel, Modern	90	175

Shotgun, Singleshot
Various Gauges, Hammer, Steel Barrel, Modern   45   75

Essex
Made by Stevens Arms

Rifle, Bolt Action
Model 50, .22 L.R.R.F., Singleshot, Takedown, Modern   30   40
Model 53, .22 L.R.R.F., Singleshot, Takedown, Modern   30   40
Model 56 Buckhorn, .22 L.R.R.F., 5 Shot Clip, Open Rear Sight, Modern   35   50

Shotgun, Double Barrel, Side by Side
Model 515, Various Gauges, Hammerless, Modern   90   140

Esteva, Pedra
Spain, C.1740

Handgun, Flintlock
Pair, Belt Pistol, Silver Inlay, Silver Furniture, Engraved, Half-Octagon
  Barrel, Antique   6,000   7,500

Evans, Stephen
Valley Forge, Pa. 1742-97. See Kentucky Rifles and U. S. Military

Evans, William
London, England 1883-1900

Shotgun, Double Barrel, Side by Side
Pair, 12 Gauge, Double Trigger, Plain, Cased Modern   4,000   5,500
Pair, 12 Gauge, Double Trigger, Straight Grip, Cased, Modern   5,000   6,500

Excam
Importers, Hialeah, Fla.

Handgun, Double Barrel, Over-under
TA-38, .38 Special, 2 Shot, Derringer, Modern   25   40

Handgun, Revolver
TA-76, .22LR/.22 WMR Combo, Western Style, Single Action, Modern   25   40
TA-76, .22 L.R.R.F., Western Style, Single Action, Modern   20   35
TA-22, .22LR/.22 WMR Combo, Western Style, Single Action, Brass
  Backstrap, Modern   35   55
TA-22, .22 L.R.R.F., Western Style, Single Action, Brass Backstrap,
  Modern   25   45

Handgun, Semi-Automatic
GT-27, .25 ACP, Clip Fed, Modern   15   25
GT-32, .32 ACP, Clip Fed, Modern   30   45
GT-380, .380 ACP, Clip Fed, Modern   35   50

Excelsior
Made by Norwich Pistol Co. C.1880

Handgun, Revolver
.32 Short R.F., 5 Shot, Spur Trigger, Solid Frame, Single Action, Antique   90   160

Excelsior
Italy

Shotgun, Double Barrel, Side by Side
Super 88, 12 Ga. Mag. 3", Boxlock, Checkered Stock, Modern   225   300

Express
Made by Bacon Arms Co. C.1880

Handgun, Revolver
.22 Short R.F., 7 Shot, Spur Trigger, Solid Frame, Single Action, Antique   90   160

Express
Spain Unknown Maker C.1920

Handgun, Semi-Automatic
.32 ACP, Clip Fed, Nickel Plated, Light Engraving, Modern   95   150

Fabrique D'Armes de Grand Precision
Spain, Unknown Maker

Handgun, Semi-Automatic
Bulwark, .25 ACP, Clip Fed, Modern   65   115

Fabrique D'Armes De Guerre
Spain, Unknown Maker. C.1900

Handgun, Semi-Automatic
Paramount, .25 ACP, Clip Fed, Modern   65   115

Fabrique d'Armes Unies de Liege
Belgium 1923-28

Handgun, Semi-Automatic
Bulwark, 32. ACP, Long Grip, Clip Fed, Modern	75	125
Helvece, .25 ACP, Clip Fed, Modern	65	110
Libia, .25 ACP, Clip Fed, Modern	75	125
Princep, .25 ACP, Clip Fed, Modern	70	120

Famars
Brescia, Italy

Shotgun, Double Barrel, Side by Side
Hammer Gun, Various Gauges, Automatic Ejector, Fancy Wood, Fancy
  Engraving, Double Triggers, Modern   3,000   4,000
Sidelock Gun, Various Gauges, Automatic Ejector, Double Trigger, Fancy
  Engraving, Fancy Wood, Modern   4,000   6 000

Farnot, Frank
Lancaster, Pa. 1779-83. See Kentucky Rifles and Pistols

Farnot, Frederick
Lancaster, Pa. 1779-82. See Kentucky Rifles and Pistols

Farrow Arms Co.
*Holyoke, Mass. Established by William Farrow 1878-85. Became Farrow Arms Co.
About 1885 and moved to Mason, Tenn., to 1904, then to Washington, D.C.
1904-17*

Rifle, Singleshot
#1, .30 Long R.F., Target Rifle, Octagon Barrel, Target Sights, Fancy
  Wood, Antique   1,200   3,000
#2, .30 Long R.F., Target Rifle, Octagon Barrel, Target Sights, Antique   950   2,250

Fast
Echave, Arizmendi y Cia. Spain

Handgun, Semi-Automatic
.380 ACP, Clip Fed, Modern   90   145

Faultless
Made by Crescent for John M. Smythe Hdw. Co., Chicago, Ill.

Shotgun, Double Barrel, Side by Side

Various Gauges, Outside Hammers, Damascus Barrel, Modern	80	150
Various Gauges, Hammerless, Steel Barrel, Modern	95	175
Various Gauges, Hammerless, Damascus Barrel, Modern	75	150
Various Gauges, Outside Hammers, Steel Barrel, Modern	90	175

Shotgun, Singleshot

Various Gauges, Hammer, Steel Barrel, Modern	45	75

Faultless Goose Gun
Made by Crescent for John M. Smythe Hdw. Co., Chicago, Ill.

Shotgun, Double Barrel, Side by Side

Various Gauges, Outside Hammers, Damascus Barrel, Modern	80	150
Various Gauges, Hammerless, Steel Barrel, Modern	95	175
Various Gauges, Hammerless, Damascus Barrel, Modern	75	150
Various Gauges, Outside Hammers, Steel Barrel, Modern	90	175

Shotgun, Singleshot

Various Gauges, Hammer, Steel Barrel, Modern	45	75

Favorite
Made by Johnson-Bye Co. C.1874-84

Handgun, Revolver

#1, .22 Short R.F., 7 Shot, Spur Trigger, Solid Frame, Single Action, Antique	90	160
#2, .32 Short R.F., 5 Shot, Spur Trigger, Solid Frame, Single Action, Antique	95	170
#3, .38 Short R.F., 5 Shot, Spur Trigger, Solid Frame, Single Action, Antique	95	190
#4, .41 Short R.F., 5 Shot, Spur Trigger, Solid Frame, Single Action, Antique	125	200

Favorite Navy
Made by Johnson-Bye Co. C.1874-84

Handgun, Revolver

.44 Short R.F., 5 Shot, Spur Trigger, Solid Frame, Single Action, Antique	175	275

Fay, Henry C.
Lancaster, Mass. C.1837

Rifle, Percussion

.58, Military, Antique	1,250	2,500

Fecht, G. Van Der
Berlin, Germany C.1733

Rifle, Flintlock

Yaeger, Half-Octagon Barrel, Brass Furniture, Engraved, Carved, Antique	2,750	4,000

Federal Arms
Made by Meriden Firearms Sold by Sears-Roebuck

Handgun, Revolver

.32 S & W, 5 Shot, Double Action, Top Break, Modern	45	95
.38 S & W, 5 Shot, Double Action, Top Break, Modern	45	95

Femaru
Hungary. Made by Femaru Fegyver es Gepgyar Pre-War; Post War Made by Femaru es Szerszamgepgyar, N. V.

Handgun, Semi-Automatic

M 37, .32 ACP, Clip Fed, Nazi-Proofed, Modern	125	200
M 37, .380 ACP, Clip Fed, Nazi-Proofed, Modern	120	185

Fenno
Lancaster, Pa. 1790-1800. See Kentucky Rifles and Pistols

Ferlach
Imported by Flaig's Lodge, Millvale, Pa.

Rifle, Double Barrel, Side by Side

Standard Grade, Various Calibers, Boxlock, Engraved, Checkered Stock, Fancy Wood, Modern	2,250	3,250
Standard Grade, Various Calibers, Sidelock, Engraved, Checkered Stock, Fancy Wood, Modern	3,500	4,250
Standard Grade, Various Calibers, Engraved, Checkered Stock, Fancy Wood, Modern	1,500	2,250

Combination Weapon, Over-Under

Turkey Gun, Various Rifle and Shotgun Calibers, Hammerless, Vent Rib, Double Set Triggers, Automatic Ejectors, Modern	400	600

Ferree, Jacob
Lancaster, Pa. 1774-84 See Kentucky Rifles and U. S. Military

Fesig, Conrad
Reading, Pa. 1779-90. See Kentucky Rifles and Pistols

Fiala
Made for Fiala Arms & Equipment Co. by Blakslee Forging Co., New Haven, Conn.

Handgun, Manual Repeater

.22 L.R.R.F., Clip Fed, Target Pistol, Curio	250	375
.22 L.R.R.F., With Shoulder Stock, 20" Barrel, add $150-$250		

F I E
Firearms Import & Export, Miami, Fla. Current

Handgun, Double Barrel, Over-Under

.38 S & W, Derringer, Modern	20	30
.38 Special, Derringer, Modern	25	35

Handgun, Flintlock

Kentucky, .44, Belt Pistol, Reproduction, Antique	35	50
Kentucky, .44, Belt Pistol, Engraved, Reproduction, Antique	40	55
Tower, .69, Antique	15	28

Handgun, Percussion

Baby Dragoon, .31, Revolver, Reproduction, Antique	25	40
Baby Dragoon, .31, Revolver, Engraved, Reproduction, Antique	30	45
Kentucky, .44, Belt Pistol, Reproduction, Antique	30	45
Kentucky, .44, Belt Pistol, Engraved, Reproduction, Antique	35	50
Navy, .36, Revolver, Reproduction, Antique	25	35
Navy, .36, Revolver, Engraved, Reproduction, Antique	30	40
Navy, .44, Revolver, Reproduction, Antique	25	40
Navy, .44, Revolver, Engraved, Reproduction, Antique	30	45
Remington, .36, Revolver, Reproduction, Antique	30	45
Remington, .36, Revolver, Engraved, Reproduction, Antique	35	55
Remington, .44, Revolver, Reproduction, Antique	30	45
Remington, .44, Revolver, Engraved, Reproduction, Antique	35	55

116

Handgun, Revolver

Arminius, .22 LR/.22 WMR Combo, Double Action, Swing-out Cylinder, Adjustable Sights, Chrome, Modern	40	60
Arminius, .22 LR/.22 WMR Combo, Double Action, Swing-out Cylinder, Adjustable Sights, Blue, Modern	40	60
Arminius, .22 LR/.22 WMR Combo, Double Action, Swing-out Cylinder, Adjustable Sights, Blue, Target, Modern	40	60
Arminius, .22 L.R.R.F., Double Action, Swing-out Cylinder, Adjustable Sights, Blue, Modern	30	50
Arminius, .22 L.R.R.F., Double Action, Swing-out Cylinder, Adjustable Sights, Chrome, Modern	30	60
Arminius, .22 L.R.R.F., Double Action, Swing-out Cylinder, Adjustable Sights, Blue, Target, Modern	30	60
Arminius, .22 L.R.R.F., Double Action, Swing-out Cylinder, Adjustable Sights, Chrome, Target, Modern	30	60
Arminius, .32 S & W, Double Action, Swing-out Cylinder, Adjustable Sights, Blue, Target, Modern	30	60
Arminius, .32 S & W, Double Action, Swing-out Cylinder, Adjustable Sights, Chrome, Target, Modern	30	60
Arminius, .357 Magnum, Double Action, Swing-out Cylinder, Adjustable Sights, Chrome, Target, Modern	55	85
Arminius, .357 Magnum, Double Action, Swing-out Cylinder, Adjustable Sights, Blue, Target, Modern	55	85
Arminius, .38 Special, Double Action, Swing-out Cylinder, Adjustable Sights, Blue, Target, Modern	35	55
Arminius, .38 Special, Double Action, Swing-out Cylinder, Adjustable Sights, Chrome, Target, Modern	35	55
Arminius, .38 Special, Double Action, Swing-out Cylinder, Blue, Modern	25	45
Arminius, .38 Special, Double Action, Swing-out Cylinder, Chrome, Modern	25	45
Buffalo Scout, .22LR/.22 WMR Combo, Single Action, Western Style, Modern	30	40
Buffalo, .22 L.R.R.F., Single Action, Western Style, Modern	25	35
Guardian, .22 L.R.R.F., Double Action, Swing-out Cylinger, Modern	25	40
Guardian, .22 L.R.R.F., Double Action, Swing-out Cylinder, Chrome, Modern	30	45
Guardian, .32 S & W, Double Action, Swing-out Cylinder, Modern	25	40
Guardian, .32 S & W, Double Action, Swing-out Cylinder, Chrome, Modern	30	45
Legend, .22LR/.22 WMR Combo, Single Action, Western Style, Steel Frame, Modern	35	50
Legend, .22 L.R.R.F., Single Action, Western Style, Steel Frame, Modern	30	45

Handgun, Semi-Automatic

Best, .25 ACP, Hammer, Steel Frame, Blue, Modern	50	75
Best, .32 ACP, Hammer, Steel Frame, Blue, Modern	60	90
Guardian, .25 ACP, Hammer, Blue, Modern	20	30
Guardian, .25 ACP, Hammer, Chrome, Modern	20	30
Guardian, .25 ACP, Hammer, Gold Plated, Modern	25	35
Titan, .25 ACP, Hammer, Blue, Modern	20	30
Titan, .25 ACP, Hammer, Chrome, Modern	20	30
Titan, .32 ACP, Hammer, Steel Frame, Blue, Modern	40	55
Titan, .32 ACP, Hammer, Steel Frame, Chrome, Modern	45	60
Titan, .32 ACP, Hammer, Steel Frame, Engraved, Chrome, Modern	55	70
Titan, .32 ACP, Hammer, Steel Frame, Engraved, Blue, Modern	50	65
Titan, .380 ACP, Hammer, Steel Frame, Blue, Modern	55	70
Titan, .380 ACP, Hammer, Steel Frame, Chrome, Modern	55	70
Titan, .380 ACP, Hammer, Steel Frame, Engraved, Blue, Modern	65	85
Titan, .380 ACP, Hammer, Steel Frame, Engraved, Chrome, Modern	65	90

Rifle, Flintlock

Kentucky, .45, Reproduction, Antique	55	85
Kentucky, .45, Engraved, Reproduction, Antique	60	85

FIE Titan .25 ACP

Rifle, Percussion

Berdan, .45, Reproduction, Antique	50	80
Kentucky, .45, Reproduction, Antique	50	80
Kentucky, .45, Engraved, Reproduction, Antique	55	80
Zoave, .58, Reproduction, Antique	60	95

Shotgun, Double Barrel, Over-Under

OU, 12 and 20 Ga., Field Grade, Vent Rib, Modern	100	150
OU 12 T, 12 Ga., Trap Grade, Vent Rib, Modern	125	160
OU-S, 12 and 20 Ga., Skeet Grade, Vent Rib, Modern	125	160

Shotgun, Double Barrel, Side by Side

DB, Various Gauges, Hammerless, Modern	65	95
DB Riot, Various Gauges, Hammerless, Modern	65	95
Brute, Various Gauges, Short Barrels, Short Stock, Modern	90	145

Shotgun, Singleshot

SB 40, 12 Ga., Hammer, Button Break, Modern	25	45
SB 41, 20 Ga., Hammer, Button Break, Modern	25	45
SB 42, .410 Ga., Hammer, Button Break, Modern	25	45
SB Youth, Various Gauges, Hammer, Modern	25	35
SB 12 16 20 .410, Various Gauges, Hammer, Modern	25	40
S.O.B., 12 and 20 Gauges, Short Barrel, Short Stock, Modern	35	55

Fiehl & Weeks Fire Arms Mfg. Co.
Philadelphia, Pa. C.1895

Handgun, Revolver

.32 S & W, 5 Shot, Top Break, Hammerless, Double Action, Modern	55	95

Figthorn, Andrew
Reading, Pa. 1779-90 See Kentucky Rifles

Finnish Lion
Made by Valmet, Finland

Rifle, Bolt Action

.22 L.R.R.F., Singleshot, Target Rifle, Target Stock, Target Sights, Modern	275	375
.22 L.R.R.F., Singleshot, Target Rifle, Thumbhole Stock, Target Sights, Modern	300	400
22 L.R.R.F., Singleshot, Target Rifle, Thumbhole Stock, Target Sights, Heavy Barrel, Modern	325	450

Firearms, Custom Made
This category covers some of the myriad special firearms that are built to an individual's specifications by a competent gunsmith, and not by the original factory. Most firearms in this class will appeal only to a person who happens to want the same special features, and because of this most of these guns sell for less than the cost of the conversion

Handgun, Revolver

P.P.C. Conversion, .38 Special, Heavy Barrel, Rib with Target Sights, Target Trigger, Target Grips, Modern	150	250
"F.B.I." Conversion, .38 Special, Cut Trigger Guard, Spurless Hammer, Short Barrel, Modern	125	200
Recoil Compensation Devices or Ports, add $20-$35		

Handgun, Semi-Automatic

Double Action Conversion, Model 1911A1, add $75-$125

Combat Conversion, Extended Trigger Guard, Ambidextrous Safety,
Special Slide Release, Ported, Combat Sights, Modern   250   350

Handgun, Singleshot

Silhouette Pistol, Various Calibers, Bolt Action, Thumbhole Stock, Target
Sights, Target Trigger, Modern   250   400

Handgun, Percussion

Target Revolver, Various Calibers, Tuned, Target Sights, Reproduction,
Antique   75   120

Rifle, Bolt Action

Sporting Rifle, Various Calibers, Checkered Stock, Recoil Pad, Simple
Military Conversion, Modern   75   125

Sporting Rifle, Various Calibers, Fancy Wood, Recoil Pad, Fancy Military
Conversion, Modern   250   375

Sporting Rifle, Various Calibers, Plain Stock, Commercial Parts, Modern   80   135

Sporting Rifle, Various Calibers, Mauser 1871 Action, Checkered Stock,
Antique   125   200

Rifle, Singleshot

Stevens 44½ Action, Heavy Barrel, Target Stock, Target Sights, Modern   200   325

Target Rifle, Centerfire Calibers, Plain, Target Sights, Built on Various
Moving Block Actions, Modern   175   275

Target Rifle, Centerfire Calibers, Fancy, Target Sights, Built on Various
Moving Block Actions, Modern   250   375

Target Rifle, Rimfire Calibers, Plain, Target Sights, Built on Various
Moving Block Actions, Modern   125   200

Shotgun, Slide Action

Combat Conversion, 12 Ga., Short Barrel, Extended Magazine Tube,
Folding Stock, Rifle Sights, Modern   135   225

Competition Conversion, Various Gauges, High Rib, Recoil Reducer in
Stock, Fancy Wood, Modern   225   350

Custom Firearm, Mauser 1871 Rifle

Custom Firearm, Stevens 44½

Firearms Specialties
Owosso, Mich. C.1972

Handgun, Revolver

.45/70 Custom Revolver, Brass Frame, Single Action, Western Style,
Modern   350   550

Firearms Co. Ltd.
England. Imported by Mandall Shooting Supplies

Rifle, Bolt Action

Alpine, Various Calibers, Checkered Stock, Recoil Pad, Open Rear Sight,
Modern 125   175

Firearms International
Washington, D.C.

Handgun, Semi-Automatic

Model D, .380 ACP, Clip Fed, Adjustable Sights, Blue, Modern	75	100
Model D, .380 ACP, Clip Fed, Adjustable Sights, Chrome Modern	80	120
Model D, .380 ACP, Clip Fed, Adjustable Sights, Matt Blue, Modern	75	110
Combo, .22 L.R.R.F., Unique Model L Pistol with Conversion Kit for Stocked Rifle, Modern	60	95

Handgun, Revolver

Regent, .22 L.R.R.F., 8 Shot, Various Barrel Lengths, Blue, Modern	25	45
Regent, .32 L.R.R.F., 7 Shot, Various Barrel Lengths, Blue, Modern	30	50

Shotgun, Double Barrel, Side by Side

Model 400, Various Gauges, Single Trigger, Checkered Stock, Modern	140	190
Model 400E, Various Gauges, Single Selective Trigger, Checkered Stock, Selective Ejector, Vent Rib, Modern	175	235
Model 400E, Various Gauges, Single Selective Trigger, Selective Ejector, Modern	150	220

Flintlock, Unknown Maker

Handgun, Flintlock

.28, English, Pocket Pistol, Queen Anne Style, Box Lock, Screw Barrel, Plain, Antique	250	400
.40, India Herdsman Pistol, Long Tapered Round Barrel, Silver Furniture, Antique 400	600	
.45, French, Mid-1700's, Screw Barrel, Long Cannon Barrel, Silver Furniture, Antique	800	1,000
.60, Continental, Early 1700's, Holster Pistol, Half-Octagon Barrel, Engraved, High Quality, Antique	1,500	2,000
.60, Oval Bore, Box Lock, Pocket Pistol, Steel Furniture, Antique	500	750
.62, Crantham English, Holster Pistol, Brass Furniture, Plain, Antique	300	375
.63, Spanish, Mid-1600's, Holster Pistol, Silver Inlay, Engraved, Antique	2,000	3,000
.68, Tower, Continental, Plain, Antique	225	300
.65, Arabian, Holster Pistol, Flared, Round Barrel, Low Quality, Antique	200	250
English Lock, Mid-1600's, Military, Holster Pistol, Iron Mounts, Plain, Antique 2,500	4,000	
English, Early 1700's, Pocket Pistol, Queen Anne Style, Box Lock, Screw Barrel, All Metal, Antique	300	500
English Early 1700's, Pocket Pistol, Box Lock Double Barrel, Screw Barrel, Low Quality, Antique	350	500
English Mid-1600's, Button Triger, Brass Barrel, Octagon Fish-tail Butt, Antique 1,200	2,000	
French Officers Type C.1650, Steel Furniture, Rifled, Antique	1,200	2,000
French Sedan Mid-1600's, Long Screw Barrel, Rifled, Plain, Antique	1,500	2,000

Rifle, Flintlock

.64, Continental, Carbine, Musket, Brass Furniture, Antique	300	450
.72, Continental, 1650, Musket, Brass Furniture, Plain, Antique	650	900

Shotgun, Flintlock

.65, American Hudson Valley, Antique	800	1,250

F.N.
Fabrique Nationale, Herstal, Belgium from 1889. Also see Browning

Automatic Weapon, Assault Rifle

FN-CAL, .223 Rem., Clip Fed, Commercial, Class 3	1,200	1,850
FN-FAL, .308 Win., Clip Fed, Commercial, Class 3	950	1,500
FN-FAL, .308 Win., Clip Fed, Folding Stock, Commercial, Class 3	1,200	1,800
FN-FAL, .308 Win., Clip Fed, Heavy Barrel, Bipod, Commercial, Class 3	1,500	2,000
FN-FAL "Para," .308 Win., Clip Fed, Folding Stock, Lightweight, Commercial, Class 3	1,300	1,750

Automatic Weapon, Light Machine Gun

FN M.A.G. 58, .308 Win., Belt Fed, Bipod, Class 3	2,750	3,400
FN M.A.G. 58, .308 Win., Belt Fed, Tripod, Class 3	4,000	4,750

Handgun, Semi-Automatic

Lithuanian Contract, 9mm Luger, Clip Fed, Tangent Sights, Military, Modern	425	550

Rifle, Bolt Action

Mauser 98 Military Style, 30/06, Military Finish, Military Stock, Commercial, Modern	110	195
Mauser 98 Military Style, Various Military Calibers, Military Finish, Military Stock, Commercial, Modern	90	150
Mauser Deluxe, Various Calibers, Sporting Rifle, Checkered Stock, Modern	300	400
Mauser Deluxe Presentation, Various Calibers, Sporting Rifle, Fancy Wood, Engraved, Modern	500	700
Mauser Supreme, Various Calibers, Sporting Rifle, Checkered Stock, Modern	275	375
Mauser Supreme, Various Calibers, Sporting Rifle, Checkered Stock, Magnum, Modern	300	425

Rifle, Semi-Automatic

Model 1949, 30/06, Clip Fed, Military, Modern	200	325
Model 1949, 7mm or 8mm Mauser, Clip Fed, Military, Modern	175	275
M-49 Egyptian, 8mm Mauser, Clip Fed, Military, Modern	195	300

Shotgun, Bolt Action

9mm Shotshell, Modern	80	120

Folger, William H.
Barnsville, Ohio 1830-54, Also See Kentucky Rifles

Folk's Gun Works
Bryan, Ohio 1860-91

Rifle, Singleshot

.32 L.R.R.F., Side Lever, Octagon Barrel, Antique	200	290

Fondersmith, John
Strasburg, Pa. 1749-1801. See Kentucky Rifles, U.S. Military

F.F. Forbes
Made by Crescent C.1900

Shotgun, Double Barrel, Side by Side

Various Gauges, Outside Hammers, Damascus Barrel, Modern	80	150
Various Gauges, Hammerless, Steel Barrel, Modern	95	175
Various Gauges, Hammerless, Damascus Barrel, Modern	75	150
Various Gauges, Outside Hammers, Steel Barrel, Modern	90	175

Forehand Arms Co. .32 S&W

Shotgun, Singleshot
Various Gauges, Hammer, Steel Barrel, Modern   45   75

Forehand Arms Co.

Handgun, Revolver
.32 S & W, 5 Shot, Double Action, Solid Frame, 2″ Barrel, Antique   45   85
.38 S & W, 5 Shot, Double Action, Solid Frame, 2″ Barrel, Antique   45   85
Perfection Automatic, .32 S & W, 5 Shot, Double Action, Top Break,
  Hammerless, Antique   65   100
Perfection Automatic, .32 S & W, 5 Shot, Double Action, Top Break,
  Antique   55   95

Forehand & Wadsworth
*Worcester, Mass. Successors and sons-in-law To Ethan Allen in 1871, in 1872
name was changed to Forehand & Wadsworth; in 1890 to Forehand Arms Co.*

Handgun, Revolver
.22 Short R.F., Single Action, Spur Trigger, Solid Frame, Side Hammer,
  Antique   85   150
.22 Short R.F., 7 Shot, Single Action, Solid Frame, Antique   75   125
.30 Short R.F., Single Action, Spur Trigger, Solid Frame, Side Hammer,
  Antique   75   140
.32 Short R.F., Single Action, Spur Trigger, Solid Frame, Side Hammer,
  Antique   80   145
.44 Short R.F., Single Action, Spur Trigger, Solid Frame, Side Hammer,
  Antique   95   175
Army, .38 Long R.F., 6 Shot, Single Action, Solid Frame, Antique   275   425
British Bulldog, .32 S & W, 7 Shot, Double Action, Solid Frame, Antique   45   85
British Bulldog, .38 S & W, 6 Shot, Double Action, Solid Frame, Antique   45   85
British Bulldog, .44 S & W, 5 Shot, Double Action, Solid Frame, Antique   60   100
Bulldog, .38 Long R.F., 5 Shot, Single Action, Solid Frame, 2″ Barrel,
  Antique   80   140
Bulldog, .44 S & W, 5 Shot Double Action, Solid Frame, 2″ Barrel, Antique   60   100
New Navy, .44 Russian, 6 Shot, Double Action, Solid Frame, 6″ Barrel,
  Antique   250   400
Old Army, .44 Russian, 6 Shot, Single Action, Solid Frame, 7″ Barrel,
  Antique   325   475
Pocket Model, .32 S & W Long, 6 Shot, Double Action, Top Break, Antique   50   95
Russian Model, .32, .32 Short R.F., 5 Shot, Single Action, Solid Frame,
  Spur Trigger, Antique   95   170
Swamp Angel, .41 Short R.F., 5 Shot, Single Action, Solid Frame, Spur
  Trigger, Antique   120   200
Terror, .32 Short R.F., 5 Shot, Single Action, Solid Frame, Spur Trigger,
  Antique   85   160

Handgun, Singleshot
.22 Short R.F., Spur Trigger, Side-Swing Barrel, Antique   150   225
.41 Short R.F., Spur Trigger, Side-swing Barrel, Antique   200   325

Forever Yours
Flaig's Lodge, Millvale, Pa.

Shotgun, Double Barrel, Over-Under
Various Gauges, Automatic Ejector, Checkered Stock, Vent Rib, Double
  Trigger, Modern   375   550
Various Gauges, Automatic Ejector, Checkered Stock, Vent Rib, Single
  Trigger, Modern   400   600

Foulkes, Adam
Easton & Allentown, Pa. 1773-94. See Kentucky Rifles, U.S. Military

Four Ace Co.
Brownsville, Texas Current

Handgun, Singleshot

Four Ace, Derringer, Presentation Case Add $8-$15

Four Ace Model 200, .22 Short R.F., Derringer, 4 Shot, Spur Trigger, Modern	25	35
Four Ace Model 200, .22 Short R.F., Derringer, 4 Shot, Spur Trigger, Nickel Plated, Gold Plated, Modern	35	50
Four Ace Model 202, .22 L.R.R.F., Derringer, 4 Shot, Spur Trigger, Nickel Plated, Gold Plated, Modern	40	55
Four Ace Model, 202, .22 L.R.R.F., Derringer, 4 Shot, Spur Trigger, Modern	30	40
Four Ace Model 204, .22 L.R.R.F., Derringer, 4 Shot, Spur Trigger, Stainless Steel, Modern	40	55
Little Ace Model 300, .22 Short R.F., Derringer, Side-swing Barrel, Spur Trigger, Modern	20	30

Fox, A.H. Gun Co.
Philadelphia, Pa. Formerly Philadelphia Arms Co., now a subsidiary of Savage Arms Co., 1930 to date. Also see Savage Arms Co.

Shotgun, Double Barrel, Side by Side

Various Gauges, Single Selective Trigger Add $150-$250
Various Gauges, For Vent Rib Add $150-$250
Various Gauges, Beavertail Forend Add 10%-15%
Various Gauges, For Single Trigger Add $100-$175
Various Grades, for 20 Ga. add 50%-75%

A Grade, Various Gauges, Box Lock, Light Engraving, Checkered Stock, Modern	475	650
AE Grade, Various Gauges, Box Lock, Light Engraving, Checkered Stock, Automatic Ejector, Modern	625	850
BE Grade, Various Gauges, Box Lock, Engraved, Checkered Stock, Automatic Ejector, Modern	700	1,000
CE Grade, Various Gauges, Box Lock, Engraved, Fancy Checkering, Automatic Ejector, Modern	950	1,400
DE Grade, Various Gauges, Box Lock, Fancy Engraving, Fancy Checkering, Fancy Wood, Automatic Ejector, Modern	3,500	5,000
FE Grade, Various Gauges, Box Lock, Fancy Engraving, Fancy Checkering, Fancy Wood, Automatic Ejector, Modern	5,500	8,500
GE Grade, Various Gauges, Box Lock, Fancy Engraving, Fancy Checkering, Fancy Wood, Automatic Ejector, Modern	9,000	14,500
HE Grade, 12 and 20 Gauge, Box Lock, Light Engraving, Checkered Stock, Automatic Ejector, Modern	600	850
Skeeter Grade, 12 and 20 Gauge, Box Lock, Skeet Grade, Beavertail Forend, Vent Rib, Automatic Ejector, Modern	850	1,250
SP Grade, Various Gauges, Box Lock, Checkered Stock, Modern	300	450
SP Grade, Various Gauges, Box Lock, Checkered Stock, Automatic Ejector, Modern	350	500
SP Grade, Various Gauges, Box Lock, Skeet Grade, Checkered Stock, Modern	350	500
SP Grade, Various Gauges, Box Lock, Skeet Grade, Automatic Ejector, Checkered Stock, Modern	400	550
Sterlingworth, Various Gauges, Box Lock, Checkered Stock, Hammerless, Modern	300	425
Various Gauges, Box Lock, Checkered Stock, Hammerless, Automatic Ejector, Modern	400	550
Sterlingworth, Various Gauges, Box Lock, Skeet Grade, Checkered Stock, Modern	350	475
Sterlingworth, Various Gauges, Box Lock, Skeet Grade, Checkered Stock, Automatic Ejector, Modern	475	700
Sterlingworth Deluxe, Various Gauges, Box Lock, Checkered Stock, Hammerless, Recoil Pad, Modern	375	500

Sterlingworth Deluxe, Various Gauges, Box Lock, Checkered Stock, Hammerless, Recoil Pad, Automatic Ejector, Modern	500	700
XE Grade, Various Gauges, Box Lock, Fancy Engraving, Fancy Checkering, Fancy Wood, Automatic Ejector, Modern	1,750	2,500

Shotgun, Singleshot

JE Grade, 12 Gauge, Trap Grade, Vent Rib, Automatic Ejector, Engraved, Fancy Checkering, Modern	1,100	1,500
KE Grade, 12 Gauge, Trap Grade, Vent Rib, Automatic Ejector, Engraved, Fancy Checkering, Modern	1,400	2,000
LE Grade, 12 Gauge, Trap Grade, Vent Rib, Automatic Ejector, Fancy Engraving, Fancy Checkering, Modern	2,000	2,750
ME Grade, 12 Gauge, Trap Grade, Vent Rib, Automatic Ejector, Fancy Engraving, Fancy Checkering, Modern	4,000	6.000

Francais
France, made by Manufacture D'Armes Automatiques Francaise

Handgun, Semi-Automatic

Prima, .25 ACP, Clip Fed, Modern	70	115

Franchi
Italy, imported by Stoeger Arms

Rifle, Semi-Automatic

Centennial, .22 L.R.R.F., Checkered Stock, Tube Feed, Takedown, Modern	95	150
Centennial Deluxe, .22 L.R.R.F., Checkered Stock, Tube Feed, Takedown, Light Engraving, Modern	150	225
Centennial Gallery, .22 Short R.F., Checkered Stock, Tube Feed, Takedown, Modern	95	160

Shotgun, Double Barrel, Over-Under

Alcione Super, 12, Vent Rib, Single Selective Trigger, Automatic Ejector, Engraved, Modern	275	375
Alcione Super Deluxe, 12, Vent Rib, Single Selective Trigger, Automatic Ejector, Engraved, Modern	375	500
Aristocrat, 12 Ga., Field Grade, Automatic Ejectors, Single Selective Trigger, Vent Rib, Modern	300	450
Aristocrat, 12 Ga., Imperial Grade, Automatic Ejectors, Single Selective Trigger, Vent Rib, Modern	950	1,450
Aristocrat, 12 Ga., Monte Carlo Grade, Automatic Ejectors, Single Selective Trigger, Vent Rib, Modern	1,300	1,950
Barrage Skeet, 12, Vent Rib, Single Selective Trigger, Automatic Ejector, Recoil Pad, Modern	500	750
Barrage Trap, 12, Vent Rib, Single Selective Trigger, Automatic Ejector, Recoil Pad, Modern	500	750
Dragon Skeet, 12, Vent Rib, Single Selective Trigger, Automatic Ejector, Recoil Pad, Modern	375	500
Dragon Trap, 12, Vent Rib, Single Selective Trigger, Automatic Ejector, Recoil Pad, Modern	375	500
Falconet Buckskin, 12 and 20 Ga., Vent Rib, Single Selective Trigger, Automatic Ejector, Modern	225	325
Falconet Ebony, 12 and 20 Ga., Vent Rib, Single Selective Trigger, Automatic Ejector, Modern	225	325
Falconet Peregrine 400, 12 and 20 Ga., Vent Rib, Single Selective Trigger, Automatic Ejector, Modern	245	325
Falconet Peregrine 451, 12 and 20 Ga., Vent Rib, Single Selective Trigger, Automatic Ejector, Modern	260	350
Falconet Pigeon, 12 Ga. Vent Rib, Single Selective Trigger, Automatic Ejector, Fancy Engraving, Fancy Checkering, Modern	800	1,100
Falconet Silver, 12 Ga., Vent Rib, Single Selective Trigger, Automatic Ejector, Modern	260	350
Falconet Super, 12, Vent Rib, Single Selective Trigger, Automatic Ejector, Modern	275	375

Falconet Super Deluxe, 12, Vent Rib, Single Selective Trigger, Automatic Ejector, Modern	350	500
Model 255, 12, Vent Rib, Single Selective Trigger, Automatic Ejector, Modern	200	300
Model 2003, 12 Ga. Trap Grade, Vent Rib, Single Selective Trigger, Automatic Ejector, Modern	600	800
Model 2005, 12 Ga., Trap Grade, Vent Rib, Single Selective Trigger, Automatic Ejector, Extra Shotgun Barrel, Modern	800	1,150

Shotgun, Double Barrel, Side by Side

Airone, 12 Ga., Box Lock, Hammerless, Checkered Stock, Automatic Ejector, Modern	425	600
Astore, 12 Ga., Box Lock, Hammerless, Checkered Stock, Modern	325	450
Astore S, 12 Ga., Box Lock, Hammerless, Checkered Stock, Light Engraving, Modern	700	950
Condor, Various Gauges, Sidelock, Engraved, Checkered Stock, Automatic Ejector, Modern	1,800	2,500
Imperial, Various Gauges, Sidelock, Engraved, Checkered Stock, Automatic Ejector, Modern	3,000	3,750
Imperial Monte Carlo #11, Various Gauges, Sidelock, Fancy Engraving, Fancy Checkering, Automatic Ejector, Modern	6,500	8,000
Imperial Monte Carlo Extra, Various Gauges, Sidelock, Fancy Engraving, Fancy Checkering, Automatic Ejector, Modern	7,750	10,000
Imperial Monte Carlo #5, Various Gauges, Sidelock, Fancy Engraving, Fancy Checkering, Automatic Ejector, Modern	6,750	8,000
Imperial S, Various Gauges, Sidelock, Engraved, Checkered Stock, Automatic Ejector, Modern	3,000	3,750

Shotgun, Semi-Automatic

Dynamic (Heavy), 12 Ga., Plain Barrel, Modern	120	175
Dynamic (Heavy), 12 Ga., Vent Rib, Modern	140	200
Dynamic (Heavy), 12 Ga., Skeet Grade, Vent Rib, Checkered Stock, Modern	150	220
Dynamic (Heavy), 12 Ga., Checkered Stock, Slug, Open Rear Sight, Modern	160	225
Eldorado, 12 and 20 Ga., Vent Rib, Engraved, Fancy Checkering, Lightweight, Modern	240	325
Hunter, 12 and 20 Ga., Vent Rib, Engraved, Checkered Stock, Lightweight, Modern	190	275
Model 500, 12 Ga., Vent Rib, Checkered Stock, Engraved, Modern	200	265
Model 500, 12 Ga., Vent Rib, Checkered Stock, Modern	180	235
Slug Gun, 12 and 20 Ga., Open Rear Sight, Sling Swivels, Modern	160	225
Standard, 12 and 20 Ga., Plain Barrel, Lightweight, Checkered Stock, Modern	145	200
Standard, 12 and 20 Ga., Solid Rib, Lightweight, Checkered Stock, Modern	150	210
Standard, 12 and 20 Ga., Vent Rib, Lightweight, Checkered Stock, Modern	160	220
Standard Magnum, 12 and 20 Gauges, Vent Rib, Lightweight, Checkered Stock, Modern	175	245
Superange (Heavy), 12 and 20 Gauges, Magnum, Plain Barrel, Checkered Stock, Modern	140	200
Superange (Heavy), 12 and 20 Gauges, Magnum, Vent Rib, Checkered Stock, Modern	160	235
Wildfowler (Heavy), 12 and 20 Gauges, Magnum, Vent Rib, Checkered Stock, Engraved, Modern	200	285

Shotgun, Singleshot

Model 2004, 12 Ga., Trap Grade, Vent Rib, Automatic Ejector, Modern	600	750

Franci, Piero Inzi
Brescia, Italy C.1640

Handgun, Wheelock

Octagon-Barrel, Dagger Handle Butt, Antique	1,750	2,700

Francotte Bulldog Revolver

Francotte, August
Belgium

Handgun, Revolver
Bulldog, Various Calibers, Double Action, Solid Frame, Curio   75   125

Handgun, Semi-Automatic
Vest Pocket, .25 ACP, Clip Fed, Curio   175   250

Rifle, Double Barrel, Side by Side
Luxury Double, .458 Win., Sidelock, Hammerless, Double Triggers, Fancy
  Engraving, Modern   9,000   13,000

Shotgun, Double Barrel, Side by Side
A & F #14, Various Gauges, Box Lock, Automatic Ejector, Checkered
  Stock, Engraved, Hammerless, Modern   2,000   2,650
A & F #20, Various Gauges, Box Lock, Automatic Ejector, Checkered
  Stock, Engraved, Hammerless, Modern   2,300   3,000
A & F #25, Various Gauges, Box Lock, Automatic Ejector, Checkered
  Stock, Engraved, Hammerless, Modern   2,800   3,500
A & F #30, Various Gauges, Box Lock, Automatic Ejector, Checkered
  Stock, Fancy Engraving, Hammerless, Modern   3,000   3,750
A & F #45, Various Gauges, Box Lock, Automatic Ejector, Checkered
  Stock, Fancy Engraving, Hammerless, Modern   3,700   4,500
A & F Jubilee, Various Gauges, Box Lock, Automatic Ejector, Checkered
  Stock, Light Engraving, Hammerless, Modern   1,750   2,500
A & F Knockabout, Various Gauges, Box Lock, Automatic Ejector,
  Checkered Stock, Hammerless, Modern   1,200   1,750
Francotte Original, Various Gauges, Box Lock, Automatic Ejector,
  Checkered Stock, Hammerless, Engraved, Modern   1,800   2,400
Francotte Special, Various Gauges, Box Lock, Automatic Ejector,
  Checkered Stock, Hammerless, Light Engraving, Modern   1,300   2,000
Model 10/18E/628, Various Gauges, Box Lock, Automatic Ejector,
  Checkered Stock, Hammerless, Light Engraving, Modern   2,600   3,250
Model 10594, Various Gauges, Box Lock, Automatic Ejector, Checkered
  Stock, Hammerless, Engraved, Modern   1,800   2,500
Model 11/18E, Various Gauges, Box Lock, Automatic Ejector, Checkered
  Stock, Hammerless, Engraved, Modern   1,800   2,500
Model 120.HE/328, Various Gauges, Sidelock, Automatic Ejector,
  Checkered Stock, Hammerless, Fancy Engraving, Modern   6,000   7,500
Model 4996, Various Gauges, Box Lock, Automatic Ejector, Checkered
  Stock, Hammerless, Light Engraving, Modern   1,300   2,000
Model 6886, Various Gauges, Box Lock, Automatic Ejector, Checkered
  Stock, Hammerless, Modern   1,250   1,900
Model 6930, Various Gauges, Box Lock, Automatic Ejector, Checkered
  Stock, Hammerless, Light Engraving, Modern   1,300   2,000
Model 6982, Various Gauges, Box Lock, Automatic Ejector, Checkered
  Stock, Hammerless, Engraved, Modern   2,000   2,800
Model 8455, Various Gauges, Box Lock, Automatic Ejector, Checkered
  Stock, Hammerless, Modern   2,100   2,850
Model 8457, Various Gauges, Box Lock, Automatic Ejector, Checkered
  Stock, Hammerless, Engraved, Modern   1,800   2,500

Model 9/40.SE, Various Gauges, Box Lock, Automatic Ejector, Checkered Stock, Hammerless, Fancy Engraving, Modern	5,500	8,000
Model 9/40E/38321, Various Gauges, Box Lock, Automatic Ejector, Checkered Stock, Hammerless, Engraved, Modern	2,800	3,400
Model SOB.E/11082, Various Gauges, Box Lock, Automatic Ejector, Checkered Stock, Hammerless, Engraved, Modern	3,500	5,000

Franklin, C. W.
Belgium, C.1900

Shotgun, Double Barrel, Side by Side
Various Gauges, Outside Hammers, Damascus Barrel, Modern	80	150
Various Gauges, Hammerless, Steel Barrel, Modern	95	175
Various Gauges, Hammerless, Damascus Barrel, Modern	75	150
Various Gauges, Outside Hammers, Steel Barrel, Modern	90	175

Shotgun, Singleshot
Various Gauges, Hammer, Steel Barrel, Modern	45	75

Frankonia
West Germany

Rifle, Singleshot
Heeren Rifle, Various Calibers, Fancy Engraving, Fancy wood, Octagon Barrel, Modern	1,200	1,800
Heeren Rifle, Various Calibers, Fancy Engraving, Fancy wood, Round Barrel, Modern	1,000	1,500

Rifle Bolt Action
Favorit, Various Calibers, Set Triggers, Checkered Stock, Modern	125	190
Favorit Deluxe, Various Calibers, Set Triggers, Checkered Stock, Modern	170	230
Favorit Leichtmodell, Various Calibers, Lightweight, Set Triggers, Checkered Stock, Modern	200	325
Safari, Various Calibers, Target Trigger, Checkered Stock, Modern	200	350
Stutzen, Various Calibers, Carbine, Set Triggers, Full Stock, Modern	165	225

Fraser, D. & J.
Edinburgh, Scotland 1870-1900

Rifle, Double Barrel, Side by Side
.360 N.E. #2, Automatic Ejector, Express Sights, Engraved, Extra Set of Barrels, Cased with Accessories, Modern	6,000	7,500

Freedom Arms
Freedom, Wyo.

Handgun, Revolver
FA-S, .22 L.R.R.F., Stainless Steel, Matt Finish, Spur Trigger, 1" Barrel, Single Action, Modern	55	80
FA-L, .22 L.R.R.F., Stainless Steel, Matt Finish, Spur Trigger, 1¾" Barrel, Single Action, Modern	60	85
FA-S, .22 W.M.R., Stainless Steel, Matt Finish, Spur Trigger, 1" Barrel, Single Action, Modern	65	95
FA-L, .22 W.M.R., Stainless Steel, Matt Finish, Spur Trigger, 1¾" Barrel, Single Action, Modern	70	100
Add for High Gloss Finish $5-$10		

French Military

Automatic Weapon, Light Machine Gun
CSRG 1915 Chauchat, 8 x 50R Lebel, Clip Fed, Bipod, Class 3	525	675

Automatic Weapon, Submachine Gun
MAS 38, 7.65 MAS, Clip Fed, Wood Stock, Dewat, Class 3	400	600
MAS 38, 7.65 MAS, Clip Fed, Wood Stock, Class 3	850	1,100

French Military Model 1777

French AN XIII

French Military Model 1873 11mm

French Model 1935-S, 7.65 MAS

Handgun, Flintlock

.69 Charleville 1810, Cavalry Pistol, Brass Furniture, Plain, Antique	450	700
.69 Charleville 1777, Cavalry Pistol, Brass Frame, Belt Hook, Antique	500	850
.69, Model 1763, Belt Pistol, Military, Antique	850	1,350

Handgun, Percussion

.69 AN XIII, Officer's Pistol, Made in France, Antique	200	350
.69 AN XIII, Officer's Pistol, Made in Occupied Country, Antique	300	450
.69 Charleville 1810 Cavalry Pistol, Brass Furniture, Converted from Flintlock, Plain, Antique	300	425

Handgun, Revolver

Model 1873, 11mm French Ordnance, Double Action, Solid Frame, Antique	95	145
Model 1892, 8mm Lebel Revolver, Double Action, Solid Frame, Modern	85	135

Handgun, Semi-Automatic

Model 1935-A, 7.65 MAS, Clip Fed, Modern	85	150
Model 1935-A, 7.65 MAS, Clip Fed, Nazi Proofed, Modern	125	195
Model 1935-S, 7.65 MAS, Clip Fed, Modern	75	120
Model 1935-S, 7.65 MAS, Clip Fed, Nazi Proofed, Modern	110	170
Model 1950, 9mm Luger, Clip Fed, Modern	250	350

French Military Model 1950 9mm

Rifle, Bolt Action

6.5 x 53.5 Daudetau, Carbine, Modern	110	170
Model 1874, 11 x 59R Gras, Antique	80	125
Model 1874, 11 x 59R Gras, Carbine, Antique	95	145
Model 1886/93 Lebel, 8 x 50R Lebel, Modern	65	115
Model 1907/15 Remington, 8 x 50R Lebel, Modern	70	120
Model 1916 St. Etienne, 8 x 50R Lebel, Carbine, Modern	85	135
Model 1936 MAS, 7.5 x 54 MAS, with Bayonet, Modern	125	175

Rifle, Flintlock

.69, Model 1763 Charleville 1st. Type, Musket, Antique	700	1,000
.69, Model 1763/66 Charleville, Musket, Antique	575	850

Frommer

Budapest, Hungary. Made by Femaru-Fegyver-Es Gepgyar R.T.

Handgun, Semi-Automatic

Baby Stop, .32 ACP, Clip Fed, Modern	95	160
Baby Stop, .380 ACP, Clip Fed, Modern	140	225
Liliput, .22 L.R.R.F., Clip Fed, Modern	250	350
Liliput, .25 ACP, Clip Fed, Modern	150	225
Model 1910, 7.65mm K, Clip Fed, Blue, Police Model, Curio	800	1,200
Roth-Frommer, 7.65mm K, Clip Fed, Curio	600	900
Stop, .32 ACP, Clip Fed, Modern	90	145
Stop, .380 ACP, Clip, Fed, Modern	110	165

Frommer "Roth-Frommer"

Frommer Stop .32 ACP

Frontier
Made by Norwich Falls Pistol Co. C.1880

Handgun, Revolver
.32 Short R.F., 5 Shot, Spur Trigger, Solid Frame, Single Action, Antique   95   170

Fryberg, Andrew
Hopkintown, Mass. C.1905

Handgun, Revolver
.32 S & W, 5 Shot, Top Break, Hammerless, Double Action, Modern   55   95
.32 S & W, 5 Shot, Top Break, Double Action, Modern   45   95
.38 S & W, 5 Shot, Top Break, Double Action, Hammerless, Modern   55   95
.38 S & W, 5 Shot, Top Break, Double Action, Modern   45   95

Frye, Martin
C.1809 Also see Kentucky Pistols and U.S. Military

FTL
Covina, Calif.

Handgun, Semi-Automatic
.22 L.R.R.F., Clip Fed, Chrome, Modern   80   120

Galef
N.Y.C. Importers

Handgun, Revolver
Stallion, .22LR/.22 WMR Combo, Western Style, Single Action, Modern   65   95

Handgun, Semi-Automatic
Brigadier, 9mm Luger, Beretta, Clip Fed, Modern   165   240
Cougar, .380 ACP, Beretta, Clip Fed, Modern   95   140
Jaguar, .22 L.R.R.F., Beretta, Clip Fed, Modern   85   140
Puma, .32 ACP, Beretta, Clip Fed, Modern   95   140
Sable, .22 L.R.R.F., Beretta, Clip Fed, Adjustable Sights, Modern   120   175

Rifle, Bolt Action
BSA Monarch, Various Calibers, Checkered Stock, Modern   125   165
BSA Monarch, Various Calibers, Checkered Stock, Magnum Action, Modern   135   180
BSA Monarch Varmint, Various Calibers, Checkered Stock, Heavy Barrel, Modern   150   195

Shotgun, Double Barrel, Over-Under
Golden Snipe, 12 Ga., Trap Grade, Single Trigger, Automatic Ejector, Engraved, Checkered Stock, Modern   325   425
Golden Snipe, 12 and 20 Gauges, Beretta, Single Trigger, Automatic Ejector, Engraved, Fancy Checkering, Modern   275   350
Golden Snipe, 12 and 20 Gauges, Beretta, Single Selective Trigger, Automatic Ejector, Engraved, Fancy Checkering, Modern   300   400
Golden Snipe, 12 and 20 Gauges, Skeet Grade, Single Trigger, Automatic Ejector, Engraved, Checkered Stock, Modern   325   425
Golden Snipe Deluxe, 12 and 20 Gauges, Beretta, Single Selective Trigger, Automatic Ejector, Fancy Engraving, Fancy Checkering, Modern   350   450
Silver Snipe, 12 Ga., Trap Grade, Single Trigger, Vent Rib, Engraved, Checkered Stock, Modern   270   350
Silver Snipe, 12 and 20 Gauges, Skeet Grade, Single Trigger, Vent Rib, Engraved, Checkered Stock, Modern   270   350
Silver Snipe, 12 and 20 Gauges, Beretta, Single Trigger, Checkered Stock, Modern   200   275
Silver Snipe, 12 and 20 Gauges, Beretta, Single Selective Trigger, Checkered Stock, Light Engraving, Modern   250   325

Zoli Golden Snipe, 12 and 20 Gauges, Vent Rib, Single Trigger,
Adjustable Choke, Engraved, Checkered Stock, Modern   290   370
Zoli Silver Snipe, 12 and 20 Gauges, Vent Rib, Single Trigger, Engraved,
Checkered Stock, Modern   240   320

Shotgun, Double Barrel, Side by Side
M213CH, 10 Ga. 3½", Double Trigger, Checkered Stock, Light Engraving,
Recoil Pad, Modern   140   200
M213CH, Various Gauges, Double Trigger, Checkered Stock, Light
Engraving, Recoil Pad, Modern   110   150
Silver Hawk, 10 Ga. 3½", Beretta, Double Trigger, Magnum, Modern   325   425
Silver Hawk, 12 and 20 Gauges, Double Trigger, Engraved, Checkered
Stock, Modern   250   325
Silver Hawk, 12 Ga. Mag. 3", Beretta, Double Trigger, Magnum, Modern   250   325
Silver Hawk, 12 Ga. Mag. 3", Beretta, Single Trigger, Magnum, Modern   300   375
Silver Hawk, Various Gauges, Beretta, Double Trigger, Lightweight,
Modern   200   275
Silver Hawk, Various Gauges, Beretta, Double Trigger, Lightweight,
Modern   250   325
Zabala 213, 10 Ga. 3½", Double Trigger, Modern   120   175
Zabala 213, 12 and 20 Gauges, Double Trigger, Modern   95   140
Zabala 213, 12 and 20 Gauges, Double Trigger, Vent Rib, Modern   100   150
Zabala Police, 12 and 20 Gauges, Double Trigger, Modern   100   150

Shotgun, Semi-Automatic
Gold Lark, 12 Ga., Beretta, Vent Rib, Light Engraving, Checkered Stock,
Modern   125   200
Ruby Lark, 12 Ga., Beretta, Vent Rib, Fancy Engraving, Fancy Checkering,
Modern   200   300
Silver Gyrfalcon, 12 Ga., Beretta, Checkered Stock, Modern   60   100
Silver Lark, 12 Ga., Beretta, Checkered Stock, Modern   90   140

Shotgun, Singleshot
Companion, Various Gauges, Folding Gun, Checkered Stock, Modern   35   50
Companion, Various Gauges, Folding Gun, Checkered Stock, Vent Rib,
Modern   45   60
Monte Carlo, 12 Ga., Trap Grade, Vent Rib, Engraved, Checkered Stock,
Modern   120   175

Shotgun, Slide Action
Gold Pigeon, 12 Ga., Beretta, Vent Rib, Fancy Engraving, Fancy
Checkering, Modern   200   300
Ruby Pigeon, 12 Ga., Beretta, Vent Rib, Fancy Engraving, Fancy
Checkering, Modern   300   400
Silver Pigeon, 12 Ga., Beretta, Light Engraving, Checkered Stock, Modern   90   125

Galesi
Brescia, Italy from 1910. Made by Industria Armi Galesi, Currently Called Armi Galesi

Handgun, Semi-Automatic
Model 506, .22 L.R.R.F., Clip Fed, Modern   65   95
Model 6, .22 Long R.F., Clip Fed, Modern   65   95
Model 6, .25 ACP, Clip Fed, Modern   60   85
Model 9, .22 L.R.R.F., Clip Fed, Modern   65   90
Model 9, .32 ACP, Clip Fed, Modern   70   110
Model 9, .380 ACP, Clip Fed, Modern   80   125

Galesi Model 9

Gallatin, Albert
See Kentucky Rifles and Pistols

Gander, Peter
Lancaster, Pa. 1779-82 See Kentucky Rifles

Garate Anitua
Eibar, Spain

Handgun, Semi-Automatic
.32 ACP, Clip Fed, Long Grip, Modern   110   165

Garrison
Made by Hopkins & Allen C.1880-90 ·

Handgun, Revolver
.22 Short R.F., 7 Shot, Spur Trigger, Solid Frame, Single Action, Antique   90   160

Garrucha
Made by Amadeo Rossi, Brazil

Handgun, Double Barrel, Side by Side
.22 L.R.R.F., Double Triggers, Outside Hammers, Modern   30   50

Gautec, Peter
Lancaster, Pa. C.1780 Kentucky Rifles & Pistols

Gavage, Armand
Leige, Belgium

Handgun, Semi-Automatic
.32 ACP, Clip Fed, Blue, Modern   150   240
.32 ACP, Clip Fed, Blue, Nazi-Proofed, Modern   200   300

Gecado
Suhl, Germany, by G. C. Dornheim

Handgun, Semi-Automatic
Model 11, .25 ACP, Clip Fed, Modern   60   95

Gem
Made by Bacon Arms Co. C.1880

Handgun, Revolver
.22 Short R.F., 7 Shot, Spur Trigger, Solid Frame, Single Action, Antique   90   160

German Military
Also See: Walther, Mauser, Luger

Automatic Weapon, Assault Rifle
FG 42 (Type 2), 8mm Mauser, Clip Fed, Wood Stock, Class 3   7,000   8,500
MP43, 8mm Mauser, Clip Fed, Class 3   500   700
MP44, 8mm Mauser, Clip Fed, Class 3   500   700

Automatic Weapon, Heavy Machine Gun
MG-08 Sledge Mount, 8mm Mauser, Belt Fed, Class 3   1,400   1,950
MG-08/15, 8mm Mauser, Belt Fed, Bipod, Class 3   700   925
MG-42, 8mm Mauser, Belt Fed, Bipod, Class 3   675   850

Automatic Weapon, Light Machine Gun
MG-34, 8mm Mauser, Belt Fed, High Quality, Bipod, Class 3   1,600   2,250

Automatic Weapon, Submachine Gun
EMP, 9mm Luger, Clip Fed, Class 3   750   1,000

German Military MP/40 Schmeisser

German Military Model 1879 Service Revolver

MP 18/1, 9mm Luger, Drum Magazine, Bergmann, Wood Stock, Military, Class 3	1,250	1,800
MP 18/1, 9mm Luger, Drum Magazine, Bergmann, Wood Stock, Military, Dewat, Class 3	300	400
MP 18/1 (Modified), 9mm Luger, Clip Fed, Bergmann, Wood Stock, Military, Class 3	800	1,200
MP 3008, 9mm Luger, Clip Fed, Military, Class 3	1,650	2,100
MP 35/1, 9mm Luger, Clip Fed, Bergmann, Wood Stock, Military, Class 3	975	1,500
MP 38, 9mm Luger, Clip Fed, Schmeisser, Military, Folding Stock, Class 3	1,500	2,000
MP 38/40, 9mm Luger, Clip Fed, Schmeisser, Military, Folding Stock, Class 3	1,500	2,250
MP 40, 9mm Luger, Clip Fed, Schmeisser, Military, Folding Stock, Class 3	750	1,000
MP 40/1, 9mm Luger, Clip Fed, Schmeisser, Military, Folding Stock, Class 3	650	900

Handgun, Revolver

Model 1879 Troopers Model, 11mm German Service, Solid Frame, Single Action, Safety, 7″ Barrel, 6 Shot, Antique	200	300
Model 1883 Officers' Model, 11mm German Service, Solid Frame, Single Action, Safety, 5″ Barrel, 6 Shot, Antique	175	275

Rifle, Bolt Action

GEW 88 Commission, 8 x 57 JRS, Clip Fed, Antique	40	65
GEW 98 (Average), 8mm Mauser, Military, Modern	95	170

German Military Model 1883 Service Revolver

GEW 98 Sniper, 8mm Mauser, Scope Mounted, Military, Curio	600	850
K98K Sniper, 8mm Mauser, Scope Mounted, Military, Curio	375	500
KAR 98 8 (Average), 8mm Mauser, Military, Carbine, Modern	95	170
KAR 98A (Average), 8mm Mauser, Military, Carbine, Modern	95	170
M-95, 8mm Mauser, Steyr-Mannlicher, German Military, Nazi-Proofed, Modern	90	160
M-95, 8mm Mauser, Steyr-Mannlicher, German Military, Carbine, Nazi-Proofed, Modern	85	145
Model 1871 Mauser, .43 Mauser, Singleshot, Military, Antique	175	260
Model 1871 Mauser, .43 Mauser, Carbine, Singleshot, Military, Antique	250	350
Model 71/84 Mauser, .43 Mauser, Tube Feed, Military, Antique	190	285
Training Rifle, .22 L.R.R.F., Military, Modern	175	225
VZ-24 BRNO, 8mm Mauser, Nazi-Proofed, Military, Modern	95	150
Needle Gun, 11mm, Singleshot, Military, Antique	250	325

Rifle, Percussion

.69, M1839, Musket, Brass Furniture, Military, Antique	225	350

Rifle, Semi-Automatic

G43, 8mm Mauser, Clip Fed, 10 Shot, Military, Curio	225	300
GEW 41, 8mm Mauser, 10 Shot, Military, Curio	325	450
GEW 41 (W), 8mm Mauser, 10 Shot, Military, Curio	300	425
KAR 43 Sniper, 8mm Mauser, Scope Mounted, Clip Fed, 10 Shot, Military, Curio	450	650
VG 2, 8mm Mauser, Clip Fed, 10 Shot, Military, Curio	275	425

Gesscer, Georg
Saxony, 1591-1611

Handgun, Wheel-Lock

Pair, Military, Inlays, Pear Pommel, Medium Ornamentation, Antique		22,000

Gevarm
Gevelot, St. Etienne, France

Rifle, Semi-Automatic

Model A3, .22 L.R.R.F., Target Sights, Clip Fed, Modern	80	145
Model A6, .22 L.R.R.F., Open Sights, Clip Fed, Modern	60	100
Model A7, .22 L.R.R.F., Target Sights, Clip Fed, Modern	90	165
Model E1, .22 L.R.R.F., Target Sights, Clip Fed, Modern	60	100

Gibralter
Possibly Meriden Firearms. Brand Name for Sears-Roebuck

Handgun, Revolver

.32 S & W, 5 Shot, Double Action, Top Break, Modern	45	95
.38 S & W, 5 Shot, Double Action, Top Break, Modern	45	95

Gibralter
Made by Stevens Arms

Shotgun, Singleshot

Model 116, Various Gauges, Hammer, Automatic Ejector, Raised Matted Rib, Modern	45	65

Gill, Thomas
London, England 1770-1812

Handgun, Flintlock

.68, Pocket Pistol, Octagon Barrel, Plain, High Quality, Antique	600	850

Glaser Waffen
Zurich, Switzerland

Handgun, Singleshot
Target Pistol, .22 L.R.R.F., Toggle Breech, Francotte, Modern　　175　　250

Rifle, Bolt Action
Custom Rifle, Various Calibers, Fancy Wood, Modern　　500　　800

Rifle, Singleshot
Heeren Rifle, Various Calibers, Engraved, Fancy Wood, Modern　　900　　1,400

Glassbrenner, David
Lancaster, Pa. See Kentucky Rifles

Glenn, Robert
Edinburgh, Scotland C.1860 Made Fine Copies of Highland Pistols

Handgun, Snaphaunce
Replica Highland, All Brass, Engraved, Ovoid Pommel, Antique　　1,750　　2,500

Glisenti
Italy 1905-10. In 1911 Became Brixia

Handgun, Semi-Automatic
M1910 Army, 9mm Glisenti, Clip Fed, Wood Grips, Modern　　165　　250
M1910 Navy, 9mm Glisenti, Clip Fed, Plastic Stock, Modern　　155　　240
M906, 7.63 Mauser, Clip Fed, Military, Modern　　200　　300

Golden Eagle
Nikko Arms Co. Ltd., Japan

Rifle, Bolt Action
Model 7000, Various Calibers, Grade 1, Checkered Stock, Modern　　200　　300
Model 7000, Various African Calibers, Grade 1, Checkered Stock, Modern　　225　　350

Shotgun, Double Barrel, Over-Under
Model 5000, 12 and 20 Gauges, Field Grade, Vent Rib, Checkered Stock,
　Light Engraving, Gold Overlay, Modern　　325　　450
Model 5000, 12 and 20 Gauges, Skeet Grade, Vent Rib, Checkered Stock,
　Light Engraving, Gold Overlay, Modern　　400　　550
Model 5000, 12 and 20 Gauges, Trap Grade, Vent Rib, Checkered Stock,
　Light Engraving, Gold Overlay, Modern　　400　　550
Model 5000, 12 and 20 Gauges, Field Grade 2, Vent Rib, Checkered Stock,
　Light Engraving, Gold Overlay, Modern　　425　　550
Model 5000, 12 and 20 Gauges, Skeet Grade 2, Vent Rib, Checkered
　Stock, Light Engraving, Gold Overlay, Modern　　475　　600
Model 5000, 12 and 20 Gauges, Trap Grade 2, Vent Rib, Checkered Stock,
　Light Engraving, Gold Overlay, Modern　　475　　600
Model 5000 Grandee, 12 and 20 Gauges, Field Grade 3, Vent Rib,
　Checkered Stock, Fancy Engraving, Gold Overlay, Modern　　1,250　　2,000
Model 5000 Grandee, 12 and 20 Gauges, Skeet Grade 3, Vent Rib,
　Checkered Stock, Fancy Engraving, Gold Overlay, Modern　　1,250　　2,000
Model 5000 Grandee, 12 Ga., Trap Grade 3, Vent Rib, Checkered Stock,
　Fancy Engraving, Gold Overlay, Modern　　1,250　　2,000

Gonter, Peter
Lancaster, Pa. 1770-78. See Kentucky Rifles

Goose Gun
Made by Stevens Arms

Shotgun, Singleshot
Model 89 Dreadnaught, Various Gauges, Hammer, Modern　　45　　60

Governor
Made by Bacon Arms Co.

Handgun, Revolver
.22 Short R.F., 7 Shot, Spur Trigger, Solid Frame, Single Action, Antique   90   160

Governor
Various Makers C.1880

Handgun, Revolver
.32 S & W, 5 Shot, Double Action, Top Break, Modern   45   95
.38 S & W, 5 Shot, Double Action, Top Break, Modern   45   95

Graeff, Wm.
Reading, Pa. 1751-84 Also See Kentucky Rifles

Grant, W. L.

Handgun, Revolver
.22 Long R.F., 6 Shot, Single Action, Solid Frame, Spur Trigger, Antique   100   175
.32 Short R.F., 6 Shot, Single Action, Solid Frame, Spur Trigger, Antique   125   200

Grave, John
Lancaster, Pa. 1769-73 See Kentucky Rifles

Great Western Gun Works
Pittsburg, Pa. 1860 to about 1923

Handgun, Revolver
.22 Short R.F., 7 Shot, Spur Trigger, Solid Frame, Single Action, Antique   90   160

Rifle, Percussion
No. 5, Various Calibers, Various Barrel Lengths, Plains Rifle, Octagon
  Barrel, Brass Fittings, Antique   350   500

Greek Military

Rifle, Bolt Action
M 1930 Greek, 8mm Mauser, Military, Modern   95   145

Greener, W. W.
Birmingham, England

Shotgun, Double Barrel, Side by Side
Various Gauges, Single Non-Selective Trigger Add $175-$250
Various Gauges, Single Selective Trigger Add $250-$350
Crown DH-55, Various Gauges, Box Lock, Automatic Ejector, Checkered
  Stock, Fancy Engraving, Modern   1,800   2,600
Empire, 12 Ga. Mag. 3", Box Lock, Hammerless, Light Engraving,
  Checkered Stock, Modern   800   1,200
Empire, 12 Ga. Mag. 3", Box Lock, Hammerless, Light Engraving,
  Checkered Stock, Automatic Ejector, Modern   950   1,500
Empire Deluxe, 12 Ga. Mag. 3", Box Lock, Hammerless, Engraved,
  Checkered Stock, Modern   950   1,500
Empire Deluxe, 12 Ga. Mag. 3", Box Lock, Hammerless, Engraved,
  Checkered Stock, Automatic Ejector, Modern   1,100   1,750
Far-Killer F35, 10 Ga. 3½", Box Lock, Hammerless, Engraved, Checkered
  Stock, Modern   1,100   1,800
Far-Killer F35, 10 Ga. 3½", Box Lock, Hammerless, Engraved, Checkered
  Stock, Automatic Ejector, Modern   1,750   2,500

Far-Killer F35, 12 Ga. Mag. 3", Box Lock, Hammerless, Engraved, Checkered Stock, Modern	1,400	2,000
Far-Killer F35, 12 Ga. Mag. 3", Box Lock, Hammerless, Engraved, Checkered Stock, Automatic Ejector, Modern	1,750	2,500
Far-Killer F35, 8 Ga., Box Lock, Hammerless, Engraved, Checkered Stock, Modern	1,200	2,000
Far-Killer F35, 8 Ga., Box Lock, Hammerless, Engraved, Checkered Stock, Automatic Ejector, Modern	1,850	2,700
Jubilee DH-35, Various Gauges, Box Lock, Automatic Ejector, Checkered Stock, Engraved, Modern	1,000	1,750
Royal DH-75, Various Gauges, Box Lock, Automatic Ejector, Checkered Stock, Fancy Engraving, Modern	2,250	3,000
Sovereign DH-40, Various Gauges, Box Lock, Automatic Ejector, Checkered Stock, Engraved, Modern	1,400	2,250

Shotgun, Singleshot

G. P. Martini, 12 Ga., Checkered Stock, Takedown, Modern	150	225

Gregory
Mt. Vernon, Ohio 1837-42. See Kentucky Rifles

Greifelt & Co.
Suhl, Germany

Combination Weapon, Double Barrel, Over-Under

Various Calibers, Solid Rib, Engraved, Checkered Stock, Modern	2,500	3,500
Various Calibers, Solid Rib, Engraved, Checkered Stock, Automatic Ejector, Modern	3,250	4,500

Combination Weapon, Drilling

Various Calibers, Fancy Wood, Fancy Checkering, Engraved, Modern	2,750	4,000
Various Calibers, Engraved, Checkered Stock, Modern	2,000	3,000

Rifle, Bolt Action

Sport, .22 Hornet, Checkered Stock, Express Sights, Modern	425	650

Shotgun, Double Barrel, Over-Under
Various Gauges, Single Trigger Add $225-$325
Various Gauges, For Vent Rib Add $175-$275

#1, .410 Ga., Automatic Ejector, Fancy Engraving, Checkered Stock, Fancy Wood, Solid Rib, Modern	3,500	5,000
#1, Various Gauges, Automatic Ejector, Fancy Engraving, Checkered Stock, Fancy Wood, Solid Rib, Modern	2,500	3,400
#3, .410 Ga., Automatic Ejector, Engraved, Checkered Stock, Solid Rib, Modern	2,600	3,350
#3, Various Gauges, Automatic Ejector, Engraved, Checkered Stock, Solid Rib, Modern	1,500	2,150
Model 143E, Various Gauges, Automatic Ejector, Engraved, Checkered Stock, Solid Rib, Double Trigger, Modern	1,000	1,750
Model 143E, Various Gauges, Automatic Ejector, Engraved, Checkered Stock, Vent Rib, Single Selective Trigger, Modern	1,400	2,000

Shotgun, Double Barrel, Side by Side

Model 103, 12 and 16 Gauges, Box Lock, Double Trigger, Checkered Stock, Light Engraving, Modern	650	900
Model 103E, 12 and 16 Gauges, Box Lock, Double Trigger, Checkered Stock, Light Engraving, Automatic Ejector, Modern	875	1,250
Model 22, 12 and 16 Gauges, Box Lock, Double Trigger, Checkered Stock, Engraved, Modern	600	900
Model 22E, 12 and 16 Gauges, Box Lock, Double Trigger, Checkered Stock, Engraved, Automatic Ejector, Modern	900	1,250

Greyhawk Arms Corp.

Rifle, Singleshot
Model 74, Various Calibers, Rolling Block, Octagon Barrel, Open Rear
  Sight, Reproduction, Modern   80   120

Groom, Richard
London, England C.1855

Handgun, Flintlock
.68, East India Company, Calvary Pistol, Military, Tapered Round Barrel,
  Brass Furniture, Antique   900   1,500

Gross Arms Co.
Tiffin, Ohio 1862-65

Handgun, Revolver
.22 Short R.F., 7 Shot, Spur Trigger, Tip-Up, Antique   300   575
.25 Short R.F., 6 Shot, Single Action, Spur Trigger, Tip-Up, Antique   325   600
.32 Short R.F., 5 Shot, Spur Trigger, Tip-Up, Antique   300   575

Guardian
Made by Bacon Arms Co. C.1880

Handgun, Revolver
.22 Short R.F., 7 Shot, Spur Trigger, Solid Frame, Single Action, Antique   90   160
.32 Short R.F., 5 Shot, Spur Trigger, Solid Frame, Single Action, Antique   95   170

Gumph, Christopher
Lancaster, Pa. 1779-1803. See Kentucky Rifles and Pistols

Gustaf, Carl
See Husqvarna

Gustloff Werke
Suhl, Germany

Handgun, Semi-Automatic
.32 ACP, Clip Fed, Hammer, Single Action, Modern   1,200   2,000

Rifle, Bolt Action
Model KKW, .22 L.R.R.F., Pre-WW2, Singleshot, Tangent Sights, Military
  Style Stock, Modern   300   425

Shotgun, Double Barrel, Side by Side
16 Ga., Engraved, Color Case Hardened Frame, Modern   375   475

Hackett, Edwin and George
London, England C.1870

Shotgun, Double Barrel, Side by Side
10 Ga. 2⅞", Damascus Barrel, Plain, Antique   125   175

Hadden, James
Philadelphia, Pa. 1769 See Kentucky Rifles and Pistols

Haeffer, John
Lancaster, Pa. C.1800 See Kentucky Rifles and Pistols

Haenel, C.G.
Suhl, Germany 1925-40

Handgun, Semi-Automatic

Schmeisser Model 1, .25 ACP, Clip Fed, Modern	95	175
Schmeisser Model 2, .25 ACP, Clip Fed, Modern	95	175

Rifle, Bolt Action

Model 88, Various Calibers, Sporting Rifle, Half-Octagon Barrel, Open' Rear Sight, Modern	200	300
Model 88 Sporter, Various Calibers, 5 Shot Clip, Half-Octagon Barrel, Open Rear Sight, Modern	225	350

Hafdasa
Hispano Argentina Fab. de Automoviles

Handgun, Singleshot

.22 L.R.R.F., Blowback, Modern	200	300

Half-Breed
Made by Hopkins & Allen C.1880

Handgun, Revolver

.32 Short R.F., 5 Shot, Spur Trigger, Solid Frame, Single Action, Antique	90	170

Hammerli
Lenzburg, Switzerland

Handgun, Revolver

Virginian, .357 Magnum, Single Action, Western Style, Modern	125	165
Virginian, .45 Colt, Single Action, Western Style, Modern	130	185

Handgun, Semi-Automatic

Model 200 Walther Olympia, .22 L.R.R.F., Target Pistol, Modern	300	425
Model 200 Walther Olympia, .22 L.R.R.F., Target Pistol, Muzzle Brake, Modern	350	475
Model 201 Walther Olympia, .22 L.R.R.F., Target Pistol, Adjustable Grips, Modern	300	425
Model 202 Walther Olympia, .22 L.R.R.F., Target Pistol, Adjustable Grips, Modern	350	475
Model 203 Walther Olympia, .22 L.R.R.F., Target Pistol, Adjustable Grips, Modern	375	500
Model 203 Walther Olympia, .22 L.R.R.F., Target Pistol, Adjustable Grips, Muzzle Brake, Modern	400	550
Model 204 Walther Olympia, .22 L.R.R.F., Target Pistol, Modern	400	550

Haenel Schmeisser Model 1 .25 ACP

Hafdasa .22

Model 204 Walther Olympia, .22 L.R.R.F., Target Pistol, Muzzle Brake, Modern	450	600
Model 205 Walther Olympia, .22 L.R.R.F., Target Pistol, Fancy Wood, Modern	450	600
Model 205 Walther Olympia, .22 L.R.R.F., Target Pistol, Fancy Wood, Muzzle Brake, Modern	500	650
Model 206, .22 L.R.R.F., Target Pistol, Modern	300	475
Model 207, .22 L.R.R.F., Target Pistol, Adjustable Grips, Modern	425	550
Model 208, .22 L.R.R.F., Target Pistol, Clip Fed, Adjustable Grips, Modern	425	600
Model 208, .22 L.R.R.F., Target Pistol, Clip Fed, Adjustable Grips, Left-Hand, Modern	450	625
Model 209, .22 Short R.F., Target Pistol, 5 Shot Clip, Muzzle Brake, Modern	400	550
Model 210, .22 L.R.R.F., Target Pistol, Modern	350	475
Model 210, .22 L.R.R.F., Target Pistol, Adjustable Grips, Modern	375	500
Model 211, .22 L.R.R.F., Target Pistol, Clip Fed, Modern	400	550
Model 230-1, .22 Short R.F., Target Pistol, 5 Shot Clip, Modern	400	550
Model 230-2, .22 Short R.F., Target Pistol, 5 Shot Clip, Adjustable Grips, Modern	450	600
Model 230-2, .22 Short R.F., Target Pistol, 5 Shot Clip, Adjustable Grips, Left-Hand, Modern	475	625
Model P-240 S I G, .22 L.R.R.F., Target Pistol, Clip Fed, Conversion Unit Only, Modern	300	425
Model P-240 S I G, .32 S & W Long, Clip Fed, Target Pistol, Cased with Accessories, Modern	525	775
Model P-240 S I G, .38 Special, Clip Fed, Target Pistol, Cased with Accessories, Modern	550	800

Handgun, Singleshot

Model 100, .22 L.R.R.F., Target Pistol, Modern	350	475
Model 100 Deluxe, .22 L.R.R.F., Target Pistol, Modern	400	525
Model 101, .22 L.R.R.F., Target Pistol, Modern	375	500
Model 102, .22 L.R.R.F., Target Pistol, Modern	350	475
Model 102 Deluxe, .22 L.R.R.F., Target Pistol, Modern	400	550
Model 103, .22 L.R.R.F., Target Pistol, Carved, Inlays, Modern	400	600
Model 103, .22 L.R.R.F., Target Pistol, Carved, Modern	350	525
Model 104, .22 L.R.R.F., Target Pistol, Round Barrel, Modern	350	475
Model 105, .22 L.R.R.F., Target Pistol, Octagon Barrel, Modern	375	525
Model 106, .22 L.R.R.F., Target Pistol, Round Barrel, Modern	350	500
Model 107, .22 L.R.R.F., Target Pistol, Octagon Barrel, Modern	425	600
Model 107 Deluxe, .22 L.R.R.F., Target Pistol, Octagon Barrel, Engraved, Modern	500	800
Model 110, .22 L.R.R.F., Target Pistol, Modern	350	500
Model 120, .22 L.R.R.F., Target Pistol, Heavy Barrel, Modern	275	400
Model 120, .22 L.R.R.F., Target Pistol, Heavy Barrel, Adjustable Grips, Modern	300	425
Model 120, .22 L.R.R.F., Target Pistol, Heavy Barrel, Left-Hand, Adjustable Grips, Modern	300	435
Model 120-1, .22 L.R.R.F., Target Pistol, Modern	275	400
Model 120-2, .22 L.R.R.F., Target Pistol, Adjustable Grips, Modern	300	425
Model 120-2, .22 L.R.R.F., Target Pistol, Adjustable Grips, Left-Hand, Modern	300	435
Model 150, .22 L.R.R.F., Target Pistol, Modern	550	850

Rifle, Bolt Action

Model 45, .22 L.R.R.F., Singleshot, Thumbhole Stock, Target Sights, with Accessories, Modern	350	500
Model 54, .22 L.R.R.F., Singleshot, Thumbhole Stock, Target Sights, with Accessories, Modern	350	500
Model 503, .22 L.R.R.F., Singleshot, Thumbhole Stock, Target Sights, with Accessories, Modern	350	500
Model 506, .22 L.R.R.F., Singleshot, Thumbhole Stock, Target Sights, with Accessories, Modern	375	525

Olympia 300 Meter, Various Calibers, Singleshot, Thumbhole Stock, Target Sights, with Accessories, Modern	400	600
Tanner, Various Calibers, Singleshot, Thumbhole Stock, Target Sights, with Accessories, Modern	425	675
Sporting Rifle, Various Calibers, Set Triggers, Fancy Wood, Checkered Stock, Open Sights, Modern	300	500

Hampton, John
Dauphin County, Pa. See Kentucky Rifles and Pistols

Hard Pan
Made by Hood Firearms C.1875

Handgun, Revolver

.22 Short R.F., 7 Shot, Spur Trigger, Solid Frame, Single Action, Antique	90	160
.32 Short R.F., 5 Shot, Spur Trigger, Solid Frame, Single Action, Antique	95	170

Harpers Ferry Arms Co.

Rifle, Flintlock

.72 Lafayette, Musket, Reproduction, Antique	175	250

Rifle, Percussion

.51 Maynard, Carbine, Breech Loader, Reproduction, Antique	120	165
.58, 1861 Springfield, Rifled, Musket, Reproduction, Antique	120	165

Harrington & Richardson Arms Co.
Worcester, Mass. Successors to Wesson & Harrington, 1874 to Date

Automatic Weapon, Assault Rifle

T-48, .308 Win., Clip Fed, Military, Class 3	2,500	3,000

Automatic Weapon, Submachine Gun

Riesing M50, .45 ACP, Commercial, Clip Fed, Class 3	250	325

Handgun, Revolver

922 (Early), .22 L.R.R.F., 9 Shot, Solid Frame, Wood Grips, Octagon Barrel, Double Action, Modern	55	80
922 (Early), .22 L.R.R.F., 9 Shot, Solid Frame, Double Action, Modern	50	75
922 (Early), .22 L.R.R.F., 9 Shot, Solid Frame, Pocket Pistol, Double Action, Modern	50	75
922 (Late), .22 L.R.R.F., 9 Shot, Solid Frame, Swing-Out Cylinder, Double Action, Modern	25	40
Abilene Anniversary, .22 L.R.R.F., Commemorative, Curio	55	95
American, Various Calibers, Double Action, Solid Frame, Modern	40	75
Auto Ejecting, Various Calibers, Top Break, Hammer, Double Action, Modern	60	100
Bobby, Various Calibers, 6 Shot, Top Break, Double Action, Modern	55	80
Defender, .38 S & W, Top Break, 6 Shot, Double Action, Adjustable Sights, Modern	55	85
Expert, .22 L.R.R.F., Top Break, 9 Shot, Double Action, Wood Grips, Modern	75	120
Expert, .22 W.R.F., Top Break, 9 Shot, Double Action, Wood Grips, Modern	80	130
Hunter (Early), .22 L.R.R.F., 7 Shot, Solid Frame, Wood Grips, Double Action, Modern	60	90
Hunter (Later), .22 L.R.R.F., 9 Shot, Solid Frame, Wood Grips, Double Action, Modern	55	80
Model 199, .22 L.R.R.F., Single Action, 9 Shot, Top Break, Adjustable Sights, Modern	45	80
Model 4, Various Calibers, Double Action, Solid Frame, Modern	40	75
Model 40, Various Calibers, Top Break, Hammerless, Double Action, Modern	60	100
Model 5, .32 S & W, Double Action, 5 Shot, Solid Frame, Modern	40	75
Model 6, .22 L.R.R.F., Double Action, 7 Shot, Solid Frame, Modern	40	75

Model 622, .22 L.R.R.F., Solid Frame, 6 Shot, Double Action, Modern	25	40
Model 632, .32 S & W Long, Solid Frame, 6 Shot, Double Action, Modern	25	40
Model 633, .32 S & W Long, Solid Frame, 6 Shot, Chrome, Double Action, Modern	30	45
Model 649, .22LR/.22 W.M.R. Combo, Western Style, 9 Shot, Double Action, Adjustable Sights, Modern	35	50
Model 650, .22LR/.22 W.M.R. Combo, Western Style, 9 Shot, Double Action, Adjustable Sights, Modern	40	55
Model 666, .22LR/.22 W.M.R. Combo, Solid Frame, 9 Shot, Double Action, Modern	25	45
Model 676, .22LR/.22 W.M.R. Combo, Western Style, 9 Shot, Double Action, Adjustable Sights, Modern	45	60
Model 676-12", .22LR/.22 W.M.R. Combo, Western Style, 9 Shot, Double Action, Adjustable Sights, Modern	50	65
Model 732, .32 S & W Long, Solid Frame, 6 Shot, Double Action, Swing-Out Cylinder, Modern	30	45
Model 733, .32 S & W Long, Solid Frame, 6 Shot, Double Action, Swing-Out Cylinder, Modern	35	50
Model 766, .22 L.R.R.F., Top Break, 7 Shot, Double Action, Wood Grips, Modern	65	110
Model 766, .22 W.R.F., Top Break, 7 Shot, Double Action, Wood Grips, Modern	75	125
Model 900, .22 L.R.R.F., Solid Frame, 9 Shot, Double Action, Modern	25	40
Model 901, .22 L.R.R.F., Solid Frame, 9 Shot, Double Action, Modern	25	40
Model 925, .22 L.R.R.F., 9 Shot, Solid Frame, Double Action, Swing-Out Cylinder, Modern	35	55
Model 925, .38 S & W, Solid Frame, 5 Shot, Adjustable Sights, Modern	40	55
Model 926, .22 L.R.R.F., 5 Shot, Solid Frame, Adjustable Sights, Modern	40	55
Model 926, .38 S & W, Solid Frame, 5 Shot, Adjustable Sights, Modern	40	55
Model 929, .22 L.R.R.F., 9 Shot, Solid Frame, Double Action, Swing-Out Cylinder, Modern	30	45
Model 930, .22 L.R.R.F., 9 Shot, Solid Frame, Double Action, Swing-Out Cylinder, Adjustable Sights, Modern	35	50
Model 939, .22 L.R.R.F., 9 Shot, Solid Frame, Double Action, Swing-Out Cylinder, Adjustable Sights, Modern	40	55
Model 940, .22 L.R.R.F., 9 Shot, Solid Frame, Double Action, Swing-Out Cylinder, Modern	35	55
Model 949, .22 L.R.R.F., 9 Shot, Western Style, Double Action, Adjustable Sights, Modern	30	45
Model 950, .22 L.R.R.F., 9 Shot, Western Style, Double Action, Adjustable Sights, Modern	35	45
Model 999 (Early), .22 L.R.R.F., 9 Shot, Top Break, Double Action, Adjustable Sights, Modern	40	70
Model 999 (Early), .22 W.R.F., Top Break, 9 Shot, Double Action, Adjustable Sights, Modern	70	120
Model 999 (Late), .22 L.R.R.F, Top Break, 9 Shot, Double Action, Adjustable Sights, Modern	40	60
New Defender, .22 L.R.R.F., Top Break, 9 Shot, Double Action, Wood Grips, Adjustable Sights, Modern	75	100
Premier, Various Calibers, Top Break, Hammer, Double Action, Modern	55	95
Special, .22 L.R.R.F., Top Break, 9 Shot, Double Action, Wood Grips, Modern	70	110
Special, .22 W.R.F., Top Break, 9 Shot, Double Action, Wood Grips, Modern	80	125
Target (Early), .22 L.R.R.F., Top Break, 9 Shot, Double Action, Wood Grips, Modern	70	100
Target (Early), .22 W.R.F., Top Break, 9 Shot, Double Action, Wood Grips, Modern	75	110
Target (Hi Speed), .22 W.R.F., Top Break, 9 Shot, Double Action, Wood Grips, Modern	80	120
Target (Hi Speed), .22 L.R.R.F., Top break, 9 Shot, Double Action, Wood Grips, Modern	75	110

Harrington & Richardson .32 Auto

Trapper, .22 L.R.R.F., 7 Shot, Solid Frame, Wood Grips, Double Action, Modern	55	80
Vest Pocket, Various Calibers, Double Action, Solid Frame, Spurless Hammer, Modern	40	75
Young America, Various Calibers, Double Action, Solid Frame, Modern	40	75

Handgun, Semi-Automatic

Self-Loading, .25 ACP, Clip Fed, Modern	125	200
Self-Loading, .32 ACP, Clip Fed, Modern	150	225

Handgun, Singleshot

U. S. R. A. Target, .22 L.R.R.F., Top Break, Adjustable Sights, Wood Grips, Modern	175	300

Rifle, Bolt Action

Model 250 Sportster, .22 L.R.R.F., 5 Shot Clip, Open Rear Sight, Modern	25	40
Model 251 Sportster, .22 L.R.R.F., 5 Shot Clip, Lyman Sights, Modern	35	50
Model 265 Reg'lar, .22 L.R.R.F., Clip Fed, Peep Sights, Modern	30	45
Model 300, Various Calibers, Cheekpiece, Monte Carlo Stock, Checkered Stock, Modern	180	250
Model 301, Various Calibers, Checkered Stock, Mannlicher, Modern	200	300
Model 317, Various Calibers, Checkered Stock, Monte Carlo Stock, Modern	180	260
Model 317P, .223 Rem., Fancy Checkering, Monte Carlo Stock, Fancy Wood, Modern	275	400
Model 330, Various Calibers, Checkered Stock, Monte Carlo Stock, Modern	145	200
Model 333, Various Calibers, Monte Carlo Stock, Modern	145	200
Model 365 ACE, .22 L.R.R.F., Singleshot, Peep Sights, Modern	20	35
Model 370, Various Calibers, Target Stock, Heavy Barrel, Modern	175	275
Model 450 Medalist, .22 L.R.R.F., 5 Shot Clip, No Sights, Target Stock, Modern	90	120
Model 451 Medalist, .22 L.R.R.F., 5 Shot Clip, Lyman Sights, Target Stock, Modern	100	140
Model 465 Targeteer, .22 L.R.R.F., Clip Fed, Peep Sights, Modern	50	70
Model 465 Targeteer Jr, .22 L.R.R.F., Clip Fed, Peep Sights, Modern	50	70
Model 750 Pioneer, .22 L.R.R.F., Singleshot, Open Rear Sight, Modern	20	35
Model 751 Pioneer, .22 L.R.R.F., Singleshot, Open Rear Sight, Mannlicher, Modern	30	45
Model 765 Pioneer, .22 L.R.R.F., Singleshot, Open Rear Sight, Modern	15	25
Model 852 Fieldsman, .22 L.R.R.F., Tube Feed, Open Rear Sight, Modern	35	50
Model 865 Plainsman, .22 L.R.R.F., 5 Shot Clip, Open Rear Sight, Modern	35	50
Model 866 Plainsman, .22 L.R.R.F., 5 Shot Clip, Open Rear Sight, Mannlicher, Modern	35	55

Rifle, Percussion

Huntsman .45, Top Break, Side Lever, Rifled, Reproduction, Antique	50	75
Huntsman .50, Top Break, Side Lever, Rifled, Reproduction, Antique	45	65
Model 175, .45 or .58 Caliber, Springfield Style, Open Sights, Reproduction, Antique	90	145
Model 175 Deluxe, .45 or .58 Caliber, Springfield Style, Open Sights, Checkered Stock, Reproduction, Antique	135	225

Rifle, Semi-Automatic

Model 150 Leatherneck, .22 L.R.R.F., 5 Shot Clip, Open Rear Sight, Modern	40	60
Model 151 Leatherneck, .22 L.R.R.F., 5 Shot Clip, Peep Sights, Modern	50	70
Model 165 Leatherneck, .22 L.R.R.F., Clip Fed, Heavy Barrel, Peep Sights, Modern 70	100	
Model 308, Various Calibers, Checkered Stock, Monte Carlo Stock, Modern	160	225
Model 360, Various Calibers, Checkered Stock, Monte Carlo Stock, Modern	160	225
Model 361, Various Calibers, Checkered Stock, Monte Carlo Stock, Modern	160	225
Model 60 Reising, .45 ACP, Clip Fed, Carbine, Open Rear Sight, Modern	225	300
Model 65 General, .22 L.R.R.F., Clip Fed, Heavy Barrel, Peep Sights, Modern	125	200
Model 700, .22 W.M.R., Monte Carlo Stock, 5 Shot Clip, Modern	75	110
Model 700 Deluxe, .22 W.M.R., Monte Carlo Stock, 5 Shot Clip, Modern	120	180
Model 755 Sahara, .22 L.R.R.F., Singleshot, Open Rear Sight, Mannlicher, Modern	25	40
Model 760 Sahara, .22 L.R.R.F., Singleshot, Open Rear Sight, Modern	20	35
Model 800 Lynx, .22 L.R.R.F., Clip Fed, Open Rear Sight, Modern	35	55

Rifle, Singleshot

1871 Springfield Deluxe, .45-70 Government, Trap Door Action, Carbine, Light Engraving, Modern	160	190
1871 Springfield Officers', .45-70 Government, Commemorative, Trap Door Action, Curio	175	300
1871 Springfield Standard, .45-70 Government, Trap Door Action, Carbine, Modern	100	160
1873 Springfield Officers', .45-70 Government, Trap Door Action, Light Engraving, Peep Sights, Modern	175	250
1873 Springfield Standard, .45-70 Government, Trap Door Action, Commemorative, Modern	175	215
Custer Memorial Enlisted Model, .45-70 Government, Commemorative, Trap Door Action, Carbine, Fancy Engraving, Fancy Wood, Curio	1,400	2,000
Custer Memorial Officers' Model, .45-70 Government, Commemorative, Trap Door Action, Carbine, Fancy Engraving, Fancy Wood, Curio	2,200	3,000
Little Big Horn Springfield Officers', .45-70 Government, Commemorative, Trap Door Action, Carbine, Curio	175	250
Little Big Horn Springfield Standard, .45-70 Government, Commemorative, Trap Door Action, Carbine, Curio	150	200
Model 172 Springfield .45-70 Government, Trap Door Action, Carbine, Engraved, Silver Plated, Tang Sights, Checkered Stock, Modern	600	800
Model 157, Various Calibers, Top Break, Side Lever, Automatic Ejector, Open Rear Sight, Mannlicher, Modern	45	60
Model 158 Topper, Various Calibers, Top Break, Side Lever, Automatic Ejector, Open Rear Sight, Modern	30	50
Model 158 Topper, Various Calibers, Top Break, Side Lever, Automatic Ejector, Open Rear Sight, Extra Set of Rifle Barrels, Modern	50	70
Model 158 Topper, Various Calibers, Top Break, Side Lever, Automatic Ejector, Open Rear Sight, Extra Shotgun Barrel, Modern	45	65
Model 163, Various Calibers, Top Break, Side Lever, Automatic Ejector, Open Rear Sight, Modern	35	50
Shikari, .44 Magnum, Top Break, Side Lever, Automatic Ejector, Modern	40	60
Shikari, .45-70 Government, Top Break, Side Lever, Automatic Ejector, Modern	45	65

Rifle, Slide Action

Model 422, .22 L.R.R.F., Tube Feed, Open Rear Sight, Modern	45	70

Shotgun, Bolt Action

Model 348 Gamemaster, 12 and 16 Gauges, Tube Feed, Takedown, Modern	25	40

Model 349 Deluxe, 12 and 16 Gauges, Tube Feed, Takedown, Adjustable Choke, Modern	35	50
Model 351 Huntsman, 12 and 16 Gauges, Tube Feed, Takedown, Monte Carlo Stock, Adjustable Choke, Modern	35	50

Shotgun, Double Barrel, Over-Under

Model 1212, 12 Ga., Field Grade, Vent Rib, Single Selective Trigger, Modern	200	300
Model 1212 Waterfowl, 12 Ga. Mag. 3″, Field Grade, Vent Rib, Single Selective Trigger, Modern	225	325

Shotgun, Double Barrel, Side by Side

Model 404, Various Gauges, Hammerless, Modern	115	150
Model 404C, Various Gauges, Hammerless, Checkered Stock, Modern	115	150

Shotgun, Percussion

Huntsman 12 Ga., Top Break, Side Lever, Reproduction, Antique	50	75

Shotgun, Semi-Automatic

Model 403, .410 Ga., Takedown, Modern	95	145

Shotgun, Singleshot

Folding Gun, Various Gauges, Top Break, Hammer, Automatic Ejector, Modern	35	55
Model #1 Harrich, 12 Ga., Vent Rib, Engraved, Fancy Checkering, Modern	1,000	1,400
Model 148, Various Gauges, Top Break, Side Lever, Automatic Ejector, Modern	25	45
Model 158, Various Gauges, Top Break, Side Lever, Automatic Ejector, Modern	25	45
Model 159, Various Gauges, Top Break, Side Lever, Automatic Ejector, Modern	30	55
Model 162 Buck, 12 Ga., Top Break, Side Lever, Automatic Ejector, Peep Sights, Modern	30	55
Model 176, 10 Ga. 3½″, Top Break, Side Lever, Automatic Ejector, Modern	30	55
Model 188 Deluxe, Various Gauges, Top Break, Side Lever, Automatic Ejector, Modern	20	40
Model 198 Deluxe, Various Gauges, Top Break, Side Lever, Automatic Ejector, Modern	20	40
Model 3, Various Gauges, Top Break, Hammerless, Automatic Ejector, Modern	30	55
Model 459 Youth, Various Gauges, Top Break, Side Lever, Automatic Ejector, Modern	25	45
Model 48, Various Gauges, Top Break, Hammer, Automatic Ejector, Modern	25	40
Model 480 Youth, Various Gauges, Top Break, Side Lever, Automatic Ejector, Modern	20	35
Model 488 Deluxe, Various Gauges, Top Break, Hammer, Automatic Ejector, Modern	30	45
Model 490 Youth, Various Gauges, Top Break, Side Lever, Automatic Ejector, Modern	25	40
Model 5, Various Gauges, Top Break, Lightweight, Automatic Ejector, Modern	40	65
Model 6, Various Gauges, Top Break, Heavyweight, Automatic Ejector, Modern	40	65
Model 7, Various Gauges, Top Break, Automatic Ejector, Modern	30	50
Model 8 Standard, Various Gauges, Top Break, Automatic Ejector, Modern	30	50
Model 9, Various Gauges, Top Break, Automatic Ejector, Modern	30	50
Model 98, Various Gauges, Top Break, Side Lever, Automatic Ejector, Modern	30	45

Shotgun, Slide Action

Model 400, Various Gauges, Solid Frame, Modern	70	120
Model 401, Various Gauges, Solid Frame, Adjustable Choke, Modern	75	125
Model 402, .410 Ga., Solid Frame, Modern	70	125
Model 440, Various Gauges, Solid Frame, Modern	75	130
Model 400, Various Gauges, Solid Frame, Vent Rib, Modern	85	145

Harris, Henry
Payton, Pa. 1779-83 See Kentucky Rifles

Harrison Arms Co.
Made in Belgium for Sickles & Davenport, Iowa

Shotgun, Double Barrel, Side by Side
Various Gauges, Outside Hammers, Damascus Barrel, Modern	80	150
Various Gauges, Hammerless, Steel Barrel, Modern	95	175
Various Gauges, Hammerless, Damascus Barrel, Modern	75	150
Various Gauges, Outside Hammers, Steel Barrel, Modern	90	175

Shotgun, Singleshot
Various Gauges, Hammer, Steel Barrel, Modern	45	75

Hartford Arms & Equipment Co.
Hartford, Conn. 1929-30

Handgun, Manual Repeater
.22 L.R.R.F., Clip Fed, Target Pistol, Curio	225	350

Handgun, Semi-Automatic
Model 1928, .22 L.R.R.F., Clip Fed, Target Pistol, Curio	200	300

Handgun, Singleshot
.22 L.R.R.F., Target Pistol, Curio	250	325

Hartford Arms Co.
Made by Norwich Falls Pistol Co. C.1880

Handgun, Revolver
.32 Short R.F., 5 Shot, Spur Trigger, Solid Frame, Single Action, Antique	90	160

Hartford Arms Co.
Made by Crescent for Simmons Hardware Co., St. Louis, Mo.

Shotgun, Double Barrel, Side by Side
Various Gauges, Outside Hammers, Damascus Barrel, Modern	80	150
Various Gauges, Hammerless, Steel Barrel, Modern	95	175
Various Gauges, Hammerless, Damascus Barrel, Modern	75	150
Various Gauges, Outside Hammers, Steel Barrel, Modern	90	175

Shotgun, Singleshot
Various Gauges, Hammer, Steel Barrel, Modern	45	75

Harvard
Made by Crescent C.1900

Shotgun, Double Barrel, Side by Side
Various Gauges, Outside Hammers, Damascus Barrel, Modern	80	150
Various Gauges, Hammerless, Steel Barrel, Modern	95	175
Various Gauges, Hammerless, Damascus Barrel, Modern	75	150
Various Gauges, Outside Hammers, Steel Barrel, Modern	90	175

Shotgun, Singleshot
Various Gauges, Hammer, Steel Barrel, Modern	45	75

Hawes Firearms
Van Nuys, Calif.

Handgun, Revolver
Montana Marshall, .22 L.R.R.F./.22 W.M.R. Combo, Western Style, Single Action, Brass Grip Frame, Modern	50	70
Montana Marshall, .22 L.R.R.F., Western Style, Single Action, Brass Grip Frame, Modern	40	60

Montana Marshall, .357 Magnum/9mm Combo, Western Style, Single Action, Brass Grip Frame, Modern	120	160
Montana Marshall, .44 Magnum, Western Style, Single Action, Brass Grip Frame, Modern	100	135
Montana Marshall, .44 Magnum/.44-40 Combo, Western Style, Single Action, Brass Grip Frame, Modern	125	170
Montana Marshall, .45 Colt, Western Style, Single Action, Brass Grip Frame, Modern	100	140
Montana Marshall, .45 Colt/.45 ACP Combo, Western Style, Single Action, Brass Grip Frame, Modern	140	185
Silver City Marshall, .22 L.R.R.F./.22 W.M.R. Combo, Western Style, Single Action, Brass Grip Frame, Modern	50	70
Silver City Marshall, .22 L.R.R.F., Western Style, Single Action, Brass Grip Frame, Modern	40	60
Silver City Marshall, .357 Magnum/9mm Combo, Western Style, Single Action, Brass Grip Frame, Modern	120	160
Silver City Marshall, .44 Magnum, Western Style, Single Action, Brass Grip Frame, Modern	100	145
Silver City Marshall, .44 Magnum/.44-40 Combo, Western Style, Single Action, Brass Grip Frame, Modern	125	170
Silver City Marshall, .45 Colt, Western Style, Single Action, Brass Grip Frame, Modern	100	145
Silver City Marshall, .45 Colt/.45 ACP Combo, Western Style, Single Action, Brass Grip Frame, Modern	140	185
Texas Marshall, .22 L.R.R.F./.22 W.M.R. Combo, Western Style, Single Action, Nickel Plated, Modern	50	70
Texas Marshall, .22 L.R.R.F., Western Style, Single Action, Nickel Plated, Modern	40	60
Texas Marshall, .357 Magnum, Western Style, Single Action, Nickel Plated, Modern	100	140
Texas Marshall, .357 Magnum/9mm Combo, Western Style, Single Action, Nickel Plated, Modern	120	170
Texas Marshall, .44 Magnum, Western Style, Single Action, Nickel Plated, Modern	115	155
Texas Marshall, .44 Magnum/.44-40 Combo, Western Style, Single Action, Nickel Plated, Modern	130	180
Texas Marshall, .45 Colt, Western Style, Single Action, Nickel Plated, Modern	100	140
Texas Marshall, .45 Colt/.45 ACP Combo, Western Style, Single Action, Nickel Plated, Modern	140	185
Denver Marshall, .22 L.R.R.F./.22 W.M.R. Combo, Western Style, Single Action, Adjustable Sights, Modern	50	70
Denver Marshall, .22 L.R.R.F., Western Style, Single Action, Brass Grip Frame, Adjustable Sights, Modern	40	60
Chief Marshall, .357 Magnum, Western Style, Single Action, Brass Grip Frame, Adjustable Sights, Modern	100	135
Chief Marshall, .44 Magnum, Western Style, Single Action, Brass Grip Frame, Adjustable Sights, Modern	100	145
Chief City Marshall, .45 Colt, Western Style, Single Action, Brass Grip Frame, Adjustable Sights, Modern	100	145

Handgun, Singleshot

Stevens Favorite Copy, .22 L.R.R.F., Tip-Up, Rosewood Grips, Modern	40	60
Stevens Favorite Copy, .22 L.R.R.F., Tip-Up, Plastic Grips, Modern	35	55
Stevens Favorite Copy, .22 L.R.R.F., Tip-Up, Plastic Grips, Target Sights, Modern	35	60

Hawkins, Henry
Schenectady, N.Y. 1769-75 See Kentucky Rifles

Heckert, Philip
York, Pa. 1769-79 See Kentucky Rifles and Pistols

Heckler & Koch
Oberndorf/Neckar, Germany

Automatic Weapon, Assault Rifle

Model G3, .308 Win., Clip Fed, Class 3	400	600
Model G3A3, .308 Win., Clip Fed, Class 3	500	700
Model G3A4, .308 Win., Clip Fed, Class 3	600	800
Model G3A4, .308 Win., Clip Fed, with Conversion Kit, Class 3	650	900
Model HK33, .223 Rem., Clip Fed, Class 3	300	400

Automatic Weapon, Submachine Gun

Model MP5A2, 9mm Luger, Clip Fed, Class 3	400	600
Model MP5A3, 9mm Luger, Clip Fed, Folding Stock, Class 3	550	750

Handgun, Semi-Automatic

HK-4, .22 L.R.R.F., Clip Fed, Double Action, Modern	125	170
HK-4, .25 ACP, Clip Fed, Double Action, Modern	110	160
HK-4, .32 ACP, Clip Fed, Double Action, Modern	125	170
HK-4, .380 ACP, Clip Fed, Double Action, Modern	130	175
HK-4, Various Calibers, Clip Fed, Conversion Kit Only, Each	30	40
HK-4, Various Calibers, Clip Fed, Double Action, with Conversion Kits All 4 Calibers, Modern	170	235
HK P-9S, .45 ACP, Clip Fed, Double Action, Modern	220	300
HK P-9S, .45 ACP, Target Model, Clip Fed, Double Action, Modern	250	335
HK P-9S, .45 ACP, with Extra 8" Barrel, Clip Fed, Double Action, Modern	260	340
P-9S Competition Kit, 9mm Luger, Clip Fed, Double Action, Extra Barrel, Target Sights, Target Grips, Modern	275	400
P-9S Target, 9mm Luger, Clip Fed, Double Action, 5 1/2" Barrel, Target Sights, Modern	190	275
P-9S Combat, 9mm Luger, Clip Fed, Double Action, 4" Barrel, Modern	220	300
P-9S Combat, 9mm Luger, Clip Fed, Double Action, 4" Barrel, with .30 Luger Conversion Kit, Modern	270	350
VP-70Z, 9mm Luger, Clip Fed, Double Action, 18 Shot Clip, Modern	135	170

Rifle, Semi-Automatic

HK 91, .22 L.R.R.F., Clip Fed, Conversion Unit Only	165	225
HK 91 A-2, .308 Win., Clip Fed, Sporting Version of Military Rifle, with Compensator, Modern	250	325

Heckler & Koch HK P9S

Heckler & Koch HK 91

Heckler & Koch HK 93 A-2

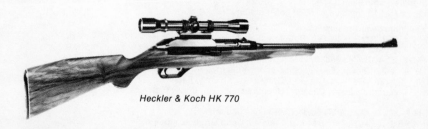

Heckler & Koch HK 770

HK 91 A-3, .308 Win., Clip Fed, Sporting Version of Military Rifle, Folding Stock with Compensator, Modern	275	375
HK 91 A-4, .308 Win., Clip Fed, Sporting Version of Military Rifle, with Compensator, Polygonal Rifling, Modern	250	350
HK 91 A-5, .308 Win., Clip Fed, Sporting Version of Military Rifle, Folding Stock with Compensator, Polygonal Rifling, Modern	300	400
HK 91/93, Light Bipod, Add $40-$55		
HK 91/93, For Scope Mount Add $55-$90		
HK 93 A-2, .223 Rem., Clip Fed, Sporting Version of Military Rifle, with Compensator, Modern	250	320
HK 93 A-3, .223 Rem., Clip Fed, Sporting Version of Military Rifle, Folding Stock, with Compensator, Modern	260	360
Model 300, .22 WMR, Clip Fed, Checkered Stock, Open Rear Sight, Modern	135	180
HK 770, Various Calibers, Sporting Rifle, Checkered Stock, Monte Carlo Stock, Modern	220	300

Hege
Germany

Combination Weapon, Double Barrel, Over-Under

President, Various Calibers, Box Lock, Solid Rib, Double Trigger, Checkered Stock, Modern	400	600

Handgun, Semi-Automatic

AP-66, .32 ACP, Clip Fed, Double Action, Modern	125	175
AP-66, .380 ACP, Clip Fed, Double Action, Modern	140	200

Hennch, Peter
Lancaster, Pa. 1770-74 See Kentucky Rifles

Henry, Alexander
Edinburgh, Scotland 1869-95

Rifle, Double Barrel, Side by Side

.500/450 Mag. BPE, Damascus Barrel, Engraved, Fancy Checkering, Ornate, Cased with Accessories, Hammerless, Antique	2,750	3,500

Henry Gun Co.
Belgium C.1900

Shotgun, Double Barrel, Side by Side

Various Gauges, Outside Hammers, Damascus Barrel, Modern	80	150
Various Gauges, Hammerless, Steel Barrel, Modern	95	175
Various Gauges, Hammerless, Damascus Barrel, Modern	75	150
Various Gauges, Outside Hammers, Steel Barrel, Modern	90	175

Shotgun, Singleshot

Various Gauges, Hammer, Steel Barrel, Modern	45	75

Hercules
Made by Stevens Arms

Shotgun, Double Barrel, Side by Side

M 315, Various Gauges, Hammerless, Steel Barrel, Modern	90	140
Model 215, 12 and 16 Gauges, Outside Hammers, Steel Barrel, Modern	85	145
Model 311, Various Gauges, Hammerless, Steel Barrel, Modern	90	145
Model 3151, Various Gauges, Hammerless, Recoil Pad, Front & Rear Bead Sights, Modern	95	165
Model 5151, Various Gauges, Hammerless, Steel Barrel, Modern	95	160

Shotgun, Singleshot

Model 94, Various Gauges, Takedown, Automatic Ejector, Plain Hammer, Modern	35	55

Hermitage
Made by Stevens Arms

Shotgun, Singleshot

Model 90, Various Gauges, Takedown, Automatic Ejector, Plain Hammer, Modern	35	55

Hermitage Arms Co.
Made by Crescent for Grey & Dudley Hdw. Co. Nashville, Tenn.

Shotgun, Double Barrel, Side by Side

Various Gauges, Outside Hammers, Damascus Barrel, Modern	80	150
Various Gauges, Hammerless, Steel Barrel, Modern	95	175
Various Gauges, Hammerless, Damascus Barrel, Modern	75	150
Various Gauges, Outside Hammers, Steel Barrel, Modern	90	175

Shotgun, Singleshot

Various Gauges, Hammer, Steel Barrel, Modern	45	75

Hermitage Gun Co.
Made by Crescent for Grey & Dudley Hdw. Co. Nashville, Tenn.

Shotgun, Double Barrel, Side by Side

Various Gauges, Outside Hammers, Damascus Barrel, Modern	80	150
Various Gauges, Hammerless, Steel Barrel, Modern	95	175
Various Gauges, Hammerless, Damascus Barrel, Modern	75	150
Various Gauges, Outside Hammers, Steel Barrel, Modern	90	175

Shotgun, Singleshot

Various Gauges, Hammer, Steel Barrel, Modern	45	75

Hero
C.1880 Made by Rupertus Arms for Tryon Bros. Co.

Handgun, Revolver

.22 Short R.F., 7 Shot, Spur Trigger, Solid Frame, Single Action, Antique	90	160
.32 Short R.F., 5 Shot, Spur Trigger, Solid Frame, Single Action, Antique	95	170

.38 Short R.F., 5 Shot, Spur Trigger, Solid Frame, Single Action, Antique	95	180
.41 Short R.F., 5 Shot, Spur Trigger, Solid Frame, Single Action, Antique	120	200

Herters
Waseca, Minn. Distributer & Importer

Handgun, Revolver

Guide, .22 L.R.R.F., Swing-Out Cylinder, Double Action, Modern	20	35
Power-Mag, .357 Magnum, Western Style, Single Action, Modern	45	70
Power-Mag, .401 Herter Mag., Western Style, Single Action,	45	70
Power-Mag, .44 Magnum, Western Style, Single Action, Modern	50	85
Western, .22 L.R.R.F., Single Action, Western Style, Modern	20	35

Rifle, Bolt Action

Model J-9 Hunter, Various Calibers, Plain, Monte Carlo Stock, Modern	120	170
Model J-9 Presentation, Various Calibers, Checkered Stock, Monte Carlo Stock, Sling Swivels, Modern	135	190
Model J-9 Supreme, Various Calibers, Checkered Stock, Monte Carlo Stock, Sling Swivels, Modern	125	180
Model U-9 Hunter, Various Calibers, Plain, Monte Carlo Stock, Modern	110	160
Model U-9 Presentation, Various Calibers, Checkered Stock, Sling Swivels, Monte Carlo Stock, Modern	125	180
Model U-9 Supreme, Various Calibers, Checkered Stock, Sling Swivels, Monte Carlo Stock, Modern	120	170

Shotgun, Singleshot

Model 151, Various Gauges, Hammer, Modern	20	35

Hess, Jacob
Stark Co., Ohio 1842-60 See Kentucky Rifles

Hess, Samuel
Lancaster, Pa. C.1771 See Kentucky Rifles

Heym
Munnerstadt, West Germany

Combination Weapon, Drilling

Model 33, Various Calibers, Hammerless, Double Triggers, Engraved, Checkered Stock, Express Sights, Modern		
Model 37, Various Calibers, Hammerless, Sidelock, Engraved, Checkered Stock, Modern	2,400	3,200
Model 37, Various Calibers, Hammerless, Sidelock, Double Rifle Barrels, Engraved, Checkered Stock, Modern	3,500	4,500

Combination Weapon, Double Barrel, Over-Under

Model 22S, Various Calibers, Single Set Trigger, Checkered Stock, Light Engraving, Modern	600	800
Model 55BF (77BF), Various Calibers, Boxlock, Double Triggers, Checkered Stock, Engraved, Modern	1,200	1,800
Model 55BFSS (77BFSS), Various Calibers, Sidelock, Double Triggers, Checkered Stock, Modern	2,500	3,400

Rifle, Double Barrel, Over-Under

Model 55B (77B), Various Calibers, Boxlock, Engraved, Checkered Stock, Modern	1,500	2,200
Model 55BSS (77BSS), Various Calibers, Sidelock, Engraved, Checkered Stock, Modern	2,900	3,750
Model 77 is 12 Ga., Model 55 is 16 or 20 Gauges		

Shotgun, Double Barrel, Over-Under

Model 55F (77F), Various Gauges, Boxlock, Engraved, Checkered Stock, Double Triggers, Modern	1,200	1,700

Model 55FSS (77FSS), Various Gauges, Sidelock, Engraved, Checkered Stock, Double Triggers, Modern	2,200	3,000
Model 77 is 12 Ga., Model 55 is 16 or 20 Gauges		

Rifle, Bolt Action
Model SR-20, Various Calibers, Fancy Wood, Double Set Triggers, Modern	250	400
Model SR-20, Various Calibers, Fancy Wood, Double Set Triggers, Left Hand, Modern	325	475

Rifle, Singleshot
Model HR-30, Various Calibers, Fancy Wood, Engraved, Single Set Trigger, Ruger Action, Round Barrel, Modern	750	1,000
Model HR-38, Various Calibers, Fancy Wood, Engraved, Single Set Trigger, Ruger Action, Octagon Barrel, Modern	900	1,200

Higgins, J. C.
Trade Name for Sears-Roebuck

Handgun, Revolver
Model 88, .22 L.R.R.F., Modern	35	50
Model 88 Fisherman, .22 L.R.R.F., Modern	35	50
Ranger, .22 L.R.R.F., Modern	35	50

Handgun, Semi-Automatic
Model 80, .22 L.R.R.F., Clip Fed, Hammerless, Modern	45	65
Model 85, .22 L.R.R.F., Clip Fed, Hammer, Modern	55	90

Rifle, Bolt Action
Model 228, .22 L.R.R.F., Clip Fed, Modern	25	40
Model 229, .22 L.R.R.F., Tube Feed, Modern	30	45
Model 245, .22 L.R.R.F., Singleshot, Modern	15	30
Model 51, Various Calibers, Checkered Stock, Modern	140	190
Model 51 Special, Various Calibers, Checkered Stock, Light Engraving, Modern	200	275

Rifle, Lever Action
.22 WMR, Modern	40	60
Model 45, Various Calibers, Tube Feed, Carbine, Modern	45	65

Rifle, Semi-Automatic
Model 25, .22 L.R.R.F., Clip Fed, Modern	25	40
Model 31, .22 L.R.R.F., Tube Feed, Modern	35	55

Rifle, Slide Action
Model 33, .22 L.R.R.F., Tube Feed, Modern	30	45

Shotgun, Bolt Action
Model 10, Various Gauges, Tube Feed, 5 Shot, Modern	30	50
Model 11, Various Gauges, Tube Feed, 3 Shot, Modern	25	45

Shotgun, Double Barrel, Side by Side
Various Calibers, Plain, Takedown, Hammerless, Modern	90	135

Shotgun, Semi-Automatic
Model 66, 12 Ga., Plain Barrel, Modern	70	125
Model 66, 12 Ga., Plain Barrel, Adjustable Choke, Modern	80	135
Model 66, 12 Ga., Vent Rib, Adjustable Choke, Modern	90	145
Model 66 Deluxe, 12 Ga., Modern	85	140

Shotgun, Singleshot
Various Calibers, Takedown, Adjustable Choke, Plain, Hammer, Modern	25	40

Shotgun, Slide Action
Model 20 Deluxe, 12 Ga., Modern	70	110
Model 20 Deluxe, 12 Ga., Vent Rib, Adjustable Choke, Modern	85	125
Model 20 Special, 12 Ga., Vent Rib, Adjustable Choke, Modern	125	175
Model 20 Standard, 12 Ga., Modern	65	100

High Standard Derringer

High Standard
New Haven, Conn.

Handgun, Double Barrel, Over-Under

Derringer, .22 L.R.R.F., Double Action, 2 Shot, Modern	40	60
Derringer, .22 WMR, Double Action, 2 Shot, Modern	40	65
Derringer, .22 L.R.R.F., Double Action, Top Break, Nickel Plated, Hammerless, Cased, Modern	45	65
Derringer, .22 WMR, Double Action, Top Break, Nickel Plated, Hammerless, Cased, Modern	50	70
Gold Derringer, .22 WMR, Double Action, 2 Shot, Modern	100	135
Presidential Derringer, .22 WMR, Double Action, Top Break, Gold Plated, Hammerless, Cased, Modern	100	150

Handgun, Percussion

.36, Griswald & Gunnison, Revolver, Commemorative, Cased, Reproduction, Antique	150	225
.36 Leech & Rigdon, Revolver, Commemorative, Cased, Reproduction, Antique	150	225
.36 Schneider & Glassick, Revolver, Commemorative, Cased, Reproduction, Antique	225	325

Handgun, Revolver

For Nickel Plating Add $5-$10

Camp Gun, .22 L.R.R.F., Double Action, Swing-Out Cylinder, Adjustable Sights, Modern	75	90
Camp Gun, .22 WMR, Double Action, Swing-Out Cylinder, Adjustable Sights, Modern	80	100
Crusader, Deluxe Pair, .44 Mag. & .45 Colt, Commemorative, Double Action, Swing-Out Cylinder, Gold Inlays, Engraved, Modern	1,400	2,950
Crusader, Standard Pair, .44 Mag. or .45 Colt, Commemorative, Double Action, Swing-Out Cylinder, Gold Inlays, Modern	650	975

High Standard Leech & Rigdon

High Standard High Sierra

Crusader, Standard Pair, .44 Mag. & .45 Colt, Commemorative, Double Action, Swing-Out Cylinder, Gold Inlays, Modern	1,300	1,900
Crusader, .44 Mag., Double Action, Swingout Cylinder, Blue, Adjustable Sights, Modern	165	230
Crusader, .45 Colt, Double Action, Swingout Cylinder, Blue, Adjustable Sights, Modern	160	220
Crusader, .357 Mag., Double Action, Swingout Cylinder, Blue, Adjustable Sights, Modern	145	200
Double-Nine, .22LR/.22 WMR Combo, Double Action, Western Style, Alloy Frame, Modern	45	70
Double-Nine, .22LR/.22 WMR Combo, Double Action, Western Style, Modern	75	100
Double-Nine, .22 L.R.R.F., Double Action, Western Style, Modern	50	80
Double-Nine Deluxe, .22LR/.22 WMR Combo, Double Action, Western Style, Adjustable Sights, Modern	80	115
Durango, .22 L.R.R.F., Double Action, Western Style, Modern	50	75
High Sierra, .22LR/.22 WMR Combo, Double Action, Western Style, Octagon Barrel, Modern	75	110
High Sierra Deluxe, .22LR/.22 WMR Combo, Double Action, Western Style, Octagon Barrel, Adjustable Sights, Modern	80	120
Longhorn, .22LR/.22 WMR Combo, Double Action, Western Style, Alloy Frame, Modern	50	75
Longhorn, .22LR/.22 WMR Combo, Double Action, Western Style, Modern	75	115
Longhorn, .22LR/.22 WMR Combo, Double Action, Adjustable Sights, Western Style, Modern	80	115
Natchez, .22LR/.22 WMR Combo, Double Action, Western Style, Birdshead Grip, Alloy Frame, Modern	45	70
Posse, .22LR/.22 WMR Combo, Double Action, Western Style, Brass Gripframe, Modern	50	70
Sentinel, .22 L.R.R.F., Double Action, Swing-Out Cylinder, Modern	35	60
Sentinel Deluxe, .22 L.R.R.F., Double Action, Swing-Out Cylinder, Modern	40	65
Sentinel Imperial, .22 L.R.R.F., Double Action, Swing-Out Cylinder, Modern	40	65
Sentinel Mk III, .357 Magnum, Double Action, Swing-Out Cylinder, Adjustable Sights, Modern	85	130
Sentinel Mk II, .357 Magnum, Double Action, Swing-Out Cylinder, Modern	75	110
Sentinel Mk. I, .22 L.R.R.F., Double Action, Swing-Out Cylinder, Modern	60	85

High Standard Sentinel Mk II

Sentinel Mk. I, .22 L.R.R.F., Double Action, Swing-Out Cylinder, Adjustable Sights, Modern	70	95
Sentinel Mk. IV, .22 WMR, Double Action, Swing-Out Cylinder, Adjustable Sights, Modern	80	110
Sentinel Mk. IV, .22 WMR, Double Action, Swing-Out Cylinder, Modern	75	100
Sentinel Snub, .22 L.R.R.F., Double Action, Swing-Out Cylinder, Modern	40	65

Handgun, Semi-Automatic
For Nickel Plating Add $10-$20

.22 L.R.R.F., Supermatic, Clip Fed, Hammerless, Modern	95	140
.22 L.R.R.F., Supermatic, Clip Fed, Hammerless, Extra Barrel, Modern	120	160
"Benner Olympic" .22 L.R.R.F., Supermatic, Military, Engraved, Curio	550	900
Citation (Early), .22 L.R.R.F., Supermatic, Clip Fed, Hammerless, Tapered Barrel, Modern	110	145
Citation (Early), .22 L.R.R.F., Supermatic, Clip Fed, Hammerless, Heavy Barrel, Modern	100	135
Citation (Late), .22 L.R.R.F., Supermatic, Military, Hammerless, Frame-Mounted Rear Sight, Fluted Barrel, Modern	125	160
Citation (Late), .22 L.R.R.F., Supermatic, Military, Hammerless, Frame-Mounted Rear Sight, Heavy Barrel, Modern	115	145
Citation (Late), .22 L.R.R.F., Supermatic, Clip Fed, Hammerless, Frame-Mounted Rear Sight, Heavy Barrel, Modern	115	150
Dura-Matic, .22 L.R.R.F., Clip Fed, Hammerless, Modern	55	85
Field King, .22 L.R.R.F., Clip Fed, Hammerless, Heavy Barrel, Modern	75	100
Flight King, .22 Short R.F., Clip Fed, Hammerless, Lightweight, Modern	65	95
Flight King, .22 Short R.F., Clip Fed, Hammerless, Lightweight, Extra Barrel, Modern	90	115
Flight King, .22 Short R.F., Clip Fed, Hammerless, Modern	65	95
Flight King, .22 Short R.F., Clip Fed, Hammerless, Extra Barrel, Modern	90	125
H-DM (O.S.S.), .22 Short R.F., Clip Fed, Silencer, Hammer, Class 3	425	600
Model A, .22 L.R.R.F., Clip Fed, Hammerless, Curio	110	155
Model B, .22 L.R.R.F., Clip Fed, Hammerless, Curio	110	175
Model C, .22 Short R.F., Clip Fed, Hammerless, Curio	115	160
Model D, .22 L.R.R.F., Clip Fed, Hammerless, Heavy Barrel, Curio	135	175
Model E, .22 L.R.R.F., Clip Fed, Hammerless, Heavy Barrel, Target Grips, Curio	150	220
Model G-380, .380 ACP, Clip Fed, Hammer, Takedown, Curio	200	275
Model G-B, .22 L.R.R.F., Clip Fed, Hammerless, Takedown, Curio	95	130
Model G-B, .22 L.R.R.F., Clip Fed, Hammerless, Takedown, Extra Barrel, Curio	120	155
Model G-D, .22 L.R.R.F., Clip Fed, Hammerless, Takedown, Curio	125	180
Model G-D, .22 L.R.R.F., Clip Fed, Hammerless, Takedown, Extra Barrel, Curio	145	215
Model G-E, .22 L.R.R.F., Clip Fed, Hammerless, Takedown, Extra Barrel, Curio	175	250
Model G-E, .22 L.R.R.F., Clip Fed, Hammerless, Takedown, Curio	150	200
Model G-O, .22 Short R.F., Clip Fed, Hammerless, Takedown, Extra Barrel, Curio	230	300
Model G-O, .22 Short R.F., Clip Fed, Hammerless, Takedown, Curio	210	265
Model H-A, .22 L.R.R.F., Clip Fed, Hammer, Curio	100	145
Model H-B, .22 L.R.R.F., Clip Fed, Hammer, Curio	95	140
Model H-D, .22 L.R.R.F., Clip Fed, Hammer, Heavy Barrel, Curio	95	175
Model H-D Military, .22 L.R.R.F., Clip Fed, Hammer, Heavy Barrel, Thumb Safety, Curio	130	200
Model H-E, .22 L.R.R.F., Clip Fed, Hammer, Heavy Barrel, Target Grips, Curio	160	225
Model SB, .22 L.R.R.F., Clip Fed, Hammerless, Smoothbore, Class 3	95	140
Olympic, .22 Short R.F., Clip Fed, Hammerless, Modern	135	170
Olympic, .22 Short R.F., Clip fed, Hammerless, Extra Barrel, Modern	155	200
Olympic I.S.U., .22 Short R.F., Supermatic, Clip Fed, Hammerless, Military, Modern	145	190
Olympic I.S.U., .22 Short R.F., Supermatic, Clip Fed, Hammerless, Modern	135	175

High Standard H-D Military .22

Olympic I.S.U., .22 Short R.F., Clip Fed, Hammerless, Military, Frame-Mounted Rear Sight, Modern	145	190
Olympic I.S.U., .22 Short R.F., Clip Fed, Hammerless, Frame-Mounted Rear Sight, Modern	145	185
Plinker, .22 L.R.R.F., Clip Fed, Hammer, Modern	40	70
Sharpshooter, .22 L.R.R.F., Clip Fed, Hammerless, Modern	80	120
Sport King, .22 L.R.R.F., Clip Fed, Hammerless, Lightweight, Modern	65	95
Sport King, .22 L.R.R.F., Clip Fed, Hammerless, Lightweight, Extra Barrel, Modern	85	125
Sport King, .22 L.R.R.F., Clip Fed, Hammerless, Modern	65	95
Sport King, .22 L.R.R.F., Clip Fed, Hammerless, Extra Barrel, Modern	85	125
Tournament, .22 L.R.R.F., Supermatic, Clip Fed, Hammerless, Modern	95	135
Tournament, .22 L.R.R.F., Supermatic, Clip Fed, Hammerless, Military, Modern	110	145
Trophy (Early), .22 L.R.R.F., Supermatic, Clip Fed, Hammerless, Modern	120	155
Trophy (Late), .22 L.R.R.F., Supermatic, Military, Hammerless, Frame-Mounted Rear Sight, Fluted Barrel, Modern	140	185
Trophy (Late), .22 L.R.R.F., Supermatic, Military, Hammerless, Frame-Mounted Rear Sight, Heavy Barrel, Modern	130	175
Victor, .22 L.R.R.F., Heavy Barrel, Military Grip, Solid Rib, Target Sights, Modern	145	200
Victor, .22 L.R.R.F., Heavy Barrel, Military Grip, Vent Rib, Target Sights, Modern	150	210

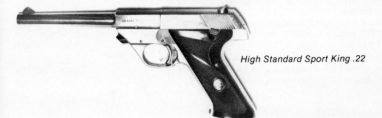

High Standard Sport King .22

High Standard Victor

High Standard Sport King Pump .22

Rifle, Bolt Action

Hi Power, Various Calibers, Field Grade, Modern	140	175
Hi Power Deluxe, Various Calibers, Monte Carlo Stock, Checkered Stock, Modern	165	215

Rifle, Slide Action

.22 L.R.R.F., Flight-King, Tube Feed, Monte Carlo Stock, Modern	45	65

Rifle, Semi-Automatic

Sport King, .22 L.R.R.F., Field Grade, Tube Feed, Modern	45	60
Sport King, .22 L.R.R.F., Field Grade, Carbine, Tube Feed, Modern	55	70
Sport King Deluxe, .22 L.R.R.F., Tube Feed, Monte Carlo Stock, Checkered Stock, Modern	55	70
Sport King Special, .22 L.R.R.F., Tube Feed, Monte Carlo Stock, Modern	50	65

Shotgun, Semi-Automatic

Trap Grade, Vent Rib, Recoil Pad, Modern	135	175
Skeet Grade, Vent Rib, Recoil Pad, Modern	135	175
12 Ga., Supermatic, Field Grade, Modern	95	140
20 Ga., Mag., Supermatic, Field Grade, Modern	95	140
20 Ga., Mag., Supermatic, Skeet Grade, Vent Rib, Modern	135	175
Deer Gun, 12 Ga., Supermatic, Open Rear Sight, Recoil Pad, Modern	120	155
Deluxe, Recoil Pad, Modern	105	145
Deluxe, Recoil Pad, Vent Rib, Modern	135	170
Deluxe, 20 Ga. Mag., Supermatic, Recoil Pad, Modern	100	145
Deluxe, 20 Ga. Mag., Supermatic, Recoil Pad, Vent Rib, Modern	133	170
Duck Gun, 12 Ga. Mag. 3″, Supermatic, Recoil Pad, Field Grade, Modern	125	155
Duck Gun, 12 Ga. Mag. 3″, Supermatic, Vent Rib, Recoil Pad, Modern	140	175
Model 10, 12 Ga., Riot Gun, Modern	165	250
Special, Field Grade, Adjustable Choke, Modern	115	155
Special, 20 Ga. Mag., Supermatic, Field Grade, Adjustable Choke, Modern	115	155
Trophy, Recoil Pad, Vent Rib, Adjustable Choke, Modern	150	185
Trophy, 20 Ga. Mag., Supermatic, Recoil Pad, Vent Rib, Adjustable Choke, Modern	155	190

Shotgun, Slide Action

.410 Ga. 3″, Flight-King, Field Grade, Modern	80	110
.410 Ga. 3″, Flight-King, Skeet Grade, Modern	100	140

High Standard Model 10 Shotgun

High Standard Flite-King Riot Shotgun

12 Ga., Flight-King, Trap Grade, Vent Rib, Recoil Pad, Modern	100	145
12 Ga., Flight-King, Skeet Grade, Vent Rib, Recoil Pad, Modern	100	140
12 and 20 Gauges, Flight-King, Field Grade, Modern	65	95
28 Ga., Flight-King, Field Grade, Modern	80	110
28 Ga., Flight-King, Skeet Grade, Vent Rib, Modern	100	145
Brush Gun, 12 Ga., Flight-King, Open Rear Sight, Modern	80	120
Deluxe, .410 Ga. 3", Flight-King, Vent Rib, Modern	90	130
Deluxe, 12 and 20 Gauges, Flight-King, Recoil Pad, Modern	65	100
Deluxe, 12 and 20 Gauges, Flight-King, Recoil Pad, Vent Rib, Modern	90	130
Deluxe, 28 Ga., Flight-King, Vent Rib, Modern	95	135
Deluxe Brush Gun, 12 Ga., Flight-King, Peep Sights, Sling Swivels, Modern	95	130
Riot, 12 Ga., Flight-King, Plain Barrel, Modern	90	130
Riot, 12 Ga., Flight-King, Open Rear Sight, Modern	100	145
Special, 12 and 20 Gauges, Flight-King, Field Grade, Adjustable Choke, Modern	85	120
Trophy, 12 and 20 Gauges, Flight-King, Recoil Pad, Vent Rib, Adjustable Choke, Modern	100	140

Shotgun, Double Barrel, Over-Under

Shadow Indy, 12 Ga., Single Selective Trigger, Selective Ejectors, Checkered Stock, Engraved, Modern	400	550
Shadow Seven, 12 Ga., Single Selective Trigger, Selective Ejectors, Checkered Stock, Light Engraving, Modern	300	450

Hi Hunter
Burbank, Calif.

Handgun, Revolver

Chicago Cub, .22 Short, 6 Shot, Folding Trigger, Modern	10	20
Detective, .22 L.R.R.F., Double Action, 6 Shot, Modern	15	25
Detective, .22 W.M.R., Double Action, 6 Shot, Modern	15	25
Frontier Six Shooter, .22 L.R.R.F., Single Action, Western Style, Modern	25	40
Frontier Six Shooter, .22 LR/.22 WRF Combo, Single Action, Western Style, Modern	30	45
Frontier Six Shooter, .357 Mag., Single Action, Western Style, Modern	50	75
Frontier Six Shooter, .44 Mag., Single Action, Western Style, Modern	80	120
Frontier Six Shooter, ".45 Mag.," Single Action, Western Style, Modern	65	100

Handgun, Semi-Automatic

Maxim, .25 ACP, Clip Fed, Modern	25	45
Militar, .22 L.R.R.F., Double Action, Hammer, Clip Fed, Blue, Modern	40	65
Militar, .32 ACP, Double Action, Hammer, Clip Fed, Blue, Modern	40	70
Militar, .380 ACP, Double Action, Hammer, Clip Fed, Blue, Modern	45	75
Panzer, .22 L.R.R.F., Clip Fed, Blue, Modern	20	40
Stingray, .25 ACP, Clip Fed, Blue, Modern	20	40
Stuka, .22 Long, Clip Fed, Blue, Modern	20	40

Handgun, Double Barrel, Over-Under

Automatic Derringer, .22 L.R.R.F., Blue, Modern	15	25

Handgun, Singleshot

Accurate Ace, .22 Short, Flobert Type, Chrome Plated, Modern	10	20
Favorite, .22 L.R.R.F., Stevens Copy, Modern	20	40
Favorite, .22 W.M.R., Stevens Copy, Modern	25	45
Gold Rush Derringer, .22 L.R.R.F., Spur Trigger, Modern	15	25

Target, .22 L.R.R.F., Bolt Action, Modern	20	30
Target, .22 W.M.R., Bolt Action, Modern	20	35

Rifle, Bolt Action

Maharaja, Various Calibers, Various Actions, Custom Made, Fancy Engraving, Fancy Wood, Fancy Inlays, Gold Plated, Modern	3,500	5,000

Hill, S.W.
See Kentucky Rifles and Pistols

Hillegas, J.
Pottsville, Pa. 1810-30 See Kentucky Rifles

Hockley, James
Chester County, Pa. 1769-71 See Kentucky Rifles

Holland & Holland
London, England

Rifle, Bolt Action

Best Quality, Various Calibers, Express Sights, Fancy Checkering, Engraved, Modern	1,500	2,500
Best Quality, Various Calibers, Express Sights, Checkered Stock, Modern	1,000	1,750

Rifle, Double Barrel, Side by Side

#2, Various Calibers, Sidelock, Checkered Stock, Engraved, Hammerless, Modern	5,000	8,000
Deluxe, Various Calibers, Sidelock, Automatic Ejector, Fancy Engraving, Fancy Checkering, Double Trigger, Modern	11,000	15,000
Royal, Various Calibers, Sidelock, Automatic Ejector, Fancy Engraving, Fancy Checkering, Double Trigger, Modern	6,000	9,000
Special Order, Various Calibers, Sidelock, Fancy Checkering, Fancy Engraving, Hammerless, Modern	11,000	16,500

Shotgun, Double Barrel, Over-Under

Deluxe Royal, 12 Ga., Sidelock, Automatic Ejector, Fancy Engraving, Fancy Checkering, Double Triggers, Modern	12,000	17,000
Deluxe Royal, 12 Ga., Sidelock Automatic Ejector, Fancy Engraving, Fancy Checkering, Single Trigger, Modern	13,000	19,000
Royal Model (Late), 12 Ga., Sidelock, Automatic Ejector, Fancy Engraving, Fancy Checkering, Double Triggers, Modern	9,000	13,500
Royal Model (Late), 12 Ga., Sidelock, Automatic Ejector, Fancy Engraving, Fancy Checkering, Single Trigger, Modern	10,000	15,000
Royal Model (Old), 12 Ga., Sidelock, Automatic Ejector, Fancy Engraving, Fancy Checkering, Double Triggers, Modern	7,500	11,000
Royal Model (Old), 12 Ga., Sidelock, Automatic Ejector, Fancy Engraving, Fancy Checkering, Single Trigger, Modern	8,500	12,500

Shotgun, Double Barrel, Side by Side

Badminton, Various Gauges, Sidelock, Automatic Ejector, Fancy Engraving, Fancy Checkering, Double Triggers, Modern	4,500	6,500
Badminton, Various Gauges, Sidelock, Automatic Ejector, Fancy Engraving, Fancy Checkering, Single Trigger, Modern	5,000	7,500
Centenary Badminton, 12 Ga. 2", Sidelock, Automatic Ejector, Fancy Engraving, Fancy Checkering, Double Triggers, Modern	4,500	6,500
Centenary Deluxe, 12 Ga. 2", Sidelock, Automatic Ejector, Fancy Engraving, Fancy Checkering, Double Triggers, Modern	8,000	12,000
Centenary Dominion, 12 Ga. 2", Sidelock, Automatic Ejector, Engraved, Checkered Stock, Double Triggers, Modern	2,500	4,000
Cententary Royal, 12 Ga. 2", Sidelock, Automatic Ejector, Fancy Engraving, Fancy Checkering, Double Triggers, Modern	7,500	10,500
Deluxe, Various Gauges, Sidelock, Automatic Ejector, Fancy Engraving, Fancy Checkering, Double Triggers, Modern	8,000	12,000
Deluxe, Various Gauges, Sidelock, Automatic Ejector, Fancy Engraving, Fancy Checkering, Single Trigger, Modern	8,500	13,000

Dominion, Various Gauges, Sidelock, Automatic Ejector, Engraved, Checkered Stock, Double Triggers, Modern	2,500	4,000
Northwood, Various Gauges, Boxlock, Automatic Ejector, Checkered Stock, Engraved, Modern	1,500	2,250
Riviera, Various Gauges, Extra Shotgun Barrel, Automatic Ejector, Fancy Engraving, Fancy Checkering, Double Triggers, Modern	5,500	9,000
Royal, Various Gauges, Sidelock, Automatic Ejector, Fancy Engraving, Fancy Checkering, Double Triggers, Modern	7,500	10,500
Royal, Various Gauges, Sidelock, Automatic Ejector, Fancy Engraving, Fancy Checkering, Single Trigger, Modern	8,000	12,000
Royal Ejector Grade, 12 Ga. Mag. 3", Single Selective Trigger, Vent Rib, Pistol-Grip Stock, Cased With Accessories, Modern	10,000	15,000

Shotgun, Singleshot

Standard Super Trap, 12 Ga., Boxlock, Automatic Ejector, Vent Rib, Fancy Engraving, Checkered Stock, Modern	5,000	7,500
Deluxe Super Trap, 12 Ga., Boxlock, Automatic Ejector, Vent Rib, Fancy Engraving, Checkered Stock, Modern	6,000	8,500
Exhibition Super Trap, 12 Ga., Boxlock, Automatic Ejector, Vent Rib, Fancy Engraving, Checkered Stock, Modern	7,000	10,500

Hollis, Chas & Sons
London, England

Shotgun, Double Barrel, Side by Side

12 Ga., Hammerless, Engraved, Fancy Checkering, Fancy Wood, Modern	2,000	2,750

Hollis, Richard
London, 1800-1850

Handgun, Flintlock

.68, Holster Pistol, Round Barrel, Brass Furniture, Plain, Antique	450	650

Shotgun, Percussion

12 Ga., Double Barrels, Double Triggers, Hook Breech, Light Engraving, Checkered Stock, Antique	275	400

Hood Fire Arms Co.
Norwich, Conn C.1875

Handgun, Revolver

.32 Short R.F., 5 Shot, Spur Trigger, Solid Frame, Single Action, Antique	90	160

Hopkins & Allen
Norwich, Conn. 1868-1917, taken over by Marlin-Rockwell in 1917. Later purchased by Numrich Arms Corp., West Hurley, N.Y. Current

Handgun, Percussion

"Boot Pistol," .36, Under-Hammer, Octagon Barrel, Reproduction, Antique, (Numrich)	25	45

Handgun, Revolver

Model 1876 Army, .44-40 WCF, Solid Frame, Single Action, 6 Shot, Finger-Rest Trigger Guard, Antique	275	450
Safety Police, .22 L.R.R.F., Top Break, Double Action, Various Barrel Lengths, Modern	60	110
Safety Police, .32 S & W, Top Break, Double Action, Various Barrel Lengths, Modern	55	95
Safety Police, .38 S & W, Top Break, Double Action, Various Barrel Lengths, Modern	55	95
XL .30 Long, .30 Long R.F., Solid Frame, Spur Trigger, Single Action, 5 Shot, Antique	85	145
XL 1 Double Action, .22 Short R.F., Solid Frame, Folding Hammer, Modern	50	90
XL 3 Double Action, .32 S & W, Solid Frame, Folding Hammer, Modern	55	85
XL Bulldog, .32 S & W, Solid Frame, Folding Hammer, Modern	55	85

Hopkins & Allen XL #3

XL Bulldog, .32 Short R.F., Solid Frame, Folding Hammer, Modern	45	75
XL Bulldog, .38 S & W, Solid Frame, Folding Hammer, Modern	55	85
XL CR .22 Short R.F., Solid Frame, Spur Trigger, Single Action, 7 Shot, Antique	85	145
XL Double Action, .32 S & W, Solid Frame, Folding Hammer, Modern	55	85
XL Double Action, .38 S & W, Solid Frame, Folding Hammer, Modern	55	85
XL Navy, .38 Short R.F., Solid Frame, Single Action, 6 Shot, Antique	250	375
XL No. 1, .22 Short R.F., Solid Frame, Spur Trigger, Single Action, 7 Shot, Antique	90	160
XL No. 2, .30 Short R.F., Solid Frame, Spur Trigger, Single Action, 5 Shot, Antique	95	170
XL No. 3, .32 Short R.F., Solid Frame, Spur Trigger, Single Action, 5 Shot, Safety Cylinder, Antique	90	175
XL No. 4, .38 Short R.F., Solid Frame, Spur Trigger, Single Action, 5 Shot, Antique	95	175
XL No. 5, .38 S & W, Solid Frame, Spur Trigger, Single Action, 5 Shot, Antique	175	300
XL No. 5, .38 Short R.F., Solid Frame, Spur Trigger, Single Action, 5 Shot, Safety Cylinder, Engraved, Antique	275	425
XL No. 6, .41 Short R.F., Solid Frame, Spur Trigger, Single Action, 5 Shot, Antique	120	195
XL No. 7, .41 Short R.F., Solid Frame, Spur Trigger, Single Action, 5 Shot, Swing-Out Cylinder, Antique	125	220
XL No. 8 (Army), .44 R.F., Solid Frame, Single Action, 6 Shot, Antique	300	475
XL Police, .38 Short R.F., Solid Frame, Single Action, 6 Shot, Antique	100	160

Handgun, Singleshot

Ladies Garter Pistol, .22 Short R.F., Tip-Up, Folding Trigger, Single Action, Antique	75	120
New Model Target, .22 L.R.R.F., Top Break, 10″ Barrel, Adjustable Sights, Target Grips, Modern	200	300
XL Derringer, .41 Short R.F., Spur Trigger, Single Action, Antique	325	500

Rifle, Bolt Action

American Military, .22 L.R.R.F., Singleshot, Takedown, Open Rear Sight, Round Barrel, Modern	120	165

Hopkins & Allen New Target Model

Rifle, Flintlock

"Kentucky," .31, Octagon Barrel, Full-Stocked, Brass Furniture, Reproduction, Antique, (Numrich)	135	180
"Kentucky," .36, Octagon Barrel, Full-Stocked, Brass Furniture, Reproduction, Antique, (Numrich)	140	180
"Kentucky," .45, Octagon Barrel, Full-Stocked, Brass Furniture, Reproduction, Antique, (Numrich)	150	190
"Minuteman Brush," .45, Octagon Barrel, Full-Stocked, Carbine, Reproduction, Antique, (Numrich)	140	190
"Minuteman Brush," .50, Octagon Barrel, Full-Stocked, Carbine, Reproduction, Antique, (Numrich)	140	190
"Minuteman," .31, Octagon Barrel, Full-Stocked, Brass Furniture, Reproduction, Antique, (Numrich)	135	180
"Minuteman," .36, Octagon Barrel, Full-Stocked, Brass Furniture, Reproduction, Antique, (Numrich)	140	180
"Minuteman," .45, Octagon Barrel, Full-Stocked, Brass Furniture, Reproduction, Antique, (Numrich)	150	190
"Minuteman," .50, Octagon Barrel, Full-Stocked, Brass Furniture, Reproduction, Antique, (Numrich)	155	190
"Pennsylvania," .31, Octagon Barrel, Half-Stocked, Brass Furniture, Reproduction, Antique, (Numrich)	130	175
"Pennsylvania," .36, Octagon Barrel, Half-Stocked, Brass Furniture, Reproduction, Antique, (Numrich)	135	175
"Pennsylvania," .45, Octagon Barrel, Half-Stocked, Brass Furniture, Reproduction, Antique, (Numrich)	135	185
"Pennsylvania," .50, Octagon Barrel, Half-Stocked, Brass Furniture, Reproduction, Antique, (Numrich)	140	185

Rifle, Percussion

"Buggy Deluxe," .36, Under-Hammer, Octagon Barrel, Carbine, Reproduction, Antique, (Numrich)	70	100
"Buggy Deluxe," .45, Under-Hammer, Octagon Barrel, Carbine, Reproduction, Antique, (Numrich)	75	110
"Deer Stalker," .58, Under-Hammer, Octagon Barrel, Reproduction, Antique, (Numrich)	75	100
"Heritage," .36, Under-Hammer, Octagon Barrel, Brass Furniture, Reproduction, Antique, (Numrich)	70	110
"Heritage," .45, Under-Hammer, Octagon Barrel, Brass Furniture, Reproduction, Antique, (Numrich)	75	115
"Kentucky," .31, Full-Stocked, Octagon Barrel, Brass Furniture, Reproduction, Antique, (Numrich)	130	175
"Kentucky," .36, Full-Stocked, Octagon Barrel, Brass Furniture, Reproduction, Antique, (Numrich)	135	175
"Kentucky," .45, Full-Stocked, Octagon Barrel, Brass Furniture, Reproduction, Antique, (Numrich)	140	180
"Minuteman Brush," .45, Full-Stocked, Octagon Barrel, Carbine, Reproduction, Antique, (Numrich)	130	180
"Minuteman Brush," .50, Full-Stocked, Octagon Barrel, Carbine, Reproduction, Antique, (Numrich)	130	180

Hopkins & Allen Buggy Deluxe Rifle
Courtesy of Numrich Arms Corp.

*Hopkins & Allen Minuteman
Courtesy of Numrich Arms Corp.*

"Minuteman," .31, Full-Stocked, Octagon Barrel, Brass Furniture, Reproduction, Antique, (Numrich)	125	175
"Minuteman," .36, Full-Stocked, Octagon Barrel, Brass Furniture, Reproduction, Antique, (Numrich)	130	175
"Minuteman," .45, Full-Stocked, Octagon Barrel, Brass Furniture, Reproduction, Antique, (Numrich)	130	180
"Minuteman," .50, Full-Stocked, Octagon Barrel, Brass Furniture, Reproduction, Antique, (Numrich)	135	180
"Offhand Deluxe," .36, Under-Hammer, Octagon Barrel, Reproduction, Antique, (Numrich)	60	100
"Offhand Deluxe," .45, Under-Hammer, Octagon Barrel, Reproduction, Antique, (Numrich)	65	100
"Offhand Deluxe," .45, Under-Hammer, Octagon Barrel, Reproduction, Antique, (Numrich)	65	100
"Pennsylvania," .31, Half-Stocked, Octagon Barrel, Brass Furniture, Reproduction, Antique, (Numrich)	125	165
"Pennsylvania," .36, Half-Stocked, Octagon Barrel, Brass Furniture, Reproduction, Antique, (Numrich)	130	165
"Pennsylvania," .45, Half-Stocked, Octagon Barrel, Brass Furniture, Reproduction, Antique, (Numrich)	130	170
"Pennsylvania," .50, Half-Stocked, Octagon Barrel, Brass Furniture, Reproduction, Antique, (Numrich)	135	170
"Target," .45, Under-Hammer, Octagon Barrel, Reproduction, Antique, (Numrich)	60	95
.45, Double Barrel, Over-Under, Swivel Breech, Brass Furniture, Reproduction, Antique, (Numrich)	80	120

Rifle, Singleshot

Model 1888 (XL), Various Calibers, Falling Block, Takedown, Lever Action, Round Barrel, Open Rear Sight, Antique	175	300
Model 1888 Junior, .22 L.R.R.F., Falling Block, Takedown, Lever Action, Round Barrel, Open Rear Sight, Antique	75	125
No. 1922 New Model Junior, .22 L.R.R.F., Falling Block, Takedown, Lever Action, Octagon Barrel, Open Rear Sight, Modern	95	175
No. 1925 New Model Junior, .25 Short R.F., Falling Block, Takedown, Lever Action, Octagon Barrel, Open Rear Sight, Modern	120	185
No. 1932 New Model Junior, .32 Long R.F., Falling Block, Takedown, Lever Action, Octagon Barrel, Open Rear Sight, Modern	115	180
No. 1938 New Model Junior, .38 S & W, Falling Block, Takedown, Lever Action, Octagon Barrel, Open Rear Sight, Modern	140	200
No. 2922 New Model Junior, .22 L.R.R.F., Falling Block, Takedown, Lever Action, Octagon Barrel, Checkered Stock, Open Rear Sight, Modern	125	185
No. 2925 New Model Junior, .25 Short R.F., Falling Block, Takedown, Lever Action, Octagon Barrel, Checkered Stock, Open Rear Sight, Modern	145	220

*Hopkins & Allen Target Model
Courtesy of Numrich Arms Corp.*

No. 2932 New Model Junior, .32 Long R.F., Falling Block, Takedown, Lever Action, Octagon Barrel, Checkered Stock, Open Rear Sight, Modern — 145 — 220

No. 2938 New Model Junior, .38 S & W, Falling Block, Takedown, Lever Action, Octagon Barrel, Checkered Stock, Open Rear Sight, Modern — 175 — 250

No. 3922 Schuetzen Target, .22 L.R.R.F., Falling Block, Takedown, Lever Action, Octagon Barrel, Checkered Stock, Swiss Buttplate, Modern — 350 — 550

No. 3925 Schuetzen Target, .25-20 WCF, Falling Block, Takedown, Lever Action, Octagon Barrel, Checkered Stock, Swiss Buttplate, Modern — 425 — 650

No. 722, .22 L.R.R.F., Rolling Block, Takedown, Round Barrel, Open Rear Sight, Modern — 60 — 95

No. 822, .22 L.R.R.F., Rolling Block, Takedown, Lever Action, Round Barrel, Open Rear Sight, Modern — 75 — 120

No. 832, .32 Short R.F., Rolling Block, Takedown, Lever Action, Round Barrel, Open Rear Sight, Modern — 80 — 130

No. 922 New Model Junior, .22 L.R.R.F., Falling Block, Takedown, Lever Action, Round Barrel, Open Rear Sight, Modern — 90 — 145

No. 925 New Model Junior, .25 Short R.F., Falling Block, Takedown, Lever Action, Round Barrel, Open Rear Sight, Modern — 85 — 140

No. 932 New Model Junior, .32 Long R.F., Falling Block, Takedown, Lever Action, Round Barrel, Open Rear Sight, Modern — 85 — 140

No. 938 New Model Junior, .38 S & W, Falling Block, Takedown, Lever Action, Round Barrel, Open Rear Sight, Modern — 120 — 175

Noiseless, .22 L.R.R.F., Falling Block, Takedown, Lever Action, Round Barrel, Silencer, Class 3 — 250 — 375

Shotgun, Double Barrel, Side by Side
No. 100, 12 and 16 Ga., Double Trigger, Outside Hammers, Checkered Stock, Steel Barrel, Modern — 90 — 135

No. 110, 12 and 16 Ga., Double Trigger, Hammerless, Checkered Stock, Steel Barrel, Modern — 100 — 150

Shotgun, Singleshot
New Model, Various Gauges, Hammer, Top Break, Steel Barrel, Modern — 40 — 60

New Model, Various Gauges, Hammer, Top Break, Steel Barrel, Automatic Ejector, Checkered Stock, Modern — 45 — 75

New Model, Various Gauges, Hammer, Top Break, Damascus Barrel, Checkered Stock, Modern — 40 — 65

Hopkins, C. W.
Made by Bacon Mfg. Co., Norwich, Conn.

Handgun, Revolver
.32 Short R.F., Single Action, Solid Frame, Swing-Out Cylinder, Antique — 200 — 325

.38 Long R.F., Single Action, Solid Frame, Swing-Out Cylinder, Antique — 350 — 600

Horolt, Lorenz
Nuremberg, C.1600

Handgun, Wheel-Lock
Long Barreled, Holster Pistol, Hexagonal Ball Pommel, Light Ornamentation, Antique — 7,500

Howard Arms
Made by Meriden Firearms Co.

Handgun, Revolver
.32 S & W, 5 Shot, Double Action, Top Break, Modern — 45 — 95
.38 S & W, 5 Shot, Double Action, Top Break, Modern — 45 — 95

Howard Arms
Made by Cresent for Fred Bifflar & Co.

Shotgun, Double Barrel, Side by Side

Various Gauges, Outside Hammers, Damascus Barrel, Modern	80	150
Various Gauges, Hammerless, Steel Barrel, Modern	95	175
Various Gauges, Hammerless, Damascus Barrel, Modern	75	150
Various Gauges, Outside Hammers, Steel Barrel, Modern	90	175

Shotgun, Singleshot

Various Gauges, Hammer, Steel Barrel, Modern	45	75

Howard Brothers
Detroit, Mich.

Rifle, Singleshot

.44 Henry R.F., Round Barrel, Antique	250	400

Humberger, Peter Jr.
Ohio 1791-1852, See Kentucky Rifles

Humberger, Peter Sr.
Pa. 1774-91, then Ohio 1791-1811. See Kentucky Rifles

Hummer
Belgium, For Lee Hdw., Kansas

Shotgun, Double Barrel, Side by Side

Various Gauges, Outside Hammers, Damascus Barrel, Modern	80	150
Various Gauges, Hammerless, Steel Barrel, Modern	95	175
Various Gauges, Hammerless, Damascus Barrel, Modern	75	150
Various Gauges, Outside Hammers, Steel Barrel, Modern	90	175

Shotgun, Singleshot

Various Gauges, Hammer, Steel Barrel, Modern	45	75

Hungarian Military

Automatic Weapon, Submachine Gun

43M, 9mm Mauser Export, Clip Fed, Retarded Blowback, Class 3	750	1,000

Handgun, Semi-Automatic

19M Frommer Stop, .380 ACP, Clip Fed, Blue, Military, Curio	110	165
29M Femaru, .380 ACP, Clip Fed, Blue, Military, Curio	150	225
37M Femaru, .380 ACP, Clip Fed, Blue, Military, Modern	125	180
Mannlicher Model 1903, 7.65mm Mannlicher, Charger Fed, Curio	165	250
Roth-Steyr Model 1907, 8mm, Charger Fed, Curio	125	200
Steyr Hahn Model 1912, 9mm Steyr, Charger Fed, Curio	135	200

Hungarian Military Femaru Model 37

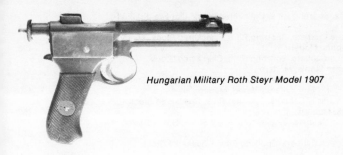

Hungarian Military Roth Steyr Model 1907

Rifle, Bolt Action
1943M, 8mm Mauser, Mannlicher, Military, Modern	100	175
8mm 1935M, Mannlicher, Military, Modern	80	125

Husqvarna Vapenfabrik Akitiebolag
Sweden

Handgun, Revolver
Model 1887 Swedish Nagent, 7.5mm, Double Action, Blue, Military, Antique	125	200

Handgun, Semi-Automatic
Model 07, 9mm Browning Long, Clip Fed, Military, Modern	125	200

Rifle, Bolt Action
Various Calibers, Sporting Rifle, Checkered Stock, Modern	175	250
1000 Super Grade, Various Calibers, Sporting Rifle, Checkered Stock, Monte Carlo Stock, Modern	200	300
1100 Deluxe, Various Calibers, Sporting Rifle, Checkered Stock, Modern	200	300
1951, Various Calibers, Sporting Rifle, Checkered Stock, Modern	175	250
3000 Crown Grade, Various Calibers, Sporting Rifle, Checkered Stock, Monte Carlo Stock, Modern	250	350
3100 Crown Grade, Various Calibers, Sporting Rifle, Checkered Stock, Modern	250	350
4000, Various Calibers, Sporting Rifle, Checkered Stock, Lightweight, Monte Carlo Stock, Modern	250	350
4100, Various Calibers, Sporting Rifle, Checkered Stock, Lightweight, Modern	250	350

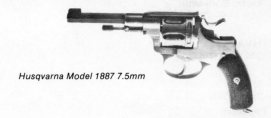

Husqvarna Model 1887 7.5mm

456, Various Calibers, Sporting Rifle, Checkered Stock, Lightweight, Full-Stocked, Modern	275	375
6000 Imperial, Various Calibers, Sporting Rifle, Checkered Stock, Fancy Wood, Express Sights, Modern	300	425
7000 Imperial, Various Calibers, Sporting Rifle, Checkered Stock, Lightweight, Express Sights, Modern	300	425
8000 Imperial Grade, Various Calibers, Sporting Rifle, Checkered Stock, Engraved, Monte Carlo Stock, Fancy Wood, Modern	325	450
9000 Crown Grade, Various Calibers, Sporting Rifle, Checkered Stock, Monte Carlo Stock, Modern	250	350
Gustav CG-T, Various Calibers, Singleshot, Target Stock, Heavy Barrel, Modern	180	240
Gustav Grade II, Various Calibers, Sporting Rifle, Checkered Stock, Modern	260	375
Gustav Grade II, Various Calibers, Sporting Rifle, Checkered Stock, Left-Hand, Modern	270	285
Gustav Grade II, Various Calibers, Sporting Rifle, Checkered Stock, Magnum Action, Modern	265	380
Gustav Grade III, Various Calibers, Sporting Rifle, Checkered Stock, Magnum Action, Left-Hand, Modern	275	400
Gustav Grade III, Various Calibers, Sporting Rifle, Checkered Stock, Magnum Action, Light Engraving, Left-Hand, Modern	300	450
Gustav Grade III, Various Calibers, Sporting Rifle, Checkered Stock, Magnum Action, Light Engraving, Modern	300	450
Gustav Grade III, Various Calibers, Sporting Rifle, Checkered Stock, Light Engraving, Modern	300	450
Gustav Grade III, Various Calibers, Sporting Rifle, Checkered Stock, Light Engraving, Left-Hand, Modern	300	450
Gustav Grade V, Various Calibers, Sporting Rifle, Checkered Stock, Engraved, Modern	400	600
Gustav Grade V, Various Calibers, Sporting Rifle, Checkered Stock, Engraved, Left-Hand, Modern	400	600
Gustav Grade V, Various Calibers, Sporting Rifle, Checkered Stock, Engraved, Magnum Action, Modern	400	600
Gustav Grade V, Various Calibers, Sporting Rifle, Checkered Stock, Engraved, Magnum Action, Left-Hand, Modern	400	600
Gustav Swede, Various Calibers, Sporting Rifle, Checkered Stock, Modern	175	275
Gustav Swede Deluxe, Various Calibers, Sporting Rifle, Checkered Stock, Light Engraving, Modern	240	300
Gustav V-T, Various Calibers, Varmint, Target Stock, Heavy Barrel, Modern	270	375
P 3000 Presentation, Various Calibers, Sporting Rifle, Checkered Stock, Engraved, Fancy Wood, Modern	425	600

Hutz, Benjamin
Lancaster, Pa. C.1802. See Kentucky Rifles

HVA
See Husqvarna

Hyper
Jenks, Okla.

Rifle, Singleshot

Hyper-Single Rifle, Various Calibers, Fancy Wood, No Sights, Falling Block, Fancy Checkering, Modern	750	1,100
Hyper-Single Rifle, Various Calibers, Fancy Wood, No Sights, Falling Block, Fancy Checkering, Stainless Steel Barrel, Modern	800	1,200

IAB
Puccinelli Co., San Anselmo, Calif.

Shotgun, Double Barrel, Over-Under
C-300 Combo, 12 Ga., Vent Rib, Single Selective Trigger, Checkered Stock, with 2 Extra Single Barrels, Modern	1,500	2,250
C-300 Super Combo, 12 Ga., Vent Rib, Single Selective Trigger, Checkered Stock, with 2 Extra Single Barrels, Modern	2,000	2,750

Shotgun, Singleshot
S-300, 12 Ga., Vent Rib, Checkered Stock, Trap Grade, Modern	800	1,200

I G
Grey, of Dundee C.1630

Handgun, Snaphaunce
Belt Pistol, Engraved, Ovoid Pommel, All Metal, Antique	20,000

Imperial
Maker Unknown C.1880

Handgun, Revolver
.22 Short R.F., 7 Shot, Spur Trigger, Solid Frame, Single Action, Antique	90	160
.32 Short R.F., 5 Shot, Spur Trigger, Solid Frame, Single Action, Antique	95	170

Imperial Arms
Made by Hopkins & Allen C.1880

Handgun, Revolver
.32 Short R.F., 5 Shot, Spur Trigger, Solid Frame, Single Action, Antique	90	160
.38 Short R.F., 5 Shot, Spur Trigger, Solid Frame, Single Action, Antique	95	175

India Military

Automatic Weapon, Heavy Machine Gun
Bira Gun, .450/.577 Martini-Henry, Drum Magazine, Carriage Mount, Twin Barrels, Antique	10,000

Indian Arms
Detroit, Mich.

Handgun, Semi-Automatic
.380 ACP, Clip Fed, Stainless Steel, Vent Rib, Double Action, Modern	175	250

Ingram
Invented by Gordon Ingram. Made by Police Ordnance Co., Los Angeles, Calif. and Military Armament Corp., Georgia

Automatic Weapon, Submachine Gun
M-10 M A C, .45 ACP, Clip Fed, Folding Stock, Commercial, Class 3	125	175
M-10 M A C, .45 ACP, Clip Fed, Folding Stock, Commercial, Silencer, Class 3	200	275
M-10 M A C, 9mm Luger, Clip Fed, Folding Stock, Commercial, Class 3	125	175
M-10 M A C, 9mm Luger, Clip Fed, Folding Stock, Commercial, Silencer, Class 3	200	275
M-11 M A C, .380 ACP, Clip Fed, Folding Stock, Commercial, Class 3	300	375
M-11 M A C, .380 ACP, Clip Fed, Folding Stock, Commercial, Silencer, Class 3	400	500
M6 Ingram, .45 ACP, Clip Fed, Commercial, Class 3	275	375

Ingram, Charles
Glasgow, Scotland C.1860

Shotgun, Double Barrel, Side by Side

Extra Set of Rifle Barrels, High Quality, Cased with Accessories, Engraved, Checkered Stock, Antique	5,000	7,000

Inhoff, Benedict
Berks County, Pa. 1781-83. See Kentucky Rifles

Interchangeable
Belgium, Trade Name Schoverlin-Daley & Gales C.1880

Shotgun, Double Barrel, Side by Side

Various Gauges, Outside Hammers, Damascus Barrel, Modern	90	150

International
Made by Hood Firearms C.1875

Handgun, Revolver

.22 Short R.F., 7 Shot, Spur Trigger, Solid Frame, Single Action, Antique	90	160
.32 Short R.F., 5 Shot, Spur Trigger, Solid Frame, Single Action, Antique	95	170

Interstate Arms Co.
Made by Crescent for Townley Metal & Hdw., Kansas City, Mo.

Shotgun, Double Barrel, Side by Side

Various Gauges, Outside Hammers, Damascus Barrel, Modern	80	150
Various Gauges, Hammerless, Steel Barrel, Modern	95	175
Various Gauges, Hammerless, Damascus Barrel, Modern	75	150
Various Gauges, Outside Hammers, Steel Barrel, Modern	90	175

Shotgun, Singleshot

Various Gauges, Hammer, Steel Barrel, Modern	45	75

I P
Probably German, 1580-1600

Rifle, Wheel-Lock

.60, German Style, Brass Furniture, Light Ornamentation, Horn Inlays, Set Trigger, Antique	3,000	4,000

Israeli Military

Automatic Weapon, Submachine Gun

UZI, 9mm Luger, Clip Fed, Silencer, Class 3	700	850
UZI, 9mm Luger, Clip Fed, Folding Stock, Class 3	500	650

Handgun, Revolver

S & W Model 10 Copy, 9mm Luger, Solid Frame, Swing-Out Cylinder, Double Action, Military, Modern	400	575

Rifle, Semi-Automatic

UZI, 9mm Luger, Clip Fed, Folding Stock, Commercial, Modern	350	475

Italian Military
Also See Beretta

Automatic Weapon, Assault Rifle

BM59, .308 Win., Clip Fed, Bipod, Class 3	450	700

Automatic Weapon, Submachine Gun

MP 38/44, 9mm Luger, Clip Fed, Military, Class 3	600	750
MP 38/49, 9mm Luger, Clip Fed, Wood Stock, Military, Class 3	250	350
MP 38A, 9mm Luger, Clip Fed, Military, Class 3	500	650

Italian Military Service Revolver

Italian Military Glisenti 9mm

Italian Military Service Revolver

Italian Military Brixia 9mm

Handgun, Revolver

Service Revolver, 10.4mm, Double Action, 6 Shot, Folding Trigger, Curio	75	125
Service Revolver, 10.4mm, Double Action, 6 Shot, Trigger Guard, Curio	75	125

Handgun, Semi-Automatic

Brixia, 9mm Glisenti, Clip Fed, Military, Curio	165	250
M 1910 Army, 9mm Glisenti, Clip Fed, Military, Curio	165	250
M 1934 Beretta, .380 ACP, Clip Fed, Military, Modern	85	140

Rifle, Bolt Action

M1891, 6.5 x 52 Mannlicher-Carcano, Military, Modern	50	85
M 38, 7.35mm Carcano, Military, Modern	50	85
M91 T.S., 6.5 x 52 Mannlicher-Carcano, Carbine, Folding Bayonet, Military, Modern	55	95
M91 T.S. (Late), 6.5 x 52 Mannlicher-Carcano, Carbine, Folding Bayonet, Military, Modern	45	80
M91/24, 6.5 x 52 Mannlicher-Carcano, Carbine, Military, Modern	45	80
M91/24, 6.5 x 52 Mannlicher-Carcano, Military, Modern	45	75
Vetterli M1870/1887, 10.4 x 47R Italian Vetterli, Antique	50	85
Vetterli M1870/87/15, 6.5 x 52 Mannlicher-Carcano, Antique	55	90

Ithaca Gun Co.
Ithaca, N.Y. 1873 to Date. Absorbed Lefever Arms Co., Syracuse Arms Co., Union Firearms Co., and Wilkes Barre Gun Co.

Combination Weapon, Double Barrel, Over-Under

LSA 55 Turkey Gun, 12 Ga./.222, Open Rear Sight, Monte Carlo Stock, Modern	250	325

Rifle, Bolt Action

BSA CF 2, Various Calibers, Magnum Action, Monte Carlo Stock, Checkered Stock, Modern	165	240
LSA 55, Various Calibers, Monte Carlo Stock, Cheekpiece, Heavy Barrel, Modern	225	300
LSA-55, Various Calibers, Monte Carlo Stock, Open Rear Sight, Modern	190	250
LSA-55 Deluxe, Various Calibers, Monte Carlo Stock, Cheekpiece, No Sights, Scope Mounts, Modern	225	290

Ithaca Turkey Gun

Ithaca LSA-55

Ithaca Model 72 Saddlegun

LSA-65, Various Calibers, Monte Carlo Stock, Open Rear Sight, Modern	190	250
LSA-65 Deluxe, Various Calibers, Monte Carlo Stock, Cheekpiece, No Sights, Scope Mounts, Modern	225	290

Rifle, Lever Action

Model 49, .22 L.R.R.F., Singleshot, Modern	25	40
Model 49, .22 WMR, Singleshot, Modern	30	45
Model 49 Deluxe, .22 L.R.R.F., Singleshot, Fancy Wood, Modern	40	55
Model 49 Presentation, .22 L.R.R.F., Singleshot, Engraved, Fancy Checkering, Modern	120	170
Model 49 R, .22 L.R.R.F., Tube Feed, Modern	45	70
Model 49 St. Louis, .22 L.R.R.F., Bicentennial, Singleshot, Fancy Wood, Curio	100	150
Model 49 Youth, .22 L.R.R.F., Singleshot, Modern	25	40
Model 72, .22 L.R.R.F., Tube Feed, Modern	75	110
Model 72, .22 WMR, Tube Feed, Modern	85	125
Model 72 Deluxe, .22 L.R.R.F., Tube Feed, Octagon Barrel, Modern	110	160

Rifle, Semi-Automatic

X-15 Lightning, .22 L.R.R.F., Clip Fed, Modern	40	60
X5 C Lightning, .22 L.R.R.F., Clip Fed, Modern	45	65
X5 T Lightning, .22 L.R.R.F., Tube Feed, Modern	45	65

Shotgun, Double Barrel, Over-Under

Model 500, 12 and 20 Gauges, Field Grade, Selective Ejector, Vent Rib, Modern	250	350
Model 500, 12 Ga. Mag. 3″, Field Grade, Selective Ejector, Vent Rib, Modern	260	360
Model 600, 12 Ga., Trap Grade, Selective Ejector, Vent Rib, Modern	360	460
Model 600, 12 Ga., Trap Grade, Selective Ejector, Vent Rib, Monte Carlo Stock, Modern	360	460
Model 600, 12 and 20 Gauges, Field Grade, Selective Ejector, Vent Rib, Modern	350	440
Model 600, 12 and 20 Gauges, Skeet Grade, Selective Ejector, Vent Rib, Modern	360	460
Model 600, 20 and .410 Gauges, Skeet Grade, Selective Ejector, Vent Rib, Modern	360	470
Model 600 Combo Set, Various Gauges, Skeet Grade, Selective Ejector, Vent Rib, Cased, Modern	800	1,100
Model 680 English, 12 and 20 Gauges, Field Grade, Selective Ejector, Vent Rib, Modern	370	460

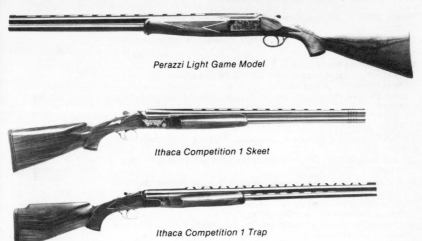

Perazzi Light Game Model

Ithaca Competition 1 Skeet

Ithaca Competition 1 Trap

Model 700, 12 Ga., Trap Grade, Selective Ejector, Vent Rib, Modern	400	550
Model 700, 12 Ga., Trap Grade, Selective Ejector, Vent Rib, Monte Carlo Stock, Modern	400	550
Model 700, 12 and 20 Gauges, Skeet Grade, Selective Ejector, Vent Rib, Modern	400	550
Model 700 Combo Set, Various Gauges, Skeet Grade, Selective Ejector, Vent Rib, Cased, Modern	900	1,450
Perazzi Light Game Model, 12 Ga., Automatic Ejector, Vent Rib, Single Trigger, Modern	800	1,200
Perazzi Competition 1, 12 Ga., Trap Grade, Automatic Ejector, Vent Rib, Single Trigger, Cased, Modern	800	1,200
Perazzi Competition 1, 12 Ga., Skeet Grade, Automatic Ejector, Vent Rib, Single Trigger, Cased, Modern	800	1,200
Perazzi Mirage, 12 Ga., Trap Grade, Automatic Ejector, Vent Rib, Cased, Modern	1,200	1,700
Perazzi Mirage 4-Barrel Set, Various Gauges, Skeet Grade, Automatic Ejector, Vent Rib, Cased, Modern	3,200	4,000
Perazzi MT-6, 12 Ga., Trap Grade, Automatic Ejector, Vent Rib, Cased, Modern	1,600	2,200
Perazzi MT-6, 12 Ga., Skeet Grade, Automatic Ejector, Vent Rib, Cased, Modern	1,600	2,200

Ithaca Mirage

Ithaca MX-8 Trap

Perazzi MX-8, 12 Ga., Trap Grade, Automatic Ejector, Vent Rib, Cased,
  Modern   1,200   1,750
Perazzi MX-8 Combo, 12 Ga., Trap Grade, Automatic Ejector, Vent Rib,
  Cased, Modern   1,800   2,500

Shotgun, Double Barrel, Side by Side
Early Model, Serial Numbers under 425,000 Deduct 50%
Outside Hammers, Deduct Another 20%-30%
Various Gauges, Field Grade, Hammerless, Magnum, Beavertail Forend,
  Modern   550   700
Various Gauges, Field Grade, Hammerless, Beavertail Forend, Double
  Trigger, Modern   500   650
Various Gauges, Field Grade, Hammerless, Double Trigger, Checkered
  Stock, Modern   325   475
Various Gauges, Field Grade, Hammerless, Magnum, Double Trigger,
  Modern   375   525
#1 E Grade, Various Gauges, Hammerless, Automatic Ejector, Beavertail
  Forend, Double Trigger, Modern   675   925
#1 E Grade, Various Gauges, Hammerless, Automatic Ejector, Magnum,
  Beavertail Forend, Double Trigger, Modern   800   1,100
#1 E Grade, Various Gauges, Hammerless, Automatic Ejector, Magnum,
  Double Trigger, Modern   700   950
#1 E Grade, Various Gauges, Hammerless, Automatic Ejector, Light
  Engraving, Checkered Stock, Double Trigger, Modern   575   800
#1 Grade, Various Gauges, Hammerless, Magnum, Double Trigger, Light
  Engraving, Checkered Stock, Modern   500   700
#1 Grade, Various Gauges, Hammerless, Double Trigger, Checkered
  Stock, Light Engraving, Modern   400   575
#1 Grade, Various Gauges, Hammerless, Magnum, Beavertail Forend,
  Double Trigger, Modern   600   850
#1 Grade, Various Gauges, Hammerless, Beavertail Forend, Light
  Engraving, Checkered Stock, Double Trigger, Modern   500   700
#2 E Grade, Various Gauges, Hammerless, Automatic Ejector, Magnum,
  Beavertail Forend, Double Trigger, Modern   900   1,200
#2 E Grade, Various Gauges, Hammerless, Automatic Ejector, Magnum,
  Double Trigger, Modern   700   1,000
#2 E Grade, Various Gauges, Hammerless, Automatic Ejector, Beavertail
  Forend, Double Trigger, Modern   750   950
#2 E Grade, Various Gauges, Hammerless, Automatic Ejector, Double
  Trigger, Engraved, Checkered Stock, Modern   650   825
#2 Grade, Various Gauges, Hammerless, Magnum, Beavertail Forend,
  Double Trigger, Modern   675   900
#2 Grade, Various Gauges, Hammerless, Beavertail Forend, Double
  Trigger, Engraved, Checkered Stock, Modern   600   750
#2 Grade, Various Gauges, Hammerless, Magnum, Double Trigger,
  Engraved, Checkered Stock, Modern   600   800
#2 Grade, Various Gauges, Hammerless, Double Trigger, Engraved,
  Checkered Stock, Modern   400   600
#3 E Grade, Various Gauges, Hammerless, Magnum, Beavertail Forend,
  Automatic Ejector, Double Trigger, Modern   1,000   1,400
#3 E Grade, Various Gauges, Hammerless, Magnum, Double Trigger,
  Engraved, Checkered Stock, Modern   900   1,275
#3 E Grade, Various Gauges, Hammerless, Beavertail Forend, Automatic
  Ejector, Double Trigger, Modern   850   1,200
#3 E Grade, Various Gauges, Hammerless, Double Trigger, Engraved,
  Checkered Stock, Automatic Ejector, Modern   775   1,100
#3 Grade, Various Gauges, Hammerless, Magnum, Beavertail Forend,
  Double Trigger, Modern   775   1,100
#3 Grade, Various Gauges, Hammerless, Magnum, Double Trigger,
  Engraved, Checkered Stock, Modern   700   1,050
#3 Grade, Various Gauges, Hammerless, Beavertail Forend, Engraved,
  Checkered Stock, Double Trigger, Modern   675   1,000

#3 Grade, Various Gauges, Hammerless, Double Trigger, Engraved, Checkered Stock, Modern — 725 — 950

#4 E Grade, Various Gauges, Hammerless, Automatic Ejector, Vent Rib, Beavertail Forend, Modern — 2,000 — 2,500

#4 E Grade, Various Gauges, Hammerless, Automatic Ejector, Vent Rib, Fancy Checkering, Fancy Engraving, Modern — 1,850 — 2,300

#4 E Grade, Various Gauges, Hammerless, Automatic Ejector, Beavertail Forend, Fancy Checkering, Fancy Engraving, Modern — 1,500 — 2,000

#4 E Grade, Various Gauges, Hammerless, Automatic Ejector, Fancy Checkering, Fancy Engraving, Double Trigger, Modern — 1,200 — 1,750

#5 E Grade, Various Gauges, Hammerless, Automatic Ejector, Vent Rib, Beavertail Forend, Modern — 2,900 — 3,600

#5 E Grade, Various Gauges, Hammerless, Automatic Ejector, Vent Rib, Fancy Checkering, Fancy Engraving, Modern — 2,700 — 3,300

#5 E Grade, Various Gauges, Hammerless, Automatic Ejector, Beavertail Forend, Fancy Checkering, Fancy Engraving, Modern — 2,600 — 3,250

#5 E Grade, Various Gauges, Hammerless, Automatic Ejector, Fancy Checkering, Fancy Engraving, Double Trigger, Modern — 2,550 — 3,100

#7 E Grade, Various Gauges, Hammerless, Automatic Ejector, Vent Rib, Beavertail Forend, Modern — 6,500 — 7,850

#7 E Grade, Various Gauges, Hammerless, Automatic Ejector, Vent Rib, Fancy Checkering, Fancy Engraving, Modern — 6,300 — 7,500

#7 E Grade, Various Gauges, Hammerless, Automatic Ejector, Beavertail Forend, Fancy Checkering, Fancy Engraving, Modern — 6,200 — 7,400

#7 E Grade, Various Gauges, Hammerless, Automatic Ejector, Fancy Checkering, Fancy Engraving, Double Trigger, Modern — 5,900 — 7,250

$2000 Grade, Various Gauges, Hammerless, Automatic Ejector, Single Selective Trigger, Ornate, Modern — 7,000 — 9,500

$2000 Grade, Various Gauges, Hammerless, Automatic Ejector, Single Selective Trigger, Vent Rib, Ornate, Modern — 7,500 — 10,000

$2000 Grade, Various Gauges, Hammerless, Automatic Ejector, Single Selective Trigger, Beavertail Forend, Ornate, Modern — 7,200 — 9,750

$2000 Grade, Various Gauges, Hammerless, Automatic Ejector, Single Selective Trigger, Vent Rib, Beavertail Forend, Modern — 7,750 — 11,000

Model 100, 12 and 20 Gauges, Hammerless, Field Grade, Modern — 175 — 250

Model 200 E, 12 and 20 Gauges, Hammerless, Selective Ejector, Field Grade, Modern — 260 — 350

Model 200 E, 12 and 20 Gauges, Hammerless, Selective Ejector, Skeet Grade, Modern — 275 — 350

Model 280 English, 12 and 20 Gauges, Hammerless, Selective Ejector, Field Grade, Modern — 270 — 350

Shotgun, Lever Action
Model 66 Supersingle, Various Gauges, Singleshot, Modern — 35 — 50
Model 66 Buck, Various Gauges, Singleshot, Open Rear Sight, Modern — 35 — 55
Model 66 Youth, Various Gauges, Singleshot, Modern — 30 — 50

Shotgun, Pistol
Auto Burglar, Various Gauges, Double Barrel, Side by Side, Short Shotgun, Class 3 — 375 — 550

Ithaca Model 66 Supersingle

Ithaca 10 Ga. Mag.

Ithaca Model 51 Deluxe Trap

Shotgun, Semi-Automatic

300 Standard, 12 and 20 Gauges, Modern	135	160
300 Standard, 12 and 20 Gauges, Vent Rib, Modern	140	170
300 XL Standard, 12 and 20 Gauges, Modern	145	180
300 XL Standard, 12 and 20 Gauges, Vent Rib, Modern	160	200
900 Deluxe, 12 and 20 Gauges, Vent Rib, Modern	150	180
900 XL, 12 Ga., Trap Grade, Modern	170	225
900 XL, 12 Ga., Trap Grade, Monte Carlo Stock, Modern	170	230
900 XL, 12 and 20 Gauges, Skeet Grade, Modern	166	215
900 XL Deluxe, 12 and 20 Gauges, Vent Rib, Modern	160	200
900 XL Slug, 12 and 20 Gauges, Open Rear Sight, Modern	150	200
Mag 10 Deluxe, 10 Ga. 3½", Takedown, Vent Rib, Fancy Wood, Checkered Stock, Modern	375	450
Mag 10 Standard, 10 Ga. 3½", Takedown, Vent Rib, Recoil Pad, Checkered Stock, Sling Swivels, Modern	275	365
Mag 10 Standard, 10 Ga. 3½", Takedown, Recoil Pad, Checkered Stock, Sling Swivels, Modern	240	320
Mag 10 Supreme, 10 Ga. 3½", Takedown, Vent Rib, Fancy Wood, Engraved, Checkered Stock, Modern	475	550
Model 51, 12 and 20 Gauges, Takedown, Vent Rib, Recoil Pad, Magnum, Modern	180	235
Model 51 Deerslayer, 12 Ga., Takedown, Open Rear Sight, Sling Swivels, Modern	175	225
Model 51 Deluxe, 12 Ga., Trap Grade, Takedown, Checkered Stock, Fancy Wood, Recoil Pad, Modern	250	295
Model 51 Deluxe, 12 Ga., Trap Grade, Monte Carlo Stock, Fancy Wood, Recoil Pad, Modern	260	310
Model 51 Deluxe, 12 and 20 Gauges, Skeet Grade, Takedown, Checkered Stock, Fancy Wood, Recoil Pad, Modern	205	255
Model 51 Standard, 12 and 20 Gauges, Takedown, Checkered Stock, Modern	150	200
Model 51 Standard, 12 and 20 Gauges, Takedown, Vent Rib, Checkered Stock, Modern	175	225

Shotgun, Singleshot

$5000 Grade, 12 Ga., Trap Grade, Automatic Ejector, Ornate, Modern	3,900	4,500
4 E Grade, 12 Gauge, Trap Grade, Automatic Ejector, Engraved, Fancy Checkering, Modern	2,000	2,650
5 E Grade, 12 Gauge, Trap Grade, Automatic Ejector, Fancy Engraving, Fancy Checkering, Modern	2,800	3,200
7 E Grade, 12 Gauge, Trap Grade, Automatic Ejector, Fancy Engraving, Fancy Checkering, Modern	3,000	3,800
Century 12 Ga., Trap Grade, Automatic Ejector, Engraved, Checkered Stock, Modern	300	400
Century II, 12 Ga., Trap Grade, Automatic Ejector, Engraved, Checkered Stock, Modern	325	450
Perazzi Competition 1, 12 Ga., Trap Grade, Automatic Ejector, Vent Rib, Cased, Modern	950	1,300

Ithaca Model 37V

Victory Grade, 12 Ga., Automatic Ejector, Checkered Stock, Vent Rib, Trap Grade, Modern	700	950

Shotgun, Slide Action
Model 37, for Extra Barrel Add $40-$65
Model 37, Extra Vent Rib Bsrrel Add $55-$80

Model 37, 12 Ga., Takedown, Bicentennial, Engraved, Fancy Wood, Checkered Stock, Modern	425	500
Model 37, Various Gauges, Takedown, Plain, Modern	80	120
Model 37 Deerslayer, Various Gauges, Takedown, Checkered Stock, Recoil Pad, Open Rear Sight, Modern	125	160
Model 37 Deerslayer, Various Gauges, Takedown, Fancy Wood, Checkered Stock, Recoil Pad, Open Rear Sight, Modern	140	185
Model 37 DSPS, 12 Ga., Takedown, Checkered Stock, 8 Shot, Open Rear Sight, Modern	125	175
Model 37 DSPS, 12 Ga., Takedown, Checkered Stock, 5 Shot, Open Rear Sight, Modern	115	160
Model 37 M & P, 12 Ga., Takedown, Parkerized, 5 Shot, Modern	100	145
Model 37 M & P, Bayonet & Adapter Add $18-$30		
Model 37-V Standard, Various Gauges, Takedown, Checkered Stock, Vent Rib, Modern	125	160
Model 37 Standard, Various Gauges, Takedown, Checkered Stock, Modern	100	135
Model 37 Supreme, Various Gauges, Takedown, Trap Grade, Fancy Wood, Checkered Stock, Modern	225	295
Model 37 Supreme, Various Gauges, Takedown, Skeet Grade, Fancy Wood, Checkered Stock, Modern	225	295
Model 37-$1000 Grade, Various Gauges, Takedown, Fancy Wood, Fancy Checkering, Fancy Engraving, Gold Inlays, Modern	2,500	3,400
Model 37-$3000 Grade, Various Gauges, Takedown, Fancy Wood, Fancy Checkering, Fancy Engraving, Gold Inlays, Modern	2,800	3,500
Model 37-D, Various Gauges, Takedown, Checkered Stock, Beavertail Forend, Modern	100	130
Model 37-Deluxe, Various Gauges, Takedown, Checkered Stock, Recoil Pad, Modern	110	145
Model 37-Deluxe, Various Gauges, Takedown, Checkered Stock, Recoil Pad, Vent Rib, Modern	140	185
Model 37-R, Various Gauges, Takedown, Solid Rib, Checkered Stock, Modern	110	140
Model 37-R, Various Gauges, Takedown, Solid Rib, Plain, Modern	95	125
Model 37-R Deluxe, Various Gauges, Takedown, Solid Rib, Fancy Wood, Checkered Stock, Modern	140	185
Model 37-S, Various Gauges, Takedown, Skeet Grade, Checkered Stock, Fancy Wood, Modern	200	275
Model 37-T, Various Gauges, Takedown, Trap Grade, Checkered Stock, Fancy Wood, Modern	200	275

Iver Johnson

Started as Johnson & Bye 1871 in Worcester, Mass. In 1883 became Iver Johnson's Arms & Cycle Works. 1891 to date at Fitchburg, Mass.

Handgun, Percussion

.36 1861 Navy, Revolver, Reproduction, Antique	50	75
.36 New Model Navy, Revolver, Reproduction, Antique	35	60
.36 Pocket Model, Revolver, Reproduction, Antique	50	75
.36 Remington Army, Revolver, Reproduction, Antique	50	75
.44 1860 Army, Revolver, Reproduction, Antique	50	75
.44 Confederate Army, Revolver, Reproduction, Antique	30	50
.44 Remington Army, Revolver, Reproduction, Antique	50	75
.44 Remington Target, Revolver, Reproduction, Antique	60	90

Handgun, Revolver

.22 Supershot, .22 L.R.R.F., 7 Shot, Blue, Wood Grips, Top Break, Double Action, Modern	45	75
Armsworth M855, .22 L.R.R.F., 8 Shot, Single Action, Top Break, Adjustable Sights, Wood Grips, Modern	55	90
Cadet, .22 WMR, 8 Shot, Solid Frame, Double Action, Plastic Stock, Blue, Modern	25	45
Cadet, .32 S & W Long, 5 Shot, Solid Frame, Double Action, Plastic Stock, Nickel Plated, Modern	30	50
Cadet, .32 S & W, 5 Shot, Solid Frame, Double Action, Plastic Stock, Blue, Modern	25	45
Cadet, .38 Special, 5 Shot, Solid Frame, Double Action, Plastic Stock, Blue, Modern	30	50
Cadet, .38 Special, 5 Shot, Solid Frame, Double Action, Plastic Stock, Nickel Plated, Modern	35	55
Cattleman, .357 Magnum, Single Action, Western Style, Color Case Hardened Frame, Various Barrel Lengths, Modern	85	120
Cattleman, .44 Magnum, Single Action, Western Style, Color Case Hardened Frame, Various Barrel Lengths, Modern	100	140
Cattleman, .45 Colt, Single Action, Western Style, Color Case Hardened Frame, Various Barrel Lengths, Modern	85	120
Cattleman Buckhorn, .357 Magnum, Single Action, Western Style, Color Case Hardened Frame, Adjustable Sights, Various Barrel Lengths, Modern	90	125
Cattleman Buckhorn, .357 Magnum, Single Action, Western Style, Color Case Hardened Frame, Adjustable Sights, 12" Barrel, Modern	100	145
Cattleman Buckhorn, .44 Magnum, Single Action, Western Style, Color Case Hardened Frame, Adjustable Sights, Various Barrel Lengths, Modern	120	150
Cattleman Buckhorn, .44 Magnum, Single Action, Western Style, Color Case Hardened Frame, Modern	115	160
Cattleman Buckhorn, .45 Colt, Single Action, Western Style, Color Case Hardened Frame, Adjustable Sights, Various Barrel Lengths, Modern	90	125
Cattleman Buckhorn, .45 Colt, Single Action, Western Style, Color Case Hardened Frame, Adjustable Sights, 12" Barrel, Modern	100	145
Cattleman Buntline, .357 Magnum, Single Action, Western Style, with Detachable Shoulder Stock, Adjustable Sights, 18" Barrel, Modern	175	240
Cattleman Buntline, .44 Magnum, Single Action, Western Style, with Detachable Shoulder Stock, Adjustable Sights, 18" Barrel, Modern	185	250
Cattleman Buntline, .45 Colt, Single Action, Western Style, with Detachable Shoulder Stock, Adjustable Sights, 18" Barrel, Modern	175	240
Cattleman Trailblazer, .22LR/.22 WMR Combo, Single Action, Western Style, Color Case Hardened Frame, Adjustable Sights, Modern	80	110
Champion Target, .22 L.R.R.F., 8 Shot, Single Action, Top Break, Adjustable Sights, Wood Grips, Modern	65	110
Model 1900, .22 L.R.R.F., 7 Shot, Blue, Double Action, Solid Frame, Modern	45	85
Model 1900, .22 L.R.R.F., 7 Shot, Nickel Plated, Double Action, Solid Frame, Modern	45	90

Model 1900, .32 S & W Long, 6 Shot, Blue, Double Action, Solid Frame, Modern	40	80
Model 1900, .32 S & W Long, 6 Shot, Nickel Plated, Double Action, Solid Frame, Modern	40	85
Model 1900, .32 Short R.F., 6 Shot, Blue, Double Action, Solid Frame, Modern	40	80
Model 1900, .32 Short RF., 6 Shot, Nickel Plated, Double Action, Solid Frame, Modern	45	90
Model 1900, .38 S & W, 5 Shot, Blue, Double Action, Solid Frame, Modern	45	85
Model 1900, .38 S & W, 5 Shot, Nickel Plated, Double Action, Solid Frame, Modern	50	95
Model 1900 Target, .22 L.R.R.F., 7 Shot, Blue, Wood Grips, Solid Frame, Double Action, Modern	55	110
Model 50A Sidewinder, .22L.R.R.F., 8 Shot, Solid Frame, Double Action, Plastic Stock, Western Style, Modern	35	50
Model 50A Sidewinder, .22L.R.R.F., 8 Shot, Solid Frame, Double Action, Wood Grips, Western Style, Modern	40	55
Model 55, .22 L.R.R.F., 8 Shot, Solid Frame, Double Action, Wood Grips, Blue, Modern	30	50
Model 55-S Cadet, .32 S & W, 5 Shot, Solid Frame, Double Action, Plastic Stock, Blue, Modern	30	50
Model 55-S Cadet, .38 S & W, 5 Shot, Solid Frame, Double Action, Plastic Stock, Blue, Modern	30	50
Model 55-SA Cadet, .22 L.R.R.F., 8 Shot, Solid Frame, Double Action, Plastic, Blue, Modern	30	50
Model 55-SA Cadet, .32 S & W, 5 Shot, Solid Frame, Double Action, Plastic Stock, Blue, Modern	30	50
Model 55-SA Cadet, .38 S & W, 5 Shot, Solid Frame, Double Action, Plastic Stock, Blue, Modern	30	50
Model 55A, .22 L.R.R.F., 8 Shot, Solid Frame, Double Action, Wood Grips, Blue, Modern	30	50
Model 55A, .22 L.R.R.F., 8 Shot, Solid Frame, Double Action, Wood Grips, Blue, Modern	30	50
Model 55A, .22 L.R.R.F., 8 Shot, Solid Frame, Double Action, Plastic Stock, Blue, Modern	30	50
Model 55S, .22 L.R.R.F., 8 Shot Solid Frame, Double Action, Plastic Stock, Blue, Modern	30	50
Model 57 Target, .22 L.R.R.F., 8 Shot, Solid Frame, Double Action, Plastic Stock, Adjustable Sights, Modern	30	50
Model 57 Target, .22 L.R.R.F., 8 Shot, Solid Frame, Double Action, Wood Grips, Adjustable Sights, Modern	30	50
Model 57-A Target, .22 L.R.R.F., 8 Shot, Solid Frame, Double Action, Plastic Stock, Adjustable Sights, Modern	35	55
Model 57-A Target, .22 L.R.R.F., 8 Shot, Solid Frame, Double Action, Wood Grips, Adjustable Sights, Modern	35	55
Model 66 Trailsman, .22 L.R.R.F., 8 Shot, Top Break, Double Action, Wood Grips, Adjustable Sights, Modern	40	55
Model 67 Viking, .22 L.R.R.F., 8 Shot, Top Break, Double Action, Plastic Stock, Adjustable Sights, Modern	45	60
Model 76S Viking, .22 L.R.R.F., 8 Shot, Top Break, Double Action, Plastic Stock, Adjustable Sights, Modern	40	55
Model 67S Viking, .32 S & W, 5 Shot, Top Break, Double Action, Plastic Stock, Adjustable Sights, Modern	40	55
Model 67S Viking, .38 S & W, 5 Shot Top Break, Double Action, Plastic Stock, Adjustable Sights, Modern	40	55
Safety, .22 L.R.R.F., 7 Shot, Top Break, Double Action, Hammer, Blue, Modern	50	85
Safety, .22 L.R.R.F., 7 Shot Top Break, Double Action, Hammer, Nickel Plated, Modern	60	95
Safety, .22 L.R.R.F., 7 Shot, Top Break, Double Action, Hammerless, Blue, Modern	60	95
Safety, .22 L.R.R.F., 7 Shot, Top Break, Double Action, Hammerless, Nickel Plated, Modern	65	110

Iver Johnson Safety .32 S & W

Iver Johnson .38 Safety Hammerless

Safety, .32 S & W, 5 Shot, Top Break, Double Action, Hammer, Nickel Plated, Modern	60	95
Safety, .32 S & W, 5 Shot, Top Break, Double Action, Hammer, Blue, Modern	50	85
Safety, .32 S & W, 5 Shot, Top Break, Double Action, Hammerless, Blue, Modern	60	95
Safety, .32 S & W, 5 Shot, Top Break, Double Action, Hammerless, Nickel Plated, Modern	65	110
Safety, .32 S & W Long, 6 Shot, Top Break, Double Action, Hammer, Blue, Modern	50	85
Safety, .32 S & W Long, 6 Shot, Top Break, Double Action, Hammer, Nickel Plated, Modern	60	95
Safety, .32 S & W Long, 6 Shot, Top Break, Double Action, Hammerless, Blue, Modern	60	95
Safety, .38 S & W, 5 Shot, Top Break, Double Action, Hammerless, Nickel Plated, Modern	65	110
Sealed 8 Protector, .22 L.R.R.F., 8 Shot, Blue Wood Grips, Top Break, Double Action, Modern	65	100
Sealed 8 Supershor, .22 L.R.R.F., Adjustable Sights, Blue, Wood Grips, Top Break, Double Action, Modern	75	110
Sealed 8 Target, .22 L.R.R.F., 8 Shot, Blue, Wood Grips, Solid Frame, Double Action, Modern	60	95
Sidewinder, .22LR/.22WMR Combo, Western Style, 4" Barrel, Adjustable Sights, Modern	55	70
Sidewinder, .22LR/.22WMR Combo, Western Style, 6" Barrel, Adjustable Sights, Modern	55	70
Supershot 9, .22 L.R.R.F., 9 Shot, Adjustable Sights, Blue, Wood Grips, Top Break, Modern	65	95
Supershot M 844, .22 L.R.R.F., 8 Shot, Double Action, Top Break, Adjustable Sights, Wood Grips, Modern	50	75
Swing Out, .22 L.R.R.F., Swing-out Cylinder, Various Barrel Lengths, Double Action, Wood Grips, Blue, Modern	55	80
Swing Out, .22 L.R.R.F., Swing-out Cylinder, 4" Barrel, Double Action, Wood Grips, Blue, Modern	60	85
Swing Out, .22 L.R.R.F., Swing-Out Cylinder, 4" Barrel, Double Action, Adjustable Sights, Blue, Modern	85	125

Swing Out, .22 L.R.R.F., Swing-out Cylinder, 6" Barrel, Double Action, Adjustable Sights, Blue, Modern	65	95
Swing Out, .22 WMR, Swing-Out Cylinder, Various Barrel Lengths, Double Action, Wood Grips, Blue, Modern	55	75
Swing Out, .22 WRM, Swing-out Cylinder, 4" Barrel, Double Action, Wood Grips, Blue, Modern	55	85
Swing Out, .22 WRM, Swing-out Cylinder, 4" Barrel, Double Action, Adjustable Sights, Blue, Modern	85	125
Swing Out, .22 WRM, Swing-Out Cylinder, 6" Barrel, Double Action, Adjustable Sights, Blue, Modern	65	95
Swing Out, .32 S & W Long, Swing-Out Cylinder, Various Barrel Lengths, Double Action, Wood Grips, Blue, Modern	55	75
Swing Out, .32 S & W Long, Swing-Out Cylinder, Various Barrel Lengths, Double Action, Wood Grips, Nickel Plated, Modern	55	85
Swing Out, .32 S & W Long, Swing-Out Cylinder, 4" Barrel, Double Action, Wood Grips, Blue, Modern	55	85
Swing Out, .32 S & W Long, Swing-Out Cylinder, 4" Barrel, Double Action, Adjustable Sights, Blue, Modern	85	125
Swing Out, .32 S & W Long, Swing-Out Cylinder, 6" Barrel, Double Action, Adjustable Sights, Blue, Modern	65	95
Swing Out, .38 Special, Swing-Out Cylinder, Various Barrel Lengths, Double Action, Wood Grips, Blue, Modern	55	80
Swing Out, .38 Special, Swing-Out Cylinder, Various Barrel Lengths, Double Action, Wood Grips, Nickel Plated, Modern	55	85
Swing Out, .38 Special, Swing-Out Cylinder, 4" Barrel, Double Action, Wood Grips, Blue, Modern	55	85
Swing Out, .38 Special, Swing-Out Cylinder, 4" Barrel, Double Action, Adjustable Sights, Blue, Modern	85	125
Swing Out, .38 Special, Swing-Out Cylinder, 6" Barrel, Double Action, Adjustable Sights, Blue, Modern	65	95
Target 9, .22 L.R.R.F., 9 Shot, Blue, Solid Frame, Wood Grips, Double Action, Modern	50	85
Trigger-Cocking, .22 L.R.R.F., 8 Shot, Single Action, Top Break, Adjustable Sights, Wood Grips, Modern	65	110

Handgun, Semi-Automatic

X-300 Pony, .380 ACP, Hammer, Clip Fed, Blue, Modern	75	110

Rifle, Bolt Action

Model 2X, .22 L.R.R.F., Singleshot, Takedown, Modern	25	45
Model X, .22 L.R.R.F., Singleshot, Takedown, Modern	20	35

Shotgun, Double Barrel, Over-Under

Silver Shadow, 12 Gauge, Single Trigger, Checkered Stock, Modern	170	225
Silver Shadow, 12 Gauge, Double Trigger, Checkered Stock, Modern	150	200
Silver Shadow, 12 Gauge, Double Trigger, Checkered Stock, Light Engraving, Vent Rib, Modern	140	200
Silver Shadow, 12 Gauge, Single Trigger, Checkered Stock, Light Engraving, Vent Rib, Modern	160	220

Shotgun, Double Barrel, Side by Side

Hercules, Various Gauges, Double Trigger, Checkered Stock, Hammerless, Modern	150	225
Hercules, Various Gauges, Double Trigger, Automatic Ejector, Hammerless, Checkered Stock, Modern	185	275
Hercules, Various Gauges, Single Trigger, Hammerless, Checkered Stock, Modern	200	300
Hercules, Various Gauges, Single Trigger, Automatic Ejector, Hammerless, Checkered Stock, Modern	250	365
Hercules, Various Gauges, Single Selective Trigger, Hammerless, Checkered Stock, Modern	250	380
Hercules, Various Gauges, Single Selective Trigger, Automatic Ejector, Hammerless, Checkered Stock, Modern	290	400
Knox-All, Various Gauges, Double Trigger, Hammer, Checkered Stock, Modern	150	225

Skeeter, Various Gauges, Double Trigger, Hammerless, Modern	225	350
Skeeter, Various Gauges, Skeet Grade, Double Trigger, Automatic Ejector, Hammerless, Modern	265	400
Skeeter, Various Gauges, Skeet Grade, Single Trigger, Hammerless, Modern	265	400
Skeeter, Various Gauges, Skeet Grade, Single Trigger, Automatic Ejector, Hammerless, Modern	320	440
Skeeter, Various Gauges, Skeet Grade, Single Selective Trigger, Hammerless, Modern	300	425
Skeeter, Various Gauges, Skeet Grade, Single Selective Trigger, Automatic Ejector, Hammerless, Modern	350	465
Super, 12 Gauge, Trap Grade, Double Trigger, Hammerless, Modern	350	500
Super, 12 Gauge, Trap Grade, Single Trigger, Hammerless, Modern	400	550
Super, 12 Gauge, Trap Grade, Single Selective Trigger, Hammerless, Modern	500	650

Shotgun, Singleshot

12 Gauge, Trap Grade, Vent Rib, Checkered Stock, Modern	65	100
Champion, Various Gauges, Automatic Ejector, Modern	35	50
Mat Rib Grade, Various Gauges, Raised Matted Rib, Automatic Ejector, Checkered Stock, Modern	40	70

Rifle, Semi-Automatic

PM 30P, .30 Carbine, Clip Fed, Telescoping Stock, Carbine, Modern	80	125
PM 30G, .30 Carbine, Clip Fed, Military Style, Carbine, Modern	70	110
PM 5.7 Spitfire, 5.7 Spitfire, Clip Fed, Military Style, Modern	80	120

Izarra
Spain Made by Bonifacio Echeverra C.1900

Handgun, Semi-Automatic

.32 ACP, Clip Fed, Long Grip, Modern	85	135

J & R
Burbank, Calif.

Rifle, Semi-Automatic

Model 68, 9mm Luger, Clip Fed, Flash Hider, Takedown, Modern	85	145

Jackson Arms Co.
Made by Crescent for C.M. McClung & Co., Knoxville, Tenn.

Shotgun, Double Barrel, Side by Side

Various Gauges, Outside Hammers, Damascus Barrel, Modern	80	150
Various Gauges, Hammerless, Steel Barrel, Modern	95	175
Various Gauges, Hammerless, Damascus Barrel, Modern	75	150
Various Gauges, Outside Hammers, Steel Barrel, Modern	90	175

Shotgun, Singleshot

Various Gauges, Hammer, Steel Barrel, Modern	45	75

Jager

Handgun, Semi-Automatic

.32 ACP, Clip Fed, Modern	185	275

Jager

Handgun, Revolver

Jager, .22LR/.22 WMR Combo, Single Action, Western Style, Adjustable Sights, Modern	60	85
Jager, .22LR/.22 WMR Combo, Single Action, Western Style, Modern	55	75
Jager Centerfire, Various Calibers, Single Action, Western Style, Adjustable Sights, Modern	75	100
Jager Centerfire, Various Calibers, Single Action, Western Style, Modern	70	90

Jager .32 ACP

Jager, F.& Co.

Rifle, Bolt Action
Herold, .22 Hornet, 5 Shot Clip Set Trigger, Checkered Stock, Modern   450   700

Janssen Freres
Liege, Belgium C.1920

Shotgun, Double Barrel, Side by Side
Various Gauges, Hammerless, Steel Barrel, Modern   90   145

Japanese Military

Automatic Weapon, Light Machine Gun

Type 92 (Lewis), 7.7mm Jap, Drum Magazine, Bipod, Military, Class 3	700	950
Type 96, 6.5 x 50 Arisaka, Clip Fed, Bipod, Military, Class 3	650	850
Type 96, 6.5 x 50 Arisaka, Clip Fed, Bipod, Military, Scope Mounted, Class 3	850	1,200
Type 99, 7.7mm Jap, Clip Fed, Bipod, Scope Mounted, Military, Class 3	1,100	1,500
Type 99, 7.7mm Jap, Clip Fed, Bipod, Military, Class 3	650	850

Automatic Weapon, Submachine Gun

Type 100, 8mm Nambu, Clip Fed, Wood Stock, Class 3	800	1,200

Handgun, Revolver

Model 26, 9mm, Military, Modern	120	160

Handgun, Semi-Automatic

Baby Nambu, 7mm Nambu, Clip Fed, Military, Curio	500	750
Baby Nambu, 7mm Nambu, Presentation, Military, Clip Fed, Military, Curio	900	1,400
Type 14 Nambu, 8mm Nambu, Clip Fed, Small Trigger Guard, Military, Curio	250	400
Type 14 Nambu, 8mm Nambu, Clip Fed, Large Trigger Guard, Military, Curio	200	300

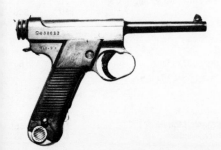

Japanese Military Nambu 8mm

Type 1904, 8mm Nambu, Clip Fed, Military, Curio	400	600
Type 94, 8mm Nambu, Clip Fed, Military, Curio	160	250

Rifle, Bolt Action

Model 38 (1905), 6.5 x 50 Arisaka, Military, Modern	70	120
Model 38 (1905), 6.5 x 50 Arisaka, Military, Carbine, Modern	70	120
Model 44 (1911), 6.5 x 50 Arisaka, Military, Carbine, Modern	70	120
Model 99 (1939), 7.7 x 58 Arisaka, Military, Open Rear Sight, Modern	70	120
Type 38, 6.5 x 50 Arisaka, Late Model, Military, Modern	60	95
Type 44, 6.5 x 50 Arisaka, Folding Bayonet, Military, Modern	70	115
Type 99, 7.7 x 58 Arisaka, Aircraft Sights Dust Cover, Military, Modern	80	130

Jewel
Made by Hood Firearms Co. C.1876

Handgun, Revolver

#1, .22 Short R.F., 7 Shot, Spur Trigger, Solid Frame, Single Action, Antique	90	160

Jo-Lo-Ar

Handgun, Semi-Automatic

.380 ACP, Tip-up, Clip Fed, Hammer Spur Trigger, Military, Modern	145	220
9mm Bergmann, Tip-up, Clip Fed, Hammer Spur Trigger, Military, Modern	100	165

Joffre
Spain, Unknown Maker, C.1900

Handgun, Semi-Automatic

M1916, .32 ACP, Clip Fed, Modern	75	110

Johnson Automatics
Also see U.S. Military

Rifle, Semi-Automatic

Model 1941, .30-06 Springfield, Military, Modern	400	600
Model 1941, 7mm Mauser, Military, Modern	550	750

Jones, Charles
Lancaster, Pa. 1780. See Kentucky Rifles

Jones, J.N. & Co.
London, England C.1760

Handgun, Flintlock

.60, George III, Navy Pistol, Brass Barrel, Brass Furniture, Military, Antique	500	800

Handgun, Percussion

.58, Holster Pistol, Converted from Flintlock, Brass Furniture, Plain, Antique	350	500

Kart

Handgun, Semi-Automatic

For Colt Government Target, .22 L.R.R.F., Conversion Unit Only	140	185

Kassnar
Harrisburg, Pa. Importers Current

Rifle, Bolt Action

Model M-14S, .22 L.R.R.F., Clip Fed, Checkered Stock, Modern	40	55
Model M-15S, .22 WMR, Clip Fed, Checkered Stock, Modern	45	65

Rifle, Semi-Automatic
Model M-16, .22 L.R.R.F., Clip Fed, Military Style, Modern .... 45 ... 65
Model M-20S, .22 L.R.R.F., 35 55

Shotgun, Double Barrel, Over-Under
Fias SK-1, 12 and 20 Gauges, Double Trigger, Checkered Stock, Modern ... 175 ... 275
Fias SK-3, 12 and 20 Gauges, Single Selective Trigger, Checkered Stock,
Modern ... 200 ... 300
Fias SK-4, 12 and 20 Gauges, Single Selective Trigger, Checkered Stock,
Automatic Ejector, Modern ... 250 ... 350
Fias SK-4D, 12 and 20 Gauges, Single Selective Trigger, Fancy
Checkering, Fancy Wood, Engraved, Automatic Ejector, Modern ... 270 ... 375
Fias SK-4T, 12 Ga., Trap Grade, Single Selective Trigger, Automatic
Ejector, Checkered Stock, Wide Vent Rib, Modern ... 275 ... 375

Shotgun, Double Barrel, Side by Side
Zabala, Various Gauges, Checkered Stock, Double Triggers, Modern ... 150 ... 225

Keffer, Jacob
Lancaster, Pa. C.1802 See Kentucky Rifles and Pistols

Keim, John
Reading, Pa. 1820-39 See Kentucky Rifles and Pistols

Kentucky Rifles and Pistols

The uniquely American "Kentucky" (or, as some prefer, "Pennsylvania") expressed in wood & metal the attitude of strength and independence that fostered our young nation. For the most part Kentuckys are custom guns, and, aside from general style similarities, virtually all are different, even those by the same maker. To add to the problem of price generalization, gunsmiths purchased parts from various makers and there may be three different names on a single gun or none at all. The main considerations in determining value are: 1. Type of ignition; 2. Quality of workmanship; 3. Decoration; 4. Orginality; 5. Condition. Except for orginality this list also applies to contemporary makers.

Rifles, Flintlock
Moderate Quality, Plain, $500-$1,000
Moderate Quality, Medium Decoration, $1,750-$3,500
High Quality, Fancy Decoration, $3,000-$5,500
Over-Under, Swivel-Breech, Plain, $700-$1,400
Over-Under, Swivel-Breech, Medium Quality, $3,000-$5,000
Over-Under, Swivel-Breech, High Quality, $4,000-$7,500
Deduct 30%-40% if Converted from Percussion

Rifles, Percussion
Moderate Quality, Plain, $500-$1,000
Moderate Quality, Medium Decoration, $800-$1,600
High Quality, Fancy Decoration, $2,500-$4,500
Over-Under, Medium Quality, Swivel Breech, Plain, $500-$1,000
Over-Under, Medium Quality, Swivel-Breech, $1,000-$2,000
Over-Under, High Quality, Swivel-Breech, $2,000-$3,500
Add 20% if converted from Flintlock to Percussion

Pistols, Flintlock
Moderate Quality, Medium Decoration, $1,500-$2,500
High Quality, Fancy Decoration, $3,000-$6,000

Pistols, Percussion (Original)
Moderate Quality, Medium Decoration $1,400-$2,000
High Quality, Fancy Decoration, $2,600-$3,500

Pistols, Percussion (Converted From Flintlock)
Moderate Quality, Medium Decoration, $800-$1,300
High Quality, Fancy Decoration, $1,400-$2,000

Arms with signatures are more desirable than those without markings. No name-deduct 10%-15%. If of recent vintage, and handmade, use this chart and deduct 50%.

Kerikkale
Turkey after 1945

Handgun, Semi-Automatic

MKE, .380 ACP, Clip Fed, Double Action, Modern	85	140

Ketland & Co.
Birmingham & London, England 1760-1831 Also See Kentucky Rifles

Handgun, Flintlock

.58, Holster Pistol, Plain, Tapered Round Barrel, Brass Furniture, Antique	500	850
.62, Belt Pistol, Brass Barrel, Brass Furniture, Light Ornamentation, Antique	550	900

Ketland, T.
Birmingham, England 1750-1829

Handgun, Flintlock

.69, Pair, Belt Pistol, Brass Furniture, Plain, Antique	1,200	1,750

Rifle, Flintlock

.65, Officers Model Brown Bess, Musket, Military, Antique	2,000	2,750
.73, 2nd. Model Brown Bess, Musket, Military, Antique	950	1,800

Ketland, William & Co.

Handgun, Flintlock

.63, Holster Pistol, Round Barrel, Plain, Antique	500	750

Kettner, Ed
Suhl, Thuringia, Germany 1922-39

Combination Weapon, Drilling

12x12, 10.75 x 65R Collath, Engraved, Checkered Stock, Sling Swivels, Modern	750	1,250

Kimball, J.M. Arms Co.
Detroit, Mich. C.1955

Handgun, Semi-Automatic

Standard Model, .30 Carbine, Clip Fed, Blue, Modern	450	700
Standard Model, .30 Carbine, Clip Fed, Blue, Grooved Chamber, Modern	500	800
Standard Model, .22 Hornet, Clip Fed, Blue, Modern	1,000	1,500
Standard Model, .38 Special, Clip Fed, Blue, Modern	800	1,200
Target Model, .30 Carbine Clip Fed, Blue, Adjustable Sights, Modern	500	800
Combat Model, .30 Carbine, Clip Fed, Blue, Short Barrel, Modern	450	700

MKE .380

Kimel Industries
Matthews, N.C. Importers

Handgun, Double Barrel, Over-Under
Twist, .22 Short R.F., Swivel Breech, Derringer, Spur Trigger, Modern   15   25

King Nitro
Made by Stevens Arms

Rifle, Bolt Action
Model 53, .22 L.R.R.F., Singleshot, Takedown, Modern   30   40

Shotgun, Double Barrel, Side by Side
M 315 Various Gauges, Hammerless, Steel Barrel, Modern   90   145

Kingland Special
Made by Crescent for Geller, Wards & Hasner St. Louis, Mo.

Shotgun, Double Barrel, Side by Side
Various Gauges, Outside Hammers, Damascus Barrel, Modern   80   150
Various Gauges, Hammerless, Steel Barrel, Modern   95   175
Various Gauges, Hammerless, Damascus Barrel, Modern   75   150
Various Gauges, Outside Hammers, Steel Barrel, Modern   90   175

Shotgun, Singleshot
Various Gauges, Hammer, Steel Barrel, Modern   45   75

Kingland 10-Star
Made by Crescent for Geller, Wards & Hasner St. Louis, Mo.

Shotgun, Double Barrel, Side by Side
Various Gauges, Outside Hammers, Damascus Barrel, Modern   80   150
Various Gauges, Hammerless, Steel Barrel, Modern   95   175
Various Gauges, Hammerless, Damascus Barrel, Modern   75   150
Various Gauges, Outside Hammers, Steel Barrel, Modern   90   175

Shotgun, Singleshot
Various Gauges, Hammer, Steel Barrel, Modern   45   75

Kittemaug
Maker Unknown, C.1880

Handgun, Revolver
.32 Short R.F., 5 Shot, Spur Trigger, Solid Frame, Single Action, Antique   90   160

Kleinguenther's
Seguin, Texas Importers, Current

Handgun, Revolver
Reck R-18, .357 Magnum, Adjustable Sights, Western Style, Single Action,
  Modern   65   90

Rifle, Bolt Action
K-14 Insta-fire, Various Calibers, Checkered Stock, No Sights, Recoil
  Pad, Modern   275   375
K-15, .22 L.R.R.F., Clip Fed, Checkered Stock, Modern   60   100

Rifle, Double Barrel, Over-Under
Model 222, .22 WMR, Plain, Modern   70   100

Shotgun, Double Barrel, Over-Under

Condor, 12 Gauge, Skeet Grade, Single Selective Trigger, Automatic
  Ejector, Wide Vent Rib, Modern   300   400
Condor, 12 Gauge, Single Selective Trigger, Automatic Ejector, Vent Rib,
  Modern   275   375

Shotgun, Double Barrel, Side by Side

Brescia, 12 Gauge, Hammerless, Light Engraving, Double Trigger,
  Modern   150   200

Klett, Simon
Probably Leipzig, C.1620

Rifle, Wheel-Lock

.54, Rifled, Octagon Barrel, Brass Furniture, Medium Ornamentation,
  Engraved, High Quality, Antique   5,500   8,500

Knickerbocker
Made by Crescent for H & D Folsom C.1900

Shotgun, Double Barrel, Side by Side

Various Gauges, Outside Hammers, Damascus Barrel, Modern   80   150
Various Gauges, Hammerless, Steel Barrel, Modern   95   175
Various Gauges, Hammerless, Damascus Barrel, Modern   75   150
Various Gauges, Outside Hammers, Steel Barrel, Modern   90   175

Shotgun, Singleshot

Various Gauges, Hammer, Steel Barrel, Modern   45   75

Knickerbocker
Made by Stevens Arms

Shotgun, Double Barrel, Side by Side

Model 311, Various Gauges, Hammerless, Steel Barrel, Modern   90   145

Knockabout
Made by Stevens Arms

Shotgun, Double Barrel, Side by Side

Model 311, Various Guages, Hammerless, Steel Barrel, Modern   90   145

Knoxall
Made by Crescent C.1900

Shotgun, Double Barrel, Side by Side

Various Gauges, Outside Hammers, Damascus Barrel, Modern   80   150
Various Gauges, Hammerless, Steel Barrel, Modern   95   175
Various Gauges, Hammerless, Damascus Barrel, Modern   75   150
Various Gauges, Outside Hammers, Steel Barrel, Modern   90   175

Shotgun, Singleshot

Various Gauges, Hammer, Steel Barrel, Modern   45   75

Kodiak Mfg. Co.
North Haven, Conn.

Rifle, Bolt Action

Model 98 Brush Carbine, Various Calibers, Checkered Stock, Modern   80   125
Model 99 Deluxe Brush Carbine, Various Calibers, Checkered Stock,
  Modern   90   135
Model 100 Deluxe Rifle, Various Calibers, Checkered Stock, Modern   90   145
Model 100M Deluxe Rifle, Various Magnum Calibers, Checkered Stock,
  Modern   100   150
Model 101 Ultra, Various Calibers, Monte Carlo Stock, Modern   120   160

Model 101M Ultra, Various Magnum Calibers, Monte Carlo Stock, Modern	130	175
Model 102 Ultra Varmint, Various Calibers, Heavy Barrel, Modern	130	175

Kohout & Spol
Czechoslovakia

Handgun, Semi-Automatic

Mars, .25 ACP, Clip Fed, Modern	70	115
Mars, .32 ACP, Clip Fed, Modern	75	120

Kommer, Theodor
Germany C.1920

Handgun, Semi-Automatic

Model I, .25 ACP, Clip Fed, Modern	225	375
Model II, .25 ACP, Clip Fed, Modern	155	250
Model III, .25 ACP, Clip Fed, Modern	225	360
Model IV, .32 ACP, Clip Fed, Modern	250	375

Kraft, Jacob
Lancaster, Pa. 1771-82. See Kentucky Rifles and Pistols

Krico
Stuttgart, West Germany

Rifle, Bolt Action

.222 Rem. Rifle, Checkered Stock, Double Set Triggers, Modern	275	425
.222 Rem. Carbine, Checkered Stock, Double Set, Triggers, Modern	300	450
Special Varmint, .222 Rem., Checkered Stock, Heavy Barrel, Double Set Triggers, Modern	275	425
Model 311, .22 L.R.R.F., Checkered Stock, Double Set Trigger, Modern	150	225
Model 351, .22 WMR, Checkered Stock, Double Set Triggers, Modern	175	250
Model 354, .22 WMR, Checkered Stock, Double Set Triggers, Modern	200	300
Model DJV, .22 Various Calibers, , Checkered Target Stock, Double Set Triggers, Modern	275	400
Model 600 Export, Various Calibers, Checkered Stock, Double Set Triggers, Modern	175	250
Model 600 Luxus, Various Calibers, Checkered Stock, Double Set Triggers, Modern	200	300
Model 620 Luxus, Various Calibers, Checkered Stock, Double Set Triggers, Modern	250	350
Model 700 Export, Various Calibers, Checkered Stock, Double Set Triggers, Modern	185	265
Model 700 Luxux, Various Calibers, Checkered Stock, Double Set Triggers, Modern	225	320
Model 720 Luxus, Various Calibers, Checkered Stock, Double Set Triggers, Modern	265	370

Krieghoff Gun Co.
Suhl, Germany

Combination Weapon, Double Barrel, Over-Under

Teck, Various Calibers, Hammerless, Engraved, Fancy Checkering, Modern	1,400	2,000
Teck Dural, Various Calibers, Hammerless, Engraved, Fancy Checkering, Lightweight, Modern	1,400	2,000
Ulm, Various Calibers, Hammerless, Engraved, Fancy Checkering, Sidelock, Modern	2,800	3,400
Ulm Dural, Various Calibers, Hammerless, Engraved, Fancy Checkering, Sidelock, Modern	2,800	3,400
Ulm Primus, Various Calibers, Hammerless, Engraved, Fancy Checkering, Sidelock, Modern	3,100	4,000

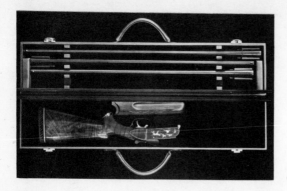

Krieghoff Crown Grade Set
Courtesy of Krieghoff Gun Co.

Ulm Primus, Various Calibers, Hammerless, Engraved, Fancy Checkering, Sidelock, Lightweight, Modern	3,500	4,500

Combination Weapon, Drilling

Neptun, Various Calibers, Hammerless, Engraved, Fancy Checkering, Sidelock, Modern	2,800	3,600
Neptun Dural, Various Calibers, Hammerless, Engraved, Fancy Checkering, Sidelock, Modern	2,800	3,600
Neptun Primus, Various Calibers, Hammerless, Fancy Checkering, Fancy Engraving, Sidelock, Modern	3,500	4,500
Neptun Primus, Various Calibers, Hammerless, Fancy Checkering, Fancy Engraving, Sidelock, Lightweight, Modern	3,500	4,500
Neptun Primus M, Various Calibers, Hammerless, Fancy Engraving, Fancy Checkering, Sidelock, Modern	8,000	12,000
Trumpf, Various Calibers, Hammerless, Engraved, Fancy Checkering, Modern	1,800	2,400
Trumpf Dural, Various Calibers, Hammerless, Engraved, Fancy Checkering, Lightweight, Modern	1,800	2,400

Rifle, Double Barrel, Over-Under

Teck, Various Calibers, Hammerless, Engraved, Fancy Checkering, Magnum, Modern	2,100	2,700
Teck, Various Calibers, Hammerless, Engraved, Fancy Checkering, Modern	1,600	2,100
Ulm, Various Calibers, Hammerless, Engraved, Fancy Checkering, Magnum, Sidelock, Modern	3,200	3,800
Ulm, Various Calibers, Hammerless, Engraved, Fancy Checkering, Sidelock, Modern	2,900	3,500
Ulm Primus, Various Calibers, Hammerless, Engraved, Fancy Checkering, Magnum, Sidelock, Modern	3,500	4,500
Ulm Primus, Various Calibers, Hammerless, Engraved, Fancy Checkering, Sidelock, Modern	3,100	4,000

Shotgun, Double Barrel, Over-Under

Extra Barrel, Add $500-$650

Crown, 12 Gauge, Trap Grade, Modern	6,500	8,500

Krieghoff San Remo Model 32
Courtesy of Krieghoff Gun Co.

Crown Combo, Various Gauges, Skeet Grade, Four Barrel Set, Modern	11,000	14,000
Exhibition, 12 Gauge, Trap Grade, Modern	17,000	20,000
Exhibition Combo, Various Gauges, Skeet Grade, Four Barrel Set, Modern	22,000	26,000
Monte Carlo, 12 Gauge, Trap Grade, Modern	6,000	8,000
Monte Carlo Combo, Various Gauges, Skeet Grade, Four Barrel Set, Modern	9,000	12,500
Munchen Combo, Various Gauges, Skeet Grade, Four Barrel Set, Modern	4,800	5,800
San Remo, 12 Gauge, Trap Grade, Modern	2,900	3,500
San Remo Combo, Various Gauges, Skeet Grade, Four Barrel Set, Modern	5,500	6,500
Standard, 12 Gauge, Trap Grade, Modern	1,200	1,500
Standard, 12 Gauge, Field Grade, Modern	1,400	1,700
Standard, Various Gauges, Skeet Grade, Modern	1,400	1,700
Standard Combo, 12 Gauge, Trap Grade, Two Barrel Set, Modern	1,800	2,200
Standard Combo, Various Gauges, Skeet Grade, Four Barrel Set, Modern	3,500	4,500
Super Crown, 12 Gauge, Trap Grade, Modern	9,000	11,000
Super Crown Combo, Various Gauges, Skeet Grade, Four Barrel Set, Modern	12,000	14,500
Teck, Various Gauges, Hammerless, Engraved, Fancy Checkering, Modern	1,400	2,000
Teck, Various Gauges, Hammerless, Engraved, Fancy Checkering, Single Trigger, Modern	1,500	2,100
Teck Dural, Various Gauges, Hammerless, Engraved, Fancy Checkering, Lightweight, Modern	1,400	2,000
Ulm, Various Gauges, Hammerless, Engraved, Fancy Checkering, Sidelock, Modern	2,300	2,900
Ulm, Various Gauges, Hammerless, Engraved, Fancy Checkering, Sidelock, Lightweight, Modern	2,300	2,900
Ulm-Primus, Various Gauges, Hammerless, Engraved, Fancy Checkering, Sidelock, Modern	3,100	3,800
Ulm-Primus, Various Gauges, Hammerless, Engraved, Fancy Checkering, Sidelock, Lightweight, Modern	3,100	3,800
Vandalia Rib, 12 Gauge, Trap Grade, Modern	1,500	2,000
Vandalia Rib Combo, Various Gauges, Skeet Grade, Four Barrel Set, Modern	2,800	3,400

Kruschitz
Vienna, Austria

Rifle, Bolt Action
Mauser 98, .30/06, Checkered Stock, Double Set Triggers, Modern	175	250

Kynoch Gun Factory
England

Handgun, Revolver
Schlund, .476 Eley, Hammerless, Top Break, Double Trigger Cocking, Antique	400	650

Kynoch H. Schlund Revolver

Lahti
Finland C.1935, Sweden 1940-44

Handgun, Semi-Automatic
L-35 Finnish, 9mm Luger, Clip Fed, Military, Curio	550	750
M 40 Swedish, 9mm Luger, Clip Fed, Military, Modern	150	225

Lakeside
Made by Crescent for Montgomery Ward & Co. C.1900

Shotgun, Double Barrel, Side by Side
Various Gauges, Outside Hammers, Damascus Barrel, Modern	80	150
Various Gauges, Hammerless, Steel Barrel, Modern	95	175
Various Gauges, Hammerless, Damascus Barrel, Modern	75	150
Various Gauges, Outside Hammers, Steel Barrel, Modern	90	175

Shotgun, Singleshot
Various Gauges, Hammer, Steel Barrel, Modern	45	75

Lames

Shotgun, Double Barrel, Over-Under
12 Gauge Mag. 3", Field Grade, Automatic Ejector, Single Selective Trigger, Vent Rib, Checkered Stock, Modern	240	325
12 Gauge Mag. 3", Skeet Grade, Automatic Ejector, Single Selective Trigger, Vent Rib, Checkered Stock, Modern	290	375
12 Gauge Mag. 3", Trap Grade, Automatic Ejector, Single Selective Trigger, Vent Rib, Checkered Stock, Modern	290	375
12 Gauge Mag. 3", Trap Grade, Automatic Ejector, Single Selective Trigger, Vent Rib, Monte Carlo Stock, Modern	300	400
California, 12 Gauge Mag. 3", Trap Grade, Automatic Ejector, Single Selective Trigger, Vent Rib, Checkered Stock, Modern	425	550

Lancaster, Charles
London 1889-1936

Rifle, Bolt Action
Various Calibers, Sporting Rifle, Modern	550	750

Lancelot

Handgun, Semi-Automatic
.25 ACP, Clip Fed, Blue, Modern	115	170

Lane & Read
Boston, Mass. 1826-35

Shotgun, Percussion
28 Gauge, Double Barrel, Side by Side, Light Engraving, Checkered Stock, Antique	300	425

Lancelot .25 ACP

Lang, Joseph
London, England Established 1821

Handgun, Percussion
Pair, Double Barrel, Over-Under, Officer's Belt Pistol, Light Engraving,
   Cased With Accessories, Antique   3,000   4,000

Shotgun, Singleshot
12 Gauge, Plain, Trap Grade, Modern   900   1,300

Langenhan
Germany, Pre-war

Handgun, Semi-Automatic
Model I, .32 ACP, Clip Fed, Military, Modern   115   175
Model II, .25 ACP, Clip Fed, Modern   175   275
Model III, .25 ACP, Clip Fed, Modern   200   300

Lasalle

Shotgun, Slide Action
12 Gauge Mag. 3", Field Grade, Plain, Modern   70   100
12 Gauge Mag. 3", Checkered Stock, Fancy Wood, Modern   90   130
20 Gauge Mag., Field Grade, Plain, Modern   70   100

Shotgun, Semi-Automatic
Custom, 12 Ga., Checkered Stock, Modern   125   175

Le Baron

Rifle, Flintlock
.69 Presentation, Silver Furniture, Fancy Wood, Fancy Checkering, Fancy
   Engraving, Antique   3,000   4,000

Le Basque

Handgun, Semi-Automatic
.32 ACP, Clip Fed, Blue, Modern   120   175

Le Francaise

Handgun, Semi-Automatic
Champion, .25 ACP, Clip Fed, Long Grip, Modern   125   185
Le Francais, .32 ACP, Clip Fed, Modern   275   400
Military Model, 9mm French Long, Clip Fed, Modern   450   600

Le Basque .32 ACP

Le Francais Armee 9mm

Le Francais Pocket .25 ACP

Le Francais Policeman .25 ACP

Pocket Model, .25 ACP, Clip Fed, Modern	120	170
Policeman, .25 ACP, Clip Fed, Modern	170	250

Le Martiny

Handgun, Semi-Automatic
.25 ACP, Clip Fed, Blue, Modern .... 75 ... 120

Le Monobloc

Handgun, Semi-Automatic
.25 ACP, Clip Fed, Modern .... 250 ... 325

Le Sans Pariel
Mre. d'Armes des Pyrenees

Handgun, Semi-Automatic
.25 ACP, Clip Fed, Blue, Modern .... 80 ... 120

Le Toutacier
Mre. d'Armes des Pyrenees

Handgun, Semi-Automatic
.25 ACP, Clip Fed, Blue, Modern .... 80 ... 125

Leader
Possibly Hopkins & Allen C.1880

Handgun, Revolver
.22 Short R.F., 7 Shot, Spur Trigger, Solid Frame, Single Action, Antique ... 90 ... 160
.32 Short R.F., 5 Shot, Spur Trigger, Solid Frame, Single Action, Antique ... 95 ... 170

Leader Gun Co.
Made by Crescent for Charles Willian Stores Inc. C.1900

Shotgun, Double Barrel, Side by Side
Various Gauges, Outside Hammers, Damascus Barrel, Modern ... 80 ... 150
Various Gauges, Hammerless, Steel Barrel, Modern ... 95 ... 175

Le Sans Pariel .25 ACP

Le Toutacier .25 ACP

| Various Gauges, Hammerless, Damascus Barrel, Modern | 75 | 150 |
| Various Gauges, Outside Hammers, Steel Barrel, Modern | 90 | 175 |

Shotgun, Singleshot
| Various Gauges, Hammer, Steel Barrel, Modern | 45 | 75 |

Leather, Jacob
York, Pa. 1779-1802. See U.S. Military, Kentucky Rifles

Lee Arms Co.
Wilkes-Barre, Pa. C.1870. Also See Red Jacket

Handgun, Revolver
.22 Short R.F., 7 Shot Spur Trigger, Solid Frame, Single Action, Antique	90	160
.32 Short R.F., Spur Trigger, Nickel Plated, Antique	85	140
.32 Short R.F., 5 Shot, Spur Trigger, Solid Frame, Single Action, Antique	90	160

Lee Special
Made by Crescent for Lee Hardware, Salina, Kans. C.1900

Shotgun, Double Barrel, Side by Side
Various Gauges, Outside Hammers, Damascus Barrel, Modern	80	150
Various Gauges, Hammerless, Steel Barrel, Modern	95	175
Various Gauges, Hammerless, Damascus Barrel, Modern	75	150
Various Gauges, Outside Hammers, Steel Barrel, Modern	90	175

Shotgun, Singleshot
| Various Gauges, Hammer, Steel Barrel, Modern | 45 | 75 |

Lee's Munner Special
Made by Crescent for Lee Hardware, Salina, Kans. C.1900

Shotgun, Double Barrel, Side by Side
Various Gauges, Outside Hammers, Damascus Barrel, Modern	80	150
Various Gauges, Hammerless, Steel Barrel, Modern	95	175
Various Gauges, Hammerless, Damascus Barrel, Modern	75	150
Various Gauges, Outside Hammers, Steel Barrel, Modern	90	175

Shotgun, Singleshot
| Various Gauges, Hammer, Steel Barrel, Modern | 45 | 75 |

Lefaucheux
Paris, France

Handgun, Revolver
9mm Pinfire, Double Action, Folding Trigger, Belgian, Antique	90	160
9mm Pinfire, Double Action, Paris, Antique	175	275
12mm Pinfire, Model 1863, Double Action, Finger Rest Trigger Guard, Antique	200	300

Lefaucheux Model 1863 12mm

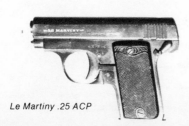

Le Martiny .25 ACP

Lefever Sons & Co.
Syracuse, N.Y. Nichols & Lefever, 1876-78, D. M. Lefever, 1879-89, Lefever Arms Co. 1889-99, Lefever, Sons & Co. 1899-1926. Purchased by Ithaca Gun Co. 1926

Shotgun, Double Barrel, Side by Side

#1000. Grade, Various Gauges, Sidelock, Hammerless, Fancy Checkering, Fancy Engraving, Monte Carlo Stock, Modern	7,500	9,500
4AA, Various Gauges, Box Lock, Hammerless, Automatic Ejector, Fancy Checkering, Fancy Engraving, Monte Carlo Stock, Modern	3,000	3,750
5BE, Various Guages, Box Lock, Hammerless, Fancy Checkering, Automatic Ejector, Fancy Engraving, Modern	2,000	2,750
6CE, Various Gauges, Box Lock, Hammerless, Fancy Checkering, Automatic Ejector, Fancy Engraving, Modern	1,500	2,000
7DE, Various Guages, Box Lock, Hammerless, Fancy Checkering, Automatic Ejector, Fancy Engraving, Modern	1,200	1,750
8EE, Various Gauges, Box Lock, Hammerless, Checkered Stock, Automatic Ejector, Engraved, Modern	950	1,400
9FE, Various Gauges, Box Lock, Hammerless, Checkered Stock, Automatic Ejector, Engraved, Modern	750	1,000
A, Various Gauges, Sidelock, Hammerless, Fancy Checkering, Fancy Engraving, Monte Carlo Stock, Modern	2,400	3,000
AA, Various Gauges, Sidelock, Hammerless, Fancy Checkering, Fancy Engraving, Monte Carlo Stock, Modern	3,000	3,700
B, Various Gauges, Sidelock, Hammerless, Fancy Checkering, Fancy Engraving, Monte Carlo Stock, Modern	1,900	2,400
BE, Various Gauges, Sidelock, Hammerless, Fancy Checkering, Fancy Engraving, Monte Carlo Stock, Automatic Ejector, Modern	2,100	2,550
C, Various Gauges, Sidelock, Hammerless, Fancy Checkering, Fancy Engraving, Monte Carlo Stock, Modern	1,400	1,900
CE, Various Gauges, Sidelock, Hammerless, Fancy Checkering, Fancy Engraving, Monte Carlo Stock, Automatic Ejector, Modern	1,500	2,000
D, Various Gauges, Sidelock, Hammerless, Fancy Checkering, Engraved, Monte Carlo Stock, Modern	1,200	1,600
DE, Various Gauges, Sidelock, Hammerless, Fancy Checkering, Engraved, Monte Carlo Stock, Automatic Ejector, Modern	1,300	1,750
D S, Various Gauges, Sidelock, Hammerless, Checkered Stock, Modern	350	450
D SE, Various Gauges, Sidelock, Hammerless, Checkered Stock, Automatic Ejector, Modern	450	600
E, Various Gauges, Sidelock, Hammerless, Fancy Checkering, Engraved, Modern	950	1,350
EE, Various Gauges, Sidelock, Hammerless, Fancy Checkering, Engraved, Modern	1,000	1,500
Excelsior, Various Gauges, Box Lock, Hammerless, Checkered Stock, Automatic Ejector, Light Engraving, Modern	650	850
F, Various Gauges, Sidelock, Hammerless, Checkered Stock, Engraved, Modern	800	1,100
FE, Various Gauges, Sidelock, Hammerless, Checkered Stock, Engraved, Automatic Ejector, Modern	900	1,250
G, Various Gauges, Sidelock, Hammerless, Checkered Stock, Light Engraving, Modern	550	700
GE, Various Gauges, Sidelock, Hammerless, Checkered Stock, Light Engraving, Automatic Ejector, Modern	650	850
H, Various Gauges, Sidelock, Hammerless, Checkered Stock, Light Engraving, Modern	450	575
HE, Various Gauges, Sidelock, Hammerless, Checkered Stock, Light Engraving, Automatic Ejector, Modern	475	700
Nitro Special, Various Gauges, Box Lock, Double Trigger, Checkered Stock, Modern	230	325
Nitro Special, Various Gauges, Box Lock, Single Trigger, Checkered Stock, Modern	275	390
Optimus, Various Gauges, Sidelock, Hammerless, Fancy Checkering, Fancy Engraving, Monte Carlo Stock, Modern	4,000	6,000

Le Page .32 ACP

Uncle Dan, Various Gauges, Box Lock, Hammerless, Automatic Ejector, Fancy Checkering, Fancy Engraving, Monte Carlo Stock, Modern	4,000	6,000

Shotgun, Singleshot

12 Gauge, Trap Grade, Hammerless, Vent Rib, Checkered Stock, Automatic Ejector, Modern	175	250
D.M. Lefever, 12 Gauge, Trap Grade, Hammerless, Vent Rib, Checkered Stock, Automatic Ejector, Modern	350	550
Long Range, Various Gauges, Field Grade, Hammerless, Checkered Stock, Modern	75	115

Lefevre, Philip
Beaver Valley, Pa. 1731-56. See Kentucky Rifles.

Lefevre, Samuel
Strasbourg, Pa. 1770-71. See Kentucky Rifles and Pistols.

Leigh, Henry
Belgium C.1890

Shotgun, Double Barrel, Side by Side

Various Gauges, Outside Hammers, Damascus Barrel, Modern	90	150

Leitner, Adam
York Co, Pa. See Kentucky Rifles and Pistols.

Lennard
Lancaster, Pa. 1770-72. See Kentucky Rifles and Pistols

Leonhardt

Handgun, Semi-Automatic

Army, .32 ACP, Clip Fed, Modern	95	150
Gering, .32 ACP, Clip Fed, Modern	125	175

LePage
Made by Manufacture D'Armes Le Page, Belgium

Handgun, Semi-Automatic

.25 ACP, Clip Fed, Modern	140	220
.32 ACP, Clip Fed, Modern	225	325
.380 ACP, Clip Fed, Adjustable Sights, Modern	250	400
9mm Browning Long, Clip Fed, Adjustable Sights, Modern	350	475
9mm Browning Long, Clip Fed, Adjustable Sights, Detachable Shoulder Stock, Class 3	575	750

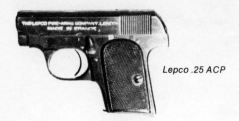

Lepco .25 ACP

Liberty .25 ACP

Lepco

Handgun, Semi-Automatic
.25 ACP, Clip Fed, Blue, Modern   80   120

Lescher
Philadelphia, Pa. C.1730. See Kentucky Rifles and Pistols

Lesconne, A.
Maybe French, C.1650

Handgun, Flintlock
Pair, Engraved, Silver Inlay, Long Screw Barrel, Rifled, Belt Hook, Antique   10,000

Liberty
Made by Hood Firearms, 1880-1900

Handgun, Revolver
.22 Short R.F., 7 Shot, Spur Trigger, Solid Frame, Single Action, Antique   90   160
.32 Short R.F., 5 Shot, Spur Trigger, Solid Frame, Single Action, Antique   95   170

Liberty
Montrose, Calif. Current

Handgun, Revolver
Mustang, .22LR/.22 WMR Combo, Single Action, Western Style,
  Adjustable Sights, Modern   20   30
Mustang, .22 L.R.R.F., Single Action, Western Style, Adjustable Sights,
  Modern   15   25

Liberty
Spain, C.1920. Unknown Maker

Handgun, Semi-Automatic
M1924, .25 ACP, Clip Fed, Long Grip, Modern   80   120
M1924, .32 ACP, Clip Fed, Long Grip, Modern   80   120
.25 ACP, Clip Fed, Blue, Modern   80   125

Libia
Made by Beistegui Hermanos

Handgun, Semi-Automatic
.25 ACP, Clip Fed, Blue, Modern   120   160

Lignitz, I. H.
Continental, C.1650

Handgun, Wheel-Lock
Brass Barrel, Holster Pistol, Medium Ornamentation, Antique   6,000

Lignose
Germany

Handgun, Semi-Automatic
Model 2, .25 ACP, Clip Fed, Modern   175   260
Model 2A, .25 ACP, Clip Fed, Einhand, Modern   165   235
Model 3, .25 ACP, Clip Fed, Long Grip, Modern   185   270
Model 3A, .25 ACP, Clip Fed, Long Grip, Einhand, Modern   165   235

Liberty Model 1924 .25 ACP

Lignose Model 2A .25 ACP

Lignose Model 3A .25 ACP

Lion
Made by Johnson Bye & Co. C.1870-80, Sold by J. P. Lovell

Handgun, Revolver

#1, .22 Short R.F., 7 Shot, Spur Trigger, Solid Frame, Single Action, Antique	90	160
#2, .32 Short R.F., 5 Shot, Spur Trigger, Solid Frame, Single Action, Antique	95	170
#3, .38 Short R.F., 5 Shot, Spur Trigger, Solid Frame, Single Action, Antique	95	175
#4, .41 Short R.F., 5 Shot, Spur Trigger, Solid Frame, Single Action, Antique	110	185

Little Giant
Made by Bacon Arms Co. C.1880

Handgun, Revolver

.22 Short R.F., 7 Shot, Spur Trigger, Solid Frame, Single Action, Antique	90	160

Little John
Made by Hood Firearms. C.1876

Handgun, Revolver

.22 Short R.F., 7 Shot, Spur Trigger, Solid Frame, Single Action, Antique	90	160

Little Joker
Made by John M. Marlin, New Haven, Conn. 1873-75

Handgun, Revolver

.22 Short R.F., 7 Shot, Spur Trigger, Solid Frame, Single Action, Antique	90	160

Little Pet
Made by Stevens Arms

Shotgun, Singleshot

Model 958, .410 Gauge, Automatic Ejector, Hammer, Modern	30	50
Model 958, 32 Gauge, Automatic Ejector, Hammer, Modern	40	60

Ljutic Industries, Inc.
Yakima, Wash. Current

Shotgun, Double Barrel, Over-Under

Bi Gun, 12 Gauge, Vent Rib, Trap Grade, Checkered Stock, Modern	3,000	3,750
Bi Gun Set, Various Calibers, Vent Rib, Skeet Grade, Checkered Stock, With 4 Sets of Barrels, Modern	6,000	8,000

Ljutic Bi-Gun Set

Ljutic Mono-Gun

Shotgun, Semi-Automatic

Bi Matic, 12 Gauge, Vent Rib, Trap Grade, Checkered Stock, Modern	1,300	1,800

Shotgun, Singleshot

Dyn-A-Trap, 12 Gauge, Trap Grade, Checkered Stock, Vent Rib, Modern	700	1,000
Dyn-A-Trap, 12 Gauge, Release Trigger Add $85-$125		
Dyn-A-Trap, 12 Gauge, for Custom Stock Add $100-$150		
Mono-Gun, 12 Gauge, Trap Grade, Checkered Stock, Vent Rib, Modern	1,600	2,300
Mono-Gun, 12 Gauge, Trap Grade, Checkered Stock, Olympic Rib, Modern	2,200	2,800
Mono-Gun, 12 Gauge, Add For Extra Barrel $300-$500		
Mono-Gun, 12 Gauge, Release Trigger Add $125-$175		
Mono-Gun, 12 Gauge, Trap Grade, Checkered Stock, Vent Rib, Adjustable Pattern, Modern	2,200	2,750
X-73, 12 Gauge, Trap Grade, Checkered Stock, Vent Rib, Modern	700	1,000
X-73, 12 Gauge, For Extra Barrel Add $275-$400		
X-73, 12 Gauge, Release Trigger Add $125-$175		

Llama
Spain from 1930 to Date. Imported by Stoeger Arms.

Handgun, Revolver

Chrome Plate Add 20%-30%
Engraving Add 25%-35%
Gold Damascening Add 300%-400%

Commanche I, .22 L.R.R.F., Swing-Out Cylinder, Double Action, Blue, Modern	95	135
Commanche II, .38 Special, Swing-Out Cylinder, Double Action, Blue, Modern	95	135
Commanche III, .357 Magnum, Swing-Out Cylinder, Double Action, Blue, Modern	95	145
Martial, .22 L.R.R.F., Swing-Out Cylinder, Double Action, Blue, Modern	85	130
Martial, .22 WMR, Swing-Out Cylinder, Double Action, Blue, Modern	95	140
Martial, .38 Special, Swing-Out Cylinder, Double Action, Blue, Modern	90	130

Handgun, Semi-Automatic

Chrome Plate Add 20%-30%
Engraving Add 25%-35%
Gold Damascening Add 300%-400%

Model I, .32 ACP, Clip Fed, Blue, Modern	80	135
Model II, .380 ACP, Clip Fed, Blue, Modern	90	145
Model III, .380 ACP, Clip Fed, Blue, Modern	95	150
Model IIIA, .380 ACP, Clip Fed, Grip Safety, Blue, Modern	95	160
Model IV, 9mm Bergmann, Clip Fed, Blue, Modern	90	145
Model IX, .45 ACP, Clip Fed, Blue, Modern	100	165
Model IXA, .45 ACP, Clip Fed, Blue, Modern	120	180
Model V, .38 ACP, Clip Fed, Blue, Modern	100	150
Model VII, .38 ACP, Clip Fed, Blue, Modern	100	150
Model VIII, .38 ACP, Grip Safety, Blue, Modern	135	175
Model X, .32 ACP, Clip Fed, Blue, Modern	95	130
Model XA, .32 ACP, Clip Fed, Grip Safety, Blue, Modern	100	145
Model XI, 9mm Luger, Clip Fed, Blue, Modern	115	165
Model XV, .22 L.R.R.F., Clip Fed, Grip Safety, Blue, Modern	95	135

Longines .32 ACP

Looking Glass .25 ACP

Lobinger, Johann
Vienna, Austria C.1780

Rifle, Flintlock
Yaeger, Smoothbore, Half-Octagon Barrel, Silver Furniture, Carved,
  Antique   2,500   3,250

Longines
Spain Unknown Maker C.1900

Handgun, Semi-Automatic
.32 ACP, Clip Fed, Modern   95   150

Long Tom
Made by Stevens Arms

Shotgun, Singleshot
Model 90, Various Gauges, Takedown, Automatic Ejector, Plain, Hammer,
  Modern   35   55
Model 95, 12 and 16 Gauges, Hammer, Automatic Ejector, Modern   35   55

Looking Glass
Spain, Unknown Maker

Handgun, Semi-Automatic
.25 ACP, Clip Fed, Modern   80   120
.32 ACP, Clip Fed, Long Grip, Modern   85   125

Lord, J.
Orwigsburg, Pa. 1842-55. See Kentucky Rifles.

Lowell Arms Co.
Lowell, Mass. 1864-68

Handgun, Revolver
.22 Short R.F., 7 Shot, Spur Trigger, Tip-up, Antique   200   300
.32 Long R.F., 6 Shot, Spur Trigger, Tip-up, Single Action, Antique   150   225
.38 Long R.F., 6 Shot, Spur Trigger, Tip-up, Single Action, Antique   225   350

Rifle, Singleshot
.38 Long R.F., Antique   200   300

Luger
Made in Various Countries for Commercial and Military Use from 1900-45. Also See Mauser Parabellum.

Handgun, Semi-Automatic

1900 Commercial, .30 Luger, Curio	750	1,900
1900 Eagle, .30 Luger, Curio	700	1,300
1900 Swiss Commercial, .30 Luger, Curio	750	1,900
1900 Swiss Military, .30 Luger, Curio	750	1,600
1900 Swiss Military, .30 Luger, Wide Trigger, Curio	850	1,900
1902, .30 Luger and 9mm Luger, Carbine, Curio	2,500	4,500
1902, 9mm Luger, Cartridge Counter, Curio	4,000	6,000
1902 Commercial, 9mm Luger, Curio	3,000	4,500
1902 Eagle, 9mm Luger, Curio	2,500	3,500
1902 Prototype, .30 Luger and 9mm Luger, Curio	6,000	12,000
1902 Test, .30 Luger, and 9mm Luger, Curio	1,800	3,500
1902-3 Presentation, .30 Luger, Carbine, Curio		30,000
1904 Navy, 9mm Luger, Curio	4,000	9,500
1906 Brazilian, .30 Luger, Curio	500	1,200
1906 Bulgarian, 9mm Luger, Curio	2,500	4,500
1906 Bulgarian, .30 Luger, Curio	3,000	5,000
1906 Commercial, .30 Luger, Curio	600	1,300
1906 Commercial, 9mm Luger, Curio	900	1,800
1906 Dutch, 9mm Luger, Curio	550	1,150
1906 Eagle, .30 Luger, Curio	550	1,400
1906 Eagle, 9mm Luger, Curio	850	1,700
1906 French, .30 Luger, Curio	3,500	6,750
1906 Navy Commercial, 9mm Luger, Curio	2,500	4,000
1906 Navy Military, 9mm Luger, Curio	850	1,750
1906 Portuguese Army, .30 Luger, Curio	650	950
1906 Portuguese Navy Crown, .30 Luger and 9mm Luger, Curio	5,000	10,000
1906 Portuguese Navy, RP, .30 Luger, Curio	2,500	4,000
1906 Russian, 9mm Luger, Curio	4,000	9,000
1906 Swiss Commercial, .30 Luger, Curio	1,000	3,000
1906 Swiss Military, .30 Luger, Curio	650	1,200
1906 Swiss Police, .30 Luger, Curio	700	1,400
1908 Bolivian, 9mm Luger, Curio	4,000	8,000
1908 Bulgarian, 9mm Luger, Curio	700	1,650
1908 DWM Commercial, 9mm Luger, Curio	450	900
1908 Military, 9mm Luger, Curio	450	750
1908 Navy Commercial, .30 Luger, Curio	1,400	3,400
1908 Navy Military, 9mm Luger, Curio	850	1,750
1913 Commercial, 9mm Luger, Curio	550	1,450
1914 Commercial, 9mm Luger, Curio	550	1,350
1914 Artillery, 9mm Luger, Curio	550	1,250
1914 Military, 9mm Luger, Curio	450	700
1914 Navy, 9mm Luger, Curio	750	1,300
1918 Spandau, 9mm Luger, Curio	2,900	5,500
1920 Abercrombie & Fitch, .30 Luger and 9mm Luger, Curio	2,500	5,000

Luger 1906 Navy 2nd. Issue

1920 Artillery, 9mm Luger, Curio	600	1,200
1920 Commercial, .30 Luger and 9mm Luger, Curio	350	750
1920 Navy, 9mm Luger, Curio	750	1,700
1920 Simson, 9mm Luger, Curio	400	800
1920 Swiss Commercial, .30 Luger and 9mm Luger, Curio	750	1,300
1920 Swiss Rework, .30 Luger and 9mm Luger, Curio	800	1,400
1920-22 .30 Luger and 9mm Luger, Curio	350	700
1921 Krieghoff, .30 Luger, Curio	600	1,300
1923 Arabian, .30 Luger, Curio	400	800
1923 Commercial, .30 Luger and 9mm Luger, Curio	350	950
1923 Commercial Krieghoff, 9mm Luger, Curio	500	950
1923 Commercial "Safe-Loaded," .30 Luger and 9mm Luger, Curio	500	1,300
1923 Dutch, 9mm Luger, Curio	550	950
1923 Russian, .30 Luger, Curio	1,100	2,400
1923 Simson Commercial, 9mm Luger, Curio	500	1,700
1923 Simson Military, 9mm Luger, Curio	750	1,900
1923 Stoeger, .30 Luger and 9mm Luger, Curio	2,400	4,500
1924 Bern, .30 Luger, Curio	1,000	2,000
1924-7 Simson, 9mm Luger, Curio	700	1,900
1929 Bern, .30 Luger and 9mm Luger, Curio	1,000	3,000
1929-33 Riff, 9mm Luger, Curio	400	800
1929-33 Sneak, 9mm Luger, Curio	450	900
1930-33 Death Head, 9mm Luger, Curio	600	1,100
1933 Finnish Army, 9mm Luger, Curio	550	1,600
1933 K.I., 9mm Luger, Curio	600	1,200
1933 Stoeger, .30 Luger and 9mm Luger, Curio	3,000	5,000
1933-35 Dutch, 9mm Luger, Curio	950	1,800
1933-35 Mauser Commercial, 9mm Luger, Curio	900	1,800
1934 P Commercial, Krieghoff, .30 Luger and 9mm Luger, Curio	1,200	2,800
1934 P Commercial, Krieghoff, 9mm Luger, Curio	1,200	2,400
1934 Sideframe, Krieghoff, 6" Barrel, 9mm Luger, Curio	3,000	6,500
1934 Sideframe, 9mm Luger, Krieghoff, 6" Barrel, Curio	2,500	4,500
1934 Simson, 9mm Luger, Curio	850	1,400
1935 Portuguese, .30 Luger, Curio	600	950
1936 Persian, 9mm Luger, Curio	3,500	7,500
1936-37, 9mm Luger, Krieghoff, Curio	850	2,000
1936-39, .30 Luger and 9mm Luger, 4" Barrel, Curio	450	900
1936-40 Dutch Banner, 9mm Luger, Curio	600	1,300
1936-9 S/42, 9mm Luger, Curio	450	750
1937-39 Banner Commercial, .30 Luger, 4" Barrel, Curio	1,200	2,000
1938, 9mm Luger, Krieghoff, Curio	2,200	3,500
1939-40 42, 9mm Luger, Curio	350	500
1940, 9mm Luger, Krieghoff, Curio	850	1,700
1940 42/42 BYF, 9mm Luger, Curio	500	1,750
1940 Mauser Banner, .30 Luger and 9mm Luger, Curio	550	1,200
1940-1 S/42, 9mm Luger, Curio	550	900
1941-2 BYF, 9mm Luger, Curio	350	600
1941-4, 9mm Luger, Krieghoff, Curio	1,500	2,400
1945, 9mm Luger, Krieghoff, Curio	2,500	4,000
36, 9mm Luger, Krieghoff, Curio	850	1,800
41 & 42 Banner, 9mm Luger, Curio	550	950
42/41, 9mm Luger, Curio	600	950
Artillery, Stock Only, Curio	175	300
Austrian Banner, 9mm Luger, Curio	500	950
Banner Commercial, .30 Luger, 4" Barrel, Curio	1,300	1,800
Bulgarian, .30 Luger, Curio	4,000	6,000
Cutaway, 9mm Luger, Curio	1,500	3,500
Double Date, 9mm Luger, Curio	400	850
Engraved, Original, 9mm Luger, Curio	3,000	5,500
Finnish Prison, .30 Luger and 9mm Luger, Curio	3,000	5,000
G-S/42, 9mm Luger, Curio	600	1,200
G-S/42, DWM, 9mm Luger, Curio	700	1,400

Luger, 1935 Portuguese, .30 Luger

Luger Mauser Parabellum Swiss .30 Luger

G.L. Baby, 9mm Luger, Curio		35,000
Ideal, Holster Stock, Curio	300	550
K U, 9mm Luger, Curio	650	1,300
K-S/42, 9mm Luger, Curio	800	1,400
K-S/42 Navy, 9mm Luger, Curio	1,200	2,300
Mauser Banner Commercial, 9mm Luger, Curio	700	1,200
Mauser Parabellum PO 8, .30 Luger, 6" Barrel, Grip Safety, Modern	375	450
Mauser Parabellum PO 8, .30 Luger, 4" Barrel, Grip Safety, Modern	400	500
Mauser Parabellum PO 8, 9mm Luger, Various Barrel Lengths, Grip Safety, Modern	375	450
Mauser Parabellum Swiss, .30 Luger, 6" Barrel, Grip Safety, Modern	300	400
Mauser Parabellum Swiss, 9mm Luger, 4" Barrel, Grip Safety, Modern	300	400
Mauser Parabellum Bulgarian, .30 Luger, Grip Safety, Commemorative, Modern	1,000	1,800
Mauser Parabellum Russian, .30 Luger, Grip Safety, Commemorative, Modern	1,000	1,800
Mauser Parabellum Kriegsmarine, 9mm Luger, Grip Safety, Commemorative, Modern	2,000	3,000
Mauser Parabellum Sport, .30 or 9mm Luger, Heavy Barrel, Target Sights, Modern	800	1,400
Navy, Stock Only, Curio	250	700
Post War, 9mm Luger, Krieghoff, Curio	850	2,000
S/42 Navy, 9mm Luger, Curio	550	1,350
Snail Drum, Magazine, Curio	200	375
Stoeger (New) STLR, .22 L.R.R.F., Clip Fed, Modern	50	75
Stoeger (New) TLR, .22 L.R.R.F., Clip Fed, Adjustable Sights, Modern	65	100

Turkish, 9mm Luger, Curio	7,000	12,000
U.S. Test Eagle, .30 Luger, Curio	1,400	2,500
Vickers Commercial, 9mm Luger, Curio	1,500	2,500
Vickers Military, 9mm Luger, Curio	750	1,700

Lyman Gun Sight Corp

Handgun, Percussion

.36 1851 Navy, Color Case Hardened Frame, Engraved Cylinder, Reproduction, Antique	65	95
.36 New Model Navy, Brass Trigger Guard, Solid Frame, Reproduction, Antique	55	85
.44 1860 Army, Color Case Hardened Frame, Engraved Cylinder, Reproduction, Antique	70	95
.44 New Model Army, Brass Trigger Guard, Solid Frame, Reproduction, Antique	70	95

Rifle, Flintlock

Plains Rifle, Various Calibers, Brass Furniture, Set Trigger, Reproduction, Antique	150	215

Rifle, Percussion

Plains Rifle, Various Calibers, Brass Furniture, Set Trigger, Reproduction, Antique	120	175
Trade Rifle, Various Calibers, Brass Furniture, Set Trigger, Reproduction, Antique	100	150

Rifle, Singleshot

Centennial, 45/70 Government, Ruger #1, Commemorative, Cased with Accessories, Modern	900	1,400

MAB
Mre. d'Armes Automatiques Bayonne, France

Handgun, Semi-Automatic
Nazi Proofs Add 20%-30%
Nazi Navy Proofs Add 40%-50%

Modele A, .25 ACP, Clip Fed, Modern	80	125
Modele B, .25 ACP, Clip Fed, Modern	125	180
Modele C, .32 ACP, Clip Fed, Modern	95	150
Modele C, .380 ACP, Clip Fed; Modern	120	180
Modele C/D, .32 ACP, Clip Fed, Modern	90	135
Modele C/D, .380 ACP, Clip Fed, Modern	95	145
Modele D, .32 ACP, Clip Fed, Modern	80	120
Modele D, .380 ACP, Clip Fed, Modern	90	135
Modele E, .25 ACP, Clip Fed, Long Grip, Modern	120	185
Modele F, .22 L.R.R.F., Clip Fed, Hammer, Modern	120	185
Modele G, .22 L.R.R.F., Clip Fed, Modern	80	125
Modele GZ, .22 L.R.R.F., Clip Fed, Blue, Modern	100	140
Modele GZ, .22 L.R.R.F., Clip Fed, Green, Modern	110	150
Modele GZ, .25 ACP, Clip Fed, Modern	120	160
Modele Le Chasseur, .22 L.R.R.F., Clip Fed, Hammer, Target Grips, Modern	125	175
Modele PA-15, 9mm Luger, Clip Fed, Hammer, Modern	200	275
Modele R (P 15), 9mm Luger, Clip Fed, Hammer, Curio	200	275
Modele R Curt, .32 ACP, Clip Fed, Hammer, Modern	150	225
Modele R Long, 7.65 MAS, Clip Fed, Hammer, Modern	140	200

M.A.C. (Military Armament Corp)
Georgia, see Ingram. Also See Ruger and Remington for Silenced Adaptations.

Automatic Weapon, Assault Rifle

M16-M.A.C.,.22 L.R.R.F., Clip Fed, Conversion Unit Only, Class 3	75	110

MAB Model B

MAB Model D

MAB Model E

MAB Model F

MAB Model GZ

Automatic Weapon, Submachine Gun

M-10 M A C, .45 ACP, Clip Fed, Folding Stock, Commercial, Class 3	125	175
M-10 M A C, .45 ACP, Clip Fed, Folding Stock, Commercial, Silencer, Class 3	200	275
M-10 M A C, 9 mm Luger, Clip Fed, Folding Stock, Commercial, Class 3	125	175
M-10 M A C, 9 mm Luger, Clip Fed, Folding Stock, Commercial, Silencer, Class 3	200	275
M-11 M A C, .380 ACP, Clip Fed, Folding Stock, Commercial, Class 3	300	375
M-11 M A C, .380 ACP, Clip Fed, Folding Stock, Commercial, Silencer, Class 3	400	500

Handgun, Semi-Automatic

Model 200 S.A.P., 9mm Luger, Clip Fed, Modern	170	250

Rifle, Bolt Action

Model 40-XB Sniper (MAC), .308 Win., Heavy Barrel, Scope Mounted, Silencer, Class 3	500	700

Macloed
Doune, Scotland 1711-50

Handgun, Flintlock

.54, All Steel, Engraved, Ram's Horn Butt, Antique	1,800	2,500

Maltby-Curtis
Agent for Norwich Pistol Co. 1875-81

Handgun, Revolver

.22 Short R.F., 7 Shot, Spur Trigger, Solid Frame, Single Action, Antique	90	160
.32 Short R.F., 5 Shot, Spur Trigger, Solid Frame, Single Action, Antique	95	170

Maltby-Henley & Co.
N.Y.C. 1878-1889 Made by Columbia Armory, Tenn.

Handgun, Revolver

.22 L.R.R.F., 7 Shot, Double Action, Hammerless, Top Break, Modern	55	95
.32 S & W, 5 Shot, Top Break, Hammerless, Double Action, Modern	55	95
.38 S & W, 5 Shot, Top Break, Hammerless, Double Action, Modern	55	95

M & N Corp.

Handgun, Repeater

C.O.P., .357 Mag., 4 Shot, Stainless Steel, Modern	135	180

Manhattan Firearms Mfg. Co.
N.Y.C. & Newark, N.J. 1849-64

Handgun, Percussion

Hero, Singleshot, Derringer, Antique	90	160
Bar Hammer, Double Action, Screw Barrel, Singleshot, Antique	120	190
Pepperbox, .28, 3 Shot, Double Action, Antique	175	400
Pepperbox, .28, 6 Shot, Double Action, Antique	150	275
Revolver, .36, Navy Model, Single Action, Antique	225	400
Revolver, .36, Pocket Model, Single Action, Antique	150	275

Mann
Germany C.1900

Handgun, Semi-Automatic

Model Wt, .25 ACP, Clip Fed, Modern	120	200
Pocket, .32 ACP, Clip Fed, Modern	150	235
Pocket, .380 ACP, Clip Fed, Modern	180	275

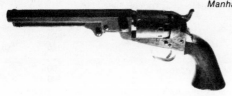

Manhattan .36 Model

Mann .32 ACP

Mann, Michel
Uhlenberg, C.1630

Handgun, Wheel-Lock
Miniature, All Metal, Gold Damascened, Ball Pommel, Antique   1,500   2,500

Mannlicher-Schoenauer

Rifle, Double Barrel, Over-Under
Safari 72, .375 H & H Mag., Checkered Stock, Engraved, Double Trigger,
   Modern   2,250   3,000
Safari 77, Various Calibers, Checkered Stock, Engraved, Double Trigger,
   Automatic Ejector, Modern   3,250   4,000

Rifle, Bolt Action
Alpine, Various Caliber, Sporting Rifle, Full-Stocked, Modern   325   425
Custom M-S, Various Calibers, Sporting Rifle, Scope Mounted, Carbine,
   Modern   350   600
Custom M-S, Various Calibers, Sporting Rifle, Scope Mounted, Modern   350   600
High Velocity, Various Calibers, Sporting Rifle, Set Trigger, Modern   450   700
High Velocity, Various Calibers, Sporting Rifle, Takedown, Set Trigger,
   Modern   475   750
M-72 LM, Various Calibers, Sporting Rifle, Full-Stocked, Modern   350   650
M-72 S, Various Calibers, Sporting Rifle, Modern   400   700
M-72 T, Various Calibers, Sporting Rifle, Modern   450   750
Magnum M-S, Various Calibers, Sporting Rifle, Monte Carlo Stock, Set
   Trigger, Modern   450   750
MCA, Various Calibers, Sporting Rifle, Carbine, Monte Carlo Stock,
   Modern   500   800
MCA, Various Calibers, Sporting Rifle, Monte Carlo Stock, Modern   500   800
Model 1903, Various Calibers, Sporting Rifle, Carbine, Set Trigger, Full-
   Stocked, Modern   475   700
Model 1905, 9 x 56 M.S., Sporting Rifle, Carbine, Set Trigger, Full-
   Stocked, Modern   400   650
Model 1908, Various Calibers, Sporting Rifle, Carbine, Set Trigger, Full-
   Stocked, Modern   375   625
Model 1910, 9.5 x 57 M.S., Sporting Rifle, Carbine, Set Trigger, Full-
   Stocked, Modern   400   650
Model 1924, .30-06 Springfield, Sporting Rifle, Carbine, Set Trigger, Full-
   Stocked, Modern   500   850
Model 1950, 6.5 x 54 M.S., Sporting Rifle, Carbine, Set Trigger, Full-
   Stocked, Modern   350   600
Model 1950, Various Calibers, Sporting Rifle, Set Trigger, Modern   375   650
Model 1950, Various Calibers, Sporting Rifle, Carbine, Set Trigger, Full-
   Stocked, Modern   375   650
Model 1952, 6.5 x 54 M.S., Sporting Rifle, Carbine, Set Trigger, Full-
   Stocked, Modern   350   650

Model 1952, Various Calibers, Sporting Rifle, Carbine, Set Trigger, Full-Stocked, Modern	350	650
Model 1952, Various Calibers, Sporting Rifle, Set Trigger, Modern	350	650
Model 1956, Various Calibers, Sporting Rifle, Carbine, Set Trigger, Full-Stocked, Modern	350	650
Model 1956, Various Calibers, Sporting Rifle, Set Trigger, Modern	350	650
Premier, Various Calibers, Sporting Rifle, Magnum Action, Fancy Checkering, Engraved, Modern	650	1,000
Premier, Various Calibers, Sporting Rifle, Fancy Checkering, Engraved, Modern	450	600
Model SSG, .308 Win., Synthetic Target Stock, Set Triggers, Modern	275	400
Model SSG Match, .308 Win., Synthetic Target Stock, Set Triggers, Walther Peep Sights, Modern	375	525
Model ML 79, Various Calibers, Checkered Stock, Set Trigger, Modern	400	600
Model L Varmint, Various Calibers, Checkered Stock, Set Trigger, Modern	275	400
Model M, Various Calibers, Checkered Stock, Set Trigger, Modern	300	475
Model M Professional, Various Calibers, Checkered Stock, Set Trigger, Modern	200	300
Model S/T Magnum, Various Calibers, Checkered Stock, Set Trigger, Modern	350	550
Model S, Various Calibers, Checkered Stock, Set Trigger, Modern	350	550

Rifle, Double Barrel, Side by Side

Mustang, Various Calibers, Standard, Checkered Stock, Sidelock, Modern	3,500	5,000
Mustang, Various Calibers, Standard, Checkered Stock, Sidelock, Engraved, Modern	4,000	5,500

Shotgun, Double Barrel, Over-Under

Edinbourgh, 12 Ga., Checkered Stock, Vent Rib, Modern	800	1,200

Shotgun, Double Barrel, Side by Side

Ambassador English, 12 and 20 Gauges, Checkered Stock, Sidelock, Automatic Ejectors, Engraved, Modern	4,500	6,500
Ambassador Extra, 12 and 20 Gauges, Checkered Stock, Sidelock, Automatic Ejectors, Engraved, Modern	4,500	6,500
Ambassador Golden Black, 12 and 20 Gauges, Checkered Stock, Sidelock, Automatic Ejectors, Engraved, Gold Inlays, Modern	5,500	8,500
Ambassador Executive, 12 and 20 Gauges, Checkered Stock, Sidelock, Automatic Ejectors, Fancy Engraving, Modern	10,000	14,000
Oxford Field, 12 and 20 Gauges, Checkered Stock, Automatic Ejectors, Engraved, Modern	700	1,000
London, 12 and 20 Gauges, Checkered Stock, Sidelock, Automatic Ejectors, Engraved, Cased, Modern	1,700	2,200

Manton, J & Co.
Belgium C.1900

Shotgun, Double Barrel, Side by Side

Various Gauges, Outside Hammers, Damascus Barrel, Modern	80	150
Various Gauges, Hammerless, Steel Barrel, Modern	95	175
Various Gauges, Hammerless, Damascus Barrel, Modern	75	150
Various Gauges, Outside Hammers, Steel Barrel, Modern	90	175

Shotgun, Singleshot

Various Gauges, Hammer, Steel Barrel, Modern	45	75

Manton, Joseph
London, England 1795-1835

Handgun, Flintlock

Pair, Octagon Barrel, Duelling Pistols, Gold Inlays, Light Engraving, Cased with Accessories, Antique	3,000	3,750

Handgun, Percussion

.55, Pair, Duelling Pistols, Octagon Barrel, Light Ornamentation, Cased with Accessories, Antique	3,500	4,200

Shotgun, Percussion
12 Ga. Double Barrel, Side by Side, Damascus Barrels, Light Engraving,
Gold Inlays, Antique   350   525

ManuFrance
St. Etienne, France Current

Rifle, Semi-Automatic
Reina, .22 L.R.R.F., Carbine, Clip Fed, Modern   50   80

Rifle, Bolt Action
Club, .22 L.R.R.F., Singleshot, Carbine, Modern   55   85
Buffalo Match, .22 L.R.R.F., Target Rifle, Modern   100   150
Rival, 375 H & H Mag., Checkered Stock, Modern   175   275

Shotgun, Double Barrel, Over-Under
Falcon, 12 Ga., Vent Rib, Automatic Ejector, Single Selective Trigger,
Checkered Stock, Modern   400   550

Shotgun, Semi-Automatic
12 Ga. Mag. 3", Checkered Stock, Modern   200   300

Shotgun, Double Barrel, Side by Side
Robust, 12 Ga. 3", Checkered Stock, Double Triggers, Modern   225   300

Mark X
Made in Zestavia, Yugoslavia Imported by Interarms

Rifle, Bolt Action
Alaskan, Various Calibers, Magnum, Open Rear Sight, Checkered Stock,
Sling Swivels, Modern   190   275
Cavalier, Various Calibers, Cheekpiece, Checkered Stock, Open Rear
Sight, Sling Swivels, Modern   175   260
Mannlicher, Various Calibers, Carbine, Full-Stocked, Checkered Stock,
Open Rear Sight, Sling Swivels, Modern   190   275
Standard, Various Calibers, Checkered Stock, Open Rear Sight, Sling
Swivels, Modern   150   225
Viscount, Various Calibers, Plain, Open Rear Sight, Checkered Stock,
Sling Swivels, Modern   125   175

Markwell Arms Co.

Handgun, Percussion
.41 Derringer, Singleshot, Brass Furniture, Reproduction, Antique   20   30
.44 C S A 1860, Revolver, 6 Shot, Brass Frame, Reproduction, Antique   40   60
.44 New Army, Revolver, 6 Shot, Brass Trigger Guard, Reproduction,
Antique   40   65
.45 Colonial, Singleshot, Brass Furniture, Reproduction, Antique   20   35
.45 Kentucky, Singleshot, Brass Furniture, Reproduction, Antique   30   45
.45 Loyalist, Singleshot, Brass Furniture, Set Trigger, Adjustable Sights,
Reproduction, Antique   45   65

Rifle, Percussion
.45 Hawken, Brass Furniture, Reproduction, Antique   60   90
.45 Kentucky, Brass Furniture, Reproduction, Antique   50   75
.45 Super Kentucky, Brass Furniture, Set Trigger, Reproduction, Antique   70   110

Marlin Firearms Co.
*New Haven, Conn. J. M. Marlin from 1870-81. Marlin Firearms from 1881-1915 Marlin-
Rockwell Corp. 1915-1926. From 1926 to Date as Marlin Firearms Co. Also See
Ballard*

Automatic Weapon, Heavy Machine Gun
M1906 Marlin, .30-06 Springfield, Belt Fed, Tripod, Potato Digger, Military,
Class 3   1,500   2,000
M1906 Marlin, .303 British, Belt Fed, Tripod, Potato Digger, Military,
Class 3   1,300   1,800

Marlin XX Standard 1873

M1906 Marlin, .308 Win., Belt Fed, Tripod, Potato Digger, Military, Class 3	1,300	1,800
M1917 Marlin, .30-06 Springfield, Belt Fed, Tripod, Potato Digger, Military, Class 3	1,500	2,000

Handgun, Revolver

Standard 1875, .30 R.F., Tip Up, Spur Trigger, Antique	90	150
XX Standard 1873, .22 R.F., Tip Up, Spur Trigger, Antique	90	160
XX Standard 1873, .22 R.F., Tip Up, Spur Trigger, Octagon Barrel, Antique	95	180
XXX Standard 1872, .30 R.F., Tip Up, Spur Trigger, Antique	90	160
XXX Standard 1872, .30 R.F., Tip Up, Spur Trigger, Octagon Barrel, Antique	95	180
Model 1887, .32 and .38, Double Action, Top Break, Antique	65	140

Rifle, Bolt Action

Glenfield M10, .22 L.R.R.F., Singleshot, Modern	15	30
Glenfield M20, .22 L.R.R.F., Clip Fed, Modern	20	35
Model 100, .22 L.R.R.F., Singleshot, Open Rear Sight, Takedown, Modern	20	30
Model 100-S, .22 L.R.R.F., Singleshot, Peep Sights, Takedown, Modern	35	55
Model 100-SB, .22 L.R.R.F., Singleshot, Smoothbore, Takedown, Modern	20	30
Model 101, .22 L.R.R.F., Singleshot, Open Rear Sight, Takedown, Beavertail Forend, Modern	20	35
Model 101-DL, .22 L.R.R.F., Singleshot, Takedown, Peep Sights, Beavertail Forend, Modern	25	35
Model 122, .22 L.R.R.F., Singleshot, Open Rear Sight, Monte Carlo Stock, Modern	20	35
Model 322 (Sako), .222 Rem., Clip Fed, Peep Sights, Checkered Stock, Modern	150	250
Model 455 (FN), Various Calibers, Peep Sights, Monte Carlo Stock, Checkered Stock, Modern	150	250
Model 65, .22 L.R.R.F., Singleshot, Open Rear Sight, Modern	20	35
Model 65E, .22 L.R.R.F., Singleshot, Peep Sights, Modern	20	35
Model 780, .22 L.R.R.F., Clip Fed, Open Rear Sight, Modern	30	45
Model 781, .22 L.R.R.F., Tube Feed, Open Rear Sight, Modern	30	45
Model 782, .22 WMR, Clip Fed, Open Rear Sight, Modern	30	50
Model 783, .22 WMR, Tube Feed, Open Rear Sight, Modern	30	50
Model 80, .22 L.R.R.F., Clip Fed, Open Rear Sight, Takedown, Modern	25	40
Model 80 DL, .22 L.R.R.F., Clip Fed, Beavertail Forend, Takedown, Peep Sights, Modern	30	45
Model 80C, .22 L.R.R.F., Clip Fed, Beavertail Forend, Takedown, Open Rear Sight, Modern	30	45
Model 80E, .22 L.R.R.F., Clip Fed, Peep Sights, Takedown, Modern	25	40
Model 81, .22 L.R.R.F., Tube Feed, Takedown, Open Rear Sight, Modern	35	50

Marlin Model 101

Marlin Model 781

Marlin Model 782

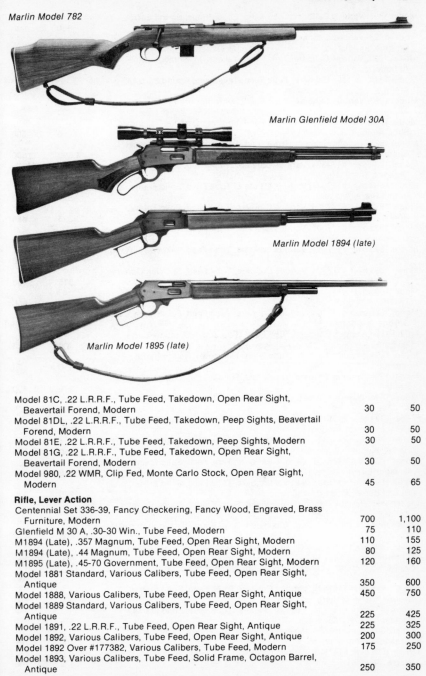

Marlin Glenfield Model 30A

Marlin Model 1894 (late)

Marlin Model 1895 (late)

Model 81C, .22 L.R.R.F., Tube Feed, Takedown, Open Rear Sight, Beavertail Forend, Modern	30	50
Model 81DL, .22 L.R.R.F., Tube Feed, Takedown, Peep Sights, Beavertail Forend, Modern	30	50
Model 81E, .22 L.R.R.F., Tube Feed, Takedown, Peep Sights, Modern	30	50
Model 81G, .22 L.R.R.F., Tube Feed, Takedown, Open Rear Sight, Beavertail Forend, Modern	30	50
Model 980, .22 WMR, Clip Fed, Monte Carlo Stock, Open Rear Sight, Modern	45	65

Rifle, Lever Action

Centennial Set 336-39, Fancy Checkering, Fancy Wood, Engraved, Brass Furniture, Modern	700	1,100
Glenfield M 30 A, .30-30 Win., Tube Feed, Modern	75	110
M1894 (Late), .357 Magnum, Tube Feed, Open Rear Sight, Modern	110	155
M1894 (Late), .44 Magnum, Tube Feed, Open Rear Sight, Modern	80	125
M1895 (Late), .45-70 Government, Tube Feed, Open Rear Sight, Modern	120	160
Model 1881 Standard, Various Calibers, Tube Feed, Open Rear Sight, Antique	350	600
Model 1888, Various Calibers, Tube Feed, Open Rear Sight, Antique	450	750
Model 1889 Standard, Various Calibers, Tube Feed, Open Rear Sight, Antique	225	425
Model 1891, .22 L.R.R.F., Tube Feed, Open Rear Sight, Antique	225	325
Model 1892, Various Calibers, Tube Feed, Open Rear Sight, Antique	200	300
Model 1892 Over #177382, Various Calibers, Tube Feed, Modern	175	250
Model 1893, Various Calibers, Tube Feed, Solid Frame, Octagon Barrel, Antique	250	350

Model 1893, Various Calibers, Tube Feed, Solid Frame, Round Barrel, Antique 200	300	
Model 1893, Various Calibers, Tube Feed, Solid Frame, Round Barrel, Carbine, Antique	350	450
Model 1893, Various Calibers, Tube Feed, Takedown, Octagon Barrel, Antique	325	450
Model 1893, Various Calibers, Tube Feed, Takedown, Round Barrel, Antique	275	400
Model 1893, Various Calibers, Tube Feed, Sporting Carbine, 5 Shot, Antique	400	550
Model 1893, Various Calibers, Tube Feed, Sporting Carbine, Takedown, 5 Shot, Antique	450	600
Model 1893, Various Calibers, Tube Feed, Full-Stocked, with Bayonet, Antique	1,500	2,500
Model 1893 over #177304, Various Calibers, Tube Feed, Solid Frame, Octagon Barrel, Modern	250	375
Model 1893 over #177304, Various Calibers, Tube Feed, Solid Frame, Round Barrel, Modern	200	300
Model 1893 over #177304, Various Calibers, Tube Feed, Solid Frame, Round Barrel, Carbine, Modern	325	425
Model 1893 over #177304, Various Calibers, Tube Feed, Takedown, Octagon Barrel, Modern	300	400
Model 1893 over #177304, Various Calibers, Tube Feed, Takedown, Round Barrel, Modern	225	300
Model 1893 over #177304, Various Calibers, Tube Feed, Sporting Carbine, 5 Shot, Modern	325	400
Model 1893 over #177304, Various Calibers, Tube Feed, Sporting Carbine, Takedown, 5 Shot, Modern	400	550
Model 1893 over #177304, Various Calibers, Tube Feed, Full-Stocked, with Bayonet, Modern	1,400	2,500
Model 1894, Various Calibers, Tube Feed, Takedown, Octagon Barrel, Antique	400	525
Model 1894, Various Calibers, Tube Feed, Takedown, Round Barrel, Antique	350	450
Model 1894, Various Calibers, Tube Feed, Solid Frame, Octagon Barrel, Antique	275	400
Model 1894, Various Calibers, Tube Feed, Solid Frame, Round Barrel, Antique	250	325
Model 1894 over #175431, Various Calibers, Tube Feed, Takedown, Octagon Barrel, Modern	400	525
Model 1894 over #175431, Various Calibers, Tube Feed, Takedown, Round Barrel, Modern	250	350
Model 1894 over #175431, Various Calibers, Tube Feed, Solid Frame, Octagon Barrel, Modern	250	350
Model 1894 over #175431, Various Calibers, Tube Feed, Solid Frame, Round Barrel, Modern	225	300
Model 1895, Various Calibers, Tube Feed, Solid Frame, Round Barrel, Antique	450	725
Model 1895, Various Calibers, Tube Feed, Solid Frame, Octagon Barrel, Antique	400	675
Model 1895, Various Calibers, Tube Feed, Takedown, Octagon Barrel, Antique	450	800
Model 1895, Various Calibers, Tube Feed, Takedown, Round Barrel, Antique	425	800
Model 1895 over #167531, Various Calibers, Tube Feed, Solid Frame, Round Barrel, Modern	300	600
Model 1895 over #167531, Various Calibers, Tube Feed, Solid Frame, Octagon Barrel, Modern	375	650
Model 1895 over #167531, Various Calibers, Tube Feed, Takedown, Octagon Barrel, Modern	400	725
Model 1895 over #167531, Various Calibers, Tube Feed, Takedown, Round Barrel, Modern	375	700

Marlin Model 1897 .22

Marlin Model 336C

Marlin Model 336T

Model 1897, .22 L.R.R.F., Tube Feed, Takedown, Antique	200	300
Model 1897 over #177197, .22 L.R.R.F., Tube Feed, Takedown, Modern	175	275
Model 336, .219 Zipper, Tube Feed, Sporting Carbine, Open Rear Sight, 5 Shot, Modern	150	250
Model 336, Various Calibers, Tube Feed, Sporting Carbine, Open Rear Sight, 5 Shot, Modern	85	125
Model 336 Marauder, Various Calibers, Tube Feed, Carbine, Open Rear Sight, Straight Grip, Modern	140	225
Model 336 Zane Grey, .30-30 Win., Tube Feed, Octagon Barrel, Open Rear Sight, Modern	125	200
Model 336A, Various Calibers, Tube Feed, Sporting Rifle, Open Rear Sight, 5 Shot, Modern	80	125
Model 336A-DL, Various Calibers, Tube Feed, Sporting Rifle, Open Rear Sight, 5 Shot, Checkered Stock, Modern	95	145
Model 336C, Various Calibers, Tube Feed, Carbine, Open Rear Sight, Modern	75	120
Model 336T, .44 Magnum, Tube Feed, Carbine, Open Rear Sight, Straight Grip, Modern	100	150
Model 336T, Various Calibers, Tube Feed, Carbine, Open Rear Sight, Straight Grip, Modern	75	120
Model 36, Various Calibers, Tube Feed, Beavertail Forend, Open Rear Sight, Carbine, Modern	125	180
Model 36, Various Calibers, Tube Feed, Beavertail Forend, Open Rear Sight, Sporting Carbine, 5 Shot, Modern	125	180
Model 36A, Various Calibers, Tube Feed, Beavertail Forend, Open Rear Sight, 5 Shot, Modern	125	180
Model 36DL, Various Calibers, Tube Feed, Fancy Checkering, Open Rear Sight, 5 Shot, Modern	150	225
Model 39, .22 L.R.R.F., Takedown, Tube Feed, Hammer, Octagon Barrel, Modern	150	235
Model 39 Article II, .22 L.R.R.F., Takedown, Tube Feed, Hammer, Octagon Barrel, Modern	125	190

Marlin Model 39M

Marlin Model 444

Marlin Model 57M

Model 39 Article II, .22 L.R.R.F., Takedown, Tube Feed, Hammer, Octagon Barrel, Carbine, Modern	125	190
Model 39 Century, .22 L.R.R.F., Takedown, Tube Feed, Hammer, Octagon Barrel, Modern	125	185
Model 39 M, .22 L.R.R.F., Takedown, Tube Feed, Hammer, Round Barrel, Carbine, Modern	70	110
Model 39A, .22 L.R.R.F., Takedown, Tube Feed, Hammer, Round Barrel, Modern	70	110
Model 39A Mountie, .22 L.R.R.F., Takedown, Tube Feed, Hammer, Round Barrel, Modern	75	115
Model 444, .444 Marlin, Tube Feed, Monte Carlo Stock, Open Rear Sight, Straight Grip, Modern	100	140
Model 56, .22 L.R.R.F., Clip Fed, Open Rear Sight, Monte Carlo Stock, Modern	40	65
Model 57, .22 L.R.R.F., Tube Feed, Open Rear Sight, Monte Carlo Stock, Modern	45	65
Model 57M, .22 WMR, Tube Feed, Open Rear Sight, Monte Carlo Stock, Modern	50	75
Model 62, Various Calibers, Clip Fed, Open Rear Sight, Monte Carlo Stock, Modern	75	125

Marlin Glenfield Model 60

Marlin Model 99C

Rifle, Semi-Automatic

Glenfield M40, .22 L.R.R.F., Tube Feed, Modern	35	50
Glenfield M60, .22 L.R.R.F., Tube Feed, Modern	25	40
Model 49 DL, .22 L.R.R.F., Tube Feed, Open Rear Sight, Modern	30	50
Model 50, .22 L.R.R.F., Clip Fed, Open Rear Sight, Takedown, Modern	30	50
Model 50E, .22 L.R.R.F., Clip Fed, Peep Sights, Takedown, Modern	30	50
Model 88C, .22 L.R.R.F., Tube Feed, Takedown, Open Rear Sight, Modern	35	50
Model 88DL, .22 L.R.R.F., Tube Feed, Takedown, Peep Sights, Modern	35	55
Model 89 DL, .22 L.R.R.F., Clip Fed, Takedown, Peep Sights, Modern	35	55
Model 89C, .22 L.R.R.F., Clip Fed, Takedown, Open Rear Sight, Modern	35	55
Model 98, .22 L.R.R.F., Tube Feed, Solid Frame, Open Rear Sight, Monte Carlo Stock, Modern	35	55
Model 989, .22 L.R.R.F., Clip Fed, Open Rear Sight, Monte Carlo Stock, Modern	35	50
Model 989 G, .22 L.R.R.F., Clip Fed, Open Rear Sight, Monte Carlo Stock, Modern	35	55
Model 990, .22 L.R.R.F., Tube Feed, Open Rear Sight, Monte Carlo Stock, Modern	35	55
Model 995, .22 L.R.R.F., Clip Fed, Open Rear Sight, Modern	35	50
Model 99, .22 L.R.R.F., Tube Feed, Open Rear Sight, Modern	30	50
Model 99 M-1, .22 L.R.R.F., Tube Feed, Open Rear Sight, Monte Carlo Stock, Modern	30	45
Model 99 M-2, .22 L.R.R.F., Clip Fed, Open Rear Sight, Modern	30	45
Model 99C, .22 L.R.R.F., Tube Feed, Open Rear Sight, Monte Carlo Stock, Modern	35	45
Model 99DL, .22 L.R.R.F., Tube Feed, Open Rear Sight, Monte Carlo Stock, Modern	35	45
Model A-1, .22 L.R.R.F., Clip Fed, Takedown, Open Rear Sight, Modern	30	45
Model A-1E, .22 L.R.R.F., Clip Fed, Takedown, Peep Sights, Modern	30	45

Rifle, Slide Action

Model 18, .22 L.R.R.F., Solid Frame, Tube Feed, Hammer, Modern	125	200
Model 20, .22 L.R.R.F., Takedown, Tube Feed, Hammer, Octagon Barrel, Modern	120	190
Model 25, .22 Short R.F., Takedown, Tube Feed, Hammer, Modern	150	250
Model 27, Various Calibers, Takedown, Tube Feed, Hammer, Octagon Barrel, Modern	145	230

Model 27-S, Various Calibers, Takedown, Tube Feed, Hammer, Round Barrel, Modern	145	235
Model 29, .22 L.R.R.F., Takedown, Tube Feed, Hammer, Round Barrel, Modern	125	200
Model 32, .22 L.R.R.F., Takedown, Tube Feed, Hammerless, Octagon Barrel, Modern	125	200
Model 38, .22 L.R.R.F., Takedown, Tube Feed, Hammerless, Octagon Barrel, Modern	125	200

Shotgun, Lever Action

Four-Tenner, .410 Ga., Tube Feed, Modern	300	450

Shotgun, Slide Action

Model 1898 Field, 12 Ga., Hammer, Tube Feed, Modern	125	275
Model 1898 B, 12 Ga., Hammer, Tube Feed, Checkered Stock, Modern	150	325
Model 1898 C, 12 Ga., Hammer, Tube Feed, Checkered Stock, Fancy Wood, Light Engraving, Modern	425	675
Model 1898 D, 12 Ga., Hammer, Tube Feed, Checkered Stock, Fancy Wood, Engraved, Modern	800	1,350
Model 19 Field, 12 Ga., Hammer, Tube Feed, Modern	100	225
Model 19 B, 12 Ga., Hammer, Tube Feed, Checkered Stock, Modern	150	325
Model 19 C, 12 Ga., Hammer, Tube Feed, Checkered Stock, Fancy Wood, Light Engraving, Modern	325	475
Model 19 D, 12 Ga., Hammer, Tube Feed, Checkered Stock, Fancy Wood, Engraved, Modern	700	1,000
Model 21 Field, 12 Ga., Hammer, Tube Feed, Modern	100	225
Model 21 B, 12 Ga., Hammer, Tube Feed, Checkered Stock, Modern	150	325
Model 21 C, 12 Ga., Hammer, Tube Feed, Checkered Stock, Fancy Wood, Light Engraving, Modern	325	475
Model 21 D, 12 Ga., Hammer, Tube Feed, Checkered Stock, Fancy Wood, Engraved, Modern	700	1,000
Model 24 Field, 12 Ga., Hammer, Tube Feed, Modern	120	250
Model 24 B, 12 Ga., Hammer, Tube Feed, Checkered Stock, Modern	200	350
Model 24 C, 12 Ga., Hammer, Tube Feed, Checkered Stock, Fancy Wood, Light Engraving, Modern	325	475
Model 24 D, 12 Ga., Hammer, Tube Feed, Checkered Stock, Fancy Wood, Engraved, Modern	700	1,100
Model 16 Field, 12 Ga., Hammer, Tube Feed, Modern	120	250
Model 16 B, 12 Ga., Hammer, Tube Feed, Checkered Stock, Modern	200	350
Model 16 C, 12 Ga., Hammer, Tube Feed, Checkered Stock, Fancy Wood, Light Engraving, Modern	325	475
Model 16 D, 12 Ga., Hammer, Tube Feed, Checkered Stock, Fancy Wood, Engraved, Modern	700	1,100
Model 30 Field, 12 Ga., Hammer, Tube Feed, Modern	120	250
Model 30 B, 12 Ga., Hammer, Tube Feed, Checkered Stock, Modern	200	350
Model 30 C, 12 Ga., Hammer, Tube Feed, Checkered Stock, Fancy Wood, Light Engraving, Modern	325	475
Model 30 D, 12 Ga., Hammer, Tube Feed, Checkered Stock, Fancy Wood, Engraved, Modern	700	1,100
Model 28 Field, 12 Ga., Hammerless, Tube Feed, Modern	140	275
Model 28 B, 12 Ga., Hammerless, Tube Feed, Checkered Stock, Modern	250	400
Model 28 C, 12 Ga., Hammerless, Tube Feed, Checkered Stock, Fancy Wood, Light Engraving, Modern	375	575
Model 28 D, 12 Ga., Hammerless, Tube Feed, Checkered Stock, Fancy Wood, Engraved, Modern	750	1,200
Model 28 Trap, 12 Ga., Hammerless, Tube Feed, Modern	275	400
Model 31 Field, 12 Ga., Hammerless, Tube Feed, Modern	140	275
Model 31 B, 12 Ga., Hammerless, Tube Feed, Checkered Stock, Modern	250	400
Model 31 C, 12 Ga., Hammerless, Tube Feed, Checkered Stock, Fancy Wood, Light Engraving, Modern	375	575
Model 31 D, 12 Ga., Hammerless, Tube Feed, Checkered Stock, Fancy Wood, Engraved, Modern	750	1,200
Model 17 Field, 12 Ga., Hammer, Tube Feed, Modern	140	275

Marlin Model 55 Goose Gun

Model 26 Field, 12 Ga., Hammer, Tube Feed, Modern	140	250
Model 44 Field, 12 Ga., Hammerless, Tube Feed, Modern	140	250
Model 63 Field, 12 Ga., Hammerless, Tube Feed, Modern	130	220
Premier Mark I, 12 Ga., Hammerless, Tube Feed, Modern	90	125
Premier Mark II, 12 Ga., Hammerless, Tube Feed, Modern	110	160
Premier Mark IV, 12 Ga., Hammerless, Tube Feed, Vent Rib, Modern	170	250
Model 120, 12 Ga. 3″, Hammerless, Tube Feed, Modern	100	145
Glenfield Model 778, 12 Ga., Hammerless, Tube Feed, Modern	75	120

Shotgun, Double Barrel, Over-Under

Model 90, 12 and 16 Gauges, Checkered Stock, Double Triggers, Modern	200	325
Model 90, 20 and .410 Gauges, Checkered Stock, Double Triggers, Modern	250	375
Model 90, 12 and 16 Gauges, Checkered Stock, Single Triggers, Modern	250	375
Model 90, 20 and 16 Gauges, Checkered Stock, Single Triggers, Modern	325	450

Shotgun, Bolt Action

Model 55, Various Gauges, Clip Fed, Modern	40	55
Model 55, Various Gauges, Clip Fed, Adjustable Choke, Modern	45	65
Model 55 Goose Gun, 12 Ga. 3″, Clip Fed, Modern	45	65
Model 55, 12 Ga. 3″, Clip Fed, Adjustable Choke, Modern	45	65
Model 55S, 12 Ga. 3″, Clip Fed, Modern	45	65
Model Super Goose, 10 Ga. 3½″, Clip Fed, Modern	75	125
Glenfield 50, 12 Ga. 3″, Clip Fed, Modern	40	60

Marquis of Lorne
Made by Hood Arms Co. Norwich, Conn. C.1880

Handgun, Revolver

.22 Short R.F., 7 Shot, Spur Trigger, Solid Frame, Single Action, Antique	90	160
.32 Short R.F., 5 Shot, Spur Trigger, Solid Frame, Single Action, Antique	95	170

Mars
Spain Unknown Maker C.1920

Handgun, Semi-Automatic

Automat Pistole Mars, .25 ACP, Clip Fed, Modern	125	180

Martian Commercial .25 ACP

Marshwood
Made by Stevens Arms

Shotgun, Double Barrel, Side by Side
M 315, Various Gauges, Hammerless, Steel Barrel, Modern   90   145

Martian
Spain C.1920

Handgun, Semi-Automatic
.25 ACP, Clip Fed, Modern   70   110

Martian Commercial

Handgun, Semi-Automatic
.25 ACP, Clip Fed, Modern   80   110

Martin, Alexander
Glasgow & Aberdeen, Scotland 1922-28

Rifle, Bolt Action
.303 British, Sporting Rifle, Express Sights, Engraved, Fancy Wood,
  Cased, Modern   700   1,000

Massachusetts Arms
Made by Stevens Arms

Shotgun, Double Barrel, Side by Side
Model 311, Various Gauges, Hammerless, Steel Barrel, Modern   90   145

Shotgun, Singleshot
Model 90, Various Gauges, Takedown, Automatic Ejector, Plain, Hammer,
  Modern   35   55
Model 94, Various Gauges, Takedown, Automatic Ejector, Plain, Hammer,
  Modern   35   55

Matchlock Arms
Unknown Maker

Rifle, Matchlock
.45, India Mid-1600's, 4 Shot, Revolving Cylinder, Light Ornamentation,
  Brass Furniture, Antique   1,000   1,500
.57, Jap Full Stock Musket, Octagon Barrel, Silver Inlay, Brass
  Furniture, Antique   350   500

Mauser
*Germany Gebruder Mauser et Cie from 1864-1890. From 1890 to Date is Known As
Mauser Werke. Also See German Military*

Automatic Weapon, Machine-Pistol
M1912, 7.63 Mauser, with Detachable Shoulder Stock, Class 3   600   900

Mauser Zig-Zag 9mm

Mauser HSc .32 ACP

Mauser Model 1896 Conehammer

M1930, 7.63 Mauser, with Detachable Shoulder Stock, Class 3	2,800	3,500
MP1932, 7.63 Mauser, with Detachable Shoulder Stock, Class 3	2,800	3,500
Handgun, Revolver		
M 78 Zig Zag, Tip-Up, Fancy Engraving, Antique	2,800	4,000
M 78 Zig Zag, 9mm Mauser, Tip-Up, Antique	1,000	1,800
M 78 Zig Zag, 10.6mm, Tip-Up, Antique	1,900	2,500
M 78 Zig Zag, 7.6mm, Tip-Up, Antique	1,500	2,200
Handgun, Semi-Automatic		
Chinese Shansei, .45 ACP, With Shoulder Stock, Curio	3,250	4,300
HSC, .32 ACP, Pre-War, Nazi-Proofed, Commercial, Modern	190	275
HSC, .32 ACP, Post-War, Blue, Modern	135	175
HSC, .32 ACP, Nickel Plated, Post-War, Modern	140	200
HSC, .380 ACP, Blue, Post-War, Modern	145	200
HSC, .380 ACP, Nickel Plated, Post-War, Modern	165	225
HSC 1 of 5,000, .380 ACP, Blue, Post-War, Cased, Modern	165	220
HSC Navy, .32 ACP, Nazi-Proofed, Curio	275	375
HSC NSDAP SA, .32 ACP, Nazi-Proofed, Curio	300	425
HSC Police, .32 ACP, Nazi-Proofed, Curio	225	300
M 1896, 7.63 Mauser, 10 Shot, Conehammer, Curio	900	1,500
M 1896, 7.63 Mauser, 10 Shot, With Loading Lever, Curio	750	1,300
M 1896, 7.63 Mauser, Conehammer, With Shoulder Stock, Curio	1,300	2,000

M 1896, 7.63 Mauser, With Loading Lever, With Shoulder Stock, Curio	950	1,700
M 1896, 7.63 Mauser, with Loading Lever, Transitional, Curio	800	1,200
M 1896, 7.63 Mauser, Slabside, Curio	600	950
M 1896 (Early), 7.63 Mauser, Small Ring, Curio	600	950
M 1896 Italian, 7.63 Mauser, Slabside, Curio	1,100	1,500
M 1896 Shallow Mill, 7.63 Mauser, With Loading Lever, Curio	750	1,100
M 1896 Turkish, 7.63 Mauser, Conehammer, Curio	1,400	2,000
M 1912, .45 ACP, Clip Fed, Modern	3,500	4,500
M 1921, .45 ACP, Clip Fed, Modern	1,800	2,500
M 1921, 9mm Luger, Clip Fed, Modern	2,700	3,500
M 1895, 7.65 Borchardt, Antique	1,800	2,500
M 1896, 6-Shot Model Add 75%-100%		
M 1896, 20-Shot Model Add 50%-80%		
M 1896, 40-Shot Model Add 100%		
M 1896, Factory Engraving Add 300%		
M 1896, Original Holster Stock Add 20%-35%		
M 1896, 7.63 Mauser, Pre-War, Commercial, Curio	550	800
M 1896 1920 Police, 7.63 Mauser, Curio	450	750
M 1896 Banner, 7.63 Mauser, Curio	700	1,000
M 1896 Bolo, 7.63 Mauser, Post-War, Curio	700	1,000
M 1896 French Police, 7.63 Mauser, Curio	1,100	1,500
M 1896 Persian, 7.63 Mauser, Curio	1,250	1,700
M 1896 WW I, 7.63 Mauser, Commercial, Curio	450	700
M 1896 WW I, 7.63 Mauser, Military, Curio	400	650
M 1896 WW I, 9mm Luger, Military, Curio	450	750
M 1906/08, 7.63 Mauser, Clip Fed, Modern	2,200	3,000
M 1910, .25 ACP, Clip Fed, Modern	170	250
M 1912, 9mm Luger, Clip Fed, Modern	1,850	2,500
M 1914, .32 ACP, Clip Fed, Modern	190	275
M 1914 Navy, .32 ACP, Clip Fed, Curio	325	400
M 1930, 7.63 Mauser, Commercial, Curio	600	900
M 1930, 9mm Luger, Commercial, Curio	550	850
M 1934, .32 ACP, Clip Fed, Modern	175	250
M 1934 Navy, .32 ACP, Clip Fed, Curio	275	350
M 1934 Police, .32 ACP, Clip Fed, Curio	250	325
Model Nickl HSV, 9mm Luger, Clip Fed, Modern	3,000	3,800
Parabellum PO 8, .30 Luger, 6" Barrel, Grip Safety, Modern	375	450
Parabellum PO 8, .30 Luger, 4" Barrel, Grip Safety, Modern	400	500
Parabellum PO 8, 9mm Luger, Various Barrel Lengths, Grip Safety, Modern	375	450
Parabellum Swiss, .30 Luger, 6" Barrel, Grip Safety, Modern	300	400
Parabellum Swiss, 9mm Luger, 4" Barrel, Grip Safety, Modern	300	400
Parabellum Bulgarian, .30 Luger, Grip Safety, Commemorative, Modern	1,000	1,800
Parabellum Russian, .30 Luger, Grip Safety, Commemorative, Modern	1,000	1,800
Parabellum Kriegsmarine, 9mm Luger, Grip Safety, Commemorative, Modern	2,000	3,000
Parabellum Sport, .30 or 9mm Luger, Heavy Barrel, Target Sights, Modern	800	1,400
W T P, .25 ACP, Clip Fed, Modern	175	250
W T P 2, .25 ACP, Clip Fed, Modern	250	325

Mauser Model 1896/1920 Police

Mauser Model 1896 WW I 9mm with Holster
Stock

Mauser Model 1914 .32 ACP

Rifle, Bolt Action

Various Calibers, Sporting Rifle, Set Trigger, Pre-WWI, Short Action, Modern	425	550
Various Calibers, Sporting Rifle, Set Trigger, Pre-WWI, Carbine, Full-Stocked, Modern	425	550
Various Calibers, Sporting Rifle, Pre-WWI, Military, Commercial, Modern	325	450
Model 10 Varminter, .22-250, Post-War, Heavy Barrel, Monte Carlo Stock, Checkered Stock, Modern	200	325
Model 2000, Various Calibers, Post-War, Monte Carlo Stock, Checkered Stock, Modern	200	300
Model 3000, Various Calibers, Post-War, Monte Carlo Stock, Modern	250	350
Model 3000, Various Calibers, Post-War, Left-Hand, Monte Carlo Stock, Checkered Stock, Modern	250	365
Model 3000, Various Calibers, Post-War, Magnum Action, Monte Carlo Stock, Checkered Stock, Modern	250	365
Model 3000, Various Calibers, Post-War, Left-Hand, Magnum Action, Monte Carlo Stock, Checkered Stock, Modern	260	375
Model 4000, Various Calibers, Varmint, Fancy Checkering, Flared, Modern	240	350
Model 660, Various Calibers, Post-War, Takedown, Monte Carlo Stock, Checkered Stock, Modern	600	750
Model 660 Safari, Various Calibers, Post-War, Takedown, Monte Carlo Stock, Checkered Stock, Magnum, Modern	650	850
Model 98, Various Calibers, Sporting Rifle, Full-Stocked, Pre-WW2, Military, Commercial, Modern	325	450
Model A, Various Calibers, Sporting Rifle, Pre-WW2, Short Action, Modern	525	675
Model A, Various Calibers, Sporting Rifle, Pre-WW2, Magnum Action, Modern	550	700
Model A British, Various Calibers, Sporting Rifle, Express Sights, Pre-WW2, Modern	375	600
Model A British, Various Calibers, Sporting Rifle, Peep Sights, Pre-WW2, Octagon Barrel, Set Trigger, Modern	600	800
Model B, Various Calibers, Sporting Rifle, Pre-WW2, Set Trigger, Express Sights, Modern	425	575
Model B, Various Calibers, Sporting Rifle, Pre-WW2, Octagon Barrel, Set Trigger, Modern	450	650
Model DSM 34, .22 L.R.R.F., Pre-WW2, Singleshot, Tangent Sights, Miltiary Style Stock, Modern	275	400
Model EL 320, .22 L.R.R.F., Pre-WW2, Singleshot, Sporting Rifle, Adjustable Sights, Modern	185	275

Model EN 310, .22 L.R.R.F., Pre-WW2, Singleshot, Open Rear Sight, Modern	150	225
Model ES 340, .22 L.R.R.F., Pre-WW2, Singleshot, Tangent Sights, Sporting Rifle, Modern	180	270
Model ES 340B, .22 L.R.R.F., Pre-WW2, Singleshot, Tangent Sights, Sporting Rifle, Modern	185	275
Model ES 350, .22 L.R.R.F., Pre-WW2, Singleshot, Target Sights, Target Stock, Modern	325	425
Model ES 350B, .22 L.R.R.F., Pre-WW2, Singleshot, Target Sights, Target Stock, Modern	275	400
Model K, Various Calibers, Sporting Rifle, Pre-WW2, Short Action, Modern	400	525
Model KKW, .22 L.R.R.F., Pre-WW2, Singleshot, Tangent Sights, Military Style Stock, Modern	300	400
Model M, Various Calibers, Sporting Rifle, Full-Stocked, Set Trigger, Express Sights, Carbine, Modern	475	625
Model M, Various Calibers, Sporting Rifle, Pre-WW2, Full-Stocked, Tangent Sights, Carbine, Modern	375	525
Model MM 410, .22 L.R.R.F., Pre-WW2, 5 Shot Clip, Tangent Sights, Sporting Rifle, Modern	225	300
Model MM 410B, .22 L.R.R.F., Pre-WW2, 5 Shot Clip, Tangent Sights, Sporting Rifle, Modern	300	425
Model MS 350B, .22 L.R.R.F., Pre-WW2, 5 Shot Clip, Target Sights, Target Stock, Modern	350	475
Model MS 420, .22 L.R.R.F., Pre-WW2, 5 Shot Clip, Tangent Sights, Sporting Rifle, Modern	225	325
Model MS 420B, .22 L.R.R.F., Pre-WW2, 5 Shot Clip, Tangent Sights, Target Stock, Modern	325	425
Model S, Various Calibers, Sporting Rifle, Pre-WW2, Full-Stocked, Set Trigger, Carbine, Modern	400	525
Standard, Various Calibers, Sporting Rifle, Set Trigger, Pre-WW1, Modern	425	600

Rifle, Double Barrel, Over-Under

Model Aristocrat, .375 H & H Magnum, Fancy Checkering, Engraved, Open Rear Sight, Cheekpiece, Double Trigger, Modern	1,100	1,700
Model Aristocrat, Various Calibers, Fancy Checkering, Engraved, Open Rear Sight, Cheekpiece, Double Trigger, Modern	900	1,300

Rifle, Semi-Automatic

M1896, 7.63 Mauser, Carbine, Curio	3,000	4.500

Shotgun, Bolt Action

16 Gauge, Modern	80	120

Shotgun, Double Barrel, Over-Under

Model 610, 12 Gauge, Trap Grade, Vent Rib, Checkered Stock, Modern	550	800
Model 610, 12 Gauge, Skeet Grade, With Conversion Kit, Vent Rib, Checkered Stock, Modern	1,000	1,300
Model 620, 12 Gauge, Automatic Ejector, Single Selective Trigger, Vent Rib, Fancy Wood, Modern	575	850
Model 620, 12 Gauge, Automatic Ejector, Single Trigger, Vent Rib, Fancy Wood, Modern	550	800
Model 620, 12 Gauge, Automatic Ejector, Double Trigger, Vent Rib, Fancy Wood, Modern	500	750
Model 71E, 12 Gauge, Field Grade, Double Trigger, Checkered Stock, Modern	250	325
Model 72E, 12 Gauge, Trap Grade, Checkered Stock, Light Engraving, Modern	300	425
Model 72E, 12 Gauge, Skeet Grade, Checkered Stock, Light Engraving, Modern	300	425

Shotgun, Double Barrel, Side by Side

Model 496, 12 Gauge, Trap Grade, Vent Rib, Single Trigger, Checkered Stock, Box Lock, Modern	325	450

Model 545, 12 and 20 Gauges, Single Trigger, Recoil Pad, Checkered Stock, Box Lock, Modern	300	400
Model 580, 12 Gauge, Engraved, Fancy Checkering, Fancy Wood, Modern	575	825

Shotgun, Singleshot

Model 496, 12 Gauge, Trap Grade, Engraved, Checkered Stock, Modern	300	425
Model 496 Competition, 12 Gauge, Trap Grade, Engraved, Fancy Wood, Fancy Checkering, Modern	425	600

Mayesch
Lancaster, Pa. 1760-70. See Kentucky Rifles and Pistols.

Mayor, Francois
Lausanne, Switzerland

Handgun, Semi-Automatic

Rochat, .25 ACP, Clip Fed, Modern	375	500

M.B. Associates
San Ramon, Calif.

Handgun, Rocket Pistol

Gyrojet Mark I, 13mm, Clip Fed, Modern	175	250
Gyrojet Mark I B, 13mm, Clip Fed, Presentation, Cased with Accessories, Modern	600	850
Gyrojet Mark II, 12mm, Clip Fed, Modern	140	200

McCoy, Alexander
Philadelphia, Pa. 1779. See Kentucky Rifles.

McCoy, Kester
Lancaster County, Pa. See Kentucky Rifles and Pistols.

McCullough, George
Lancaster, Pa. 1770-73. See Kentucky Rifles.

Meier, Adolphus
St. Louis, Mo. 1845-50.

Rifle, Percussion

.58 Plains Type, Double Barrel, Side by Side, Half-Octagon Barrel, Rifled, Plain, Antique	1,200	1,500

Melior
Liege, Belgium. Made by Robar et Cie. 1900-59.

Handgun, Semi-Automatic

New Model Pocket, .22 L.R.R.F., Clip Fed, Modern	120	175
New Model Pocket, .32 ACP, Clip Fed, Modern	90	145
New Model Pocket, .380 ACP, Clip Fed, Modern	95	160
New Model Vest Pocket, .22 Long R.F., Clip Fed, Modern	90	140
New Model Vest Pocket, .25 ACP, Clip Fed, Modern	90	140
Old Model Pocket, .32 ACP, Clip Fed, Modern	95	150
Old Model Vest Pocket, .25 ACP, Clip Fed, Modern	90	145
Target, .22 L.R.R.F., Clip Fed, Long Barrel, Modern	135	200

Mendoza
Mexico City, Mexico

Handgun, Singleshot

K-62, .22 L.R.R.F., Modern	60	100

Menz Model 2

Rifle, Bolt Action

Modelo Conejo, .22 L.R.R.F., 2 Shot, Modern   90   145

Menta

.25 ACP, Clip Fed, Modern   225   325
.32 ACP, Clip Fed, Modern   120   175

Menz, August
Suhl, Germany. 1912-24

Handgun, Semi-Automtic

Lilliput, .25 ACP, Clip Fed. Modern   140   200
Model 1, .25 ACP, Clip Fed, Modern   140   200
Model 2, .25 ACP, Clip Fed, Modern   175   250

Mercury
Belgium

Handgun, Semi-Automatic

M 622 VP, .22 L.R.R.F., Clip Fed, Modern   80   125

Shotgun, Double Barrel, Side by Side

Mercury, 10 Gauge 3″, Hammerless, Magnum, Checkered Stock, Double
  Trigger, Modern   150   225
Mercury, 12 and 20 Gauges, Hammerless, Magnum, Checkered Stock,
  Double Trigger, Modern   130   185

Meriden Fire Arms Co.
Meriden, Conn. 1907-09

Handgun, Revolver

.38 S & W, 5 Shot, Top Break, Hammerless, Double Action, Modern   55   95

Rifle, Singleshot

Model 10, .22 L.R.R.F., Modern   25   40

Rifle, Slide Action

Model 15, .22 L.R.R.F., Tube Feed, Modern   100   175

Merkel
Suhl, Germany from 1920.

Combination Weapon, Double Barrel, Over-Under

Model 210, Various Calibers, Pre-WW2, Engraved, Checkered Stock,
  Modern   750   950
Model 210E, Various Calibers, Engraved, Checkered Stock, Automatic
  Ejector, Modern   900   1,200
Model 211, Various Calibers, Pre-WW2, Engraved, Checkered Stock,
  Modern   850   1,200
Model 211E, Various Calibers, Engraved, Checkered Stock, Automatic
  Ejector, Modern   1,200   1,500
Model 212, Various Calibers, Pre-WW2, Fancy Engraving, Fancy
  Checkering, Modern   1,200   1,500

Model 212E, Various Calibers, Pre-WW2, Fancy Engraving, Fancy Checkering, Automatic Ejector, Modern	1,500	2,000
Model 213E, Various Calibers, Sidelock, Fancy Checkering, Fancy Engraving, Automatic Ejector, Modern	2,100	2,700
Model 214E, Various Calibers, Pre-WW2, Sidelock, Fancy Checkering, Fancy Engraving, Automatic Ejector, Modern	2,100	2,700
Model 310, Various Calibers, Pre-WW2, Engraved, Checkered Stock, Modern	1,200	1,600
Model 310E, Various Calibers, Pre-WW2, Engraved, Checkered Stock, Automatic Ejector, Modern	1,500	2,000
Model 311, Various Calibers, Pre-WW2, Fancy Engraving, Fancy Checkering, Modern	1,350	1,800
Model 311E, Various Calibers, Pre-WW2, Fancy Engraving, Fancy Checkering, Automatic Ejector, Modern	1,500	2,100
Model 312, Various Calibers, Pre-WW2, Fancy Engraving, Fancy Checkering, Automatic Ejector, Modern	1,800	2,400
Model 313, Various Calibers, Sidelock, Fancy Checkering, Fancy Engraving, Automatic Ejector, Modern	3,500	4,800
Model 314, Various Calibers, Sidelock, Fancy Checkering, Fancy Engraving, Automatic Ejector, Modern	5,000	6,500
Model 410, Various Calibers, Pre-WW2, Engraved, Checkered Stock, Modern	700	950
Model 410E, Various Calibers, Pre-WW2, Engraved, Checkered Stock, Automatic Ejector, Modern	750	1,000
Model 411, Various Calibers, Pre-WW2, Engraved, Checkered Stock, Modern	875	1,100
Model 411E, Various Calibers, Pre-WW2, Engraved, Checkered Stock, Automatic Ejector, Modern	1,000	1,400

Combination Weapon, Drilling

Model 142, Various Calibers, Pre-WW2, Double Trigger, Engraved, Checkered Stock, Modern	2,750	3,300
Model 144, Various Calibers, Pre-WW2, Double Trigger, Engraved, Checkered Stock, Modern	2,800	3,350
Model 145, Various Calibers, Pre-WW2, Double Trigger, Engraved, Checkered Stock, Modern	2,500	3,100

Rifle, Double Barrel, Over-Under

Model 220, Various Calibers, Pre-WW2, Checkered Stock, Engraved, Modern	750	1,000
Model 220E, Various Calibers, Engraved, Checkered Stock, Automatic Ejector, Modern	850	1,100
Model 221, Various Calibers, Pre-WW2, Checkered Stock, Engraved, Modern	850	1,100
Model 221E, Various Calibers, Engraved, Checkered Stock, Automatic Ejector, Modern	1,200	1,600
Model 320, Various Calibers, Pre-WW2, Checkered Stock, Engraved, Modern	1,200	1,600
Model 320E, Various Calibers, Pre-WW2, Checkered Stock, Engraved, Automatic Ejector, Modern	1,500	2,000
Model 321, Various Calibers, Pre-WW2, Fancy Engraving, Fancy Checkering, Modern	1,400	1,850
Model 321E, Various Calibers, Pre-WW2, Fancy Engraving, Fancy Checkering, Automatic Ejector, Modern	1,600	2,100
Model 322, Various Calibers, Pre-WW2, Fancy Engraving, Fancy Checkering, Automatic Ejector, Modern	1,800	2,400
Model 323, Various Calibers, Sidelock, Fancy Checkering, Fancy Engraving, Automatic Ejector, Modern	3,600	5,000
Model 324, Various Calibers, Sidelock, Fancy Checkering, Fancy Engraving, Automatic Ejector, Modern	5,500	6,500

Shotgun, Double Barrel, Over-Under

Model 100, Various Gauges, Pre-WW2, Plain Barrel, Checkered Stock, Modern	475	600

Model 100, Various Gauges, Pre-WW2, Raised Matted Rib, Checkered
Stock, Modern ... 525 ... 650
Model 101, Various Gauges, Pre-WW2, Raised Matted Rib, Checkered
Stock, Light Engraving, Modern ... 575 ... 750
Model 101E, Various Gauges, Pre-WW2, Raised Matted Rib, Checkered
Stock, Light Engraving, Automatic Ejector, Modern ... 650 ... 850
Model 200, Various Gauges, Pre-WW2, Raised Matted Rib, Checkered
Stock, Light Engraving, Modern ... 800 ... 1,100
Model, 200E, Various Gauges, Pre-WW2, Raised Matted Rib, Checkered
Stock, Light Engraving, Automatic Ejector, Modern ... 1,000 ... 1,350
Model 201, Various Gauges, Pre-WW2, Raised Matted Rib, Checkered
Stock, Engraved, Modern ... 900 ... 1,300
Model 201E, Various Gauges, Pre-WW2, Raised Matted Rib, Checkered
Stock, Engraved, Automatic Ejector, Modern ... 1,100 ... 1,500
Model 202, Various Gauges, Pre-WW2, Raised Matted Rib, Fancy
Checkering, Fancy Engraving, Modern ... 1,200 ... 1,550
Model 202E, Various Gauges, Pre-WW2, Raised Matted Rib, Fancy
Checkering, Fancy Engraving, Automatic Ejector, Modern ... 1,500 ... 2,000
Model 203E, Various Gauges, Sidelock, Fancy Checkering, Fancy
Engraving, Automatic Ejector, Modern ... 2,100 ... 2,800
Model 203E, Various Gauges, Sidelock, Single Selective Trigger,
Automatic Ejector, Fancy Checkering, Fancy Engraving, Modern ... 3,000 ... 3,900
Model 204E, Various Gauges, Pre-WW2, Sidelock, Fancy   Checkering,
Fancy Engraving, Automatic Ejector, Modern ... 2,200 ... 2,900
Model 300, Various Gauges, Pre-WW2, Raised Matted Rib,   Checkered
Stock, Engraved, Modern ... 1,200 ... 1,600
Model 300E, Various Gauges, Pre-WW2, Raised Matted Rib, Checkered
Stock, Engraved, Automatic Ejector, Modern ... 1,500 ... 2,000
Model 301, Various Gauges, Pre-WW2, Raised Matted Rib, Fancy
Checkering, Engraved, Modern ... 1,400 ... 1,900
Model 301E, Various Gauges, Pre-WW2, Raised Matted Rib, Fancy
Checkering, Engraved, Automatic Ejector, Modern ... 1,700 ... 2,100
Model 302, Various Gauges, Pre-WW2, Raised Matted Rib, Fancy
Checkering, Fancy Engraving, Automatic Ejector, Modern ... 2,000 ... 2,750
Model 303E, Various Gauges, Sidelock, Single Selective Trigger,
Automatic Ejector, Fancy Engraving, Fancy Checkering, Modern ... 3,500 ... 4,700
Model 304E, Various Gauges, Sidelock, Single Selective Trigger,
Automatic Ejector, Fancy Engraving, Fancy Checkering, Modern ... 5,500 ... 6,500
Model 400, Various Gauges, Pre-WW2, Raised Matted Rib, Checkered
Stock, Engraved, Modern ... 675 ... 850
Model 400E, Various Gauges, Pre-WW2, Raised Matted Rib, Checkered
Stock, Engraved, Automatic Ejector, Modern ... 750 ... 1,100
Model 401, Various Gauges, Pre-WW2, Raised Matted Rib, Checkered
Stock, Fancy Engraving, Modern ... 875 ... 1,200
Model 401E, Various Gauges, Pre WW-2, Raised Matted Rib, Checkered
Stock, Fancy Engraving, Automatic Ejector, Modern ... 975 ... 1,350

Shotgun, Double Barrel, Side by Side
Model 127, Various Gauges, Pre-WW2, Sidelock, Fancy Engraving, Fancy
Checkering, Automatic Ejector, Modern ... 4,500 ... 5,900
Model 130, Various Gauges, Pre-WW2, Fancy Engraving, Fancy
Checkering, Automatic Ejector, Modern ... 2,500 ... 3,200
Model 147E, Various Gauges, Fancy Checkering, Fancy Engraving,
Modern ... 750 ... 950
Model 147E, Various Gauges, Fancy Checkering, Fancy Engraving,
Single Selective Trigger, Modern ... 825 ... 1,150
Model 147S, Various Gauges, Fancy Checkering, Fancy Engraving,
Sidelock, Modern ... 1,600 ... 2,100
Model 147S, Various Gauges, Fancy Checkering, Fancy Engraving,
Sidelock, Single Selective Trigger, Modern ... 1,700 ... 2,400
Model 47E, Various Gauges, Checkered Stock, Engraved, Modern ... 550 ... 750
Model 47E, Various Gauges, Single Selective Trigger, Checkered Stock,
Engraved, Modern ... 650 ... 850

Model 47S, Various Gauges, Sidelock, Checkered Stock, Engraved, Modern	1,100	1,500
Model 47S, Various Gauges, Sidelock, Single Selective Trigger, Checkered Stock, Engraved, Modern	1,200	1,600

Merrill Co.
Rockwell City, Iowa. Current

Handgun, Singleshot

Sportsman, For Extra Barrel Add $35-$50		
Sportsman, Wrist Attachment Add $10-$15		
Sportsman, Various Calibers, Target Pistol, Top Break, Adjustable Sights, Vent Rib, Modern	125	175

Merrimac Arms & Mfg. Co.
Newburyport, Mass. Absorbed by Brown Mfg. Co. Worcester, Mass. 1861-66

Handgun, Singleshot

Southerner, .41 Short R.F., Derringer, Iron Frame, Light Engraving, Antique	300	375

Rifle, Double Barrel, Side by Side

Various Calibers, Octagon Barrel, Antique	700	900

Rifle, Singleshot

Ballard, .44 Long R.F., Falling Block, Carbine, Antique	450	650
Ballard, .46 Long R.F., Falling Block, Military, Antique	550	700
Ballard, .56-52 Spencer R.F., Falling Block, Carbine, Antique	525	700
Ballard, Various Rimfires, Falling Block, Sporting Rifle, Antique	425	600

Shotgun, Singleshot

20 Gauge, Falling Block, Antique	175	250

Merwin & Bray
Worcester, Mass. 1864-68. Became Merwin & Simpkins in 1868 and Also Merwin-Taylor & Simpkins Same Year and Also within Same Year became Merwin and Hulbert

Handgun, Revolver

.22 Short R.F., 7 Shot, Single Action, Solid Frame, Spur Trigger, Antique	95	150
.28 Cup Primed Cartridge, 6 Shot, Single Action, Spur Trigger, Solid Frame, Antique	95	160
.30 Cup Primed Cartridge, 6 Shot, Single Action, Spur Trigger, Solid Frame, Antique	95	170
.31 R.F., 6 Shot, Single Action, Solid Frame, Spur Trigger, Antique	95	150
.32 Short R.F., 6 Shot, Single Action, Solid Frame, Spur Trigger, Antique	95	150
.42 Cup Primed Cartridge, 6 Shot, Single Action, Spur Trigger, Solid Frame, Antique	130	195
.42 Cup Primed Cartridge, 6 Shot, Single Action, Spur Trigger, Solid Frame, 6" Barrel, Antique	220	340
"Navy," .32 Short R.F., 6 Shot, Single Action, Solid Frame, Finger-Rest Trigger Guard, Antique	250	375
"Navy," .38 Short R.F., 6 Shot, Single Action, Solid Frame, Finger-Rest Trigger Guard, Antique	300	400
"Original," .28 Cup Primed Cartridge, 6 Shot, Single Action, Spur Trigger, Tip-Up, Antique	400	550
"Original," .30 Cup Primed Cartridge, 6 Shot, Single Action, Spur Trigger, Tip-Up, Antique	425	575
"Original," .42 Cup Primed Cartridge, 6 Shot, Single Action, Spur Trigger, Tip-Up, Antique	475	625
"Original," Various Cup-Primed Calibers, Extra Cylinder, Percussion, Add $90-$150		

Merwin & Bray .42 Cup Fire with Extra Cylinder

Reynolds, .25 Short R.F., 5 Shot, Single Action, Spur Trigger, 3" Barrel,
Antique 90 160

Handgun, Singleshot
.32 Short R.F., Side-Swing Barrel, Brass Frame, 3" Barrel, Spur Trigger,
Antique 95 150

Rifle, Singleshot
Ballard, .54 Ballard R.F., Military, Carbine, Falling Block, Antique 450 600
Ballard, Various Rimfires, Falling Block, Sporting Rifle, Antique 375 500

Merwin, Hulbert & Co.

Handgun, Revolver
Army Model, Extra Barrel, Add $125-$175
Army Model, "Safety Hammer," Add $30-$50
Army Model, .44-40 WCF, Belt Pistol, 7" Barrel, Double Action, Round
Butt, 6 Shot, Antique 275 475
Army Model, .44-40 WCF, Belt Pistol, 7" Barrel, Single Action, Square-
Butt, 6 Shot, Antique 300 525
Army Model, .44-40 WCF, Pocket Pistol, 3½" Barrel, Double Action,
Round Butt, 6 Shot, Antique 250 400
Army Model, .44-40 WCF, Pocket Pistol, 3½" Barrel, Single Action,
Square-Butt, 6 Shot, Antique 275 425
Pocket Model, .32 S & W, 5 Shot, Double Action, Antique 110 190
Pocket Model, .38 S & W, 5 Shot, Double Action, Antique 120 200
Target Model, .32 S & W, 7 Shot, Double Action, Antique 145 225

Messersmith, Jacob
Lancaster, Pa. 1779-82. See Kentucky Rifles & Pistols

Meteor
Made by Stevens Arms

Rifle, Bolt Action
Model 52, .22 L.R.R.F., Singleshot, Takedown, Modern 30 35

Metropolitan
Made by Crescent for Siegel Cooper Co., N.Y. C.1900

Shotgun, Double Barrel, Side by Side
Various Gauges, Outside Hammers, Damascus Barrel, Modern 80 150
Various Gauges, Hammerless, Steel Barrel, Modern 95 175
Various Gauges, Hammerless, Damascus Barrel, Modern 75 150
Various Gauges, Outside Hammers, Steel Barrel, Modern 90 175

Shotgun, Singleshot
Various Gauges, Hammer, Steel Barrel, Modern 45 75

Metropolitan Police
Made by Norwich Falls Pistol Co. Norwich, Conn. 1885

Handgun, Revolver
.32 Short R.F., 5 Shot, Spur Trigger, Solid Frame, Single Action, Antique 90 160

Metzger, J.
Lancaster, Pa. 1728 See Kentucky Rifles

Meuhirter, S.
See Kentucky Rifles

Mexican Military

Handgun, Semi-Automatic
Obregon, .45 ACP, Clip Fed, Military, Modern   190   275

Rifle, Bolt Action
M1936 Mauser, 7mm, Military, Modern   125   165

Miida

Shotgun, Double Barrel, Over-Under

Model 2100, 12 Gauge, Skeet Grade, Checkered Stock, Engraved, Single Selective Trigger, Vent Rib, Modern	340	425
Model 2200 S, 12 Gauge, Skeet Grade, Checkered Stock, Engraved, Single Selective Trigger, Wide Vent Rib, Modern	350	475
Model 2200 T, 12 Gauge, Trap Grade, Checkered Stock, Engraved, Single Selective Trigger, Wide Vent Rib, Modern	400	550
Model 2300 S, 12 Gauge, Skeet Grade, Fancy Wood, Engraved, Single Selective Trigger, Vent Rib, Modern	400	550
Model 2300 T, 12 Gauge, Trap Grade, Fancy Wood, Engraved, Single Selective Trigger, Vent Rib, Modern	425	600
Model 612, 12 Gauge, Field Grade, Checkered Stock, Light Engraving, Single Selective Trigger, Vent Rib, Modern	325	425
Model Grandee, 12 Gauge, Fancy Engraving, Fancy Wood, Gold Inlays, Single Selective Trigger, Vent Rib, Modern	850	1,250

Mikros

Tradename of Manufacture D'Armes Des Pyrenees Heydaye, France, 1934-39, 1958-Current

Handgun, Semi-Automatic

.25 ACP, Clip Fed, Magazine Disconnect, Modern	95	145
.32 ACP, Clip Fed, Magazine Disconncet, Modern	95	145
KE, .22 Short R.F., Clip Fed, Hammer, Magazine Disconnect, 2" Barrel, Modern 65	110	
KE, .22 Short R.F., Clip Fed, Hammer, Magazine Disconnect, 4" Barrel, Modern	75	120
KE, .22 Short R.F., Clip Fed, Hammer, Magazine Disconnect, 2" Barrel, Lightweight, Modern	70	100
KE, .22 Short R.F., Clip Fed, Hammer, Magazine Disconnect, 4" Barrel, Lightweight, Modern	65	95
KN, .25 ACP, Clip Fed, Hammer, Magazine Disconnect, 2" Barrel, Modern	70	100
KN, .25 ACP, Clip Fed, Hammer, Magazine Disconncet, 2" Barrel, Lightweight, Modern	70	110

Military

Handgun, Semi-Automatic
Model 1914, .32 ACP, Clip Fed, Modern   70   110

Military Model 1914 .32 ACP

Miller, Mathias
Easton, Pa. 1771-88 See Kentucky Rifles

Mills, Benjamin
Charlottesville, N.C. 1784-90 1790-1814 at Harrodsburg, Ky. See Kentucky Rifles, U.S. Military

Minneapolis Firearms Co.
Minneapolis, Minn. C.1883

Handgun, Palm Pistol

The Protector, .32 Extra Short R.F., Nickel Plated, Antique	350	550

Miquelet-Lock
Unknown Maker

Handgun, Miquelet-Lock

.52 Arabian, Holster Pistol, Tapered Round Barrel, Low Quality, Antique	200	300
.55, Russian Cossack Type, Tapered Round Barrel, Steel Furniture, Silver Furniture, Antique	500	750
Central Italian 1700's, Holster Pistol, Brass Furniture, Brass Overlay Stock, Medium Quality, Antique	1,500	2,200
Pair Late 1700's, Pocket Pistol, Medium Quality, Brass Furniture, Light Ornamentation, Antique	1,000	1,500
Pair Spanish Late 1600's, Belt Hook, Brass Overlay Stock, High Quality, Antique		20,000
Pair Cominazzo Early 1700's, Steel Inlay, Medium Quality, Holster Pistol, Antique	2,200	3,000
Ripoll Type Late 1600's, Blunderbuss, Brass Inlay, Antique	3,300	4,000
Ripoll Type Late 1600's, Blunderbuss, Silver Inlay, Antique	5,000	6,000

Rifle, Miquelet-Lock

Mid-Eastern, Gold Inlays, Cannon Barrel, Front & Rear Bead Sights, Silver Overlay Stock, Silver Furniture, Antique	2,000	3,000
Mid-Eastern 1700's, Damascus Barrel, Gold Inlays, Many Semi-Precious Gem Inlays, Silver Furniture, Ornate, Antique	3,000	5,000

Miroku
Tokyo, Japan

Handgun, Revolver

.38 Special, Double Action, Swingout Cylinder, Blue, Modern	70	125

Also See Browning for Similar Models

Mississippi Valley Arms Co.
Made by Crescent for Shapleigh Hardware, St. Louis, Mo.

Shotgun, Double Barrel, Side by Side

Various Gauges, Outside Hammers, Damascus Barrel, Modern	80	150
Various Gauges, Hammerless, Steel Barrel, Modern	95	175
Various Gauges, Hammerless, Damascus Barrel, Modern	75	150
Various Gauges, Outside Hammers, Steel Barrel, Modern	90	175

Shotgun, Singleshot

Various Gauges, Hammer, Steel Barrel, Modern	45	75

Mitchell Arms

Handgun, Double Barrel, Over-Under

Derringer, .357 Mag., Spur Trigger, Modern	55	80

Handgun, Revolver

Army Target, Various Calibers, Single Action, Western Style, Modern	95	140

Mohawk
Made by Crescent for Blish, Mize & Stillman. C.1900

Shotgun, Double Barrel, Side by Side

Various Gauges, Outside Hammers, Damascus Barrel, Modern	80	150
Various Gauges, Hammerless, Steel Barrel, Modern	95	175
Various Gauges, Hammerless, Damascus Barrel, Modern	75	150
Various Gauges, Outside Hammers, Steel Barrel, Modern	90	175

Shotgun, Singleshot

Various Gauges, Hammer, Steel Barrel, Modern	45	75

Moll, David
Hellerstown, Pa. 1814-1833. See Kentucky Rifles

Moll, John
Hellerstown, Pa. 1770-94. See Kentucky Rifles.

Moll, John III
Hellerstown, Pa. 1824-63. See Kentucky Rifles.

Moll, John, Jr.
Hellerstown, Pa. 1794-1824. See Kentucky Rifles

Moll, Peter
Hellerstown, Pa. 1804-33 with Brother John Moll Jr. Made Some of the Finest Kentucky Rifles in Pa. See Kentucky Rifles.

Monarch
Maker Unknown C.1880

Handgun, Revolver

.32 Short R.F., 5 Shot, Spur Trigger, Solid Frame, Single Action, Antique	90	160

Monarch
Made by Hopkins & Allen C.1880

Handgun, Revolver

#1, .22 Short R.F., 7 Shot, Spur Trigger, Solid Frame, Single Action, Antique	90	160
#2, .32 Short R.F., 5 Shot, Spur Trigger, Solid Frame, Single Action, Antique	95	170
#3, .38 Short R.F., 5 Shot, Spur Trigger, Solid Frame, Single Action, Antique	95	175
#4, .41 Short R.F., 5 Shot, Spur Trigger, Solid Frame, Single Action, Antique	110	190

Mondial
Gaspar Arizaga

Handgun, Semi-Automatic

.25 ACP, Clip Fed, Modern	100	145

Mondial .25 ACP

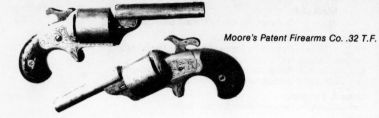

Moore's Patent Firearms Co. .32 T.F.

Monitor
Made by Stevens Arms

Shotgun, Double Barrel, Side by Side
Model 311, Various Gauges, Hammerless, Steel Barrel, Modern 90 145
Shotgun, Singleshot
Model 90, Various Gauges, Takedown, Automatic Ejector, Plain, Hammer,
Modern 35 55

Moore Patent Fire Arms Co.
Brooklyn, N.Y. 1863-83

Handgun, Singleshot
.41 Short R.F., Derringer, Brass Frame, Antique 300 375

Handgun, Revolver
Williamson's Patent, .32 T.F., Brass Frame, Hook Extractor, Antique 165 240
.32 T.F., Spur Trigger, Single Action, Brass Frame, No Extractor, Antique 150 250
.32 T.F., Spur Trigger, Single Action, Brass Frame, Hook Extractor,
Antique 175 275

Morrone
Rhode Island Arms Co., Hope Valley, R.I.

Shotgun, Double Barrel, Over-Under
Model 46, 12 Ga., Single Trigger, Plain Barrels, Checkered Stock, Modern 400 600
Model 46, 20 Ga., Single Trigger, Vent Rib, Checkered Stock, Modern 650 900

Mortimer, H. W. & Son
London, England 1800-02

Handgun, Flintlock
.45, 4 Barrel Duckfoot, Pocket Pistol, Steel Barrel and Frame, Plain,
Antique 3,000 3,750

Mossberg, O. F. & Sons
*New Haven, Conn. 1919 to Date Fitchburg & Chicopee Falls, Mass. 1892-1919 as
Oscar F. Mossberg*

Handgun, Manual Repeater
Brownie, .22 L.R.R.F., Top Break, Double Action, Rotating Firing Pin, 4
Barrels, 4 Shot, Modern 130 200

Rifle, Bolt Action
Model 10, .22 L.R.R.F., Singleshot, Takedown, Modern 35 50
Model 14, .22 L.R.R.F., Singleshot, Takedown, Peep Sights, Modern 40 55
Model 14OB, .22 L.R.R.F., Clip Fed, Peep Sights, Monte Carlo Stock,
Modern 35 60
Model 14OK, .22 L.R.R.F., Clip Fed, Open Rear Sight, Monte Carlo Stock,
Modern 35 60
Model 142A, .22 L.R.R.F., Clip Fed, Peep Sights, Modern 40 65
Model 142A, .22 L.R.R.F., Clip Fed, Carbine, Monte Carlo Stock, Peep
Sights, Modern 35 65

Model 142K, .22 L.R.R.F., Clip Fed, Open Rear Sight, Modern	40	65
Model 142K, .22 L.R.R.F., Clip Fed, Carbine, Monte Carlo Stock, Modern	30	55
Model 144, .22 L.R.R.F., Clip Fed, Heavy Barrel, Target Stock, Target Sights, Modern	65	90
Model 144LS, .22 L.R.R.F., Clip Fed, Heavy Barrel, Lyman Sights, Target Stock, Modern	70	95
Model 146B, .22 L.R.R.F., Takedown, Tube Feed, Monte Carlo Stock, Peep Sights, Modern	40	65
Model 20, .22 L.R.R.F., Singleshot, Takedown, Modern	35	50
Model 25, .22 L.R.R.F., Singleshot, Takedown, Peep Sights, Modern	35	55
Model 25A, .22 L.R.R.F., Singleshot, Takedown, Peep Sights, Modern	40	60
Model 268, .22 L.R.R.F., Singleshot, Takedown, Peep Sights, Modern	30	50
Model 26C, .22 L.R.R.F., Singleshot, Takedown, Open Rear Sight, Modern	30	45
Model 30, .22 L.R.R.F., Singleshot, Takedown, Peep Sights, Modern	35	55
Model 32OB, .22 L.R.R.F., Singleshot, Peep Sights, Modern	40	60
Model 320K, .22 L.R.R.F., Singleshot, Open Rear Sight, Monte Carlo Stock, Modern	30	45
Model 321K, .22 L.R.R.F., Singleshot, Open Rear Sight, Modern	25	45
Model 340B, .22 L.R.R.F., Clip Fed, Peep Sights, Modern	40	60
Model 340K, .22 L.R.R.F., Clip Fed, Open Rear Sight, Modern	35	55
Model 340M, .22 L.R.R.F., Clip Fed, Full-Stocked, Carbine, Modern	45	70
Model 341, .22 L.R.R.F., Clip Fed, Open Rear Sight, Modern	35	55
Model 342K, .22 L.R.R.F., Clip Fed, Open Rear Sight, Modern	35	55
Model 346B, .22 L.R.R.F., Tube Feed, Peep Sights, Monte Carlo Stock, Modern	40	65
Model 346K, .22 L.R.R.F., Tube Feed, Monte Carlo Stock, Open Rear Sight, Modern	40	60
Model 35, .22 L.R.R.F., Singleshot, Target Stock, Target Sights, Modern	65	95
Model 35A, .22 L.R.R.F., Singleshot, Target Stock, Target Sights, Modern	55	95
Model 35A-LS, .22 L.R.R.F., Singleshot, Target Stock, Lyman Sights, Modern	65	100
Model 35B, .22 L.R.R.F., Singleshot, Target Sights, Heavy Barrel, Target Stock, Modern	65	95
Model 40, .22 L.R.R.F., Takedown, Tube Feed, Open Rear Sight, Modern	40	55
Model 42, .22 L.R.R.F., Takedown, Clip Fed, Open Rear Sight, Modern	35	55
Model 42A, .22 L.R.R.F., Takedown, Clip Fed, Peep Sights, Modern	35	55
Model 42B, .22 L.R.R.F., Takedown, 5 Shot Clip, Peep Sights, Modern	35	60
Model 42C, .22 L.R.R.F., Takedown, 5 Shot Clip, Open Rear Sight, Modern	35	55
Model 42M, .22 L.R.R.F., Takedown, Clip Fed, Full-Stocked, Peep Sights, Modern	40	65
Model 42MB (British), .22 L.R.R.F., Takedown, Clip Fed, Full-Stocked, Peep Sights, Modern	60	80
Model 43, .22 L.R.R.F., Clip Fed, Heavy Barrel, Target Sights, Target Stock, Modern	60	90
Model 44, .22 L.R.R.F., Takedown, Tube Feed, Open Rear Sight, Modern	40	60
Model 44 US, .22 L.R.R.F., Clip Fed, Target Sights, Target Stock, Heavy Barrel, Modern	75	110
Model 448, .22 L.R.R.F., Target Stock, Clip Fed, Target Sights, Modern	60	95
Model 45, .22 L.R.R.F., Takedown, Tube Feed, Peep Sights, Modern	40	55
Model 45A, .22 L.R.R.F., Takedown, Tube Feed, Peep Sights, Modern	40	55
Model 45AC, .22 L.R.R.F., Takedown, Tube Feed, Open Rear Sight, Modern	40	55
Model 45B, .22 L.R.R.F., Takedown, Tube Feed, Open Rear Sight, Modern	40	60
Model 45B, .22 L.R.R.F., Takedown, Tube Feed, Open Rear Sight, Modern	45	65
Model 45C, .22 L.R.R.F., Takedown, Tube Feed, no Sights, Modern	40	60
Model 46, .22 L.R.R.F., Takedown, Tube Feed, Peep Sights, Modern	50	75
Model 46A-LS, .22 L.R.R.F., Takedown, Tube Feed, Lyman Sights, Modern	50	85
Model 46AC, .22 L.R.R.F., Takedown, Tube Feed, Open Rear Sight, Modern	40	60
Model 46B, .22 L.R.R.F., Takedown, Tube Feed, Peep Sights, Modern	40	60
Model 46M, .22 L.R.R.F., Takedown, Tube Feed, Full-Stocked, Peep Sights, Modern	45	85

Model 46T, .22 L.R.R.F., Takedown, Tube Feed, Heavy Barrel, Target
 Stock, Peep Sights, Modern 50 85
Model 64OK, .22 WMR, 5 Shot Clip, Monte Carlo Stock, Open Rear Sight,
 Modern 50 65
Model 800, Various Calibers, Open Rear Sight, Monte Carlo Stock,
 Modern 115 150
Model 800D, Various Calibers, Monte Carlo Stock, Cheekpiece,
 Checkered Stock, Open Rear Sight, Modern 130 160
Model 800M, Various Calibers, Open Rear Sight, Full-Stocked, Modern 115 160
Model 800SM, Various Calibers, Scope Mounted, Monte Carlo Stock,
 Modern 130 175
Model 800V, Various Calibers, no Sights, Monte Carlo Stock, Heavy
 Barrel, Modern 120 155
Model 810, Various Calibers, Magnum Action, Open Rear Sight, Monte
 Carlo Stock, Modern 125 165
Model 810, Various Calibers, Open Rear Sight, Long Action, Monte Carlo
 Stock, Modern 125 165
Model B, .22 L.R.R.F., Singleshot, Takedown, Modern 25 45
Model L42A, .22 L.R.R.F., Takedown, Clip Fed, Peep Sights, Left-Hand,
 Modern 40 65
Model L43, .22 L.R.R.F., Clip Fed, Heavy Barrel, Target Sights, Target
 Stock, Left-Hand, Modern 70 95
Model L45A, .22 L.R.R.F., Takedown, Tube Feed, Peep Sights, Modern 45 65
Model L46A-LS, .22 L.R.R.F., Takedown, Tube Feed, Lyman Sights, Left-
 Hand, Modern 55 95
Model R, .22 L.R.R.F., Takedown, Tube Feed, Open Rear Sight, Modern 30 45

Rifle, Lever Action
Model 400, .22 L.R.R.F., Tube Feed, Open Rear Sight, Modern 40 60
Model 402, .22 L.R.R.F., Tube Feed, Open Rear Sight, Monte Carlo Stock,
 Modern 45 65
Model 472C, Various Calibers, Straight Grip, Tube Feed, Open Rear Sight,
 Carbine, Modern 75 110
Model 472P, Various Calibers, Pistol-Grip Stock, Tube Feed, Open Rear
 Sight, Carbine, Modern 75 110
RM-7, Various Calibers, Open Sights, Modern 120 160

Rifle, Semi-Automatic
Model 151K, .22 L.R.R.F., Takedown, Tube Feed, Open Rear Sight,
 Modern 45 65
Model 151M, .22 L.R.R.F., Takedown, Tube Feed, Peep Sights, Full-
 Stocked, Modern 50 75
Model 152, .22 L.R.R.F., Clip Fed, Monte Carlo Stock, Peep Sights,
 Carbine, Modern 50 75
Model 152K, .22 L.R.R.F., Clip Fed, Monte Carlo Stock, Open Rear Sight,
 Carbine, Modern 45 70
Model 350K, .22 L.R.R.F., Clip Fed, Monte Carlo Stock, Open Rear Sight,
 Modern 40 60
Model 351C, .22 L.R.R.F., Tube Feed, Monte Carlo Stock, Open Rear
 Sight, Carbine, Modern 40 60
Model 351K, .22 L.R.R.F., Tube Feed, Monte Carlo Stock, Open Rear
 Sight, Modern 35 55
Model 352K, .22 L.R.R.F., Clip Fed, Monte Carlo Stock, Open Rear Sight,
 Carbine, Modern 40 60
Model 450, .22 L.R.R.F., Tube Feed, Monte Carlo Stock, Checkered Stock,
 Open Rear Sight, Modern 40 55
Model 432, .22 L.R.R.F., Tube Feed, Western Style, Carbine, Modern 40 60
Model 50, .22 L.R.R.F., Takedown, Tube Feed, Open Rear Sight, Modern 40 60
Model 51, .22 L.R.R.F., Takedown, Tube Feed, Peep Sight, Modern 50 65
Model 51M, .22 L.R.R.F., Takedown, Tube Feed, Peep Sight, Full-Stocked,
 Modern 50 65

Rifle, Singleshot
Model L, .22 L.R.R.F., Lever Action, Falling Block, Takedown, Modern 130 185

Rifle, Slide Action
Model K, .22 L.R.R.F., Takedown, Tube Feed, Hammerless, Modern   45   65
Model M, .22 L.R.R.F., Takedown, Tube Feed, Hammerless, Octagon
  Barrel, Modern   60   85

Shotgun, Bolt Action
Model 173, .410 Ga., Takedown, Singleshot, Modern   25   40
Model 173Y, .410 Ga., Clip Fed, Singleshot, Modern   25   40
Model 183D, .410 Ga., Takedown, 3 Shot, Modern   30   45
Model 183K, .410 Ga., Takedown, Adjustable Choke, Clip Fed, Modern   30   45
Model 183T, .410 Ga., Clip Fed, Modern   30   50
Model 185D, 20 Ga., Takedown, 3 Shot, Modern   30   45
Model 185K, 20 Ga., Takedown, 3 Shot, Adjustable Choke, Modern   30   45
Model 19OD, 16 Ga., Takedown, Clip Fed, Modern   30   45
Model 19OK, 16 Ga., Takedown, Adjustable Choke, Clip Fed, Modern   30   45
Model 195D, 12 Ga., Takedown, Clip Fed, Modern   35   50
Model 195K, 12 Ga., Takedown, Adjustable Choke, Clip Fed, Modern   35   50
Model 385K, 20 Ga., Clip Fed, Adjustable Choke, Modern   40   55
Model 385T, 20 Ga., Clip Fed, Modern   35   50
Model 39OK, 16 Ga., Clip Fed, Adjustable Choke, Modern   40   55
Model 39OT, 16 Ga., Clip Fed, Modern   35   50
Model 395K, 12 Ga. Mag. 3", Clip Fed, Adjustable Choke, Modern   40   55
Model 395S, 12 Ga. Mag. 3", Clip Fed, Open Rear Sight, Modern   40   55
Model 395T, 12 Ga., Clip Fed, Modern   35   50
Model 73, .410 Ga., Takedown, Singleshot, Modern   25   35
Model 83D, .410 Ga., Takedown, 3 Shot, Modern   30   45
Model 85D, 20 Ga., Takedown, 3 Shot, Adjustable Choke, Modern   30   45

Shotgun, Slide Action
Model 200D, 12 Ga., Clip Fed, Adjustable Choke, Modern   40   70
Model 200K, 12 Ga., Clip Fed, Adjustable Choke, Modern   45   75
Model 500 Super, Checkered Stock, Vent Rib, Modern   85   125
Model 500A, 12 Ga. Mag. 3", Field Grade, Modern   75   100
Model 500AA, 12 Ga. Mag. 3", Trap Grade, Modern   100   135
Model 500AK, Field Grade, Adjustable Choke, Modern   75   110
Model 500AKR, Field Grade, Adjustable Choke, Vent Rib, Modern   85   115
Model 500AM, Field Grade, Magnum, Modern   75   100
Model 500AMR, Field Grade, Magnum, Vent Rib, Modern   90   115
Model 500AR, Field Grade, Vent Rib, Modern   85   110
Model 500AS, Field Grade, Open Rear Sight, Modern   85   110
Model 500ATR, Trap Grade, Vent Rib, Modern   90   130
Model 500B, 16 Ga., Field Grade, Modern   65   95
Model 500BK, 16 Ga., Adjustable Choke, Modern   65   95
Model 500BS, 16 Ga., Open Rear Sight, Modern   70   100
Model 500C, 20 Ga., Field Grade, Modern   70   95
Model 500CK, 20 Ga., Field Grade, Adjustable Choke, Modern   70   100
Model 500CKR, 20 Ga., Field Grade, Vent Rib, Adjustable Choke, Modern   70   110
Model 500CR, 20 Ga., Field Grade, Vent Rib, Modern   70   100
Model 500CS, 20 Ga., Field Grade, Open Rear Sight, Modern   70   100
Model 500E, .410 Ga., Field Grade, Modern   65   95
Model 500EK, .410 Ga., Field Grade, Adjustable Choke, Modern   70   100
Model 500EKR, .410 Ga., Field Grade, Vent Rib, Adjustable Choke,
  Modern   75   110
Model 500ER, .410 Ga., Field Grade, Vent Rib, Modern   70   100

Moster, Geo.
Lancaster, Pa. 1771-79. See Kentucky Rifles and Pistols

Mt. Vernon Arms
Belgium C.1900

Shotgun, Double Barrel, Side by Side
Various Gauges, Outside Hammers, Damascus Barrel, Modern   80   150

Various Gauges, Hammerless, Steel Barrel, Modern	95	175
Various Gauges, Hammerless, Damascus Barrel, Modern	75	150
Various Gauges, Outside Hammers, Steel Barrel, Modern	90	175

Shotgun, Singleshot
Various Gauges, Hammer, Steel Barrel, Modern	45	75

Mountain Eagle
Made by Hopkins & Allen C.1880

Handgun, Revolver
.32 Short R.F., 5 Shot, Spur Trigger, Solid Frame, Single Action, Antique	90	160

Musgrave
South Africa

Rifle, Bolt Action
Valiant NR6, Various Calibers, Checkered Stock, Modern	100	160
Premier NR5, Various Calibers, Checkered Stock, Modern	160	220

Musketeer

Rifle, Bolt Action
Carbine, Various Calibers, Monte Carlo Stock, Checkered Stock, Sling Swivels, Modern	150	200
Deluxe, Various Calibers, Monte Carlo Stock, Checkered Stock, Sling Swivels, Modern	175	225
Sporter, Various Calibers, Monte Carlo Stock, Checkered Stock, Sling Swivels, Modern	150	200
Mannlicher, Various Calibers, Full Stock, Modern	130	200

Mutti, Gerolimo
Brescia, C.1680

Handgun, Snaphaunce
Pair, Belt Pistol, Brass Mounts, Engraved, Ornate, Antique	12,000+

Mutti, Giesu
Brescia, C.1790

Handgun, Snaphaunce
Pair, Engraved, Belt Hook, Medium Ornamentation, Antique	8,500+

Napoleon
Made by Thomas Ryan, Jr., Pistol Mfg. Co. C.1870-76

Handgun, Revolver
.22 Short R.F., 7 Shot, Spur Trigger, Solid Frame, Single Action, Antique	90	160
.32 Short R.F., 5 Shot, Spur Trigger, Solid Frame, Single Action, Antique	95	170

National
Made by Norwich Falls Pistol Co. C.1880

Handgun, Revolver
.32 Short R.F., 5 Shot, Spur Trigger, Solid Frame, Single Action, Antique	90	160
.38 Short R.F., 5 Shot, Spur Trigger, Solid Frame, Single Action, Antique	95	170

Handgun, Singleshot
.41 Short R.F., Derringer, all Metal, Light Engraving, Antique	175	235

National Arms Co.
Made by Crescent C.1900

Shotgun, Double Barrel, Side by Side

Various Gauges, Outside Hammers, Damascus Barrel, Modern	80	150
Various Gauges, Hammerless, Steel Barrel, Modern	95	175
Various Gauges, Hammerless, Damascus Barrel, Modern	75	150
Various Gauges, Outside Hammers, Steel Barrel, Modern	90	175

Shotgun, Singleshot

Various Gauges, Hammer, Steel Barrel, Modern	45	75

National Ordnance
South El Monte, Calif.

Rifle, Bolt Action

1903A3, .30-06 Springfield, Military, Modern	65	95

Rifle, Semi-Automatic

Garand, .30-06 Springfield, Military, Modern	175	275
M-1 Carbine, .30 Carbine, Clip Fed, Modern	60	110
M-1 Carbine, .30 Carbine, Clip Fed, Folding Stock, Modern	85	120
Tanker Garand, .308 Win., Military, Modern	175	275

Navy Arms
Ridgefield, N.J. Importers

Presentation Case only $10-$18
A. Engraving Pistol, Add $60-$75
B. Engraving Pistol, Add $70-$110
C. Engraving Pistol, Add $160-$225
A Engraving Rifle, Add $70-$110
B Engraving Rifle, Add $125-$165
C Engraving Rifle, Add $300-$400
Tiffany Grips only $75-$120
Silver Plating, Add $50-$90

Handgun, Flintlock

.44 "Kentucky," Belt Pistol, Reproduction, Brass Furniture, Antique	55	75
.44 "Kentucky," Belt Pistol, Reproduction, Brass Furniture, Brass Barrel, Antique	55	75
.577 Scotch Black Watch, Military, Reproduction, Belt Pistol, all Metal, Antique	55	85
.69 M1763 Charleville, Military, Reproduction, Belt Pistol, Antique	150	200
.69 M1763 Charleville, Military, Reproduction, Belt Pistol, Antique	50	80
.69 M1777 Charleville, Military, Reproduction, Belt Pistol, Antique	50	80
.69 Tower, Military, Reproduction, Belt Pistol, Antique	25	35

Handgun, Percussion

.36 M1851 New Navy, Revolver, Reproduction, Brass Grip Frame, Antique	50	75
.36 M1851 New Navy, Revolver, Reproduction, Silver-Plated Grip Frame, Antique	50	75
.36 M1853, Revolver, Reproduction, Pocket Pistol, 4½" Barrel, Antique	50	75
.36 M1853, Revolver, Reproduction, Pocket Pistol, 5½" Barrel, Antique	50	75
.36 M1853, Revolver, Reproduction, Pocket Pistol, 6½" Barrel, Antique	50	75
.36 M1860 Reb, Revolver, Reproduction, Brass Frame, Antique	35	45
.36 M1860 Sheriff, Revolver, Reproduction, Brass Frame, Antique	35	45
.36 M1861, Revolver, Reproduction, Sheriff's Model, with Short Barrel, Antique	50	75
.36 M1861 Navy, Revolver, Reproduction, Fluted Cylinder, Antique	50	75
.36 M1861 Navy, Revolver, Reproduction, Engraved Cylinder, Antique	45	70

Navy Arms .44 M1847 Walker
Courtesy of Navy Arms

Navy Arms .44 M1860 Army
Courtesy of Navy Arms

.36 M1862 Police, Revolver, Reproduction, 5 Shot, Brass Grip Frame, Cased with Accessories, Antique	75	100
.36 M1862 Police, Revolver, Reproduction, 5 Shot, Brass Grip Frame, 4½" Barrel, Antique	50	70
.36 M1862 Police, Revolver, Reproduction, 5 Shot, Brass Grip Frame, 5½" Barrel, Antique	50	70
.36 M1862 Police, Revolver, Reproduction, 5 Shot, Brass Grip Frame, 6½" Barrel, Antique	50	70
.36 M1862 Police, Revolver, Reproduction, Fancy Engraving, Silver Plated, Gold Plated, Antique	300	400
.36 M1863, Revolver, Reproduction, Sheriff's Model, with Short Barrel, Antique	50	75
.36 Remington, Revolver, Reproduction, Target Pistol, Adjustable Sights, Antique	65	90
.36 Remington, Revolver, Reproduction, Solid Frame, Antique	50	75
.36 Spiller & Burr, Revolver, Reproduction, Solid Frame, Antique	40	55
.44 "Kentucky," Belt Pistol, Reproduction, Brass Furniture, Antique	50	70
.44 "Kentucky," Belt Pistol, Reproduction, Brass Furniture, Brass Barrel, Antique	60	80
.44 First Model Dragoon, Revolver, Reproduction, Brass Grip Frame, Antique	65	90
.44 M1847 Walker, Revolver, Reproduction, Brass Grip Frame, Antique	70	100
.44 M1847 Walker, Revolver, Reproduction, Brass Grip Frame, Engraved, Gold Inlays, Antique	150	200
.44 M1860, Revolver, Reproduction, Sheriff's Model, with Short Barrel, Antique	50	75
.44 M1860 Army, Revolver, Reproduction, Fluted Cylinder, Antique	50	75
.44 M1860 Army, Revolver, Reproduction, Engraved Cylinder, Antique	50	75
.44 M1860 Reb, Revolver, Reproduction, Brass Frame, Antique	35	45
.44 M1860 Reb, Revolver, Reproduction, Shoulder Stock Only	25	30
.44 M1860 Sheriff, Revolver, Reproduction, Brass Frame, Antique	35	45
.44 Remington, Revolver, Reproduction, Target Pistol, Adjustable Sights, Antique	65	90
.44 Remington, Revolver, Reproduction, Solid Frame, Antique	50	75
.44 Remington, Revolver, Reproduction, Stainless Steel, Antique	80	120
.44 Remington Army, Revolver, Reproduction, Nickel Plated, Antique	65	95
.44 Second Model, Dragoon, Revolver, Reproduction, Brass Grip Frame, Antique	65	90
.44 Third Model Dragoon, Revolver, Reproduction, Buntline, with Detachable Shoulder Stock, Antique	110	145

Navy Arms .44 Remington Army
Courtesy of Navy Arms

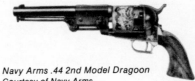

Navy Arms .44 2nd Model Dragoon
Courtesy of Navy Arms

.44 Third Model Dragoon, Revolver, Reproduction, Brass Grip Frame,
   Antique   70   100
.44 Third Model Dragoon, Revolver, Reproduction, Brass Grip Frame, with
   Detachable Shoulder Stock, Antique   100   135
.58 M1806, Harper's Ferry, Reproduction, Brass Furniture, Military, Belt
   Pistol, Antique   50   70
.58 M1855, Harper's Ferry, Reproduction, Holster Pistol, Military, with
   Detachable Shoulder Stock, Antique   75   100
.58 M1855, Harper's Ferry, Shoulder Stock Only   20   25

Handgun, Revolver
Frontier, Various Calibers, Color Case Hardened Frame, Single Action,
   Western Style, Modern   85   125
Frontier Target, .357 Magnum, Color Case Hardened Frame, Single
   Action, Western Style, Adjustable Sights, with Detachable Shoulder
   Stock, Modern   130   175
Frontier Target, .45 Colt, Color Case Hardened Frame, Single Action,
   Western Style, Adjustable Sights, with Detachable Shoulder Stock,
   Modern   135   170
Frontier Target, Various Calibers, Color Case Hardened Frame, Single
   Action, Western Style, Adjustable Sights, Modern   90   135
M1875 Remington, .357 Magnum, Color Case Hardened Frame, Western
   Style, Single Action, Modern   100   135
M1875 Remington, .357 Magnum, Nickel Plated, Western Style, Single
   Action, Modern   115   150
M1875 Remington, .44-40 WCF, Color Case Hardened Frame, Western
   Style, Single Action, Modern   90   130

Navy Arms .58 Model 1806
Courtesy of Navy Arms

Navy Arms .58 M1855
Courtesy of Navy Arms

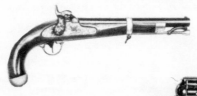

Navy Arms 1875 Remington Revolver
Courtesy of Navy Arms

Navy Arms Rolling Block Pistol
Courtesy of Navy Arms

M1875 Remington, .44-40 WCF, Nickel Plated, Western Style, Single Action, Modern	110	145
M1875 Reming.on, .45 Colt, Color Case Hardened Frame, Western Style, Single Action, Modern	100	135
M1875 Remington, .45 Colt, Stainless Steel, Western Style, Single Action, Modern	110	140
M1875 Remington, .45 Colt, Nickel Plated, Western Style, Single Action, Modern	115	150

Handgun, Singleshot

Rolling Block, .22 Hornet, Half-Octagon Barrel, Color Case Hardened Frame, Adjustable Sights, Modern	70	110
Rolling Block, .22 L.R.R.F., Half-Octagon Barrel, Color Case Hardened Frame, Adjustable Sights, Modern	55	85
Rolling Block, .357 Magnum, Half-Octagon Barrel, Color Case Hardened Frame, Adjustable Sights, Modern	70	100

Rifle, Bolt Action

Mauser '98, .45-70 Government, Checkered Stock, Modern	80	115
Mauser '98, .45-70 Government, Carbine, Checkered Stock, Modern	80	115

Rifle, Flintlock

.45 "Kentucky," Long Rifle, Reproduction, Brass Furniture, Antique	100	140
.45 "Kentucky," Carbine, Reproduction, Brass Furniture, Antique	100	135
.58 M1803, Harper's Ferry, Reproduction, Brass Furniture, Military, Antique	110	150
.69 M1795 Springfield, Modern, Reproduction, Musket, Antique	150	200
.69 M1809 Springfield, Modern, Reproduction, Musket, Antique	150	200
.75 Brown Bess, Modern, Reproduction, Musket, Antique	175	225
.75 Brown Bess, Modern, Reproduction, Carbine, Antique	175	225
.75 Brown Bess (Jap), Modern, Reproduction, Musket, Antique	140	175

Rifle, Lever Action

M1873 1 of 1000, .44-40 WCF, Blue Tube, Octagon Barrel, Steel Buttplate, Engraved, Modern	500	700
M1873-"101," .22 L.R.R.F., Color Case Hardened Frame, Tube Feed, Round Barrel, Steel Buttplate, Carbine, Modern	130	160
M1873-"101," .44-40 WCF, Color Case Hardened Frame, Tube Feed, Octagon Barrel, Steel Buttplate, Modern	145	180
M1873-"101", .44-40 WCF, Color Case Hardened Frame, Tube Feed, Round Barrel, Steel Buttplate, Carbine, Modern	130	160
M1873-"101", Trapper, .22 L.R.R.F., Color Case Hardened Frame, Tube Feed, Round Barrel, Steel Buttplate, Modern	130	160
M1873-"101", Trapper, .44-40 WCF, Color Case Hardened Frame, Tube Feed, Round Barrel, Steel Buttplate, Modern	130	160
Yellowboy, .22 L.R.R.F., Brass Frame, Tube Feed, Round Barrel, Brass Buttplate, Saddle-Ring Carbine, Modern	110	150

Navy Arms .58 M1803 Harper's Ferry
Courtesy of Navy Arms

Navy Arms .75 Brown Bess
Courtesy of Navy Arms

Navy Arms Yellowboy
Courtesy of Navy Arms

Yellowboy, .38 Special, Brass Frame, Tube Feed, Octagon Barrel, Brass Buttplate, Modern	130	160
Yellowboy, .38 Special, Brass Frame, Tube Feed, Round Barrel, Brass Buttplate, Saddle-Ring Carbine, Modern	110	150
Yellowboy, .44-40 WCF, Brass Frame, Tube Feed, Octagon Barrel, Brass Buttplate, Modern	130	160
Yellowboy, .44-40 WCF, Brass Frame, Tube Feed, Round Barrel, Brass Buttplate, Saddle-Ring Carbine, Modern	110	150
Yellowboy Trapper, .22 L.R.R.F., Brass Frame, Tube Feed, Round Barrel, Brass Buttplate, Modern	110	150
Yellowboy Trapper, .38 Special, Brass Frame, Tube Feed, Round Barrel, Brass Buttplate, Modern	110	150
Yellowboy Trapper, .44-40 WCF, Brass Frame, Tube Feed, Round Barrel, Brass Buttplate, Modern	110	150

Rifle, Percussion

.44 Remington, Revolver, Reproduction, Carbine, Brass Furniture, Antique	80	120
.45 "Kentucky," Long Rifle, Reproduction, Brass Furniture, Antique	95	135
.45 "Kentucky," Carbine, Reproduction, Brass Furniture, Antique	95	130
.45 "Kentucky," Carbine, Reproduction, Brass Furniture, Antique	95	130
.45 Hawken Hurricane, Octagon Barrel, Brass Furniture, Reproduction, Antique	115	145
.45 Morse, Octagon Barrel, Brass Frame, Reproduction, Antique	65	90
.50 Hawken Hurricane, Octagon Barrel, Brass Furniture, Reproduction, Antique	115	145
.50 Morse, Octagon Barrel, Brass Frame, Reproduction, Antique	65	90
.54 Gallagher, Carbine, Reproduction, Military, Steel Furniture, Antique	125	160
.577 M1853 3-Band, Military, Reproduction, Musket, Antique (Parker-Hale)	150	200
.577 M1858 2-Band, Military, Reproduction, Rifled, Antique (Parker-Hale)	115	150
.577 M1861, Military, Reproduction, Musketoon, Antique (Parker-Hale)	115	150
.58, J.P. Murray Artillery Carbine, Reproduction, Brass Furniture, Military, Antique	75	100
.58 Buffalo Hunter, Round Barrel, Brass Furniture, Reproduction, Antique	90	125
.58 Hawken Hunter, Octagon Barrel, Brass Furniture, Reproduction, Antique	115	145
.58 M1841, Mississippi Rifle, Reproduction, Brass Furniture, Military, Antique	85	120
.58 M1863 Springfield, Military, Reproduction, Rifled, Musket, Antique	100	140
.58 M1864 Springfield, Military, Reproduction, Rifled, Musket, Antique	120	150
.58 Morse, Octagon Barrel, Brass Frame, Reproduction, Antique	65	90
.58 Zouave, Military, Reproduction, Antique	90	120
.58 Zouave 1864, Military, Reproduction, Carbine, Brass Furniture, Antique	90	120

Navy Arms .58 M1863 Springfield
Courtesy of Navy Arms

Navy Arms .58 Morse
Courtesy of Navy Arms

Navy Arms Remington Rolling Block
Creedmore
Courtesy of Navy Arms

Rifle, Revolver
M1875 Remington, .357 Magnum, Color Case Hardened Frame, Carbine,
 Single Action, Brass Furniture, Modern   110   150
M1875 Remington, .44-40 WCF, Color Case Hardened Frame, Carbine,
 Single Action, Brass Furniture, Modern   110   150
M1875 Remington, .45 Colt, Color Case Hardened Frame, Carbine, Single
 Action, Brass Furniture, Modern   110   150

Rifle, Semi-Aitomatic
AP-74, .22 L.R.R.F., Clip Fed, Plastic Stock, Modern   50   75
AP-74, .22 L.R.R.F., Clip Fed, Wood Stock, Modern   55   85
AP-74, .32 ACP, Clip Fed, Plastic Stock, Modern   55   85
AP-74 Commando, .22 L.R.R.F., Clip Fed, Wood Stock, Modern   55   85

Rifle, Singleshot
Buffalo, .45-70 Government, Rolling Block, Color Case Hardened Frame,
 Octagon Barrel, Open Rear Sight, Various Barrel Lengths, Modern   100   130
Buffalo, .45-70 Government, Rolling Block, Color Case Hardened Frame,
 Half-Octagon Barrel, Open Rear Sight, Various Barrel Lengths, Modern   95   125
Buffalo, .50 U.S. Carbine, Rolling Block, Color Case Hardened Frame,
 Octagon Barrel, Open Rear Sight, Various Barrel Lengths, Modern   90   120
Buffalo, .50 U.S. Carbine, Rolling Block, Color Case Hardened Frame,
 Half-Octagon Barrel, Open Rear Sight, Various Barrel Lengths, Modern   85   110
Creedmore, .45-70 Government, Rolling Block, Color Case Hardened
 Frame, Octagon Barrel, Vernier Sights, 30" Barrel, Modern   120   165
Creedmore, .45-70 Government, Rolling Block, Color Case Hardened
 Frame, Half-Octagon Barrel, Vernier Sights, 30" Barrel, Modern   115   160
Creedmore, .50 U.S. Carbine, Rolling Block, Color Case Hardened Frame,
 Octagon Barrel, Vernier Sights, 30" Barrel, Modern   110   150
Creedmore, .50 U.S. Carbine, Rolling Block, Color Case Hardened Frame,
 Half-Octagon Barrel, Vernier Sights, 30" Barrel, Modern   110   150
Creedmore, .50-140 Sharps, Rolling Block, Color Case Hardened Frame,
 Octagon Barrel, Vernier Sights, 30" Barrel, Modern   . 100   145
Martini, .45-70 Government, Color Case Hardened Frame, Half-Octagon
 Barrel, Open Rear Sight, Checkered Stock, Modern   140   185
Martini, .45-70 Government, Color Case Hardened Frame, Octagon Barrel,
 Open Rear Sight, Checkered Stock, Modern   135   180
Rolling Block, .22 Hornet, Carbine, Color Case Hardened Frame,
 Adjustable Sights, Modern   80   110
Rolling Block, .22 L.R.R.F., Carbine, Color Case Hardened Frame,
 Adjustable Sights, Modern   70   95
Rolling Block, .357 Magnum, Carbine, Color Case Hardened Frame,
 Adjustable Sights, Modern   85   110

Shotgun, Percussion
Magnum Deluxe, 12 Ga., Double Barrel, Side by Side, Reproduction,
 Outside Hammers, Checkered Stock, Antique   135   175
Morse/Navy, 12 Ga., Singleshot, Reproduction, Brass Frame, Antique   65   95
Upland Deluxe, 12 Ga., Double Barrel, Side by Side, Reproduction,
 Outside Hammers, Checkered Stock, Antique   75   110
Zouave, 12 Ga., Brass Furniture, Reproduction, Antique   80   110

Neihard, Peter
Northhampton, Pa. 1785-87, See Kentucky Rifles

Nero
Made by J. Rupertus Arms Co. C.1880. Sold by E. Tryon Co.

Handgun, Revolver
.22 Short R.F., 7 Shot, Spur Trigger, Solid Frame, Single Action, Antique   90   160
.32 Short R.F., 5 Shot, Spur Trigger, Solid Frame, Single Action, Antique   95   170

Nero
Made by Hopkins & Allen. C.1880. Sold by C.L. Riker

Handgun, Revolver
.22 Short R.F., 7 Shot, Spur Trigger, Solid Frame, Single Action, Antique   90   160
.32 Short R.F., 5 Shot, Spur Trigger, Solid Frame, Single Action, Antique   95   170

New Chieftain
Made by Stevens Arms

Shotgun, Singleshot
Model 94, Various Gauges, Takedown, Automatic Ejector, Plain, Hammer,
Modern   35   55

New Rival
Made by Crescent for Van Camp Hardwore & Iron Co., Indianapolis, Ind.

Shotgun, Double Barrel, Side by Side
Various Gauges, Outside Hammers, Damascus Barrel, Modern   80   150
Various Gauges, Hammerless, Steel Barrel, Modern   95   175
Various Gauges, Hammerless, Damascus Barrel, Modern   75   150
Various Gauges, Outside Hammers, Steel Barrel, Modern   90   175

Shotgun, Singleshot
Various Gauges, Hammer, Steel Barrel, Modern   45   75

New York Arms Co.
Made by Crescent for Garnet Carter Co. Tenn. C.1900

Shotgun, Double Barrel, Side by Side
Various Gauges, Outside Hammers, Damascus Barrel, Modern   80   150
Various Gauges, Hammerless, Steel Barrel, Modern   95   175
Various Gauges, Hammerless, Damascus Barrel, Modern   75   150
Various Gauges, Outside Hammers, Steel Barrel, Modern   90   175

Shotgun, Singleshot
Various Gauges, Hammer, Steel Barrel, Modern   45   75

New York Pistol Co.
N.Y.C. C.1870

Handgun, Revolver
.22 Short R.F., 7 Shot, Spur Trigger, Solid Frame, Single Action, Antique   90   160
.32 Short R.F., 5 Shot, Spur Trigger, Solid Frame, Single Action, Antique   90   165

Newcomer, John
Lancaster, Pa. 1770-72. See Kentucky Rifles

Newhardt, Jacob
Allentown, Pa. 1770-77. See Kentucky Rifles.

Newport
Made by Stevens Arms

Shotgun, Double Barrel, Side by Side
Model 311, Various Gauges, Hammerless, Steel Barrel, Modern   90   145

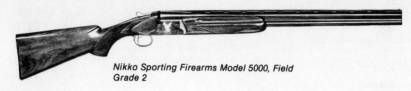

Nikko Sporting Firearms Model 5000, Field Grade 2

Newton Arms Co.
Buffalo, N.Y. 1914-18, Reorganized 1918-30 as Newton Rifle Corp.

Rifle, Bolt Action

1st Type, Various Calibers, Sporting Rifle, Set Trigger, Checkered Stock, Open Rear Sight, Modern	350	475
2nd Type, Various Calibers, Sporting Rifle, Set Trigger, Checkered Stock, Open Rear Sight, Modern	375	550
Newton-Mauser, Various Calibers, Sporting Rifle, Set Trigger, Checkered Stock, Open Rear Sight, Modern	275	400

Nichols, John
Oxford, England 1730-75

Handgun, Flintlock

Holster Pistol, Engraved, Brass Furniture, High Quality, Antique	2,000	2,750

Nikko Sporting Firearms
Japan Imported by Kanematsu-Gosho U.S.A. Inc. Arlington Heights, Ill.

Rifle, Bolt Action

Model 7000, Various Calibers, Grade 1, Checkered Stock, Modern	200	300
Model 7000, Various African Calibers, Grade 1, Checkered Stock, Modern	225	350

Shotgun, Double Barrel, Over-Under

Model 5000, 12 and 20 Gauges, Field Grade, Vent Rib, Checkered Stock, Light Engraving, Gold Overlay, Modern	325	450
Model 5000, 12 and 20 Gauges, Skeet Grade, Vent Rib, Checkered Stock, Light Engraving, Gold Overlay, Modern	400	550
Model 5000, 12 and 20 Gauges, Trap Grade, Vent Rib, Checkered Stock, Light Engraving, Gold Overlay, Modern	400	550
Model 5000, 12 and 20 Gauges, Field Grade 2, Vent Rib, Checkered Stock, Light Engraving, Gold Overlay, Modern	425	550
Model 5000, 12 and 20 Gauges, Skeet Grade 2, Vent Rib, Checkered Stock, Light Engraving, Gold Overlay, Modern	475	600
Model 5000, 12 and 20 Gauges, Trap Grade 2, Vent Rib, Checkered Stock, Light Engraving, Gold Overlay, Modern	475	600
Model 5000 Grandee, 12 and 20 Gauges, Field Grade 3, Vent Rib, Checkered Stock, Fancy Engraving, Gold Overlay, Modern	1,250	2,000
Model 5000 Grandee, 12 and 20 Gauges, Skeet Grade 3, Vent Rib, Checkered Stock, Fancy Engraving, Gold Overlay, Modern	1,250	2,000
Model 5000 Grandee, 12 Ga., Trap Grade 3, Vent Rib, Checkered Stock, Fancy Engraving, Gold Overlay, Modern	1,250	2,000

Nitro Proof
Made by Stevens Arms

Shotgun, Singleshot

Model 115, Various Gauges, Hammer, Automatic Ejector, Modern	40	55

Noble
Haydenville, Mass.

Rifle, Bolt Action

98 Mauser, .30-06 Springfield, Monte Carlo Stock, Open Rear Sight, Modern	75	100
Model 10, .22 L.R.R.F., Singleshot, Modern	20	30
Model 20, .22 L.R.R.F., Singleshot, Modern	20	30
Model 222, .22 L.R.R.F., Singleshot, Modern	25	40

Rifle, Lever Action

Model 275, .22 L.R.R.F., Tube Fed, Modern	40	60

Rifle, Semi-Automatic

Model 285, .22 L.R.R.F., Tube Fed, Modern	45	65

Rifle, Slide Action

Model 235, .22 L.R.R.F., Wood Stock, Modern	45	65
Model 33, .22 L.R.R.F., Plastic Stock, Modern	35	50
Model 33A, .22 L.R.R.F., Wood Stock, Modern	40	65

Shotgun, Double Barrel, Side by Side

Model 420, Various Gauges, Hammerless, Checkered Stock, Recoil Pad, Modern	110	150
Model 420EK, Various Gauges, Hammerless, Checkered Stock, Recoil Pad, Fancy Wood, Modern	125	185
Model 450E, Various Gauges, Hammerless, Checkered Stock, Recoil Pad, Modern	135	285

Shotgun, Semi-Automatic

Model 80, .410 Ga., Modern	90	135

Shotgun, Slide Action

Model 160 Deergun, 12 and 20 Gauges, Peep Sights, Modern	65	120
Model 166L Deergun, 12 and 16 Gauges, Peep Sights, Modern	75	120
Model 166LP Deergun, 12 and 16 Gauges, Peep Sights, Modern	75	115
Model 200, 20 Ga., Vent Rib, Adjustable Choke, Modern	70	110
Model 200, 20 Ga., Adjustable Choke, Modern	70	100
Model 200, 20 Ga., Modern	65	95
Model 200, 20 Ga., Trap Grade, Modern	80	125
Model 300, 12 Ga., Vent Rib, Adjustable Choke, Modern	90	130
Model 300, 12 Ga., Adjustable Choke, Modern	80	110
Model 300, 12 Ga., Modern	75	110
Model 300, 12 Ga., Trap Grade, Modern	90	130
Model 390, 12 Ga., Peep Sights, Modern	75	110
Model 40, 12 Ga., Hammerless, Solid Frame, Adjustable Choke, Modern	60	90
Model 400, .410 Ga., Trap Grade, Modern	70	95
Model 400, .410 Ga., Adjustable Choke, Modern	70	95
Model 400, .410 Ga., Trap Grade, Adjustable Choke, Modern	75	100
Model 400, .410 Ga., Modern	65	100
Model 50, 12 Ga., Hammerless, Solid Frame, Modern	45	90
Model 60, 12 and 16 Gauges, Hammerless, Solid Frame, Adjustable Choke, Modern	65	100
Model 602, 20 Ga., Modern	70	100
Model 602CLP, 20 Ga., Adjustable Choke, Modern	80	115
Model 602RCLP, 20 Ga., Adjustable Choke, Vent Rib, Modern	95	135
Model 602 RLP, 20 Ga., Vent Rib, Modern	75	110
Model 60ACP, 12 and 16 Gauges, Hammerless, Solid Frame, Adjustable Choke, Vent Rib, Modern	60	90
Model 60AF, 12 and 16 Gauges, Hammerless, Solid Frame, Vent Rib, Adjustable Choke, Modern	65	95
Model 60 RCLP, 12 and 16 Gauges, Hammerless, Solid Frame, Vent Rib, Adjustable Choke, Checkered Stock, Modern	65	95
Model 65, 12 and 16 Gauges, Hammerless, Solid Frame, Modern	44	70
Model 662CR, 20 Ga., Vent Rib, Modern	85	125
Model 66CLP, 12 and 16 Gauges, Adjustable Choke, Modern	90	130
Model 66RCLP, 12 and 16 Gauges, Hammerless, Solid Frame, Adjustable Choke, Vent Rib, Modern	90	130
Model 66RLP, 12 and 16 Gauges, Hammerless, Solid Frame, Vent Rib, Modern	80	135

Model 66XLP, 12 and 16 Gauges, Hammerless, Solid Frame, Modern	70	110
Model 70, .410 Ga., Modern	50	80
Model 70CLP, .410 Ga., Hammerless, Solid Frame, Adjustable Choke, Modern	75	115
Model 70RL, .410 Ga., Modern	70	100
Model 70X, .410 Ga., Modern	65	95
Model 70XL, .410 Ga., Modern	60	90
Model 757, 20 Ga., Adjustable Choke, Lightweight, Modern	95	145

Nock, Henry
London & Birmingham, England 1760-1810

Rifle, Flintlock

.65, Ellett Carbine, Musket, Military, Antique	950	1,300

Shotgun, Percussion

Fowler, Converted from Flintlock, Patent Breech, Antique	375	600

Nonpareil
Made by Norwich Falls Pistols Co. 1880

Handgun, Revolver

.32 Short R.F., 5 Shot, Spur Trigger, Solid Frame, Single Action, Antique	90	160

North American Arms Co.
Freedom, Wyo. Current

Handgun, Revolver

.454 Casull Magnum, Single Action, Western Style, Stainless Steel, 5 Shot, Modern	300	400
Mini, .22 L.R.R.F., 5 Shot, Single Action, Spur Trigger, 1⅛" Barrel, Derringer, Modern	60	85
Mini, .22 L.R.R.F., 5 Shot, Single Action, Spur Trigger, 1⅝" Barrel, Derringer, Modern	65	95

North Vietnam Military

Automatic Weapon, Submachine Gun

K50M, 7.62mm Tokarev, Clip Fed, Folding Stock, Class 3	1,000	1,500

Northwesterner
Made by Stevens Arms

Rifle, Bolt Action

Model 52, .22 L.R.R.F., Single Action, Takedown, Modern	35	35

Shotgun, Singleshot

Model 94, Various Gauges, Takedown, Automatic Ejector, Plain, Hammer, Modern	35	50

Norton
Americarms, Miami, Fla.

Handgun, Semi-Automatic

TP-70, .22 L.R.R.F., Clip Fed, Stainless Steel, Modern	135	200
TP-70, .25 ACP, Clip Fed, Stainless Steel, Modern	120	175

Norwegian Military

Handgun, Semi-Automatic

Mauser Model 1914, .32 ACP, Blue, Clip Fed, Modern	500	750
Model 1914, .45 ACP, Military, Clip Fed, Modern	175	275
Model 1914, .45 ACP, Military, Clip Fed, Nazi-Proofed, Modern	275	375

Norwegian Mauser Model 1914 .32 ACP

Norwich Arms Co.
Probably made by Norwich Falls Pistols Co.

Handgun, Revolver
.22 Short R.F., 7 Shot, Spur Trigger, Solid Frame, Single Action, Antique   90   160
.32 Short R.F., 5 Shot, Spur Trigger, Solid Frame, Single Action, Antique   95   170

Norwich Arms Co.
Made by Crescent C.1900

Shotgun, Double Barrel, Side by Side
Various Gauges, Outside Hammers, Damascus Barrel, Modern   80   150
Various Gauges, Hammerless, Steel Barrel, Modern   95   175
Various Gauges, Hammerless, Damascus Barrel, Modern   75   150
Various Gauges, Outside Hammers, Steel Barrel, Modern   90   175

Shotgun, Singleshot
Various Gauges, Hammer, Steel Barrel, Modern   45   75

Not-Nac Mfg. Co.
Made by Crescent for Belknap Hardware Co., Louisville, Ky.

Shotgun, Double Barrel, Side by Side
Various Gauges, Outside Hammers, Damascus Barrel, Modern   80   150
Various Gauges, Hammerless, Steel Barrel, Modern   95   175
Various Gauges, Hammerless, Damascus Barrel, Modern   75   150
Various Gauges, Outside Hammers, Steel Barrel, Modern   90   175

Shotgun, Singleshot
Various Gauges, Hammer, Steel Barrel, Modern   45   75

Noys, R.
Wiltshire, England 1800-30

Handgun, Flintlock
Pocket Pistol, Screw Barrel, Box Lock, Steel Barrel and Frame, Plain,
  Antique   400   550

Numrich Arms Co.
West Hurley, N.Y. Also see Thompson, Hopkins & Allen, and Auto-Ordnance

Handgun, Semi-Automatic
Model 27A5, .45 ACP, Clip Fed, Finned Barrel, Adjustable Sights, with
  Compensator, Modern, (Numrich)   225   325

Rifle, Semi-Automatic
Model 27A1, .45 ACP, Clip Fed, without Compensator, Modern, (Numrich)   200   300

Model 27A1, .45 ACP, Clip Fed, without Compensator, Cased with Accessories, Modern, (Numrich)	375	450
Model 27A1 Deluxe, .45 ACP, Clip Fed, Finned Barrel, Adjustable Sights, with Compensator, Modern, (Numrich)	240	345
Model 27A3, .22 L.R.R.F., Clip Fed, Finned Barrel, Adjustable Sights, with Compensator, Modern, (Numrich)	200	325

Nunnemacher, Abraham
York, Pa. 1779-83, See Kentucky Rifles

Oak Leaf
Made by Stevens Arms

Shotgun, Singleshot

Model 90, Various Gauges, Takedown, Automatic Ejector, Plain, Hammer, Modern	35	50

Occidental
Belgium, C.1880

Shotgun, Double Barrel, Side by Side

Various Gauges, Outside Hammers, Damascus Barrel, Modern	90	150

Old Timer
Made by Stevens Arms

Shotgun, Singleshot

Model 94, Various Gauges, Takedown, Automatic Ejector, Plain, Hammer, Modern	35	50

Olympic
Made by Stevens Arms

Shotgun, Double Barrel, Side by Side

M 315, Various Gauges, Hammerless, Steel Barrel, Modern	90	145
Model 311, Various Gauges, Hammerless, Steel Barrel, Modern	90	145

Shotgun, Singleshot

Model 94, Various Gauges, Takedown, Automatic Ejector, Plain, Hammer, Modern	35	50

Omega
Spain Industria Obrera

Handgun, Semi-Automatic

.25 ACP, Clip Fed, Modern	60	90
.32 ACP, Clip Fed, Grip Safety, Modern	70	110

Omega
Torrance, Calif. Made by Hi-Shear Corp. Current

Rifle, Bolt Action

Omega III, Various Calibers, no Sights, Fancy Wood, Adjustable Trigger, Modern	255	375

Ortgies
Germany, 1918-20, 1920 Taken over by Deutsche-Werke

Handgun, Semi-Automatic

D Pocket, .380 ACP, Clip Fed, Modern	90	125
H O Pocket, .380 ACP, Clip Fed, Modern	80	115
D Pocket , .32 ACP, Clip Fed, Modern	70	110
H O Pocket, .32 ACP, Clip Fed, Modern	80	120

Ortgies .32 ACP

D Vest Pocket, .25 ACP, Clip Fed, Modern	90	130
H O Vest Pocket, .25 ACP, Clip Fed, Modern	85	120

Our Jake

Handgun, Revolver
.32 R.F., Spur Trigger, Solid Frame, Hammer, Antique   85   140

OWA
Austria C.1920

Handgun, Semi-Automatic

Model 1921 Standard, .25 ACP, Clip Fed, Modern	85	130
Model 1924, .25 ACP, Clip Fed, Lightweight, Modern	110	165

Oxford Arms
Made by Stevens Arms

Shotgun, Double Barrel, Side by Side
Model 311, Various Gauges, Hammerless, Steel Barrel, Modern   90   145

Page, T.
Norwich, England, 1766-76

Handgun, Flintlock
.60, Queen Anne Style, Pocket Pistol, Screw Barrel, Box Lock, Brass
  Furniture, Engraved, Antique   850   1,200

Page-Lewis Arms Co.
See Stevens, J. Arms & Tool Co. for Similar Listings

Palmer, Thomas
Philadelphia, Pa. 1772-76. See Kentucky Rifles and U.S. Military

Palmetto
Made by Stevens Arms

Shotgun, Singleshot

Model 90, Various Gauges, Takedown, Automatic Ejector, Plain, Hammer, Modern	35	50
Model 94, Various Gauges, Takedown, Automatic Ejector, Plain, Hammer, Modern	35	50

Pannabecker, Jefferson
Lancaster, Pa. 1790-1810. See Kentucky Rifles

Pannabecker, Jesse
Lancaster, Pa. 1833-60. See Kentucky Rifles and Percussion Kentucky

Paragon
Made by Stevens Arms

Shotgun, Double Barrel, Side by Side
Model 311, Various Gauges, Hammerless, Steel Barrel, Modern	90	145

Paragon
Possibly made by Hopkins & Allen, C.1880

Handgun, Revolver
.32 Short R.F., 5 Shot, Spur Trigger, Solid Frame, Single Action, Antique	90	160

Paramount
Spain. Retolaza Hermanos, C.1900

Handgun, Semi-Automatic
.32 ACP, Clip Fed, Modern	75	110
M 1914, .32 ACP, Clip Fed, Long Grip, Modern	70	115
Vest Pocket, .25 ACP, Clip Fed, Modern	65	95

Parker Brothers
Meriden, Conn. 1868-1934. In 1934 Parker Bros. was taken over by Remington Arms

Shotgun, Double Barrel, Side by Side
Deduct 25%-30% for Upgrades
Deduct 30%-45% for Plain Extractor
Deduct 60%-75% for Damascus Barrel
Single Selective Trigger, Add $200-$325
Beavertail Forend, for BHE through A-1, Add $250-$350
Beavertail Forend, VHE through CHE, Add $200-$300
Extra Barrel, Add 30%-40%
Vent Rib, Add $275-$350
Trap Grade, Add 15%-25%
Skeet Grade, Add 15%-25%
Outside Hammers with Steel Barrels, Deduct 20%-30%

A-1 Special, 12 Ga., Hammerless, Double Trigger, Automatic Ejector, Modern	15,000	25,000
A-1 Special, 16 Ga., Hammerless, Double Trigger, Automatic Ejector, Modern	12,000	18,000
A-1 Special, 20 Ga., Hammerless, Double Trigger, Automatic Ejector, Modern	20,000	30,000
A-1 Special, 28 Ga., Hammerless, Double Trigger, Automatic Ejector, Modern	40,000	60,000
A-1 Upgrade, .410 Ga., Hammerless, Double Trigger, Automatic Ejector, Modern	8,000	15,000
A-1 Upgrade, 12 and 16 Gauges, Hammerless, Double Trigger, Automatic Ejector, Modern	7,000	10,000
A-1 Upgrade, 20 Ga., Hammerless, Double Trigger, Automatic Ejector, Modern	6,000	9,000
A-1 Upgrade, 28 Ga., Hammerless, Double Trigger, Automatic Ejector, Modern	9,000	15,000
AAHE, 10 Ga., Hammerless, Double Trigger, Automatic Ejector, Modern	23,000	28,000
AAHE, 12 Ga., Hammerless, Double Trigger, Automatic Ejector, Modern	9,500	15,000
AAHE, 16 Ga., Hammerless, Double Trigger, Automatic Ejector, Modern	9,500	15,000
AAHE, 20 Ga., Hammerless, Double Trigger, Automatic Ejector, Modern	12,000	18,000
AAHE, 28 Ga., Hammerless, Double Trigger, Automatic Ejector, Modern	24,000	30,000
AHE, .410 Ga., Hammerless, Double Trigger, Automatic Ejector, Modern	15,000	20,000
AHE, 10 Ga., Hammerless, Double Trigger, Automatic Ejector, Modern	15,000	20,000
AHE, 12 Ga., Hammerless, Double Trigger, Automatic Ejector, Modern	9,000	13,000
AHE, 16 Ga., Hammerless, Double Trigger, Automatic Ejector, Modern	8,500	12,000
AHE, 20 Ga., Hammerless, Double Trigger, Automatic Ejector, Modern	11,000	18,000
AHE, 28 Ga., Hammerless, Double Trigger, Automatic Ejector, Modern	14,000	21,000
BHE, .410 Ga., Hammerless, Double Trigger, Automatic Ejector, Modern	13,000	19,000
BHE, 10 Ga., Hammerless, Double Trigger, Automatic Ejector, Modern	12,000	18,000

Description		
BHE, 12 Ga., Hammerless, Double Trigger, Automatic Ejector, Modern	7,500	11,000
BHE, 16 Ga., Hammerless, Double Trigger, Automatic Ejector, Modern	7,000	10,500
BHE, 20 Ga., Hammerless, Double Trigger, Automatic Ejector, Modern	10,000	15,000
BHE, 28 Ga., Hammerless, Double Trigger, Automatic Ejector, Modern	15,000	22,000
CHE, .410 Ga., Hammerless, Double Trigger, Automatic Ejector, Modern	8,500	13,000
CHE, 10 Ga., Hammerless, Double Trigger, Automatic Ejector, Modern	8,500	13,000
CHE, 12 Ga., Hammerless, Double Trigger, Automatic Ejector, Modern	6,500	9,500
CHE, 16 Ga., Hammerless, Double Trigger, Automatic Ejector, Modern	6,000	9,000
CHE, 20 Ga., Hammerless, Double Trigger, Automatic Ejector, Modern	8,000	11,000
CHE, 28 Ga., Hammerless, Double Trigger, Automatic Ejector, Modern	9,500	14,000
DHE, .410 Ga., Hammerless, Double Trigger, Automatic Ejector, Modern	6,500	10,000
DHE, 10 Ga., Hammerless, Double Trigger, Automatic Ejector, Modern	5,500	9,000
DHE, 12 Ga., Hammerless, Double Trigger, Automatic Ejector, Modern	5,000	8,500
DHE, 16 Ga., Hammerless, Double Trigger, Automatic Ejector, Modern	4,500	8,000
DHE, 20 Ga., Hammerless, Double Trigger, Automatic Ejector, Modern	7,000	10,500
DHE, 28 Ga., Hammerless, Double Trigger, Automatic Ejector, Modern	9,500	14,000
Early Model, Various Gauges, Outside Hammers, Damascus Barrel, Under-Lever, Antique	650	1,100
GHE, .410 Ga., Hammerless, Double Trigger, Automatic Ejector, Modern	4,500	9,000
GHE, 10 Ga. 3½", Hammerless, Double Trigger, Automatic Ejector, Modern	4,500	8,000
GHE, 12 Ga., Hammerless, Double Trigger, Automatic Ejector, Modern	2,800	4,000
GHE, 16 Ga., Hammerless, Double Trigger, Automatic Ejector, Modern	2,800	4,000
GHE, 20 Ga., Hammerless, Double Trigger, Automatic Ejector, Modern	5,000	9,500
GHE, 28 Ga., Hammerless, Double Trigger, Automatic Ejector, Modern	6,500	10,000
Invincible, 12 Ga., Hammerless, Double Trigger, Automatic Ejector, Modern		120,000+
Invincible, 16 Ga., Hammerless, Double Trigger, Automatic Ejector, Modern		65,000+
Trojan, 12 and 16 Gauges, Hammerless, Double Trigger, Modern	600	950
Trojan, 20 Ga., Hammerless, Double Trigger, Modern	900	1,500
Trojan, 24 Ga., Hammerless, Double Trigger, Modern		20,000+
VHE, .410 Ga., Hammerless, Double Trigger, Automatic Ejector, Modern	4,500	8,000
VHE, 10 Ga. 3½", Hammerless, Double Trigger, Automatic Ejector, Modern	3,500	7,000
VHE, 12 Ga., Hammerless, Double Trigger, Automatic Ejector, Modern	1,500	2,300
VHE, 16 Ga., Hammerless, Double Trigger, Automatic Ejector, Modern	1,500	2,200
VHE, 20 Ga., Hammerless, Double Trigger, Automatic Ejector, Modern	4,000	8,000
VHE, 28 Ga., Hammerless, Double Trigger, Automatic Ejector, Modern	4,500	8,500

Shotgun, Singleshot

Description		
S.A., 12 Ga., Hammerless, Vent Rib, Automatic Ejector, Modern	5,000	7,500
S.A.-1 Special, 12 Ga., Hammerless, Vent Rib, Automatic Ejector, Modern	8,000	12,000
S.A.A., 12 Ga., Hammerless, Vent Rib, Automatic Ejector, Modern	6,000	9,000
S.B., 12 Ga., Hammerless, Vent Rib, Automatic Ejector, Modern	4,500	6,500
S.C. 12 Ga., Hammerless, Vent Rib, Automatic Ejector, Modern	3,500	5,500

Parker Brothers
Imported from Italy by Jana International

Shotgun, Double Barrel, Over-Under

Description		
Field Model, 12 Ga. 3", Single Selective Trigger, Automatic Ejectors, Checkered Stock, Engraved, Vent Rib, Modern	200	300
Skeet Model, 12 Ga., Single Selective Trigger, Automatic Ejectors, Checkered Stock, Engraved, Vent Rib, Modern	230	325
Monte Carlo Trap Model, 12 Ga., Single Selective Trigger, Automatic Ejectors, Checkered Stock, Engraved, Vent Rib, Modern	250	350
California Trap Model, 12 Ga., Single Selective Trigger, Automatic Ejectors, Checkered Stock, Engraved, Double Vent Ribs, Modern	350	500

Parker-Hale
Birmingham, England Imported by Jana. Current

Rifle, Bolt Action

Description		
Model 1200, Various Calibers, Checkered Stock, Open Rear Sight, Monte Carlo Stock, Modern	150	195

Model 1200M, Various Calibers, Magnum, Checkered Stock, Open Rear Sight, Monte Carlo Stock, Modern	160	220
Model 1200V, Various Calibers, Heavy Barrel, Checkered Stock, no Sights, Monte Carlo Stock, Modern	160	220

Rifle, Percussion

.54 Gallagher, Breech Loader, Carbine, Brass Furniture, Reproduction, Antique	120	170
.58 M1853 Enfield, Musket, Rifled, 2 Bands, Brass Furniture, Reproduction, Antique	135	185
.58 M1858 Enfield Rifle, Rifled, Brass Furniture, Reproduction, Antique	130	190
.58 M1861 Enfield, Musketoon, Rifled, 2 Bands, Brass Furniture, Reproduction, Antique	120	170
.451, Whitworth Military Target Rifle, 3 Bands, Target Sights, Checkered Stock, Reproduction, Antique	250	350

Shotgun, Semi-Automatic

Model 900, 12 Ga., Checkered Stock, Vent Rib, Modern	140	200
Model 900, 12 Ga. 3", Checkered Stock, Vent Rib, Modern	150	220

Parker Safety Hamerless
Made by Columbia Armory, Tenn. C.1890

Handgun, Revolver

.32 S & W, 5 Shot, Top Break, Hammerless, Double Action, Modern	55	95

Parker, William
London, England 1790-1840

Shotgun, Flintlock

16 Ga., Double Barrel, Side by Side, Engraved, High Quality, Antique	2,000	3,500

Shotgun, Percussion

14 Ga., Single Barrel, Smoothbore, High Quality, Cased with Accessories, Antique	800	1,250

Parkhill, Andrew
Phila., Pa. 1778-85. See Kentucky Rifles and Pistols

Parole
Made by Hopkins & Allen C.1880

Handgun, Revolver

.22 Short R.F., 7 Shot, Spur Trigger, Solid Frame, Single Action, Antique	90	160

Parr, J.
Liverpool C.1810

Rifle, Flintlock

.75, 3rd Model Brown Bess, Musket, Military, Antique	775	1,300

Parsons, Hiram
Baltimore, Md. C.1819. See Kentucky Rifles

Patriot
Made by Norwich Falls Pistol Co. C.1880

Handgun, Revolver

.32 Short R.F., 5 Shot, Spur Trigger, Solid Frame, Single Action, Antique	90	160

Peck, Abijah
Hartford, Conn. See U. S. Military

Peerless
Made by Stevens

Rifle, Bolt Action

Model 056 Buckhorn, .22 L.R.R.F., 5 Shot Clip, Peep Sights, Modern	45	60
Model 066 Buckhorn, .22 L.R.R.F., Tube Feed, Peep Sights, Modern	45	60
Model 53, .22 L.R.R.F., Singleshot, Takedown, Modern	30	40

Peerless
Made by Crescent H. & D. Folsom C.1900

Shotgun, Double Barrel, Side by Side

Various Gauges, Outside Hammers, Damascus Barrel, Modern	80	150
Various Gauges, Hammerless, Steel Barrel, Modern	95	175
Various Gauges, Hammerless, Damascus Barrel, Modern	75	150
Various Gauges, Outside Hammers, Steel Barrel, Modern	90	175

Shotgun, Singleshot

Various Gauges, Hammer, Steel Barrel, Modern	45	75

Pence, Jacob
Lancaster, Pa. 1771. See Kentucky Rifles and Pistols

Penetrator
Made by Norwich Falls Pistol Co. C.1880

Handgun, Revolver

.32 Short R.F., 5 Shot, Spur Trigger, Solid Frame, Single Action, Modern	90	160

Pennypacker, Daniel
Berks County, Pa. 1773-1808. See Kentucky Rifles and Pistols

Pennypacker, Wm.
Berks County, Pa. 1808-58. See Kentucky Rifles and Pistols

Percussion, Unknown Maker

Handgun, Percussion

.40 English, 6 Shot, Pepperbox, Pocket Pistol, Light Engraving, German Silver Frame, Steel Barrel, Antique	225	350
.45, Pair French, Target Pistol, Octagon Barrel, Single Set Trigger, Brass Furniture, Cased with Accessories, Antique	2,000	2,500
.70, French Sotiau, Belt Pistol, Steel Furniture, Rifled, Octagon Barrel, Antique	400	550
Boot Pistol, Bar Hammer, Screw Barrel, Antique	90	150
Boot Pistol, Boxlock, Screw Barrel, Antique	85	140
Boot Pistol, Sidelock, Derringer Style, Antique	100	160
Pair, Duelling Pistols, Octagon Barrel, Single Set Trigger, German Silver Furniture, Medium Quality, Cased with Accessories, Antique	1,400	2,000

Percussion Arms Unknown Maker Boot Pistol

Percussion Firearms, Unknown Maker
Benchrest Rifle

Handgun, Revolver

.36, Navy Colt Type, Belgian Make, Medium Quality, Antique	100	175
.45, Adams Type, Double Action, Octagon Barrel, Plain, Cased with Accessories, Antique	600	900

Rifle, Percussion

American Indian Trade Gun, Belgian, Converted from Flintlock, Brass Furniture, Antique	500	900
Benchrest, Various Calibers, Heavy Barrel, Set Triggers, Target Sights, Light Decoration, Antique	400	750
Benchrest, Various Calibers, Heavy Barrel, Set Triggers, Target Sights, Medium Decoration, Antique	500	950
German, Schutzen Rifle, Rifled, Ivory Inlays, Gold Inlays, Ornate, Antique	4,500	5,000

Shotgun, Percussion

English, 12 Ga., Double Barrel, Side by Side, Light Ornamentation, Medium Quality, Antique	300	450
English, 12 Ga., Double Barrel, Side by Side, Light Ornamentation, High Quality, Cased with Accessories, Antique	500	800

Perfect
Made by Foehl & Weeks. Phila, Pa. C.1890

Handgun, Revolver

.38 S & W, 5 Shot, Double Action, Top Break, Modern	45	95

Perfection
Made by Crescent for H. & G. Lipscomb & Co. Nashville, Tenn.

Shotgun, Double Barrel, Side by Side

Various Gauges, Outside Hammers, Damascus Barrel, Modern	80	150
Various Gauges, Hammerless, Steel Barrel, Modern	95	175
Various Gauges, Hammerless, Damascus Barrel, Modern	75	150
Various Gauges, Outside Hammers, Steel Barrel, Modern	90	175

Shotgun, Singleshot

Various Gauges, Hammer, Steel Barrel, Modern	45	75

Perfection Automatic Revolver
Made by Forehand Arms Co.

Handgun, Revolver

.32 S & W, 5 Shot, Double Action, Top Break, Antique	55	85
.32 S & W, 5 Shot, Double Action, Top Break, Hammerless, Antique	60	95

Pettibone, Daniel
Philadelphia, Pa. 1799-1814.

Phillipine Military

Shotgun, Singleshot

WW 2 Guerrilla Weapon, 12 Ga., Modern	55	95

Phoenix Arms .25 ACP

Phoenix
Spain, Tomas de Urizar y Cia C.1920

Handgun, Semi-Automatic
Vest Pocket, .25 ACP, Clip Fed, Modern 70 100

Phoenix Arms Co.
Lowell, Mass. Lowell Arms Co. C.1920

Handgun, Semi-Automatic
Vest Pocket, .25 ACP, Clip Fed, Curio 250 375

Pic
Germany

Handgun, Semi-Automatic
Vest Pocket, .25 ACP, Clip Fed, Modern 45 65
Vest Pocket, .22 Short R.F., Clip Fed, Modern 45 65

Pickfatt, Humphrey
London, England 1714-30

Handgun, Flintlock
Pair, Queen Anne Style, Box Lock, Pocket Pistol, Silver Furniture, Antique 2,000 2,500
Pair, Holster Pistol, Engraved, Brass Furniture, High Quality, Antique 7,500+

Piedmont
Made by Crescent for Piedmont Hdw. Danville, Pa.

Shotgun, Double Barrel, Side by Side
Various Gauges, Outside Hammers, Damascus Barrel, Modern 80 150
Various Gauges, Hammerless, Steel Barrel, Modern 95 175
Various Gauges, Hammerless, Damascus Barrel, Modern 75 150
Various Gauges, Outside Hammers, Steel Barrel, Modern 90 175

Shotgun, Singleshot
Various Gauges, Hammer, Steel Barrel, Modern 45 75

Pieper
Herstal, Belgium (N. Pieper) 1906-23

Combination Weapon, Double Barrel, Side by Side
Various Calibers, Hammer, Open Rear Sight, Checkered Stock, Plain,
Modern 275 375

Handgun, Semi-Automatic
Bayard Model 1908 Pocket, .25 ACP, Blue, Clip Fed, Modern 95 165
Bayard Model 1908 Pocket, .380 ACP, Blue, Clip Fed, Modern 85 145
Bayard Model 1923 Pocket, .25 ACP, Blue, Clip Fed, Modern 85 150
Bayard Model 1923 Pocket, .32 ACP, Blue, Clip Fed, Modern 100 185
Bayard Model 1930 Pocket, .25 ACP, Blue, Clip Fed, Modern 100 185

Model A (Army), .32 ACP, Clip Fed, 7 Shot, Modern 80 120
Model B, .32 ACP, Clip Fed, 6 Shot, Modern 70 100

Model C, .25 ACP, Clip Fed, Long Grip, Modern	100	135
Model C, .25 ACP, Clip Fed, Modern	85	120
Model D (1920), .25 ACP, Clip Fed, Tip-Up, Modern	100	140
Model Legia, .25 ACP, Clip Fed, Modern	75	110
Model Legia, .25 ACP, Clip Fed, Long Grip, Modern	85	125
Model N, .32 ACP, Clip Fed, Tip-Up, 7 Shot, Modern	85	125
Model O, .32 ACP, Clip Fed, Tip-Up, 6 Shot, Modern	75	110
Model P, .25 ACP, Clip Fed, Tip-Up, Modern	100	145

Rifle, Semi-Automatic

Pieper/Bayard Carbine, .22 Short, Checkered Stock, Pistol Grip, Curio	40	70
Pieper/Bayard Carbine, .22 Long, Checkered Stock, Pistol Grip, Curio	50	85
Pieper Carbine, .22 L.R.R.F., Checkered Stock, English Grip, Curio	50	85
Pieper Musket, .22 L.R.R.F., Military Style Stock, Curio	60	90
Pieper Musket, .22 L.R.R.F., Military Style Stock, with Bayonet, Curio	75	110

Shotgun, Double Barrel, Side by Side

Bayard, Various Gauges, Hammerless, Boxlock, Light Engraving, Checkered Stock, Modern	100	175
Hammer Gun, Various Gauges, Plain, Steel Barrels, Modern	75	135
Hammer Gun, Various Gauges, Plain, Damascus Barrels, Modern	65	125
Hammer Gun, Various Gauges, Light Engraving, Steel Barrels, Modern	95	165

Pieper, Abraham
Lancaster, Pa. 1801-03 See Kentucky Rifles and Pistols

Pieper, Henri

Combination Weapon, Double Barrel, Side by Side

Various Calibers, Double Trigger, Outside Hammers, Side Lever, Antique	250	325

Pinafore
Made by Norwich Falls Pistol Co. C.1880

Handgun, Revolver

.22 Short R.F., 7 Shot, Spur Trigger, Solid Frame, Single Action, Antique	90	160

Pioneer
Made by Stevens Arms

Rifle, Semi-Automatic

Model 87, .22 L.R.R.F., Tube Feed, Open Rear Sight, Modern	45	65

Pioneer
Maker Unknown C.1880

Handgun, Revolver

.38 Short R.F., 5 Shot, Spur Trigger, Solid Frame, Single Action, Antique	95	170

Pieper Model C Demontant .25 ACP

Pioneer Arms Co.
Made by Crescent for Kruse Hardware Co. Cincinnati, Ohio

Shotgun, Double Barrel, Side by Side

Various Gauges, Outside Hammers, Damascus Barrel, Modern	80	150
Various Gauges, Hammerless, Steel Barrel, Modern	95	175
Various Gauges, Hammerless, Damascus Barrel, Modern	75	150
Various Gauges, Outside Hammers, Steel Barrel, Modern	90	175

Shotgun, Singleshot

Various Gauges, Hammer, Steel Barrel, Modern	45	75

Piotti
Brescia, Italy. Currently Imported by Ventura Imports

Shotgun, Double Barrel, Side by Side

Gardone, 12 and 20 Gauges, Sidelock, Automatic Ejector, Double Trigger, Fancy Checkering, Fancy Engraving, Modern	1,200	1,700
Val Trompia Crown, 12 and 20 Gauges, Sidelock, Automatic Ejector, Single Selective Trigger, Fancy Checkering, Fancy Engraving, Modern	2,500	3,500

PJK
Bradbury, Calif.

Rifle, Semi-Automatic

M-68, 9mm Luger, Clip Fed, Carbine, Frash Hider, Modern	125	175

Plainfield Machine Co.
Dunellen, N.J. Current

Automatic Weapon, Submachine Gun

M-2, .30 Carbine, Carbine, Commercial, Class 3	140	175

Handgun, Semi-Automatic

Super Enforcer, .30 Carbine, Clip Fed, Modern	95	140

Rifle, Semi-Automatic

M-1, .30 Carbine, Carbine, Modern	80	120
M-1, .30 Carbine, Carbine, Sporting Rifle, Modern	80	120
M-1, 5.7mm Carbine, Carbine, Modern	80	110
M-1 Deluxe, .30 Carbine, Carbine, Sporting Rifle, Monte Carlo Stock, Checkered Stock, Modern	95	125
M-1 Paratrooper, .30 Carbine, Carbine, Folding Stock, Modern	100	130
M-1 Presentation, .30 Carbine, Carbine, Sporting Rifle, Monte Carlo Stock, Fancy Wood, Modern	95	125

Plainfield Ordnance Co.
Middlesex, N.J.

Handgun, Semi-Automatic

Model 71, .22 L.R.R.F., Clip Fed, Stainless Steel, Modern	50	70
Model 71, .22 L.R.R.F. and .25 ACP, Clip Fed, Stainless Steel, with Conversion Kit, Modern	60	90
Model 71, .25 ACP, Clip Fed, Stainless Steel, Modern	40	65
Model 72, .22 L.R.R.F., Clip Fed, Lightweight, Modern	45	70
Model 72, .22 L.R.R.F. and .25 ACP, Clip Fed, Lightweight, with Conversion Kit, Modern	60	90
Model 72, .25 ACP, Clip Fed, Lightweight, Modern	40	65

Plant's Mfg. Co.

Handgun, Revolver

.28 Cup Primed Cartridge, 6 Shot, Single Action, Spur Trigger, Solid Frame, Antique	95	160
.30 Cup Primed Cartridge, 6 Shot, Single Action, Spur Trigger, Solid Frame, Antique	95	170

Plant's Mfg. Co. Cup-Fires - .42; .30

Plus Ultra .32 ACP

.31 R.F., 6 Shot, Single Action, Solid Frame, Spur Trigger, Antique	95	150
.32 Short R.F., 6 Shot, Single Action, Solid Frame, Spur Trigger, Antique	95	150
.42 Cup Primed Cartridge, 6 Shot, Single Action, Spur Trigger, Solid Frame, Antique	130	195
.42 Cup Primed Cartridge, 6 Shot, Single Action, Spur Trigger, Solid Frame, 6" Barrel, Antique	220	340
"Original," .28 Cup Primed Cartridge, 6 Shot, Single Action, Spur Trigger, Tip-Up, Antique	400	550
"Original," .30 Cup Primed Cartridge, 6 Shot, Single Action, Spur Trigger, Tip-Up, Antique	425	575
"Original," .42 Cup Primed Cartridge, 6 Shot, Single Action, Spur Trigger, Tip-Up, Antique	475	625
"Original," Various Cup-Primed Calibers, Extra Cylinder, Percussion, Add $90-$150		
Reynolds, .25 Short R.F., 5 Shot, Single Action, Spur Trigger, 3" Barrel, Antique	90	160

Plus Ultra
Gabilondo y Cia., Spain

Handgun, Semi-Automatic

.32 ACP, Extra Long Grip, Military, Modern	350	500

Pous, Eudal
Spain, C.1790

Handgun, Miquelet-Lock

Pair, Holster Pistol, Low Quality, Light Brass Furniture, Antique	1,500	2,300

Praga "Praha" .32 ACP

Praga
Zbrojovka Praga

Handgun, Semi-Automatic
Praha, .32 ACP, Clip Fed, Modern 175 225

Prairie King
Made by Norwich Falls Pistol Co. C.1880

Handgun, Revolver
.22 Short R.F., 7 Shot, Spur Trigger, Solid Frame, Single Action, Antique 75 130

Premier
Brooklyn, N.Y.

Shotgun, Double Barrel, Side by Side
Ambassador, Various Calibers, Checkered Stock, Hammerless, Double Trigger, Modern 165 220
Brush King, 12 and 20 Gauges, Checkered Stock, Hammerless, Double Trigger, Modern 125 165
Continental, Various Calibers, Checkered Stock, Outside Hammers, Double Trigger, Modern 135 185
Magnum, 10 Ga. 3½", Checkered Stock, Hammerless, Double Trigger, Modern 150 200
Magnum, 12 Ga. Mag. 3", Checkered Stock, Hammerless, Double Trigger, Modern 135 180
Monarch, Various Calibers, Hammerless, Double Trigger, Checkered Stock, Engraved, Adjustable Choke, Modern 250 350
Presentation, Various Calibers, Hammerless, Double Trigger, Fancy Engraving, Fancy Checkering, Adjustable Choke, Modern 450 675
Presentation, Various Calibers, Adjustable Choke, Double Trigger, Fancy Engraving, Fancy Checkering, Extra Shotgun Barrel, Modern 650 900
Regent, Various Calibers, Checkered Stock, Hammerless, Double Trigger, Modern 110 155
Regent, Various Calibers, Checkered Stock, Hammerless, Double Trigger, Extra Shotgun Barrel,Modern 200 300

Premier
Made by Stevens Arms

Rifle, Bolt Action
Model 52, .22 L.R.R.F., Singleshot, Takedown, Modern 25 35
Model 53, .22 L.R.R.F., Singleshot, Takedown, Modern 25 40
Model 66 Buckhorn, .22 L.R.R.F., Tube Feed, Open Rear Sight, Modern 30 50

Rifle, Slide Action
Model 75, .22 L.R.R.F., Tube Feed, Hammerless, Modern 85 160

Premier
Made by Thomas E. Ryan, Norwich, Conn. C.1870-76

Handgun, Revolver
.22 Short R.F., 7 Shot, Spur Trigger, Solid Frame, Single Action, Antique 90 160
.38 Long R.F., 6 Shot, Spur Trigger, Solid Frame, Single Action, Antique 90 160

Premier Trail Blazer
Made by Stevens Arms

Rifle, Pump
Model 75, .22 L.R.R.F., Tube Feed, Hammerless, Modern 85 160

Prima .25 ACP

Princep .25 ACP

Prescott, E. A.

Handgun, Revolver

.22 Short R.F., 7 Shot, Spur Trigger, Solid Frame, Single Action, Antique   90   150
.30 R.F., 6 Shot, Spur Trigger, Solid Frame, Single Action, Antique   95   155
.32 Short R.F., 6 Shot, Spur Trigger, Solid Frame, Single Action, Antique   95   155
"Navy" .32 Short R.F., 6 Shot, Single Action, Solid Frame, Finger-Rest
   Trigger Guard, Antique   220   300
"Navy" .38 Short R.F., 6 Shot, Single Action, Solid Frame, Finger-Rest
   Trigger Guard, Antique   250   325

Price, J. W.
Made by Stevens Arms

Shotgun, Singleshot

Model 90, Various Gauges, Takedown, Automatic Ejector, Plain, Hammer,
   Modern   35   50

Prima

Handgun, Semi-Automatic

.25 ACP, Clip Fed, Modern   80   110

Princep

Handgun, Semi-Automatic

.25 ACP, Clip Fed, Blue, Modern   85   125
.32 ACP, Clip Fed, Modern   80   125

Princess
Unknown Maker C.1880

Handgun, Revolver

.22 Short R.F., 7 Shot, Spur Trigger, Solid Frame, Single Action,   Antique   90   160

Protector
Made by Norwich Falls Pistol Co. C.1880

Handgun, Revolver

.22 Short R.F., 7 Shot, Spur Trigger, Solid Frame, Single Action, Antique   90   160
.32 Short R.F., 5 Shot, Spur Trigger, Solid Frame, Single Action, Antique   95   170

Protector Arms Co.
Spain C.1900

Handgun, Semi-Automatic
M 1918, .25 ACP, Clip Fed, Modern   80   120

Purdey, James

Rifle, Double Barrel, Side by Side
.500 #2 Express, Damascus Barrel, Outside Hammers, Under-Lever,
  Engraved, Ornate, Antique   2,500   3,500

Rifle, Percussion
.52, Double Barrel, Side by Side, Damascus Barrel, Engraved, Fancy
  Wood, Gold Inlays, Cased with Accessories, Antique   5,000   6,000

Purdey, Jas & Sons
London, England 1816 to Date

Rifle, Double Barrel, Side by Side
Various Calibers, Sidelock, Fancy Engraving, Fancy Checkering, Fancy
Wood, Modern   8,000   14,500

Rifle, Bolt Action
Sporting Rifle, Various Calibers, Fancy Wood, Checkered Stock, Express
Sights, Modern   1,300   2,000

Shotgun, Double Barrel, Over-Under
12 Ga., Vent Rib, Single Selective Trigger, Pistol-Grip Stock, Modern   9,000   16,000
Various Gauges, Extra Barrels Only $3000-$5000
Purdy, Various Gauges, Sidelock, Automatic Ejector, Double Trigger,
  Fancy Engraving, Fancy Checkering, Modern   7,500   12,000
Purdy, Various Gauges, Sidelock, Automatic Ejector, Single Trigger,
  Fancy Engraving, Fancy Checkering, Modern   9,500   14,000
Woodward, Various Gauges, Sidelock, Automatic Ejector, Double Trigger,
  Fancy Engraving, Fancy Checkering, Modern   7,500   10,000
Woodward, Various Gauges, Sidelock, Automatic Ejector, Single Trigger,
  Fancy Engraving, Fancy Checkering, Modern   11,000   17,000

Shotgun, Double Barrel, Side by Side
12 Ga., Extra Barrel, Vent Rib, Single Selective Trigger, Engraved, Cased
  with Accessories, Modern   12,000   18,000
12 Ga., Extra Barrels, 10 Ga., Pistol-Grip Stock, Cased with Accessories,
  Modern   12,000   18,000
Various Gauges, Extra Barrels Only $2,500-$3,500
Featherweight, Various Gauges, Sidelock, Automatic Ejector, Double
  Trigger, Fancy Engraving, Fancy Checkering, Modern   8,500   12,000
Featherweight, Various Gauges, Sidelock, Automatic Ejector, Single
  Trigger, Fancy Engraving, Fancy Checkering, Modern   9,000   15,000
Game Gun, Various Gauges, Sidelock, Automatic Ejector, Double Trigger,
  Fancy Engraving, Fancy Checkering, Modern   8,000   13,000

Purdey Game Gun

Game Gun, Various Gauges, Sidelock, Automatic Ejector, Single Trigger, Fancy Engraving, Fancy Checkering, Modern	9,000	15,000
Pigeon Gun, 12 Ga., Single Selective Trigger, Vent Rib, Cased Straight Grip, Modern	9,000	15,000
Pigeon Gun, Various Gauges, Sidelock, Automatic Ejector, Double Trigger, Fancy Engraving, Fancy Checkering, Modern	7,000	12,000
Pigeon Gun, Various Gauges, Sidelock, Automatic Ejector, Single Trigger, Fancy Engraving, Fancy Checkering, Modern	8,000	13,000
Two-Inch, 12 Ga. 2″, Sidelock, Automatic Ejector, Double Trigger, Fancy Engraving, Fancy Checkering, Modern	7,000	10,000
Two-Inch, 12 Ga. 2″, Sidelock, Automatic Ejector, Single Trigger, Fancy Engraving, Fancy Checkering, Modern	8,500	12,500

Shotgun, Singleshot

12 Ga., Vent Rib, Plain, Trap Grade, Modern	6,000	9,500

Quackenbush
Herkimer, N.Y.

Rifle, Singleshot

.22 R.F., Side Swing Breech, Nickel Plated, Takedown, Modern	90	125

Quail
Made by Crescent C.1900

Shotgun, Double Barrel, Side by Side

Various Gauges, Outside Hammers, Damascus Barrel, Modern	80	150
Various Gauges, Hammerless, Steel Barrel, Modern	95	175
Various Gauges, Hammerless, Damascus Barrel, Modern	75	150
Various Gauges, Outside Hammers, Steel Barrel, Modern	90	175

Shotgun, Singleshot

Various Gauges, Hammer, Steel Barrel, Modern	45	75

Quail's Fargo

Shotgun, Double Barrel, Side by Side

12 Ga., Checkered Stock, Plain, Modern	110	150

Queen City
Made by Crescent for Elmira Arms Co. C.1900

Shotgun, Double Barrel, Side by Side

Various Gauges, Outside Hammers, Damascus Barrel, Modern	80	150
Various Gauges, Hammerless, Steel Barrel, Modern	95	175
Various Gauges, Hammerless, Damascus Barrel, Modern	75	150
Various Gauges, Outside Hammers, Steel Barrel, Modern	90	175

Shotgun, Singleshot

Various Gauges, Hammer, Steel Barrel, Modern	45	75

Radom
Poland 1935-48

Handgun, Semi-Automatic

VIS 1935, 9mm Luger, Clip Fed, Military, Nazi-Proofed, Early Type, Modern	140	200
VIS 1935, 9mm Luger, Clip Fed, Military, Nazi-Proofed, Late Type, Modern	120	175
VIS 1935 Navy, 9mm Luger, Clip Fed, Military, Nazi-Proofed, Curio	200	325
VIS 1935 Polish, 9mm Luger, Clip Fed, Military, Curio	225	350

Raffsnyder, John
Berks County, Pa. 1779-85. See Kentucky Rifles

Radoms - Polish; Early German; Late German

Ranger
Made by E. L. Dickinson, Springfield, Mass.

Handgun, Revolver

#2, .32 Short R.F., 5 Shot, Spur Trigger, Solid Frame, Single Action, Antique	90	160

Ranger
Made by Stevens Arms

Rifle, Slide Action

Model 70, .22 L.R.R.F., Hammer, Solid Frame, Modern	85	130
Model 75, .22 L.R.R.F., Tube Feed, Hammerless, Modern	95	160

Shotgun, Double Barrel, Side by Side

M 315, Various Gauges, Hammerless, Steel Barrel, Modern	90	145
Model 215, 12 and 16 Gauges, Outside Hammers, Steel Barrel, Modern	95	145

Shotgun, Singleshot

Model 89 Dreadnaught, Various Gauges, Hammer, Modern	40	55

Ranger Arms, Inc.
Gainesville, Tex.

Rifle, Bolt Action

Bench Rest/Varminter, Various Calibers, Singleshot, Target Rifle, Thumbhole Stock, Heavy Barrel, Recoil Pad, Modern	325	475
Governor Grade, Various Calibers, Sporting Rifle, Fancy Checkering, Fancy Wood, Recoil Pad, Sling Swivels, Modern	300	400
Governor Grade Magnum, Various Calibers, Sporting Rifle, Fancy Checkering, Fancy Wood, Recoil Pad, Sling Swivels, Modern	325	475
Senator Grade, Various Calibers, Sporting Rifle, Fancy Checkering, Recoil Pad, Sling Swivels, Modern	250	375
Senator Grade Magnum, Various Calibers, Sporting Rifle, Fancy Checkering, Recoil Pad, Sling Swivels, Modern	260	375
Statesman Grade, Various Calibers, Sporting Rifle, Checkered Stock, Recoil Pad, Sling Swivels, Modern	185	295
Statesman Grade Magnum, Various Calibers, Sporting Rifle, Checkered Stock, Recoil Pad, Sling Swivels, Modern	250	350

Ranger Revolvers
Made by Hopkins & Allen C.1880

Handgun, Revolver

.22 Short R.F., 7 Shot, Spur Trigger, Solid Frame, Single Action, Antique	90	160
.32 Short R.F., 5 Shot, Spur Trigger, Solid Frame, Single Action, Antique	95	160

Rasch
Brunswick, Germany 1790-1810

Rifle, Flintlock
Yaeger, Octagon Barrel, Brass Furniture, Engraved, Carved, Target
  Sights, Antique   2,400   3,250

Rathfong, George
Lancaster, Pa. 1774-1809. See U.S. Military, Kentucky Rifles

Rathfong, Jacob
Lancaster, Pa. 1810-39. See Kentucky Rifles and Pistols

Raven

Handgun, Semi-Automatic
.25 ACP, Blue, Clip Fed, Modern	30	40
.25 ACP, Nickel, Clip Fed, Modern	30	40
.25 ACP, Chrome, Clip Fed, Modern	30	40

Reasor, David
Lancaster, Pa. 1749-80. See Kentucky Rifles and Pistols

Reck
Germany

Handgun, Semi-Automatic
P-8, .25 ACP, Clip Fed, Modern   35   55

Red Cloud

Handgun, Revolver
.32 Long R.F., 5 Shot, Single Action, Solid Frame, Spur Trigger, Antique   90   160

Red Jacket
Made by Lee Arms Wilkes-Barre, Pa. C.1870

Handgun, Revolver
.22 L.R.R.F., 7 Shot, Spur Trigger, Solid Frame, Single Action, Antique	90	160
.32 Short R.F., 5 Shot, Spur Trigger, Solid Frame, Single Action, Antique	95	165

Red Mountain Arsenal
Parowen, Utah

Automatic Weapon, Submachinegun
Model 80C, 9mm and .45 ACP Combo, Clip Fed, with Conversion Kit,
  Class 3   225   300

Reed, James
Lancaster, Pa. 1778-80. See Kentucky Rifles

Reform

Handgun, Repeater
.25 ACP, 4 Barrels, Spur Trigger, Hammer, Modern   60   100

Regina
Eibar, Spain Gregorio Bolumburu C.1900

Handgun, Semi-Automatic
Pocket, .32 ACP, Clip Fed, Modern	70	100
Vest Pocket, .25 ACP, Clip Fed, Modern	60	90

Regina .25 ACP

Regnum

Handgun, Repeater
.25 ACP, 4 Barrels, Spur Trigger, Hammerless, Modern　　　　　　　　　65　　110

Reid Patent Revolvers
Made by W. Irving for James Reid, N.Y. 1862-84

Handgun, Revolver

.22 Short R.F., 7 Shot, Spur Trigger, Solid Frame, Single Action, Antique	125	250
.32 Short R.F., 7 Shot, Spur Trigger, Solid Frame, Single Action, Antique	175	325
.41 Short R.F., 5 Shot, Spur Trigger, Solid Frame, Single Action, Antique	375	525
My Friend, .22 R.F., Knuckleduster, 7 Shot, Antique	200	350
My Friend, .32 R.F., Knuckleduster, 7 Shot, Antique	275	425

Reims
Azanza y Arrizabalaga

Handgun, Semi-Automatic
1914 Model, .32 ACP, Clip Fed, Modern　　　　　　　　　　　　　　　70　　110

Reising
Hartford, Conn. 1916-24

Automatic Weapon, Submachine Gun

M50 Reising, .45 ACP, Clip Fed, Wood Stock, Military, Cased with Accessories, Class 3	225	325
M50 Reising, .45 ACP, Clip Fed, Wood Stock, Military, Class 3	140	225
M55 Reising, .45 ACP, Clip Fed, Folding Stock, Military, Class 3	225	325

Reims Model 1914 .32 ACP

Handgun, Semi-Automatic

Target (Hartford), .22 L.R.R.F., Clip Fed, Hammer, Modern	200	300
Target (N.Y.), .22 L.R.R.F., Clip Fed, Hammer, Modern	300	425

Remington Arms Co.
Eliphalet Remington, Herkimer County, N.Y. 1816-31. Ilion, N.Y. 1831 to Date. 1856-E. Remington & Sons. 1888- Remington Arms Co. 1910- Remington Arms U.M.C. Co. 1925 to Date Remington Arms Co.

Handgun, Double Barrel, Over-Under

Elliot Derringer, 1st. Model, .41 Short R.F., Spur Trigger, Tip-Up, no Extractor, Markings on Sides of Barrel, E. Remington & Sons, Antique	300	575
Elliot Derringer, 2nd. Model, .41 Short R.F., Spur Trigger, Tip-Up, with Extractor, Markings on Sides of Barrel, E. Remington & Sons, Antique	275	550
Elliot Derringer, 3rd. Model, .41 Short R.F., Spur Trigger, Tip-Up, with Extractor, Markings on Top of Barrel, E. Remington & Sons, Antique	200	375
Elliot Derringer, 4th Model, .41 Short R.F., Spur Trigger, Tip-Up, with Extractor, Markings on Top of Barrel, Remington Arms Co., Modern	175	300
Elliot Derringer, 5th Model, .41 Short R.F., Spur Trigger, Tip-Up, with Extractor, Markings on Top of Barrel, Modern	175	300
Elliot Derringer, 6th Model, .41 Short R.F., Spur Trigger, Tip-Up, with Extractor, Remington Arms Co. #'s L75925-L99941, Modern	150	275

Handgun, Manual Repeater

Elliot Derringer, .22 Short R.F., 5 Shot, Double Action, Ring Trigger, Rotating Firing Block, Antique	275	400
Elliot Derringer, .32 Short R.F., 4 Shot, Double Action, Ring Trigger, Rotating Firing Block, Antique	250	375
Rider Magazine Pistol, .32 Extra Short R.F., Tube Feed, Spur Trigger, 5 Shot, Antique	300	475

Handgun Percussion

.31, Beals #1, Revolver, Pocket Pistol, 5 Shot, Octagon Barrel, 3" Barrel, Antique	250	400
.31, Beals #2, Revolver, Pocket Pistol, 5 Shot, Octagon Barrel, 3" Barrel, Spur Trigger, Antique	950	1,850
.31, Beals #3, Revolver, Octagon Barrel, 4" Barrel, Spur Trigger, with Loading Lever, Antique	600	1,100
.31, New Model Pocket, Revolver, Safety Notches on Cylinder, Spur Trigger, 5 Shot, Octagon Barrel, Antique	275	525
.31, Rider Pocket, Revolver, Double Action, 5 Shot, Octagon Barrel, 3" Barrel, Antique	225	450
.36, Beals Navy, Revolver, Single Action, Octagon Barrel, 7½" Barrel Antique	375	650
.36, Belt Model, Revolver, Safety Notches on Cylinder, Single Action, Octagon Barrel, 6½" Barrel, Antique	325	575
.36, Belt Model, Revolver, Safety Notches on Cylinder, Double Action, Octagon Barrel, 6½" Barrel, Antique	450	900
.36, Model 1861 Navy, Revolver, Channeled Loading Level, Single Action, Octagon Barrel, 7½" Barrel, Antique	375	650
.36, New Model Navy, Revolver, Safety Notches on Cylinder, Single Action, Octagon Barrel, 7½" Barrel, Antique	425	700
.36, Police Model, Revolver, Single Action, Octagon Barrel, Various Barrel Lengths, 5 Shot, Antique	300	525

Remington Elliot Derringer, Ring Trigger

Remington Beals Army Model

Remington .44, New Model Army

.44, Beals Army, Revolver, Single Action, Octagon Barrel, 8" Barrel, Antique	525	900
.44, Model 1861 Army, Revolver, Channeled Loading Lever, Single Action, Octagon Barrel, 8" Barrel, Antique	400	650
.44, New Model Army, Revolver, Safety Notches on Cylinder, Single Action, Octagon Barrel, 7½" Barrel, Antique	375	625

Handgun Revolver

Iroquois, .22 L.R.R.F., 7 Shot, Solid Frame, Spur Trigger, Single Action, Fluted Cylinder, Antique	175	275
Iroquois, .22 L.R.R.F., 7 Shot, Solid Frame, Spur Trigger, Single Action, Unfluted Cylinder, Antique	250	375
Model 1875, .44-40 WCF, Single Action, Western Style, Solid Frame, Antique	550	950
Model 1875, .45 Colt, Single Action, Western Style, Solid Frame, Antique	500	900
Model 1890, .44-40 WCF, Single Action, Western Style, Solid Frame, Antique	850	1,500
Smoot #1, .30 Short R.F., 5 Shot, Solid Frame, Spur Trigger, Single Action, Antique	145	225
Smoot #2, .32 Short R.F., 5 Shot, Solid Frame, Spur Trigger, Single Action, Antique	115	190
Smoot #3, .38 Long R.F., 5 Shot, Solid Frame, Spur Trigger, Single Action, Birdhead Grip, Antique	150	275

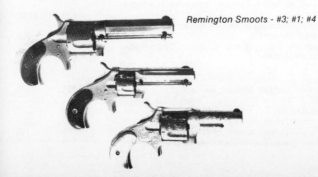

Remington Smoots - #3; #1; #4

Remington Model 51 .32 ACP

Smoot #3, .38 Long R.F., 5 Shot, Solid Frame, Spur Trigger, Single Action,
   Saw Handle Grip, Antique   165   300
Smoot #4, .38 S & W, 5 Shot, Solid Frame, Spur Trigger, Single Action, no
   Ejector Housing, Antique   120   180
Smoot #4, .41 Short R.F., 5 Shot, Solid Frame, Spur Trigger, Single
   Action, no Ejector Housing, Antique   95   160
Zig-Zag Derringer, .22 Short R.F., Pepperbox, Double Action, 6 Shot, Ring
   Trigger, Antique   675   1,200

Handgun, Semi-Automatic
Model 51, .32 ACP, Clip Fed, Grip Safety, Modern   135   225
Model 51, .380 ACP, Clip Fed, Grip Safety, Modern   150   260

Handgun, Singleshot
#1 Vest Pocket, .22 Short R.F., Iron Frame, no Breech Bolt, Spur Trigger,
   Antique   175   275
#2 Vest Pocket, .30 Short R.F., Iron Frame, "Split Breech" Model, Spur
   Trigger, Antique   275   450
#2 Vest Pocket, .41 Short R.F., Iron Frame, "Split Breech" Model, Spur
   Trigger, Antique   225   375
Elliot Derringer, .41 Short R.F., Iron Frame, Birdhead Grip, no Breech
   Bolt, Antique   275   450
Model 1865 Navy, .50 Rem. Navy R.F., Rolling Block, Spur Trigger, 8½"
   Barrel, Antique   800   1,300
Model 1867 Navy, .50 Rem., Rolling Block, 7" Barrel, Antique   425   700
Model 1891 Target, Rolling Block, 12" Barrel, Add 15%-20%
Model 1891 Target, Rolling Block, 10" Barrel, Add 15%-20%
Model 1891 Target, .22 L.R.R.F., Rolling Block, 8" Barrel, Half-Octagon
   Barrel, Plain Barrel, Antique   575   975
Model 1891 Target, .25 Short R.F., Rolling Block, 8" Barrel, Half-Octagon
   Barrel, Plain Barrel, Antique   400   600
Model 1891 Target, .32 Long R.F., Rolling Block, 8" Barrel, Half-Octagon
   Barrel, Plain Barrel, Antique   425   750
Model 1891 Target, .32 S & W, Rolling Block, 8" Barrel, Half-Octagon
   Barrel, Plain Barrel, Antique   525   950
Model 1891 Target, .32-20 WCF, Rolling Block, 8" Barrel, Half-Octagon
   Barrel, Plain Barrel, Antique   650   1,000
Model 1901 Target, .22 L.R.R.F., Rolling Block, 10" Barrel, Checkered
   Stock, Half-Octagon Barrel, Modern   550   900
Model 1901 Target, .44 Russian, Rolling Block, 10" Barrel, Checkered
   Stock, Half-Octagon Barrel, Modern   550   975

Rifle, Bolt Action
Enfield 1914, .303 British, Full-Stocked, Military, Modern   125   175
International (1961), Various Calibers, Singleshot, Target Stock, no
   Sights, with Accessories, Modern   250   375
Model 1907/15 French, 8 x 50R Lebel, Military, Modern   85   150
Model 1907/15 French, 8 x 50R Lebel, Carbine, Military, Modern   85   150
Model 1917 U.S., .30-06 Springfield, Full-Stocked, Military, Modern   110   175

Model 30A, Various Calibers, Sporting Rifle, Plain, Open Rear Sight, Modern	145	200
Model 30F Premier, Various Calibers, Sporting Rifle, Fancy Checkering, Fancy Engraving, Fancy Wood, Modern	450	575
Model 30R, Various Calibers, Sporting Rifle, Plain, Carbine, Open Rear Sight, Modern	150	210
Model 30S, Various Calibers, Sporting Rifle, Checkered Stock, Peep Sights, Modern	200	275
Model 33A, .22 L.R.R.F., Plain, Singleshot, Open Rear Sight, Modern	30	45
Model 33A, .22 L.R.R.F., Plain, Singleshot, Peep Sights, Modern	30	45
Model 33NRA, .22 L.R.R.F., Plain, Singleshot, Peep Sights, Sling Swivels, Modern	35	55
Model 341A, .22 L.R.R.F., Tube Feed, Takedown, Open Rear Sight, Modern	50	80
Model 341P, .22 L.R.R.F., Tube Feed, Takedown, Peep Sights, Modern	55	85
Model 341SB. .22 L.R.R.F., Tube Feed, Takedown, Smoothbore, Modern	45	60
Model 34A, .22 L.R.R.F., Tube Feed, Takedown, Open Rear Sight, Modern	50	75
Model 34A, .22 L.R.R.F., Tube Feed, Takedown, Lyman Sights, Modern	50	75
Model 34NRA, .22 L.R.R.F., Tube Feed, Takedown, Lyman Sights, Target, Modern	60	85
Model 37A, .22 L.R.R.F., 5 Shot Clip, Target Stock, Target Sights, Target Barrel, Modern	200	275
Model 37A, .22 L.R.R.F., 5 Shot Clip, Target Stock, Target Sights, Target Barrel, Fancy Wood, Modern	225	300
Model 37AX, .22 L.R.R.F., 5 Shot Clip, Target Stock, no Sights, Target Barrels, Modern	170	225
Model 40-XB CF-H2, Various Calibers, Stainless Steel Barrel, Heavy Barrel, Target Stock, no Sights, Modern	225	345
Model 40-XB CF-S2, Various Calibers, Stainless Steel Barrel, Target Stock, no Sights, Modern	235	340
Model 40-XB RF-H2, .22 L.R.R.F., Heavy Barrel, Target Stock, no Sights, Modern	150	225
Model 40-XB RF-S2, .22 L.R.R.F., Target Stock, no Sights, Modern	150	225
Model 40-XB-BR, Add $30-$40 for 2 oz. Trigger		
Model 40-XB-BR, Various Calibers, Stainless Steel Barrel, Heavy Barrel, Target Stock, no Sights, Modern	275	350
Model 40-XB-CF, Add $25 for Repeater		
Model 40X-CFH2, Various Calibers, Singleshot, Target Stock, no Sights, Heavy Barrel, Modern	155	220
Model 40X-CFS2, Various Calibers, Singleshot, Target Stock, no Sights, Modern	145	200
Model 40X-H1, .22 L.R.R.F., Singleshot, Target Stock, Target Sights, Heavy Barrel, Modern	140	185
Model 40X-H2, .22 L.R.R.F., Singleshot, Target Stock, no Sights, Heavy Barrel, Modern	115	160
Model 40X-S1, .22 L.R.R.F., Singleshot, Target Stock, Target Sights, Modern	140	175
Model 40X-S2, .22 L.R.R.F., Singleshot, Target Stock, no Sights, Modern	110	150
Model 40XB Sporter, .22 L.R.R.F., Modern	300	375
Model 40XC National Match, .308 Winchester, Target Stock, Target Sights, Modern	250	325
Model 40XR Position, .22 L.R.R.F., Target Stock, no Sights, Modern	175	275
Model 41A, .22 L.R.R.F., Takedown, Singleshot, Plain, Open Rear Sight, Modern	30	45
Model 41AS, .22 WRF, Takedown, Singleshot, Plain, Open Rear Sight, Modern	35	50
Model 41P, .22 L.R.R.F., Takedown, Singleshot, Plain, Target Sights, Modern	35	45
Model 41SB, .22 L.R.R.F., Takedown, Singleshot, Plain, Smoothbore, Modern	30	45
Model 510A, .22 L.R.R.F., Singleshot, Open Rear Sight, Plain, Takedown, Modern	30	50
Model 510C, .22 L.R.R.F., Singleshot, Carbine, Plain, Takedown, Modern	30	50

Model 51OP, .22 L.R.R.F., Singleshot, Peep Sights, Plain, Takedown, Modern	30	50
Model 510SB, .22 L.R.R.F., Singleshot, Smoothbore, Plain, Takedown, Modern	25	45
Model 510X, .22 L.R.R.F., Singleshot, Plain, Modern	20	35
Model 510X, .22 L.R.R.F., Singleshot, Plain, Smoothbore, Modern	20	35
Model 511A, .22 L.R.R.F., Clip Fed, Open Rear Sight, Plain, Takedown, Modern	40	60
Model 511P, .22 L.R.R.F., Clip Fed, Peep Sights, Plain, Takedown, Modern	40	65
Model 511SB, .22 L.R.R.F., Clip Fed, Smoothbore, Plain, Takedown, Modern	30	50
Model 511X, .22 L.R.R.F., Clip Fed, Plain, Modern	35	45
Model 512A, .22 L.R.R.F., Tube Feed, Plain, Open Rear Sight, Modern	40	60
Model 512P, .22 L.R.R.F., Tube Feed, Plain, Peep Sights, Modern	40	60
Model 512SB, .22 L.R.R.F., Tube Feed, Plain, Smoothbore, Modern	35	50
Model 512X. .22 L.R.R.F., Tube Feed, Plain, Modern	35	45
Model 513SA, .22 L.R.R.F., Clip Fed, Sporting Rifle, Open Rear Sight, Takedown, Checkered Stock, Modern	60	100
Model 513SP, .22 L.R.R.F., Clip Fed, Sporting Rifle, Peep Sights, Takedown, Checkered Stock, Modern	60	100
Model 513TR, .22 L.R.R.F., Clip Fed, Target Stock, Target Sights, Takedown, Modern	80	125
Model 513TX, .22 L.R.R.F., Clip Fed, Target Stock, no Sights, Takedown, Modern	60	100
Model 514, .22 L.R.R.F., Singleshot, Plain, Open Rear Sight, Modern	20	35
Model 514BR (Youth), .22 L.R.R.F., Singleshot, Plain, Open Rear Sight, Modern	20	35
Model 514P, .22 L.R.R.F., Singleshot, Plain, Peep Sights, Modern	25	40
Model 521TL, .22 L.R.R.F., Takedown, Clip Fed, Target Stock, Lyman Sights, Modern	55	80
Model 540XR Position, .22 L.R.R.F., Target Stock, no Sights, Modern	85	150
Model 540XRJR Position, .22 L.R.R.F., Target Stock, no Sights, Modern	85	150
Model 541-S, .22 L.R.R.F., Clip Fed, Checkered Stock, Fancy Wood, Modern	80	120
Model 580, .22 L.R.R.F., Singleshot, Plain, Modern	25	45
Model 580 BR (Youth), .22 L.R.R.F., Singleshot, Plain, Modern	25	45
Model 580 SB, .22 L.R.R.F., Singleshot, Plain, Smoothbore, Modern	25	40
Model 581, .22 L.R.R.F., Clip Fed, Plain, Modern	35	60
Model 581, .22 L.R.R.F., Clip Fed, Plain, Left-Hand, Modern	40	65
Model 582, .22 L.R.R.F., Tube Feed, Plain, Modern	40	65
Model 591, 5mm Rem. RFM, Clip Fed, Monte Carlo Stock, Plain, Modern	60	110
Model 592, 5mm Rem. RFM, Tube Feed, Monte Carlo Stock, Plain, Modern	60	110
Model 600, Various Calibers, Vent Rib, Carbine, Checkered Stock, Modern	125	175
Model 600, Various Calibers, Vent Rib, Carbine, Magnum, Recoil Pad, Checkered Stock, Modern	155	200
Model 600 Montana Centennial, Trap Grade, Carbine, Checkered Stock, Commemorative, Curio	175	245
Model 660, Various Calibers, Carbine, Checkered Stock, Modern	135	180
Model 660, Various Calibers, Carbine, Magnum, Recoil Pad, Checkered Stock, Modern	165	235
Model 700 Safari, Various Calibers, Magnum, Checkered Stock, Fancy Wood, Modern	300	425
Model 700ADL, Various Calibers, Checkered Stock, Modern	135	190
Model 700ADL, Various Calibers, Magnum, Checkered Stock, Modern	150	200
Model 700BDL, Various Calibers, Checkered Stock, Fancy Wood, Modern	170	225
Model 700BDL, Various Calibers, Magnum, Checkered Stock, Fancy Wood, Modern	190	240
Model 700BDL, Various Calibers, Heavy Barrel, Varmint, Checkered Stock, Fancy Wood, Modern	180	275
Model 700BDL, Various Calibers, Checkered Stock, Fancy Wood, Magnum, Left-Hand, Modern	200	280

Model 700BDL, Various Calibers, Checkered Stock, Fancy Wood, Left-Hand, Modern	180	255
Model 700C Custom, Various Calibers, Checkered Stock, Fancy Wood, Modern	300	425
Model 700D Peerless, Various Calibers, Fancy Checkering, Fancy Wood, Engraved, Modern	500	700
Model 700F Premier, Various Calibers, Fancy Checkering, Fancy Wood, Fancy Engraving, Modern	950	1,350
Model 720A, Various Calibers, Sporting Rifle, Open Rear Sight, Modern	140	190
Model 720A, Various Calibers, Sporting Rifle, Target Sights, Modern	170	225
Model 720R, Various Calibers, Sporting Rifle, Open Rear Sight, Carbine, Modern	140	200
Model 720R, Various Calibers, Sporting Rifle, Target Sights, Carbine, Modern	170	220
Model 720S, Various Calibers, Sporting Rifle, Target Sights, Modern	170	220
Model 721, Add $10-$20 for .300 H & H Magnum		
Model 721 Peerless, Various Calibers, Long Action, Sporting Rifle, Fancy Wood, Engraved, Fancy Checkering, Modern	450	600
Model 721 Premier, Various Calibers, Long Action, Sporting Rifle, Fancy Wood, Fancy Engraving, Fancy Checkering, Modern	750	1,100
Model 721 Special, Various Calibers, Long Action, Sporting Rifle, Checkered Stock, Fancy Wood, Modern	115	160
Model 721A, Various Calibers, Long Action, Sporting Rifle, Plain, Modern	90	140
Model 721ADL, Various Calibers, Long Action, Sporting Rifle, Checkered Stock, Modern	100	155
Model 721BDL, Various Calibers, Long Action, Sporting Rifle, Monte Carlo Stock, Checkered Stock, Fancy Wood, Modern	115	160
Model 722, Add $15-$25 for .222 Rem. Model 722A, Various Calibers, Short Action, Sporting Rifle, Plain, Modern	95	145
Model 722ADL, Various Calibers, Short Action, Sporting Rifle, Checkered Stock, Modern	115	160
Model 722BDL, Various Calibers, Short Action, Sporting Rifle, Checkered Stock, Fancy Wood, Modern	120	175
Model 722D Peerless, Various Calibers, Short Action, Sporting Rifle, Fancy Wood, Fancy Checkering, Engraved, Modern	450	600
Model 722F Premier, Various Calibers, Short Action, Sporting Rifle, Fancy Wood, Fancy Engraving, Fancy Checkering, Modern	700	900
Model 725ADL, Various Calibers, Long Action, Sporting Rifle, Checkered Stock, Fancy Wood, Modern	160	225
Model 725ADL, Various Calibers, Long Action, Magnum, Sporting Rifle, Checkered Stock, Fancy Wood, Modern	300	425
Model 725D Peerless, Various Calibers, Long Action, Sporting Rifle, Engraved, Fancy Checkering, Fancy Wood, Modern	450	600
Model 725F Premier, Various Calibers, Long Action, Sporting Rifle, Fancy Engraving, Fancy Checkering, Fancy Wood, Modern	800	1,100
Model 788, Various Calibers, Clip Fed, Plain, Modern	100	140
Model 788, Various Calibers, Clip Fed, Left-Hand, Plain, Modern	110	150
Nylon 10, .22 L.R.R.F., Singleshot, Plastic Stock, Modern	30	45
Nylon 10-SB, .22 L.R.R.F., Singleshot, Plastic Stock, Smoothbore, Modern	20	35
Nylon 12, .22 L.R.R.F., Tube Feed, Plastic, Modern	40	65

Rifle, Lever Action

Nylon 76, .22 L.R.R.F., Tube Feed, Plastic Stock, Modern	50	85

Rifle, Semi-Automatic

Model 10C Mohawk, 22 L.R.R.F., Clip Fed, Plastic Stock, Modern	30	50
Model 16, .22 Rem. Automatic R.F., Takedown, Tube Feed, Modern	100	175
Model 16D, .22 Rem. Automatic R.F., Takedown, Tube Feed, Checkered Stock, Engraved, Modern	275	350
Model 16F, .22 Rem. Automatic R.F., Takedown, Tube Feed, Fancy Checkering, Fancy Engraving, Modern	600	750
Model 241A, .22 L.R.R.F., Tube Feed, Takedown, Open Rear Sight, Modern	150	220

Model 241A, .22 Short R.F., Tube Feed, Takedown, Open Rear Sight, Modern	140	200
Model 241D, .22 L.R.R.F., Takedown, Tube Feed, Fancy Checkering, Engraved, Modern	275	350
Model 241F, .22 L.R.R.F., Takedown, Tube Feed, Fancy Checkering, Fancy Engraving, Modern	675	750
Model 24A, .22 L.R.R.F., Takedown, Plain, Modern	90	140
Model 24A, .22 Short R.F., Takedown, Plain, Modern	90	140
Model 24C, .22 L.R.R.F., Takedown, Checkered Stock, Modern	95	150
Model 24D Peerless, .22 L.R.R.F., Takedown, Fancy Checkering, Engraved, Modern	300	400
Model 24F Premier, .22 L.R.R.F., Takedown, Fancy Checkering, Fancy Engraving, Modern	675	800
Model 550-2G, .22 Short R.F., Takedown, Open Rear Sight, Plain, Modern	45	75
Model 550A, .22 L.R.R.F., Takedown, Open Rear Sight, Plain, Modern	45	75
Model 550P, .22 L.R.R.F., Takedown, Peep Sights, Plain, Modern	50	85
Model 552A, .22 L.R.R.F., Tube Feed, Plain, Modern	50	80
Model 552BDL, .22 L.R.R.F., Tube Feed, Checkered Stock, Modern	55	85
Model 552C, .22 L.R.R.F., Tube Feed, Carbine, Plain, Modern	50	80
Model 552GS, .22 Short R.F., Tube Feed, Plain, Modern	55	85
Model 740A, Various Calibers, Clip Fed. Sporting Rifle, Open Rear Sight, Plain, Modern	120	180
Model 740ADL, Various Calibers, Clip Fed, Sporting Rifle, Open Rear Sight, Checkered Stock, Modern	135	190
Model 740BDL., Various Calibers, Clip Fed, Sporting Rifle, Open Rear Sight, Checkered Stock, Fancy Wood, Modern	150	210
Model 740D Peerless, Various Calibers, Clip Fed, Sporting Rifle, Open Rear Sight, Fancy Checkering, Engraved, Modern	600	800
Model 740F Premier, Various Calibers, Clip Fed, Sporting Rifle, Open Rear Sight, Fancy Checkering, Fancy Engraving, Modern	950	1,300
Model 742, .30-06 Springfield, Bicentennial, Clip Fed, Modern	175	250
Model 742, Various Calibers, Clip Fed, Sporting Rifle, Open Rear Sight, Checkered Stock, Modern	160	240
Model 742 Canadian Centennial, Clip Fed, Sporting Rifle, Open Rear Sight, Checkered Stock, Commemorative, Curio	175	300
Model 742ADL, Various Calibers, Clip Fed, Sporting Rifle, Open Rear Sight, Checkered Stock, Modern	150	225
Model 742BDL, Various Calibers, Clip Fed, Sporting Rifle, Open Rear Sight, Checkered Stock, Fancy Wood, Modern	165	260
Model 742C, Various Calibers, Clip Fed, Sporting Rifle, Open Rear Sight, Carbine, Checkered Stock, Modern	160	240
Model 742CDL, Various Calibers, Clip Fed, Sporting Rifle, Open Rear Sight, Carbine, Fancy Wood, Modern	165	255
Model 742D Peerless, Various Calibers, Clip Fed, Sporting Rifle, Open Rear Sight, Fancy Checkering, Engraved, Modern	600	800
Model 742F Premier, Various Calibers, Clip Fed, Sporting Rifle, Open Rear Sights, Fancy Checkering, Engraved, Modern	1,200	1,600
Model 81A, Various Calibers, Plain, Takedown, Modern	175	275
Model 81D Peerless, Various Calibers, Takedown, Fancy Checkering, Engraved, Modern	475	600
Model 81F Premier, Various Calibers, Takedown, Fancy Checkering, Fancy Engraving, Fancy Wood, Modern	800	1,100
Model 8A Standard, Various Calibers, Plain, Modern	175	250
Model 8C Special, Various Calibers, Checkered Stock, Modern	200	300
Model 8D Peerless, Various Calibers, Fancy Checkering, Light Engraving, Modern	400	550
Model 8E Expert, Various Calibers, Fancy Checkering, Engraved, Modern	550	800
Model 8F Premier, Various Calibers, Fancy Checkering, Fancy Engraving, Fancy Wood, Modern	800	1,000
Nylon 11, .22 L.R.R.F., Clip Fed, Plastic Stock, Modern	35	50
Nylon 66, .22 L.R.R.F., Tube Feed, Plastic Stock, Modern	45	70
Nylon 66, .22 L.R.R.F., Tube Feed, Bicentennial, Plastic Stock, Modern	45	70

Nylon 66 GS, .22 Short R.F., Tube Feed, Plastic Stock, Modern	45	70
Model 77, .22 L.R.R.F., Clip Fed, Plastic Stock, Modern	40	65

Rifle, Singleshot

Model 4S Boy Scout, .22 L.R.R.F., Rolling Block, Full-Stocked, Modern	125	200
Model 4S Boy Scout, .22 L.R.R.F., Rolling Block, Full-Stocked, with Bayonet, Modern	175	235
Model 6, .22 L.R.R.F., Rolling Block, Takedown, Modern	80	125
Model 6, .32 Long Rifle, Rolling Block, Takedown, Modern	80	120
Model 7, Various Rimfires, Rolling Block, Target, Adjustable Sights, Checkered Stock, Modern	275	425
Model 7, Various Rimfires, Rolling Block, Target, Swiss Buttplate, Checkered Stock, Adjustable Sights, Modern	350	500
Model 7, Various Rimfires, Rolling Block, Target, Swiss Buttplate, Checkered Stock, Peep Sights, Modern	375	525

Rifle, Slide Action

Model 121A, .22 L.R.R.F., Takedown, Tube Feed, Plain, Modern	150	225
Model 121A, .22 Short R.F., Takedown, Tube Feed, Plain, Modern	125	180
Model 121D Peerless, .22 L.R.R.F., Takedown, Tube Feed, Fancy Checkering, Engraved, Modern	450	600
Model 121F Premier, .22 L.R.R.F., Takedown, Tube Feed, Fancy Checkering, Fancy Engraving, Modern	750	900
Model 121S, .22 WRF, Takedown, Tube Feed, Plain, Modern	135	190
Model 121SB, .22 L.R.R.F., Takedown, Tube Feed, Plain, Smoothbore, Modern	140	175
Model 12A Standard, .22 L.R.R.F., Plain Round Barrel, Tube Feed, Modern	110	160
Model 12B Gallery, .22 Short R.F., Plain, Round Barrel, Tube Feed, Modern	100	150
Model 12C, .22 L.R.R.F., Plain, Octagon Barrel, Tube Feed, Target, Modern	125	200
Model 12C-NRA, .22 L.R.R.F., Plain, Octagon Barrel, Tube Feed, Peep Sights, Modern	165	240
Model 12CS Special, .22 WRF, Plain, Octagon Barrel, Tube Feed, Modern	125	200
Model 12D Peerless, .22 L.R.R.F., Checkered Stock, Octagon Barrel, Tube Feed, Light Engraving, Modern	325	425
Model 12E Expert, .22 L.R.R.F., Fancy Checkering, Octagon Barrel, Tube Feed, Engraved, Modern	450	600
Model 12F Premier, .22 L.R.R.F., Fancy Checkering, Octagon Barrel, Tube Feed, Fancy Engraving, Fancy Wood, Modern	700	850
Model 14½ A, Various Calibers, Tube Feed, Short Action, Plain, Modern	175	250
Model 14½ R, Various Calibers, Tube Feed, Short Action, Carbine, Plain Barrel, Modern	235	310
Model 141A, Various Calibers, Takedown, Tube Feed, Plain, Modern	175	250
Model 141D Peerless, Various Calibers, Takedown, Tube Feed, Fancy Checkering, Engraved, Modern	450	600
Model 141F Premier, Various Calibers, Takedown, Tube Feed, Fancy Checkering, Fancy Engraving, Modern	850	1,050
Model 141R, Various Calibers, Takedown, Tube Feed, Plain, Carbine, Modern	175	250
Model 14A, Various Calibers, Tube Feed, Plain, Modern	150	225
Model 14C Special, Various Calibers, Tube Feed, Checkered Stock, Modern	180	250

Remington Model 12C

Model 14D Peerless, Various Calibers, Tube Feed, Fancy Checkering, Engraved, Modern	425	550
Model 14F Premier, Various Calibers, Tube Feed, Fancy Checkering, Fancy Wood, Fancy Engraving, Modern	750	1,000
Model 14R, Various Calibers, Tube Feed, Carbine, Plain, Modern	190	275
Model 25A, Various Calibers, Takedown, Plain, Modern	150	225
Model 25D Peerless, Various Calibers, Takedown, Checkered Stock, Engraved, Modern	450	600
Model 25F Premier, Various Calibers, Takedown, Fancy Checkering, Fancy Engraving, Modern	800	1,050
Model 25R, Various Calibers, Takedown, Plain, Carbine, Modern	175	250
Model 572, .22 L.R.R.F., Tube Feed, Open Rear Sight, Lightweight, Fancy Checkering, Chrome, Modern	35	55
Model 572 BDL, .22 L.R.R.F., Tube Feed, Checkered Stock, Modern	60	95
Model 572 SB, .22 L.R.R.F., Tube Feed, Smoothbore, Modern	55	85
Model 572A, .22 L.R.R.F., Tube Feed, Open Rear Sight, Plain, Modern	50	80
Model 572BDL, .22 L.R.R.F., Tube Feed, Open Rear Sight, Checkered Stock, Modern	55	85
Model 572SB, .22 L.R.R.F., Tube Feed, Plain, Smoothbore, Modern	50	80
Model 760, .30-06 Springfield, Bicentennial, Clip Fed, Modern	150	210
Model 760A, Various Calibers, Clip Fed, Sporting Rifle, Open Rear Sight, Plain, Modern	130	175
Model 760ADL, Various Calibers, Clip Fed, Sporting Rifle, Open Rear Sight, Monte Carlo Stock, Checkered Stock, Modern	150	220
Model 760BDL, Various Calibers, Clip Fed, Sporting Rifle, Open Rear Sight, Monte Carlo Stock, Checkered Stock, Modern	165	235
Model 760C, Various Calibers, Clip Fed, Sporting Rifle, Open Rear Sight, Carbine, Plain, Modern	140	210
Model 760CDL, Various Calibers, Clip Fed, Sporting Rifle, Open Rear Sight, Carbine, Checkered Stock, Modern	165	235
Model 760D Peerless, Various Calibers, Clip Fed, Sporting Rifle, Open Rear Sight, Fancy Checkering, Engraved, Modern	550	800
Model 760F Premier, Various Calibers, Clip Fed, Sporting Rifle, Open Rear Sight, Fancy Checkering, Fancy Engraving, Modern	1,100	1,600

Shotgun, Double Barrel, Over-Under

Model 32, Raised Solid Rib, Add $40-$60		
Model 32, for Vent Rib, Add $80-$100		
Model 32, 12 Ga., Skeet Grade, Engraved, Fancy Checkering, Modern	800	1,000
Model 3200, 12 Ga., Field Grade, Automatic Ejector, Single Selective Trigger, Vent Rib, Checkered Stock, Modern	475	675
Model 3200, 12 Ga., Skeet Grade, Automatic Ejector, Single Selective Trigger, Vent Rib, Checkered Stock, Modern	550	775
Model 3200, 12 Ga., Trap Grade, Automatic Ejector, Single Selective Trigger, Vent Rib, Checkered Stock, Modern	550	775
Model 3200, 12 Ga. Mag. 3″, Field Grade, Automatic Ejector, Single Selective Trigger, Vent Rib, Checkered Stock, Modern	500	750
Model 3200 Competition, 12 Ga., Skeet Grade, Automatic Ejector, Single Selective Trigger, Vent Rib, Engraved, Modern	650	900
Model 3200 Competition, 12 Ga., Trap Grade, Automatic Ejector, Single Selective Trigger, Vent Rib, Engraved, Modern	650	900
Model 32A, 12 Ga., Double Trigger, Automatic Ejector, Plain Barrel, Engraved, Checkered Stock, Modern	450	600
Model 32A, 12 Ga., Single Selective Trigger, Automatic Ejector, Plain Barrel, Engraved, Checkered Stock, Modern	625	850
Model 32D, 12 Ga., Fancy Checkering, Fancy Wood, Fancy Engraving, Modern	1,400	1,900
Model 32E, 12 Ga., Fancy Checkering, Fancy Wood, Fancy Engraving, Modern	2,000	2,600
Model 32F, 12 Ga., Fancy Checkering, Fancy Wood, Fancy Checkering, Modern	2,800	3,500
Model 32TC, 12 Ga., Trap Grade, Single Selective Trigger, Engraved, Fancy Checkering, Modern	1,000	1,400

Shotgun, Double Barrel, Side by Side

Model 1894 A E, Various Gauges, Hammerless, Damascus Barrel, Automatic Ejector, Checkered Stock, Double Trigger, Modern	175	300
Model 1894 A E O, Various Gauges, Hammerless, Steel Barrel, Automatic Ejector, Checkered Stock, Double Trigger, Modern	375	500
Model 1894 A O, Various Gauges, Hammerless, Steel Barrel, Plain, Checkered Stock, Double Trigger, Modern	325	450
Model 1894 B, Various Gauges, Hammerless, Damascus Barrel, Light Engraving, Checkered Stock, Double Trigger, Modern	150	225
Model 1894 B E, Various Gauges, Hammerless, Damascus Barrel, Automatic Ejector, Light Engraving, Checkered Stock, Modern	250	375
Model 1894 B E O, Various Gauges, Hammerless, Steel Barrel, Automatic Ejector, Light Engraving, Checkered Stock, Modern	475	700
Model 1894 B O, Various Gauges, Hammerless, Steel Barrel, Light Engraving, Checkered Stock, Double Trigger, Modern	375	500
Model 1894 C, Various Gauges, Hammerless, Damascus Barrel, Engraved, Checkered Stock, Double Trigger, Modern	275	400
Model 1894 C E, Various Gauges, Hammerless, Damascus Barrel, Automatic Ejector, Engraved, Checkered Stock, Modern	350	475
Model 1894 C E O, Various Gauges, Hammerless, Steel Barrel, Automatic Ejector, Engraved, Checkered Stock, Modern	675	950
Model 1894 C O, Various Gauges, Hammerless, Steel Barrel, Engraved, Checkered Stock, Double Trigger, Modern	550	750
Model 1894 D, Various Gauges, Hammerless, Damascus Barrel, Fancy Engraving, Fancy Checkering, Fancy Wood, Modern	475	650
Model 1894 D E, Various Gauges, Hammerless, Damascus Barrel, Automatic Ejector, Fancy Engraving, Fancy Checkering, Modern	550	750
Model 1894 D E O, Various Gauges, Hammerless, Steel Barrel, Automatic Ejector, Fancy Engraving, Fancy Checkering, Modern	850	1,400
Model 1894 D O, Various Gauges, Hammerless, Steel Barrel, Fancy Engraving, Fancy Checkering, Fancy Wood, Modern	675	1,250
Model 1894 E, Various Gauges, Hammerless, Damascus Barrel, Fancy Engraving, Fancy Checkering, Fancy Wood, Modern	700	950
Model 1894 E E, Various Gauges, Hammerless, Damascus Barrel, Automatic Ejector, Fancy Engraving, Fancy Checkering, Modern	775	1,100
Model 1894 E E O, Various Gauges, Hammerless, Steel Barrel, Automatic Ejector, Fancy Engraving, Fancy Checkering, Modern	1,800	2,500
Model 1894 E O, Various Gauges, Hammerless, Steel Barrel, Fancy Engraving, Fancy Checkering, Fancy Wood, Modern	1,600	2,300
Model 1894 Special, Various Gauges, Hammerless, Steel Barrel, Automatic Ejector, Fancy Engraving, Fancy Checkering, Modern	4,000	6,500
Model 1894-A, Various Gauges, Hammerless, Damascus Barrel, Plain, Checkered Stock, Double Trigger, Modern	95	175
Model 1900 K, 12 and 16 Gauges, Hammerless, Steel Barrel, Plain, Checkered Stock, Modern	175	300
Model 1900 K D, 12 and 16 Gauges, Hammerless, Damascus Barrel, Plain, Checkered Stock, Modern	100	200
Model 1900 K E D, 12 and 16 Gauges, Hammerless, Damascus Barrel, Automatic Ejector, Palm Rest, Checkered Stock, Modern	150	250
Model 1900 KE, 12 and 16 Gauges, Hammerless, Steel Barrel, Automatic Ejector, Plain, Checkered Stock, Modern	250	375
Model Parker 920, 12 Ga., Double Trigger, Checkered Stock, Modern	450	700

Shotgun, Semi-Automatic

Autoloading, 12 Ga., Add $15-$20 for Solid Rib		
Autoloading-0, 12 Ga., Takedown, Riot Gun, Plain, Modern	95	150
Autoloading-1, 12 Ga., Takedown, Plain, Modern	110	160
Autoloading-2, 12 Ga., Takedown, Checkered Stock, Modern	145	200
Autoloading-4, 12 Ga., Takedown, Fancy Checkering, Fancy Wood, Engraved, Modern	400	525
Autoloading-6, 12 Ga., Takedown, Fancy Checkering, Fancy Wood, Fancy Engraving, Modern	700	950
Model 11, for Vent Rib, Add $30-$40		

Model 11, Raised Solid Rib, Add $10-$20

Model 11 Sportsman, Various Gauges, Skeet Grade, Vent Rib, Light Engraving, Checkered Stock, Modern	200	300
Model 11-48 D Tournament, Various Gauges, Vent Rib, Fancy Wood, Fancy Engraving, Fancy Checkering, Modern	400	525
Model 11-48 Duck, Various Gauges, Vent Rib, Checkered Stock, Modern	130	185
Model 11-48 R, 12 Ga., Riot Gun, Plain Barrel, Modern	90	135
Model 11-48 RSS, 12 Ga., Open Rear Sight, Slug, Checkered Stock, Modern	135	190
Model 11-48 SA, Various Gauges, Skeet Grade, Vent Rib, Checkered Stock, Modern	135	200
Model 11-48A, Various Gauges, Plain Barrel, Modern	100	160
Model 11-48B, Various Gauges, Vent Rib, Checkered Stock, Fancy Wood, Modern	115	165
Model 11-48F Premier, Various Gauges, Vent Rib, Fancy Wood, Fancy Engraving, Fancy Checkering, Modern	800	1,100

Model 1100, Add $15-$25 for Left Hand
Model 1100, 2 Ga. Lightweight, Add $5-$10
Model 1100, for .28 Ga. or .410 Ga., Add $5-$10

Model 1100, 12 Ga., Bicentennial, Skeet Grade, Vent Rib, Checkered Stock, Modern	180	225
Model 1100, Various Gauges, Plain Barrel, Checkered Stock, Modern	160	210
Model 1100, Various Gauges, Vent Rib, Checkered Stock, Modern	175	215
Model 1100, Various Gauges, Plain Barrel, Magnum, Checkered Stock, Modern	175	215
Model 1100, Various Gauges, Vent Rib, Magnum, Checkered Stock, Modern	180	230
Model 1100, Various Gauges, Skeet Grade, Vent Rib, Checkered Stock, Modern	160	210
Model 1100 Cutts, Various Gauges, Skeet Grade, Vent Rib, Checkered Stock, Modern	200	245
Model 1100 D Tournament, Various Gauges, Vent Rib, Fancy Checkering, Fancy Wood, Fancy Engraving, Modern	500	800
Model 1100 Deer Gun, Various Gauges, Open Rear Sight, Checkered Stock, Modern	175	230
Model 1100 F Premier, Various Gauges, Vent Rib, Fancy Checkering, Fancy Wood, Fancy Engraving, Modern	1,250	1,650
Model 1100 TB, 12 Ga., Bicentennial, Trap Grade, Vent Rib, Checkered Stock, Modern	210	265
Model 1100 TB, 12 Ga., Bicentennial, Trap Grade, Vent Rib, Monte Carlo Stock, Checkered Stock, Modern	230	270
Model 1100 TB, 12 Ga., Trap Grade, Vent Rib, Checkered Stock, Modern	210	265
Model 1100 TB, 12 Ga., Trap Grade, Vent Rib, Checkered Stock, Monte Carlo Stock, Modern	210	275
Model 11A, 12 Ga., Plain Barrel, Modern	110	165
Model 11A, Sportsman, Various Gauges, Plain Barrel, Light Engraving, Modern	125	175
Model 11B, 12 Ga., Plain Barrel, Fancy Wood, Checkered Stock, Modern	160	200
Model 11B Sportsman, Various Gauges, Plain Barrel, Light Engraving, Checkered Stock, Modern	170	235
Model 11C, 12 Ga., Plain Barrel, Trap Grade, Fancy Checkering, Fancy Wood, Modern	200	300
Model 11D, 12 Ga., Plain Barrel, Fancy Checkering, Fancy Wood, Fancy Engraving, Modern	500	550
Model 11D Sportsman, Various Gauges, Plain Barrel, Engraved, Fancy Checkering, Modern	400	550
Model 11E, 12 Ga., Plain Barrel, Fancy Checkering, Fancy Wood, Fancy Engraving, Modern	575	700
Model 11E Sportsman, Various Gauges, Plain Barrel, Fancy Checkering, Fancy Wood, Fancy Engraving, Modern	575	725
Model 11F, 12 Ga., Plain Barrel, Fancy Checkering, Fancy Wood, Fancy Engraving, Modern	700	950

Model 11F Sportsman, Various Gauges, Plain Barrel, Fancy Checkering, Fancy Wood, Fancy Engraving, Modern	700	950
Model 11R, 12 Ga., Riot Gun, Military, Modern	110	160
Model 11R, 12 Ga., Riot Gun, Commercial, Modern	100	150
Model 48-D Sportsman, Various Gauges, Vent Rib, Fancy Checkering, Fancy Wood, Fancy Engraving, Modern	450	600
Model 48-F Sportsman, Various Gauges, Vent Rib, Fancy Checkering, Fancy Wood, Fancy Engraving, Modern	825	1,100
Model 48-SA Sportsman, Various Gauges, Skeet Grade, Vent Rib, Checkered Stock, Modern	140	190
Model 48A Sportsman, Various Gauges, Plain Barrel, Modern	100	150
Model 48B Sportsman, Various Gauges, Vent Rib, Checkered Stock, Modern	115	170
Model 58 ADL, 12 and 20 Gauges, Vent Rib, Recoil Pad, Checkered Stock, Magnum, Modern	160	210
Model 58 ADL, Various Gauges, Plain Barrel, Checkered Stock, Modern	130	175
Model 58 ADL, Various Gauges, Vent Rib, Checkered Stock, Modern	150	215
Model 58 ADX, Various Gauges, Vent Rib, Checkered Stock, Fancy Wood, Modern	150	210
Model 58 BDL, Various Gauges, Plain Barrel, Checkered Stock, Fancy Wood, Modern	150	210
Model 58 BDL, Various Gauges, Vent Rib, Checkered Stock, Fancy Wood, Modern	165	225
Model 58 D Tournament, Various Gauges, Vent Rib, Fancy Checkering, Fancy Wood, Fancy Engraving, Modern	450	600
Model 58 F Premier, Various Gauges, Vent Rib, Fancy Checkering, Fancy Wood, Fancy Engraving, Modern	950	1,200
Model 58 RSS, 12 Ga., Slug, Open Rear Sight, Checkered Stock, Modern	140	190
Model 58 SA, Various Gauges, Skeet Grade, Vent Rib, Checkered Stock, Modern	175	235
Model 58 TB, 12 Ga., Trap Grade, Vent Rib, Checkered Stock, Modern	175	235
Model 878 A, 12 Ga., Plain Barrel, Modern	90	140
Model 878 A, 12 Ga., Vent Rib, Modern	110	160
Model 878 ADL, 12 Ga., Plain Barrel, Checkered Stock, Modern	110	160
Model 878 ADL, 12 Ga., Vent Rib, Checkered Stock, Modern	130	185
Model 878 D, 12 Ga., Vent Rib, Fancy Checkering, Fancy Wood, Fancy Engraving, Modern	450	525
Model 878 F, 12 Ga., Vent Rib, Fancy Checkering, Fancy Wood, Fancy Engraving, Modern	750	975
Model 878 SA, 12 Ga., Skeet Grade, Checkered Stock, Vent Rib, Modern	140	200

Shotgun, Singleshot

Model 3 (M1893), 12 Ga., 24 Ga., 28 Ga., Add $25		
Model 3 (M1893), Various Gauges, Takedown, Plain, Modern	80	115
Model 9 (M1902), Various Gauges, Automatic Ejector, Plain, Modern	75	110
Model Parker 930, 12 Ga., Trap Grade, Vent Rib, Automatic Ejector, Fancy Checkering, Modern	850	1,200
Model Parker 930, 12 Ga., Trap Grade, Vent Rib, Fancy Checkering, Fancy Engraving, Modern	1,600	2,400

Shotgun, Slide Action

Model 10A, 12 Ga., Takedown, Plain, Modern	140	185
Model 108, 12 Ga., Takedown, Checkered Stock, Fancy Wood, Modern	165	225
Model 10C, 12 Ga., Takedown, Fancy Wood, Checkered Stock, Modern	180	250
Model 10D, 12 Ga., Takedown, Fancy Checkering, Fancy Wood, Engraved, Modern	425	550
Model 10E, 12 Ga., Takedown, Fancy Checkering, Fancy Wood, Fancy Engraving, Modern	575	725
Model 10F, 12 Ga., Takedown, Fancy Checkering, Fancy Engraving, Fancy Wood, Modern	700	950
Model 10R, 12 Ga., Takedown, Riot Gun, Plain, Modern	95	150
Model 10S, 12 Ga., Takedown, Trap Grade, Checkered Stock, Modern	150	200
Model 17, 20 Ga., for Solid Rib, Add $20-$35		

Model 17A, 20 Ga., Takedown, Plain, Modern	155	200
Model 17B, 20 Ga., Takedown, Checkered Stock, Modern	180	250
Model 17C, 20 Ga., Takedown, Fancy Wood, Checkered Stock, Modern	240	325
Model 17D, 20 Ga., Takedown, Fancy Wood, Fancy Checkering, Engraved, Modern	400	525
Model 17E, 20 Ga., Takedown, Fancy Wood, Fancy Checkering, Fancy Engraving, Modern	550	750
Model 17F, 20 Ga., Takedown, Fancy Wood, Fancy Checkering, Fancy Engraving, Modern	800	975
Model 17R, 20 Ga., Takedown, Riot Gun, Plain, Modern	115	170
Model 1908-0, 12 Ga., Takedown, Riot Gun, Plain, Modern	115	170
Model 1908-1, 12 Ga., Takedown, Plain, Modern	135	190
Model 1908-3, 12 Ga., Takedown, Checkered Stock, Fancy Wood, Modern	165	225
Model 1908-4, 12 Ga., Takedown, Fancy Checkering, Fancy Wood, Engraved, Modern	400	525
Model 1908-6, 12 Ga., Takedown, Fancy Checkering, Fancy Wood, Fancy Engraving, Modern	650	900
Model 29, for Solid Rib, Add $20-$30		
Model 29, for Vent Rib, Add $30-55		
Model 29A Sportsman, 12 Ga., Plain Barrel, Takedown, Modern	140	210
Model 29B, 12 Ga., Checkered Stock, Takedown, Modern	150	225
Model 29C, 12 Ga., Trap Grade, Takedown, Modern	150	225
Model 29R, 12 Ga., Riot Gun, Plain Barrel, Modern	100	150
Model 29S, 12 Ga., Trap Grade, Plain Barrel, Checkered Stock, Modern	140	200
Model 29TA, 12 Ga., Trap Grade, Vent Rib, Checkered Stock, Modern	175	250
Model 29TC, 12 Ga., Trap Grade, Vent Rib, Checkered Stock, Fancy Wood, Modern	225	325
Model 29TD, 12 Ga., Trap Grade, Vent Rib, Fancy Checkering, Fancy Wood, Engraved, Modern	350	475
Model 29TE, 12 Ga., Trap Grade, Vent Rib, Fancy Checkering, Fancy Wood, Fancy Engraving, Modern	550	700
Model 29TF, 12 Ga., Trap Grade, Vent Rib, Fancy Checkering, Fancy Wood, Fancy Engraving, Modern	700	900
Model 31, for Vent Rib, Add $45-$60		
Model 31, for Solid Rib, Add $15-$30		
Model 31, Various Gauges, Skeet Grade, Vent Rib, Checkered Stock, Fancy Wood, Modern	325	450
Model 31A, Various Gauges, Plain Barrel, Modern	135	190
Model 31B, Various Gauges, Plain Barrel, Checkered Stock, Fancy Wood, Modern	210	325
Model 31D Tournament, Various Gauges, Plain Barrel, Checkered Stock, Fancy Wood, Engraved, Modern	500	650
Model 31E Expert, Various Gauges, Plain Barrel, Fancy Checkering, Fancy Wood, Fancy Engraving, Modern	600	775
Model 31F Premier, Various Gauges, Plain Barrel, Fancy Checkering, Fancy Wood, Fancy Engraving, Modern	850	1,200
Model 31H Hunter, Various Gauges, Checkered Stock, Fancy Wood, Plain Barrel, Modern	250	335
Model 31R, 12 Ga., Plain Barrel, Riot Gun, Modern	120	175
Model 31S, 12 Ga., Raised Matted Rib, Checkered Stock, Fancy Wood, Modern	300	425
Model 31TC, 12 Ga., Trap Grade, Vent Rib, Recoil Pad, Modern	325	425
Model 870, for Lightweight 20, Add $10-$15		
Model 870, for .28 Ga. or .410 Ga., Add $10-$15		
Model 870, for Left-Hand, Add $5-$10		
Model 870, Various Gauges, Plain Barrel, Checkered Stock, Modern	135	185
Model 870, Various Gauges, Vent Rib, Checkered Stock, Modern	150	215
Model 870, Various Gauges, Plain Barrel, Magnum, Checkered Stock, Modern	155	220
Model 870, Various Gauges, Vent Rib, Magnum, Checkered Stock, Modern	165	230
Model 870 All American, 12 Ga., Trap Grade, Vent Rib, Fancy Checkering, Engraved, Modern	375	500

Model 870 Brushmaster, 12 and 20 Gauges, Open Rear Sight, Recoil Pad, Checkered Stock, Modern	140	200
Model 870 D Tournament, Various Gauges, Vent Rib, Fancy Checkering, Fancy Wood, Fancy Engraving, Modern	500	775
Model 870 Deergun, 12 Ga., Open Rear Sight, Checkered Stock, Modern	130	190
Model 870 F Premier, Various Gauges, Vent Rib, Fancy Checkering, Fancy Wood, Fancy Engraving, Modern	1,300	1,700
Model 870 Police, 12 Ga., Open Rear Sight, Modern	140	185
Model 870 Police, 12 Ga., Plain Barrel, Modern	120	165
Model 870 SA, 12 Ga., Bicentennial, Skeet Grade, Vent Rib, Checkered Stock, Modern	160	225
Model 870SA, Various Gauges, Skeet Grade, Vent Rib, Checkered Stock, Modern	155	230
Model 870SA Cutts, Various Gauges, Skeet Grade, Vent Rib, Checkered Stock, Modern	160	220
Model 870SC, Various Gauges, Skeet Grade, Vent Rib, Checkered Stock, Modern	165	230
Model 870TB, 12 Ga., Trap Grade, Vent Rib, Checkered Stock, Modern	160	215
Model 870TB, 12 Ga., Trap Grade, Vent Rib, Checkered Stock, Monte Carlo Stock, Modern	165	225
Model 870TB, 12 Ga., Bicentennial, Trap Grade, Vent Rib, Checkered Stock, Modern	160	225
Model 870TB, 12 Ga., Bicentennial, Trap Grade, Vent Rib, Checkered Stock, Monte Carlo Stock, Modern	160	225
Model 870TC, 12 Ga., Trap Grade, Vent Rib, Checkered Stock, Modern	200	265
Model 870TC, 12 Ga., Trap Grade, Vent Rib, Checkered Stock, Monte Carlo Stock, Modern	210	275

Silenced Weapon, Rifle

Rem. 40XB Sniper, .308 Win., Heavy Barrel, Scope Mounted, Silencer, Class 3	550	750

Republic
Spain, Unknown Maker

Handgun, Semi-Automatic

.25 ACP, Clip Fed, Blue, Modern	80	120
.32 ACP, Clip Fed, Long Grip, Modern	85	125

Retriever
Made by Thomas Ryan 1870-76 Norwich, Conn.

Handgun, Revolver

.32 Short R.F., 5 Shot, Spur Trigger, Solid Frame, Single Action, Antique	90	160

Revelation
Trade Name for Western Auto

Rifle, Bolt Action

Model 107, .22 WMR, Clip Fed, Modern	35	55
Model 210B, 7mm Rem. Mag., Checkered Stock, Monte Carlo Stock, Modern	120	160

Republic .25 ACP

Model 220A, .308 Win., Checkered Stock, Monte Carlo Stock, Modern	105	145
Model 220AD, .308 Win., Checkered Stock, Monte Carlo Stock, Fancy Wood, Modern	130	180
Model 220B, .243 Win., Checkered Stock, Monte Carlo Stock, Modern	105	145
Model 220BD, .243 Win., Checkered Stock, Monte Carlo Stock, Fancy Wood, Modern	130	180
Model 220C, .22-250, Checkered Stock, Monte Carlo Stock, Modern	105	145
Model 220CD, .22-250, Checkered Stock, Monte Carlo Stock, Fancy Wood, Modern	130	180

Rifle, Lever Action

Model 117, .22 L.R.R.F., Tube Feed, Modern	35	55

Rifle, Semi-Automatic

Model 125, .22 L.R.R.F., Clip Fed, Modern	30	50

Rifle, Singleshot

Model 100, .22 L.R.R.F., Modern	15	30

Shotgun, Bolt Action

Model 312B, 12 Ga., Clip Fed, Modern	30	45
Model 312BK, 12 Ga., Clip Fed, Adjustable Choke, Modern	35	55
Model 316B, 16 Ga., Clip Fed, Modern	25	40
Model 316BK, 16 Ga., Clip Fed, Adjustable Choke, Modern	25	45
Model 325B, 20 Ga., Clip Fed, Modern	30	45
Model 325BK, 20 Ga., Clip Fed, Adjustable Choke, Modern	35	50
Model 330, .410 Ga., Clip Fed, Modern	25	40

Shotgun, Slide Action

Model 310, Various Gauges, Plain Barrel, Takedown, Modern	75	115
Model 31OR, Various Gauges, Vent Rib, Takedown, Modern	80	120

Rev-O-Noc
Made by Crescent for Hibbard-Spencer-Bartlett Co., Chicago

Shotgun, Double Barrel, Side by Side

Various Gauges, Outside Hammers, Damascus Barrel, Modern	80	150
Various Gauges, Hammerless, Steel Barrel, Modern	95	175
Various Gauges, Hammerless, Damascus Barrel, Modern	75	150
Various Gauges, Outside Hammers, Steel Barrel, Modern	90	175

Shotgun, Singleshot

Various Gauges, Hammer, Steel Barrel, Modern	45	75

Reynolds, Plant & Hotchkiss

Handgun, Revolver

.25 Short R.F., 5 Shot, Single Action, Spur Trigger, 3″ Barrel, Antique	95	145

R. G. Industries
Made in Miami, Fla.

Handgun, Double Barrel, Over-Under

RG-16, .22 WMR, 2 Shot, Derringer, Modern	15	25
RG-17, .38 Special, 2 Shot, Derringer, Modern	15	25

Handgun, Revolver

RG-14, .22 L.R.R.F., 6 Shot, Double Action, Modern	10	20
RG-23, .22 L.R.R.F., 6 Shot, Double Action, Modern	15	25
RG-30, .22LR/.22 WMR Combo, 6 Shot, Double Action, Swing-Out Cylinder, Modern	25	40
RG-30, .22 L.R.R.F., 6 Shot, Double Action, Swing-Out Cylinder, Modern	20	30
RG-30, .22 WMR, 6 Shot, Double Action, Swing-Out Cylinder, Modern	15	30
RG-30, .32 S & W Long, 6 Shot, Double Action, Swing-Out Cylinder, Modern	15	30
RG-31, .32 S & W Long, 6 Shot, Double Action, Modern	15	30
RG-31, .38 Special, 5 Shot, Double Action, Modern	15	30

RG-38S, .38 Special, 6 Shot, Double Action, Blue, Modern 25 45
RG-38S, .38 Special, 6 Shot, Double Action, Nickel Plated, Modern 25 45
RG-40, .38 Special, 6 Shot, Double Action, Swing-Out Cylinder, Modern 25 45
RG-57, .357 Magnum, 6 Shot, Double Action, Swing-Out Cylinder,
  Modern 45 75
RG-57, .44 Magnum, 6 Shot, Double Action, Swing-Out Cylinder, Modern 60 95
RG-63, .22 L.R.R.F., 6 Shot, Double Action, Western Style, Modern 15 25
RG-66, .22LR/.22 WMR Combo, 6 Shot, Single Action, Western Style,
  Modern 15 30
RG-66T, .22LR/.22 WMR Combo, 6 Shot, Single Action, Western Style,
  Adjustable Sights, Modern 20 35
RG-88, .357 Magnum, 6 Shot, Double Action, Swing-Out Cylinder,
  Modern 55 80

Handgun, Semi-Automatic
RG-25, .25 ACP, Modern 15 25

Rheinmetall
Germany, Rheinsche Metallwaren Fabrik

Handgun, Semi-Automatic
.32 ACP, Clip Fed, Modern 175 300

Richards, John
London & Birmingham, England 1745-1810

Shotgun, Flintlock
Blunderbuss, Half-Octagon, Cannon, Steel Barrel, Folding Bayonet,
  Antique 600 850

Richards, W.
Belgium C.1900

Shotgun, Double Barrel, Side by Side
Various Gauges, Outside Hammers, Damascus Barrel, Modern 80 150
Various Gauges, Hammerless, Steel Barrel, Modern 95 175
Various Gauges, Hammerless, Damascus Barrel, Modern 75 150
Various Gauges, Outside Hammers, Steel Barrel, Modern 90 175

Shotgun, Singleshot
Various Gauges, Hammer, Steel Barrel, Modern 45 75

Richland Arms Co.
Bussfield, Mich. Importers

Shotgun, Double Barrel, Over-Under
Model 808, 12 Ga., Single Trigger, Checkered Stock, Vent Rib, Modern 200 325
Model 810, 10 Ga. 3½", Double Trigger, Checkered Stock, Vent Rib,
  Modern 320 425
Model 828, 28 Ga., Single Trigger, Checkered Stock, Modern 225 290
Model 844, 12 Ga., Single Trigger, Checkered Stock, Modern 160 200

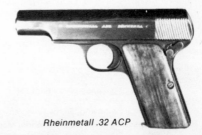

Rheinmetall .32 ACP

Shotgun, Double Barrel, Side by Side

Model 200, Various Gauges, Double Trigger, Checkered Stock, Modern	175	240
Model 202, Various Gauges, Double Trigger, Extra Shotgun Barrel, Modern	250	325
Model 707 Deluxe, 12 and 20 Gauges, Double Trigger, Modern	200	275
Model 707 Deluxe, 12 and 20 Gauges, Double Trigger, Checkered Stock, Extra Shotgun Barrel, Modern	250	350
Model 711, 10 Ga. 3½", Double Trigger, Modern	190	265
Model 711, 12 Ga. Mag. 3", Double Trigger, Modern	180	225

Rifle, Percussion

Wesson Rifle, .50, Set Triggers, Target Sights, Reproduction, Antique	125	190

Richter, Charles
Made by Crescent for New York Sporting Goods Co. C.1900

Shotgun, Double Barrel, Side by Side

Various Gauges, Outside Hammers, Damascus Barrel, Modern	80	150
Various Gauges, Hammerless, Steel Barrel, Modern	95	175
Various Gauges, Hammerless, Damascus Barrel, Modern	75	150
Various Gauges, Outside Hammers, Steel Barrel, Modern	90	175

Shotgun, Singleshot

Various Gauges, Hammer, Steel Barrel, Modern	45	75

Rickard Arms
Made by Crescent for J. A. Rickard Co. Schenectady, N.Y.

Shotgun, Double Barrel, Side by Side

Various Gauges, Outside Hammers, Damascus Barrel, Modern	80	150
Various Gauges, Hammerless, Steel Barrel, Modern	95	175
Various Gauges, Hammerless, Damascus Barrel, Modern	75	150
Various Gauges, Outside Hammers, Steel Barrel, Modern	90	175

Shotgun, Singleshot

Various Gauges, Hammer, Steel Barrel, Modern	45	75

Rigarmi
Italy, Current

Handgun, Semi-Automatic

Militar, .22 L.R.R.F., Clip Fed, Hammer, Double Action, Modern	90	135
Pocket, .32 ACP, Clip Fed, Hammer, Double Action, Modern	95	130
RG-217, .22 Long R.F., Clip Fed, Modern	50	80
RG-218, .22 L.R.R.F., Clip Fed, Modern	70	100
RG-219, .25 ACP, Clip Fed, Modern	50	80

Rigby, John & Co.
Dublin & London from 1867

Rifle, Bolt Action

.275 Rigby, Sporting Rifle, Express Sights, Checkered Stock, Modern	1,250	1,900
.275 Rigby, Sporting Rifle, Lightweight, Express Sights, Checkered Stock, Modern	1,250	1,900
.350 Rigby, Sporting Rifle, Express Sights, Checkered Stock, Modern	1,250	1,900
Big Game, .416 Rigby, Sporting Rifle, Express Sights, Checkered Stock, Modern	1,250	1,900

Rifle, Double Barrel, Side by Side

Best Grade, Various Calibers, Sidelock, Double Trigger, Express Sights, Fancy Engraving, Fancy Checkering, Modern	7,500	13,000
Second Grade, Various Calibers, Box Lock, Double Trigger, Express Sights, Fancy Engraving, Fancy Checkering, Modern	5,500	8,500
Third Grade, Various Calibers, Box Lock, Double Trigger, Express Sights, Engraved, Checkered Stock, Modern	4,000	5,500

Shotgun, Double Barrel, Side by Side
Chatsworth, Various Gauges, Box Lock, Automatic Ejector, Double
  Trigger, Fancy Engraving, Fancy Checkering, Modern   1,750   2,500
Regal, Various Gauges, Sidelock, Automatic Ejector, Double Trigger,
  Fancy Engraving, Fancy Checkering, Modern   5,500   9,000
Sackville, Various Gauges, Box Lock, Automatic Ejector, Double Trigger,
  Fancy Engraving, Fancy Checkering, Modern   2,000   3,000
Sandringham, Various Gauges, Sidelock, Automatic Ejector, Double
  Trigger, Fancy Engraving, Fancy Checkering, Modern 4,000 6,500

Riot
Made by Stevens Arms

Shotgun, Pump
Model 520, 12 Ga., Takedown, Modern   90   125
Model 620, Various Gauges, Takedown, Modern   95   135

Ripoli

Handgun, Miquelot-Lock
Ball Butt, Brass Inlay, Light Ornamentation, Antique   1,500   2,000
Pair, Fluted Barrel, Pocket Pistol, Engraved, Silver Furniture, Antique   5,000   6,500

Ritter, Jacob
Phila., Pa. 1775-83. See Kentucky Rifles and Pistols

Riverside Arms Co.
Made by Stevens Arms & Tool Co.

Shotgun, Double Barrel, Side by Side
Model 215, 12 and 16 Gauges, Outside Hammers, Steel Barrel, Modern   90   145

Rob Roy
Made by Hood Firearms Norwich, Conn. C.1880

Handgun, Revolver
.22 Short R.F., 7 Shot, Spur Trigger, Solid Frame, Single Action, Antique   90   160

Robin Hood
Made by Hood Firearms Norwich, Conn. C.1875

Handgun, Revolver
.22 Short R.F., 7 Shot, Spur Trigger, Solid Frame, Single Action, Antique   90   160
.32 Short R.F., 5 Shot, Spur Trigger, Solid Frame, Single Action, Antique   95   170

Roesser, Peter
Lancaster, Pa. 1741-82, See Kentucky Rifles and Pistols

Rogers & Spencer
Willowvale, N.Y.

Handgun, Percussion
.44 Army, Single Action, Antique   450   700

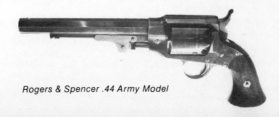

Rogers & Spencer .44 Army Model

Rome Revolver and Novelty Works
Rome, N.Y. C.1880

Handgun, Revolver

.32 Short R.F., 5 Shot, Spur Trigger, Solid Frame, Single Action, Antique	90	160

Roop, John
Allentown, Pa. C.1775, See Kentucky Rifles

Rossi
Amade Rossi S.A., S. Leopoldo, Brazil

Handgun, Revolver

.22 L.R.R.F., Solid Frame, Swing-Out Cylinder, Adjustable Sights, 5 Shot, 3″ Barrel, Modern	65	85
.32 S & W Long, Solid Frame, Swing-Out Cylinder, Adjustable Sights, 5 Shot, 3″ Barrel, Modern	60	80
.38 Special, Solid Frame, Swing-Out Cylinder, Adjustable Sights, 5 Shot, 3″ Barrel, Modern	70	95

Handgun, Singleshot

.22 Short R.F., Derringer, Modern	35	50

Rifle, Slide Action

Gallery, .22 L.R.R.F., Tube Feed, Takedown, Hammer, Modern	50	80
Gallery, .22 L.R.R.F., Tube Feed, Takedown, Hammer, Carbine, Modern	120	80

Shotgun, Double Barrel, Side by Side

12 Ga. Mag. 3″, Checkered Stock, Hammerless, Double Trigger, Modern	125	180
12 Ga. Mag. 3″, Hammerless, Double Trigger, Modern	120	175
Overland, 12 and 20 Gauges, Checkered Stock, Outside Hammers, Double Trigger, Modern	120	160
Overland, 12 and 20 Gauges, Outside Hammers, Double Trigger, Modern	120	160

Ross Rifle Co.
Quebec, Canada

Rifle, Bolt Action

Canadian Issue, .303 British, Military, Modern	125	190
Model 1903 MK I, .303 British, Sporting Rifle, Open Rear Sight, Modern	220	300
Model 1905 MK II, Various Calibers, Sporting Rifle, Open Rear Sight, Modern	190	280
Model 1910 MK III, Various Calibers, Sporting Rifle, Open Rear Sight, Checkered Stock, Modern	160	225

Rottweil
Germany, Imported by Eastern Sports Milford, N.H.

Rifle, Double Barrel, Over-Under

Standard Grade, Various Calibers, Engraved, Fancy Checkering, Open Rear Sight, Modern	1,400	2,000

Shotgun, Double Barrel, Over-Under

Montreal, 12 Ga., Trap Grade, Vent Rib, Single Selective Trigger, Checkered Stock, Modern	1,150	1,600
Olympia, 12 Ga., Skeet Grade, Single Selective Trigger, Automatic Ejector, Vent Rib, Engraved, Modern	1,300	1,900
Olympia, 12 Ga., Trap Grade, Single Selective Trigger, Automatic Ejector, Vent Rib, Engraved, Modern	1,300	1,900
Olympia 72, 12 Ga., Skeet Grade, Trap Grade, Single Selective Trigger, Checkered Stock, Modern	1,150	1,600
Supreme, 12 Ga., Vent Rib, Single Selective Trigger, Checkered Stock, Modern	1,000	1,500

Supreme, 12 Ga., Field Grade, Single Selective Trigger, Automatic
   Ejector, Vent Rib, Engraved, Modern   1,300   1,900
American, 12 Ga., Trap Grade, Single Selective Trigger, Automatic
   Ejector, Vent Rib, Engraved, Modern   1,300   1,900

Roviro, Antonio
Iqualada, Spain, C.1790

Handgun, Miquelet-Lock
Pair, Belt Pistol, Belt Hook, Engraved, Light Ornamentation, Antique   4,000+

Royal
Possibly Hopkins & Allen C.1880

Handgun, Revolver
.22 Short R.F., 7 Shot, Spur Trigger, Solid Frame, Single Action, Antique   90   160
.32 Short R.F., 5 Shot, Spur Trigger, Solid Frame, Single Action, Antique   95   170

Royal
Spain, Zulaika y Cia

Handgun, Semi-Automatic
.32 ACP, Clip Fed, Long Grip, Modern   95   150
12 Shot, .32 ACP, Clip Fed, Long Grip, Modern   125   175

Ruby
Various Manufacturers, for WW-1 French Army Use

Handgun, Semi-Automatic
.32 ACP, Clip Fed, Military, Curio   75   115

Ruby .32 ACP

Royal .32 ACP

Royal Long Grip .32 ACP

Ruger Model AC-556

Ruger Model AC-556K

Ruger
Sturm, Ruger & Co., Southport, Conn.

Add for Bicentennial Stamping 5%-10%

Automatic Weapon, Submachine Gun

AC-556, .223 Rem., Clip Fed, Wood Stock, with Compensator, Class 3	150	250
AC-556K, .223 Rem., Clip Fed, Folding Stock, with Compensator, Class 3	200	325

Handgun, Revolver

Brass Gripframe, Add $15-20

.22 L.R.R.F., Western Style, Single Action, Blue, Lightweight, Early Model, Modern	225	275
"Magna-port IV," .44 Magnum, Western Style, Single Action, Commemorative, Modern	950	1,400
Bearcat, .22 L.R.R.F., Western Style, Single Action, Blue, Brass Grip Frame, Modern	135	190
Bearcat, .22 L.R.R.F., Western Style, Single Action, Blue, Aluminum Gripframe, Early Model, Modern	150	225
Blackhawk, .30 Carbine, Western Style, Single Action, Blue, New Model, Modern	95	140
Blackhawk, .30 Carbine, Western Style, Single Action, Blue, Modern	130	180
Blackhawk, .357 Magnum, Western Style, Single Action, Blue, New Model, Modern	95	140
Blackhawk, .357 Magnum, Western Style, Single Action, Blue, Modern	130	170
Blackhawk, .357 Magnum, Western Style, Single Action, Blue, Flat-Top Frame, Early Model, Modern	250	350
Blackhawk, .357 Magnum, Western Style, Single Action, Blue, 10" Barrel, Modern	450	600
Blackhawk, .357 Magnum, Western Style, Single Action, Stainless Steel, New Model, Modern	120	150

Ruger Blackhawk

Ruger Stainless Blackhawk

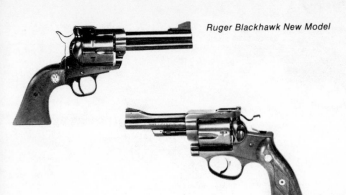

Ruger Blackhawk New Model

Ruger Security

Ruger Service-Six

Blackhawk, .357 Magnum/9mm Combo, Western Style, Single Action, Blue, New Model, Modern	100	145
Blackhawk, .357 Magnum/9mm Combo, Western Style, Single Action, Blue, Modern	150	185
Blackhawk, .41 Magnum, Western Style, Single Action, Blue, New Model, Modern	95	135
Blackhawk, .41 Magnum, Western Style, Single Action, Blue, Modern	125	170
Blackhawk, .45 Colt, Western Style, Single Action, Blue, Modern	130	180
Blackhawk, .45 Colt, Western Style, Single Action, Blue, New Model, Modern	95	135
Blackhawk, .45 Colt/.45 ACP Combo, Western Style, Single Action, Blue, Modern	125	170
Blackhawk, .45 Colt/.45 ACP Combo, Western Style, Single Action, Blue, Modern	165	220
Security-Six, .357 Magnum, Double Action, Swing-Out Cylinder, Stainless Steel, Adjustable Sights, Modern	125	160
Security-Six, .357 Magnum, Double Action, Swing-Out Cylinder, Blue, Adjustable Sights, Modern	110	140
Service-Six, .357 Magnum, Double Action, Swing-Out Cylinder, Blue, Modern	100	130
Service-Six, .357 Magnum, Double Action, Swing-Out Cylinder, Stainless Steel, Modern	115	145
Service-Six, .38 Special, Double Action, Swing-Out Cylinder, Blue, Modern	80	100
Service-Six, .38 Special, Double Action, Swing-Out Cylinder, Stainless Steel, Modern	100	130
Service-Six, 9mm Luger, Double Action, Swing-Out Cylinder, Blue, Modern	100	125
Single-Six, .22 L.R.R.F., Western Style, Single Action, Blue, Engraved, Cased, Modern	550	700
Single-Six, .22 L.R.R.F., Western Style, Single Action, Blue, Flat Loading Gate, Early Model, Modern	175	240

Ruger Speed

Ruger New Model Super Blackhawk

Single-Six Colorado Centennial, .22 L.R.R.F., Commemorative, Cased, Curio	175	275
Speed-Six, .357 Magnum, Double Action, Swing-Out Cylinder, Blue, Modern	90	120
Speed-Six, .357 Magnum, Double Action, Swing-Out Cylinder, Stainless Steel, Modern	115	145
Speed-Six .38 Special, Double Action, Swing-Out Cylinder, Blue, Modern	80	100
Speed-Six, .38 Special, Double Action, Swing-Out Cylinder, Stainless Steel, Modern	100	130
Speed-Six, 9mm Luger, Double Action, Swing-Out Cylinder, Blue, Modern	90	120
Super Blackhawk, .44 Magnum, Western Style, Single Action, Blue, New Model, Modern	120	160
Super Blackhawk, .44 Magnum, Western Style, Single Action, Blue, Modern	165	225
Super Blackhawk, .44 Magnum, Western Style, Single Action, Blue, Flat-Top Frame, Early Model, Modern	450	600
Super Blackhawk, .44 Magnum, Western Style, Single Action, Blue, 10" Barrel, Modern	450	600
Super Single Six, .22LR/.22 WMR Combo, Western Style, Single Action, Blue, New Model, Modern	60	95
Super Single Six, .22LR/.22 WMR Combo, Western Style, Single Action, Blue, New Model, 9½" Barrel, Modern	70	110
Super Single Six, .22LR/.22 WMR Combo, Western Style, Single Action, Blue, Modern	95	150
Super Single Six, .22LR/.22 WMR Combo, Western Style, Single Action, Blue, 9½" Barrel, Modern	120	155
Super Single Six, .22LR/.22 WMR Combo, Western Style, Single Action, Stainless Steel, New Model, Modern	110	140

Handgun, Semi-Automatic

MK I, .22 L.R.R.F., Clip Fed, Adjustable Sights, Target Pistol, Modern	60	85
MK I, .22 L.R.R.F., Clip Fed, Adjustable Sights, Target Pistol, Wood Grips, Modern	65	90

Ruger Super Single

Ruger Mk.I Auto

Ruger Standard Auto

Ruger Model 77 Rifle

Standard, .22 L.R.R.F., Clip Fed, Modern	45	65
Standard (Under #25600), .22 L.R.R.F., Clip Fed, Early Model, Blue, Modern	170	235

Handgun, Singleshot

Hawkeye, .256 Win. Mag., Western Style, Single Action, Blue, Modern	350	500

Rifle, Bolt Action

M-77, for .338 Win. Mag., Add $10-$15
M-77, for .458 Win. Mag., Add $40-$50

M-77R, Various Calibers, Checkered Stock, Scope Mounts, no Sights, Modern	140	190
M-77RS, Various Calibers, Checkered Stock, Open Rear Sight, Scope Mounts, Modern	150	200
M-77ST, Various Calibers, Checkered Stock, Open Rear Sight, Modern	150	200
M-77V, Various Calibers, Heavy Barrel, Varmint, no Sights, Scope Mounts, Checkered Stock, Modern	150	200

Rifle, Semi-Automatic

10/22, .22 L.R.R.F., Clip Fed, Plain, Modern	45	60
10/22 Canadian Centennial, .22 L.R.R.F., Commemorative, Curio	60	120
10/22 International, .22 L.R.R.F., Clip Fed, Full-Stocked, Modern	80	120
10/22 Sporter I, .22 L.R.R.F., Clip Fed, Monte Carlo Stock, Modern	50	75
10/22 Sporter II, .22 L.R.R.F., Clip Fed, Checkered Stock, Modern	55	80
Mini-14, .223 Rem., Clip Fed, Carbine, Modern	115	150
Mini-14, .223 Rem., Clip Fed, Carbine, Stainless, Modern	150	200
Model 44 Deluxe, .44 Magnum, Tube Feed, Clip Fed, Plain, Peep Sights, Sling Swivels, Modern	120	160

Ruger 10-22

Ruger Mini-14

290

Ruger Model 44 Carbine

Ruger #1 Tropical

Ruger #3 Carbine

Model 44 International, .44 Magnum, Tube Feed, Clip Fed, Full-Stocked,
Modern 150 190
Model 44 Sporter, .44 Magnum, Tube Feed, Clip Fed, Monte Carlo Stock,
Modern 125 170
Model 44 Standard, .44 Magnum, Tube Feed, Clip Fed, Plain, Open Rear
Sight, Modern 110 150

Rifle, Singleshot
#1 Canadian Centennial Deluxe, Commemorative, Curio 500 800
#1 Light Sporter, Various Calibers, Open Rear Sight, Checkered Stock,
Modern 150 225
#1 Medium Sporter, Various Calibers, Open Rear Sight, Checkered Stock,
Modern 150 225
#1 Standard Sporter, Various Calibers, no Sights, Scope Mounts,
Checkered Stock, Modern 145 215
#1 Tropical, Various Calibers, Open Rear Sight, Checkered Stock, Modern 175 230
#1 Varminter, Various Calibers, Heavy Barrel, no Sights, Checkered Stock,
Modern 160 235
#2 Canadian Centennial Set, Commemorative, Curio 375 500
#3 Canadian Centennial Set, Commemorative, Curio 265 375
#3 Carbine, Various Calibers, Open Rear Sight, Modern 120 160

Silenced Weapon, Pistol
MK I (Mac), .22 L.R.R.F., Semi-Automatic, Adjustable Sights, Clip Fed,
Target Pistol, Class 3 .... 350 500

Silenced Weapon, Rifle
10/22 (Mac), .22 L.R.R.F., Semi-Automatic, Clip Fed, Military, Class 3 600 800

Rummel
Made by Crescent for A.J. Rummel Arms Co., Toledo, Ohio

Shotgun, Double Barrel, Side by Side
Various Gauges, Outside Hammers, Damascus Barrel, Modern 80 150
Various Gauges, Hammerless, Steel Barrel, Modern 95 175
Various Gauges, Hammerless, Damascus Barrel, Modern 75 150
Various Gauges, Outside Hammers, Steel Barrel, Modern 90 175

Shotgun, Singleshot
Various Gauges, Hammer, Steel Barrel, Modern 45 75

Rupertus, Jacob
Philadelphia, Pa. 1858-99

Handgun, Double Barrel, Side by Side
.22 Short R.F., Derringer, Side-Swing Barrel, Iron Frame, Spur Trigger,
  Antique   250   375

Handgun, Revolver
.22 Short R.F., Pepperbox, 8 Shot, Iron Frame, Spur Trigger, Antique   225   350
.22 Short R.F., 7 Shot, Spur Trigger, Solid Frame, Single Action, Antique   90   160
.32 Short R.F., 5 Shot, Spur Trigger, Solid Frame, Single Action, Antique   90   160
.38 Short R.F., 5 Shot, Spur Trigger, Solid Frame, Single Action, Antique   95   170
.41 Short R.F., 5 Shot, Spur Trigger, Solid Frame, Single Action, Antique   125   190

Handgun, Singleshot
.22 Short R.F., Derringer, Side-Swing Barrel, Iron Frame, Spur Trigger,
  Antique   120   210
.32 Short R.F., Derringer, Side-Swing Barrel, Iron Frame, Spur Trigger,
  Antique   110   170
.38 Short R.F., Derringer, Side-Swing Barrel, Iron Frame, Spur Trigger,
  Antique   115   175

Rupp, Herman
Pa. 1784. See Kentucky Rifles.

Rupp, John
Allentown, Pa. See U.S. Military, Kentucky Rifles and Pistols

Ruppert, William
Lancaster, Pa. C.1776. See U.S. Military, Kentucky Rifles and Pistols

Rush, John
Philadelphia, Pa. 1740-50. See Kentucky Rifles and Pistols

Russian Military

Automatic Weapon, Assault Rifle
AVS 36 Simonava, 7.62 X 39 Russian, Clip Fed, Wood Stock, Class 3   700   950

Automatic Weapon, Heavy Machine Gun
Goryunov SG-43, 7.62 X 39 Russian, Belt Fed, Heavy Barrel, Class 3   1,200   1,600

Automatic Weapon, Light Machine Gun
Degtyarov DP, 7.62 X54R Russian, Drum Magazine, Bipod, Class 3   950   1,500

Automatic Weapon, Submachine Gun
PPS-43, 7.62mm Tokarev, Clip Fed, Folding Stock, Class 3   650   900
PPSH-41, 7.62mm Tokarev, Clip Fed, Wood Stock, Class 3   475   700

Handgun, Free Pistol
Vostok M-T03-35, .22 L.R.R.F., Cased with Accessories, Modern   550   750

Handgun, Percussion
.50, Officer's Belt Pistol, Military, Belt Hook, Antique   350   500

Russian Military Percussion Pistol

Russian Military Model 1890 Nagent

Russian Military Nagent 7.62mm

Russian Military Makarov 9mm

Russian Military Tokarev Pistol

Handgun, Revolver

M1890, 7.62mm Nagent, Gas-Seal Cylinder, Imperial, Modern	70	120
M1890, 7.62mm Nagent, Gas-Seal Cylinder, Communist, Modern	90	145

Handgun, Semi-Automatic

Makarov, 9mm Makarov, Clip Fed, Double Action, Modern	500	750
Tokarev, 7.62mm Tokarev, Clip Fed, Modern	140	200

Rifle, Bolt Action

M1891 Moisin-Nagent, 7.62 X 54R Russian, Military, Modern	50	85
M1891 Remington, 7.62 X 54R Russian, Military, Modern	80	120
M1910, 7.62 X 54R Russian, Military, Carbine, Modern	55	95

Rifle, Semi-Automatic

M1940 Tokarev, 7.62 X 54R Russian, Clip Fed, Military, Modern	110	200
SKS, 7.62 X 39 Russian, Carbine, Military, Modern	150	225

Ryan, Thomas
Norwich, Conn.

Handgun, Revolver

.22 Short R.F., 7 Shot, Spur Trigger, Solid Frame, Single Action, Antique	90	160
.32 Short R.F., 5 Shot, Spur Trigger, Solid Frame, Single Action, Antique	95	170

Sable

Handgun, Revolver
Baby Hammerless, .22 Short R.F., Folding Trigger, Modern   60   90

Sako
Finland, Imported by Garcia, Current

Rifle, Bolt Action

Deluxe (Garcia), Various Calibers, Sporting Rifle, Monte Carlo Stock,
  Fancy Checkering, Long Action, Modern   320   425

Deluxe (Garcia), Various Calibers, Sporting Rifle, Monte Carlo Stock,
  Fancy Checkering, Medium Action, Modern   325   425

Deluxe (Garcia), Various Calibers, Sporting Rifle, Monte Carlo Stock,
  Fancy Checkering, Short Action, Modern   325   425

Finnbear, Various Calibers, Sporting Rifle, Monte Carlo Stock, Checkered
  Stock, Long Action, Modern   325   425

Finnbear Carbine, Various Calibers, Sporting Rifle, Monte Carlo Stock,
  Checkered Stock, Long Action, Full-Stocked, Modern   340   450

Forester, Various Calibers, Sporting Rifle, Monte Carlo Stock, Checkered
  Stock, Medium Action, Modern   300   400

Forester, Various Calibers, Sporting Rifle, Monte Carlo Stock, Checkered
  Stock, Medium Action, Heavy Barrel, Modern   300   400

Forester Carbine, Various Calibers, Sporting Rifle, Monte Carlo Stock,
  Checkered Stock, Medium Action, Full-Stocked, Modern   325   450

Hi-Power Mauser (FN), Various Calibers, Sporting Rifle, Monte Carlo
  Stock, Checkered Stock, Modern   275   375

Magnum Mauser (FN), Various Calibers, Sporting Rifle, Monte Carlo
  Stock, Checkered Stock, Modern   300   420

Model 74 (Garcia), Various Calibers, Sporting Rifle, Monte Carlo Stock,
  Checkered Stock, Long Action, Modern   250   350

Model 74 (Garcia), Various Calibers, Sporting Rifle, Monte Carlo Stock,
  Checkered Stock, Medium Action, Modern   250   350

Model 74 (Garcia), Various Calibers, Sporting Rifle, Monte Carlo Stock,
  Checkered Stock, Short Action, Modern   250   350

Model 74 (Garcia), Various Calibers, Sporting Rifle, Monte Carlo Stock,
  Checkered Stock, Heavy Barrel, Medium Action, Modern   270   365

Model 74 (Garcia), Various Calibers, Sporting Rifle, Monte Carlo Stock,
  Checkered Stock, Heavy Barrel, Short Action, Modern   270   365

Vixen, Various Calibers, Sporting Rifle, Monte Carlo Stock, Checkered
  Stock, Short Action, Modern   240   335

Vixen, Various Calibers, Sporting Rifle, Monte Carlo Stock, Checkered
  Stock, Short Action, Heavy Barrel, Modern   250   360

Vixen Carbine, Various Calibers, Sporting Rifle, Monte Carlo Stock,
  Checkered Stock, Short Action, Full-Stocked, Modern   275   380

Rifle, Lever Action

Finnwolf, Various Calibers, Sporting Rifle, Monte Carlo Stock, Checkered
  Stock, Modern   250   375

St. Louis Arms Co.
Belgium for Shapleigh Hardware Co. C.1900

Shotgun, Double Barrel, Side by Side
Various Gauges, Outside Hammers, Damascus Barrel, Modern   80   150
Various Gauges, Hammerless, Steel Barrel, Modern   95   175
Various Gauges, Hammerless, Damascus Barrel, Modern   75   150
Various Gauges, Outside Hammers, Steel Barrel, Modern   90   175

Shotgun, Singleshot
Various Gauges, Hammer, Steel Barrel, Modern   45   75

Samples, Bethuel
Urbana, Ohio. See Kentucky Rifles and Pistols

Sarasqueta, Victor
Victor Sarasqueta, Eibar, Spain, from 1934

Rifle, Double Barrel, Side by Side

Various Calibers, Sidelock, Automatic Ejector, Fancy Engraving, Fancy Checkering, Modern	1,750	2,400

Shotgun, Double Barrel, Side by Side

#10, Various Gauges, Sidelock, Fancy Checkering, Fancy Engraving, Modern	650	950
#11, Various Gauges, Sidelock, Fancy Checkering, Fancy Engraving, Modern	850	1,100
#12, Various Gauges, Sidelock, Fancy Checkering, Fancy Engraving, Modern	1,100	1,350
#2, Various Gauges, Double Trigger, Checkered Stock, Light Engraving, Modern	125	175
#3, Various Gauges, Double Trigger, Checkered Stock, Light Engraving, Modern	175	275
#4, Various Gauges, Sidelock, Checkered Stock, Light Engraving, Modern	225	325
#4E, Various Gauges, Sidelock, Checkered Stock, Light Engraving, Modern	250	385
#5, Various Gauges, Sidelock, Checkered Stock, Light Engraving, Modern	225	325
#5E, Various Gauges, Sidelock, Checkered Stock, Light Engraving, Modern	275	400
#6, Various Gauges, Sidelock, Fancy Checkering, Engraved, Modern	250	365
#6E, Various Gauges, Sidelock, Fancy Checkering, Engraved, Modern	350	475
#7, Various Gauges, Sidelock, Fancy Checkering, Engraved, Modern	350	475
#7E, Various Gauges, Sidelock, Fancy Checkering, Engraved, Modern	400	550
#8, Various Gauges, Sidelock, Fancy Checkering, Fancy Engraving, Modern	525	650
#9, Various Gauges, Sidelock, Fancy Checkering, Fancy Engraving, Modern	625	750
Super Deluxe, Various Gauges, Sidelock, Fancy Checkering, Fancy Engraving, Modern	1,800	2,200

Sauer, J.P.
Suhl, Germany, 1855 to Date

Combination Weapon, Double Barrel, Over-Under

BBF, Various Calibers, Double Trigger, Set Trigger, Engraved, Checkered Stock, Modern	850	1,300
BBF Deluxe, Various Calibers, Double Trigger, Set Trigger, Fancy Engraving, Fancy Checkering, Modern	950	1,450

Sauer Behorden .32 ACP

Sauer Model 1913 .25 ACP

Sauer Model 1913 .32 ACP (late)

Sauer H 38 .32 ACP

Combination Weapon, Drilling

Model 3000 E, Various Calibers, Double Trigger, Engraved, Checkered Stock, Modern	950	1,350
Model 3000 E Deluxe, Various Calibers, Double Trigger, Fancy Engraving, Fancy Checkering, Modern	1,200	1,700

Handgun, Semi-Automatic

Behorden, .32 ACP, Clip Fed, Modern	150	225
Behorden, .32 ACP, Clip Fed, Lightweight, Modern	275	375
Behorden 4mm, .32 ACP, Clip Fed, Extra Barrel, Modern	475	650
Behorden Dutch Navy, .32 ACP, Clip Fed, Military, Modern	240	350
Model 1913, .25 ACP, Clip Fed, Modern	125	200
Model 1913, .32 ACP, Clip Fed, Modern	115	170
Model 28, .25 ACP, Clip Fed, Modern	160	225
Model H 38, .25 ACP, Double Action, Clip Fed, Hammer, Modern	175	275
Model H 38, .32 ACP, Double Action, Clip Fed, Hammer, Commercial, Modern	145	200
Model H 38, .32 ACP, Double Action, Clip Fed, Hammer, Nazi-Proofed, Military, Modern	160	220
Model H 38, .32 ACP, Double Action, Clip Fed, Hammer, Lightweight, Modern	375	500
Model H 38, Double Action, Clip Fed, Hammer, Modern	220	350
Model H 38 Police, .32 ACP, Double Action, Clip Fed, Hammer, Nazi-Proofed, Curio	325	450
W.T.M., .25 ACP, Clip Fed, Modern	160	225
Roth-Sauer, 8mm, Clip Fed, Curio	500	800

Rifle, Bolt Action

Mauser Custom, Various Calibers, Set Trigger, Checkered Stock, Octagon Barrel, Modern	300	425

Shotgun, Double Barrel, Over-Under

Model 66 GR I, 12 Ga., Single Selective Trigger, Selective Ejector, Hammerless, Sidelock, Engraved, Modern	850	1,200

Roth-Sauer 8mm

Model 66 GR I, 12 Ga., Skeet Grade, Selective Ejector, Hammerless, Sidelock, Engraved, Modern	700	1,000
Model 66 GR II, 12 Ga., Single Selective Trigger, Selective Ejector, Hammerless, Sidelock, Fancy Engraving, Modern	950	1,400
Model 66 GR II, 12 Ga., Skeet Grade, Selective Ejector, Hammerless, Sidelock, Fancy Engraving, Modern	850	1,100
Model 66 GR II, 12 Ga., Trap Grade, Selective Ejector, Hammerless, Sidelock, Fancy Engraving, Modern	850	1,100
Model 66 GR III, 12 Ga., Single Selective Trigger, Selective Ejector, Hammerless, Sidelock, Fancy Engraving, Modern	1,500	2,000
Model 66 GR III, 12 Ga., Skeet Grade, Selective Ejector, Hammerless, Sidelock, Fancy Engraving, Modern	1,000	1,550
Model 66 GR III, 12 Ga., Trap Grade, Selective Ejector, Hammerless, Sidelock, Fancy Engraving, Modern	1,000	1,550
Model GR I, 12 Ga., Trap Grade, Selective Ejector, Hammerless, Sidelock, Engraved, Modern	700	1,000

Shotgun, Double Barrel, Side by Side

.410 Gauge, Double Trigger, Light Engraving, Modern	400	550
Artemis I, 12 Ga., Single Selective Trigger, Engraved, Checkered Stock, Modern	2,300	3,250
Artemis II, 12 Ga., Single Selective Trigger, Fancy Engraving, Fancy Checkering, Modern	2,800	3,750
Royal, 12 and 20 Gauges, Single Selective Trigger, Engraved, Checkered Stock, Modern	475	800

Savage Arms Co.

Utica, N.Y., 1893-99. Renamed Savage Arms Co. 1899. J. Stevens Arms Co. Springfield Arms Co. and A.H. Fox are all part of Savage. Also See U.S. Military.

Automatic Weapon, Heavy Machine Gun

M2 Browning (Sav), .50 BMG, Belt Fed, Tripod, Class 3	2,900	3,500

Automatic Weapon, Submachine Gun

Thompson M1928A1, .45 ACP, Clip Fed, with Compensator, Lyman Sights, Class 3	1,000	1,400

Combination Weapon, Double Barrel, Over-Under

Model 24, Various Calibers, Hammer, Modern	45	75
Model 24-C, .22-20 Ga., Hammer, Modern	65	90
Model 24-D, Various Calibers, Hammer, Modern	65	95
Model 24-V, Various Calibers, Checkered Stock, Hammer, Modern	85	110
Model 2400, Various Calibers, Checkered Stock, Hammer, Modern	350	450

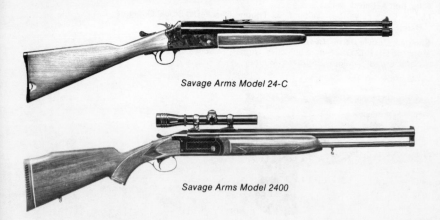

Savage Arms Model 24-C

Savage Arms Model 2400

Savage Arms Model 1907 .32 ACP

Savage Model 1917 .32 ACP

Handgun, Semi-Automatic

Model 1907, Factory Nickel, Add $30-$40		
Model 1907, Grade A Engraving (Light), Add $60-$75		
Model 1907, Grade C Engraving (Fancy), Add $175-$225		
Model 1907 (1908), .32 ACP, Clip Fed, Burr Cocking Piece, Modern, (under #70500)	125	185
Model 1907 (1909), .32 ACP, Clip Fed, Burr Cocking Piece, Modern, (#'s- 10,900-70,499)	110	150
Model 1907 (1912), .32 ACP, Clip Fed, Burr Cocking Piece, Modern, (Higher # than 70500)	105	145
Model 1907 (1913), .380 ACP, Clip Fed, Burr Cocking Piece, Modern	160	200
Model 1907 (1914), .32 ACP, Spur Cocking Piece, Modern	90	130
Model 1907 (1914), .380 ACP, Spur Cocking Piece, Modern	110	150
Model 1907 (1918), .32 ACP, Clip Fed, no Cartridge Indicator, Burr Cocking Piece, Modern, (After # 175,000)	80	120
Model 1907 (1918), .32 ACP, Clip Fed, Spur Cocking Piece, Modern, (After # 195000)	110	150
Model 1907 (1918), .380 ACP, Clip Fed, Burr Cocking Piece, Modern, (After # 10000B)	170	225
Model 1907 Military, .32 ACP, Clip Fed, Burr Cocking Piece, Modern	85	125
Model 1907 Military, .32 ACP, Clip Fed, Burr Cocking Piece, Modern, (Portuguese Contract)	225	300
Model 1915, .32 ACP, Clip Fed, Hammerless, Grip Safety, Modern	150	200
Model 1915, .380 ACP, Clip Fed, Hammerless, Grip Safety, Modern	200	275
Model 1917, .32 ACP, Clip Fed, Spur Cocking Piece, Flared Grip, Modern	135	175
Model 1917, .380 ACP, Clip Fed, Spur Cocking Piece, Flared Grip, Modern	155	200

Handgun, Singleshot

Model 101, .22 L.R.R.F., Western Style, Single Action, Swing-Out Cylinder, Modern	60	85

Rifle, Bolt Action

Model 10, .22 L.R.R.F., Target Sights, Modern, (Anschutz)	75	110
Model 110, Magnum Calibers, Add $10		
Model 110, Various Calibers, Open Rear Sight, Checkered Stock, Modern	110	150
Model 110-B, Various Calibers, Open Rear Sight, Modern	115	160
Model 110-BL, Various Calibers, Open Rear Sight, Left-Hand, Modern	120	165
Model 110-C, Various Calibers, Clip Fed, Open Rear Sight, Modern	115	160
Model 110-CL, Various Calibers, Clip Fed, Open Rear Sight, Left-Hand, Modern	120	165

Savage Arms Model 110-CL

Savage Arms Model 111

Savage Arms Model 112-V

Model 110-E, Various Calibers, Open Rear Sight, Modern	100	150
Model 110-EL, Various Calibers, Open Rear Sight, Left-Hand, Modern	110	155
Model 110-M, Various Calibers, Open Rear Sight, Monte Carlo Stock, Checkered Stock, Magnum Action, Modern	135	170
Model 110-MC, Various Calibers, Open Rear Sight, Monte Carlo Stock, Checkered Stock, Modern	100	145
Model 110-MCL, Various Calibers, Open Rear Sight, Monte Carlo Stock, Checkered Stock, Left-Hand, Modern	110	150
Model 110-ML, Various Calibers, Open Rear Sight, Monte Carlo Stock, Checkered Stock, Magnum Action, Left-Hand, Modern	145	185
Model 110-P, Various Calibers, Open Rear Sight, Fancy Wood, Monte Carlo Stock, Fancy Checkering, Sling Swivels, Modern	225	300
Model 110-PE, Various Calibers, Engraved, Fancy Checkering, Fancy Wood, Sling Swivels, Modern	400	500
Model 110-PEL, Various Calibers, Engraved, Fancy Checkering, Fancy Wood, Sling Swivels, Left-Hand, Modern	400	500
Model 110-PL, Various Calibers, Fancy Wood, Monte Carlo Stock, Fancy Checkering, Sling Swivels, Left-Hand, Modern	250	325
Model 111, Various Calibers, Clip Fed, Monte Carlo Stock, Checkered Stock, Modern	150	195
Model 112-V, Various Calibers, Singleshot, no Sights, Modern	140	190
Model 1407, Sights Only, $45-$65		
Model 1407 "I.S.U.," .22 L.R.R.F., Heavy Barrel, no Sights, Modern, (Anschutz)	220	290
Modle 1407-L "I.S.U.," .22 L.R.R.F., Heavy Barrel, no Sights, Left-Hand, Modern, (Anschutz)	240	310
Model 1408, .22 L.R.R.F., Heavy Barrel, no Sights, Modern, (Anschutz)	220	300
Model 1408-ED, .22 L.R.R.F., Heavy Barrel, no Sights, Modern, (Anschutz)	345	410
Model 1408-L .22 L.R.R.F., Heavy Barrel, no Sights, Left-Hand, Modern, (Anschutz)	225	310
Model 1411, Sights Only, $45-$65		
Model 1411, "Prone," .22 L.R.R.F., Heavy Barrel, no Sights, Modern, (Anschutz)	250	350
Model 1411-L "Prone," .22 L.R.R.F., Heavy Barrel, no Sights, Left-Hand, Modern, (Anschutz)	250	360
Model 1413, .22 L.R.R.F., Sights Only, $45-$65		
Model 1413 "Match," .22 L.R.R.F., Heavy Barrel, no Sights, Modern, (Anschutz)	450	525
Model 1413-L "Match," .22 L.R.R.F., Heavy Barrel, no Sights, Left-Hand, Modern, (Anschutz)	440	550
Model 1418, .22 L.R.R.F., Clip Fed, Mannlicher, Fancy Checkering, Modern, (Anschutz)	180	235
Model 1432, .22 Hornet, Sporting Rifle, Clip Fed, Fancy Checkering, Modern, (Anschutz)	275	350

Savage-Anschutz Model 1413 Match

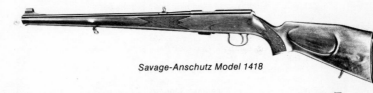

Savage-Anschutz Model 1418

Savage-Anschutz Model 1432

Model 1433, .22 Hornet, Mannlicher, Clip Fed, Fancy Checkering, Modern, (Anschutz)	340	435
Model 1518, .22 WMR, Clip Fed, Mannlicher, Fancy Checkering, Modern, (Anschutz)	200	260
Model 1533, .222 Rem., Mannlicher, Clip Fed, Fancy Checkering, Modern, (Anschutz)	340	445
Model 164, .22 L.R.R.F., Sporting Rifle, Clip Fed, Checkered Stock, Modern, (Anschutz)	145	185
Model 164-M, .22 WMR, Sporting Rifle, Clip Fed, Checkered Stock, Modern, (Anschutz)	155	210
Model 19-H, .22 Hornet, 5 Shot Clip, Peep Sights, Modern	170	230
Model 19-L, .22 L.R.R.F., 5 Shot Clip, Lyman Sights, Modern	110	135
Model 19-M, .22 L.R.R.F., 5 Shot Clip, Heavy Barrel, Modern	105	140
Model 19-N.R.A., .22 L.R.R.F., 5 Shot Clip, Full-Stocked, Peep Sights, Modern	75	110
Model 19-Speed Lock, .22 L.R.R.F., 5 Shot Clip, Peep Sights, Modern	95	120
Model 1904, .22 L.R.R.F., Singleshot, Takedown, Modern	35	55
Model 1904-Special, .22 L.R.R.F., Singleshot, Takedown, Fancy Wood, Modern	60	85
Model 1905, .22 L.R.R.F., Target, Singleshot, Takedown, Swiss Buttplate, Modern	45	65
Model 1905-B, .22 L.R.R.F., Modern	35	55
Model 1905-Special, .22 L.R.R.F., Fancy Wood, Modern	75	110
Model 1911, .22 Short R.F., Target, Singleshot, Takedown, Modern	35	55
Model 20, Various Calibers, Open Rear Sight, Modern	145	190
Model 20, Various Calibers, Peep Sights, Modern	170	225

Savage-Anschutz Model 164

Model 23A, .22 L.R.R.F., 5 Shot Clip, Open Rear Sight, Modern	95	125
Model 23AA, .22 L.R.R.F., 5 Shot Clip, Open Rear Sight, Monte Carlo Stock, Modern	110	135
Model 23B, .25-20 WCF, 5 Shot Clip, Open Rear Sight, Monte Carlo Stock, Modern	120	155
Model 23C, .32-20 WCF, 5 Shot Clip, Open Rear Sight, Monte Carlo Stock, Modern	120	155
Model 23D, .22 Hornet, 5 Shot Clip, Open Rear Sight, Monte Carlo Stock, Modern	175	220
Model 3, .22 L.R.R.F., Singleshot, Takedown, Open Rear Sight, Modern	25	40
Model 3-S, .22 L.R.R.F., Singleshot, Takedown, Peep Sights, Modern	25	40
Model 3-ST, .22 L.R.R.F., Singleshot, Takedown, Peep Sights, Sling Swivels, Modern	30	45
Model 340, Various Calibers, Clip Fed, Modern	75	110
Model 340-C, Various Calibers, Clip Fed, Carbine, Modern	75	110
Model 340-S Deluxe, Various Calibers, Clip Fed, Peep Sights, Modern	85	120
Model 342, .22 Hornet, Clip Fed, Modern	75	110
Model 342-S, .22 Hornet, Clip Fed, Peep Sights, Modern	85	130
Model 4, .22 L.R.R.F., 5 Shot Clip, Takedown, Modern	30	50
Model 4-M, .22 WMR, 5 Shot Clip, Takedown, Modern	45	65
Model 4-S, .22 L.R.R.F., 5 Shot Clip, Takedown, Peep Sights, Modern	40	55
Model 40, Various Calibers, Open Rear Sight, Modern	140	190
Model 45 Super, Various Calibers, Peep Sights, Checkered Stock, Modern	160	220
Model 5, .22 L.R.R.F., Tube Feed, Takedown, Open Rear Sight, Modern	40	60
Model 5-S, .22 L.R.R.F., Tube Feed, Takedown, Peep Sights, Modern	40	60
Model 54, .22 L.R.R.F., Sporting Rifle, Clip Fed, Fancy Checkering, Modern, (Anschutz)	200	280
Model 54-M, .22 WMR, Sporting Rifle, Clip Fed, Fancy Checkering, Modern, (Anschutz)	215	285
Model 63, .22 L.R.R.F., Singleshot, Open Rear Sight, Modern	25	40
Model 63-K, .22 L.R.R.F., Singleshot, Open Rear Sight, Modern	25	40
Model 63-M, .22 WMR, Singleshot, Open Rear Sight, Modern	30	50
Model 64, .22 L.R.R.F., Sights Only, $25-$45		
Model 64, .22 L.R.R.F., Heavy Barrel, no Sights, Modern, (Anschutz)	115	150
Model 64-CS, .22 L.R.R.F., Heavy Barrel, no Sights, Lightweight, Modern, (Anschutz)	150	200
Model 64-CSL, .22 L.R.R.F., Heavy Barrel, no Sights, Left-Hand, Lightweight, Modern, (Anschutz)	165	215
Model 64-L, .22 L.R.R.F., Heavy Barrel, no Sights, Left-Hand, Modern, (Anschutz)	120	170
Model 64-S, .22 L.R.R.F., Heavy Barrel, no Sights, Modern, (Anschutz)	150	200
Model 64-SL, .22 L.R.R.F., Heavy Barrel, no Sights, Left-Hand, Modern, (Anschutz)	165	220
Model 65-M, .22 WMR, Clip Fed, Open Rear Sight, Modern	45	65
Model 73, .22 L.R.R.F., Singleshot, Modern	20	35
Model 73-Y Boys, .22 L.R.R.F., Singleshot, Modern	20	35

Rifle, Lever Action

Model 1892, .30-40 Krag, Hammerless, Rotary Magazine, Military, Antique	750	1,100
Model 1895, .303 Savage, Hammerless, Rotary Magazine, Open Rear Sight, Antique	400	600

Savage-Anschutz Model 64

Savage Model 65-M

Savage Arms Model 73

Model 1899, .30-30 Win., Hammerless, Rotary Magazine, Full-Stocked, Military, Modern	200	280
Model 1899, Various Calibers, Hammerless, Rotary Magazine, Open Rear Sight, Modern	120	160
Model 1899 A2, Various Calibers, Hammerless, Rotary Magazine, Checkered Stock, Modern	125	165
Model 1899 AB, Various Calibers, Light Engraving, Checkered Stock, Hammerless, Rotary Magazine, Modern	235	325
Model 1899 BC, Various Calibers, Light Engraving, Checkered Stock, Hammerless, Rotary Magazine, Modern	220	285
Model 1899 Excelsior, Various Calibers, Light Engraving, Checkered Stock, Featherweight, Hammerless, Rotary Magazine, Modern	400	575
Model 1899 Leader, Various Calibers, Engraved, Checkered Stock, Hammerless, Rotary Magazine, Modern	400	550
Model 1899 Monarch, Various Calibers, Fancy Engraving, Fancy Checkering, Ornate, Hammerless, Rotary Magazine, Modern	1,750	2,350
Model 1899 Premier, Various Calibers, Fancy Engraving, Fancy Checkering, Takedown, Hammerless, Rotary Magazine, Modern	1,100	1,400
Model 1899 Rival, Various Calibers, Fancy Engraving, Fancy Checkering, Hammerless, Rotary Magazine, Modern	900	1,300
Model 1899 Victor, Various Calibers, Engraved, Fancy Checkering, Hammerless, Rotary Magazine, Modern	550	800
Model 89, .22 L.R.R.F., Singleshot, Open Rear Sight, Modern	30	45
Model 99, for Extra Barrel, Add $50-$75		
Model 99 E, Various Calibers, Solid Frame, Carbine, Hammerless, Rotary Magazine, Modern	120	165
Model 99-1895 Anniversary, .308 Win., Octagon Barrel, Hammerless, Rotary Magazine, Modern	190	240
Model 99-358, .358 Win., Solid Frame, Hammerless, Rotary Magazine, Modern	140	200

Savage Arms Model 89

Savage Arms Model 99-358

Savage Arms Model 99-A

Model 99-A, Various Calibers, Solid Frame, Hammerless, Rotary Magazine, Modern	110	170
Model 99-B, Various Calibers, Takedown, Hammerless, Rotary Magazine, Modern	150	200
Model 99-C, Various Calibers, Clip Fed, Solid Frame, Featherweight, Hammerless, Modern	135	185
Model 99-CD, Various Calibers, Hammerless, Clip Fed, Solid Frame, Monte Carlo Stock, Modern	175	225
Model 99-DE, Various Calibers, Solid Frame, Monte Carlo Stock, Light Engraving, Hammerless, Rotary Magazine, Modern	200	275
Model 99-DL, Various Calibers, Solid Frame, Monte Carlo Stock, Hammerless, Rotary Magazine, Modern	135	170
Model 99-E, Various Calibers, Solid Frame, Hammerless, Rotary Magazine, Modern	130	180
Model 99-EG, Various Calibers, Takedown, Checkered Stock, Hammerless, Rotary Magazine, Modern	100	145
Model 99-F, Various Calibers, Featherweight, Takedown, Hammerless, Rotary Magazine, Modern	180	250
Model 99-F, Various Calibers, Solid Frame, Featherweight, Hammerless, Rotary Magazine, Modern	145	200
Model 99-G, Various Calibers, Takedown, Checkered Stock, Hammerless, Rotary Magazine, Modern	150	210
Model 99-H, Various Calibers, Carbine, Solid Frame, Hammerless, Rotary Magazine, Modern	140	200
Model 99-K, Various Calibers, Takedown, Light Engraving, Checkered Stock, Hammerless, Rotary Magazine, Modern	450	650
Model 99-PE, Various Calibers, Solid Frame, Monte Carlo Stock, Engraved, Hammerless, Rotary Magazine, Modern	275	375
Model 99-R, Various Calibers, Solid Frame, Checkered Stock, Pre-War, Hammerless, Rotary Magazine, Modern	175	230
Model 99-R, Various Calibers, Solid Frame, Checkered Stock, Hammerless, Rotary Magazine, Modern	135	185
Model 99-RS, Various Calibers, Solid Frame, Peep Sights, Pre-War, Hammerless, Rotary Magazine, Modern	185	235
Model 99-RS, Various Calibers, Solid Frame, Peep Sights, Hammerless, Rotary Magazine, Modern	150	200
Model 99-T, Various Calibers, Solid Frame, Featherweight, Hammerless, Rotary Magazine, Modern	170	245

Rifle, Semi-Automatic

Model 1912, .22 L.R.R.F., Half-Octagon Barrel, Takedown, Clip Fed, Modern	75	110
Model 6, .22 L.R.R.F., Takedown, Tube Feed, Open Rear Sight, Modern	50	65
Model 6-S, .22 L.R.R.F., Takedown, Tube Feed, Peep Sights, Modern	55	70
Model 60, .22 L.R.R.F., Monte Carlo Stock, Checkered Stock, Tube Feed, Modern	55	75
Model 7, .22 L.R.R.F., 5 Shot Clip, Takedown, Open Rear Sight, Modern	45	55
Model 7-S, .22 L.R.R.F., 5 Shot Clip, Takedown, Open Rear Sight, Modern	50	65
Model 80, .22 L.R.R.F., Tube Feed, Modern	35	50
Model 88, .22 L.R.R.F., Tube Feed, Modern	35	50
Model 90, .22 L.R.R.F., Carbine, Tube Feed, Modern	35	55

Rifle, Singleshot

Model 219, Various Calibers, Hammerless, Top Break, Open Rear Sight, Modern	45	65
Model 219L, Various Calibers, Hammerless, Top Break, Open Rear Sight, Side Lever, Modern	40	60
Model 221, .30-30 Win., Hammerless, Top Break, Extra Shotgun Barrel, Modern	50	80
Model 222, .30-30 Win., Hammerless, Top Break, Extra Shotgun Barrel, Modern	50	80
Model 223, .30-30 Win., Hammerless, Top Break, Extra Shotgun Barrel, Modern	50	80
Model 227, .30-30 Win., Hammerless, Top Break, Extra Shotgun Barrel, Modern	50	80
Model 228, .30-30 Win., Hammerless, Top Break, Extra Shotgun Barrel, Modern	50	80
Model 229, .30-30 Win., Hammerless, Top Break, Extra Shotgun Barrel, Modern	50	80
Model 71 Stevens Favorite, .22 L.R.R.F., Lever Action, Falling Block, Favorite, Modern	75	135
Model 72, .22 L.R.R.F., Lever Action, Falling Block, Modern	45	65

Rifle, Slide Action

Model 170, Various Calibers, Open Rear Sight, Modern	80	110
Model 170-C, .30-30 Win., Carbine, Open Rear Sight, Modern	80	110
Model 1903, .22 L.R.R.F., Hammerless, Clip Fed, Octagon Barrel, Modern	60	90
Model 1903-EF, .22 L.R.R.F., Hammerless, Clip Fed, Octagon Barrel, Fancy Wood, Engraved, Modern	325	425
Model 1903-Expert, .22 L.R.R.F., Hammerless, Clip Fed, Octagon Barrel, Checkered Stock, Light Engraving, Modern	150	225
Model 1909, .22 L.R.R.F., Half-Octagon Barrel, Takedown, Clip Fed, Modern	60	85
Model 1914, .22 L.R.R.F., Half-Octagon Barrel, Takedown, Tube Feed, Modern	90	130
Model 1914-E.F., .22 L.R.R.F., Half-Octagon Barrel, Takedown, Tube Feed, Fancy Engraving, Modern	425	550
Model 1914-Expert, .22 L.R.R.F., Half-Octagon Barrel, Takedown, Tube Feed, Light Engraving, Modern	300	375
Model 1914-Gold Medal, .22 L.R.R.F., Half-Octagon Barrel, Takedown, Tube Feed, Checkered Stock, Light Engraving, Modern	190	245
Model 25, .22 L.R.R.F., Tube Feed, Octagon Barrel, Open Rear Sight, Monte Carlo Stock, Modern	75	110
Model 29, .22 L.R.R.F., Tube Feed, Octagon Barrel, Open Rear Sight, Monte Carlo Stock, Modern	120	170
Model 29, .22 L.R.R.F., Tube Feed, Round Barrel, Open Rear Sight, Modern	110	140
Model 29-G, .22 Short R.F., Tube Feed, Modern	115	150

Shotgun, Bolt Action

Model 58, .410 Ga., Singleshot, Modern	35	50

Shotgun, Double Barrel, Over-Under

Model 242, .410 Ga., Hammer, Single Trigger, Modern	75	110

Savage Arms Model 72

Savage Arms Model 330

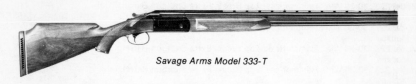

Savage Arms Model 333-T

Model 330, 12 and 20 Gauges, Hammerless, Single Selective Trigger, Modern	245	300
Model 330, 12 and 20 Gauges, Hammerless, Extra Shotgun Barrel, Cased, Modern	340	400
Model 333, 12 and 20 Gauges, Hammerless, Vent Rib, Single Selective Trigger, Modern	320	400
Model 333-T, 12 Ga., Hammerless, Vent Rib, Trap Grade, Single Selective Trigger, Modern	300	385
Model 420, Various Gauges, Hammerless, Takedown, Double Trigger, Modern	190	225
Model 420, Various Gauges, Hammerless, Takedown, Single Trigger, Modern	220	275
Model 430, Various Gauges, Hammerless, Takedown, Checkered Stock, Recoil Pad, Double Trigger, Modern	220	250
Model 430, Various Gauges, Hammerless, Takedown, Checkered Stock, Recoil Pad, Single Trigger, Modern	260	300
Model 440, 12 Ga., Hammerless, Vent Rib, Single Selective Trigger, Checkered Stock, Modern	175	220
Model 440-B, 20 Ga., Hammerless, Vent Rib, Checkered Stock, Modern	200	250
Model 444, 12 Ga., Hammerless, Vent Rib, Single Selective Trigger, Checkered Stock, Selective Ejector, Modern	210	260
Model 444-T, 12 Ga., Hammerless, Trap Grade, Modern	210	260

Shotgun, Double Barrel, Side by Side

Model B Fox, Various Gauges, Hammerless, Vent Rib, Double Trigger, Modern	130	160
Model B-SE Fox, Various Gauges, Hammerless, Vent Rib, Selective Ejector, Single Trigger, Modern	140	185

Shotgun, Semi-Automatic

Model 720, 12 Ga., Tube Feed, Checkered Stock, Plain Barrel, Modern	100	125
Model 720-P, 12 Ga., Checkered Stock, Adjustable Choke, Modern	110	135
Model 720-R, 12 Ga., Riot Gun, Modern	85	120
Model 721, 12 Ga., Tube Feed, Checkered Stock, Raised Matted Rib, Modern	120	150
Model 722, 12 Ga., Tube Feed, Checkered Stock, Vent Rib, Modern	140	175
Model 723, 16 Ga., Tube Feed, Checkered Stock, Plain Barrel, Modern	85	100
Model 724, 16 Ga., Tube Feed, Checkered Stock, Raised Matted Rib, Modern	95	120

Savage Arms Model B-SE Fox

Model 725, 16 Ga., Tube Feed, Checkered Stock, Vent Rib, Modern	100	130
Model 726, 12 and 16 Gauges, 3 Shot, Checkered Stock, Plain Barrel, Modern	100	125
Model 727, 12 and 16 Gauges, 3 Shot, Checkered Stock, Raised Matted Rib, Modern	110	130
Model 728, 12 and 16 Gauges, 3 Shot, Checkered Stock, Vent Rib, Modern	115	140
Model 740-C, 12 and 16 Gauges, Skeet Grade, Modern	140	175
Model 745, 12 Ga., Lightweight, Modern	120	150
Model 750, 12 Ga., Modern	140	175
Model 750-AC, 12 Ga., Adjustable Choke, Modern	140	175
Model 750-SC, 12 Ga., Adjustable Choke, Modern	145	180
Model 755, 12 and 16 Gauges, Modern	120	145
Model 755-SC, 12 and 16 Gauges, Adjustable Choke, Modern	125	150
Model 775, 12 and 16 Gauges, Lightweight, Modern	140	165
Model 775-SC, 12 and 16 Gauges, Adjustable Choke, Lightweight, Modern	145	170

Shotgun, Singleshot

Model 220, Various Gauges, Hammerless, Takedown, Modern	30	45
Model 220-AC, Various Gauges, Hammerless, Takedown, Adjustable Choke, Modern	35	50
Model 220-P, Various Gauges, Hammerless, Takedown, Adjustable Choke, Modern	45	60
Model 94-C, Various Gauges, Hammer, Takedown, Modern	30	45
Model 94-Y, Youth, Various Gauges, Hammer, Takedown, Modern	30	45

Shotgun, Slide Action

Model 21-A, 12 Ga., Hammerless, Takedown, Modern	100	125
Model 21-B, 12 Ga., Hammerless, Takedown, Raised Matted Rib, Modern	110	135
Model 21-C, 12 Ga., Hammerless, Takedown, Riot Gun, Modern	85	110
Model 21-D, 12 Ga., Hammerless, Takedown, Trap Grade, Modern	150	200
Model 21-E, 12 Ga., Hammerless, Takedown, Fancy Wood, Fancy Checkering, Vent Rib, Modern	200	250
Model 28-A, 12 Ga., Hammerless, Takedown, Modern	100	125
Model 28-B, 12 Ga., Hammerless, Takedown, Raised Matted Rib, Modern	110	135
Model 28-C, 12 Ga., Hammerless, Takedown, Riot Gun, Modern	85	110
Model 28-D, 12 Ga., Hammerless, Takedown, Trap Grade, Modern	150	200
Model 28-S, 12 Ga., Hammerless, Takedown, Fancy Checkering, Modern	140	185
Model 30, Add for Vent Rib, $15-$20		
Model 30, Various Gauges, Hammerless, Solid Frame, Modern	85	100
Model 30-AC, Various Gauges, Hammerless, Solid Frame, Adjustable Choke, Modern	85	100
Model 30-ACL, Various Gauges, Hammerless, Solid Frame, Left-Hand, Adjustable Choke, Modern	95	110
Model 30-D, Various Gauges, Hammerless, Solid Frame, Light Engraving, Recoil Pad, Modern	100	130
Model 30-L, Various Gauges, Hammerless, Solid Frame, Left-Hand, Modern	95	110
Model 30-Slug, 12 Ga., Hammerless, Solid Frame, Modern	95	115
Model 30-T, 12 Ga., Hammerless, Solid Frame, Monte Carlo Stock, Recoil Pad, Vent Rib, Modern	110	140

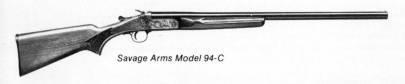

Savage Arms Model 94-C

Savage Arms Model 30-D

Schall
Hartford, Conn.

Handgun, Manual Repeater
.22 L.R.R.F., Target Pistol, Clip Fed, Curio   225   300

Scheaner, Wm.
Reading, Pa. 1779-90. See Kentucky Rifles

Schmid, Ernst
Suhl, Germany

Rifle, Singleshot
8mm Roth-Steyr, Schutzen Rifle, Engraved, Set Trigger, Takedown,
Octagon Barrel, Modern   550   750

Schmidt & Habermann
Suhl, Germany, 1920-40

Combination Weapon, Double Barrel, Over-Under
Various Calibers, Pre-WW2, Engraved, Checkered Stock, Modern   425   600

Schouboe

Handgun, Semi-Automatic
Model 1902/07, 11.35mm Sch., Curio   2,800   3,750
Model 1902/10, 11.35mm Sch., Curio   2,800   3,750

Schultz & Larsen
Otterup, Denmark

Handgun, Singleshot
Free Pistol, .22 L.R.R.F., Bolt Action, Target Trigger, Target Sights,
Modern   180   275

Rifle, Bolt Action
M54, Various Calibers, Modern   375   525
Model 61, .22 L.R.R.F., Target Rifle, Thumbhole Stock, Adjustable Trigger,
Singleshot, Modern   275   375
Model 62, Various Calibers, Target Rifle, Thumbhole Stock, Adjustable
Trigger, Singleshot, Modern   300   425
Model 65DL, Various Calibers, Sporting Rifle, Checkered Stock,
Adjustable Trigger, no Sights, Repeater, Modern   225   350
Model 68DL, .458 Win. Mag., Sporting Rifle, Checkered Stock, Adjustable
Trigger, no Sights, Repeater, Modern   375   550
Model 68DL, Various Calibers, Sporting Rifle, Checkered Stock,
Adjustable Trigger, no Sights, Repeater, Modern   325   450

Schutzen Rifles, Unknown Maker

Rifle, Singleshot
Aydt System, Various Calibers, Dropping Block, Plain Tyrol Stock, Light
Engraving, Target Sights, Modern   300   550
Aydt System, Various Calibers, Dropping Block, Fancy Tyrol Stock, Fancy
Engraving, Target Sights, Modern   550   850
Martini System, Various Calibers, Dropping Block, Fancy Tyrol Stock,
Fancy Engraving, Target Sights, Modern   500   800

Schwarzlose
Austria C.1900

Handgun, Semi-Automatic
M 1908 Pocket, .32 ACP, Clip Fed, Grip Safety, Modern   300   450

Schwarzlose .32 ACP

Scott Arms Co.
Probably Norwich Fall Pistol Co. C.1880

Handgun, Revolver

.32 Short R.F., 5 Shot, Spur Trigger, Solid Frame, Single Action, Antique	90	160

Scott Revolver-Rifle
Hopkins & Allen C.1880

Handgun, Revolver

24½″ Brass Barrel, .38 Short R.F., 5 Shot, Spur Trigger, Solid Frame, Single Action, Antique	120	210

Scout
Made by Stevens

Shotgun, Double Barrel, Side by Side

Model 311, Various Gauges, Hammerless, Steel Barrel, Modern	90	145

Secret Service Special
Made for Fred Biffar, Chicago. Made by Iver-Johnson and Meriden

Handgun, Revolver

.32 S & W, 5 Shot, Top Break, Hammerless, Double Action, Modern	55	95
.38 S & W, 5 Shot, Top Break, Hammerless, Double Action, Modern	55	95

Security Industries of America
Little Ferry, N.J.

Handgun, Revolver

Police Pocket, .357 Magnum, Stainless Steel, 2″ Barrel, Swing-Out Cylinder, Double Action, Spurless Hammer, Modern	110	150
Police Security Spec, .38 Special, Stainless Steel, 2″ Barrel, Swing-Out Cylinder, Double Action, Modern	90	125
Security Undercover, .357 Magnum, Stainless Steel, 2½″ Barrel, Swing-Out Cylinder, Double Action, Modern	110	150

Sedgley, R.F., Inc.
Philadelphia, Pa. 1911-38. Successor to Henry Knob

Handgun, Revolver

Baby Hammerless, .22 L.R.R.F., Double Action, Folding Trigger, Modern	60	90

Rifle, Bolt Action

Springfield, Various Calibers, Sporting Rifle, Lyman Sights, Checkered Stock, Modern	275	350
Springfield, Various Calibers, Sporting Rifle, Lyman Sights, Checkered Stock, Left-Hand, Modern	300	400
Springfield, Various Calibers, Sporting Rifle, Lyman Sights, Checkered Stock, Full-Stocked, Modern	325	450
Springfield, Various Calibers, Sporting Rifle, Lyman Sights, Checkered Stock, Full-Stocked, Left-Hand, Modern	325	450

Selecta
Spain Echave y Arizmendi

Handgun, Semi-Automatic

M 1918, .25 ACP, Clip Fed, Modern	85	125

Semmerling

Handgun, Manual Repeater

LM-4, .45 ACP, Double Action, Clip Fed, Modern	400	600

Shakanoosa Arms Mfg. Co.
1862-64, See Confederate Military

Rifle, Percussion

.58, Military, Carbine, Antique, (C S A)	1,200	1,700
.58, Military, Antique, (C S A)	950	1,300

Sharpe
English, 1670-80

Handgun, Flintlock

Pair, Pocket Pistol, Screw Barrel, Octagon, High Quality, Antique	1,750	2,800

Sharps
Made by Shiloh Products Farmingdale, N.Y. Current

Rifle, Percussion

Model 1859 New Model Cavalry Carbine, .54, Reproduction, Antique	200	300
Model 1863 Cavalry Carbine, .54, Reproduction, Antique	175	275
Model 1863 Sporting Rifle #3, .54, Reproduction, Antique	220	325
Model 1863 Sporting Rifle #2, .54, Reproduction, Antique	250	340
Model 1862 Robinson Confederate Cavalry Carbine, .54, Reproduction, Antique	200	300
Model 1863 New Model Military Rifle, .54, Reproduction, Antique	220	325

Rifle, Singleshot

Model 1874 Military Rifle, Various Calibers, Reproduction, Modern	225	350
Model 1874 Military Carbine, Various Calibers, Reproduction, Modern	200	300
Model 1874 Hunter's Rifle, Various Calibers, Reproduction, Modern	215	320
Model 1874 Business Rifle, Various Calibers, Reproduction, Modern	220	320
Model 1874 Sporting Rifle #2, Various Calibers, Reproduction, Modern	275	400
Model 1874 Sporting Rifle #3, Various Calibers, Reproduction, Modern	225	350

Sharps, Christian

Handgun, Multi-Barrel

.22 R.F., Model 1, 4 Barreled Pistol, Frame to Muzzle Distance ⅛", Antique	175	275
.22 R.F., Model 2, 4 Barreled Pistol, Frame to Muzzle Distance ½", Antique	165	250
.22 R.F., Model 3, 4 Barreled Pistol, Frame to Muzzle Distance ¼", Antique	185	300
.22 R.F., Model 4, 4 Barreled Pistol, Frame to Muzzle Distance ¼", Iron Frame, Antique	300	425
.30 R.F., Model 1, 4 Barreled Pistol, Frame to Muzzle Distance ⅝", Antique	175	275

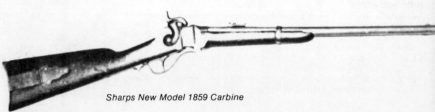

Sharps New Model 1859 Carbine

.30 R.F., Model 2, 4 Barreled Pistol, Frame to Muzzle Distance ¾", Antique	200	350
.32 R.F., Model 1, 4 Barreled Pistol, Mechanism in Frame, Antique	225	375
.32 R.F., Model 2, 4 Barreled Pistol, Mechanism on Hammer, Antique	200	300
.32 R.F. Bulldog, Model 1, 4 Barreled Pistol, Screw Under Frame, Antique	200	300
.32 R.F. Bulldog, Model 2, 4 Barreled Pistol, Pin on Side of Frame, Antique	225	350

Rifle, Percussion

1851 Carbine, .52, Maynard Primer, Antique	1,200	2,000
1852 Carbine, .52, Pellet Primer, Antique	500	750
1853 Carbine, .52, Pellet Primer, Antique	500	800
1855 Carbine, .52, Maynard Primer, Antique	700	1,200
1855 Rifle, .52, Maynard Primer, Antique	1,000	1,750
1859 Carbine, .52, Pellet Primer, Antique	550	900
1863 Carbine, .52, Lawrence Cut-off, Antique	400	650
1863 Rifle, .52, Lawrence Cut-off, Antique	800	1,200

Rifle, Singleshot

1874 Sporting Rifle, Various Calibers, Set Trigger, Target Sights, Antique	900	1,500
1874 Hunting Rifle, Various Calibers, Open Sights, Antique	500	1,000
Long Range Rifle, Various Calibers, Target Sights, Antique	1,500	2,500

Shaw, John
London, England C.1688

Handgun, Flintlock

Holster Pistol, Engraved, Steel Mounts, High Quality, Antique	1,300	1,750

Shell, John
Leslie County, Ky. 1810-80. See Kentucky Rifles

Shilen
Ennis, Tex.

Rifle, Bolt Action

DGA Sporter, Various Calibers, Blind Magazine, Plain Stock, Modern	350	475
DGA Benchrest, Various Calibers, Target Rifle, Modern	400	525
DGA Varmint, Various Calibers, Heavy Barrel, Modern	350	475

Shorer, Andrew
Northampton, Pa. 1775-76. See Kentucky Rifles

Sickel's Arms Co.
Belgium for Robert Sickels & Preston Co., Davenport, Iowa

Shotgun, Double Barrel, Side by Side

Various Gauges, Outside Hammers, Damascus Barrel, Modern	80	150
Various Gauges, Hammerless, Steel Barrel, Modern	95	175
Various Gauges, Hammerless, Damascus Barrel, Modern	75	150
Various Gauges, Outside Hammers, Steel Barrel, Modern	90	175

Shotgun, Singleshot

Various Gauges, Hammer, Steel Barrel, Modern	45	75

S. I. G.
Swiss Industrial Co., Current

Automatic Weapon, Assault Rifle

SIG 510, .308 Win., Clip Fed, Bipod, Class 3	850	1,200

Handgun, Semi-Automatic

P210-1, .22 L.R.R.F., Clip Fed, Blue, High-Polish Finish, Wood Grips, Modern	525	850
P210-1, .30 Luger, Clip Fed, Blue, High-Polish Finish, Wood Grips, Modern	500	775

SIG P.210-6 9mm

P210-1, 9mm Luger, Clip Fed, Blue, High-Polish Finish, Wood Grips, Modern	525	775
P210-1, Various Calibers, Clip Fed, High-Polish Finish, with 3 Caliber Conv. Units, Wood Grips, Modern	800	1,200
P210-2, .30 Luger, Clip Fed, Blue, Plastic Stock, Modern	475	700
P210-2, 9mm Luger, Clip Fed, Blue, Plastic Stock, Modern	475	700
P210-5, .30 Luger, Clip Fed, Blue, Plastic Stock, Target Pistol, 6" Barrel, Modern	500	800
P210-5, 9mm Luger, Clip Fed, Blue, Plastic Stock, Target Pistol, 6" Barrel, Modern	500	800
P210-6, .30 Luger, Clip Fed, Blue, Plastic Stock, Target Pistol, 4¾" Barrel, Modern	525	825
P210-6, 9mm Luger, Clip Fed, Blue, Plastic Stock, Target Pistol, 4¾" Barrel, Modern	525	825

Rifle, Semi-Automatic

SIG AMT, .308 Win., Clip Fed, Bipod, Modern	650	1,000
SIG STG-57, 7.5 Swiss, Clip Fed, Bipod, Modern	750	1,100

Sile

Handgun, Semi-Automatic

Seecamp, .25 ACP, Double Action, Clip Fed, Stainless Steel, Modern	80	115

Simson & Co.
Germany, Waffenfabrik Simson & Co.

Handgun, Semi-Automatic

Vest Pocket, .25 ACP, Clip Fed, Modern	250	375

Singer
Spain, Arizmendi

Handgun, Semi-Automatic

Vest Pocket, .25 ACP, Clip Fed, Modern	95	125

Simson .25 ACP

Singer .25 ACP

SKB
Tokyo, Japan

Shotgun, Double Barrel, Over-Under

Model 500, 12 and 20 Gauges, Field Grade, Selective Ejector, Vent Rib, Modern	250	350
Model 500, 12 Ga. Mag. 3", Field Grade, Selective Ejector, Vent Rib, Modern	260	360
Model 600, 12 Ga., Trap Grade, Selective Ejector, Vent Rib, Modern	360	460
Model 600, 12 Ga., Trap Grade, Selective Ejector, Vent Rib, Monte Carlo Stock, Modern	360	460
Model 600, 12 and 20 Gauges, Field Grade, Selective Ejector, Vent Rib, Modern	350	440
Model 600, 12 and 20 Gauges, Skeet Grade, Selective Ejector, Vent Rib, Modern	360	460
Model 600, 20 and .410 Gauges, Skeet Grade, Selective Ejector, Vent Rib, Modern	360	470
Model 600 Combo Set, Various Gauges, Skeet Grade, Selective Ejector, Vent Rib, Cased, Modern	800	1,100
Model 680 English, 12 and 20 Gauges, Field Grade, Selective Ejector, Vent Rib, Modern	370	460
Model 700, 12 Ga., Trap Grade, Selective Ejector, Vent Rib, Modern	400	550
Model 700, 12 Ga., Trap Grade, Selective Ejector, Vent Rib, Monte Carlo Stock, Modern	400	550
Model 700, 12 and 20 Gauges, Skeet Grade, Selective Ejector, Vent Rib, Modern	400	550
Model 700 Combo Set, Various Gauges, Skeet Grade, Selective Ejector, Vent Rib, Cased, Modern	900	1,450

Shotgun, Semi-Automatic

900 Deluxe, 12 and 20 Gauges, Vent Rib, Modern	150	180
900 XL, 12 Ga., Trap Grade, Modern	170	225
900 XL, 12 Ga., Trap Grade, Monte Carlo Stock, Modern	170	230
900 XL, 12 and 20 Gauges, Skeet Grade, Modern	166	215
900 XL Deluxe, 12 and 20 Gauges, Vent Rib, Modern	160	200
900 XL Slug, 12 and 20 Gauges, Open Rear Sight, Modern	150	200

Sloans
Importers, N.Y.C. Also see Charles Daly

Shotgun, Double Barrel, Side by Side

POS, .410 Ga., Checkered Stock, Hammerless, Double Trigger, Modern	95	145
POS, 10 Ga., 3½", Checkered Stock, Hammerless, Double Trigger, Modern	110	155
POS, 12 and 20 Gauges, Checkered Stock, Hammerless, Double Trigger, Modern	90	130
POS Coach Gun, 12 and 20 Gauges, Checkered Stock, Outside Hammers, Double Trigger, Modern	95	140

Smith & Wesson

Norwich, Conn. 1855 as Volcanic Repeating Arms Co., reorganized at Springfield, Mass. as Smith & Wesson in 1857 (Volcanic Repeating Arms moved to New Haven, Conn. in 1856. It was purchased in 1857 by Winchester Repeating Arms Co.). Smith & Wesson at Springfield, Mass. to date. Also see U.S. Military

Automatic Weapon, Submachine Gun

Model 76, 9mm Luger, Clip Fed, Commercial, Class 3	375	475

Handgun, Revolver

.32 Double Action, .32 S & W, 2nd Model, Top Break, 5 Shot, Irregularly-Cut Sideplate, Rocker Cylinder Stop, Antique	100	175
.32 Double Action, .32 S & W, 1st Model, Top Break, 5 Shot, Straight-Cut Sideplate, Rocker Cylinder Stop, Antique 800	1,350	
.32 Double Action, .32 S & W, 3rd Model, Top Break, 5 Shot, Irregularly-Cut Sideplate, Antique	95	165
.32 Double Action, .32 S & W, 4th Model, Round-Back Trigger Guard, Top Break, 5 Shot, Irregularly-Cut Sideplate, Modern	75	140
.32 Double Action, .32 S & W, 5th Model, Round-Back Trigger Guard, Top Break, 5 Shot, Irregularly-Cut Sideplate, Front Sight Forged on Barrel, Modern	85	155
.32 Hand Ejector, .32 S & W Long, 1st Model, Solid Frame, Swing-Out Cylinder, Hammer Actuated Cylinder Stop, 6 Shot, Modern	225	375
.32 Hand Ejector, .32 S & W Long, Solid Frame, Swing-Out Cylinder, 6 Shot, Target Sights, Double Action, Modern	200	350
.32 Hand Ejector 1903, .32 S & W Long, Solid Frame, Swing-Out Cylinder, 6 Shot, Double Action, Modern	90	175
.32 Regulation Police, .32 S & W Long, Solid Frame, Swing-Out Cylinder, 6 Shot, Double Action, Modern	85	145
.32 Safety Hammerless, .32 S & W, 1st Model, Double Action, Top Break, 5 Shot, Push-Button Latch, Modern	125	225
.32 Safety Hammerless, .32 S & W, 2nd Model, Double Action, Top Break, 5 Shot, T Latch, Modern	95	150
.32 Safety Hammerless, .32 S & W, 3rd Model, Double Action, Top Break, 5 Shot, Over #170,000, Modern	90	160
.32 Single Action, .32 S & W, Top Break, Spur Trigger, 5 Shot, Antique	200	325
.32 Single Action, .32 S & W, 6" or 8" Barrel, Add 50%-75%		
.32 Single Action, .32 S & W, 10" Barrel, Add 75%-100%		
.38 D A Perfected, .38 S & W, Solid Trigger Guard, Thumbpiece, Hand-Ejector Action, Top Break, Double Action, Modern	165	275
.38 D A Perfected, .38 S & W, made without Thumbpiece, Hand-Ejector Action, Top Break, Double Action, Modern	300	425
.38 Double Action, .38 S & W, 1st Model, Straight-Cut Sideplate, Rocker Cylinder Stop, Double Action, Top Break, 5 Shot, Antique	375	650
.38 Double Action, .38 S & W, 2nd Model, Irregularly-Cut Sideplate, Rocker Cylinder Stop, Double Action, Top Break, 5 Shot, Antique	100	175

Smith & Wesson .32 Hand Ejector First Issue

Smith & Wesson .38 D.A.

Smith & Wesson Perfected

Smith & Wesson .38 Safety Hammerless

.38 Double Action, .38 S & W, 3rd Model, Irregularly-Cut Sideplate, Double Action, Top Break, 5 Shot, Antique	100	175
.38 Double Action, .38 S & W, 4th Model, #'s 322,701-539,000, Double Action, Top Break, 5 Shot, Modern	90	150
.38 Double Action, .38 S & W, 5th Model, #'s 539-001-554,077, Double Action, Top Break, 5 Shot, Modern	80	145
.38 Double Action, .38 S & W, 4th Model, #'s 322,701-539,000, Double Action, Top Break, 5 Shot, Adjustable Sights, Modern	265	375
.38 Double Action, .38 S & W, 5th Model, #'s 539,001-554,077, Double Action, Top Break, 5 Shot, Adjustable Sights, Modern	250	350
.38 Hand Ejector, .38 Long Colt, 1st Model, Solid Frame, Swing-Out Cylinder, no Cylinder-Pin Front-Lock, U.S. Army Model, Modern	375	650
.38 Hand Ejector, .38 Long Colt, 1st Model, Solid Frame, Swing-Out Cylinder, no Cylinder-Pin Front-Lock, U.S. Navy Model, Modern	375	600
.38 Hand Ejector, .38 Long Colt, 2nd Model, Solid Frame, Swing-Out Cylinder, U.S. Navy Model, Modern	350	575
.38 Hand Ejector, .38 Special, 1st Model, Solid Frame, Swing-Out Cylinder, no Cylinder-Pin Front-Lock, Modern	175	300
.38 Hand Ejector, .38 Special, 1st Model, Solid Frame, Swing-Out Cylinder, no Cylinder-Pin Front-Lock, Adjustable Sights, Modern	350	500
.38 Hand Ejector, .38 Special, 2nd Model, Solid Frame, Swing-Out Cylinder, Modern	150	250
.38 Hand Ejector, .38 Special, 2nd Model, Solid Frame, Swing-Out Cylinder, Adjustable Sights, Modern	350	500
.38 Hand Ejector 1902, .38 Special, Military and Police, Solid Frame, Swing-Out Cylinder, Double Action, Modern	140	220
.38 Hand Ejector 1902, .38 Special, Military and Police, Solid Frame, Swing-Out Cylinder, Double Action, Adjustable Sights, Modern	250	375
.38 Hand Ejector 1905, .38 Special, Military and Police, Solid Frame, Swing-Out Cylinder, Double Action, Modern	135	225
.38 Hand Ejector 1905, .38 Special, Military and Police, Solid Frame, Swing-Out Cylinder, Double Action, Adjustable Sights, Modern	275	400
.38 Safety Hammerless, .38 S & W, 1st Model-Button Latch, Release on Left Topstrap, Top Break, Double Action, Antique	200	325
.38 Safety Hammerless, .38 S & W, 2nd Model-Button Latch, Release on Top of Frame, Top Break, Double Action, Antique	150	250
.38 Safety Hammerless, .38 S & W, 3rd Model-Button Latch, Release on Rear Topstrap, Top Break, Double Action, Antique	120	200
.38 Safety Hammerless, .38 S & W, 4th Model T-Shaped Latch, Top Break, Double Action, Modern	100	190
.38 Safety Hammerless, .38 S & W, 5th Model T-Shaped Latch, Top Break, Double Action, Front Sight Forged on Barrel, Modern	95	175

.38 Single Action, .38 S & W, 1st Model, Baby Russian, Top Break, Spur Trigger, Antique	200	300
.38 Single Action, .38 S & W, 2nd Model, Top Break, Spur Trigger, Short Ejector Housing, Antique	125	200
.38 Single Action, .38 S & W, 3rd Model, Top Break, with Trigger Guard, Modern	350	500
.38 Single Action, .38 S & W, 3rd Model, Top Break, with Trigger Guard, with Extra Single-Shot Barrel, Modern	550	800
.38 Single Action, .38 S & W, Mexican Model, Top Break, Spur Trigger, 5 Shot, Modern	1,000	1,500
.38 Win. Double Action, .38-40 WCF, Top Break, Modern	600	900
.44 Double Action, for Target Sights, Add 20%-30%		
.44 Double Action, .44 Russian, 1st Model, Top Break, 6 Shot, Antique	325	450
.44 Double Action, .44 Russian, Wesson Favorite, 6 Shot, Lightweight, Top Break, Antique	900	1,500
.44 Double Action Frontier, for Target Sights, Add 20%-30%		
.44 Double Action Frontier, .44-40 WCF, Top Break, 6 Shot, Antique	400	550
.44 Hand Ejector, Calibers other than .44 Spec., Add 15%-25%		
.44 Hand Ejector, 1st Model, for Target Sights, Add 20%-30%		
.44 Hand Ejector, Calibers other than .44 Spec., Add 15%-25%		
.44 Hand Ejector, 2nd Model, for Target Sights, Add 20%-30%		
.44 Hand Ejector, 3rd Model, for Target Sights, Add 20%-30%		
.44 Hand Ejector, .44 Special, 1st Model, Triple-Lock, Solid Frame, Swing-Out Cylinder, Modern, New Century	400	600
.44 Hand Ejector, .44 Special, 2nd Model, Un-Shrouded Ejector Rod, Solid Frame, Swing-Out Cylinder, Modern	275	400
.44 Hand Ejector, .44 Special, 3rd Model, Shrouded Ejector Rod, Solid Frame, Swing-Out Cylinder, Modern	250	350
.455 MK II Hand Ejector, Solid Frame, Swing-Out Cylinder, Double Action, Military, Modern	200	375
22/32 Bekeart Model, .22 L.R.R.F., #'s 138,220-139,275, Target Pistol, Double Action, Adjustable Sights, 6" Barrel, Modern	300	450
22/32 Hand Ejector, .22 L.R.R.F., Target Pistol, Double Action, Adjustable Sights, 6" Barrel, Modern	165	250
22/32 Kit Gun, .22 L.R.R.F., Early Model, Double Action, Adjustable Sights, 4" Barrel, Modern	125	200
32/20 Hand Ejector, .32-20 WCF, 1st Model, Solid Frame, Swing-Out Cylinder, 6 Shot, no Cylinder-Pin Front-Lock, Modern	175	275
32/20 Hand Ejector 1902, .32-20 WCF, 2nd Model, Solid Frame, Swing-Out Cylinder, 6 Shot, Modern	175	275
32/20 Hand Ejector 1902, .32-20 WCF, 2nd Model, Solid Frame, Swing-Out Cylinder, 6 Shot, Adjustable Sights, Modern	275	400
32/20 Hand Ejector 1905, .32-20 WCF, Solid Frame, Swing-Out Cylinder, 6 Shot, Adjustable Sights, Modern	250	350
32/20 Hand Ejector 1905, .32-20 WCF, Solid Frame, Swing-Out Cylinder, 6 Shot, Modern	150	250
38/200 British, .38 S & W, Military & Police, Solid Frame, Swing-Out Cylinder, Double Action, Military, Modern	90	160
First Model Schofield, .45 S & W, Top Break, Single Action, Military, Antique	700	1,250
First Model Schofield, .45 S & W, Top Break, Single Action, Commercial, Antique	1,300	2,000
First Model Schofield, .45 S & W, Wells Fargo, Top Break, Single Action, Antique	750	1,000
K-22 Hand Ejector, .22 L.R.R.F., 1st Model, Double Action, Adjustable Sights, 6" Barrel, Modern	150	225
K-22 Masterpiece, .22 L.R.R.F., 2nd Model K-22 Hand Ejector, Speed Lock Action, Double Action, Adjustable Sights, 6" Barrel, Modern	250	375
K-32 Hand Ejector, .32 S & W Long, 1st Model, Pre-War, 6 Shot, Adjustable Sights, Target Pistol, Modern	375	525
K-32 Hand Ejector, .32 S & W Long, 2nd Model, Post-War, 6 Shot, Adjustable Sights, Target Pistol, Modern	130	200

Smith & Wesson #1 Third Issue

Model #1, .22 Short R.F., 1st Issue, Tip-Up, Spur Trigger, 7 Shot, Antique	1,500	2,500
Model #1, .22 Short R.F., 2nd Issue, Tip-Up, Spur Trigger, 7 Shot, Antique	675	1,100
Model #1, .22 Short R.F., 3rd Issue, Tip-Up, Spur Trigger, 7 Shot, Antique	400	750
Model #1½, .32 Short R.F., 1st Issue, Tip-Up, Spur Trigger, 5 Shot Clip, Non-Fluted Cylinder, Antique	175	300
Model #1½, .32 Short R.F., 2nd Issue, Tip-Up, Spur Trigger, 5 Shot Clip, Fluted Cylinder, Antique	175	300
Model #2 Old Army, .32 Long R.F., Tip-Up, Spur Trigger, 6 Shot, Antique	275	400
Model #3 American, .44 Henry, 1st Model, Single Action, Top Break, 6 Shot, Antique	850	1,500
Model #3 American, .44 Henry, 2nd Model, #'s 8,000-32,800, Single Action, Top Break, 6 Shot, Antique	700	1,275
Model #3 American, .44 S & W, 1st Model, Single Action, Top Break, 6 Shot, Antique	550	800
Model #3 American, .44 S & W, 2nd Model #'s 8,000-32,800, Single Action, Top Break, 6 Shot, Antique	450	700
Model #3 Frontier, .44-40 WCF, Single Action, Top Break, 6 Shot, Antique	650	950
Model #3 New Model, Calibers other than .44 Russian, Add 40%-60%		
Model #3 New Model, .44 Russian, Australian Police with Shoulder Stock, Add 200%-225%		
Model #3 New Model, .44 Russian, Single Action, Top Break, 6 Shot, Antique	400	600
Model #3 New Model, .44 Russian Japanese Navy Issue, Add 30%-45%		
Model #3 New Model, .44 Russian, Australian Police with Shoulder Stock, Add 200%-225%		
Model #3 New Model, .44 Russian, Argentine Model, Add 25%-35%		
Model #3 New Model, .44 S & W, Turkish Model, Add 15%-25%		
Model #3 New Model, Various Calibers, Calibers other than .44 Russian, Add 40%-60%		
Model #3 Russian, .44 Russian, 1st Model, Single Action, Top Break, 6 Shot, Antique, Military	475	700
Model #3 Russian, .44 Russian, 2nd Model, Finger-Rest Trigger Guard, Single Action, Top Break, 6 Shot, Antique	400	650
Model #3 Russian, .44 Russian, 2nd Model, Finger-Rest Trigger Guard, Single Action, Top Break, with Shoulder Stock, Antique	700	1,100
Model #3 Russian, .44 Russian, 3rd Model, Front Sight Forged on Barrel, Single Action, Top Break, 6 Shot, Antique	525	750
Model #3 Target, .32-44 S & W, .38-44 S & W, New Model #3, Single Action, Top Break, Modern	400	600
Model 10, .38 Special, Double Action, Blue, Various Barrel Lengths, Swing-Out Cylinder, Modern	80	120
Model 10, .38 Special, Double Action, Swing-Out Cylinder, 4″ Barrel, Heavy Barrel, Blue, Modern	85	125
Model 10, .38 Special, Double Action, Swing-Out Cylinder, 4″ Barrel, Heavy Barrel, Nickel Plated, Modern	90	130
Model 10, .38 Special, Double Action, Swing-Out Cylinder, Various Barrel Lengths, Nickel Plated, Modern	90	125
Model 11, .38 S & W, Double Action, Swing-Out Cylinder, Modern	160	200
Model 12, .38 Special, Double Action, Swing-Out Cylinder, Various Barrel Lengths, Blue, Modern	95	150

Model 12, .38 Special, Double Action, Swing-Out Cylinder, Various Barrel
  Lengths, Nickel Plated, Modern   110   160
Model 12 USAF, .38 Special, Double Action, Swing-Out Cylinder,
  Lightweight, Modern   200   275
Model 13, .357 Magnum, Double Action, Swing-Out Cylinder, 4" Barrel,
  Heavy Barrel, Blue, Modern   95   130
Model 13, .357 Magnum, Double Action, Swing-Out Cylinder, 4" Barrel,
  Nickel Plated, Heavy Barrel, Modern   105   140
Model 14, .38 Special, Double Action, Swing-Out Cylinder, 6" Barrel,
  Blue, Adjustable Sights, Modern   95   140
Model 14, .38 Special, Double Action, Swing-Out Cylinder, 8⅜" Barrel,
  Blue, Adjustable Sights, Modern   110   150
Model 14 SA, .38 Special, Single Action, Swing-Out Cylinder, 6" Barrel,
  Blue, Adjustable Sights, Modern   110   150
Model 14 SA, .38 Special, Single Action, Swing-Out Cylinder, 8⅜" Barrel,
  Blue, Adjustable Sights, Modern   115   160
Model 15, .38 Special, Double Action, Swing-Out Cylinder, Various Barrel
  Lengths, Blue, Adjustable Sights, Modern   110   140
Model 15, .38 Special, Double Action, Swing-Out Cylinder, Various Barrel
  Lengths, Nickel Plated, Adjustable Sights, Modern   110   150
Model 16, .32 S & W Long, Double Action, Swing-Out Cylinder, Adjustable
  Sights, Target Pistol, Modern   180   225
Model 17, .22 L.R.R.F., Double Action, Swing-Out Cylinder, 6" Barrel,
  Adjustable Sights, Blue, Modern   125   165
Model 17, .22 L.R.R.F., Double Action, Swing-Out Cylinder, 8⅜" Barrel,
  Adjustable Sights, Blue, Modern   130   170
Model 18, .22 L.R.R.F., Double Action, Swing-Out Cylinder, 4" Barrel,
  Adjustable Sights, Blue, Modern   130   165
Model 19, .357 Magnum, Double Action, Swing-Out Cylinder, Various
  Barrel Lengths, Adjustable Sights, Blue, Modern   145   180
Model 19, .357 Magnum, Double Action, Swing-Out Cylinder, Various
  Barrel Lengths, Adjustable Sights, Nickel Plated, Modern   150   185
Model 19 Texas Ranger, .357 Magnum, Commemorative, Blue, Cased,
  with Knife, Curio   375   525
Model 1917, .45 Auto-Rim, Double Action, Swing-Out Cylinder, Modern   250   350
Model 1917, .45 Auto-Rim, Double Action, Swing-Out Cylinder, Military,
  Modern   200   275
Model 20, .38 Special, Double Action, Swing-Out Cylinder, Modern   195   275
Model 21, .44 Special, Double Action, Swing-Out Cylinder, Various Barrel
  Lengths, Modern   275   350
Model 22, .45 Auto-Rim, Double Action, Swing-Out Cylinder, Modern   190   270
Model 23, .38 Special, Double Action, Swing-Out Cylinder, Adjustable
  Sights, Target Pistol, Modern   250   325
Model 24, .44 Special, Double Action, Swing-Out Cylinder, Various Barrel
  Lengths, Adjustable Sights, Modern   275   325
Model 25, .45 Auto-Rim, Double Action, Swing-Out Cylinder, Target
  Pistol, Blue, Cased with Accessories, Modern   225   290
Model 25, .45 Auto-Rim, Double Action, Swing-Out Cylinder, Target
  Pistol, Blue, Modern   190   250
Model 26, .45 Auto-Rim, Double Action, Swing-Out Cylinder, Modern   250   325
Model 27, .357 Magnum, Double Action, Swing-Out Cylinder, Pre-War,
  Adjustable Sights, Modern   300   475
Model 27, .357 Magnum, Double Action, Swing-Out Cylinder, Various
  Barrel Lengths, Adjustable Sights, Blue, Modern   160   240
Model 27, .357 Magnum, Double Action, Swing-Out Cylinder, Nickel
  Plated, Modern   170   250
Model 27, .357 Magnum, Double Action, Swing-Out Cylinder, 8⅜" Barrel,
  Blue, Modern   165   245
Model 27, .357 Magnum, Double Action, Swing-Out Cylinder, 8⅜" Barrel,
  Nickel Plated, Modern   170   250
Model 27, .357 Magnum, Double Action, Various Barrel Lengths,
  Adjustable Sights, Cased with Accessories, Blue, Modern   200   270

Model 27, .357 Magnum, Double Action, 8⅜" Barrel, Adjustable Sights, Cased with Accessories, Nickel Plated, Modern	210	275
Model 27, .357 Magnum, Double Action, Various Barrel Lengths, Adjustable Sights, Cased with Accessories, Blue, Modern	200	270
Model 27, .357 Magnum, Double Action, 8⅜" Barrel, Adjustable Sights, Cased with Accessories, Nickel Plated, Modern	210	280
Model 27 with Registration, .357 Magnum, Double Action, Swing-Out Cylinder, Pre-War, Adjustable Sights, Modern	550	750
Model 28, .357 Magnum, Double Action, Various Barrel Lengths, Adjustable Sights, Blue, Modern	135	165
Model 28, .357 Magnum, Double Action, Various Barrel Lengths, Target Grips, Adjustable Sights, Blue, Modern	140	175
Model 29, .44 Magnum, Double Action, Various Barrel Lengths, Adjustable Sights, Swing-Out Cylinder, Blue, Modern	200	265
Model 29, .44 Magnum, Double Action, Various Barrel Lengths, Adjustable Sights, Swing-Out Cylinder, Nickel Plated, Modern	210	270
Model 29, .44 Magnum, Double Action, 8⅜" Barrel, Adjustable Sights, Swing-Out Cylinder, Blue, Modern	220	275
Model 29, .44 Magnum, Double Action, 8⅜" Barrel, Adjustable Sights, Swing-Out Cylinder, Nickel Plated, Modern	220	280
Model 29, .44 Magnum, Double Action, Various Barrel Lengths, Adjustable Sights, Cased with Accessories, Blue, Modern	225	285
Model 29, .44 Magnum, Double Action, Various Barrel Lengths, Adjustable Sights, Cased with Accessories, Nickel Plated, Modern	225	295
Model 29, .44 Magnum, Double Action, 8⅜" Barrel, Adjustable Sights, Cased with Accessories, Blue, Modern	230	300
Model 29, .44 Magnum, Double Action, 8⅜" Barrel, Adjustable Sights, Cased with Accessories, Nickel Plated, Modern	240	315
Model 30, .32 S & W Long, Double Action, Swing-Out Cylinder, Modern	115	160
Model 31, .32 S & W Long, Double Action, Swing-Out Cylinder, Various Barrel Lengths, Nickel Plated, Modern	120	165
Model 31, .32 S & W Long, Double Action, Swing-Out Cylinder, Various Barrel Lengths, Blue, Modern	95	155
Model 32, .38 S & W, Double Action, Swing-Out Cylinder, 2" Barrel, Modern	130	180
Model 33, .38 S & W, Double Action, Swing-Out Cylinder, Modern	150	200
Model 34, .22 L.R.R.F., Double Action, Swing-Out Cylinder, Various Barrel Lengths, Adjustable Sights, Blue, Modern	135	180
Model 34, .22 L.R.R.F., Double Action, Swing-Out Cylinder, Various Barrel Lengths, Adjustable Sights, Nickel Plated, Modern	140	190
Model 35, .22 L.R.R.F., Double Action, Swing-Out Cylinder, Target Pistol, Adjustable Sights, Modern	175	250
Model 36, .38 Special, Double Action, Swing-Out Cylinder, Various Barrel Lengths, Blue, Modern	120	165
Model 36, .38 Special, Double Action, Swing-Out Cylinder, Various Barrel Lengths, Nickel Plated, Modern	125	175
Model 36, .38 Special, Double Action, Swing-Out Cylinder, 3" Barrel, Heavy Barrel, Blue, Modern	115	165
Model 36, .38 Special, Double Action, Swing-Out Cylinder, 3" Barrel, Heavy Barrel, Nickel Plated, Modern	125	170
Model 37, .38 Special, Double Action, Swing-Out Cylinder, Various Barrel Lengths, Lightweight, Blue, Modern	120	165
Model 37, .38 Special, Double Action, Swing-Out Cylinder, Various Barrel Lengths, Lightweight, Nickel Plated, Modern	130	170
Model 38, .38 Special, Swing-Out Cylinder, 2" Barrel, Hammer Shroud, Nickel Plated, Double Action, Modern	145	195
Model 38, .38 Special, Double Action, Swing-Out Cylinder, 2" Barrel, Hammer Shroud, Blue, Modern	140	190
Model 40, .38 Special, Double Action, Swing-Out Cylinder, Hammerless, Modern	200	300
Model 42, .38 Special, Double Action, Swing-Out Cylinder, Hammerless, Lightweight, Modern	250	375

Model 43, .22 L.R.R.F., Double Action, Swing-Out Cylinder, Adjustable Sights, Lightweight, Modern	225	300
Model 45, .22 L.R.R.F., Double Action, Swing-Out Cylinder, Modern	170	235
Model 45 USPO, .22 L.R.R.F., Double Action, Swing-Out Cylinder, Modern	350	450
Model 48, .22 WMR, Double Action, Swing-Out Cylinder, Various Barrel Lengths, Blue, Adjustable Sights, Modern	140	185
Model 48, .22 WMR, Double Action, Swing-Out Cylinder, 8⅜" Barrel, Blue, Adjustable Sights, Modern	150	190
Model 49, .38 Special, Double Action, Swing-Out Cylinder, 2" Barrel, Hammer Shroud, Nickel Plated, Modern	140	190
Model 49, .38 Special, Double Action, Swing-Out Cylinder, 2" Barrel, Hammer Shroud, Blue, Modern 135 180		
Model 50, .38 Special, Double Action, Swing-Out Cylinder, Adjustable Sights, Modern	450	700
Model 51, .22LR/.22 WMR Combo, Double Action, Swing-Out Cylinder, Adjustable Sights, Modern	325	400
Model 51, .22 WMR, Double Action, Swing-Out Cylinder, Adjustable Sights, Modern	250	325
Model 53, .22 Rem. Jet, Double Action, Swing-Out Cylinder, Adjustable Sights, Modern	325	475
Model 53, .22 Rem. Jet, Double Action, Swing-Out Cylinder, Adjustable Sights, Extra Cylinder, Modern	375	550
Model 56, .38 Special, Double Action, Swing-Out Cylinder, 2" Barrel, Adjustable Sights, Modern	500	750
Model 57, .41 Magnum, Double Action, Swing-Out Cylinder, Various Barrel Lengths, Blue, Adjustable Sights, Modern	200	255
Model, 57, .41 Magnum, Double Action, Swing-Out Cylinder, Various Barrel Lengths, Nickel Plated, Adjustable Sights, Modern	210	260
Model 57, .41 Magnum, Double Action, Swing-Out Cylinder, 8⅜" Barrel, Blue, Adjustable Sights, Modern	210	265
Model 57, .41 Magnum, Double Action, Swing-Out Cylinder, 8⅜" Barrel, Nickel Plated, Adjustable Sights, Modern	220	270
Model 57, .41 Magnum, Double Action, Swing-Out Cylinder, Various Barrel Lengths, Blue, Cased with Accessories, Modern	225	280
Model 57, .41 Magnum, Double Action, Swing-Out Cylinder, Various Barrel Lengths, Nickel Plated, Cased with Accessories, Modern	230	285
Model 57, .41 Magnum, Double Action, Swing-Out Cylinder, 8⅜" Barrel, Blue, Cased with Accessories, Modern	235	285
Model 57, .41 Magnum, Double Action, Swing-Out Cylinder, 8⅜" Barrel, Blue, Cased with Accessories, Modern	230	280
Model 58, .41 Magnum, Double Action, Swing-Out Cylinder, 4" Barrel, Blue, Modern	175	260
Model 58, .41 Magnum, Double Action, Swing-Out Cylinder, 4" Barrel, Nickel Plated, Modern	180	270
Model 60, .38 Special, Double Action, Swing-Out Cylinder, Stainless Steel, Adjustable Sights, Modern	550	750
Model 60, .38 Special, Double Action, Swing-Out Cylinder, Stainless Steel, 4" Barrel, Modern	165	225

Smith & Wesson Model 60

Smith & Wesson Model 66

Model 64, .38 Special, Double Action, Swing-Out Cylinder, Stainless Steel, Various Barrel Lengths, Modern	140	190
Model 65, .357 Magnum, Double Action, Swing-Out Cylinder, Stainless Steel, 4″ Barrel, Heavy Barrel, Modern	125	155
Model 66, .357 Magnum, Double Action, Swing-Out Cylinder, Stainless Steel, Various Barrel Lengths, Modern	175	240
Model 67, .38 Special, Double Action, Swing-Out Cylinder, Stainless Steel, 4″ Barrel, Modern	140	175
Model M Hand Ejector, .22 Long R.F., 1st Model Ladysmith, Solid Frame, Swing-Out Cylinder, Double Action, Curio	425	675
Model M Hand Ejector, .22 Long R.F., 2nd Model Ladysmith, Solid Frame, Swing-Out Cylinder, Double Action, Curio	400	600
Model M Hand Ejector, .22 Long R.F., 3rd Model Ladysmith, Solid Frame, Swing-Out Cylinder, Double Action, Curio	350	550
Model M Hand Ejector, .22 Long R.F., 3rd Model Ladysmith, Solid Frame, Swing-Out Cylinder, Double Action, Adjustable Sights, Curio	550	775
Second Model Schofield, .45 S & W, Knurled Latch, Top Break, Single Action, Military, Antique	550	750
Second Model Schofield, .45 S & W, Knurled Latch, Top Break, Single Action, Commercial, Antique	800	1,100
Second Model Schofield, .45 S & W, Wells Fargo, Knurled Latch, Top Break, Single Action, Antique	650	900
Victory, .38 Special, Military & Police, Solid Frame, Swing-Out Cylinder, Double Action, Military, Modern	80	135

Handgun, Semi-Automatic

.32 ACP, Blue, Curio	400	850
.32 ACP, Nickel Plated, Curio	525	950
.35 S & W Automatic, Blue, Curio	350	450
.35 S & W Automatic, Nickel Plated, Curio	375	500
Model 39, 9mm Luger, Double Action, Steel Frame, Curio	750	1,200
Model 39, 9mm Luger, Double Action, Blue, Modern	150	190
Model 39, 9mm Luger, Double Action, Nickel Plated, Modern	165	215
Model 39-1, .38 AMU, Double Action, Curio	750	1,200
Model 41, .22 L.R.R.F., Various Barrel Lengths, Modern	160	225

Smith & Wesson .35 Auto

Smith & Wesson Model 61 .22

Model 41-1, .22 Short R.F., Various Barrel Lengths, Modern	225	320
Model 44, 9mm Luger, Single Action, Modern	1,200	1,500
Model 46, .22 L.R.R.F., Various Barrel Lengths, Modern	180	275
Model 52, .38 Special, Blue, Modern	250	325
Model 59, 9mm Luger, Double Action, Blue, Modern	175	225
Model 59, 9mm Luger, Double Action, Nickel Plated, Modern	185	235
Model 61-1, .22 L.R.R.F., Clip Fed, Nickel Plated, Modern	150	220
Model 61-1, .22 L.R.R.F., Clip Fed, Blue, Modern	125	190
Model 61-2, .22 L.R.R.F., Clip Fed, Nickel Plated, Modern	130	185
Model 61-2, .22 L.R.R.F., Clip Fed, Blue, Modern	110	165
Model 61-3, .22 L.R.R.F., Clip Fed, Nickel Plated, Modern	120	170
Model 61-3, .22 L.R.R.F., Clip Fed, Blue, Modern	110	145

Handgun, Singleshot

Model 1891, .22 L.R.R.F., Target Pistol, Single Action, 1st Model, Various Barrel Lengths, Antique	175	325
Model 1891, .22 L.R.R.F., Target Pistol, Single Action, 2nd Model, no Hand or Cylinder Stop, Modern	175	300
Model 1891 Set, Various Calibers, Extra Cylinder, Extra Barrel, Target Pistol, Single Action, 1st Model, Antique	400	675
Perfected, .22 L.R.R.F., Double Action, Top Break, Target Pistol, Modern	200	300
Perfected Olympic, .22 L.R.R.F., Double Action, Top Break, Tight Bore and Chamber, Target Pistol, Modern	400	575
Straight Line, .22 L.R.R.F., Cased, Curio	400	650

Rifle, Bolt Action

Model 125 Deluxe, Various Calibers, Monte Carlo Stock, Modern	125	170
Model 125 STD, Various Calibers, Monte Carlo Stock, Modern	120	155
Model A, Various Calibers, Monte Carlo Stock, Checkered Stock, Modern	200	300
Model B, Various Calibers, Monte Carlo Stock, Checkered Stock, Modern	180	275
Model C, Various Calibers, Sporting Rifle, Checkered Stock, Modern	180	275
Model D, Various Calibers, Mannicher, Checkered Stock, Modern	200	300
Model E, Various Calibers, Monte Carlo Stock, Mannlicher, Modern	210	320

Rifle, Revolver

Model 320, .320 S & W Rifle, Single Action, Top Break, 6 Shot, Adjustable Sights, Cased with Accessories, Antique	2,000	3,500

Rifle, Semi-Automatic

Light Rifle, MK I, 9mm Luger, Clip Fed, Carbine, Curio	1,300	1,700
Light Rifle MK II, 9mm Luger, Clip Fed, Carbine, Curio	1,800	2,400

Shotgun, Semi-Automatic

Model 1000, 12 Ga., Vent Rib, Modern	150	200

Shotgun, Slide Action

Model 916 Eastfield, Various Gauges, Vent Rib, Recoil Pad, Modern	70	115
Model 916 Eastfield, Various Gauges, Plain Barrel, Modern	70	110
Model 916 Eastfield, Various Gauges, Plain Barrel, Recoil Pad, Modern	70	100

Smith, Anthony
Northampton, Pa., 1770-79. See Kentucky Rifles and Pistols

Smith, L. C. Gun Co.
Syracuse, N.Y., 1877-90, 1890 became Hunter Arms. 1948 became a division of Marlin

Shotgun, Double Barrel, Side by Side

Crown Grade, Various Calibers, Sidelock, Single Selective Trigger, Automatic Ejector, Fancy Engraving, Fancy Checkering, Modern	2,500	3,500
Crown Grade, Various Calibers, Sidelock, Double Trigger, Automatic Ejector, Fancy Engraving, Fancy Checkering, Modern	2,300	3,200
Field Grade, Various Calibers, Sidelock, Double Trigger, Checkered Stock, Light Engraving, Modern	450	650
Field Grade, Various Calibers, Sidelock, Double Trigger, Automatic Ejector, Checkered Stock, Light Engraving, Modern	400	550
Field Grade, Various Calibers, Sidelock, Single Trigger, Checkered Stock, Light Engraving, Modern	425	550
Field Grade, Various Calibers, Sidelock, Single Trigger, Automatic Ejector, Checkered Stock, Light Engraving, Modern	400	600
Ideal Grade, Various Calibers, Sidelock, Double Trigger, Checkered Stock, Engraved, Modern	400	600
Ideal Grade, Various Calibers, Sidelock, Double Trigger, Automatic Ejector, Checkered Stock, Engraved, Modern	500	750
Ideal Grade, Various Calibers, Sidelock, Single Selective Trigger, Checkered Stock, Engraved, Modern	600	950
Ideal Grade, Various Calibers, Sidelock, Single Selective Trigger, Automatic Ejector, Engraved, Checkered Stock, Modern	675	1,000
Marlin Deluxe, 12 Ga., Double Trigger, Checkered Stock, Vent Rib, Modern	350	450
Marlin Field, 12 Ga., Double Trigger, Checkered Stock, Modern	250	375
Monogram Grade, Various Calibers, Sidelock, Single Selective Trigger, Automatic Ejector, Fancy Engraving, Fancy Checkering, Modern	3,700	6,000
Olympic Grade, Various Calibers, Sidelock, Single Selective Trigger, Automatic Ejector, Engraved, Checkered Stock, Modern	650	850
Premier Grade, Various Calibers, Sidelock, Single Selective Trigger, Automatic Ejector, Fancy Engraving, Fancy Checkering, Modern	6,500	9,500
Skeet Grade, Various Calibers, Sidelock, Single Selective Trigger, Automatic Ejector, Engraved, Checkered Stock, Modern	700	950
Skeet Grade, Various Calibers, Sidelock, Single Trigger, Automatic Ejector, Engraved, Checkered Stock, Modern	650	900
Specialty Grade, Various Calibers, Sidelock, Double Trigger, Engraved, Checkered Stock, Modern	700	950
Specialty Grade, Various Calibers, Sidelock, Single Selective Trigger, Automatic Ejector, Engraved, Checkered Stock, Modern	800	1,100
Trap Grade, 12 Ga., Sidelock, Single Selective Trigger, Automatic Ejector, Engraved, Checkered Stock, Modern	700	1,000

Shotgun, Singleshot

Crown Grade, 12 Ga., Trap Grade, Vent Rib, Automatic Ejector, Fancy Engraving, Fancy Checkering, Modern	2,000	2,500
Olympic Grade, 12 Ga., Trap Grade, Vent Rib, Automatic Ejector, Engraved, Fancy Checkering, Modern	700	1,000
Specialty Grade, 12 Ga., Trap Grade, Vent Rib, Automatic Ejector, Engraved, Fancy Checkering, Modern	1,200	1,500

Smith, Otis A.
Middlefield & Rockfall, Conn. 1873-90

Handgun, Revolver

.22 Short R.F., 7 Shot, Spur Trigger, Solid Frame, Single Action, Antique	90	160
.32 S & W, 5 Shot, Single Action, Top Break, Spur Trigger, Antique	80	135
.32 Short R.F., 5 Shot, Spur Trigger, Solid Frame, Single Action, Antique	90	160
.38 Short R.F., 5 Shot, Spur Trigger, Solid Frame, Single Action, Antique	95	170
.41 Short R.F., 5 Shot, Spur Trigger, Solid Frame, Single Action, Antique	120	195

Smith, Stoeffel
Pa. 1790-1800. See Kentucky Rifles and Pistols

Smith, Thomas
London, England, C.1850

Rifle, Percussion

16 Ga., Smoothbore, Anson-Deeley Lock, Octagon Barrel, Fancy Wood, Cased with Accessories, Antique	2,000	2,800

Smoker
Made by Johnson Bye & Co. 1875-84

Handgun, Revolver

#1, .22 Short R.F., 7 Shot, Spur Trigger, Solid Frame, Single Action, Antique	90	160
#2, .32 Short R.F., 5 Shot, Spur Trigger, Solid Frame, Single Action, Antique	95	170
#3, .38 Short R.F., 5 Shot, Spur Trigger, Solid Frame, Single Action, Antique	95	170
#4, .41 Short R.F., 5 Shot, Spur Trigger, Solid Frame, Single Action, Antique	120	195

Snaphaunce, Unknown Maker

Handgun, Snaphaunce

.45 Italian Early 1700's, Holster Pistol, Half-Octagon Barrel, Engraved, Carved, High Quality, Steel Furiture, Antique	2,000	2,500
Early 1800's Small, Plain, Antique	600	1,000
English Late 1500's, Ovoid Pommel, Engraved, Gold Damascened, High Quality, Antique		20,000+
Italian Early 1700's, Medium Quality, Brass Furniture, Plain, Antique	750	1,000
Italian 1700's, High Quality, Belt Pistol, Light Ornamentation, Antique	1,800	2,800

Rifle, Snaphaunce

Italian Mid-1600's, Half-Octagon Barrel, Carved, Engraved, Silver Inlay, Steel Furniture, Ornate, Antique		10,000+

Sneider, C. W.

Handgun, Snaphaunce

Pair Tuscan Mid-1700's, Medium Quality, Belt Pistol, Light Ornamentation, Antique	3,200	3,500

Sodia, Franz
Ferlach, Austria

Combination Weapon, Multi-Barrel

Bochdrilling, Various Calibers, Fancy Wood, Fancy Checkering, Fancy Engraving, Modern	2,000	3,500
Doppelbuchse, Various Calibers, Fancy Wood, Fancy Checkering, Fancy Engraving, Modern	1,500	2,500
Over-Under Rifle, Various Calibers, Fancy Wood, Fancy Checkering, Fancy Engraving, Modern	1,400	2,200

Soler
Ripoll, Spain, C.1625

Handgun, Wheel-Lock

Enclosed Mid-1600's, Ball Pommel, Ornate, Antique		10,000+

Southern Arms Co.
Made by Crescent for H. & D. Folsom, N.Y.C.

Shotgun, Double Barrel, Side by Side

Various Gauges, Outside Hammers, Damascus Barrel, Modern	80	150

Spanish Military Campo Giro Model 1913/16

Various Gauges, Hammerless, Steel Barrel, Modern	95	175
Various Gauges, Hammerless, Damascus Barrel, Modern	75	150
Various Gauges, Outside Hammers, Steel Barrel, Modern	90	175

Shotgun, Singleshot
Various Gauges, Hammer, Steel Barrel, Modern	45	75

Spaarman, Andreas
Berlin, C.1680

Rifle, Flintlock
.72, Jaeger, Octagon Barrel, Swamped, Rifled, Iron Mounts, Ornate, Set Trigger, Antique	3,000	3,500

Spanish Military
Also see Astra, Star

Automatic Weapon, Submachine Gun
Star Z-63, 9mm Luger, Clip Fed, Class 3	450	650

Handgun, Semi-Automatic
Jo-Lo-Ar, 9mm Bergmann, Clip Fed, Military, Hammer, Modern	145	225
M1913-16 Campo-Giro, 9mm Bergmann, Clip Fed, Military, Modern	155	235

Rifle, Bolt Action
Destroyer, 9mm Bayard Long, Clip Fed, Carbine, Modern	75	135
M98 La Caruna, 8mm Mauser, Military, Modern	55	95

Spencer Gun Co.
Made by Crescent for Hibbard & Spencer Bartlett, C.1900

Shotgun, Double Barrel, Side by Side
Various Gauges, Outside Hammers, Damascus Barrel, Modern	80	150
Various Gauges, Hammerless, Steel Barrel, Modern	95	175
Various Gauges, Hammerless, Damascus Barrel, Modern	75	150
Various Gauges, Outside Hammers, Steel Barrel, Modern	90	175

Shotgun, Singleshot
Various Gauges, Hammer, Steel Barrel, Modern	45	75

Spencer Safety Hammerless
Made by Columbia Armory, Tenn. C.1892

Handgun, Revolver
.38 S & W, 5 Shot, Top Break, Hammerless, Double Action, Modern	55	95

Spitfire
Arizona

Automatic Weapon, Submachine Gun
Spitfire, .45 ACP, Clip Fed, Wood Stock, Class 3   140   200

Sportsman
Made by Steven Arms

Shotgun, Double Barrel, Side by Side
M 315, Various Gauges, Hammerless, Steel Barrel, Modern   90   145

Shotgun, Singleshot
Model 90, Various Gauges, Takedown, Automatic Ejector, Plain, Hammer,
  Modern   30   50

Sportsman
Made by Crescent for W. Bingham Co. Cleveland, Ohio, C.1900

Shotgun, Double Barrel, Side by Side
Various Gauges, Outside Hammers, Damascus Barrel, Modern   80   150
Various Gauges, Hammerless, Steel Barrel, Modern   95   175
Various Gauges, Hammerless, Damascus Barrel, Modern   75   150
Various Gauges, Outside Hammers, Steel Barrel, Modern   90   175

Shotgun, Singleshot
Various Gauges, Hammer, Steel Barrel, Modern   45   75

Springfield Armory

Automatic Weapon, Assault Rifle
M1A, .308 Win., Clip Fed, Silencer, Class 3   750   1,000
M1A (M-14), .308 Win., Clip Fed, Commercial, Class 3   525   650

Rifle, Semi-Automatic
M1A Match Grade, .308 Win., Clip Fed, Version of M-14, Modern   325   400

Springfield Arms
Made by Crescent, C.1900

Shotgun, Double Barrel, Side by Side
Various Gauges, Outside Hammers, Damascus Barrel, Modern   80   150
Various Gauges, Hammerless, Steel Barrel, Modern   95   175
Various Gauges, Hammerless, Damascus Barrel, Modern   75   150
Various Gauges, Outside Hammers, Steel Barrel, Modern   90   175

Shotgun, Singleshot
Various Gauges, Hammer, Steel Barrel, Modern   45   75

Spy
Made by Norwich Falls Pistol Co. C.1880

Handgun, Revolver
.22 Short R.F., 7 Shot, Spur Trigger, Solid Frame, Single Action, Antique   90   160

Square Deal
Made by Crescent for Stratton-Warren Hdw. Co., Memphis, Tenn.

Shotgun, Double Barrel, Side by Side
Various Gauges, Outside Hammers, Damascus Barrel, Modern   80   150
Various Gauges, Hammerless, Steel Barrel, Modern   95   175
Various Gauges, Hammerless, Damascus Barrel, Modern   75   150
Various Gauges, Outside Hammers, Steel Barrel, Modern   90   175

Shotgun, Singleshot
Various Gauges, Hammer, Steel Barrel, Modern   45   75

Squires Bingham
Made by Squibman in the Phillipines

Handgun, Revolver
M 100-D, .22LR/.22 WMR Combo, Double Action, Solid Frame, Swing-Out
  Cylinder, Adjustable Sights, Modern   40   65

Rifle, Bolt Action
M 14D, .22 L.R.R.F., Clip Fed, Checkered Stock, Modern   30   45
M 15, .22 WMR, Clip Fed, Checkered Stock, Modern   50   65

Rifle, Semi-Automatic
M-16, .22 L.R.R.F., Clip Fed, Flash Hider, Modern   35   55
M20D, .22 L.R.R.F., Clip Fed, Checkered Stock, Modern   35   55

Shotgun, Slide Action
M 30/28, 12 Ga., Plain, Modern   60   95

Standard Arms Co.
Wilmington, Del., 1909-11

Rifle, Semi-Automatic
Model G, Various Calibers, Takedown, Tube Feed, Hammerless, Modern   200   300

Rifle, Slide Action
Model M, Various Calibers, Takedown, Tube Feed, Hammerless, Modern   175   250

Stanley
Belgium, C.1900

Shotgun, Double Barrel, Side by Side
Various Gauges, Outside Hammers, Damascus Barrel, Modern   80   150
Various Gauges, Hammerless, Steel Barrel, Modern   95   175
Various Gauges, Hammerless, Damascus Barrel, Modern   75   150
Various Gauges, Outside Hammers, Steel Barrel, Modern   90   175

Shotgun, Singleshot
Various Gauges, Hammer, Steel Barrel, Modern   45   75

Stanton
London, England C.1778

Handgun, Flintlock
.55 Officers, Belt Pistol, Screw Barrel, Box Lock, Brass, Antique   900   1,500

Star
Made by Bonifacio Echeverria, Eibar, Spain 1911 to date

Automatic Weapon, Machine-Pistol
Model MD, .45 ACP, Clip Fed, Holster Stock, Class 3   600   750
Model MD, 7.63 Mauser, Clip Fed, Holster Stock, Class 3   500   650
Model MD, 9mm Luger, Clip Fed, Holster Stock, Class 3   550   700

Automatic Weapon, Submachine Gun
Model Z-45, 9mm Luger, Clip Fed, Folding Stock, Class 3   350   450
Model Z-62, 9mm Luger, Clip Fed, Folding Stock, Class 3   375   500
Model Z-63, 9mm Luger, Clip Fed, Folding Stock, Class 3   475   600

Handgun, Semi-Automatic
Model A, .25 ACP, Clip Fed, Modern   125   175
Model A, .38 ACP, Clip Fed, Modern   90   125
Model A, .45 ACP, Clip Fed, Early Model, Adjustable Sights, Various
  Barrel Lengths, Modern   120   170
Model A, 7.63 Mauser, Clip Fed, Early Model, Adjustable Sights, Various
  Barrel Lengths, Modern   95   135
Model A, 9mm Bergmann, Clip Fed, Early Model, Adjustable Sights,
  Various Barrel Lengths, Modern   95   135

Model A, Various Calibers, Holster Stock, Add $150-$250

Model AS, .38 Super, Clip Fed, Modern	95	135
Model B, 9mm Luger, Clip Fed, Modern	95	135
Model B, 9mm Luger, Clip Fed, Early Model, Various Barrel Lengths, Modern	95	135
Model, BKS-Starlight, 9mm Luger, Clip Fed, Lightweight, Modern	100	140
Model C, 9mm Bayard Long, Clip Fed, 8 Shot, Modern	95	130
Model C O, .25 ACP, Clip Fed, Modern	85	120
Model C U, .25 ACP, Clip Fed, Lightweight, Modern	70	95
Model D, .380 ACP, Clip Fed, 6 Shot, Modern	95	130
Model D, .380 ACP, Clip Fed, 15 Shot Clip, Modern	110	145
Model DK, .380 ACP, Clip Fed, Lightweight, Modern	85	120
Model E Vest Pocket, .25 ACP, Clip Fed, Modern	90	125
Model F, .22 L.R.R.F., Clip Fed, Modern	75	115
Model F R S, .22 L.R.R.F., Clip Fed, Target Pistol, Adjustable Sights, Modern	70	110
Model F T B, .22 L.R.R.F., Clip Fed, Target Pistol, Modern	65	95
Model F-Olympic, .22 Short R.F., Clip Fed, Target Pistol, Modern	120	160
Model F-Sport, .22 L.R.R.F., Clip Fed, 6" Barrel, Modern	70	95
Model FR, .22 L.R.R.F., Clip Fed, Modern	70	110
Model H, .32 ACP, Clip Fed, 7 Shot, Modern	85	120
Model HF, .22 L.R.R.F., Clip Fed, Modern	120	160
Model HN, .380 ACP, Clip Fed, Modern	80	120
Model I, .32 ACP, Clip Fed, 9 Shot, Modern	85	115
Model Lancer, .22 L.R.R.F., Clip Fed, Lightweight, Modern	80	110
Model M, .38 ACP, Clip Fed, Modern	90	125
Model Militar, 9mm, Clip Fed, Modern	120	155
Model NZ, .25 ACP, Clip Fed, Modern	275	375
Model 1, .25 ACP, Clip Fed, Modern	140	200
Model 1, .32 ACP, Clip Fed, Modern	140	200
Model 1914, .32 ACP, Mannlicher Style, Clip Fed, Modern	190	290
Model 1919, .32 ACP, Clip Fed, Modern	160	225
Model 1920, .32 ACP, Clip Fed, Modern	175	250
Model 1920, .380 ACP, Clip Fed, Modern	135	200
Model P, .45 ACP, Clip Fed, Modern	95	135
Model PD, .45 ACP, Clip Fed, Modern	120	160
Model S, .380 ACP, Clip Fed, Modern	75	120
Model S I, .32 ACP, Clip Fed, Modern	65	95
Model SM, .380 ACP, Clip Fed, Modern	80	110
Model Starfire, .380 ACP, Clip Fed, Lightweight, Modern	85	120
Model Starlet, .25 ACP, Clip Fed, Lightweight, Modern	60	95
Model Super A, .38 ACP, Clip Fed, Modern	95	135
Model Super B, 9mm Luger, Clip Fed, Modern	95	140
Model Super M, .38 Super, Clip Fed, Modern	95	140
Model Super P, .45 ACP, Clip Fed, Modern	110	160
Model Super S, .380 ACP, Clip Fed, Modern	80	125
Model Super S I, .32 ACP, Clip Fed, Modern	75	120

Star Model 1 .32 ACP

Star Gauge
Spain, Imported by Interarms Current

Shotgun, Double Barrel, Side by Side
12 and 20 Gauges, Checkered Stock, Adjustable Choke, Double Trigger,
Modern 150 215

State Arms Co.
Made by Crescent for J. H. Lau & Co. C.1900

Shotgun, Double Barrel, Side by Side
Various Gauges, Outside Hammers, Damascus Barrel, Modern 80 150
Various Gauges, Hammerless, Steel Barrel, Modern 95 175
Various Gauges, Hammerless, Damascus Barrel, Modern 75 150
Various Gauges, Outside Hammers, Steel Barrel, Modern 90 175

Shotgun, Singleshot
Various Gauges, Hammer, Steel Barrel, Modern 45 75

Steigleder, Ernst
Suhl & Berlin, Germany 1921-35

Rifle, Double Barrel, Side by Side
Various Calibers, Box Lock, Engraved, Checkered Stock, Color Case
Hardened Frame, Modern 1,800 2,400

Stenda
Germany Stenda Werke Waffenfabrik C.1900

Handgun, Semi-Automatic
.32 ACP, Clip Fed, Modern 95 160

Sterling
Gasport, N.Y. Current

Handgun, Semi-Automatic
#283 Target 300, .22 L.R.R.F., Hammer, Adjustable Sights, Various Barrel
Lengths, Modern 70 95
#284 Target 300 L, .22 L.R.R.F., Hammer, Adjustable Sights, Tapered
Barrel, Modern 65 95
#285 Huskey, .22 L.R.R.F., Hammer, Heavy Barrel, Modern 65 85
#286 Trapper, .22 L.R.R.F., Hammer, Tapered Barrel, Modern 65 85
Model 300B, .25 ACP, Blue, Modern 45 55
Model 300N, .25 ACP, Nickel Plated, Modern 45 60
Model 300S, .25 ACP, Stainless Steel, Modern 55 85
Model 302B, .22 L.R.R.F., Blue, Modern 45 60
Model 302N, .22 L.R.R.F., Nickel Plated, Modern 45 60
Model 302S, .22 L.R.R.F., Stainless Steel, Modern 60 80
Model 400B, .380 ACP, Blue, Clip Fed, Modern 80 110
Model 400N, .380 ACP, Nickel Plated, Clip Fed, Modern 85 120
Model 402, .22 L.R.R.F., Blue, Clip Fed, Modern 75 110
Model 402, .22 L.R.R.F., Nickel Plated, Clip Fed, Modern 75 110
Model 450, .45 ACP, Clip Fed, Double Action, Adjustable Sights, Blue,
Modern 150 225
Model PPL, .380 ACP, Short Barrel, Clip Fed, Modern 90 130

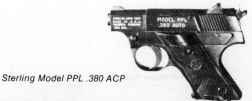

Sterling Model PPL .380 ACP

Sterling Arms Corp.
Made by Crescent for H. & D. Folsom C.1900

Shotgun, Double Barrel, Side by Side

Various Gauges, Outside Hammers, Damascus Barrel, Modern	80	150
Various Gauges, Hammerless, Steel Barrel, Modern	95	175
Various Gauges, Hammerless, Damascus Barrel, Modern	75	150
Various Gauges, Outside Hammers, Steel Barrel, Modern	90	175

Shotgun, Singleshot

Various Gauges, Hammer, Steel Barrel, Modern	45	75

Sterling Revolvers
Maker Unknown C.1880

Handgun, Revolver

.22 Short R.F., 7 Shot, Spur Trigger, Solid Frame, Single Action, Antique	90	160
.32 Short R.F., 5 Shot, Spur Trigger, Solid Frame, Single Action, Antique	95	170

Stevens, J. Arms & Tool Co.
Chicopee Falls, Mass. 1864-86. Became J. Stevens Arms & Tools Co. 1886. Absorbed Page-Lewis Arms Co., Davis-Warner Arms Co., and Crescent Firearms Co. in 1926. Became a subsidiary of Savage in 1936.

Combination Weapon, Double Barrel, Over-Under

Model 22-410, .22-.410 Ga., Hammer, Plastic Stock, Modern	40	65
Model 22-410, .22-.410 Ga., Hammer, Wood Stock, Modern	60	80

Handgun, Singleshot

1888 #1, Various Calibers, Tip-Up, Octagon Barrel, Open Rear Sight, Antique	85	120
1888 #2 "Gallery," .22 L.R.R.F., Tip-Up, Octagon Barrel, Open Rear Sight, Antique	80	120
1888 #3 "Combined Sight", Various Calibers, Tip-Up, Octagon Barrel, Antique	95	135
1888 #4 "Combined Sight," .22 L.R.R.F., Tip-Up, Octagon Barrel, Antique	85	120
1888 #5 "Expert," Various Calibers, Tip-Up, Half Octagon Barrel, Antique	90	130
1894 "New Ideal," Various Calibers, Level Action, Falling Block, Vernier Sights, Antique	175	245
Model 23 "Sure-Shot," .22 L.R.R.F., Side-Swing Barrel, Hammer, Antique	60	85
Model 34 "Hunters Pet," Various Rimfires, Tip-Up, Octagon Barrel, with Shoulder Stock, Curio	250	325
Model 39 New Model Pocket Shotgun, Various Calibers, Tip-Up, Smoothbore, with Shoulder Stock, Class 3	90	130
Model 40 New Model Pocket Rifle, Various Calibers, Tip-Up, with Shoulder Stock, Curio	250	325
Model 42 Reliable Pocket Rifle, .22 L.R.R.F., Tip-Up, with Shoulder Stock, Curio	150	195
Model "Offhand," .410 Ga., Tip-Up, Class 3	150	200
Model 10, .22 L.R.R.F., Tip-Up, Target, Various Barrel Lengths, Modern	75	120
Model 34 "Hunters Pet," Various Rimfires, Tip-Up, Half-Octagon Barrel, with Shoulder Stock, Vernier Sights, Curio	275	345
Model 35 "Offhand," .22 L.R.R.F., Tip-Up, Target, Various Barrel Lengths, Modern	175	235
Model 35 "Offhand," .22 L.R.R.F., Tip-Up, Target, Ivory Grips, Various Barrel Lengths, Modern	200	290
Model 35 Autoshot, .410 Ga., Tip-Up, Various Barrel Lengths, Class 3	150	200
Model 37 "Gould," Various Calibers, Tip-Up, Modern	175	225
Model 38 "Conlin," .22 L.R.R.F., Tip-Up, Modern	200	275
Model 41, .22 L.R.R.F., Tip-Up, Pocket Pistol, Modern	90	125
Model 43 "Diamond," .22 L.R.R.F., Tip-Up, Spur Trigger, 6" Barrel, Octagon Barrel, Modern	100	145
Model 43 "Diamond," .22 L.R.R.F., Tip-Up, Spur Trigger, 10" Barrel, Octagon Barrel, Modern	115	150

Model 43 "Diamond," .22 L.R.R.F., Tip-Up, Spur Trigger, 6" Barrel, Globe
  Sights, Modern 120   160
Model 43 "Diamond," .22 L.R.R.F., Tip-Up, Spur Trigger, 10" Barrel, Globe
  Sights, Modern 135   175

Rifle, Bolt Action

Model 053 Buckhorn, Various Rimfires, Singleshot, Peep Sights, Modern	30	45
Model 056 Buckhorn, .22 L.R.R.F., 5 Shot Clip, Peep Sights, Modern	40	60
Model 066 Buckhorn, .22 L.R.R.F., Tube Feed, Peep Sights, Modern	40	60
Model 083, .22 L.R.R.F., Singleshot, Peep Sights, Takedown, Modern	25	45
Model 084, .22 L.R.R.F., 5 Shot Clip, Peep Sights, Takedown, Modern	35	55
Model 086, .22 L.R.R.F., Tube Feed, Takedown, Peep Sights, Modern	40	60
Model 15, .22 L.R.R.F., Singleshot, Modern, (Springfield)	20	35
Model 15Y, .22 L.R.R.F., Singleshot, Modern	25	35
Model 322, .22 Hornet, Clip Fed, Carbine, Open Rear Sight, Modern	70	95
Model 322-S, .22 Hornet, Clip Fed, Carbine, Peep Sights, Modern	75	95
Model 325, .30-30 Win., Clip Fed, Carbine, Open Rear Sight, Modern	60	80
Model 325-S, .30-30 Win., Clip Fed, Carbine, Peep Sights, Modern	65	85
Model 416, .22 L.R.R.F., 5 Shot Clip, Peep Sights, Target Stock, Modern	90	145
Model 419, .22 L.R.R.F., Singleshot, Peep Sights, Modern	35	55
Model 48, .22 L.R.R.F., Singleshot, Takedown, Modern	25	35
Model 49, .22 L.R.R.F., Singleshot, Takedown, Modern	25	35
Model 50, .22 L.R.R.F., Singleshot, Takedown, Modern	25	35
Model 51, .22 L.R.R.F., Singleshot, Takedown, Modern 25 30		
Model 52, .22 L.R.R.F., Singleshot, Takedown, Modern	25	35
Model 53, .22 L.R.R.F., Singleshot, Takedown, Modern	25	35
Model 56 Buckhorn, .22 L.R.R.F., 5 Shot Clip, Open Rear Sight, Modern	30	45
Model 65 "Little Krag," .22 L.R.R.F., Singleshot, Takedown, Modern	35	50
Model 66 Buckhorn, .22 L.R.R.F., Tube Feed, Open Rear Sight, Modern	30	45
Model 82, .22 L.R.R.F., Singleshot, Peep Sights, Modern (Springfield)	25	35
Model 83, .22 L.R.R.F., Singleshot, Open Rear Sight, Takedown, Modern	20	35
Model 84, .22 L.R.R.F., 5 Shot Clip, Open Rear Sight, Takedown, Modern	30	45
Model 86, .22 L.R.R.F., Tube Feed, Takedown, Open Rear Sight, Modern	35	50

Rifle, Lever Action

Model 425, Various Calibers, Hammer, Modern	75	100
Model 430, Various Calibers, Hammer, Checkered Stock, Modern	75	110
Model 435, Various Calibers, Hammer, Light Engraving, Fancy Checkering, Modern	125	175
Model 440, Various Calibers, Hammer, Fancy Checkering, Fancy Engraving, Fancy Wood, Modern	325	400

Rifle, Semi-Automatic

Model 057 Buckhorn, .22 L.R.R.F., 5 Shot Clip, Peep Sights, Modern	45	60
Model 076 Buckhorn, .22 L.R.R.F., Peep Sights, Tube Feed, Modern	45	65
Model 085 Springfield, .22 L.R.R.F., 5 Shot Clip, Peep Sights, Modern	45	65
Model 57 Buckhorn, .22 L.R.R.F., 5 Shot Clip, Open Rear Sight, Modern	40	55
Model 76 Buckhorn, .22 L.R.R.F., Open Rear Sight, Tube Feed, Modern	40	60
Model 85 Springfield, .22 L.R.R.F., 5 Shot Clip, Open Rear Sight, Modern	40	60
Model 87, .22 L.R.R.F., Tube Feed, Open Rear Sight, Modern	40	60
Model 87-S, .22 L.R.R.F., Peep Sights, Tube Feed, Modern	45	65
Model 87K Scout, .22 L.R.R.F., Tube Feed, Open Rear Sight, Carbine, Modern	45	65

Rifle, Singleshot

1888 #10 "Range," Various Calibers, Tip-Up, Half-Octagon Barrel, Fancy Wood, Vernier Sights, Antique	140	175
1888 #11 "Ladies," Various Calibers, Tip-Up, Half-Octagon Barrel, Open Rear Sight, Antique	110	135
1888 #12 "Ladies," Various Calibers, Tip-Up, Half-Octagon Barrel, Open Rear Sight, Fancy Wood, Antique	150	195
1888 #13 "Ladies," Various Calibers, Tip-Up, Half-Octagon Barrel, Vernier Sights, Antique	140	175

1888 #14 "Ladies," Various Calibers, Tip-Up, Half-Octagon Barrel, Vernier Sights, Fancy Wood, Antique	175	220
1888 #15 "Crack Shot," Various Calibers, Tip-Up, Half-Octagon Barrel, Peep Sights, Antique	135	160
1888 #16 "Crack Shot," Various Calibers, Tip-Up, Half-Octagon Barrel, Peep Sights, Fancy Wood, Antique	150	185
1888 #6 "Expert," Various Calibers, Tip-Up, Half-Octagon Barrel, Fancy Wood, Antique	120	145
1888 #7 "Premier," Various Calibers, Tip-Up, Half-Octagon Barrel, Globe Sights, Antique	110	135
1888 #8 "Premier," Various Calibers, Tip-Up, Half-Octagon Barrel, Fancy Wood, Globe Sights, Antique	130	160
1888 #9 "Range," Various Calibers, Tip-Up, Half-Octagon Barrel, Vernier Sights, Antique	125	150
Model 14½ "Little Scout," .22 L.R.R.F., Hammer, Rolling Block, Modern	45	70
Model 101 Featherweight, .44-40 WCF, Lever Action, Tip-Up, Smoothbore, Takedown, Half-Octagon Barrel, Modern	75	100
Model 101, with Extra 22 Barrel, .44-40 WCF, Lever Action, Tip-Up, Smoothbore, Takedown, Half-Octagon Barrel, Modern	125	150
Model 11 "Ladies," Various Rimfires, Tip-Up, Open Rear Sight, Modern	100	140
Model 12 "Marksman," Various Rimfires, Hammer, Lever Action, Tip-Up, Modern	60	75
Model 13 "Ladies," Various Rimfires, Tip-Up, Vernier Sights, Modern	120	160
Model 14 "Little Scout," .22 L.R.R.F., Hammer, Rolling Block, Modern	45	70
Model 15 "Maynard Jr.," .22 L.R.R.F., Lever Action, Tip-Up, Modern	55	70
Model 15½ "Maynard Jr.," .22 L.R.R.F., Lever Action, Tip-Up, Modern	55	70
Model 17, Various Rimfires, Lever Action, Takedown, Favorite, Open Rear Sight, Modern	60	90
Model 18, Various Rimfires, Lever Action, Takedown, Favorite, Vernier Sights, Modern	65	95
Model 19, Various Rimfires, Lever Action, Takedown, Favorite, Lyman Sights, Modern	65	95
Model 2, Various Rimfires, Tip-Up, Open Rear Sight, Modern	115	150
Model 20, Various Rimfires, Lever Action, Takedown, Favorite, Smoothbore, Curio	60	75
Model 26, Crack-Shot, Various Rimfires, Lever Action, Takedown, Open Rear Sight, Modern	60	85
Model 26½, Various Rimfires, Lever Action, Takedown, Smoothbore, Modern	60	80
Model 27, Various Rimfires, Lever Action, Takedown, Favorite, Octagon Barrel, Open Rear Sight, Modern	80	100
Model 28, Various Rimfires, Lever Action, Takedown, Favorite, Octagon Barrel, Vernier Sights, Modern	85	110
Model 29, Various Rimfires, Lever Action, Takedown, Favorite, Octagon Barrel, Lyman Sights, Modern	85	110
Model 404, .22 L.R.R.F., Hammer, Falling Block, Target Sights, Full-Stocked, Modern 325	425	
Model 414, "Armory," .22 L.R.R.F., Lever Action, Lyman Sights, Modern	180	275
Model 417½, Various Calibers, Lever Action, Walnut Hill, Modern	290	350
Model 417-0, Various Calibers, Lever Action, Walnut Hill, Modern	290	350
Model 417-1, Various Calibers, Lever Action, Lyman Sights, Walnut Hill, Modern	290	375
Model 417-2, Various Calibers, Lever Action, Vernier Sights, Walnut Hill, Modern	300	380
Model 417-3, Various Calibers, Lever Action, no Sights, Walnut Hill, Modern	280	350
Model 418, .22 L.R.R.F., Lever Action, Takedown, Walnut Hill, Modern	160	225
Model 418½, Various Rimfires, Lever Action, Takedown, Walnut Hill, Modern	150	215
Model 44 "Ideal," Various Calibers, Lever Action, Rolling Block, Modern	175	245
Model 44½ "Ideal," Various Calibers, Lever Action, Falling Block, Modern	250	335
Model 49 "Ideal," Various Calibers, Walnut Hill, Lever Action, Falling Block, Engraved, Fancy Checkering, Modern	375	460

Model 5, Various Rimfires, Tip-Up, Vernier Sights, Modern   120   175

Model 51 "Pope," Various Calibers, Schutzen Rifle, Lever Action, Falling
   Block, Engraved, Fancy Checkering, Modern   400   550

Model 52 "Pope, Jr.," Various Calibers, Schutzen Rifle, Lever Action,
   Falling Block, Engraved, Fancy Checkering, Modern   400   575

Model 54 "Pope," Various Calibers, Schutzen Rifle, Lever Action, Falling
   Block, Fancy Engraving, Fancy Checkering, Modern   500   600

Model 56 "Pope Ladies," Various Calibers, Schutzen Rifle, Lever Action,
   Falling Block, Fancy Checkering, Modern   220   350

Model 7 "Swiss Butt.", Various Rimfires, Tip-Up, Vernier Sights, Modern   125   185

Rifle, Slide Action

Model 70, .22 L.R.R.F., Hammer, Solid Frame, Modern   75   120

Model 71, .22 L.R.R.F., Hammer, Solid Frame, Modern   75   120

Model 75, .22 L.R.R.F., Tube Feed, Hammerless, Modern   85   160

Model 80, Various Rimfires, Tube Feed, Takedown, Modern   60   85

Shotgun, Bolt Action

Model 237, 20 Ga., Takedown, Singleshot, Modern, (Springfield)   20   35

Model 258, 20 Ga., Takedown, Clip Fed, Modern   35   50

Model 37, .410 Ga., Takedown, Singleshot, Modern (Springfield)   20   35

Model 235, Various Gauges, Outside Hammers, Checkered Stock, Steel
   Barrel, Modern   90   140

Model 250, Various Gauges, Outside Hammers, Checkered Stock, Steel
   Barrel, Modern   90   140

Model 255, 12 and 16 Gauges, Outside Hammers, Checkered Stock, Steel
   Barrel, Modern   90   140

Model 260 "Twist," Various Gauges, Outside Hammers, Checkered Stock,
   Damascus Barrel, Modern   75   115

Model 265 "Krupp," 12 and 16 Gauges, Outside Hammers, Checkered
   Stock, Steel Barrel, Modern   90   140

Model 270 "Nitro," Various Gauges, Outside Hammers, Checkered Stock,
   Damascus Barrel, Modern   95   145

Model 311, Various Gauges, Hammerless, Steel Barrel, Modern   95   155

Model 311 ST, Various Gauges, Hammerless, Steel Barrel, Single Trigger,
   Modern   120   155

Stevens Model 80

Stevens Model 58

Stevens Model 311

Model 3151, Various Gauges, Hammerless, Recoil Pad, Front and Rear Bead Sights, Modern	95	155
Model 330, Various Gauges, Hammerless, Checkered Stock, Modern	85	145
Model 335, 12 and 16 Gauges, Hammerless, Steel Barrel, Checkered Stock, Double Trigger, Modern	95	145
Model 345, 20 Ga., Hammerless, Checkered Stock, Steel Barrel, Double Trigger, Modern	95	145
Model 355, 12 and 16 Gauges, Hammerless, Steel Barrel, Checkered Stock, Double Trigger, Modern	90	140
Model 365 "Krupp," 12 and 16 Gauges, Hammerless, Checkered Stock, Steel Barrel, Double Trigger, Modern	95	155
Model 375 "Krupp," 12 and 16 Gauges, Hammerless, Light Engraving, Fancy Checkering, Double Trigger, Steel Barrel, Modern	100	140
Model 385 "Krupp," 12 and 16 Gauges, Hammerless, Fancy Checkering, Fancy Engraving, Double Trigger, Steel Barrel, Modern	150	185
Model 515, Various Gauges, Hammerless, Modern	80	125
Model 5151, Various Gauges, Hammerless, Steel Barrel, Modern	95	140
Model 530, Various Gauges, Hammerless, Steel Barrel, Double Trigger, Modern	80	135
Model 530 ST, Various Gauges, Hammerless, Steel Barrel, Single Trigger, Modern	120	150
Model 530M, Various Gauges, Hammerless, Plastic Stock, Modern	65	100
Model 58, .410 Ga., Takedown, Clip Fed, Modern	30	45

Shotgun, Pump

Model 520, 12 Ga., Takedown, Modern	85	125
Model 620, Various Gauges, Takedown, Modern	80	120

Shotgun, Semi-Automatic

Model 124, 12 Ga., Plastic Stock, Modern	50	80

Shotgun, Singleshot

Various Gauges, Hammer, Automatic Ejector, Modern	35	55
Various Gauges, Hammer, Automatic Ejector, Raised Matted Rib, Modern	40	60
1888 "New Style," Various Gauges, Tip-Up, Hammer, Damascus Barrel, Antique	150	200
Model 100, Various Gauges, Selective Ejector, Hammer, Modern	25	45
Model 102, .410 Ga., Hammer, Featherweight, Modern	25	40
Model 102, 24, 28, and 32 Gauges, Hammer, Featherweight, Modern	30	45
Model 104, .410 Ga., Hammer, Featherweight, Automatic Ejector, Modern	35	45
Model 104, 24, 28, and 32 Gauges, Hammer, Automatic Ejector, Featherweight, Modern	45	60
Model 105, 20 Ga., Hammer, Modern	25	35
Model 105, 28 Ga., Hammer, Modern	30	40
Model 106, .410 Ga. 2½", Hammer, Modern	20	30
Model 106, .44-40 WCF, Hammer, Smoothbore, Modern	30	40
Model 106, 32 Ga., Hammer, Modern	25	35
Model 107, Various Gauges, Hammer, Automatic Ejector, Modern	35	50
Model 108, .410 Ga. 2½", Hammer, Automatic Ejector, Modern	25	35
Model 108, .44-40 WCF, Hammer, Automatic Ejector, Smoothbore, Modern	35	45
Model 108, 32 Ga., Hammer, Automatic Ejector, Modern	30	40
Model 110, Various Gauges, Selective Ejector, Checkered Stock, Hammer, Modern	30	45
Model 120, Various Gauges, Selective Ejector, Fancy Checkering, Hammer, Modern	35	50
Model 125 Ladies, 20 Ga., Automatic Ejector, Hammer, Modern	35	50
Model 125 Ladies, 28 Ga., Automatic Ejector, Hammer, Modern	40	60
Model 140, Various Gauges, Selective Ejector, Hammerless, Checkered Stock, Modern	40	60
Model 160, Various Gauges, Hammer, Modern	25	35
Model 165, Various Gauges, Automatic Ejector, Hammer, Modern	25	40
Model 170, Various Gauges, Automatic Ejector, Hammer, Checkered Stock, Modern	30	40

Model 180, Various Gauges, Hammerless, Automatic Ejector, Checkered Stock, Round Barrel, Modern	50	75
Model 182, 12 Ga., Hammerless, Automatic Ejector, Light Engraving, Checkered Stock, Trap Grade, Modern	65	95
Model 185, Deduct 25% for Damascus Barrel		
Model 185, Add 20% for 16 or 20 Gauge		
Model 185, 12 Ga., Hammerless, Automatic Ejector, Checkered Stock, Half-Octagon Barrel, Modern	85	115
Model 190, Deduct 25% for Damascus Barrel		
Model 190, Add 20% for 16 or 20 Gauge		
Model 190, 12 Ga., Hammerless, Automatic Ejector, Fancy Checkering, Light Engraving, Half-Octagon Barrel, Modern	95	135
Model 195, Deduct 25% for Damascus Barrel		
Model 195, Add 20% for 16 or 20 Gauge		
Model 195, 12 Ga., Hammerless, Automatic Ejector, Fancy Checkering, Fancy Engraving, Half-Octagon Barrel, Modern	150	175
Model 89 Dreadnaught, Various Gauges, Hammer, Modern	40	55
Model 90, Various Gauges, Takedown, Automatic Ejector, Plain, Hammer, Modern	30	45
Model 93, 12 and 16 Gauges, Hammer, Modern	25	40
Model 94, Various Gauges, Takedown, Automatic Ejector, Plain, Hammer, Modern	30	45
Model 944, .410 Ga., Hammer, Automatic Ejector, Modern (Springfield)	30	45
Model 94A, Various Gauges, Hammer, Automatic Ejector, Modern	30	45
Model 94C, Various Gauges, Hammer, Automatic Ejector, Modern	30	45
Model 95, 12 and 16 Gauges, Modern	30	45
Model 958, .410 Ga., Automatic Ejector, Hammer, Modern	30	45
Model 958, 32 Ga., Automatic Ejector, Hammer, Modern	40	55
Model 97, 12 and 16 Gauges, Hammer, Automatic Ejector, Modern	30	40
Model 970, 12 Ga., Hammer, Automatic Ejector, Checkered Stock, Half-Octagon Barrel, Modern	40	50

Shotgun, Slide-Action

Model 522, 12 Ga., Trap Grade, Takedown, Raised Matted Rib, Modern	90	130
Model 621, Various Gauges, Hammerless, Checkered Stock, Raised Matted Rib, Takedown, Modern	90	135
Model 67, Various Gauges, Hammerless, Solid Frame, Modern (Springfield)	60	80
Model 67-VR, Various Gauges, Hammerless, Solid Frame, Vent Rib, Modern (Springfield)	75	95
Model 77, for Vent Rib, Add $10-$15		
Model 77, 12 and 16 Gauges, Hammerless, Solid Frame, Modern	85	130
Model 77, Various Gauges, Hammerless, Solid Frame, Modern	65	90
Model 77 S C, 12 and 16 Gauges, Hammerless, Solid Frame, Recoil Pad, Adjustable Choke, Modern	100	140
Model 77-AC, Various Gauges, Hammerless, Solid Frame, Adjustable Choke, Modern	65	90
Model 77-M, 12 Ga., Hammerless, Solid Frame, Adjustable Choke, Modern	70	100
Model 820, 12 Ga., Hammerless, Solid Frame, Modern	65	90

Stevens, James

Shotgun, Percussion

14 Ga., Double Barrel, Side by Side, Engraved, Light Ornamentation, Antique	300	450

Steyr
Austria 1911-39

Automatic Weapon, Submachine Gun

MP Solothurn 34, 9mm Mauser, Clip Fed, Class 3	800	1,200

Handgun, Semi-Automatic

Model 1908, .32 ACP, Clip Fed, Tip-Up, Modern	95	150
Model 1909, .32 ACP, Clip Fed, Tip-Up, Modern	90	145

Steyr - Model 1908 .32 ACP; Solothurn .32 ACP

Steyr Model 1909 "Baby" .25 ACP

Steyr Model SP .32 ACP

Steyr Model 1912 Military

Stock, Franz .25 ACP

Model 1911, 9mm Steyr, Commercial, Curio	225	300
Model 1912, 9mm Luger, Nazi-Proofed, Military, Curio	135	195
Model 1912, 9mm Steyr, Military, Curio	125	180
Model 1912 Roumanian, 9mm Steyr, Military, Curio	135	200
Model SP, .32 ACP, Clip Fed, Double Action, Modern	150	250
Solothurn, .32 ACP, Clip Fed, Modern	100	150

Stock, Franz
Germany 1920-40

Handgun, Semi-Automatic

.22 L.R.R.F., Clip Fed, Modern	140	200
.25 ACP, Clip Fed, Modern	110	155
.32 ACP, Clip Fed, Modern	110	155

Stockman, Hans
Dresden 1590-1621

Handgun, Wheel-Lock

Pair, Holster Pistol, Pear Pommel, Horn Inlays, Light Ornamentation, Antique	15,000+

Stock, Franz .32 ACP

Stosel Model 1913 .25 ACP

Stosel

Handgun, Semi-Automatic
Model 1913, .25 ACP, Clip Fed, Modern   80   110

Stuart, Johan
Edinburgh, Scotland 1701-50

Handgun, Snaphaunce
All Steel Highland, Engraved, Scroll Butt, Ball Trigger, Antique   10,000+

Sullivan Arms Co.
Made by Crescent for Sullivan Hardware, Anderson, S.C. C.1900

Shotgun, Double Barrel, Side by Side

Various Gauges, Outside Hammers, Damascus Barrel, Modern	80	150
Various Gauges, Hammerless, Steel Barrel, Modern	95	175
Various Gauges, Hammerless, Damascus Barrel, Modern	75	150
Various Gauges, Outside Hammers, Steel Barrel, Modern	90	175

Shotgun, Singleshot
Various Gauges, Hammer, Steel Barrel, Modern   45   75

Super Dreadnaught
Made by Stevens Arms

Shotgun, Singleshot
Model 89 Dreadnaught, Various Gauges, Hammer, Modern   40   55

Super Range Goose
Made by Stevens Arms

Rifle, Semi-Automatic
Model 85 Springfield, .22 L.R.R.F., 5 Shot Clip, Open Rear Sight, Modern   40   60

Sutherland, James
Edinburgh, Scotland C.1790

Handgun, Flintlock
.50, all Steel, Engraved, Ram's Horn Butt, Antique   1,600   2,000

Sutherland, Ramsey
London and Birmingham, 1790-1827

Handgun, Flintlock
.67, George III, Calvary Pistol, Military, Tapered Round Barrel, Brass
  Furniture, Antique   650   900

Rifle, Flintlock
.75, 3rd Model Brown Bess, Musket, Military, Antique   800   1,200

Swiss Military Vetterli Rifle

Swamp Angel
Made by Forehand & Wadsworth, Worcester, Mass C.1871

Handgun, Revolver
.41 Short R.F., 5 Shot, Spur Trigger, Solid Frame, Single Action, Antique   120   195

Sweitzer, Daniel & Co.
Lancaster, Pa. 1808-14

Swift
Made by Iver Johnson, Fitchburg, Mass. 1890-1900

Handgun, Revolver
.38 S & W, 5 Shot, Top Break, Hammerless, Double Action, Modern   55   95
.38 S & W, 5 Shot, Double Action, Top Break, Modern   45   95

Swiss Military

Automatic Weapon, Submachine Gun
MP Solothurn 34, 9mm Mauser, Clip Fed, Class 3   800   1,200

Handgun, Revolver
Swiss Ordnance, 7.5mm, Double Action, Blue, Military, Antique   100   140

Rifle, Bolt Action
Vetterli, Bern 1878, .41 Swiss R.F., Tube Feed, Military, Antique   80   130
M 1889, 7.5 x 55 Swiss, Military, Modern   95   145
M1911 Schmidt Rubin, 7.5 x 55 Swiss, Clip Fed, Military, Modern   75   125
M1911 Schmidt Rubin, 7.5 x 55 Swiss, Clip Fed, Carbine, Military, Modern   85   125

Talleries
Argentina

Handgun, Semi-Automatic
T.A.L.A., .22 L.R.R.F., Clip Fed, Modern   50   85

Tanarmi
Italy, Imported by Excam, Current

Handgun, Revolver
E-15, for Chrome, Add $5
E-15, .22LR/.22 WMR Combo, Single Action, Western Style, Modern   20   30
E-15, .22 L.R.R.F., Single Action, Western Style, Modern   17   20
TA-22, for Chrome, Add $5
TA-22, .22LR/.22 WMR Combo, Single Action, Western Style, Brass Grip
  Frame, Modern   25   45
TA-22, .22 L.R.R.F., Single Action, Western Style, Brass Grip Frame,
  Modern   20   35

Tanke .25 ACP

Tanke

Handgun, Semi-Automatic

.25 ACP, Clip Fed, Modern	80	110

Taurus
Made in Brazil

Handgun, Revolver

Model 74, .32 S & W Long, Solid Frame, Swing-Out Cylinder, Double Action, Adjustable Sights, Modern	40	75
Model 80, .38 Special, Solid Frame, Swing-Out Cylinder, Double Action, Modern	45	67
Model 82, .38 Special, Solid Frame, Swing-Out Cylinder, Double Action, Heavy Barrel, Modern	40	65
Model 84, .38 Special, Solid Frame, Swing-Out Cylinder, Double Action, Adjustable Sights, Modern	40	60
Model 86, .38 Special, Solid Frame, Swing-Out Cylinder, Double Action, Adjustable Sights, 6" Barrel, Modern	45	70
Model 94, .22 L.R.R.F., Solid Frame, Swing-Out Cylinder, Double Action, Adjustable Sights, Modern	40	60
Model 96, .22 L.R.R.F., Solid Frame, Swing-Out Cylinder, Double Action, Adjustable Sights, 6" Barrel, Modern	45	75

T.D.E.
El Monte, Calif. Also see Auto-Mag

Handgun, Semi-Automatic

Pistol, Modern	120	150

Ted Williams
Trade name of Sears Roebuck

Rifle, Bolt Action

Model 52703, .22 L.R.R.F., Singleshot, Plain, Modern	20	35
Model 52774, .22 L.R.R.F., Clip Fed, Plain, Modern	30	45
Model 53, Various Calibers, Checkered Stock, Modern	110	140

Ted Williams Model 52703
Courtesy of Sears, Roebuck & Co.

Ted Williams Model 53
Courtesy of Sears, Roebuck & Co.

Ted Williams Model 34
Courtesy of Sears, Roebuck & Co.

Rifle, Lever Action
Model 120, .30-30 Win., Carbine, Modern   40   65

Rifle, Semi-Automatic
Model 34, .22 L.R.R.F., Modern   30   45
Model 34, .22 L.R.R.F., Carbine, Modern   30   45
Model 3T, .22 L.R.R.F., Checkered Stock, Modern   60   75
Model 52811, .22 L.R.R.F., Plain, Tube Feed, Takedown, Modern   35   50
Model 52814, .22 L.R.R.F., Checkered Stock, Clip Fed, Takedown, Modern   65   100

Shotgun, Bolt Action
Model 51106, 12 and 20 Gauges, Clip Fed, Adjustable Choke, Modern   40   55
Model 51142, .410 Ga., Clip Fed, Plain, Modern   35   45

Shotgun, Double Barrel, Over-Under
Model Laurona, 12 Ga., Checkered Stock, Light Engraving, Double
   Trigger, Vent Rib, Modern   220   295
Model Zoli, 12 Ga., Checkered Stock, Light Engraving, Double Trigger,
   Vent Rib, Automatic Ejector, Modern   121   255
Model Zoli, 12 and 20 Gauges, Checkered Stock, Light Engraving, Double
   Trigger, Vent Rib, Modern   175   250

Shotgun, Double Barrel, Side by Side
Model 51226, 12 and 20 Gauges, Plain, Double Trigger, Modern   70   100
Model Laurona, 12 and 20 Gauges, Checkered Stock, Light Engraving,
   Hammerless, Modern   95   135

Shotgun, Semi-Automatic
Model 300, 12 Ga., Plain, Modern   95   135
Model 300, 12 and 20 Gauges, Checkered Stock, Vent Rib, Adjustable
   Choke, Modern   125   160
Model 300, 12 and 20 Gauges, Checkered Stock, Vent Rib, Modern   115   145

Ted Williams Model 51106
Courtesy of Sears, Roebuck & Co.

Ted Williams Model 300
Courtesy of Sears, Roebuck & Co.

340

Ted Williams Model 200
Courtesy of Sears, Roebuck & Co.

Shotgun, Singleshot
Model 5108, Various Gauges, Plain, Modern   30   40

Shotgun, Slide Action
Model 200, 12 and 20 Gauges, Checkered Stock, Vent Rib, Adjustable
  Choke, Modern   115   145
Model 200, 12 and 20 Gauges, Checkered Stock, Vent Rib, Modern   100   125
Model 200, 12 and 20 Gauges, Plain, Modern   70   90
Model 200, 12 and 20 Gauges, Checkered Stock, Plain Barrel, Modern   80   110
Model 51454, .410 Ga., Plain, Modern   55   75

Ten Star
Belgium C.1900

Shotgun, Double Barrel, Side by Side
Various Gauges, Outside Hammers, Damascus Barrel, Modern   80   150
Various Gauges, Hammerless, Steel Barrel, Modern   95   175
Various Gauges, Hammerless, Damascus Barrel, Modern   75   150
Various Gauges, Outside Hammers, Steel Barrel, Modern   90   175

Shotgun, Singleshot
Various Gauges, Hammer, Steel Barrel, Modern   45   75

Terrier
Made by J. Rupertus, Philadelphia, Pa. Sold by Tryon Bros. C.1880

Handgun, Revolver
.22 Short R.F., 7 Shot, Spur Trigger, Solid Frame, Single Action, Antique   90   160
.32 Short R.F., 5 Shot, Spur Trigger, Solid Frame, Single Action, Antique   95   170
.38 Short R.F., 5 Shot, Spur Trigger, Solid Frame, Single Action, Antique   95   170
.41 Short R.F., 5 Shot, Spur Trigger, Solid Frame, Single Action, Antique   120   195

Terror
Made by Forehand & Wadsworth C.1870

Handgun, Revolver
6 Shots or, .32 Short R.F., 5 Shot, Spur Trigger, Solid Frame, Single
  Action, Antique   90   160

Texas Ranger
Made by Stevens Arms

Shotgun, Singleshot
Model 95, 12 and 16 Gauges, Modern   30   45

Thames Arms Co.
Norwich, Conn. C.1907

Handgun, Revolver
.22 L.R.R.F., 7 Shot, Double Action, Top Break, Modern   45   95
.32 S & W, 5 Shot, Double Action, Top Break, Modern   45   95
.38 S & W, 5 Shot, Double Action, Top Break, Modern   45   95

Thayer, Robertson & Cary
Norwich, Conn. C.1907

Handgun, Revolver

.32 S & W, 5 Shot, Double Action, Top Break, Modern	45	95
.38 S & W, 5 Shot, Double Action, Top Break, Modern	45	95

Thompson
Developed by Auto-Ordnance, Invented by Gen. John T. Thompson. Made by various companies.

Automatic Weapon, Submachine Gun

M1, .45 ACP, Clip Fed, with Compensator, Military, Plain Barrel, Class 3	600	900
M1921A, .45 ACP, Early Model, Clip Fed, without Compensator, Lyman Sights, Curio, Class 3	2,000	2,500
M1921AC, .45 ACP, Early Model, Clip Fed, with Compensator, Lyman Sights, Curio, Class 3	2,300	2,800
M1921AC, .45 ACP, Early Model, Clip Fed, with Compensator, Cased with Accessories, Curio, Class 3	3,400	4,000
M1921AC, .45 ACP, Early Model, Clip Fed, with Compensator, Metric Lyman Sights, Curio, Class 3	2,800	3,500
M1928 (Numrich), .45 ACP, Clip Fed, with Compensator, Lyman Sights, Class 3	400	500
M1928 Navy, .45 ACP, Clip Fed, with Compensator, Lyman Sights, Finned Barrel, Class 3	1,900	2,400
M1928 Navy, .45 ACP, Clip Fed, with Compensator, Lyman Sights, Finned Barrel, British Proofs, Class 3	2,300	2,750
M1928 Navy, .45 ACP, Clip Fed, with Compensator, Lyman Sights, Finned Barrel, Cased with Accessories, Class 3	2,500	3,000
M1928A1 (AO), .45 ACP, Clip Fed, with Compensator, Adjustable Sights, Finned Barrel, Military, Class 3	1,200	1,600
M1928A1 (AO), .45 ACP, Clip Fed, with Compensator, Military, Plain Barrel, Class 3	800	1,100
M1928A1 (S), .45 ACP, Clip Fed, with Compensator, Lyman Sights, Class 3	1,000	1,400
M1A1, .45 ACP, Clip Fed, with Compensator, Military, Plain Barrel, Class 3	550	850

Handgun, Semi-Automatic

Model 27A5, .45 ACP, Clip Fed, Finned Barrel, Adjustable Sights, with Compensator, Modern, (Numrich)	145	225

Rifle, Semi-Automatic

M1927, .45 ACP, Clip Fed, with Compensator, Short Barreled Rifle, Lyman Sights, Curio, Class 3	4,000	5,000
Model 27A1, .45 ACP, Clip Fed, without Compensator, Modern, (Numrich)	275	350
Model 27A1, .45 ACP, Clip Fed, without Compensator, Cased with Accessories, (Numrich)	225	325

Thompson Model 27A5
Courtesy of Auto Ordnance

Thompson Model 27A1
Courtesy of Auto Ordnance

Model 27A1 Deluxe, .45 ACP, Clip Fed, Finned Barrel, Adjustable Sights, with Compensator, Modern, (Numrich)	225	315
Model 27A1 Deluxe, .45 ACP, Clip Fed, Finned Barrel, Adjustable Sights, with Compensator, Cased with Accessories, Modern	320	375
Model 27A3, .22 L.R.R.F., Clip Fed, Finned Barrel, Adjustable Sights, with Compensator, Modern, (Numrich)	275	350

Thompson, Samuel
Columbus, Ohio 1820-22. See Kentucky Rifles

Thompson/Center
Rochester, N.H.

Handgun, Singleshot

Contender, Various Calibers, Adjustable Sights, Modern	90	145
Contender, Various Calibers, Adjustable Sights, Vent Rib, Modern	95	155
Contender, Various Calibers, Adjustable Sights, Heavy Barrel, Modern	95	150
Contender, Various Calibers, Heavy Barrel, no Sights, Modern	95	140

Rifle, Flintlock

.45 Hawken, Set Trigger, Octagon Barrel, with Accessories, Reproduction, Antique	150	190
.45 Hawken, Set Trigger, Octagon Barrel, Reproduction, Antique	135	170
.50 Hawken, Set Trigger, Octagon Barrel, with Accessories, Reproduction, Antique	150	190
.50 Hawken, Set Trigger, Octagon Barrel, Reproduction, Antique	135	170

Handgun, Percussion

.45 Patriot, Set Trigger, Octagon Barrel, Reproduction, Antique	55	80
.45 Patriot, Set Trigger, Octagon Barrel, with Accessories, Reproduction, Antique	70	100

Rifle, Percussion

.36 Seneca, Set Trigger, Octagon Barrel, with Accessories, Reproduction, Antique	145	180
.36 Seneca, Set Trigger, Octagon Barrel, Reproduction, Antique	130	160
.45 Hawken, Set Trigger, Octagon Barrel, with Accessories, Reproduction, Antique	145	180
.45 Hawken, Set Trigger, Octagon Barrel, Reproduction, Antique	130	160
.45 Seneca, Set Trigger, Octagon Barrel, with Accessories, Reproduction, Antique	145	180
.45 Seneca, Set Trigger, Octagon Barrel, Reproduction, Antique	130	160

Thompson/Center Arms .45 Patriot
Courtesy of Thompson/Center

Thompson/Center Arms Contender
Courtesy of Thompson/Center

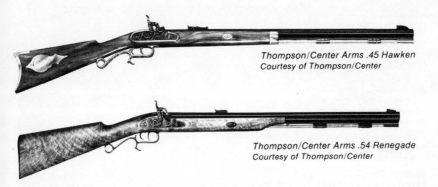

Thompson/Center Arms .45 Hawken
Courtesy of Thompson/Center

Thompson/Center Arms .54 Renegade
Courtesy of Thompson/Center

.50 Hawken, Set Trigger, Octagon Barrel, with Accessories, Reproduction,
  Antique   145   180
.50 Hawken, Set Trigger, Octagon Barrel, Reproduction, Antique   130   160
.54 Renegade, Set Trigger, Octagon Barrel, with Accessories,
  Reproduction, Antique   90   125
.54 Renegade, Set Trigger, Octagon Barrel, Reproduction, Antique   75   110

Three-Barrel Gun Co.
Moundsville, W.Va., 1906-08. Also at Wheeling, W.Va. as Royal Gun Co. and as Hollenbeck Gun Co.

Combination Weapon, Drilling
Various Calibers, Damascus Barrel, Antique   600   895

Thunder
Spain, M. Bascaran, made for Alberdi, Teleria y Cia 1912-19

Handgun, Semi-Automatic
M 1919, .25 ACP, Clip Fed, Modern   70   110

Tiger
Maker unknown C.1880

Handgun, Revolver
#2, .32 Short R.F., 5 Shot, Spur Trigger, Solid Frame, Single Action,
  Antique   90   160

Tiger
Made by Crescent for J. H. Hill Co. Nashville, Tenn. C.1900

Shotgun, Double Barrel, Side by Side
Various Gauges, Outside Hammers, Damascus Barrel, Modern   80   150

Thunder Model 1919 .25 ACP

Various Gauges, Outside Hammers, Steel Barrel, Modern	90	175
Shotgun, Singleshot		
Various Gauges, Hammer, Steel Barrel, Modern	45	75

Tindall & Dutton
Shelbyville, Ind. Modern

Tingle Mfg. Co.

Handgun, Percussion

Model 1960 Target, Octagon Barrel, Rifled, Reproduction, Antique	80	120

Rifle, Percussion

Model 1962 Target, Octagon Barrel, Brass Furniture, Rifled, Reproduction, Antique	125	185

Shotgun, Percussion

Model 1960, 10 or 12 Gauges, Vent Rib, Double Barrel, Over-Under, Reproduction, Antique	140	200

Titan
Italy

Handgun, Semi-Automatic

Vest Pocket (Italy), .25 ACP, Clip Fed, Hammer, Modern	25	40

Titanic
Spain, made by Retoloza Hermanos C.1900

Handgun, Semi-Automatic

M 1914, .32 ACP, Clip Fed, Modern	60	90

Tower's Police Safety
Made by Hopkins & Allen Norwich, Conn. C.1875

Handgun, Revolver

.38 Short R.F., 5 Shot, Spur Trigger, Solid Frame, Single Action, Antique	95	170

Tradewinds, Inc.
Tacoma, Wash. Importers. Also see HVA

Rifle, Bolt Action

Husky (Early), Various Calibers, Checkered Stock, Monte Carlo Stock, Modern	200	300
Husky M-5000, Various Calibers, Checkered Stock, Clip Fed, Modern	115	175
Husqvarna, Various Calibers, Checkered Stock, Monte Carlo Stock, Lightweight, Modern	275	400
Husqvarna, Various Calibers, Checkered Stock, Monte Carlo Stock, Lightweight, Full-Stocked, Modern	300	425
Husqvarna Crown Grade, Various Calibers, Checkered Stock, Monte Carlo Stock, Modern	300	450
Husqvarna Imperial, Various Calibers, Checkered Stock, Monte Carlo Stock, Lightweight, Modern	275	400
Husqvarna Imperial Custom, Various Calibers, Checkered Stock, Monte Carlo Stock, Modern	275	400
Husqvarna Presentation, Various Calibers, Checkered Stock, Monte Carlo Stock, Modern	400	575
Model 1998, .222 Rem., no Sights, Heavy Barrel, Target Stock, Modern	240	350
Model 600K, Various Calibers, Clip Fed, no Sights, Heavy Barrel, Set Trigger, Modern	150	225
Model 600S, Various Calibers, Clip Fed, Heavy Barrel, Octagon Barrel, Modern	140	180

Rifle, Semi-Automatic
Model 260A, .22 L.R.R.F., 5 Shot Clip, Checkered Stock, Modern   75   120

Shotgun, Double Barrel, Over-Under
Gold Shadow Indy, 12 Ga., Field Grade, Engraved, Fancy Checkering,
   Automatic Ejector, Vent Rib, Modern   1,000   1,400
Gold Shadow Indy, 12 Ga., Skeet Grade, Engraved, Fancy Checkering,
   Automatic Ejector, Vent Rib, Modern   1,000   1,400
Gold Shadow Indy, 12 Ga., Trap Grade, Engraved, Fancy Checkering,
   Automatic Ejector, Vent Rib, Modern   1,000   1,400
Shadow Indy, 12 Ga., Field Grade, Automatic Ejector, Vent Rib,
   Checkered Stock, Modern   325   425
Shadow Indy, 12 Ga., Skeet Grade, Automatic Ejector, Vent Rib,
   Checkered Stock, Modern   325   425
Shadow Indy, 12 Ga., Trap Grade, Automatic Ejector, Vent Rib,
   Checkered Stock, Modern   325   425
Shadow-7, 12 Ga., Field Grade, Automatic Ejector, Vent Rib, Modern   200   300
Shadow-7, 12 Ga., Skeet Grade, Automatic Ejector, Vent Rib, Modern   200   300
Shadow-7, 12 Ga., Trap Grade, Automatic Ejector, Vent Rib, Modern   200   300

Shotgun, Double Barrel, Side by Side
Model G-1032, 10 Ga. 3½", Checkered Stock, Modern   125   160
Model G-1228, 12 Ga. Mag. 3", Checkered Stock, Modern   110   140
Model G-2028, 20 Ga. Mag., Checkered Stock, Modern   110   140
Shotgun, Semi-Automatic
Model D-200, 12 Ga., Field Grade, Vent Rib, Engraved, Modern   145   180
Model H-150, 12 Ga., Field Grade, Modern   115   140
Model H-170, 12 Ga., Field Grade, Vent Rib, Modern   125   160
Model T-220, 12 Ga., Trap Grade, Vent Rib, Engraved, Modern   145   180

Shotgun, Singleshot
Model M50, 10 Ga., 3½" Barrel, Checkered Stock, Modern   75   100

Tramps Terror
Made by Hoods Firearms Co. Norwich, Conn. C.1870

Handgun, Revolver
.22 Short R.F., 7 Shot, Spur Trigger, Solid Frame, Single Action, Antique   90   160

Triumph
Made by Stevens Arms

Shotgun, Double Barrel, Side by Side
Model 311, Various Gauges, Hammerless, Steel Barrel, Modern   95   145

True Blue
Made by Norwich Falls Pistols Co. C.1880

Handgun, Revolver
.32 Short R.F., 5 Shot, Spur Trigger, Solid Frame, Single Action, Antique   90   165

Trust

Handgun, Semi-Automatic
.25 ACP, Clip Fed, Modern   80   110

Trust .25 ACP

Turner
Dublin, C.1820

Handgun, Flintlock

.62, Double Barrel, Pocket Pistol, Platinum Furniture, Plain, Antique	850	1,200

Turner & Ross
Made by Hood Firearms, Norwich, Conn. C.1875

Handgun, Revolver

.22 Short R.F., 7 Shot, Spur Trigger, Solid Frame, Single Action, Antique	90	160

Twigg
London, England 1760-1813

Handgun, Flintlock

.58, Pair, Belt Pistol, Flared, Octagon Barrel, Cased with Accessories, Plain, Antique	2,500	3,200

Tycoon
Made by Johnson-Bye, Worcester, Mass. 1873-87

Handgun, Revolver

#1, .22 Short R.F., 7 Shot, Spur Trigger, Solid Frame, Single Action, Antique	90	160
#2, .32 Short R.F., 5 Shot, Spur Trigger, Solid Frame, Single Action, Antique	145	190
#3, .38 Short R.F., 5 Shot, Spur Trigger, Solid Frame, Single Action, Antique	95	160
#4, .41 Short R.F., 5 Shot, Spur Trigger, Solid Frame, Single Action, Antique	105	140
#5, .44 Short R.F., 5 Shot, Spur Trigger, Solid Frame, Single Action, Antique	150	225

U.M.C. Arms Co.
Probably Norwich Arms Co. C.1880

Handgun, Revolver

.32 Short R.F., 5 Shot, Spur Trigger, Solid Frame, Single Action, Antique	90	160

Union
Fab. Francaise

Handgun, Semi-Automatic

.32 ACP, Ruby Style, Clip Fed, Modern	100	150
.32 ACP, Ruby Style, with Horseshoe Magazine, Modern	600	850

Union
France, M. Seytres

Handgun, Semi-Automatic

.25 ACP, Clip Fed, Long Grip, Modern	75	120
.32 ACP, Clip Fed, Long Grip, Modern	75	120

Union Firearms Co.
Toledo, Ohio

Handgun, Semi-Automatic, Revolver

Lefever Patent, .32 S & W, 5 Shot, Top Break, Modern	450	800
Reifgraber Patent, .32 S & W, 8 Shot, Modern	500	800

Union .25 ACP (Fab. Francaise)

Union Jack
Made by Hood Firearms Norwich, Conn. 1880

Handgun, Revolver

.22 Short R.F., 7 Shot, Spur Trigger, Solid Frame, Single Action, Antique	90	160
.32 Short R.F., 5 Shot, Spur Trigger, Solid Frame, Single Action, Antique	95	170

Union Revolver
Maker Unknown C.1880

Handgun, Revolver

.22 Short R.F., 7 Shot, Spur Trigger, Solid Frame, Single Action, Antique	90	160
.32 Short R.F., 5 Shot, Spur Trigger, Solid Frame, Single Action, Antique	95	170

Unique
Made by C. S. Shattuck C.1880

Handgun, Revolver

.32 Short R.F., 5 Shot, Spur Trigger, Solid Frame, Single Action, Antique	95	190
.38 Short R.F., 5 Shot, Spur Trigger, Solid Frame, Single Action, Antique	95	190

Handgun, Repeater

Shattuck Palm Pistol, Various Calibers, 4 Shot, Curio	300	500

Unique
France, 1923 to Date

Handgun, Semi-Automatic

Kriegsmodell, .32 ACP, Clip Fed, Magazine Disconnect, 9 Shot, Nazi-Proofed, Hammer, Curio	150	200
Model 10, .25 ACP, Clip Fed, Magazine Disconnect, Modern	60	95
Model 11, .25 ACP, Clip Fed, Magazine Disconnect, Grip Safety, Cartridge Indicator, Modern	110	150
Model 12, .25 ACP, Clip Fed, Magazine Disconnect, Grip Safety, Modern	80	115
Model 13, .25 ACP, Clip Fed, Magazine Disconnect, Grip Safety, 7 Shot, Modern	80	120
Model 14, .25 ACP, Clip Fed, Magazine Disconnect, Grip Safety, 9 Shot, Modern	85	125
Model 15, .32 ACP, Clip Fed, Magazine Disconnect, 6 Shot, Modern	75	115
Model 16, .32 ACP, Clip Fed, Magazine Disconnect, 7 Shot, Modern	75	115
Model 17, .32 ACP, Clip Fed, Magazine Disconnect, 9 Shot, Nazi-Proofed, Curio	135	185
Model 17, .32 ACP, Clip Fed, Magazine Disconnect, 9 Shot, Modern	80	120
Model 18, .32 ACP, Clip Fed, Magazine Disconnect, 6 Shot, Modern	80	120
Model 19, .32 ACP, Clip Fed, Magazine Disconnect, 7 Shot, Modern	75	115
Model 20, .32 ACP, Clip Fed, Magazine Disconnect, 9 Shot, Modern	95	135
Model 21, .380 ACP, Clip Fed, Magazine Disconnect, 6 Shot, Modern	95	135
Model 52, .22 L.R.R.F., Clip Fed, Hammer, Various Barrel Lengths, Modern	65	95

Model C, .32 ACP, Clip Fed, 9 Shot, Hammer, Modern	65	95
Model D-1, .22 L.R.R.F., Clip Fed, Hammer, 3" Barrel, Modern	65	90
Model D-2, .22 L.R.R.F., Clip Fed, Hammer, Adjustable Sights, 4" Barrel, Modern	85	120
Model D-3, .22 L.R.R.F., Clip Fed, Hammer, Adjustable Sights, 8" Barrel, Modern	85	125
Model D-4, .22 L.R.R.F., Clip Fed, Hammer, Muzzle Brake, Adjustable Sights, 9½" Barrel, Modern	90	150
Model E-1, .22 Short R.F., Clip Fed, Hammer, 3" Barrel, Modern	55	75
Model E-2, .22 Short R.F., Clip Fed, Hammer, Adjustable Sights, 4" Barrel, Modern	75	100
Model E-3, .22 Short R.F., Clip Fed, Hammer, Adjustable Sights, 8" Barrel, Modern	80	110
Model E-4, .22 Short R.F., Clip Fed, Hammer, Muzzle Brake, Adjustable Sights, 9½" Barrel, Modern	90	140
Model F, .380 ACP, Clip Fed, 8 Shot, Hammer, Modern	70	110
Model L (Corsair), .22 L.R.R.F., Clip Fed, Hammer, Lightweight, Modern	65	110
Model L (Corsair), .22 L.R.R.F., Clip Fed, Hammer, Modern	70	110
Model L (Corsair), .32 ACP, Clip Fed, Hammer, Lightweight, Modern	70	110
Model L (Corsair), .32 ACP, Clip Fed, Hammer, Modern	70	110
Model L (Corsair), .380 ACP, Clip Fed, Hammer, Lightweight, Modern	80	125
Model L (Corsair), .380 ACP, Clip Fed, Hammer, Modern	80	120
Model RD (Ranger), .22 L.R.R.F., Clip Fed, Hammer, Modern	40	60
Model RD (Ranger), .22 L.R.R.F., Clip Fed, Muzzle Brake, Hammer, Modern	55	80
Model DES/69, .22 L.R.R.F., Clip Fed, Target Pistol, Modern	225	325
Model DES/VO, .22 L.R.R.F., Clip Fed, Rapid Fire Target Pistol, Modern	250	350
Model DES/VO 79, .22 L.R.R.F., Clip Fed, Rapid Fire Target Pistol, Gas Ports, Modern	275	400

United States Arms
Riverhead, N.Y. Current

Handgun, Revolver

Abilene, .44 Magnum, Single Action, Western Style, Adjustable Sights, Modern	110	150
Abilene, .44 Magnum, Stainless Steel, Single Action, Western Style, Adjustable Sights, Modern	145	200
Abilene, Various Calibers, Single Action, Western Style, Adjustable Sights, Modern	95	135
Abilene, Various Calibers, Single Action, Western Style, Adjustable Sights, Stainless Steel, Modern	110	165

Universal
Made by Hopkins & Allen, Norwich, Conn. C.1890

Handgun, Revolver

.32 S & W, 5 Shot, Double Action, Solid Frame, Modern	45	75

Universal
Hialeah, Fla. Current

Handgun, Semi-Automatic

Model 3000 Enforcer, .30 Carbine, Clip Fed, Modern	110	150
Model 3005 Enforcer, .30 Carbine, Clip Fed, Nickel Plated, Modern	135	165
Model 3010 Enforcer, .30 Carbine, Clip Fed, Gold Plated, Modern	140	170

Rifle, Semi-Automatic

Model 1001, .30 Carbine, Carbine, Clip Fed, Modern	80	110
Model 1002, .30 Carbine, Carbine, Clip Fed, Bayonet Lug, Modern	85	115
Model 1003, .30 Carbine, Carbine, Clip Fed, Walnut Stock, Modern	80	110
Model 1004, .30 Carbine, Carbine, Clip Fed, Scope Mounted, Modern	90	120
Model 1010, .30 Carbine, Carbine, Clip Fed, Nickel Plated, Modern	110	150

Model 1011 Deluxe, .30 Carbine, Carbine, Clip Fed, Nickel Plated, Monte
Carbine Stock, Modern   115   160
Model 1015, .30 Carbine, Carbine, Clip Fed, Gold Plated, Modern   115   160
Model 1016 Deluxe, .30 Carbine, Carbine, Clip Fed, Gold Plated, Monte
Carlo Stock, Modern   130   170
Model 1025 Ferret, .256 Win. Mag., Carbine, Clip Fed, Sporting Rifle,
Modern   95   130
Model 1025 Ferret, .30 Carbine, Carbine, Clip Fed, Sporting Rifle, Modern   100   135
Model 1941 Field Commander, .30 Carbine, Carbine, Clip Fed, Fancy
Wood, Modern   100   140

Rifle, Slide Action
Vulcan 440, .44 Magnum, Clip Fed, Sporting Rifle, Open Rear Sight,
Modern   115   150

Shotgun, Double Barrel, Over-Under
Baikal 1J-27, 12 Ga., Double Trigger, Vent Rib, Engraved, Checkered
Stock, Modern   150   200
Baikal 1J-27, 12 Ga., Double Trigger, Vent Rib, Engraved, Checkered
Stock, Automatic Ejector, Modern   160   220
Baikal MC-5, 20 Ga., Double Trigger, Engraved, Checkered Stock, Solid
Rib, Modern   300   400
Baikal MC-6, 20 Ga., Skeet Grade, Extra Shotgun Barrel, Single Trigger,
Engraved, Checkered Stock, Modern   450   650
Baikal MC-7, 12 and 20 Gauges, Single Selective Trigger, Solid Rib, Fancy
Engraving, Fancy Checkering, Selective Ejector, Modern   900   1,300
Baikal MC-8, 12 Ga., Double Trigger, Monte Carlo Stock, Checkered
Stock, Modern   400   600
Model 7312, 12 Ga., Trap Grade, Vent Rib, Engraved, Checkered Stock,
Monte Carlo Stock, Modern   700   900
Model 7312, 12 Ga., Skeet Grade, Vent Rib, Engraved, Checkered Stock,
Monte Carlo Stock, Modern   700   900
Model 7412, 12 Ga., Trap Grade, Vent Rib, Fancy Engraving, Checkered
Stock, Single Selective Trigger, Modern   600   800
Model 7412, 12 Ga., Skeet Grade, Vent Rib, Fancy Engraving, Checkered
Stock, Single Selective Trigger, Modern   600   800

Universal Model 3000 Enforcer

Universal Model 7312

Universal Model 1004

Universal Model 7712

Universal Model 7112

Universal Model TOZ 66/54

Universal Model 7512

Model 7712, 12 Ga. Mag. 3″, Recoil Pad, Checkered Stock, Single Trigger,
    Vent Rib, Modern   175   225
Model 7812, 12 Ga. Mag. 3″, Automatic Ejector, Recoil Pad, Checkered
    Stock, Single Trigger, Vent Rib, Modern   275   350
Model 7912, 12 Ga. Mag. 3″, Automatic Ejector, Engraved, Checkered
    Stock, Single Trigger, Vent Rib, Modern   500   650
Over-Wing, 12 and 20 Gauges, Field Grade, Vent Rib, Double Trigger,
    Checkered Stock, Magnum, Modern   135   185

Shotgun, Double Barrel, Side by Side
Model 2030, 10 Ga., 3½″, Field Grade, Hammerless, Light Engraving,
    Checkered Stock, Modern   140   175
Model 7112, 12 Ga., Field Grade, Hammerless, Light Engraving,
    Checkered Stock, Modern   115   150
Model IJ58M, 12 Ga., Hammerless, Recoil Pad, Checkered Stock, Modern   95   130
Model TOZ 66/54, 12 Ga., Outside Hammers, Checkered Stock, Modern   85   120
Model TOZ67, 12 Ga., Outside Hammers, Riot Gun, Nickel Plated, Gold
    Plated, Modern   135   175

Shotgun, Semi-Automatic
Model 7512, 12 Ga., Checkered Stock, Vent Rib, Modern   155   200
Model 7512, 12 Ga. Mag. 3″, Checkered Stock, Vent Rib, Modern   165   210
Model 7512, 12 Ga. Mag. 3″, Checkered Stock, Monte Carlo Stock, Vent
    Rib, Modern   165   210

Shotgun, Singleshot
Model 7212, 12 Ga., Trap Grade, Vent Rib, Engraved, Checkered Stock,
    Monte Carlo Stock, Modern   475   600
Model IJ18, 12 Ga., Hammerless, Modern   30   40

Unwin & Rogers
Yorkshire, England 1850

Handgun, Percussion
Knife Pistol with Ramrod and Mould, Cased with Accessories, Antique   750   1,000

U.S. Arms Co.
Brooklyn, N.Y. 1874-78

Handgun, Revolver

.22 Short R.F., 7 Shot, Spur Trigger, Solid Frame, Single Action, Antique	90	160
.32 Short R.F., 5 Shot, Spur Trigger, Solid Frame, Single Action, Antique	95	170
.38 Short R.F., 5 Shot, Spur Trigger, Solid Frame, Single Action, Antique	95	170
.41 Short R.F., 5 Shot, Spur Trigger, Solid Frame, Single Action, Antique	120	195

U.S. Arms Co.
Made by Crescent for H & D Folsom C.1900

Shotgun, Double Barrel, Side by Side

Various Gauges, Outside Hammers, Damascus Barrel, Modern	80	150
Various Gauges, Hammerless, Steel Barrel, Modern	95	175
Various Gauges, Hammerless, Damascus Barrel, Modern	75	150
Various Gauges, Outside Hammers, Steel Barrel, Modern	90	175

Shotgun, Singleshot
Various Gauges, Hammer, Steel Barrel, Modern   45   75

U.S. Military

Automatic Weapon, Assault Rifle

AR-15, .223 Rem., Clip Fed, Early Model, Class 3	600	850
M-1 Garand (Win), .30-06 Springfield, Clip Fed, Experimental, Class 3		5,000+
M14, .308 Win., Clip Fed, Wood Stock, Class 3	1,000	1,400
M16, .223 Rem., Clip Fed, Military, Class 3	600	800
M16-M A C, .22 L.R.R.F., Clip Fed, Conversion Unit Only, Class 3	65	100
M16A1, .223 Rem., Clip Fed, Military, Class 3	650	875
M1918 Bar (Winchester), .30-06 Springfield, Clip Fed, Bipod, Modern, Class 3	1,000	1,400
M63 Stoner, .308 Win., Clip Fed, Military, Class 3	1,500	2,000
T-48, .308 Win., Clip Fed, Military, Class 3	2,200	2,750

Automatic Weapon, Heavy Machine Gun

M1906 Colt, .30-06 Springfield, Belt Fed, Tripod, Potato Digger, Military, Class 3	1,200	1,600
M1906 Marlin, .30-06 Springfield, Belt Fed, Tripod, Potato Digger, Military, Class 3	1,200	1,600
M1906 Marlin, .308 Win., Belt Fed, Tripot, Potato Digger, Military, Class 3	1,100	1,500
M1917, .30-06 Springfield, Belt Fed, Tripod, Class 3	5,750	6,500
M1917 Marlin, .30-06 Springfield, Belt Fed, Tripod, Potato Digger, Military, Class 3	1,200	1,600
M1917A1, .30-06 Springfield, Belt Fed, Tripod, Class 3	3,200	4,000
M2 Browning, .50 Bmg, Belt Fed, Heavy Barrel, Military, Class 3	1,600	2,000
M2 Browning (Sav), .50 Bmg, Belt Fed, Tripod, Class 3	2,900	3,500

U.S. Arms Co. .41 Bulldog

Automatic Weapon, Light Machine Gun

Benet-Mercie U. S. N. 1912, .30-06 Springfield, Clip Fed, Dewat, Class 3	2,000	2,500
M1919A6, .30-06 Springfield, Belt Fed, Wood Stock, Bipod, Class 3	800	1,100
M1941 Johnson, .30-06 Springfield, Clip Fed, Military, Bipod, Class 3	1,200	1,600
M1944 Johnson, .30-06 Springfield, Belt Fed, Monopod, Class 3	2,400	2,700
M1946 Johnson, .30-06 Springfield, Belt Fed, Class 3	2,400	3,000
M60, .308 Win., Belt Fed, Bipod, Class 3	2,500	3,000

Automatic Weapon, Submachine Gun

M-180, .22 L.R.R.F., 177 Round Drum Magazine, Class 3	200	275
M-2 (Win), .30 Carbine, Clip Fed, Military, Class 3	375	500
M-3, .45 ACP, Clip Fed, Military, Class 3	375	500
M1 Thompson, .45 ACP, Clip Fed, with Compensator, Military, Plain Barrel, Class 3	600	900
M1A1 Thompson, .45 ACP, Clip Fed, with Compensator, Military, Plain Barrel, Class 3	550	850
M2, .30 Carbine, Clip Fed, Military, Carbine, Class 3	300	400
M3, 9mm Luger, Clip Fed, Military, Class 3	450	600
M3 Grease Gun, .45 ACP, Clip Fed, Military, Silencer, Class 3	700	900
M3A1 Grease Gun, .45 ACP, Clip Fed, Military, Flash Hider, Class 3	550	750
M50 Reising, .45 ACP, Clip Fed, Wood Stock, Military, Class 3	140	200
M50 Reising, .45 ACP, Clip Fed, Wood Stock, Military, Cased with Accessories, Class 3	225	300
M55 Reising, .45 ACP, Clip Fed, Folding Stock, Military, Class 3	225	300
XM177E2, .223 Rem., Clip Fed, Folding Stock, Silencer, Short Rifle, Military, Class 3	900	1,400

Handgun, Flintlock

.54 M1805 (06), Singleshot, Smoothbore, Brass Mounts, Antique, Dated 1806	1,200	1,800
.54 M1805 (06), Singleshot, Smoothbore, Brass Mounts, Antique, Dated 1807	1,000	1,350
.54 M1805 (06), Singleshot, Smoothbore, Brass Mounts, Antique, Dated 1808	1,150	1,550
.54 M1807-8, Singleshot, Smoothbore, Brass Mounts, Various Contractors, Antique	2,300	2,900
.54 M1816, Singleshot, Smoothbore, S North Army, Brass Furniture, Antique	400	625
.54 M1819, Singleshot, Smoothbore, S North Army, Iron Mounts, Antique	575	875
.54 M1826, Singleshot, Smoothbore, S North Army, Iron Mounts, Antique	700	1,000
.54 M1836, Singleshot, Smoothbore, R Johnson Army, Iron Mounts, Antique	550	725
.64 M1808, Singleshot, Smoothbore, S North Army, Brass Furniture, Antique	1,200	1,600
.69 M1799, Singleshot, North & Cheney, Brass Furniture, Brass Frame, Antique	10,000	14,000
.69 M1811, Singleshot, Smoothbore, S North Army, Brass Furniture, Antique	1,250	1,800
.69 M1817 (18), Singleshot, Smoothbore, Springfield, Iron Mounts, Antique	1,500	2,000

Handgun, Percussion

.54 M1836, Singleshot, Smoothbore, Gedney Conversion from Flintlock, Iron Mounts, Antique	625	875
.54 M1842 Aston, Singleshot, Smoothbore, Brass Mounts, Antique	325	450
.54 M1842 Johnson, Singleshot, Smoothbore, Brass Mounts, Antique	325	450
.54 M1843 Deringer Army, Singleshot, Smoothbore, Brass Mounts, Antique	525	675
.54 M1843 Deringer Army, Singleshot, Rifled, Brass Mounts, Antique	650	900
.54 M1843 Deringer Navy, Singleshot, Smoothbore, Brass Mounts, Antique	600	800
.54 M1843 N P Ames, Singleshot, Smoothbore, Brass Mounts, Antique	525	675
.58 M1855 Springfield, Singleshot, Rifled, Brass Mounts, with Shoulder Stock, Antique	525	675
.58 M1855 Springfield, Singleshot, Rifled, Brass Mounts, Antique	1,300	1,700

U.S. Military Colt Model 1903 Pocket .32 ACP

Handgun, Revolver

M1889 Navy Colt, .39 Long Colt, 6 Shot, 6" Barrel, Double Action, Swing-Out Cylinder, Antique	175	350
M1892 New Army Colt, .38 Long Colt, 6 Shot, 6" Barrel, Double Action, Swing-Out Cylinder, Antique	175	275
M1892 New Navy Colt, .38 Long Colt, 6 Shot, 6" Barrel, Double Action, Swing-Out Cylinder, Antique	175	250
M1896 New Army Colt, .38 Long Colt, 6 Shot, 6" Barrel, Double Action, Swing-Out Cylinder, Antique	150	225
M1902 Army Colt, .45 Colt, 6 Shot, 6" Barrel, Double Action, Modern	350	500
M1905 U.S.M.C. Colt, .38 Long Colt, 6 Shot, 6" Barrel, Double Action, Swing-Out Cylinder, Modern	650	950
M1905 U.S.M.C. Colt, .38 Special, 6 Shot, 6" Barrel, Double Action, Swing-Out Cylinder, Modern	600	900
M1909 Army Colt, .45 Colt, 6 Shot 5½" Barrel, Double Action, Modern	200	375
M1909 U.S.M.C. Colt, .45 Colt, 6 Shot, 5½" Barrel, Double Action, Modern	400	675
M1909 U.S.N. Colt, .45 Colt, 6 Shot 5½" Barrel, Double Action, Modern	300	475
M1917 Army Colt, .45 Auto-Rim, 6 Shot, 5½" Barrel, Double Action, Modern	200	350
M1917 S & W, .45 Auto-Rim, Double Action, Swing-Out Cylinder, Modern	225	350

Handgun, Semi-Automatic

Hi Standard H-D M/O.S.S., .22 L.R.R.F., Clip Fed, Silencer, Hammer, Class 3	375	550
M1900 Colt, .38 ACP, Clip Fed, 6" Barrel, Military, Curio	500	850
M1902 Colt, .38 ACP, Clip Fed, 6" Barrel, Military, Curio	375	550
M1903 Colt, .32 ACP, Clip Fed, Modern, Curio	300	450
M1903 Colt, .380 ACP, Clip Fed, Modern, Curio	300	450
M1905/07 Colt, .45 Colt, Clip Fed, Blue, Military, Modern	1,300	1,800
M1908 Colt, .32 ACP, Clip Fed, Military, Curio	300	450
M1908 Colt, .32 ACP, Clip Fed, Military, Magazine Disconnect, Curio	275	400
M1908 Colt, .380 ACP, Clip Fed, Military, Curio	300	450
M1908 Colt, .380 ACP, Clip Fed, Military, Magazine Disconnect, Curio	275	400
M1911, .45 ACP, Clip Fed, Modern	200	275
M1911, Springfield, .45 ACP, Clip Fed, Modern	375	600
M1911A1, .45 ACP, Clip Fed, Modern	175	275
M1911A1 Ithaca, .45 ACP, Clip Fed, Modern	200	300
M1911A Remington, .45 ACP, Clip Fed, Modern	200	300
M1911A1 Singer, .45 ACP, Clip Fed, Modern	1,750	2,500
M1911A1 U.S. & S., .45 ACP, Clip Fed, Modern	225	350

Handgun, Singleshot

Liberator, .45 ACP, Military, Curio	150	225
Liberator, .45 ACP, Silencer, Militaary, Class 3	300	375

Rifle, Bolt Action

M1892 Krag, .30-40 Krag, Antique	200	325
M1895 Lee Straight Pull, 6mm Lee Navy, Musket, Antique	550	700
M1896 Krag, .30-40 Krag, Antique	200	350
M1896 Krag, .30-40 Krag, Carbine, Antique	325	500
M1898 Krag, .30-40 Krag, Carbine, Modern	450	700

U.S. Military Model 1819 Hall

M1898 Krag, .30-40 Krag, Modern	150	300
M1899 Krag, .30-40 Krag, Carbine, Modern	150	225
M1903, .30-06 Springfield, Machined Parts, Modern	200	325
M1903A1, .30-06 Springfield, Parkerized, Checkered Butt, Machined Parts, Modern	120	200
M1903A1 National Match, .30-06 Springfield, Target Rifle, Modern	300	575
M1903A3, .30-06 Springfield, Stamped Parts, Modern	120	175
M1903A4 Sniper, .30-06 Springfield, Scope Mounts, Modern	450	800
M1917 Eddystone, .30-06 Springfield, Modern	110	175
M1917 Remington, .30-06 Springfield, Modern	115	180
M1917 Winchester, .30-06 Springfield, Modern	120	200
M1922 Trainer, .22 L.R.R.F., Target Rifle, Modern	450	750
M1922M2 Trainer, .22 L.R.R.F., Target Rifle, Modern	350	500
M40-XB Sniper (Rem.), .308 Win., Heavy Barrel, Scope Mounted, Silencer, Class 3	500	700

Rifle, Flintlock

.52, M1819 Hall, Rifled, Breech Loader, 32½" Barrel, 3 Bands, Antique	1,400	2,200
.52, M1819 Hall Whitney, Rifled, Breech Loader, 32½" Barrel, 3 Bands, Antique	1,200	2,000
.54, M1803 Harper's Ferry, Rifled, 32½" Barrel, Antique	1,000	1,800
.54, M1807 Springfield, Indian, Carbine, 27¾" Barrel, Antique	1,200	2,000
.54, M1814 Ghriskey, Rifled, 36" Barrel, Antique	1,200	2,200
.54, M1814 Harper's Ferry, Rifled, 36" Barrel, Antique	700	1,300
.54, M1817 (Common Rifle), Rifled, 36" Barrel, 3 Bands, Antique	1,000	1,800
.54, M1839 Springfield, Cadet Musket, 40½" or 36" Barrel, 3 Bands, Antique	900	1,800
.64, M1837 Hall, Carbine, 23" Barrel, 2 Bands, Antique	850	1,600
.64, M1837 Jenks, Musketoon, 25⅝" or 19½" Barrel, 2 Bands, Antique	850	1,500
.69, M1795 Penn. Contract, Musket, 3 Bands, 44½" Barrel, Antique	800	1,500
.69, M1795 Springfield, Musket, 3 Bands, 44½" Barrel, Antique	800	1,500
.69, M1795 U.S. Contract, Musket, 3 Bands, 44½" Barrel, Antique	800	1,500
.69, M1795 Va. Contract, Musket, 3 Bands, 44½" Barrel, Antique	800	1,500
.69, M1795/98 Whitney, Musket, 3 Bands, 43" Barrel, Antique	1,000	1,600
.69, M1808 Harper's Ferry, Musket, 3 Bands, 44½" Barrel, Antique	600	1,000
.69, M1808 N.Y. Contract, Musket, 40" Barrel, 3 Bands, Antique	600	1,200
.69, M1808 Springfield, Musket, 3 Bands, 44½" Barrel, Antique	600	1,000
.69, M1808 U.S. Contract, Musket, 42" Barrel, 3 Bands, Antique	500	900
.69, M1812 Contract, Musket, 40" Barrel, 3 Bands, Antique	550	1,100
.69, M1812 Springfield, Musket, 42" Barrel, 3 Bands, Antique	650	1,200
.69, M1813 (Conversion), Short Musket, 32½" Barrel, 2 Bands, Antique	550	1,000
.69, M1816 Contract, Musket, 42" Barrel, 3 Bands, Antique	500	1,000
.69, M1816 State Militia, Musket, 42" Barrel, 3 Bands, Antique	400	900
.69, M1816 U.S. Musket, 42" Barrel, 3 Bands, Antique	350	850
.69, M1817 U.S., Cadet Musket, 36" Barrel, 3 Bands, Antique	500	1,000
.69, M1835 Contract, Adjustable, 42" Barrel, 3 Bands, Antique	800	1,700
.69, M1835 U.S., Musket, 42" Barrel, 3 Bands, Antique	800	1,700
.69, M1840 U.S., Musketoon, 26" Barrel, 2 Bands, Antique	950	1,700
M1808 Harper's Ferry, Blunderbuss, 27¾" Barrel, Antique	4,500	6,000

Rifle, Lever Action

Ball Repeating Carbine, .56-56 Spencer R.F., Tube Feed, Antique	650	900
Spencer, .56-50 Spencer R.F., Repeater, Carbine, 7 Shot, Falling Block, Antique	400	625

U.S. Military Spencer Carbine

Spencer, .56–52 Spencer R.F., Repeater, Carbine, 7 Shot, Falling Block,
  Antique   425   650
Spencer, .56–56 Spencer R.F., Repeater, 7 Shot, Falling Block, Antique 475   675
Spencer, .56–56 Spencer R.F., Repeater, Carbine, 7 Shot, Falling Block,
  Antique   425   625

Rifle, Percussion
.44, M1841 Colt, Revolver, Carbine, 8 Shot, Antique   5,000   7,500
.50 Gallagher, Breech Loader, Carbine, Military, Antique   400   575
.50 Joslyn, Breech Loader, Carbine, Antique   850   1,300
.50 Maynard, Breech Loader, Carbine, without Tape Priming System,
  Antique   475   650
.50 Maynard, Breech Loader, Carbine, Antique   525   775
.52 Smith, Breech Loader, Carbine, Antique   400   675
.52, M1838 Hall-North, Carbine, 21″ Barrel, 2 Bands, Antique   850   1,500
.52, M1840 Hall-North, Breech Loader, Carbine, 21″ Barrel, 2 Bands,
  Antique   750   1,400
.52, M1843 Hall-North, Breech Loader, 21″ Barrel, 2 Bands, Antique   650   1,350
.53 Greene, Breech Loader, Carbine, Antique   500   800
.54 Gibbs, Breech Loader, Carbine, Antique, Marked William F. Brooks
  · Mfg. Co.   650   950
.54 Greene, Breech Loader, Under-Hammer, Bolt Action, Antique   525   775
.54 Merrill, Breech Loader, Carbine, Antique   475   625
.54 Merrill Navy, Breech Loader, Brass Furniture, Antique   525   750
.54 Starr, Breech Loader, Carbine, Antique   475   625
.54, M1836 Hall-North, Rifled, Breech Loader, Carbine, 21″ Barrel, 2
  Bands, Antique   850   1,300
.54, M1839 Jenks, Breech Loader, Rifled, 35⅜″ Barrel, 3 Bands, Antique 800 1,400
.54, M1841 U.S., Rifled, 33″ Barrel, 2 Bands, Antique   600   850
.56 Sharps, Breech Loader, Carbine, Brass Furniture, Antique, U.S. 1852 650   900
.56 Sharps, Breech Loader, Carbine, Pellet Priming System, Brass
  Furniture, Adjustable Sights, Antique   550   775
.56 Sharps, Breech Loader, Carbine, with Tape Priming System, Brass
  Furniture, Antique   625   800
.57, M1841 U.S., Cadet Musket, 40″ Barrel, 2 Bands, Antique   600   950
.57, M1851 U.S., Cadet Musket, Rifled, 40″ Barrel, 2 Bands, Antique 650   1,000
.57, M1851 U.S., Cadet Musket, Smoothbore, 40″ Barrel, 2 Bands, Antique 600   900
.58 Lindner, Breech Loader, Carbine, Rising Block, Antique   575   950
.58, M1841 Contract, Rifled, 33″ Barrel, 2 Bands, Antique, (Mississippi
  Rifle)   500   850
.58, M1855 U.S., Rifled, 40″ Barrel, 3 Bands, with Tape Priming System,
  Antique   800   1,350

U.S. Military .50 Joslyn Carbine

U.S. Military Starr Carbine

.58, M1855 U.S., Carbine, Rifled, 22″ Barrel, 1 Band, with Tape Priming System, Antique	850	1,400
.64, M1833 Hall-North, Rifled, Breech Loader, Carbine, 26⅛″ Barrel, 2 Bands, Antique	700	1,200
.69, M1842 U.S., Musket, 42″ Barrel, 3 Bands, Antique	425	650
.69, M1842 U.S., Musket, 42″ Barrel, 3 Bands, Antique	450	700
.69, M1847 Artillery, Musketoon, 26″ Barrel, 2 Bands, Steel Furniture, Antique	550	850
.69, M1847 Cavalry, Musketoon, 26″ Barrel, 2 Bands, Brass Furniture, Antique	450	700
.69, M1847 Sappers, Musketoon, 26″ Barrel, 2 Bands, Bayonet Stud on Right Side, Antique	750	1,200
Burnside .54 Cal., Breech Loader, Carbine, 1st Model, Singleshot, Antique	850	1,650
Burnside, .54 Cal., Breech Loader, Carbine, 2nd Model, Singleshot, Antique	450	850
Burnside, .54 Cal., Breech Loader, Carbine, 3rd Model, Singleshot, Antique	375	575
Burnside, .54 Cal., Breech Loader, Carbine, 4th Model, Singleshot, Antique	375	550
Gwyn & Cambell, .50 Cal., Breech Loader, Carbine, Cosmopolitan, Antique	425	600
M 1864 Training Rifle, Military, Wood Barrel, Antique	60	95

Rifle, Semi-Automatic

M-1 Carbine, .30 Carbine, Clip Fed, Modern	100	150
M-1 Carbine Irwin-Pedersen, .30 Carbine, Clip Fed, Modern	325	450
M-1 Carbine Quality Hdw., .30 Carbine, Clip Fed, Modern	350	475

U.S. Revolver Co.
Made by Iver Johnson. Trade Name

Handgun, Revolver

.22 L.R.R.F., 7 Shot, Top Break, Double Action, Modern	55	90
.22 Short R.F., 7 Shot, Spur Trigger, Solid Frame, Single Action, Antique	90	150
.32 S & W, 5 Shot, Double Action, Solid Frame, Modern	45	80
.32 S & W, 5 Shot, Top Break, Hammerless, Double Action, Modern	55	95
.32 S & W, 5 Shot, Double Action, Top Break, Modern	45	95
.32 Short R.F., 5 Shot, Spur Trigger, Solid Frame, Single Action, Antique	90	160
.38 S & W, 5 Shot, Double Action, Solid Frame, Modern	45	70
.38 S & W, 5 Shot, Top Break, Hammerless, Double Action, Modern	55	95
.38 S & W, 5 Shot, Double Action, Top Break, Modern	45	95

Valiant
Made by Stevens Arms

Rifle, Bolt Action

Model 51, .22 L.R.R.F., Singleshot, Takedown, Modern	25	35

Valmet
Made in Finland, Imported by Interarms

Automatic Weapon, Assault Rifle

Model 718S, .223 Rem., Clip Fed, Commercial, Class 3	450	650

Rifle, Semi-Automatic
M-62S, 7.62 x 39 Russian, Clip Fed, AK-47 Type, Sporting Version of
   Military Rifle, Modern   250   350
M-72S, .223 Rem., Clip Fed, AK-47 Type, Sporting Version of Military
   Rifle, Modern   275   400

Valor Arms
Importers Miami, Fla.

Handgun, Revolver
.22 L.R.R.F., Double Action, Lightweight, Modern   8   15

Vanderfrift, Isaac and Jeremiah
Philadelphia, Pa. 1809-15. See Kentucky Rifles and Pistols

Vega
Pacific International

Handgun, Semi-Automatic
Vega 1911a1, .45 ACP, Stainless Steel, Clip Fed, Modern   175   250
Vega 1911a1, .45 ACP, Adjustable Sights, Stainless Steel, Clip Fed,
   Modern   190   270

Ventura Imports (Contento)
Seal Beach, Calif. Also see Bertuzzi and Piotti

Shotgun, Double Barrel, Over-Under
MK-1 Contento, 12 Ga., Field Grade, Automatic Ejector, Single Selective
   Trigger, Engraved, Checkered Stock, Modern   325   450
MK-2 Contento, 12 Ga., Field Grade, Automatic Ejector, Single Selective
   Trigger, Engraved, Checkered Stock, Modern   450   650
MK-2 Contento, 12 Ga., Trap Grade, with Extra Single Trap Barrel,
   Engraved, Checkered Stock, Modern   750   1,100
MK-2 Luxe Contento, 12 Ga., Field Grade, Automatic Ejector, Single
   Selective Trigger, Engraved, Checkered Stock, Modern   625   800
MK-2 Luxe Contento, 12 Ga., Trap Grade, with Extra Single Trap Barrel,
   Engraved, Checkered Stock, Modern   950   1,300
MK-3 Contento, 12 Ga., Field Grade, Automatic Ejector, Single Selective
   Trigger, Engraved, Checkered Stock, Modern   750   1,000
MK-3 Contento, 12 Ga., Trap Grade, with Extra Single Trap Barrel,
   Engraved, Checkered Stock, Modern   1,200   1,700
MK-3 Luxe Contento, 12 Ga., Field Grade, Automatic Ejector, Single
   Selective Trigger, Engraved, Checkered Stock, Modern   950   1,300
MK-3 Luxe Contento, 12 Ga., Trap Grade, with Extra Single Trap Barrel,
   Engraved, Checkered Stock, Modern   1,450   2,000
Nettuno Contento, 12 Ga., Field Grade, Automatic Ejector, Single
   Selective Trigger, Engraved, Checkered Stock, Modern   250   375

Ventura Imports Contento Mk.III
Courtesy of Ventura Imports

Shotgun, Double Barrel, Side by Side
Ventura Model 51, 12 and 20 Gauges, Boxlock, Checkered Stock, Modern 250 375
Ventura Model 62 Standard, 12 and 20 Gauges, Sidelock, Checkered
   Stock, Engraved, Modern 475 700
Ventura Model 64 Standard, 12 and 20 Gauges, Sidelock, Checkered
   Stock, Engraved, Modern 475 700

Venus
Spain, Made by Tomas de Urizar y Cia

Handgun, Semi-Automatic
.32 ACP, Clip Fed, Modern 65 95

Verney-Carron
St. Etienne, France

Shotgun, Double Barrel, Uver-Under
Field Grade, 12 Ga., Automatic Ejectors, Checkered Stock, Engraved,
   Modern 450 675

Vesta
Spain

Handgun, Semi-Automatic
Pocket, .32 ACP, Clip Fed, Long Grip, Modern 70 110
Vest Pocket, .25 ACP, Clip Fed, Modern 70 100

Veteran
Made by Norwich Falls Pistol Co. 1880

Handgun, Revolver
.32 Short R.F., 5 Shot, Spur Trigger, Solid Frame, Single Action, Antique 90 160

Veto
Unknown Maker C.1880

Handgun, Revolver
.32 Short R.F., 5 Shot, Spur Trigger, Solid Frame, Single Action, Antique 90 160

Vici

Handgun, Semi-Automatic
.25 ACP, Clip Fed, Modern 80 110

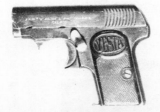

Vesta .25 ACP

Vici .25 ACP

Victor
Made by Crescent C.1900

Shotgun, Double Barrel, Side by Side
Various Gauges, Outside Hammers, Damascus Barrel, Modern	80	150
Various Gauges, Hammerless, Steel Barrel, Modern	95	175
Various Gauges, Hammerless, Damascus Barrel, Modern	75	150
Various Gauges, Outside Hammers, Steel Barrel, Modern	90	175

Shotgun, Singleshot
Various Gauges, Hammer, Steel Barrel, Modern	45	75

Victor Bernedo
Spain, C.1920

Handgun, Semi-Automatic
Pocket, .32 ACP, Clip Fed, Modern	90	140
Vest Pocket, .25 ACP, Clip Fed, Modern	80	130

Victor #1
Made by Harrington & Richardson 1876

Handgun, Revolver
.32 S & W, 5 Shot, Single Action, Solid Frame, Antique	55	95
#1, .22 Short R.F., 7 Shot, Spur Trigger, Solid Frame, Single Action, Antique	90	160
#2, .32 Short R.F., 5 Shot, Spur Trigger, Solid Frame, Single Action, Antique	90	160

Victor Special
Made by Crescent for Hibbard-Spencer-Bartlett Co. C.1900

Shotgun, Double Barrel, Side by Side
Various Gauges, Outside Hammers, Damascus Barrel, Modern	80	150
Various Gauges, Hammerless, Steel Barrel, Modern	95	175
Various Gauges, Hammerless, Damascus Barrel, Modern	75	150
Various Gauges, Outside Hammers, Steel Barrel, Modern	90	175

Shotgun, Singleshot
Various Gauges, Hammer, Steel Barrel, Modern	45	75

Victoria
Made by Hood Firearms C.1875

Handgun, Revolver
.32 Short R.F., 5 Shot, Spur Trigger, Solid Frame, Single Action, Antique   90   160

Victoria
Spain Esperanza y Unceta C.1900

Handgun, Semi-Automatic
M1911, .32 ACP, Clip Fed, Modern   70   110

.25 ACP, Clip Fed, Modern   80   110

Victory

Handgun, Semi-Automatic
.25 ACP, Clip Fed, Modern   80   110

Vilar
Spain, Unknown Maker 1920-38

Handgun, Semi-Automatic
Pocket, .32 ACP, Clip Fed, Long Grip, Modern   70   100

Virginia Arms Co.
Made by Crescent for Virginia-Caroline Co. C.1900

Shotgun, Double Barrel, Side by Side
Various Gauges, Outside Hammers, Damascus Barrel, Modern   80   150
Various Gauges, Hammerless, Steel Barrel, Modern   95   175
Various Gauges, Hammerless, Damascus Barrel, Modern   75   150
Various Gauges, Outside Hammers, Steel Barrel, Modern   90   175

Shotgun, Singleshot
Various Gauges, Hammer, Steel Barrel, Modern   45   75

Voere

Combination Weapon, Double Barrel, Over-Under
Various Calibers, Single Trigger, Checkered Stock, Cheekpiece, Sling
  Swivels, Modern   175   300

Victoria .25 ACP

Victory .25 ACP

Rifle, Bolt Action
Premier Mauser, Various Calibers, Sporting Rifle, Checkered Stock,
   Recoil Pad, Open Rear Sight, Modern   145   195
Shikar, Various Calibers, Sporting Rifle, Fancy Checkering, Fancy Wood,
   Recoil Pad, no Sights, Modern   225   340

Shotgun, Double Barrel, Over-Under
Lames, 12 Ga., Vent Rib, Fancy Checkering, Fancy Wood, Single Selective
   Trigger, Recoil Pad, Modern   245   370

Volunteer
Made by Stevens Arms

Shotgun, Singleshot
Model 94, Various Gauges, Takedown, Automatic Ejector, Plain, Hammer,
   Modern   30   50

Vulcan Arms Co.
Made by Crescent C.1900

Shotgun, Double Barrel, Side by Side
Various Gauges, Outside Hammers, Damascus Barrel, Modern   80   150
Various Gauges, Hammerless, Steel Barrel, Modern   95   175
Various Gauges, Hammerless, Damascus Barrel, Modern   75   150
Various Gauges, Outside Hammers, Steel Barrel, Modern   90   175

Shotgun, Singleshot
Various Gauges, Hammer, Steel Barrel, Modern   45   75

Walman
Spain, Made by F. Arizmendi Y Goenaga

Handgun, Semi-Automatic
.25 ACP, Clip Fed, Modern   75   110

Walsh, James
Philadelphia, Pa. 1775-79. See Kentucky Rifles and Pistols and U.S. Military

*Walther .25 ACP's, clockwise from top:
#5; #5/2; #2*

Walther
*Germany, First started in 1886 by Carl Walther. After his death in 1915 the firm was
operated by his sons Fritz, George, and Erich. In business to date. Also see German
Military*

Handgun, Semi-Automatic

Model 1, .25 ACP, Blue, Modern	140	220
Model 2, .25 ACP, Pop-Up Rear Sight, Blue, Modern	300	550
Model 3, .32 ACP, Blue, Modern	350	500
Model 3/4, .32 ACP, Takedown Lever, Blue, Modern	150	225

Walther #1 .25 ACP

Walther #3/4 .32 ACP

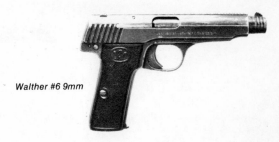

Walther #6 9mm

Model 4, .32 ACP, Blue, Modern	125	175
Model 5/2, .25 ACP, no Sights, Blue, Modern	120	175
Model 5, .25 ACP, Solid Rib, Blue, Modern	120	175
Model 6, 9mm Luger, Blue, Curio	700	1,100
Model 7, .25 ACP, Blue, Modern	150	225
Model 8, .25 ACP, Blue, Modern	125	185
Model 8, .25 ACP, Blue, Lightweight, Modern	175	250
Model 9, .25 ACP, Blue, Modern	125	185
Model GSP, .22 L.R.R.F., 5 Shot Clip, Target Pistol, Modern	450	625
Model GSP C, .22 Short, 5 Shot Clip, Target Pistol, Modern	500	700
Model GSP C, .22 Short, 5 Shot Clip, Target Pistol, with .22 L.R. Conversion Kit, Modern	750	1,200
Model HP, .30 Luger, Single Action, Modern	3,000	4,000

Walther #7 .25 ACP

Walther #9 .25 ACP

Walther PP Sport

Walther OSP .22 Short

Model HP, .30 Luger, Single Action, Wood Grips, Modern	3,000	4,200
Model HP, Commercial Finish, 9mm Luger, Double Action, Lightweight, Modern	2,000	2,750
Model HP Croation, 9mm Luger, Double Action, Military, Modern	2,500	3,200
Model HP Exposed Extractor, 9mm Luger, Double Action, Military, Modern	800	1,250
Model HP Late Military, 9mm Luger, Double Action, Military, Modern	550	700
Model HP Late Serial # Placement, 9mm Luger, Action, Military, Modern	550	700
Model HP Round Pin Early, 9mm Luger, Double Action, Military, Modern	700	900
Model HP Swedish, 9mm Luger, Double Action, Military, Modern	800	1,000
Model HP Waffenampt, 9mm Luger, Double Action, Military, Modern	450	600
Model OSP, .22 Short R.F., 5 Shot Clip, Target Pistol, Modern	475	650
Model PP Sport, .22 L.R.R.F., Target Pistol, Clip Fed, Modern	175	300
Olympia Funkamph, .22 L.R.R.F., Target Pistol, Modern	600	850
Olympia Hunting, .22 L.R.R.F., Target Pistol, Modern	350	475
Olympia Rapid Fire, .22 L.R.R.F., Target Pistol, Modern	400	600
Olympia Sport, .22 L.R.R.F., Target Pistol, Modern	325	450
P.38, 9mm Luger, Double Action, Military, Modern	250	375
P.38, (Current), .22 L.R.R.F., Double Action, Modern	350	450
P.38, (Current), .30 Luger, Double Action, Blue, Modern	300	400

Walther Olympia Sport

Walther P 38 9mm

P.38, (Current), 9mm Luger, Double Action, Modern	275	400
P.38, "480," 9mm Luger, Double Action, Military, Modern	550	775
P.38 1st. Model Zero Series, 9mm Luger, Double Action, Modern	700	950
P.38 2nd. Model Zero Series, 9mm Luger, Double Action, Military, Modern	550	800
P.38 3rd. Model Zero Series, 9mm Luger, Double Action, Military, Modern	400	700
P.38 ac no Date, 9mm Luger, Double Action, Military, Modern	600	850
P.38 ac-45 Zero Series, 9mm Luger, Double Action, Military, Modern	300	450
P.38 ac-40, 9mm Luger, Double Action, Military, Modern	375	475
P.38 ac-41, 9mm Luger, Double Action, Military, Modern	340	450
P.38 ac-41 Military Finish, 9mm Luger, Double Action, Military, Modern	275	375
P.38 ac-42, 9mm Luger, Double Action, Military, Modern	200	300
P.38 ac-43 Double Line, 9mm Luger, Double Action, Military, Modern	200	300
P.38 ac-43 Police, 9mm Luger, Double Action, Military, Modern	650	900
P.38 ac-43 Single Line, 9mm Luger, Double Action, Military, Modern	240	350
P.38 ac-43 WaA135, 9mm Luger, Double Action, Military, Modern	250	350
P.38 ac-44, 9mm Luger, Double Action, Military, Modern	250	325
P.38 ac-44 Police, 9mm Luger, Double Action, Military, Modern	650	900
P.38 ac-44 WaA140, 9mm Luger, Double Action, Military, Modern	275	375
P.38 ac-45, 9mm Luger, Double Action, Military, Modern	200	275
P.38 ac-45 Mismatch, 9mm Luger, Double Action, Military, Modern	200	275
P.38 byf-42, 9mm Luger, Double Action, Military, Modern	325	450
P.38 byf-43, 9mm Luger, Double Action, Military, Modern	200	275
P.38 byf-43 Police, 9mm Luger, Double Action, Military, Modern	600	800
P.38 byf-44, 9mm Luger, Double Action, Military, Modern	200	275
P.38 byf-44 Police F Dual T, 9mm Luger, Double Action, Military, Modern	450	650
P.38 byf-44 Police L Dual T, 9mm Luger, Double Action, Military, Modern	800	1,100
P.38 byf-44 Police L, 9mm Luger, Double Action, Military, Modern	550	750
P.38 cyq, 9mm Luger, Double Action, Military, Modern	200	275
P.38 cyq 1945, 9mm Luger, Double Action, Military, Modern	250	350
P.38 cyq Zero Series, 9mm Luger, Double Action, Military, Modern	225	325
P.38 svw-45, 9mm Luger, Double Action, Military, Modern	300	425
P.38 svw-45 French, 9mm Luger, Double Action, Military, Modern	350	450
P.38 svw-45 Police, 9mm Luger, Double Action, Military, Modern	750	950
P.38 svw-46, 9mm Luger, Double Action, Military, Modern	425	550
P.38k, 9mm Luger, Double Action, Short Barrel, Modern	300	400
P.38-IV (P.4), 9mm Luger, Double Action, Modern	320	425
P.5, 9mm Luger, Interarms, Double Action, Blue, Modern	450	700
PP, .22 L.R.R.F., Double Action, Pre-War, Commercial, Nickel Plated, Curio	325	475
PP, .22 L.R.R.F., Double Action, Pre-War, Commercial, Nickel Plated, Nazi-Proofed, Curio	300	450
PP, .22 L.R.R.F., Double Action, Pre-War, Commercial, High-Polish Finish, Modern	240	375
PP, .22 L.R.R.F., Double Action, Pre-War, Commercial, High-Polish Finish, Nazi-Proofed, Modern	275	400
PP, .22 L.R.R.F., Double Action, Lightweight, Modern	250	400

Walther P 5 9mm

PP, .25 ACP, Double Action, Pre-War, Commercial, High-Polish Finish,
Curio 850   1,300
PP, .32 ACP, Double Action, Pre-War, Commercial, Lightweight, High-
Polish Finish, Curio 325   450
PP, .32 ACP, Double Action, Pre-War, Nazi-Proofed, Lightweight, High-
Polish Finish, Curio 325   450
PP, .32 ACP, Double Action, Pre-War, Nazi-Proofed, Lightweight, Curio ... 275   375
PP, .32 ACP, Double Action, Pre-War, Commercial, Nickel Plated, Curio ... 275   400
PP, .32 ACP, Double Action, Pre-War, Commercial, Nickel Plated, Nazi-
Proofed, Curio 275   400
PP, .32 ACP, Double Action, Pre-War, Commercial, High-Polish Finish,
Modern 200   275
PP, .32 ACP, Double Action, Pre-War, Commercial, High-Polish Finish,
Nazi-Proofed, Modern 225   300
PP, .32 ACP, Double Action, Pre-War, Commercial, Nazi-Proofed, Modern ... 200   275
PP, .32 ACP, Double Action, Lightweight, Modern 220   375
PP, .380 ACP, Double Action, Pre-War, Commercial, High-Polish Finish,
Modern 275   375
PP, .38 ACP, Double Action, Pre-War, Commercial, High-Polish Finish,
Nazi-Proofed, Modern 300   400
PP, .380 ACP, Double Action, Pre-War, Commercial, Nickel Plated, Curio ... 650   800
PP, .380 ACP, Double Action, Pre-War, Commercial, Nickel Plated, Nazi-
Proofed, Curio 600   750
PP, .380 ACP, Double Action, Lightweight, Modern 220   375
PP "Nairobi," .32 ACP, Double Action, Pre-War, High-Polish Finish, Curio ... 500   700
PP (Current), .22 L.R.R.F., Double Action, Modern 225   325
PP (Current), .32 ACP, Double Action, Blue, Modern 175   250
PP (Current), .380 ACP, Double Action, Blue, Modern 175   250
PP (Early) 90 Degree Safety, .32 ACP, Double Action, Pre-War,
Commercial, High-Polish Finish, Modern 225   350
PP (Early) Bottom Magazine Release, .380 ACP, Double Action, Pre-War,
Commercial, High-Polish Finish, Curio 750   1,200
PP AC, .380 ACP, Double Action, Pre-War, Nazi-Proofed, Modern 450   650
PP AC Police F, .32 ACP, Double Action, Pre-War, Nazi-Proofed, Curio ... 225   300
PP AC Waffenamt, .32 ACP, Double Action, Pre-War, Nazi-Proofed, Curio ... 225   325
PP Bottom Magazine Release, .32 ACP, Double Action, Pre-War,
Commercial, High-Polish Finish, Curio 325   425
PP Bottom Magazine Release, .32 ACP, Double Action, Pre-War,
Commercial, High-Polish Finish, Lightweight, Curio 325   425
PP Czech, .32 ACP, Double Action, Pre-War, Commercial, High-Polish
Finish, Curio 550   700
PP Mark II "Manurhin," .22 L.R.R.F., Double Action, High-Polish Finish,
Blue, Curio 275   400
PP Mark II "Manurhin," .32 ACP, Double Action, High-Polish Finish, Blue,
Curio 250   350
PP Mark II "Manurhin," .380 ACP, Double Action, High-Polish Finish,
Blue, Curio 275   375
PP NSKK, .32 ACP, Double Action, Pre-War, High-Polish Finish, Nazi-
Proofed, Curio 675   900
PP PDM, .32 ACP, Double Action, Pre-War, High-Polish Finish, Curio 400   500

Walther Manurhin PP .32 ACP

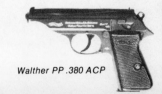

Walther PP .380 ACP

PP Persian, .380 ACP, Double Action, Pre-War, Commercial, High-Polish Finish, Curio	1,300	1,750
PP Police C, .32 ACP, Double Action, Pre-War, High-Polish Finish, Nazi-Proofed, Curio	275	375
PP Police C, .32 ACP, Double Action, Pre-War, Nazi-Proofed, Curio	250	350
PP Police F, .32 ACP, Double Action, Pre-War, Nazi-Proofed, Curio	225	300
PP Presentation, Double Action, Lightweight, Modern	450	625
PP RFV, .32 ACP, Double Action, Pre-War, High-Polish, Curio	350	425
PP RFV, .32 ACP, Double Action, Pre-War, Nazi-Proofed, Curio	300	400
PP RJ, .32 ACP, Double Action, Pre-War, High-Polish Finish, Curio	325	400
PP SS, .22 L.R.R.F., Double Action, Pre-War, High-Polish Finish, Curio	600	750
PP SA, .32 ACP, Double Action, Pre-War, High-Polish Finish, Curio	500	650
PP Stoeger, .32 ACP, Double Action, Pre-War, High-Polish Finish, Curio	400	550
PP Super, 9 x 18mm, Clip Fed, Blue, Modern	300	400
PP Verchromt, .32 ACP, Double Action, Pre-War, Commercial, Curio	500	650
PP Verchromt, .380 ACP, Double Action, Pre-War, Commercial, Curio	650	800
PP with Lanyard Loop, .32 ACP, Double Action, Pre-War, Commercial, High-Polish Finish, Nazi-Proofed, Modern	300	400
PP Waffenamt, .32 ACP, Double Action, Pre-War, High-Polish Finish, Nazi-Proofed, Curio	225	325
PP Waffenamt, .32 ACP, Double Action, Pre-War, Nazi-Proofed, Curio	200	300
PP Waffenamt, .380 ACP, Double Action, Pre-War, High-Polish Finish, Nazi-Proofed, Curio	375	475
PPK, .22 L.R.R.F., Double Action, Pre-War, Commercial, Nickel Plated, Curio	375	475
PPK, .22 L.R.R.F., Double Action, Pre-War, Commercial, Nickel Plated, Nazi-Proofed, Curio	325	425
PPK, .22 L.R.R.F., Double Action, Pre-War, Commercial, High-Polish Finish, Modern	275	350
PPK, .22 L.R.R.F., Double Action, Pre-War, Commercial, High-Polish Finish, Nazi-Proofed, Modern	300	400
PPK, .22 L.R.R.F., Double Action, Post-War, Modern	250	350
PPK, .22 L.R.R.F., Double Action, Lightweight, Post-War, Modern	275	400
PPK, .25 ACP, Double Action, Pre-War, Commercial, High-Polish Finish, Curio	1,100	1,400
PPK, .32 ACP, Double Action, Pre-War, Commercial, Nickel Plated, Curio	300	400
PPK, .32 ACP, Double Action, Pre-War, Commercial, Nazi-Proofed, Nickel Plated, Curio	300	400
PPK, .32 ACP, Double Action, Pre-War, Commercial, Lightweight, High-Polish Finish, Curio	350	450
PPK, .32 ACP, Double Action, Pre-War, Nazi-Proofed, Lightweight, High-Polish Finish, Curio	350	450
PPK, .32 ACP, Double Action, Pre-War, Nazi-Proofed, Lightweight, Curio	275	375

Walther PP Super 9x18mm

Walther PPk

PPK, .32 ACP, Double Action, Pre-War, Commercial, High-Polish Finish, Modern	200	275
PPK, .32 ACP, Double Action, Pre-War, Commercial, High-Polish Finish, Nazi-Proofed, Modern	220	300
PPK, .32 ACP, Double Action, Pre-War, Commercial, Nazi-Proofed, Modern	200	275
PPK, .32 ACP, Double Action, Post-War, Modern	225	300
PPK, .32 ACP, Double Action, Lightweight, Post-War, Modern	275	400
PPK, .380 ACP, Double Action, Pre-War, Commercial, Nickel Plated, Curio	775	950
PPK, .380 ACP, Double Action, Pre-War, Commercial, Nickel Plated, Nazi-Proofed, Curio	800	1,200
PPK, .380 ACP, Double Action, Pre-War, Commercial, High-Polish Finish, Modern	575	750
PPK, .380 ACP, Double Action, Pre-War, Commercial, High-Polish Finish, Nazi-Proofed, Modern	650	850
PPK, .380 ACP, Double Action, Post-War, Modern	225	300
PPK, .380 ACP, Double Action, Lightweight, Post-War, Modern	275	400
PPK "Nairobi," .32 ACP, Double Action, Pre-War, High-Polish Finish, Curio	600	800
PPK (Early) 90 Degree Safety, .32 ACP, Double Action, Pre-War, Commercial, High-Polish Finish, Modern	250	350
PPK (Early) Bottom Magazine Release, .380 ACP, Double Action, Pre-War, Commercial, High-Polish Finish, Curio	750	1,100
PPK Czech, .32 ACP, Double Action, Pre-War, Commercial, High-Polish Finish, Curio	600	750
PPK DRP, .32 ACP, Double Action, Pre-War, High-Polish Finish, Curio	400	500
PPK DRP, .32 ACP, Double Action, Pre-War, High-Polish Finish, Nickel Plated, Curio	500	700
PPK Mark II "Manurhin,", .22 L.R.R.F., Double Action, High-Polish Finish, Blue, Curio	400	550
PPK Mark II "Manurhin," .22 L.R.R.F., Double Action, High-Polish Finish, Blue, Lightweight, Curio	500	650
PPK Mark II "Manurhin," .32 ACP, Double Action, High-Polish Finish, Blue, Curio	350	450
PPK Mark II "Manurhin," .32 ACP, Double Action, High-Polish Finish, Blue, Lightweight, Curio	400	550
PPK Mark II "Manurhin," .380 ACP, Double Action, High-Polish Finish, Blue, Curio	375	475
PPK Mark II "Manhurin," .380 ACP, Double Action, High-Polish Finish, Blue, Lightweight, Curio	450	550
PPK Model PP, .32 ACP, Double Action, Pre-War, Commercial, High-Polish Finish, Curio	1,000	1,350
PPK Party Leader, .32 ACP, Double Action, Pre-War, High-Polish Finish, Curio	850	1,150
PPK PDM, .32 ACP, Double Action, Pre-War, High-Polish Finish, Lightweight, Curio	750	900
PPK Police C, .32 ACP, Double Action, Pre-War, High-Polish Finish, Nazi-Proofed, Curio	300	400
PPK Police C, .32 ACP, Double Action, Pre-War, Nazi-Proofed, Curio	275	375
PPK Police F, .32 ACP, Double Action, Pre-War, Nazi-Proofed, Curio	250	350
PPK RFV, .32 ACP, Double Action, Pre-War, High-Polish Finish, Curio	500	700
PPK RZM, .32 ACP, Double Action, Pre-War, High-Polish Finish, Curio	350	450
PPK RZM, .32 ACP, Double Action, Pre-War, High-Polish Finish, Nickel Plated, Curio	550	700
PPK Stoeger, .32 ACP, Double Action, Pre-War, High-Polish Finish, Curio	450	650
PPK Verchromt, .32 ACP, Double Action, Pre-War, Commercial, Curio	600	750
PPK Verchromt, .32 ACP, Double Action, Pre-War, Commercial, Lightweight, Curio	1,000	1,400
PPK Verchromt, .380 ACP, Double Action, Pre-War, Commercial, Curio	750	1,000
PPK Waffenamt, .32 ACP, Double Action, Pre-War, High-Polish Finish, Nazi-Proofed, Curio	375	475

PPK Waffenamt, .32 ACP, Double Action, Pre-War, Nazi-Proofed, Curio	275	375
PPK Waffenamt, .380 ACP, Double Action, Pre-War, High-Polish Finish, Nazi-Proofed, Curio	750	1,100
PPKS (Current), .22 L.R.R.F., Double Action, Modern	225	325
PPKS (Current), .32 ACP, Double Action, Blue, Modern	200	275
PPKS (Current), .380 ACP, Double Action, Blue, Modern	200	275
Self-Loading, .22 L.R.R.F., Target Pistol, Modern	250	350
T P H, .22 L.R.R.F., Double Action, Clip Fed, Modern	250	375

Rifle, Bolt Action

GX-1 Match, .22 L.R.R.F., Singleshot, Target Stock, with Accessories, Modern	575	775
KKJ, .22 Hornet, 5 Shot Clip, Open Rear Sight, Checkered Stock, Modern	240	325
KKJ, .22 Hornet, 5 Shot Clip, Open Rear Sight, Checkered Stock, Set Trigger, Modern	260	350
KKJ, .22 L.R.R.F., 5 Shot Clip, Open Rear Sight, Checkered Stock, Modern	175	275
KKJ, .22 L.R.R.F., 5 Shot Clip, Open Rear Sight, Checkered Stock, Set Trigger, Modern	210	285
KKJ, .22 WMR, 5 Shot Clip, Open Rear Sight, Checkered Stock, Modern	195	270
KKJ, .22 WMR, 5 Shot Clip, Open Rear Sight, Checkered Stock, Set Trigger, Modern	220	300
KKJ International Match, .22 L.R.R.F., Singleshot, Target Stock, with Accessories, Modern	400	575
Model KKW, .22 L.R.R.F., Pre-WW2, Singleshot, Tangent Sights, Military Style Stock, Modern	300	425
Model V, Singleshot, Sporting Rifle, Open Rear Sight, Modern	175	250
Model V "Meisterbushse," Singleshot, Pistol-Grip Stock, Target Sights, Modern	190	275
Moving Target, .22 L.R.R.F., Singleshot, Target Stock, with Accessories, Modern	425	575
Olympic, .22 L.R.R.F., Singleshot, Target Stock, with Accessories, Modern	300	450
Prone "400," .22 L.R.R.F., Singleshot, Target Stock, with Accessories, Modern	275	375
U I T Match, .22 L.R.R.F., Singleshot, Target Stock, with Accessories, Modern	450	625
U I T Super, .22 L.R.R.F., Singleshot, Target Stock, with Accessories, Modern	400	550

Rifle, Semi-Automatic

Model 1, Clip Fed, Carbine, Modern	175	250
Model 2, .22 L.R.R.F., Clip Fed, Modern	175	250

Warner

Handgun, Semi-Automatic

Infallable, .32 ACP, Clip Fed, Modern	90	140
The Infallable, .32 ACP, Clip Fed, Modern	120	160

Warren Arms Corp.
Belgium C.1900

Shotgun, Double Barrel, Side by Side

Various Gauges, Outside Hammers, Damascus Barrel, Modern	80	150
Various Gauges, Hammerless, Steel Barrel, Modern	95	175
Various Gauges, Hammerless, Damascus Barrel, Modern	75	150
Various Gauges, Outside Hammers, Steel Barrel, Modern	90	175

Shotgun, Singleshot

Various Gauges, Hammer, Steel Barrel, Modern	45	75

Weatherby's Inc. Mk V

Weatherby's Inc. Vanguard

Watson Bros.
London, England 1885-1931

Rifle, Bolt Action

.303 British, Express Sights, Sporting Rifle, Checkered Stock, Modern	425	600

Rifle, Double Barrel, Side by Side

.450/.400 N.E. 3", Double Trigger, Recoil Pad, Plain, Cased, Modern	2,750	3,500

Watters, John
Carlisle, Pa. 1778-85

Weatherby's, Inc.
South Gate, Calif.

Rifle, Bolt Action
For German Manufacture add 30%-50%

Deluxe, .378 Wby. Mag., Magnum, Checkered Stock, Modern	250	350
Deluxe, Various Calibers, Checkered Stock, Modern	180	240
Deluxe, Various Calibers, Magnum, Checkered Stock, Modern	210	300
Mark V, .378 Wby. Mag., Checkered Stock, Modern	375	425
Mark V, .460 Wby. Mag., Checkered Stock, Modern	450	535
Mark V, Various Calibers, Varmint, Checkered Stock, Modern	260	350
Mark V, Various Calibers, Checkered Stock, Modern	285	350
Vanguard, Various Calibers, Checkered Stock, Modern	210	275

Rifle, Semi-Automatic

Mark XXII, .22 L.R.R.F., Clip Fed, Checkered Stock, Modern	125	175
Mark XXII, .22 L.R.R.F., Tube Feed, Checkered Stock, Modern	140	200

Shotgun, Double Barrel, Over-Under

Regency, 12 Ga., Trap Grade, Vent Rib, Checkered Stock, Engraved, Single Selective Trigger, Modern	530	625
Regency, Field Grade, 12 and 20 Gauges, Vent Rib, Checkered Stock, Engraved, Single Selective Trigger, Modern	500	600

Shotgun, Semi-Automatic

Centurion, 12 Ga., Field Grade, Vent Rib, Checkered Stock, Modern	150	200
Centurion, 12 Ga., Trap Grade, Checkered Stock, Vent Rib, Modern	175	225
Centurion Deluxe, 12 Ga., Checkered Stock, Vent Rib, Light Engraving, Fancy Wood, Modern	200	250

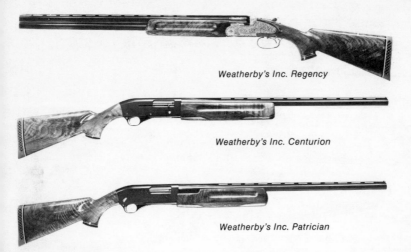

Weatherby's Inc. Regency

Weatherby's Inc. Centurion

Weatherby's Inc. Patrician

Shotgun, Slide Action

Patrician, 12 Ga., Field Grade, Checkered Stock, Vent Rib, Modern	125	175
Patrician, 12 Ga., Trap Grade, Checkered Stock, Vent Rib, Modern	150	200
Patrician, Deluxe, 12 Ga., Checkered Stock, Light Engraving, Fancy Wood, Vent Rib, Modern	180	215

Weaver, Crypret
Pa. C.1818. See Kentucky Rifles

Webley & Scott Revolver Arms Co.
Birmingham & London from 1898. Also see British Military

Handgun, Revolver

Webley British Bulldog, Various Calibers, Solid Frame, Double Action, Modern	80	120
Webley Kaufmann, .45 Colt, Top Break, Square-Butt, Commercial, Antique	350	450
Webley Mk 1, .455 Revolver Mk 1, Top Break, Round Butt, Military, Antique	150	200
Webley Mk 6, Detachable Buttstock Only	125	200

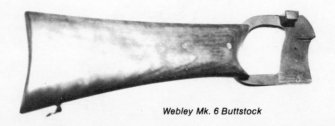

Webley Mk. 6 Buttstock

Webley Model 1913 Mk. 1 .455 Auto

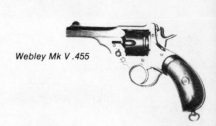

Webley Mk V .455

Webley Mk 1*, .455 Revolver Mk 1, Top Break, Round Butt, Military, Antique — 140 — 180

Webley Mk 1** Navy, .455 Revolver Mk 1, Top Break, Round Butt, Military, Modern — 110 — 150

Webley Mk 2, .455 Revolver Mk 1, Top Break, Round Butt, Military, Antique — 140 — 175

Webley Mk 2*, .455 Revolver Mk 1, Top Break, Round Butt, Military, Modern — 110 — 150

Webley Mk 2**, .455 Revolver Mk 1, Top Break, Round Butt, Military, Modern — 110 — 150

Webley Mk 3, .455 Revolver Mk 1, Top Break, Round Butt, Military, Modern — 140 — 175

Webley Mk 4, .455 Revolver Mk 1, Top Break, Round Butt, Military, Modern — 130 — 160

Webley Mk 5, .455 Revolver Mk 1, Top Break, Round Butt, Military, Modern — 140 — 175

Webley Mk 6, .455 Revolver Mk 1, Top Break, Square-Butt, Military, Modern — 110 — 150

Webley Mk III M & P, .38 S & W, Top Break, Square-Butt, Commercial, Modern — 90 — 140

Webley Mk IV, .22 L.R.R.F., Top Break, Square-Butt, Commercial, Modern — 125 — 175

Webley Mk IV, .38 S & W, Top Break, Square-Butt, Military, Modern — 85 — 130

Webley Mk VI, .22 L.R.R.F., Top Break, Square-Butt, Commercial, Modern — 125 — 175

Webley British Bulldog .44

Webley RIC Revolver

Webley-Green Revolver

Webley Model 1909 9mm

Webley R I C, .455 Revolver Mk 1, Solid Frame, Square-Butt, Commercial, Antique	90	125
Webley-Green, .455 Revolver Mk 1, Top Break, Square-Butt, Commercial, Target Pistol, Antique	250	325
Webley-Green, .476 Enfield Mk 3, Top Break, Square-Butt, Commercial, Target Pistol, Antique	300	400
Handgun, Semi-Automatic		
Model 1904, .455 Webley Auto., Clip Fed, Grip Safety, Hammer, Curio	400	500
Model 1906, .25 ACP, Clip Fed, Hammer, Modern	110	150
Model 1909, .25 ACP, Clip Fed, Hammerless, Modern	150	200
Model 1909 M & P, 9mm Browning Long, Clip Fed, Hammer, Curio	300	400
1911 Automatic, .22 L.R.R.F., Hammer, Modern	175	250
Model 1911 Metro Police, .32 ACP, Clip Fed, Hammer, Modern	125	200
Model 1911 Metro Police, .380 ACP, Clip Fed, Hammer, Modern	170	250
Model 1913 Mk 1, .455 Webley Auto., Clip Fed, Grip Safety, Military, Hammer, Curio	225	325
Model 1913 Mk 1 #2, .455 Webley Auto., Clip Fed, Grip Safety, Adjustable Sights, Hammer, Curio	450	600
Handgun, Semi-Automatic Revolver		
Webley-Fosbery, .455 Revolver Mk 1, Top Break, Military, Modern	600	900
Webley-Fosbery (Union Arms), .32 S & W, Top Break, Military, Modern	450	800
Webley-Fosbery .38 Cal., Top Break, Military, Modern	575	850
Handgun, Singleshot		
Single Shot Target, .22 L.R.R.F., Adjustable Sights, Target Grips, Tip-Up, Modern	150	200

Shotgun, Double Barrel, Side by Side

Model 700, 12 and 20 Gauges, Box Lock, Hammerless, Checkered Stock, Light Engraving, Double Trigger, Modern	300	400
Model 700, 12 and 20 Gauges, Box Lock, Hammerless, Checkered Stock, Light Engraving, Single Trigger, Modern	350	450
Model 701, 12 and 20 Gauges, Box Lock, Hammerless, Checkered Stock, Fancy Engraving, Double Trigger, Modern	600	750
Model 701, 12 and 20 Gauges, Box Lock, Hammerless, Checkered Stock, Fancy Engraving, Single Trigger, Modern	650	800
Model 702, 12 and 20 Gauges, Box Lock, Hammerless, Checkered Stock, Engraved, Double Trigger Modern	425	550
Model 702, 12 and 20 Gauges, Box Lock, Hammerless, Checkered Stock, Engraved, Single Trigger, Modern	475	600

Welshantz, David
York, Pa. 1780-83. See Kentucky Rifles, U.S. Military

Welshantz, Jacob
York, Pa. 1777-92. See Kentucky Rifles, U.S. Military

Welshantz, Joseph
York, Pa. 1779-83. See Kentucky Rifles, U.S. Military

Wesson & Harrington
Worcester, Mass. 1871-74. Succeeded by Harrington and Richardson

Handgun, Revolver

.22 Short R.F., 7 Shot, Spur Trigger, Solid Frame, Single Action, Antique	90	160
.32 Short R.F., 5 Shot, Spur Trigger, Solid Frame, Single Action, Antique	90	160
.38 Short R.F., 5 Shot, Spur Trigger, Solid Frame, Single Action, Antique	95	180

Wesson, Frank
Worcester, Mass. 1854 to 1865. 1865-75 at Springfield, Mass. Also see U.S. Military

Rifle, Singleshot

.32 Long R.F., Antique	350	475

Western Arms Co.

Handgun, Revolver

.32 Long R.F., 5 Shot, Folding Trigger, Double Action, Antique	55	95

Western Field
Trade name for Montgomery Ward

Rifle, Bolt Action

Model 56 Buckhorn, .22 L.R.R.F., 5 Shot Clip, Open Rear Sight, Modern	30	50
Model 724, .30-06 Springfield, Checkered Stock, Full-Stocked, Modern	125	170
Model 732, .30-06 Springfield, Checkered Stock, Recoil Pad, Modern	135	175
Model 734, 7mm Rem. Mag., Checkered Stock, Recoil Pad, Modern	140	190
Model 770, Various Calibers, Checkered Stock, Sling Swivels, Modern	135	175
Model 780, Various Calibers, Checkered Stock, Sling Swivels, Modern	125	160
Model 815, .22 L.R.R.F., Singleshot, Modern	15	25
Model 822, .22 WMR, Clip Fed, Modern	35	55
Model 83, .22 L.R.R.F., Singleshot, Open Rear Sight, Modern	20	40
Model 830, .22 L.R.R.F., Clip Fed, Modern	30	45
Model 832, .22 L.R.R.F., Clip Fed, Checkered Stock, Modern	30	45
Model 84, .22 L.R.R.F., 5 Shot Clip, Open Rear Sight, Takedown, Modern	30	45
Model 842, .22 L.R.R.F., Tube Feed, Modern	35	45
Model 86, .22 L.R.R.F., Tube Feed, Takedown, Open Rear Sight, Modern	35	55

Rifle, Lever Action

Model 72, .30-30 Win., Pistol-Grip Stock, Plain, Tube Feed, Modern	65	95
Model 72C, .30-30 Win., Straight Grip, Plain, Tube Feed, Modern	65	95
Model 865, .22 L.R.R.F., Tube Feed, Sling Swivels, Modern	40	55
Model 895, .22 L.R.R.F., Tube Feed, Carbine, Modern	35	55

Rifle, Semi-Automatic

Model 808, .22 L.R.R.F., Tube Feed, Modern	25	40
Model 828, .22 L.R.R.F., Clip Fed, Checkered Stock, Modern	35	45
Model 836, .22 L.R.R.F., Tube Feed, Modern	35	45
Model 846, .22 L.R.R.F., Tube Feed, Modern	35	45
Model 850, .22 L.R.R.F., Clip Fed, Modern	30	40
Model 880, .22 L.R.R.F., Tube Feed, Modern	30	40
Model M-1, .30 Carbine, Clip Fed, Modern	75	115

Shotgun, Bolt Action

Model 150, .410 Ga., Clip Fed, Modern	30	40
Model 172-5, 12 and 20 Gauges, Magnum, Clip Fed, Adjustable Choke, Modern	35	45

Shotgun, Double Barrel, Side by Side

12 and 20 Gauges, Single Trigger, Hammerless, Checkered Stock, Modern	100	135
Various Gauges, Hammerless, Plain, Modern	70	95
Long-Range, Various Gauges, Double Trigger, Hammerless, Modern	110	150
Long-Range, Various Gauges, Single Trigger, Hammerless, Modern	130	175
Model 330, Various Gauges, Hammerless, Checkered Stock, Modern	80	125
Model 5151, Various Gauges, Hammerless, Steel Barrel, Modern	90	140

Shotgun, Semi-Automatic

Model 600, 12 Ga., Takedown, Plain Barrel, Checkered Stock, Modern	90	120
Model 600, 12 Ga., Takedown, Vent Rib, Checkered Stock, Modern	100	135

Shotgun, Singleshot

Model 100, Various Gauges, Hammerless, Adjustable Choke, Modern	30	40
Trap, 12 Ga., Hammer, Solid Rib, Checkered Stock, Modern	50	75

Shotgun, Slide Action

Model 500, .410 Ga., Plain, Takedown, Modern	75	115
Model 502, .410 Ga., Checkered Stock, Light Engraving, Takedown, Vent Rib, Modern	90	120
Model 520, 12 Ga., Takedown, Modern	85	125
Model 550, 12 and 20 Gauges, Checkered Stock, Light Engraving, Vent Rib, Takedown, Modern	90	120
Model 550, 12 and 20 Gauges, Checkered Stock, Light Engraving, Vent Rib, Takedown, Adjustable Choke, Modern	95	135
Model 550, 12 and 20 Gauges, Plain, Takedown, Modern	85	115
Model 620, Various Gauges, Takedown, Modern	85	130

Westley Richards
London, England. From 1812 to Date

Rifle, Bolt Action

Best Quality, Various Calibers, Express Sights, Fancy Wood, Fancy Checkering, Repeater, Modern	1,500	2,100

Rifle, Double Barrel, Over-Under

Ovundo, 12 Ga., Ventilated Barrels, Vent Rib, Single Selective Trigger, Extra Barrel, Detachable Side Lock, Modern	10,000	15,500

Rifle, Double Barrel, Side by Side

Best Quality, Various Calibers, Box Lock, Double Trigger, Fancy Engraving, Fancy Checkering, Express Sights, Modern	3,500	5,500
Best Quality, Various Calibers, Sidelock, Double Trigger, Fancy Engraving, Fancy Checkering, Express Sights, Modern	8,500	12,000

Shotgun, Double Barrel, Over-Under
Ovundo, 12 Ga., Sidelock, Single Selective Trigger, Selective Ejector,
Fancy Engraving, Fancy Checkering, Modern ... 10,000 17,500

Shotgun, Double Barrel, Side by Side
10 Ga. Pinfire, Engraved, Carbine, Antique ... 450 700
Best Quality, Various Gauges, Sidelock, Hammerless, Fancy Engraving,
Fancy Checkering, Double Trigger, Modern ... 7,500 10,000
Best Quality, Various Gauges, Sidelock, Hammerless, Fancy Engraving,
Fancy Checkering, Single Selective Trigger, Modern ... 8,000 12,000
Best Quality, Various Gauges, Box Lock, Hammerless, Fancy Engraving,
Fancy Checkering, Double Trigger, Modern ... 5,500 8,000
Best Quality, Various Gauges, Box Lock, Hammerless, Fancy Engraving,
Fancy Checkering, Single Selective Trigger, Modern ... 6,000 9,000
Best, Pigeon, 12 Ga. Mag. 3", Sidelock, Hammerless, Fancy Engraving,
Fancy Checkering, Double Trigger, Modern ... 11,500 18,000
Best, Pigeon, 12 Ga. Mag. 3", Sidelock, Hammerless, Fancy Engraving,
Fancy Checkering, Single Selective Trigger, Modern ... 13,500 19,000
Deluxe Quality, Various Gauges, Sidelock, Hammerless, Fancy Engraving,
Fancy Checkering, Double Trigger, Modern ... 8,500 12,000
Deluxe Quality, Various Gauges, Sidelock, Hammerless, Fancy Engraving,
Fancy Checkering, Single Selective Trigger, Modern ... 9,000 13,000
Deluxe Quality, Various Gauges, Box Lock, Hammerless, Fancy
Engraving, Fancy Checkering, Double Trigger, Modern ... 5,500 7,500
Deluxe Quality, Various Gauges, Box Lock, Hammerless, Fancy
Engraving, Fancy Checkering, Single Selective Trigger, Modern ... 6,500 8,500
Model E, Various Gauges, Box Lock, Hammerless, Engraved, Double
Trigger, Selective Ejector, Modern ... 3,500 5,000
Model E, Various Gauges, Box Lock, Hammerless, Engraved, Double
Trigger, Modern ... 2,800 3,500
Model E Pigeon, 12 Ga. Mag. 3", Box Lock, Hammerless, Engraved,
Double Trigger, Selective Ejector, Modern ... 4,000 5,500
Model E Pigeon, 12 Ga. Mag 3", Box Lock, Hammerless, Engraved,
Double Trigger, Modern ... 3,300 4,000

Shotgun, Singleshot
12 Ga., Trap Grade, Vent Rib, Fancy Engraving, Fancy Checkering,
Hammerless, Modern ... 5,500 8,000
12 Ga., Vent Rib, Plain, Monte Carlo Stock, Trap Grade, Modern ... 1,800 2,600

Weston, Edward
Sussex, England 1800-35

Handgun, Flintlock
.67, Pair, Duelling Pistols, Octagon Barrel, Silver Furniture, Plain, Antique ... 1,500 2,000

Wheel-Lock, Unknown Maker

Combination Weapon, Pistol
German, 1500's War-Hammer, all Metal, Antique ... 15,000+

Handgun, Wheel-Lock
Augsburg, Late 1500's, Ball Pommel, Engraved, Ornate, Antique ... 20,000+
Brescian, Mid-1600's, Military, Fish-Tail Butt, Plain, Antique ... 1,500 2,000
Embellished Original, Ornate, Antique ... 2,500 3,500
Enclosed Lock German, Mid-1600's, Engraved, Holster Pistol, Antique ... 3,000 3,500
Enclosed Lock, Late 1600's, Military, Plain, Antique ... 1,500 2,500
English, Mid-1600's, Ornate, Antique ... 20,000+
English, Mid-1600's, Military, Holster Pistol, Plain, Antique ... 1,500 2,500
French, Early 1600's, Military, Silver Inlay, Antique ... 2,500 3,500
German, 1600, Dagger-Handle Butt, Military, Plain, Antique ... 2,000 2,750
German, Late 1500's, Carved, Horn Inlays, Ball Pommel, Flattened,
Antique ... 18,000+

German, Mid-1500's, Horn Inlays, Dagger-Handle Butt, Gold and Silver Damascened, Ornate, Antique		50,000+
German, Mid-1600's, Military, Fish-Tail Butt, Plain, Antique	1,000	2,000
German Puffer, Late 1500's, Horn Inlays, Ball Pommel, Antique		10,000+
German Style, Reproduction, Engraved, Inlays, High Quality, Antique	1,400	1,700
Italian, 1500's, Dagger-Handle, External Mechanism, Antique		15,000+
Late 1500's Odd Butt, all Metal, Engraved, Ornate, Antique	7,000	10,000
Old Reproduction, High Quality, Antique	1,000	1,500
Pair Brescian, Mid-1600's, Inlays, Engraved, Ornate, Fish-Tail Butt, Antique		25,000+
Pair Dutch, Mid-1600's, Holster Pistol, Gold Damascened, Inlays, Ornate, Antique		25,000+
Pair Saxon, Late 1500's, Ball Pommel, Medium Ornamentation, Antique		20,000+
Pair Saxon, Late 1500's, Ball Pommel, Light Ornamentation, Antique		15,000+
Pair Saxon, Late 1500's, Ball Pommel, Inlays, Engraved, Antique		30,000+
Saxon, Double Barrel, Over-Under, Inlays, Ornate, Ball Pommel, Antique		30,000
Saxon, Dated 1579, Horn Inlays, Engraved, Ball Pommel, Antique		10,000+
Saxon, Late 1500's, Ball Pommel, Checkered Stock, Military, Plain, Antique	4,000	5,000

Whippet
Made by Stevens Arms

Shotgun, Singleshot

Model 94A, Various Gauges, Hammer, Automatic Ejector, Modern	30	50

White Powder Wonder
Made by Stevens Arms

Shotgun, Singleshot

Model 90, Various Gauges, Takedown, Automatic Ejector, Plain, Hammer, Modern	30	50

White, Rollin, Arms Co.
Hartford, Conn. 1849-58 Lowell, Mass. 1864-92

Handgun, Revolver

.22 Short R.F., 7 Shot, Spur Trigger, Tip-Up, Antique	175	275
.32 Short R.F., 5 Shot, Spur Trigger, Tip-Up, Antique	200	300

White Star
Maker Unknown C.1880

Handgun, Revolver

.32 Short R.F., 5 Shot, Spur Trigger, Solid Frame, Single Action, Antique	90	160

Handgun, Revolver

.32 Short R.F., 5 Shot, Spur Trigger, Solid Frame, Single Action, Antique	95	170

Whitney Arms Co.
New Haven, Conn. 1866-76

Handgun, Revolver

.22 Short R.F., 7 Shot, Spur Trigger, Solid Frame, Single Action, Antique	90	160

Whitney Arms .32 R.F.

Wichita Engineering & Supply "Classic Rifle"
Courtesy of Nolen Jackson

.38 Short R.F., 5 Shot, Spur Trigger, Solid Frame, Single Action, Antique	90	160
.32 Short R.F., 5 or 6 Shots, Spur Trigger, Solid Frame, Single Action, Antique	95	170

Shotgun, Double Barrel, Side by Side
12 Ga., Damascus Barrel, Outside Hammers, Antique	175	250

Whitneyville Armory
See Whitney Arms Co.

Wichita Engineering & Supply
Wichita, Kans.

Handgun, Singleshot
Silhouette Pistol, Various Calibers, Bolt Action, Modern	300	400

Rifle, Bolt Action
Classic, Various Calibers, Singleshot, Target, Modern	425	650
Classic, Various Calibers, Repeater, Modern	425	650

Wickliffe
Triple-S Development, Wickliffe, Ohio

Rifle, Singleshot
Stinger Standard, Various Calibers, Falling Block, Modern	140	200
Stinger Deluxe, Various Calibers, Falling Block, Modern	175	250
'76 Standard, Various Calibers, Falling Block, Modern	140	200
'76 Deluxe, Various Calibers, Falling Block, Modern	175	250
Traditional, Various Calibers, Falling Block, Modern	140	200

Wickliffe '76 Rifle

Wide Awake
Made by Hood Fire Arms, Norwich, Conn. 1875

Handgun, Revolver
.32 Short R.F., 5 Shot, Spur Trigger, Solid Frame, Single Action, Antique   90   160

Wilkinson Arms Co.
Belgium for Richmond Hardware Co. Richmond, Va. C.1900

Shotgun, Double Barrel, Side by Side
Various Gauges, Outside Hammers, Damascus Barrel, Modern	80	150
Various Gauges, Hammerless, Steel Barrel, Modern	95	175
Various Gauges, Hammerless, Damascus Barrel, Modern	75	150
Various Gauges, Outside Hammers, Steel Barrel, Modern	90	175

Shotgun, Singleshot
Various Gauges, Hammer, Steel Barrel, Modern   45   75

Williams, Frederick
Birmingham, England 1893-1929

Shotgun, Double Barrel, Side by Side
12 Ga., Damascus Barrel, Outside Hammers, Checkered Stock, Engraved,
Antique   300   450

Williamson, David
Brooklyn, N.Y. and Greenville, N.J. 1864-74. Also see Moore's Patent Firearms Co.

Handgun, Singleshot
.41 Short R.F., Derringer, Nickel Plated, Antique   185   300

Willis, Richard
Lancaster, Pa. C.1776. See Kentucky Rifles and Pistols

Wilmont Arms Co.
Belgium C.1900

Shotgun, Double Barrel, Side by Side
Various Gauges, Outside Hammers, Damascus Barrel, Modern	80	150
Various Gauges, Hammerless, Steel Barrel, Modern	95	175
Various Gauges, Hammerless, Damascus Barrel, Modern	75	150
Various Gauges, Outside Hammers, Steel Barrel, Modern	90	175

Shotgun, Singleshot
Various Gauges, Hammer, Steel Barrel, Modern   45   75

Wilson, R.
London, England 1720-50

Shotgun, Flintlock
Fowling, 9 Ga., Queen Anne Style, Half-Stock, Antique   1,000   1,500

Wiltshire Arms Co.
Belgium C.1900

Shotgun, Double Barrel, Side by Side
Various Gauges, Outside Hammers, Damascus Barrel, Modern	80	150
Various Gauges, Hammerless, Steel Barrel, Modern	95	175
Various Gauges, Hammerless, Damascus Barrel, Modern	75	150
Various Gauges, Outside Hammers, Steel Barrel, Modern	90	175

Shotgun, Singleshot
Various Gauges, Hammer, Steel Barrel, Modern   45   75

Winchester Repeating Arms Co.

New Haven, Conn. 1866 to date. In 1857 Oliver Winchester reorganized the Volcanic Repeating Arms Co. into the New Haven Arms Co., and it became Winchester Repeating Arms Co. in 1866. In 1869 Winchester absorbed Fogerty Repeating Rifle Co., and the American Rifle Co. The Spencer Repeating Arms Co. in 1870 and Adironack Arms Co. in 1874. Also see U.S. Military

Add for Custom Features, 50%-100%
Add for Special Sights, 25%-50%

Automatic Weapon, Assault Rifle

M-1 Garand (Win), .30-06 Springfield, Clip Fed, Experimental, Class 3		8,000+
M1918 BAR, .30-06 Springfield, Clip Fed, Bipod, Modern, Class 3	1,000	1,400

Automatic Weapon, Submachine Gun

M-2 (Win), .30 Carbine, Clip Fed, Military, Class 3	375	500

Rifle, Bolt Action

Hotchkiss, .40-65 Win., Sporting Rifle, Antique	750	1,000
Hotchkiss 1st Model Fancy, .45-70 Government, Sporting Rifle, Antique	500	850
Hotchkiss 1st Model, .45-70 Government, Military, Rifle, Antique	300	600
Hotchkiss 1st Model, .45-70 Government, Military, Carbine, Antique	350	650
Hotchkiss 1st Model, .45-70 Government, Sporting Rifle, Antique	400	700
Hotchkiss 2nd Model, .45-70 Government, Military, Rifle, Antique	400	700
Hotchkiss 2nd Model, .45-70 Government, Military, Carbine, Antique	450	750
Hotchkiss 2nd Model, .45-70 Government, Sporting Rifle, Antique	500	800
Hotchkiss 3rd Model, .45-70 Government, Military, Rifle, Antique	350	700
Hotchkiss 3rd Model, .45-70 Government, Military, Carbine, Antique	450	800
Hotchkiss 3rd Model, .45-70 Government, Sporting Rifle, Antique	550	900
Lee Straight-Pull, 6mm Lee Navy, Musket, Antique	450	600
Lee Straight-Pull, 6mm Lee Navy, Sporting Rifle, Antique	500	750
M131, .22 L.R.R.F., Clip Fed, Open Rear Sight, Modern	35	55
M135, .22 WMR, Modern	45	70
M145, Modern	45	70
M1900, .22 Long R.F., Singleshot, Modern	60	110
M1902, Various Rimfires, Singleshot, Modern	75	150
M1904, Various Rimfires, Singleshot, Modern	75	150
M43, Various Calibers, Sporting Rifle, Modern	150	225
M43 Special Grade, Various Calibers, Modern	175	275
M47, .22 L.R.R.F., Singleshot, Modern	50	80
M52, .22 L.R.R.F., Heavy Barrel, Modern	190	300
M52 Slow-Lock, .22 L.R.R.F., Modern	125	200
M52 Speed-Lock, .22 L.R.R.F., Modern	170	250
M52 Sporting, .22 L.R.R.F., Rifle, Modern	450	700
M52-B, .22 L.R.R.F., Modern	175	275
M52-B, .22 L.R.R.F., Heavy Barrel, Modern	200	300
M52-B, .22 L.R.R.F., Bull Gun, Modern	200	325
M52-B, .22 L.R.R.F., Sporting Rifle, Modern	450	675
M52-C, .22 L.R.R.F., Modern	190	250
M52-C, .22 L.R.R.F., Standard Barrel, Modern	175	250
M52-C, .22 L.R.R.F., Bull Gun, Modern	200	325
M52-D, .22 L.R.R.F., Modern	200	325
M54, .270 Win., Carbine, Curio	450	650
M54, .30-06 Springfield, Sniper Rifle, Modern	375	525
M54, Various Calibers, Carbine, Modern	300	450
M54, Various Calibers, Sporting Rifle, Modern	325	450
M54 Match, Various Calibers, Sniper Rifle, Modern	375	550
M54 National Match, Various Calibers, Modern	325	450
M54 Super Grade, Various Calibers, Modern	325	450
M54 Target, Various Calibers, Modern	350	525
M56, .22 L.R.R.F., Sporting Rifle, Clip Fed, Modern	75	150
M57, Various Rimfires, Target, Modern	100	200
M58, .22 L.R.R.F., Singleshot, Modern	50	100
M59, .22 L.R.R.F., Singleshot, Modern	65	115

M60, .22 L.R.R.F., Singleshot, Modern	50	80
M60-A, .22 L.R.R.F., Target, Singleshot, Modern	65	100
M67, Various Rimfires, Singleshot, Modern	50	80
M67 Boy's Rifle, Various Rimfires, Singleshot, Modern	50	80
M68, Various Rimfires, Singleshot, Modern	60	90
M69, .22 L.R.R.F., Clip Fed, Modern	75	100
M69 Match, .22 L.R.R.F., Clip Fed, Modern	90	125
M69 Target, .22 L.R.R.F., Clip Fed, Modern	80	110
M70 Action Only, Various Calibers, Pre'64, Modern	150	200
M70, Add for Pre-War, 25%-50%		
M70, Add for Mint Unfired, Pre'64, 50%-100%		
M70 African, .458 Win. Mag., Pre'64, Modern	450	700
M70 Alaskan, Various Calibers, Pre'64, Checkered Stock, Modern	275	450
M70 Barreled Action Only, Various Calibers, Pre'64, Checkered Stock, Modern	175	300
M70 Bull Gun, Various Calibers, Pre'64, Checkered Stock, Modern	375	625
M70 Carbine, Various Calibers, Pre'64, Checkered Stock, Modern	375	600
M70 Featherweight Sporter Grade, Various Calibers, Pre'64, Checkered Stock, Modern	350	600
M70 Featherweight, Various Calibers, Pre'64, Checkered Stock, Modern	250	400
M70 National Match, .30-06 Springfield, Pre'64, Modern	350	550
M70 Standard, Various Calibers, Pre'64, Checkered Stock, Modern	250	450
M70 Target, Various Calibers, Pre'64, Checkered Stock, Modern	375	600
M70 Varmint, Various Calibers, Pre'64, Checkered Stock, Modern	275	450
M70 Westerner, Various Calibers, Pre'64, Checkered Stock, Modern	275	450
M72, .22 L.R.R.F., Tube Feed, Modern	60	90
M75, .22 L.R.R.F., Sporting Rifle, Clip Fed, Modern	125	200
M75 Target, .22 L.R.R.F., Clip Fed, Modern	100	175
M99 Thumb Trigger, Various Rimfires, Singleshot, Modern	150	325
Model 52 I.M., .22 L.R.R.F., Post '64, Heavy Barrel, Target Stock, Modern	350	450
Model 52 I.M.I.S.U., .22 L.R.R.F., Post '64, Heavy Barrel, Target Stock, Modern	375	500
Model 52 I.M. Kenyon, .22 L.R.R.F., Post '64, Heavy Barrel, Target Stock, Modern	375	500
Model 52 International Prone, .22 L.R.R.F., Post '64, Heavy Barrel, Target Stock, Modern	250	350
Model 52D, .22 L.R.R.F., Post '64, Heavy Barrel, Target Stock, Modern	150	225
Model 670, Various Calibers, Post '64, Scope Mounted, Modern	120	170
Model 70, Various Calibers, Post '64, Checkered Stock, Open Rear Sight, Magnum Action, Modern	150	190
Model 70 African, .458 Win. Mag., Post '64, Checkered Stock, Open Rear Sight, Magnum Action, Modern	250	325
Model 70 International Match, .308 Win., Post '64, Checkered Stock, Target Stock, Modern	300	400

Winchester Model 52-D

Winchester Model 670

Winchester Model 70 Standard Post-64

Winchester Model 70A Standard

Model 70 Standard, Various Calibers, Post '64, Checkered Stock, Open Rear Sight, Modern	140	185
Model 70 Target, Various Calibers, Post '64, Checkered Stock, Target Stock, Modern	225	300
Model 70 Varmint, Various Calibers, Post '64, Checkered Stock, Heavy Barrel, Modern	150	190
Model 70A, Various Calibers, Post '64, Magnum Action, Modern	125	175
Model 70A Police, Various Calibers, Post '64, Modern	120	170
Model 70A Standard, Various Calibers, Post '64, Modern	120	165
M70 Super Grade, Various Calibers, Pre'64, Modern	350	600

Rifle, Double Barrel, Side by Side

Model 21, .405 Win., Checkered Stock, Fancy Wood, Modern		10,000+

Rifle, Lever Action

Henry, .44 Henry, Brass Frame, Rifle, Antique	3,000	5,000
Henry, .44 Henry, Brass Frame, Military, Rifle, Antique	3,500	6,000
Henry, .44 Henry, Iron Frame, Rifle, Antique	4,500	7,000
M 88, Various Calibers, Clip Fed, Checkered Stock, Open Rear Sight, Modern	150	225
M1866, .44 Henry, Musket, Antique	800	1,450
M1866, .44 Henry, Rifle, Antique	850	1,500
M1866, .44 Henry, Carbine, Antique	750	1,400
M1866 Improved Henry, .44 Henry, Carbine, Antique	750	1,500
M1866 Improved Henry, .44 Henry, Rifle, Antique	850	1,750
M1873, Various Calibers, Rifle, Modern	400	900
M1873, Various Calibers, Musket, Modern	500	1,000
M1873, Various Calibers, Carbine, Modern	400	800
M1873 1 of 1,000, Various Calibers, Rifle, Antique		10,000+
M1873, Add for Deluxe	250	400
M1873, Add for Extra Fancy Deluxe	2,000	5,000
M1873 Special, under #525,299, Various Calibers, Sporting Rifle, Antique	750	1,500
M1973 Special, Various Calibers, Sporting Rifle, Modern	600	1,400
M1873, under #525,299, Various Calibers, Musket, Antique	600	1,100
M1873, under #525,299, Various Calibers, Carbine, Antique	500	900
M1873, under #525,299, Various Calibers, Rifle, Antique	700	1,100
M1876, Various Calibers, Carbine, Antique	600	1,200
M1876, Various Calibers, Octagon Barrel, Rifle, Antique	450	1,000
M1876, Various Calibers, Round Barrel, Rifle, Antique	400	900
M1876, Various Calibers, Musket, Antique	1,000	1,800
M1876, Add for Deluxe	300	450
M1876, Add for Extra Fancy Deluxe	2,000	5,000
M1876 RCMP, Various Calibers, Carbine, Antique	800	1,200
M1886, Various Calibers, Rifle, Modern	300	500
M1886, Various Calibers, Carbine, Modern	400	700
M1886, Various Calibers, Musket, Modern	400	750
M1886, Add for Deluxe	150	300
M1886, Add for Extra Fancy Deluxe	1,000	3,000
M1886, under #118,443, Various Calibers, Musket, Antique	500	950
M1886, under #118,443, Various Calibers, Rifle, Antique	350	575
M1886, under #118,443, Various Calibers, Carbine, Antique	500	900
M250, .22 L.R.R.F., Tube Feed, Modern	40	70

Winchester Model 94

M250 Deluxe, .22 L.R.R.F., Tube Feed, Modern	60	90
M255, .22 WMR, Tube Feed, Modern	60	90
M255 Deluxe, .22 WMR, Tube Feed, Modern	75	100
M53, Various Calibers, Modern	250	375
M55, Various Calibers, Modern	300	425
M64, .219 Zipper, Pre'64, Modern	350	450
M64, .30-30 Win., Current Mfg., Modern	100	175
M64, Various Calibers, Pre'64, Modern	225	325
M64 Deer Rifle, Various Calibers, Pre'64, Modern	300	375
M65, .218 Bee, Modern	500	750
M65, Various Calibers, Modern	250	375
M71, .348 Win., Tube Feed, Modern	300	450
M71 Special, .348 Win., Tube Feed, Modern	400	*550
M92, Various Calibers, Rifle, Modern	250	350
M92, Various Calibers, Carbine, Modern	275	375
M92, Various Calibers, Musket, Modern	350	500
M92, Add for Takedown	50	100
M92, under #103316, Various Calibers, Rifle, Antique	175	400
M92, under #103316, Various Calibers, Carbine, Antique	300	450
M92, under #103316, Various Calibers, Musket, Antique	400	600
M94, .30-30 Win., Carbine, Current Mfg., Modern	55	95
M94, .44 Magnum, Carbine, Modern	150	250
M94, Various Calibers, Carbine, Pre'64, Modern	150	250
M94, Various Calibers, Carbine, Pre-War, Modern	200	350
M94, Various Calibers, Rifle, Pre-War, Modern	200	350
M94, Various Calibers, Rifle, Takedown, Pre-War, Modern	225	450
M94 Alaska Centennial, .30-30 Win., Commemorative, Carbine, Curio	500	725
M94 Antique, .30-30 Win., Carbine, Modern	65	100
M94 Bicentennial, .30-30 Win., Commemorative, Curio	400	650
M94 Buffalo Bill, .30-30 Win., Commemorative, Rifle, Curio	140	240
M94 Buffalo Bill, .30-30 Win., Commemorative, Carbine, Curio	140	240
M94 Buffalo Bill Set, .30-30 Win., Commemorative, Curio	375	500
M94 Canadian Centennial, .30-30 Win., Commemorative, Rifle, Curio	140	240
M94 Canadian Centennial, .30-30 Win., Commemorative, Carbine, Curio	140	240
M94 Canadian Centennial Set, .30-30 Win., Commemorative, Curio	400	525
M94 Centennial 66, .30-30 Win., Commemorative, Rifle, Curio	150	225
M94 Centennial 66, .30-30 Win., Commemorative, Carbine, Curio	150	225
M94 Centennial 66 Set, .30-30 Win., Commemorative, Curio	400	600
M94 Classic, .30-30 Win., Carbine, Modern	85	150
M94 Classic, .30-30 Win., Rifle, Modern	85	150
M94 Cowboy, .30-30 Win., Commemorative, Carbine, Curio	140	240
M94 Deluxe, Various Calibers, Pre-War, Modern	750	1,000
M94 Golden Spike, .30-30 Win., Commemorative, Carbine, Curio	140	240
M94 Illinois, .30-30 Win., Commemorative, Carbine, Curio	140	240
M94 Klondike, .30-30 Win., Commemorative, Curio	300	425
M94 Lone Star, .30-30 Win., Commemorative, Rifle, Curio	140	240
M94 Lone Star, .30-30 Win., Commemorative, Carbine, Curio	140	240
M94 Lone Star Set, .30-30 Win., Commemorative, Curio	375	500
M94 Nebraska Centennial, .30-30 Win., Commemorative, Carbine, Curio	500	625
M94 NRA, .30-30 Win., Commemorative, Musket, Curio	150	230
M94 NRA, .30-30 Win., Commemorative, Rifle, Curio	140	240

Winchester Model 9422

M94 NRA Set, .30-30 Win., Commemorative, Curio	400	525
M94 RCMP, .30-30 Win., Commemorative, Curio	400	650
M94 Texas Ranger, .30-30 Win., Commemorative, Curio	400	525
M94 Theodore Roosevelt, .30-30 Win., Commemorative, Rifle, Curio	140	240
M94 Theodore Roosevelt, .30-30 Win., Commemorative, Carbine, Curio	140	240
M94 Theodore Roosevelt Set, .30-30 Win., Commemorative, Curio	375	500
M94, under #50,000, Various Calibers, Carbine, Antique	225	375
M94, under #50,000, Various Calibers, Rifle, Antique	225	400
M94 Wyoming Diamond Jubilee, .30-30 Win., Commemorative, Carbine, Curio	525	700
M95, Various Calibers, Rifle, Modern	300	400
M95, Various Calibers, Carbine, Modern	400	650
M95, Various Calibers, Musket, Modern	350	550
M95, Add for Takedown	75	150
M95, under #19,477, Various Calibers, Rifle, Antique	325	650
M95, under #19,477, Various Calibers, Carbine, Antique	450	750
Model 9422, .22 L.R.R.F., Tube Feed, Modern	95	130
Model 9422M, .22 WMR, Tube Feed, Modern	100	135
Rifle, Semi-Automatic		
M100, Various Calibers, Clip Fed, Modern	125	200
M1903, .22 Win. Auto. R.F., Tube Feed, Modern	125	250
M1905, Various Calibers, Clip Fed, Modern	200	400
M1907, .351 Win. Self-Loading, Clip Fed, Modern	175	325
M1907 Police, .351 Win. Self-Loading, Clip Fed, Modern	200	375
M1910, .401 Win. Self-Loading, Clip Fed, Modern	175	325
M190, .22 L.R.R.F., Tube Feed, Modern	35	50
M190 Deluxe, .22 L.R.R.F., Tube Feed, Modern	40	60
M290, .22 L.R.R.F., Tube Feed, Modern	45	70
M290 Deluxe, .22 L.R.R.F., Tube Feed, Modern	60	90
M63, .22 L.R.R.F., Tube Feed, Modern	200	325
M77, .22 L.R.R.F., Clip Fed, Modern	65	100
M77, .22 L.R.R.F., Tube Feed, Modern	65	100

Winchester Model 290

Rifle, Singleshot

High-Wall, Various Calibers, Sporting Rifle, Modern	275	400
High-Wall, Various Calibers, Sporting Rifle, Takedown, Modern	300	450
High-Wall, Various Calibers, Schutzen Rifle, Takedown, Modern	900	1,400
High-Wall, Various Calibers, Schutzen Rifle, Modern	750	1,100
Low-Wall, .22 Long R.F., Musket, Modern	175	250
Low-Wall, Various Calibers, Sporting Rifle, Modern	150	250
M55 Automatic, .22 L.R.R.F., Modern	60	90
Winder, .22 Long R.F., Musket, Takedown, Modern	250	350
Winder, .22 Long R.F.; Musket, Modern	200	300

Rifle, Slide Action

M1890, Various Rimfires, Modern	100	200
M1890, Various Rimfires, Solid Frame, Modern	150	225
M1890, under #64,521, Various Rimfires, Antique	140	200
M1906, .22 L.R.R.F., Tube Feed, Hammer, Modern	150	250
M270, .22 L.R.R.F., Tube Feed, Modern	40	65
M270 Deluxe, .22 L.R.R.F., Tube Feed, Modern	55	80
M275, .22 WMR, Tube Feed, Modern	50	75
M275 Deluxe, .22 WMR, Tube Feed, Modern	60	100
M61, .22 L.R.R.F., Tube Feed, Modern	150	275
M61, Various Rimfires, Tube Feed, Octagon Barrel, Modern	200	325
M61 Magnum, .22 WMR, Tube Feed, Modern	225	350
M62, .22 L.R.R.F., Tube Feed, Hammer, Modern	150	250
M62 Gallery, .22 Short R.F., Tube Feed, Hammer, Modern	175	275

Shotgun, Bolt Action

Model 36, 9mm Shotshell, Takedown, Singleshot, Modern	75	150
Model 41, .410 Ga., Takedown, Singleshot, Modern	75	150
Model 41, .410 Ga., Takedown, Singleshot, Checkered Stock, Modern	100	175

Shotgun, Double Barrel, Over-Under

Model 101, 12 Ga., Trap Grade, Monte Carlo Stock, Single Trigger, Automatic Ejector, Engraved, Modern	325	450
Model 101, 12 Ga., Trap Grade, Single Trigger, Automatic Ejector, Checkered Stock, Engraved, Modern	325	450
Model 101, 12 Ga. Mag. 3″, Vent Rib, Single Trigger, Automatic Ejector, Checkered Stock, Engraved, Modern	300	425
Model 101, Various Gauges, Skeet Grade, Single Trigger, Automatic Ejector, Checkered Stock, Engraved, Modern	325	450
Model 101 3 Ga. Set, Various Gauges, Skeet Grade, Single Trigger, Automatic Ejector, Checkered Stock, Engraved, Modern	700	1,000
Model 101 Field, Various Gauges, Vent Rib, Single Trigger, Automatic Ejector, Checkered Stock, Engraved, Modern	300	425

Winchester Model 101 Field

Winchester Model 101 Pigeon

Winchester Model 21 Custom

Model 101 Pigeon, 12 Ga., Trap Grade, Single Trigger, Automatic Ejector, Checkered Stock, Engraved, Modern	400	525
Model 101 Pigeon, 12 Ga., Trap Grade, Monte Carlo Stock, Single Trigger, Automatic Ejector, Engraved, Modern	400	525
Model 101 Pigeon, 12 and 20 Gauges, Skeet Grade, Single Trigger, Automatic Ejector, Checkered Stock, Engraved, Modern	375	500
Model 101 Pigeon, Various Gauges, Field Grade, Single Trigger, Automatic Ejector, Checkered Stock, Engraved, Modern	375	500
Model 96, 12 Ga., Trap Grade, Vent Rib, Checkered Stock, Modern	295	375
Model 92, 12 Ga., Trap Grade, Vent Rib, Monte Carlo Stock, Modern	295	375
Model 96, 12 and 20 Gauges, Field Grade, Vent Rib, Checkered Stock, Modern	280	360
Model 96, 12 and 20 Gauges, Skeet Grade, Vent Rib, Checkered Stock, Modern	290	370

Shotgun, Double Barrel, Side by Side

Model 21, for Vent Rib, Add $250		
Model 21, .410 Ga., Checkered Stock, Fancy Wood, Modern		6,000+
Model 21, 12 Ga., Trap Grade, Hammerless, Single Selective Trigger, Selective Ejector, Vent Rib, Modern	1,800	2,500
Model 21, 12 Ga., Trap Grade, Hammerless, Single Selective Trigger, Selective Ejector, Raised Matted Rib, Modern	1,500	2,300
Model 21, 12 and 16 Gauges, Skeet Grade, Hammerless, Single Selective Trigger, Selective Ejector, Vent Rib, Modern	1,500	2,000
Model 21, 12 and 16 Gauges, Skeet Grade, Hammerless, Single Selective Trigger, Selective Ejector, Raised Matted Rib, Modern	1,800	2,500
Model 21, 12 and 16 Gauges, Field Grade, Double Trigger, Automatic Ejector, Hammerless, Modern	950	1.500
Model 21, 12 and 16 Gauges, Field Grade, Double Trigger, Selective Ejector, Hammerless, Modern	1,150	1,750
Model 21, 12 and 16 Gauges, Field Grade, Single Selective Trigger, Automatic Ejector, Hammerless, Modern	1,150	1,700
Model 21, 12 and 16 Gauges, Field Grade, Single Selective Trigger, Selective Ejector, Hammerless, Modern	1,500	2,000
Model 21, 20 Ga., Skeet Grade, Hammerless, Single Selective Trigger, Selective Ejector, Vent Rib, Modern	1,850	2,500
Model 21, 20 Ga., Skeet Grade, Hammerless, Single Selective Trigger, Selective Ejector, Raised Matted Rib, Modern	2,000	2,800
Model 21, 20 Ga., Field Grade, Double Trigger, Automatic Ejector, Hammerless, Modern	1,600	2,400
Model 21, 20 Ga., Field Grade, Double Trigger, Selective Ejector, Hammerless, Modern	1,450	1,900
Model 21, 20 Ga., Field Grade, Single Selective Trigger, Automatic Ejector, Hammerless, Modern	1,500	1,950
Model 21, 20 Ga., Field Grade, Single Selective Trigger, Selective Ejector, Hammerless, Modern	2,000	2,700
Model 21 Custom, 12 Ga., Hammerless, Single Selective Trigger, Selective Ejector, Fancy Engraving, Fancy Checkering, Modern	2,700	3,500
Model 21 Custom, 20 Ga., Hammerless, Single Selective Trigger, Selective Ejector, Fancy Checkering, Fancy Engraving, Modern	3,000	4,000

Model 21 Duck, 12 Ga. Mag. 3″, Hammerless, Single Selective Trigger, Selective Ejector, Raised Matted Rib, Modern	1,300	1,900
Model 21 Duck, 12 Ga. Mag. 3″, Hammerless, Single Selective Trigger, Selective Ejector, Vent Rib, Modern	1,500	1,950
Model 21 Grand American, 12 Ga., Hammerless, Single Selective Trigger, Selective Ejector, Fancy Engraving, Fancy Checkering, Modern	5,000	6,500
Model 21 Grand American, 20 Ga., Hammerless, Single Selective Trigger, Selective Ejector, Fancy Engraving, Fancy Checkering, Modern	5,500	7,000
Model 21 Pigeon, 12 Ga., Hammerless, Single Selective Trigger, Selective Ejector, Fancy Engraving, Fancy Checkering, Modern	3,500	4,250
Model 21 Pigeon, 12 Ga., Hammerless, Single Selective Trigger, Selective Ejector, Fancy Engraving, Fancy Checkering, Modern	3,800	5,000
Model 24, Various Gauges, Double Trigger, Automatic Ejector, Modern	175	275

Shotgun, Lever Action

M1887, Various Gauges, Antique	275	400
M1887 Deluxe Grade, Various Gauges, Antique	350	500
M1901, 10 Ga. 2⅞″, Tube Feed, Damascus Barrel, Modern	250	350
Model 1887, 10 Ga. 2⅞″, Tube Feed, Checkered Stock, Damascus Barrel, Modern	275	400
Model 1887, 10 Ga. 2⅞″, Tube Feed, Plain, Modern	225	350
Model 1887, 12 Ga., Damascus Barrel, Checkered Stock, Tube Feed, Modern	300	425
Model 1887, 12 Ga., Tube Feed, Plain, Modern	225	350
Model 1887, under #64842, 10 Ga. 2⅞″, Damascus Barrel, Checkered Stock, Tube Feed, Antique	300	425
Model 1887, under #64842, 10 Ga. 2⅞″, Tube Feed, Plain, Antique	225	350
Model 1887, under #64842, 12 Ga., Tube Feed, Plain, Antique	250	375
Model 1887, under #64842, 12 Ga., Tube Feed, Checkered Stock, Damascus Barrel, Antique	325	450
Model 1901, 10 Ga. 2⅞″, Tube Feed, Plain, Modern	200	300

Shotgun, Semi-Automatic

Model 1400 Field, 12 and 20 Gauges, Adjustable Choke Modern	130	170
Model 1400 Field, 12 and 20 Gauges, Adjustable Choke Vent Rib, Modern	145	190
Model 1911, 12 Ga., Takedown, Plain, Modern	150	250
Model 1911, 12 Ga., Takedown, Checkered Stock, Modern	200	325
Model 40, 12 Ga., Takedown, Field Grade, Modern	150	225
Model 40, 12 Ga., Takedown, Skeet Grade, Adjustable Choke, Modern	175	250
Model 50, 12 Ga., Trap Grade, Vent Rib, Monte Carlo Stock, Modern	200	300
Model 50, 12 and 20 Gauges, Field Grade, Plain Barrel, Checkered Stock, Modern	150	225
Model 50, 12 and 20 Gauges, Field Grade, Vent Rib, Checkered Stock, Modern	160	235
Model 50, 12 and 20 Gauges, Skeet Grade, Vent Rib, Checkered Stock, Modern	190	260
Model 59, 12 Ga., Lightweight, Adjustable Choke, Modern	225	300
Model Super-X, 12 Ga., Vent Rib, Field Grade, Modern	160	225
Model Super-X, 12 Ga., Trap Grade, Vent Rib, Modern	225	300
Model Super-X, 12 Ga., Trap Grade, Vent Rib, Monte Carlo Stock, Modern	235	315
Model Super-X, 12 Ga., Skeet Grade, Vent Rib, Modern	225	300

Shotgun, Singleshot

Model 101, 12 Ga., Trap Grade, Vent Rib, Modern	275	375
Model 20, .410 Ga. 2½″, Takedown, Hammer, Checkered Stock, Modern	125	200
Model 36, 9mm Shotshell, Modern	135	160
Model 37, .410 Ga., Takedown, Automatic Ejector, Plain Barrel, Modern	70	100
Model 37, 12 Ga., Takedown, Automatic Ejector, Plain Barrel, Modern	55	85
Model 37, 16 Ga., Takedown, Automatic Ejector, Plain Barrel, Modern	50	65
Model 37, 20 Ga., Takedown, Automatic Ejector, Plain Barrel, Modern	55	80
Model 37, 28 Ga., Takedown, Automatic Ejector, Plain Barrel, Modern	80	120
Model 37A, Various Gauges, Modern	35	50
Model 37A Youth, Various Gauges, Modern	35	50

Winchester Model 12

Shotgun, Slide Action

Model 12, 12 Ga., Pre'64, Takedown, Trap Grade, Raised Matted Rib, Modern	350	425
Model 12, 12 Ga., Pre'64, Takedown, Trap Grade, Vent Rib, Modern	400	500
Model 12, 12 Ga., Pre'64, Takedown, Trap Grade, Vent Rib, Monte Carlo Stock, Modern	425	525
Model 12, 12 Ga., Pre-War, Takedown, Vent Rib, Modern	375	450
Model 12, 12 Ga., Pre-War, Takedown, Riot Gun, Modern	175	250
Model 12, 12 Ga., Post '64, Trap Grade, Checkered Stock, Modern	350	425
Model 12, 12 Ga., Post '64, Trap Grade, Monte Carlo Stock, Modern	350	425
Model 12, Various Gauges, Pre'64, Takedown, Skeet Grade, Raised Matted Rib, Modern	375	450
Model 12, Various Gauges, Pre'64, Takedown, Skeet Grade, Vent Rib, Modern	400	475
Model 12, Various Gauges, Pre'64, Takedown, Skeet Grade, Plain Barrel, Modern	300	400
Model 12, Various Gauges, Pre'64, Takedown, Skeet Grade, Plain Barrel, Adjustable Choke, Modern	325	425
Model 12, Various Gauges, Pre'64, Takedown, Raised Matted Rib, Modern	325	400
Model 12, Featherweight, Various Gauges, Pre'64, Takedown, Modern	225	300
Model 12, Heavy Duck, 12 Ga. Mag. 3", Pre'64, Takedown, Vent Rib, Modern	375	500
Model 12, Heavy Duck, 12 Ga. Mag. 3", Pre'64, Takedown, Modern	325	450
Model 12, Heavy Duck, 12 Ga. Mag. 3", Pre'64, Takedown, Raised Matted Rib, Modern	325	450
Model 12, Pigeon Grade, 12 Ga., Pre'64, Takedown, Trap Grade, Vent Rib, Modern	700	850
Model 12, Pigeon Grade, 12 Ga., Pre'64, Takedown, Trap Grade, Raised Matted Rib, Modern	600	750
Model 12, Pigeon Grade, Various Gauges, Pre'64, Takedown, Skeet Grade, Raised Matted Rib, Modern	500	625
Model 12, Pigeon Grade, Various Gauges, Pre'64, Takedown, Skeet Grade, Vent Rib, Modern	675	800
Model 12, Pigeon Grade, Various Gauges, Pre'64, Takedown, Skeet Grade, Plain Barrel, Adjustable Choke, Modern	500	600
Model 12, Pigeon Grade, Various Gauges, Pre'64, Takedown, Field Grade, Plain Barrel, Modern	425	550
Model 12, Pigeon Grade, Various Gauges, Pre'64, Takedown, Field Grade, Vent Rib, Modern	500	625
Model 12, Standard, Various Gauges, Pre'64, Takedown, Modern	275	375
Model 12, Super Pigeon, 12 Ga., Post '64, Takedown, Vent Rib, Engraved, Checkered Stock, Modern		1,000+
Model 1200 Field, 12 and 20 Gauges, Adjustable Choke, Modern	85	125
Model 1200 Field, 12 and 20 Gauges, Adjustable Choke, Vent Rib, Modern	110	150
Model 1200 Field, 12 and 20 Gauges, Modern	80	120
Model 1200 Field, 12 and 20 Gauges, Vent Rib, Modern	100	145
Model 1200 Field, 12 Ga. Mag. 3", Modern	95	135
Model 1200 Field, 12 Ga. Mag. 3", Vent Rib, Modern	115	155
Model 1200 Riot, 12 Ga., Modern	90	120
Model 25, 12 Ga., Solid Frame, Plain Barrel, Modern	125	200
Model 25, 12 Ga., Solid Frame, Riot Gun, Modern	100	150

Winchester Model 1200 Field

Model 72, .410 Ga., Field Grade, Takedown, Modern	275	350
Model 42, .410 Ga., Field Grade, Takedown, Raised Matted Rib, Modern	325	400
Model 42, .410 Ga., Skeet Grade, Takedown, Raised Matted Rib, Modern	425	525
Model 42 Deluxe, .410 Ga., Takedown, Vent Rib, Fancy Checkering, Fancy Wood, Modern	550	700
Model 97, 12 Ga., Solid Frame, Plain, Modern	125	185
Model 97, 12 Ga., Takedown, Plain, Modern	125	200
Model 97, 12 Ga., Takedown, Riot Gun, Modern	125	200
Model 97, 12 Ga., Solid Frame, Riot Gun, Modern	125	175
Model 97, 16 Ga., Solid Frame, Plain, Modern	110	165
Model 97, 16 Ga., Takedown, Plain, Modern	110	180
Model 97 Pigeon, 12 Ga., Takedown, Checkered Stock, Modern	600	750
Model 97 Tournament, 12 Ga., Takedown, Checkered Stock, Modern	350	500
Model 97 Trap, 12 Ga., Takedown, Checkered Stock, Modern	265	350
Model 97 Trench, 12 Ga., Solid Frame, Riot Gun, Military, Modern	225	300
Model 97 Trench, 12 Ga., Solid Frame, Riot Gun, Military, with Bayonet, Modern	250	330

Winfield Arms Co.
Made by Norwich Falls Pistol Co. C.1880

Handgun, Revolver
.32 Short R.F., 5 Shot, Spur Trigger, Solid Frame, Single Action, Antique	90	160

Winfield Arms Co.
Made by Crescent C.1900

Shotgun, Double Barrel, Side by Side
Various Gauges, Outside Hammers, Damascus Barrel, Modern	80	150
Various Gauges, Hammerless, Steel Barrel, Modern	95	175
Various Gauges, Hammerless, Damascus Barrel, Modern	75	150
Various Gauges, Outside Hammers, Steel Barrel, Modern	90	175

Shotgun, Singleshot
Various Gauges, Hammer, Steel Barrel, Modern	45	75

Wingert, Richard
Lancaster, Pa. 1775-77. See Kentucky Rifles, U.S. Military

Winoca Arms Co.
Made by Crescent for Jacobi Hardware Co., Philadelphia, Pa.

Shotgun, Double Barrel, Side by Side
Various Gauges, Outside Hammers, Damascus Barrel, Modern	80	150
Various Gauges, Hammerless, Steel Barrel, Modern	95	175
Various Gauges, Hammerless, Damascus Barrel, Modern	75	150
Various Gauges, Outside Hammers, Steel Barrel, Modern	90	175

Shotgun, Singleshot
Various Gauges, Hammer, Steel Barrel, Modern	45	75

Winslow Arms Co.

Rifle, Bolt Action
Add for Left-Hand Act $35-$50

Crown, Various Calibers, Carved, Fancy Wood, Inlays, Modern	600	850
Emperor, Various Calibers, Carved, Fancy Engraving, Ornate, Fancy Wood, Inlays, Modern	3,400	4,200
Imperial, Various Calibers, Carved, Engraved, Fancy Wood, Inlays, Modern	1,650	2,400
Regal, Various Calibers, Fancy Checkering, Inlays, Modern	300	425
Regent, Various Calibers, Inlays, Carved, Fancy Wood, Modern	375	500
Regimental, Various Calibers, Carved, Inlays, Modern	450	650
Royal, Various Calibers, Carved, Fancy Wood, Inlays, Modern	850	1,200
Varmint, Various Calibers, Fancy Checkering, Inlays, Modern	350	525

Shotgun, Double Barrel, Side by Side

Hammerless, 12 Ga., Single Trigger, Checkered Stock, Inlays, Modern	400	600

Shotgun, Double Barrel, Over-Under

Hammerless, 12 and 20 Gauges, Single Trigger, Checkered Stock, Inlays, Modern	500	800

Withers, Michael
Lancaster, Pa. 1774-1805. See Kentucky Rifles, U.S. Military

Wittes Hdw. Co.
Made by Stevens Arms

Shotgun, Double Barrel, Side by Side

Model 311, Various Gauges, Hammerless, Steel Barrel, Modern	90	145

Shotgun, Singleshot

Model 90, Various Gauges, Takedown, Automatic Ejector, Plain, Hammer, Modern	30	50
Model 94, Various Gauges, Takedown, Automatic Ejector, Plain, Hammer, Modern	30	50

Wogdon
London & Dublin 1760-97

Handgun, Flintlock

.56, Officers, Holster Pistol, Flared, Octagon Barrel, Steel Furniture, Engraved, High Quality, Antique	1,500	2,000

Wolf
Spain C.1900

Handgun, Semi-Automatic

.25 ACP, Clip Fed, Modern	75	110

Wolf, A. W.
Suhl, Germany C.1930

Shotgun, Double Barrel, Side by Side

12 Ga., Engraved, Platinium Inlays, Ivory Inlays, Ornate, Cased, Modern	5,000	6,000

Wolfheimer, Philip
Lancaster, Pa. C.1774. See Kentucky Rifles

Wolverine Arms Co.
Made by Crescent for Fletcher Hardware Co. C.1900

Shotgun, Double Barrel, Side by Side

Various Gauges, Outside Hammers, Damascus Barrel, Modern	80	150

Various Gauges, Hammerless, Steel Barrel, Modern	95	175
Various Gauges, Hammerless, Damascus Barrel, Modern	75	150
Various Gauges, Outside Hammers, Steel Barrel, Modern	90	175

Shotgun, Singleshot

Various Gauges, Hammer, Steel Barrel, Modern	45	75

Woodward, James & Sons
London, England

Shotgun, Double Barrel, Over-Under

Best Quality, Various Gauges, Sidelock, Automatic Ejector, Double Trigger, Fancy Engraving, Fancy Checkering, Modern	10,000	15,000
Best Quality, Various Gauges, Sidelock, Automatic Ejector, Single Trigger, Fancy Engraving, Fancy Checkering, Modern	11,000	17,000

Shotgun, Double Barrel, Side by Side

Best Quality, Various Gauges, Sidelock, Automatic Ejector, Double Trigger, Fancy Engraving, Fancy Checkering, Modern	8,500	12,000
Best Quality, Various Gauges, Sidelock, Automatic Ejector, Single Trigger, Fancy Engraving, Fancy Checkering, Modern	9,000	13,500

Shotgun, Singleshot

12 Ga., Trap Grade, Vent Rib, Hammerless, Fancy Engraving, Fancy Checkering, Modern	8,000	14,000

Worthington Arms
Made by Stevens Arms

Shotgun, Double Barrel, Side by Side

M 315, Various Gauges, Hammerless, Steel Barrel, Modern	90	145
Model 215, 12 and 16 Gauges, Outside Hammers, Steel Barrel, Modern	85	140

Worthington Arms Co.
Made by Crescent for Geo. Worthington Co. Cleveland, Ohio

Shotgun, Double Barrel, Side by Side

Various Gauges, Outside Hammers, Damascus Barrel, Modern	80	150
Various Gauges, Hammerless, Steel Barrel, Modern	95	175
Various Gauges, Hammerless, Damascus Barrel, Modern	75	150
Various Gauges, Outside Hammers, Steel Barrel, Modern	90	175

Shotgun, Singleshot

Various Gauges, Hammer, Steel Barrel, Modern	45	75

Worthington, George
Made by Stevens Arms

Shotgun, Double Barrel, Side by Side

M 315, Various Gauges, Hammerless, Steel Barrel, Modern	80	125
Model 215, 12 and 16 Gauges, Outside Hammers, Steel Barrel, Modern	75	125
Model 311, Various Gauges, Hammerless, Steel Barrel, Modern	80	125

Yato-Hamada
Japan

Handgun, Semi-Automatic

Yato, .32 ACP, Clip Fed, Pre-War, Curio	1,400	2,000
Yato, .32 ACP, Clip Fed, Military, Curio	900	1,500

Ydeal
Spain, Made by Francisco Arizmendi

Handgun, Semi-Automatic
.25 ACP, Clip Fed, Modern   70   100

You Bet
Made by Hopkins & Allen C.1880

Handgun, Revolver
.22 Short R.F., 7 Shot, Spur Trigger, Solid Frame, Single Action, Antique   90   160

Young America
See Harrington & Richardson Arms Co.

Young, Henry
Easton, Pa. 1774-80. See Kentucky Rifles

Young, John
Easton, Pa. 1775-88. See Kentucky Rifles, U.S. Military

Z
Czechoslovakia, Made by F. Dusek

Handgun, Semi-Automatic
Vest Pocket, .25 ACP, Clip Fed, Modern   75   110

Z-B

Automatic Weapon, Light Machine Gun
VZ-26, 8mm Mauser, Finned Barrel, Clip Fed, Bipod, Class 3   2,100   2,500

Zehna
Germany, Made by E. Zehner 1919-28

Handgun, Semi-Automatic
Vest Pocket, .25 ACP, Clip Fed, Modern   95   150

Zoli, Angelo
Brescia, Italy

Rifle, Percussion
.50 Hawkin, Brass Furniture, Reproduction, Antique   100   150

Zehna .25 ACP

Zonda .22

Shotgun, Double Barrel, Over-Under
Angel, 12 Ga., Trap Grade, Single Selective Trigger, Engraved, Checkered
   Stock, Modern   350   450
Angel, 12 and 20 Gauges, Field Grade, Single Selective Trigger, Engraved,
   Checkered Stock, Modern   325   400
Condor, 12 Ga., Trap Grade, Single Selective Trigger, Engraved,
   Checkered Stock, Modern   300   375
Condor, 12 and 20 Gauges, Single Selective Trigger, Field Grade,
   Checkered Stock, Engraved, Modern   275   350
Monte Carlo, 12 Ga., Trap Grade, Single Selective Trigger, Engraved,
   Checkered Stock, Modern   425   525
Monte Carlo, 12 and 20 Gauges, Field Grade, Single Selective Trigger,
   Engraved, Checkered Stock, Modern   400   500

Zoli, Antonio
Gardone, V.T., Italy

Shotgun, Double Barrel, Over-Under
Golden Snipe, 12 Ga., Trap Grade, Single Trigger, Automatic Ejector,
   Engraved, Checkered Stock, Modern   325   425
Golden Snipe, 12 and 20 Gauges, Vent Rib, Single Trigger, Automatic
   Ejector, Engraved, Checkered Stock, Modern   290   370
Golden Snipe, 12 and 20 Gauges, Skeet Grade, Single Trigger, Automatic
   Ejector, Engraved, Checkered Stock, Modern   325   425
Silver Snipe, 12 Ga., Trap Grade, Single Trigger, Vent Rib, Engraved,
   Checkered Stock, Modern   270   350
Silver Snipe, 12 and 20 Gauges, Vent Rib, Single Trigger, Engraved,
   Checkered Stock, Modern   240   320
Silver Snipe, 12 and 20 Gauges, Skeet Grade, Single Trigger, Vent Rib,
   Engraved, Checkered Stock, Modern   270   350

Shotgun, Double Barrel, Side by Side
Silver Hawk, 12 and 20 Gauges, Double Trigger, Engraved, Checkered
   Stock, Modern   250   325

Zonda
Hispano Argentina Fab. de Automiviles

Handgun, Singleshot
.22 L.R.R.F., Blue, Modern   175   250

CARTRIDGE PRICES

The newcomers joining the swelling ranks of cartridge collectors have made prices in this specialized field quite volatile because of increased demand. This trend will continue for the foreseeable future.

The prices shown are based on the average value of a single cartridge with (unless otherwise noted) a common headstamp ranging from very good to excellent condition. Rare headstamps, unusual bullets, scarce case construction, will add to the value of the item. Fired cases, dummies, and blanks all have the same value. On common cartridges, empty cases are worth about 20% to 25% of the value shown; with rare calibers the empties should bring about 75% to 80% of the price of the loaded round. Dummies and blanks are worth about the same as the value shown. Full boxes of ammunition of common type should earn a discount of 15% to 20% per cartridge, whereas full boxes of rare ammo will command a premium because of the collectability of the box itself.

.17 Rem., Jacketed Bullet, Modern	.35	.40
.218 Bee, Various Makers, Modern	.35	.40
.219 Zipper, Various Makers, Modern	.55	.85
.22 BB Cap R.F., Lead Bullet Antique	.05	.10
.22 CB Cap R.F., Lead Bullet Antique	.05	.10
.22 CB Cap R.F., Two Piece Case, Antique	.10	.15
.22 Extra Long R.F., Various Makers, Curio	.60	.70
.22 Hi-Power, Various Makers, Modern	.60	.70
.22 Hornet, Various Makers, Modern	.25	.35
.22 L.R.R.F., Various Makers, Modern	.04	.07
.22 L.R.R.F., Shotshell, Various Makers, Modern	.07	.10
.22 L.R.R.F., Brass Case Russian, Antique	.30	.35
.22 L.R.R.F., Brass Case Austrian, Antique	.25	.30
.22 L.R.R.F., British Raised K, Antique	2.10	2.25
.22 L.R.R.F., Wadcutter, Modern	.25	.30
.22 L.R.R.F., Tracer, U.M.C., Modern	.45	.55
.22 L.R.R.F., Tracer, Gevelot, Modern	.10	.15
.22 L.R.R.F., U.M.C., "S & W Long," Modern	2.75	3.50
.22 Long R.F., Various Makers, Modern	.03	.05
.22 Long R.F., Lead Bullet Antique	.10	.15
.22 Maynard Extra Long, Various Makers, Curio	.50	1.00
.22 Newton, Soft Point Bullet, Modern	8.00	10.00
.22 Rem. Auto. R.F., Various Makers, Modern	.10	.15
.22 Rem. Jet, Jacketed Bullet, Modern	.30	.35
.22 Short R.F., Various Makers, Modern	.03	.05
.22 Short R.F., Blank Cartridge, Various Makers, Modern	.05	.10
.22 Short R.F., Copper Case Raised "U," Antique	2.50	2.75
.22 Short R.F., Copper Case Raised "H," Antique	2.00	2.25

.22 Short R.F., Lead Bullet Antique	.10	.15
.22 WCF, Various Makers, Modern	.30	.50
.22 Win. Auto. R.F., Various Makers, Modern	.08	.12
.22 WMR, Various Makers, Modern	.07	.10
.22 WMR, Shotshell, Various Makers, Modern	.12	.16
.22 WRF, Various Makers, Modern	.07	.10
.22-15-60 Stevens, Lead Bullet Curio	2.25	2.75
.22-3000 G & H, Soft Point Bullet, Modern	1.00	1.40
.220 Swift, Various Makers, Modern	.50	.60
.221 Rem. Fireball, Various Makers, Modern	.35	.40
.222 Rem., Various Makers, Modern	.35	.40
.222 Rem. Mag., Various Makers, Modern	.35	.40
.22-250, Various Makers, Modern	.35	.40
.223 Rem., Various Makers, Modern	.35	.40
.223 Rem., Military, Various Makers, Modern	.15	.20
.224 Wby., Varmintmaster, Modern	.45	.60
.225 Win., Various Makers, Modern	.35	.40
.230 Long, Various Makers, Modern	.75	1.00
.230 Short, Various Makers, Modern	.45	.60
.240 Belted N.E., Jacketed Bullet, Modern	.50	.80
.240 Flanged N.E., Various Makers, Modern	1.50	2.00
.240 Wby. Mag., Modern	.60	.80
.242 Rimless N.E., Various Makers, Modern	2.25	3.75
.243 Win., Various Makers, Modern	.40	.50
.244 H & H Mag., Jacketed Bullet, Modern	2.00	2.75
.244 Halger Mag., Various Makers, Modern	15.00	20.00
.244 Rem., Various Makers, Modern	.50	.75
.246 Purdey, Soft Point Bullet, Modern	2.00	2.75
.247 Wby. Mag., Modern	.65	.90
.25 ACP, Various Makers, Modern	.15	.20
.25 L.F., Various Makers, #50 Allen, Curio	3.00	3.50
.25 Rem., Various Makers, Modern	.70	.95
.25 Short R.F., Lead Bullet Antique	.20	.30
.25 Stevens R.F., Wood Shotshell Bullet, Modern	.50	.75
.25 Stevens Short R.F., Various Makers, Modern	.18	.25
.25 Stevens Long R.F., Various Makers, Modern	.20	.25
.25-06 Rem., Various Makers, Modern	.45	.55
.25-20 WCF, Lead Bullet, Various Makers, Modern	.20	.30
.25-20 WCF, Jacketed Bullet, Various Makers, Modern	.25	.35
.25-21, Jacketed Bullet, Curio	2.25	3.00
.25-25, Various Makers, Modern	2.00	2.75
.25-35 WCF, Various Makers, Modern	.45	.55
.25-36, Jacketed Bullet, Curio	1.15	1.50
.250 Savage, Various Makers, Modern	.40	.50

.255 Roof, Various Makers, Curio	.60	.80
.256 Gibbs Mag., Various Makers, Modern	2.50	3.25
.256 Newton, Soft Point Bullet, Modern	1.15	1.50
.256 Win. Mag., Various Makers, Modern	.30	.40
.257 Roberts, Various Makers, Modern	.40	.50
.257 Wby. Mag., Modern	.80	1.20
.26 BSA, Soft Point Bullet, Modern	2.25	3.00
.264 Win. Mag., Various Makers, Modern	.50	.60
.267 Rem. R.F., Experimental, Curio	7.00	7.75
.270 Wby. Mag., Modern	.65	.90
.270 Win., Various Makers, Modern	.45	.50
.270 Win., Flare Cartridge, Various Makers, Modern	1.40	1.75
.275 Flanged Mag., Various Makers, Modern	1.00	1.50
.275 H & H Mag., Various Makers, Modern	2.50	3.00
.275 Rigby, Various Makers, Modern	1.75	2.50
.276 Pederson, Various Makers, Miliary, Curio	1.00	2.00
.276 Garand, Military, Experimental, Curio	1.25	2.00
.276 Enfield, Various Makers, Miliary, Modern	5.00	6.00
.28 Cup Primed Cartridge, Various Makers, Curio	7.50	8.00
.28-30-120 Stevens, Lead Bullet, Curio	2.50	3.25
.280 Flanged N.E., Various Makers, Modern	2.50	3.00
.280 Halgar Mag., Various Makers, Modern	2.75	3.50
.280 Jeffery, Various Makers, Modern	3.50	4.50
.280 Rem., Various Makers, Modern	.45	.55
.280 Ross, Various Makers, Modern	1.25	2.50
.280/30 Experimental, Various Makers, Miliary, Modern	4.00	7.50
.284 Win., Various Makers, Modern	.45	.55
.295 Rook, Various Makers, Modern	.50	.75
.297/.230 Morris, Various Makers, Modern	.40	.65
.297/.230 Morris Short, Various Makers, Modern	.30	.50
.297/.250 Rook, Various Makers, Modern	.40	.65
.297 R. F. Revolver, Various Makers, Modern	2.00	3.00
.30 Carbine, Various Makers, Modern	.30	.35
.30 Carbine, Various Makers, Military, Modern	.15	.20
.30 Cup Primed Cartridge, Various Makers, Curio	5.00	6.00
.30 H & H Super Mag. Flanged, Various Makers, Moder:	1.50	2.50
.30 Long R.F., Merwin Cone Base, Antique	20.00	22.50
.30 Long R.F., Various Makers, Antique	1.00	1.50
.30 Luger, Various Makers, Modern	.25	.30
.30 Newton, Soft Point Bullet, Modern	1.50	2.00
.30 Pederson, Various Makers, Military, Modern	1.00	2.00
.30 Rem., Various Makers, Modern	.45	.55
.30 Short R.F., Various Makers, Curio	2.50	3.50
.30-03 Springfield, Various Makers, Curio	1.00	1.50

.30-06 Springfield, Various Makers, Modern	.45	.50
.30-06 Springfield, Various Makers, Military, Modern	.15	.20
.30-06 Springfield, Flare Cartridge, Various Makers, Modern	1.40	1.75
.30-30 Wesson, Lead Bullet, Curio	16.00	20.00
.30-30 Win., Various Makers, Modern	.35	.40
.30-30 Win., Bicentennial, Various Makers, Modern	.40	.50
.30-30 Win., Flare Cartridge, Various Makers, Modern	1.40	1.75
.30-40 Krag, Various Makers, Modern	.45	.55
.300 AMU Mag., Various Makers, Military, Modern	1.75	2.25
.300 Hoffman Mag., Soft Point Bullet, Modern	1.75	2.50
.300 H & H Mag., Various Makers, Modern	.55	.65
.300 Rook, Various Makers, Modern	.50	.75
.300 Savage, Various Makers, Modern	.45	.50
.300 Sherwood, Various Makers, Modern	1.25	2.25
.300 Wby. Mag., Modern	.70	1.00
.300 Win. Mag., Various Makers, Modern	.55	.65
.303/.22, Soft Point Bullet, Modern	5.75	7.00
.303 British, Various Makers, Modern	.45	.55
.303 Lewis Rimless, Various Makers, Military, Modern	2.50	3.50
.303 Mag., Various Makers, Modern	2.00	3.00
.303 Savage, Various Makers, Modern	.45	.55
.305 Rook, Various Makers, Modern	.75	1.00
.308 Norma Mag., Various Makers, Modern	.75	.85
.308 Win., Various Makers, Modern	.45	.50
.308 Win., Various Makers, Military, Modern	.15	.20
.308 Win., Flare Cartridge, Various Makers, Modern	1.40	1.75
.31 Eley R.F., Lead Bullet, Dished Base, Modern	8.50	11.00
.31 Crispin, Patent Ignition, Antique	100.00	130.00
.31 Milbank, Patent Ignition, Antique	30.00	40.00
.31 Theur, Patent Ignition, Antique	7.00	10.00
.31 Volcanic, Patent Ignition, Antique	9.00	12.00
.310 Cadet, Various Makers, Modern	.65	.90
.318 Rimless N.E., Various Makers, Modern	1.00	1.25
.32 ACP, Various Makers, Modern	.20	.25
.32 Ballard Extra Long, Lead Bullet, Curio	.65	.85
.32 Colt New Police, Various Makers, Modern	.20	.25
.32 Extra Long R.F., Various Makers, Curio	4.00	5.00
.32 Extra Short R.F., Lead Bullet, Antique	.45	.65
.32 Ideal, Lead Bullet, Curio	.65	.85
.32 Teat-Fire Cartridge, Various Makers, Curio	2.00	2.50
.32 L.F., Various Makers, #52 Allen, Curio	5.00	6.00
.32 Long Colt, Various Makers, Modern	.15	.20
.32 Long R.F., Various Makers, Modern	5.00	6.00
.32 Long R.F., Shotshell, Curio	.20	.35
.32 Long Rifle, Lead Bullet, Antique	2.50	3.50

.32 Rem., Various Makers, Modern	.45	.55
.32 Rem. Rimless, Various Makers, Modern	.50	.60
.32 S & W, Various Makers, Modern	.15	.20
.32 S & W, Shotshell, Various Makers, Modern	.10	.15
.32 S & W, Blank Cartridge, Various Makers, Modern	.10	.15
.32 S & W Long, Various Makers, Modern	.15	.20
.32 Short Colt, Various Makers, Modern	.15	.20
.32 Short R.F., Various Makers, Modern	.20	.25
.32 Win. Self-Loading, Various Makers, Modern	.40	.50
.32 Win. Special, Various Makers, Modern	.35	.45
.32-20 WCF, Lead Bullet, Various Makers, Modern	.50	.60
.32-20 WCF, Jacketed Bullet, Various Makers, Modern	.65	.75
.32-30 Rem., Lead Bullet, Curio	2.70	3.30
.32-35 Stevens & Maynard, Lead Bullet, Curio	2.60	3.25
.32-40 Bullard, Lead Bullet, Curio	1.40	1.75
.32-40 Rem., Lead Bullet, Curio	1.20	1.65
.32-40 WCF, Various Makers, Modern	.30	.40
.320 Rook, Various Makers, Modern	.50	.75
.320 Extra Long Rifle, Various Makers, Modern	1.35	1.75
.322 Swift, Various Makers, Modern	4.00	4.50
.33 BSA, Soft Point Bullet, Modern	2.00	2.75
.33 Win., Soft Point Bullet, Modern	.75	1.25
.333 Flanged N.E., Various Makers, Modern	2.25	3.50
.333 Rimless N.E., Various Makers, Modern	2.25	3.50
.338 Win. Mag., Various Makers, Modern	.60	.70
.340 Wby. Mag., Modern	.70	1.00
.340 R.F. Revolver, Various Makers, Modern	1.25	1.75
.348 Win., Various Makers, Modern	.75	.85
.35 Allen R.F., Lead Bullet, Curio	9.00	12.00
.35 Newton, Soft Point Bullet, Modern	2.25	3.00
.35 Rem., Various Makers, Modern	.40	.50
.35 S & W Auto., Jacketed Bullet, Curio	.40	.55
.35 Win., Various Makers, Modern	1.75	2.10
.35 Win. Self-Loading, Various Makers, Modern	.45	.55
.35-30 Maynard, Lead Bullet, with Riveted Head, Curio	7.00	9.00
.35-30 Maynard, Lead Bullet, without Riveted Head, Curio	4.00	5.00
.35-40 Maynard, Various Makers, Curio	7.50	10.00
.350 Rem. Mag., Various Makers, Modern	.65	.75
.350 Rigby, Various Makers, Modern	2.00	2.75
.351 Win. Self-Loading, Various Makers, Modern	1.00	1.20
.357 Magnum, Lead Bullet, Various Makers, Modern	.20	.25
.357 Magnum, Jacketed Bullet, Various Makers, Modern	.25	.35
.358 Norma Mag., Various Makers, Modern	.75	.90
.358 Win., Various Makers, Modern	.55	.65
.36 L. F., #56 Allen, Various Makers, Curio	5.00	6.00

.36 Crispin, Patent Ignition, Antique	130.00	165.00
.36 Theur Navy, Patent Ignition, Antique	7.00	10.00
.360 #5 Rook, Various Makers, Modern	7.00	10.00
.360 N.E., Various Makers, Modern	.70	1.00
.360 N.E. #2, Various Makers, Curio	1.50	2.00
.369 Purdey, Soft Point Bullet, Curio	4.25	5.00
.370 Flanged, Various Makers, Modern	.70	1.00
.375 Flanged Mag. N.E., Various Makers, Modern	1.50	1.75
.375 Flanged N.E., Various Makers, Modern	1.80	2.25
.375 H & H Mag., Various Makers, Modern	1.50	2.00
.375 Rimless N.E. 2¼", Various Makers, Curio	.70	.80
.375/.303 Axite, Various Makers, Curio	1.50	2.00
.378 Wby. Mag., Modern	2.00	3.00
.38 ACP, Various Makers, Modern	.20	.25
.38 AMU, Various Makers, Military, Modern	.25	.35
.38 Ballard Extra Long, Lead Bullet, Curio	1.00	1.40
.38 Extra Long R.F., Lead Bullet, Curio	3.00	4.00
.38 Long CF, Lead Bullet, Curio	.40	.55
.38 Long Colt, Various Makers, Modern	.25	.30
.38 Long R.F., Various Makers, Curio	2.00	3.25
.38 S & W, Various Makers, Modern	.20	.25
.38 S & W, Blank Cartridge, Various Makers, Modern	.15	.20
.38 Short R.F., Various Makers, Modern	2.00	3.00
.38 Short R.F., Shotshell, Curio	.25	.40
.38 Short Colt, Various Makers, Modern	.15	.20
.38 Special, Lead Bullet, Various Makers, Modern	.25	.30
.38 Special, Flare Cartridge, Various Makers, Modern	1.40	1.75
.38 Special, Sub-Velocity Ammo, Various Makers, Modern	.10	.15
.38 Special, Shotshell, Various Makers, Modern	.25	.30
.38 Special, Blank Cartridge, Various Makers, Modern	.15	.20
.38 Special, Tracer, Military, Modern	.25	.35
.38 Super, Various Makers, Modern	.20	.25
.38-40 Rem. Hepburn, Various Makers, Curio	1.50	2.50
.38-40 WCF, Various Makers, Modern	.30	.40
.38-44, Various Makers, Modern	.20	.25
.38-45 Bullard, Lead Bullet, Curio	3.25	4.25
.38-50 Ballard, Lead Bullet, Curio	3.75	4.50
.38-50 Maynard, Various Makers, Curio	7.50	10.00
.38-50 Rem. Hepburn, Lead Bullet, Curio	1.60	2.25
.38-55 Win. & Ballard, Various Makers, Modern	.75	1.00
.38-56 Win., Lead Bullet, Curio	1.50	2.00
2mm Rimfire, Blank Cartridge, Modern	.08	.14
2mm Rimfire, Lead Bullet, Modern	.25	.30
2.7mm Kolibri, Jacketed Bullet, Curio	11.00	14.00
3mm Kolibri, Various Makers, Curio	12.00	15.00

4mm R.F., Lead Bullet, Antique	.10	.15
4.25mm Liliput, Jacketed Bullet, Curio	4.50	6.00
5.5mm Soemmerda, Various Makers, Modern	2.00	2.75
5.5mm Velo Dog, Lead Bullet, Curio	.35	.55
5.6 x 33 Rook, Various Makers, Modern	1.00	1.40
5.6 x 35R Vierling, Various Makers, Modern	.40	.60
5.6 x 50R Mag., Various Makers, Modern	.80	1.00
5.6 x 50 Mag., Various Makers, Modern	.80	1.00
5.6 x 52R, Various Makers, Modern	.65	.80
5.6 x 57, Various Makers, Modern	.95	1.20
5.6 x 61 Vom Hofe Express, Soft Point Bullet, Modern	3.25	4.25
5.6 x 57R, Various Makers, Modern	.95	1.20
5.6 x 61R Vom Hofe Express, Various Makers, Modern	3.00	4.00
5.7mm Target Pistol, Various Makers, Modern	3.00	3.75
5.75mm Velo-Dog, Various Makers, Modern	.80	1.10
5.75mm Velo-Dog Short, Various Makers, Modern	1.50	2.00
5mm Bergmann, Various Makers, Curio	6.00	8.00
5mm Bergmann, Grooved, Various Makers, Curio	4.00	6.00
5mm Brun, Various Makers, Modern	10.00	14.00
5mm Clement, Soft Point Bullet, Curio	3.00	3.75
5mm French Revolver, Various Makers, Modern	.45	.70
5mm Pickert, Various Makers, Modern	12.00	16.00
5mm Rem. RFM, Jacketed Bullet, Modern	.12	.18
6 x 58 Forster, Various Makers, Curio	6.00	8.00
6 x 58R Forster, Various Makers, Curio	2.50	3.50
6.35mm Pickert, Various Makers, Modern	3.25	4.50
6.5 x 48R Sauer, Various Makers, Curio	2.00	2.50
6.5 x 52 Mannlicher-Carcano, Various Makers, Modern	.60	.70
6.5 x 54 M.S., Various Makers, Modern	.95	1.20
6.5 x 54 Mauser, Soft Point Bullet, Modern	2.00	2.50
6.5 x 55 Swedish, Various Makers, Modern	.60	.70
6.5 x 57, Various Makers, Modern	.85	1.15
6.5 x 57R, Various Makers, Modern	.85	1.15
6.5 x 58 Vergueiro, Various Makers, Military, Modern	3.50	4.50
6.5mm Dutch, Various Makers, Military, Modern	.05	.10
6.5 x 58R Sauer, Jacketed Bullet, Modern	1.50	2.25
6.5mm Jap, Various Makers, Modern	.60	.70
6.5 x 68 Schuler, Various Makers, Modern	1.15	1.40
6.5 x 68R, Various Makers, Modern	1.40	1.75
6.5mm Bergmann, Various Makers, Curio	7.00	9.00
6.5mm Bergmann Grooved, Various Makers, Curio	5.00	6.00
6.50mm Mannlicher, Various Makers, Modern	4.75	6.00
6.8mm Gasser, Various Makers, Modern	3.75	4.75
6.8mm Schulhof, Various Makers, Modern	2.50	3.25

6mm Lee Navy, Various Makers, Military, Modern	1.50	2.50
6mm Loron, Patent Ignition, Antique	2.50	3.25
6mm Flobert, 2 Piece Case, Antique	.35	.40
6mm Merveilleux, Various Makers, Modern	1.50	2.00
6mm Protector, Various Makers, Modern	1.00	1.50
6mm Rem., Various Makers, Modern	.40	.50
6.5mm Reg. Mag., Various Makers, Modern	.70	.80
7 x 57R, Various Makers, Modern	.80	1.00
7 x 61 Norma, Various Makers, Modern	.65	.75
7 x 64 Brenneke, Various Makers, Modern	.90	1.10
7 x 64, Various Makers, Modern	.95	1.20
7 x 65R, Various Makers, Modern	.95	1.25
7 x 72R, Various Makers, Modern	2.00	3.00
7 x 72R, Dummy Cartridge, Curio	2.00	2.50
7 x 73 Vom Hofe, Soft Point Bullet, Modern	7.50	8.50
7.25mm Adler, Various Makers, Modern	60.00	85.00
7.35mm Carcano, Various Makers, Military, Modern	.05	.10
7.5 x 54 MAS, Various Makers, Military, Modern	.10	.15
7.5 x 55 Swiss, Military, Modern	.50	.70
7.5mm Swedish Nagent, Various Makers, Modern	.60	.70
7.5mm Swiss Nagent, Modern	.70	.90
7.6mm Mauser Revolver, Various Makers, Modern	5.50	8.00
7.62 x 39 Russian, Various Makers, Military, Modern	.20	.30
7.62 x 39 Russian, Various Makers, Modern	.40	.50
7.62 x 54R Russian, Various Makers, Modern	.60	.70
7.62mm Nagent, Various Makers, Military, Modern	1.25	1.75
7.62mm Tokarev, Various Makers, Military, Modern	.30	.50
7.63 Mannlicher, Various Makers, Military, Modern	.10	.15
7.63 Mauser, Various Makers, Modern	.10	.15
7.65 Borchardt, Various Makers, Modern	2.00	2.75
7.65mm Francotte, Various Makers, Modern	18.00	23.00
7.65mm Glisenti, Various Makers, Modern	75.00	90.00
7.65mm Pickert, Various Makers, Modern	2.75	3.50
7.65 Roth-Sauer, Various Makers, Curio	2.00	3.00
7.65 x 53 Mauser, Military, Modern	.45	.60
7.65 Argentine, Various Makers, Modern	.55	.65
7.65 Argentine Navy Match, Military, Curio	25.00	30.00
7.7mm Jap, Various Makers, Modern	.55	.65
7.7mm Bittner, Various Makers, Modern	24.00	30.00
7.8mm Bergmann #5, Various Makers, Modern	4.00	6.50
7.92 x 33 Kurz, Various Makers, Military, Modern	.60	1.00
7mm Baer, Various Makers, Modern	1.50	2.00
7mm Charola, Various Makers, Modern	4.75	6.00
7mm Flobert, Lead Bullet, Antique	.35	.40

7mm French Revolver, Various Makers, Modern	.90	1.35
7mm H & H, Soft Point Bullet, Modern	1.40	2.00
7mm Mauser, Various Makers, Modern	.45	.50
7mm Mauser, Various Makers, Military, Modern	.10	.15
7mm Nambu,Various Makers, Curio	6.00	8.50
7mm Rem. Mag., Various Makers, Modern	.55	.65
7mm Rem. Mag., Various Makers, Flare Cartridge, Modern	1.40	1.75
7mm Rigby Mag., Soft Point Bullet, Modern	1.75	2.50
7mm Target Pistol, Various Makers, Modern	1.50	2.00
7mm Vom Hofe S.E., Various Makers, Modern	7.00	8.00
7mm Wby. Mag., Modern	.65	.90
8 x 48R Sauer, Various Makers, Curio	3.00	4.00
8 x 50R Lebel, Various Makers, Military, Modern	.07	.15
8 x 50R Mannlicher, Various Makers, Modern	1.25	1.50
8 x 51 Mauser, Various Makers, Curio	.75	1.00
8 x 51R Mauser, Various Makers, Curio	4.00	5.50
8 x 56R Mannlicher, Various Makers, Military, Modern	4.00	5.00
8 x 56R Kripatschek, Various Makers, Military, Curio	.15	.20
8 x 57 Jrs, Various Makers, Modern	.75	.95
8 x 575, Various Makers, Modern	.55	.65
8 x 58R Krag, Jacketed Bullet, Military, Modern	2.00	2.75
8 x 58R Saver, Various Makers, Curio	2.75	3.50
8 x 60 Mauser, Various Makers, Modern	1.30	2.00
8 x 60S, Various Makers, Modern	1.20	1.50
8 x 64 Brenneke, Various Makers, Modern	1.30	1.75
8 x 68S, Various Makers, Modern	1.15	1.35
8 x 75, Various Makers, Curio	3.00	3.77
8 x 75R, Various Makers, Curio	2.25	3.00
8.1 x 72R, Lead Bullet, Modern	2.40	2.75
8.15 x 46R, Lead Bullet, Modern	.75	1.00
8.15 x 46R, Soft Point Bullet, Modern	1.30	1.60

AFTERWORD

The prices listed in this guide have been gathered from reliable sources, and every effort has been made to ensure their accuracy. However, as with all things, one man's trash is another's treasure, and the opinions of individuals and the machinations of a free market may during the life of this guide swing some prices widely. Over this I exercise no control, but rather wish the phenomenon Godspeed, for it sometimes turns the sedate art of collecting into a wild treasure hunt.